Police Reform
in China

Advances in Police Theory and Practice Series

Series Editor: Dilip K. Das

Police Reform
in China

Kam C. Wong

CRC Press
Taylor & Francis Group
Boca Raton London New York

CRC Press is an imprint of the
Taylor & Francis Group, an **informa** business

CRC Press
Taylor & Francis Group
6000 Broken Sound Parkway NW, Suite 300
Boca Raton, FL 33487-2742

First issued in paperback 2017

© 2012 by Taylor and Francis Group, LLC
CRC Press is an imprint of Taylor & Francis Group, an Informa business

No claim to original U.S. Government works

ISBN-13: 978-1-4398-1969-2 (hbk)
ISBN-13: 978-1-138-11186-8 (pbk)

Library of Congress Cataloging-in-Publication Data

Wong, Kam C.
    Police reform in China / Kam C. Wong.
        p. cm. -- (Advances in police theory and practice ; 9)
    Includes index.
    ISBN 978-1-4398-1969-2 (hardcover : alk. paper)
    1. Police administration--China. I. Title.

HV7935.W66 2011
363.20951--dc22

                                                                              2011010492

Visit the Taylor & Francis Web site at
http://www.taylorandfrancis.com

and the CRC Press Web site at
http://www.crcpress.com

To my brother, Dr. Kam Shing Wong, for taking care of the Wong family, and me, all his life

Contents

5   Reform Measures   217

Contents

Series Editor Preface

While the literature on police and allied subjects is growing exponentially, its impact upon day-to-day policing remains small. The two worlds of research and practice of policing remain disconnected even though cooperation between the two is growing. A major reason is that the two groups speak in different languages. The research work is published in hard-to-access journals and presented in a manner that is difficult to comprehend for a layperson. On the other hand, the police practitioners tend not to mix with researchers and remain secretive about their work; consequently, there is little dialog between the two and almost no attempt to learn from one another. Dialog across the globe, among researchers and practitioners situated in different continents, is of course even more limited.

I attempted to address this problem by starting the International Police Executive Symposium (IPES), www.ipes.info, where a common platform has brought the two together. IPES is now in its 17th year. The annual meetings, which constitute most of the organization's major events, have been hosted in all parts of the world. Several publications have come out of these deliberations, and a new collaborative community of scholars and police officers has been created whose membership runs into several hundreds.

Another attempt to foster better communication between researchers and practitioners was to begin a new journal, aptly called *Police Practice and Research: An International Journal* (PPR), which has opened the gate for practitioners to share their work and experiences. The journal has attempted to focus upon issues that help bring the two onto a single platform. PPR completed its 12th year of publication in 2011. It is certainly evidence of the growing collaboration between police research and practice that PPR, which initially published four issues a year, expanded to five issues in its fourth year and now is issued six times a year.

Clearly, these attempts, despite their success, remain limited. Conferences and journal publications do help create a body of knowledge and an association of police activists but cannot address substantial issues in depth. The limitations of time and space preclude larger discussions and more authoritative expositions that can provide stronger and broader linkages between the two worlds.

It is this realization of the increasing dialog between police research and practice that has encouraged many of us—my colleagues and I, connected closely with IPES and PPR across the world—to conceive and implement a new attempt in this direction. I am now embarking on a book series, Advances in Police Theory and Practice, that seeks to attract writers from all parts of the world, particularly practitioner contributors. The objective is to make a serious contribution to our knowledge of the police as well as to improve police practices through this series. The focus is not only on work that describes the best and successful police practices but also on work that challenges current paradigms and breaks new ground to prepare a police for the 21st century. The series seeks comparative analyses that highlight achievements in distant parts of the world as well as in-depth examinations of specific problems confronting a particular police force.

Kam Wong's *Police Reform in China* does just that. It is a pioneering, defining, foundational, must-read resource for anyone who wants to learn about Chinese policing. It is the first book to investigate Chinese police reform in a systematic and comprehensive way. The author had access to Ministry of Public Security officers and data and consulted with professors and students of the Chinese People's Public Security University. The research results are supported by Chinese indigenous theories and by local empirical data.

Findings on the impact of the Hu–Wen vs. Deng administrations on policing, contradictions arising due to the entrenched Lei Feng spirit, aspirations of the emerging post-1980s generation, and how the public "thinks" and "feels" about their police with regard to corruption, abuses, and female police officers, among other issues, all contribute to our understanding of Chinese policing in new and radical ways. Dr. Wong establishes a necessary foundation for the development of Chinese police research and discourse by debunking myths, proposing methods, offering perspectives, raising issues, providing data, expounding on findings, and looking ahead to the future. His groundbreaking book is an important contribution to this series.

It is hoped that this series will make it possible to accelerate the process of building knowledge about policing and help bridge the gap between the two worlds of police research and police practice. This is an invitation to police scholars and practitioners across the world to come join in this venture.

Dilip K. Das, PhD
Founding President, International Police Executive Symposium (IPES),
www.ipes.info

Founding editor-in-chief, Police Practice and Research: An International Journal (PPR),
www.tandf.co.uk/journals

Foreword

Three years ago, a well-traveled colleague who was visiting Shanghai for the first time related his impression in one sentence: "I have seen the future, and it is here." Shanghai, of course, is not representative of all China, but recent developments there hint at wider changes in the Middle Kingdom. And these are truly massive. Economic development is occurring on a scale that is unprecedented. Scores of millions of people have risen from poverty, with many more to follow. Internal population movements number in the hundreds of millions, as people seek a better life in urban areas. By 2025, China is expected to have 220 cities with populations of a million or more inhabitants. Social changes of which Chairman Mao would almost certainly disapprove, such as the pursuit of individual wealth, appear indomitable. With nearly 20% of the world's population, what happens in China is by definition worthy of note. Policing is no exception. Managing such massive change, while maintaining political stability, economic growth, and social harmony, is a daunting task. If, as routine activity theorists suggest, "crime follows opportunity," criminal opportunities have never been greater and will inevitably increase. A significant proportion of the responsibility for crime control falls on the shoulders of the Chinese police. This book provides a rare and insightful glimpse of policing in China in the midst of such change.

The book is far from a sugarcoated view of policing in China. The formidable challenges posed by the profound social and economic changes noted above are daunting enough. Moreover, any reversal in current and anticipated economic fortunes could lead to massive social dislocation, with dire consequences. In addition, the latent centrifugal forces in Chinese society, from separatists to cults, and the potential impact of state collapse in North Korea cannot be ignored. Challenges such as these would test even a police force from heaven. But Chinese police are far from perfect.

One of the key issues confronting police in any country is that of legitimacy. This is usually defined in terms of public acceptance of the role and conduct of the police as right and proper. Readers will learn that Chinese police are not universally revered by their public. Anti-police graffiti appears on walls. Surveys of police reveal deteriorating relations with the public, especially with unemployed and floating populations. Citizens appear disinclined to report crimes to police or to assist police officers. Verbal insults from citizens are not uncommon, nor are acts of physical resistance. There have been over a thousand deliberate killings of police officers since the year 2000. All of this would have been unimaginable in Chairman Mao's time.

Sociologists of law have long been familiar with the distinction between law "on the books" and law in action. In other words, what looks good on paper may not play out that way in practice. The Chinese law relating to detention during investigation seems to follow this story line, with the spirit of the law not being honored. Such outcomes flow from failures on the part of senior police and of external authorities, such as the procuracy, to supervise implementation of the Criminal Procedure Law. The problem is compounded by police culture, with its characteristic properties of solidarity, defensiveness, and cover-up. Of course, these problems are hardly unique to China.

It is not surprising that what many in China regard as progress comes at a price. Displacement of populations and expropriation of property without fair compensation bring people into the streets. Thus, one sees increasing public protest, or what Chinese authorities refer to as "mass incidents." The ways in which such activities are managed are of course crucial to public perceptions of the police. Provincial governments are discouraged from allowing their citizens to travel to Beijing to petition their government for a redress of grievances. Needless to say, authorities would prefer to avoid another Tiananmen incident.

China is large and diverse. It is hardly a monolithic state. A great deal of governance takes place at the provincial or municipal level, and not all provinces are well endowed with resources. Chapter 5 reports that some of the less well-resourced provincial police agencies resort to fines as a means of revenue enhancement and that some police agencies actually borrow funds in order to finance investigations. The potential for distortion of enforcement priorities is self-evident. Moreover, inadequate funding increases the vulnerability of police to corruption. It is a recipe for disaster. Chapter 5 also calls our attention to risks that can arise when police are called upon to perform extraneous duties. Tax collection, enforcement of the one-child policy, and forced relocation of displaced citizens are but three examples of tasks performed by Chinese police from time to time that will hardly endear them to the public they serve.

In some Western nations, automatic cameras identify vehicles exceeding the speed limit or drivers who ignore stop signs and stop lights. Offenders are notified of their transgression by mail and are asked to pay their fine by credit card or automatic funds transfer. Police have no role to play in the process, thereby sparing citizens the burdens of interacting with police under unpleasant circumstances. Whether there are technological or administrative solutions that might serve to reduce friction between police and the public is well worth exploring.

Many of those at the beginning of a career, whether in the practice of law or medicine, or in academia generally, are idealistic. Over time, they tend to become more cynical. This process in China may take less time than one would wish. In 1996, I lectured a group of Chinese police cadets on the concepts of efficiency and effectiveness in policing. At the end of my presentation, the first question posed by a student related to the annual salary of an Australian police officer. More recent surveys of early career Chinese police officers seem to reflect something other than starry-eyed idealism. When asked about their reasons for joining the police, income and employment security were cited more frequently than altruism or even excitement. Fewer still profess to having been motivated by communist ideology. At the end of Chapter 4, the reader will find some interesting manifestations of police cynicism in a section that reports "32 Classical Police Sayings." Officers caution each other not to be too zealous in their work and not to volunteer. So much for selfless dedication to duty. Lest there be any doubt, officers are warned, "Do not expect your leaders to support you."

It is therefore perhaps not surprising that corruption is a serious problem in China and is regarded as such by the public. Whether the political will exists to address this problem remains to be seen, but there is no dearth of examples of reform. The former colonizers of Hong Kong presided over police corruption on a grand scale. They were able to address the problem to a significant extent, without drastically curtailing human rights and the rule of law, prior to the handover of sovereignty. Authorities in contemporary China might have something to learn from this experience.

The book does report some positive signs. These entail a continuation of trends that began two decades ago on the other side of the world. On March 3, 1991, an African American named Rodney King was beaten savagely by several officers of the Los Angeles Police Department. Unbeknownst to the officers at the time, the beating was recorded with a handheld video camera by a resident of a nearby apartment. Consumer electronics have since enabled unprecedented public scrutiny, widespread dissemination, and robust discussion of untoward police activities. Today, cell phones can serve as video cameras; images that they capture can reach millions within minutes.

The potential for the application of such technologies to policing is great indeed. Bloggers routinely comment on incidents of police misconduct. Already one has seen examples of mass mobilization of public indignation over corruption and abuse of power and of repugnant private conduct such as cruelty to animals. The term "human flesh search engines" (renrou sousuo) applies to online campaigns to punish abhorrent behavior.

Policing in China is fraught with contradictions and ironies. What was once a totalitarian state, groaning with excessive formalism and bureaucratism, has sought to develop a degree of "customer focus." Chinese authorities are beginning to appreciate the importance of transparency as a means of enhancing legitimacy. Police museums have been established, police departments sponsor "open days," and they use the World Wide Web to present a friendly public face. A 110 contact number has been established to facilitate public reporting of emergency situations.

This book cites some fascinating examples of these progressive tendencies in furtherance of transparency—innovations that would make Western government "spin doctors" recoil in horror. The city of Dalian, for example, encourages local news media to report on the activities of government agencies and enterprises and urges them to expose shortcomings and to identify problems. City officials are required to cooperate with the media and are forbidden from interfering in media work.

Readers will note that rhetoric has yielded to a professed commitment to evidence-based policing. Among the book's most significant contributions are the data sources that it makes accessible to a Western readership. These include publications in professional policing journals, longitudinal data from successive crime victim surveys and surveys of police personnel, and excerpts from conversations in online chat rooms. This book is richly documented, a resource in its own right.

Content analyses of policing journals over time reveal that the earlier emphasis on ideology has given way to problem solving. China is not averse to experimentation. The city of Shenzhen was established as an experiment in economic reform. Chinese police educators are well aware of, and keenly interested in, international developments in policing. They are familiar with the vocabularies of human rights, the rule of law, and community policing. The opportunity exists for them to learn from the successes and the mistakes of their counterparts elsewhere and to develop a world-class policing system. Whether or not they will be capable of overcoming the bureaucratic inertia characteristic of many police organizations around the world remains to be seen, as does their ability to harness the individualism that appears to be growing in their own ranks no less than in Chinese society as a whole. Kam C. Wong's intriguing book provides us with a valuable vantage point from which to view the unfolding of this drama.

Peter Grabosky
Australian National University
Vice President, Asian Criminological Society

Acknowledgments

In completing this project, I have a lot of people to thank. This is a lifetime project and a project of a lifetime. As a lifetime project, this book started when I was a young police inspector with the Royal Hong Kong Police (HKP). During this time, I learned much about being a police officer. This experience is where I first confronted many of the issues raised in this book, chief of which is the need to "think" and "feel" like locals as a (colonial) police officer.

Over the years, many wonderful colleagues from the HKP, past and present, have helped me to think through a number of issues appearing in this book, whether it was over a beer, talking inside quarters, or watching sunsets. Some of the notable ones include Douglas Tsui, Chief Superintendent, retired; Chu Wing Hong, Senior Superintendent, retired; David Hodson, Assistant Commissioner, retired; Douglas Lau, Deputy Commission, retired; and Dick Lee, Commissioner, retired. A special thanks goes to the many HKP officers I have taught and mentored through the years, including David Ng Ka-sing and Albert Cheuk Chun-yin, both Assistant Commissioners of Police. Finally, I would be remiss if I did not mention ICAC Commissioner Timothy Tong, who shared with me his long experience and penetrating insights on many law and order issues. They are a part of me as I am a part of them. When I was lost in my thoughts, they would suddenly appear just in time to salvage a sure to be unproductive night.

Much of the research for this project was conducted in four academic institutions or libraries: Universities Service Centre for Chinese Studies, Hong Kong University, City University of Hong Kong, and Chinese People's Public Security University (PSU). I owe the staffs there for their unfailing support. They are the unsung heroes of this book.

As to Chinese colleagues or researchers, there are hundreds I could acknowledge. Most of them are aspiring police cadets, in-service officers, and staff members from the PSU, Chinese Armed Police Force Academy, Zhejiang Provincial Police College (ZPC), Hubei Provincial Police College, and Hunan Police Officer College. Others are those whom I have met along the way during my many travels throughout China. In the last decade, I have visited these colleges as an expert consultant (Ministry of Public Security and Hubei Provincial Police College), visiting professor (PSU), or foreign editor (ZPC), all the while attending conferences, giving lectures, providing consultation, and giving advice. Upon each visit, I learned a bit more about China from the faculty and students. Truth be told, they are the true authors of this book; I am but a ghostwriter.

A very special thanks goes out to two persons who introduced me to the inner workings of Chinese policing. The first is Dr. Mei Jianming, a wonderful colleague and knowledge-able professor from PSU who specializes in international police cooperation and terrorism. We have spent long hours together trying to find ways to make Chinese policing one of the best policing systems in the world. We communicated frequently while I was writing this book. The other is Dr. Wang Daiwei, the Graduate Director at PSU. Wang is a learned scholar from the old school who is as comfortable discussing Chinese ideological treatises as he is expounding on police practices. I spent many nights drinking *mao-tai* in his PSU office, with a foldaway bed handy by the desk.

I also must make note of an intellectual debt that I cannot hope to ever fully repay, a debt of the highest order. I have been blessed with learned, demanding, and inspirational teachers from the School of Criminal Justice, State University of New York, Albany. David Bayley introduced me to comparative policing and taught me all I know about the subject. I am a slow learner, and he was my patient teacher—a perfect match. Hans Toch molded me into an inquisitive and unrelenting scholar. He never let me off with the first answer until it was time to go to class or to return home. In his cigar-smoke-filled room I fell in love with knowledge long before I knew what it is. The one who gave me courage and tenacity in dealing with tough legal issues and taught me to be humble and self-effacing as a person was James Acker. My only excuse for not being able to learn as much as I could from him is that his expectations were always high and fast moving. To this day, I am playing a game of catch-up. Thanks to these individuals, I finally understand what "standing on the shoulders of giants" means in everyday life. As a summary of what I learned from all these giants, I offer you this phrase: "Knowledge never rests; people do."

Finally, I want to thank the editorial staff at Taylor & Francis for their support and particularly Sarah Nicely Fortener of Nicely Creative Services, who edited my manuscript. Without Sarah's attention to detail and facility with editing, I doubt if this book would look or read as professionally as it does.

In closing, I want to share with my colleagues and readers what I have learned from this research exercise. The research into Chinese policing has humbled me. The more I learn about Chinese policing, the more questions I have and the less I feel I know. Chinese police research is a project of a lifetime.

Kam C. Wong
Xavier University

Author

Kam C. Wong, JD, PhD, teaches in and has served as chairperson of the Department of Criminal Justice, Xavier University, Cincinnati, Ohio. He is also a Faculty Fellow with the School of Criminal Justice, University at Albany–State University of New York. Professor Wong earned his bachelor's degree and doctor of jurisprudence degree from Indiana University, Bloomington, and his doctorate in criminal justice from the University at Albany–SUNY. He was awarded the Remington Award for Distinguished Work in Law and Social Science. A black-belt karate instructor for over 20 years, Professor Wong served as an Inspector of Police in Hong Kong and was the director of the Chinese Law program at the Chinese University of Hong Kong. He also served as the vice president of the Hong Kong Society of Criminology. He is currently an honorary fellow of the Center of Criminology, Hong Kong University. Professor Wong was on the advisory board of the China Law Center at Yale and has been a visiting scholar at the Scarman Centre, University of Leicester; Institute of Criminology, Cambridge University; Cyberspace Policy Institute, George Washington University; Chinese People's Public Security University; Zhejiang Provincial Police College; Hubei Provincial Police College; Hunan Police Officer College; and Chinese Armed Police Force College.

Professor Wong was an organizer and founding member of the Asian Association of Police Studies, of which he was a past president. He is a board member of the Asia Criminological Society, Pakistan Society of Criminology, Asian School of Management and Technology (India), and South Asian Society of Criminology and Victimology. He is a legal consultant to the Immigration and Refugee Board of Canada on Chinese policing and criminal process issues; a consultant to the United Nations Office on Drugs and Crime; an expert observer at the United Nations Congress on the Prevention of Crime and the Treatment of Offenders; a foreign expert to the PRC Ministry of Public Security; and a consultant to the Hong Kong Police.

Professor's Wong's publications (over 100 articles and book chapters) have appeared in *Police Quarterly*; *Columbia Journal of Asian Law*; *Georgetown Journal of Law & Public Policy*; *Australian and New Zealand Journal of Criminology*; *British Journal of Criminology*; *Asian Journal of Criminology*; *Australian Journal of Law and Society*; *China Perspective* (France); *Crime Review* (Korea); *Herald of Law* (Yugoslavia); *International Journal of the Sociology of Law*; *Criminal Law Bulletin*; *Journal of Information, Law, and Technology*; *Pacific Rim Law & Policy Journal*; *John Marshall Journal of Computer and Information Law*; *Education & Law Journal*; *Asia-Pacific Journal on Human Rights and the Law*; and *Michigan Journal of Race & Law*, among others. Professor Wong was managing editor for *Police Practice and Research: An International Journal*; editor-in-chief of the Working Paper Series of the International Police Executive Symposium; and editor of *Crime & Delinquency, Zhejiang Police College Journal,* and a web-based journal produced by Korea National Police University. He is currently on the editorial board of the *International Journal of Comparative Criminology, Open Journal of Law, Open Journal of Sociology,* and *Asian Policing.* Professor Wong's latest books include *The Impact of USA Patriot Act on American Society: An Evidence Based Assessment* (Nova, 2007); *The Making of USA Patriot Act: Legislation, Implementation, Impact* (China Law Press, 2008); *Chinese Policing: History and Reform* (Peter Lang, 2009); *Cyberspace Governance in China* (Nova, 2011); and *Policing in Hong Kong* (Ashgate, 2011). Professor Wong has been a regular columnist and contributor on law and order issues for *The Standard (Hong Kong), South China Morning Post, Hong Kong Economic Journal, Far Eastern Economic Review,* and *Apple Daily.*

Introduction

1

> Henan province is witnessing a new surge in police reforms....Henan will repeal the more than 60-year-old "public security bureau—sub-bureau—local police station" system of organization.
>
> **Henan Public Security Bureau (2010)**[1]

Crime in China

In 1979, China sought reform through the modernization of four aspects of its economy.[2] The "central kingdom" aggressively pursued an open-door policy to attract foreign investment, expand international trade, build domestic industries, and develop the local economy.[3] The reform process was as successful in creating wealth as in breeding criminality. Historically, the People's Republic of China (PRC) has enjoyed exceptionally low crime rates[4] due to its closed society,[5] static economy,[6] administrative control,[7] family discipline, and individual cultivation. It was Confucius who first observed: "Wishing to govern well in their states, they would first regulate their families. Wishing to regulate their families, they would first cultivate their persons. Wishing to cultivate their persons, they would first rectify their minds."[8] Famously, this philosophy represents the internal, informal, and communal crime control model[9] being challenged by the reform process.

The Arrival of Crime

With the onslaught of a market economy,[10] free trade,[11] open borders,[12] global communication,[13] and a mobile population,[14] the once crime-free society is today afflicted with all kinds of antisocial behaviors and is populated by many new criminal elements.[15] The most troublesome criminal elements of the reform era are drifters (*mang liu*);[16] juvenile offenders (*qing shaonian zuifan*);[17] organized criminals (*you zuzhi zuifan*);[18] secret society members (*heishehui fenzi*);[19] economic criminals (*jingji zuifan*), including white-collar criminals;[20] computer criminals (*jixuanji zuifan*);[21] terrorists (*kongbu fenzi*);[22] cult members (*xiejiao fenzi*);[23] cross-border criminals;[24] and, of late, mass incident mobilizers and organizers.[25] Beyond the increase in criminality, individual grievances (*xinfang*), mass incidents (*qunzhong shijian*),[26] and civil disturbances are on the rise, reflecting deep-seated personal grievances and widespread public discontent.[27]

Since 1978, Chinese economic reform has brought with it crime waves of tsunami proportions.[28] In 1950, the PRC recorded 513,416 crimes, or 9.3 crimes per 10,000 people. The crime rate was reduced to 56,300 crimes (5.9/10,000) and 57,482 crimes (4.2/10,000) in 1951 and 1952, respectively,[29] and it remained low until the reform era.

In 1981, only 3 years into the reform, the crime rate rose to 8.9/10,000 people (see Table 1.1).[30] Since then, the overall crime rate in China has increased. Between 1981 and 2001, robberies grew 18 times, from 22,266 to 352,216.[31] In 2007, there were 80,000 juvenile arrests, up from 30,000 in 1998.[32] (Note that crime rate figures are subject to variation due to central crime fighting campaigns and local underreporting of crime). In 2005, there were 4585 cases of arson (21.3% decrease over the same period the previous year), 543 bombings (17.7% decrease), 11,000 murders (13.6% decrease), 15,000 rapes (5.8% decrease), and 65,000 assaults and batteries (0.1% decrease).[33] The Ministry of Public Security (MPS) has reported more street crimes, with the criminals being younger in age and their victims wealthier, and the nature of the crimes has changed (e.g., car thefts, con games, blackmail, and e-prostitution).[34] Most of the crimes reported were perpetrated by youth,[35] migrants,[36] and gangs.[37] Crimes of major concern are economic,[38] violent, official misconduct,[39] and Internet.[40]

Though not entirely unanticipated and still very low by international standards, the increase in crime in a communist state poses ideological challenges and practical problems.[41] Party leaders from Deng to Jiang have insisted on stability at all costs.[42] Resolute and forceful actions were necessary to protect the rights of the people, maintain the stability of the nation, make possible economic reform under socialism, and strengthen the rule of law.[43] The Chinese Communist Party responded with draconian "Strike Hard" (*yanda*) campaigns.[44] In September 1983, the National People's Congress issued the "Decision of the Standing Committee of the National People's Congress regarding the Severe Punishment of Criminals Who Seriously Endanger Public Security." In 1984, the campaign reduced the number of crimes to 7.48 million, or 5.0/10,000 people. Such campaigns were repeated in 1990, 1996, and 2001[45] and were somewhat successful in temporarily reducing crime.[46] The police resorted to pervasive and invasive comprehensive crime control programs,[47] but such control measures were found to be difficult to maintain and were only marginal in effect.[48]

Causes of Crime

In the 1990s, and in desperation, the Party turned to scientific research for answers; that is, they sought to strengthen the country through science and technology (*kexue qiang guo*). Police studies and criminological research came to the rescue of a besieged nation, promising hope for the disillusioned masses and addressing concerns of anxious investors. Western theories were borrowed and scientific research mounted to understand the nature, prevalence, patterns, causes, and cures for the nation's runaway crime problem.[49]

With regard to the causes of crime and disorder, leading Chinese policing experts pointed to the changing economic structure, deteriorating social conditions, and destruction of traditional cultural values. The rapidly diversifying market was at odds with a centralized police administration, and the country's increasingly diversified and mobile population was making collective communal surveillance difficult. Also, the robust and open market was providing criminal opportunities by attracting potential offenders, creating vulnerable victims, and fostering risky situations. Elements of the traditional static order management system (*jingtai zhian guangli*), such as household registration, were no longer effective at keeping criminals at bay. Too many people were coming and going (*mangliu*, or "blind flowing population"), and they escaped monitoring and close supervision. Fierce market competition tended to attenuate personal relationship, destroy communal bonds, and accentuate interpersonal conflicts.[50] Anomie set in, fostering greed and minimizing the importance of self-discipline.[51]

TABLE 1.1 Crime Rates in China, 1950–2002 (per 100,000 population)

Year	Crime Rate	Year	Crime Rate	Year	Crime Rate
1950	93.0	1972	46.2	1988	77.4
1951	59.1	1973	60.1	1989	181.5
1952	42.3	1974	56.8	1990	200.9
1953	49.7	1975	51.4	1991	209.4
1954	65.1	1976	52.2	1992	138.6
1955	53.0	1977	57.7	1993	140.3
1956	28.7	1978	55.7	1994	142.9
1957	46.1	1979	65.2	1995	144.0
1958	32.0	1980	76.7	1996	135.1
1959	31.3	1981	89.4	1997	135.0
1960	33.6	1982	73.7	1998	159.1
1961	64.1	1983	60.0	1999	178.6
1962	48.2	1984	49.9	2000	287.3
1963	36.3	1985	52.1	2001	349.3
1964	30.5	1986	51.9	2002	337.6
1965	29.8	1987	54.1		

Source: Wong, K.C., *China Report*, 44(3), 213–231, 2008. With permission.

Chinese criminologists have given many reasons for the precipitous and substantial increase in crimes, chief of which are the demise of communist ideology,[52] a decline in personal morality,[53] dilution of social control,[54] creation of criminal opportunities,[55] an increase in economic incentives,[56] and development of a corrupting culture.[57] Foreign observers have attributed Chinese crime and disorder problems to strain[58] and anomie,[59] more generally to social disorganization and political discontentment. Globalization has also played a part.

From the perspective of the Communist Party and Chinese authorities, foreign countries are actively destabilizing the Chinese political economy and corrupting the minds of Chinese youth in order to advance their economic interests (open market), political agenda (liberal ideology), and cultural dominance (corrupt lifestyle). Foreigners (mainly Americans)[60] are blamed for corrupting the Chinese people with their materialism and consumerism, brainwashing Chinese youth with the decadent Western culture (e.g., sex and drugs), encouraging dissidents (Falun Gong), and supporting secessionists (Taiwan, Tibet).[61]

Market reform has facilitated the spread of a countercriminal culture[62] while at the same time undermining traditional values and indigenous culture (e.g., replacing respect for authority and commitment to self-discipline with individualism, egoism, and materialism).[63] Finally, globalization has opened China to cross-border crime due to increasing ease of travel, faster communications, anonymous online identities, and ample criminal opportunities.[64]

The Discovery of Fear

The proliferation of crime led to a fear of crime. Between May and June 1991, the MPS Public Safety Research Institute conducted a second national survey on the nation's feelings of safety.[65] The first survey was conducted in 1988. Both surveys covered 15 provinces, autonomous districts, and direct municipalities (Beijing, Shanghai, Tianjin, Liaoning, Hebei, Shandong, Jiangsu, Zhejiang, Jiangxi, Hubei, Guangdong, Guizhou, Sichuan, Shanxi, and Xinjiang), totaling 150 city-districts, 75 counties, 375 streets (townships), and 750 residential committees. The surveys were sent to 15,000 residents over 16 years old. Out of all of the surveys distributed, 14,951 were returned (99.67%); of those, 14,860 were usable (99.39%).

The survey sought to evaluate the public's feeling of safety (*gongzhong anquan gan*) by analyzing the people's subjective feelings, expectations, attitudes, and evaluations of social safety conditions. Overall, the survey showed that 7% of the respondents felt completely safe, and 62% felt "relatively safe" or "average safe," but a sizable minority (31%) felt "not very safe" or "not safe." The survey was based on two global items of safety.

First, respondents were asked, "With the current public safety condition, what is your personal feeling of safety?" Responses were "safe," 1085 (7%); "relatively safe," 6500 (44%); "average safe," 2660 (18%); "not very safe," 3412 (23%); and "not safe," 1111 (8%). The assessment scoring for feeling of safety was as follows: "safe," 1 point; "relatively safe," 0.75 point; "average safe," 0.5 point; "relatively not safe," 0.25 point; and "not safe," 0 point. The statistical aggregated average safety score was 0.550; compared with the 1988 survey result of 0.473, this represented a slight increase of 0.077 point, or about 14%.

Second, respondents were asked, "What is your assessment of current public safety conditions in the society?" Responses were "very good," 788 (5%); "relatively good," 4755 (32%); "average," 6188 (42%); "relatively bad," 2543 (17%); and "very bad," 52 (4%). The assessment scoring for safety conditions was as follows: "good," 1 point; "relatively good," 0.75 point; "average," 0.5 point; "relatively not good," 0.25 point; and "not good," 0 point. The statistical aggregated average safety conditions score was 0.545; compared with the 1988 survey result of 0.484, this represented a slight increase of 0.061 point, or about 11%.

The Return of the Police

Confronted with rising crime, spreading disorder, decreasing safety, and increasing fear, the PRC adopted draconian measures, such as capital punishment,[66] and mounted mass campaigns ("Strike Hard" campaigns, from 1983 to 1987 and in 1996, 2001, 2005, 2009,[67] and 2010[68])[69] to pacify the nation.[70] This was at the urging of Deng Xiaoping, the master engineer of all reform policies.[71] It was Deng who said, famously: "We should not leave criminals fearless. This is a people's dictatorship, and here we protect the safety of the majority. This is humanitarianism."[72]

The police were resurrected from the ashes of the Cultural Revolution[73] to provide order, security, and stability.[74] Since then, the police have struggled to find their rightful place and proper role in a rapidly changing[75] and fast-moving Chinese political economy.[76,77] This is how Ren Yinxun at the MPS, Fourth Research Institute, summed up the situation and the challenges confronted by the MPS in 1999, which remains very much relevant today:

> Public security work…seeks to protect the nation's political stability and social order with all its might, providing a favorable public order environment for economic development.

> Since the reform, the public security agency is faced with an all-new social environment. The social structure has substantially changed; many kinds of collective ownership co-exist, business enterprises are increasingly separated from government ownership and control, there is great mobility with people and property, social life has become more and more complex and diverse, every aspect of the original management system is substantially weakened.

The mindset and ideas of society have radically changed; social values and standards have become diversified, and people's attitudes towards democracy and law have increased by the day, resulting in heightened expectations for police work. The society's public order situation has become more complex; all kinds of social evils have manifested themselves, public security management responsibilities have become more complex and burdensome, there is a continuous increase in crime, many kinds of new criminality have surfaced, and crimes and criminals have become more violent, intelligent, and regionalized. Black society crimes proliferate, and serious economic crimes are running amok.

The new social environment is posing serious and severe challenges to the traditional police work style. Public security must adapt to the needs of such new situations to create a new and appropriate operating system.[78]

    This book investigates police reform in China in the face of the challenges (*wei*) and opportunities (*ji*)[79] offered up by the reform process. Particularly, this book documents how the PRC political leaders and police managers are dealing with various political, social, legal, and other issues confronting the public security bureaus (PSBs) as a whole, including an erosion of ideology, abuse of powers,[80] corruption in office,[81] a loss of legitimacy, and a lack of resources, among others.

    We begin our discussion with a brief history of police reform in China. In a country with a long history and lasting memory, knowing the past is necessary to understand the present, especially police reform. The message here is that history matters.[82] This discussion is followed by an examination of political leadership and policing reform. China is still very much a one-party state. At the epicenter of police reform is the president of the state, secretary of the Party, and premier of the country; thus, it is important to explore the governing philosophy and management style of President Hu Jintao and Premier Wen Jiabao's (Hu–Wen) administration for evidence of the direction and content of today's police reform. The message here is that political leadership counts. The text then explores some of the more salient issues to be investigated in this book.[83] Chinese police, reformers, and officers alike have major concerns and reservations about the goals, processes, and sustainability of police reform that have rarely been expressed to outsiders.

    The next section addresses the impact of police reform on the public and police. First it looks into the impact of reform on police–public relationships by reporting on findings of a 1999 survey on police–public relationships. The survey found that police–public relationships are not as close as they should be ideologically (e.g., mass line policing, "from the mass to the mass") and certainly not as good as they had been under Mao (the spirit of Lei Feng) or as good as the Hu–Wen administration would wish (e.g., people-first policing). Such surveys and findings provide much food for thought when examining where the country has been and mapping where it should be headed for police reform. The discussion then looks at the impact of police reform on police working conditions and front-line officers. The point here is that police reform has an impact on and implications for China's police officers.

History

Since 1978, the public security apparatus has changed its role and functions, core values, leadership, organization structure and processes, management philosophy, and operational procedures and practices.[84]

Change in Police Role and Mission

Traditionally, the primary missions of the police in the West have been law enforcement, order maintenance, and public service. In mid-century China, Mao Tse-tung added a political dimension to this conventional idea of policing.[85] Following Marx, he observed that the police were a political instrument of the state employed to suppress and oppress the enemy class. In the Mao era, the public security bureaus (PSBs) fulfilled dual political and social roles—that is, suppressing the class enemies (landlords, capitalists, reactionaries, and counterrevolutionaries) and serving the people. But, under Deng Xiaoping, the role, mission, and function of the PSBs have changed.

The PSBs Have Become Less Concerned with Political Matters and More Involved with Law Enforcement and Order Maintenance Activities

The mission statement of the Ministry of Public Security is most revealing with regard to the new roles and responsibilities of the PSBs:

> Take charge of and administer public security according to law; guard against and deal with criminal activities; take charge of and manage road traffic, exit and entry formalities, and fire-fighting; take charge of People's Armed Police Force, border defense, and internal security; be responsible for education, training, and management of public security officials and policemen.[86]

The mission statement clearly sets law and order as the primary duties of police. It limits the political function of police to enforcing internal security laws (e.g., the investigation of counterrevolutionaries). The newly established Ministry of State Security has assumed much of the sensitive political work involved with national security. The People's Armed Police (*Renmin wuzhuang jingcha budui*) have been made responsible for curbing political disorders or civil disturbances, while the people's police (*minjing*) are solely responsible for maintaining law and order. This is a far cry from the 1950s when the PSBs were preoccupied with purging internal political threats, real or imagined. The very first public security organization law, the Police Act of 1957, set forth the basic missions of the people's police (*minjing*).[87] They included: (1) suppressing counterrevolutionaries, (2) preventing the destructive activity of criminal elements, (3) preserving public security and social order, (4) protecting public property and citizens' rights and interests, (5) defending the people's democracy, and (6) safeguarding the socioeconomic construction. The tone and texture of the Police Act of 1957 were unmistakably belligerent, with its "suppressing counterrevolutionaries" and "defending the people's democracy."

The role and function of police work have in large part been defined by Party ideology, public expectations, and community needs. The changed nature of police work can be gauged from police responses to the public's calls for assistance. In 1993, Shanghai's PSB introduced an emergency 110 telephone service.[88] In 2 months, from May 1 to June 30, the station received a total of 39,000 calls, of which 4700 (12%) were actually calls for assistance. Of these calls, 526 (11.2%) were criminal cases, 2550 (54.3%) were order maintenance cases, 1176 (25.1%) were road traffic cases, 440 (9.4%) were for emergency services, and the rest were unclassified. In essence, the police were involved with order maintenance work over 50% of the time.[89]

The PSBs Are Less Concerned with Providing Service and More Focused on Controlling Crime

Economic reform caused an explosion in criminality in China, and the country's crime problem was getting out of hand, requiring swift and decisive countermeasures.[90] Concerns about crime were raised as early as 1978 at a PSB work meeting (*zhian gongzuo huiyi*) held in Beijing. The participants at the meeting observed that the most urgent public security task facing the country was to "resolutely strike at criminal elements who engage in destructive activities" (*jianjue daji xingshi fanzui fenzi de pohuai huodong*). The targets were murderers, arsonists, robbers, rapists, thieves, fraud perpetrators, hooligan gangs, and other bad elements bent on seriously damaging society (*yanzhong pohuai shehui zhixu de huaifenzi*). Participants also recognized the need for an overall plan (*tongchou*) to educate and reform these offenders. Security administration must be institutionalized, beginning with educating young people about the law by introducing legal education to primary and middle schools, the Communist Youth League (*Gongqingtuan*), and Young Pioneers (*Shaoxiandui*). The conference also requested that PSB administrative work (*zhian guanli qunzhong gongzuo*) be stepped up, especially consolidation of the Public Security Committee (*Zhian baowei weiyuanhui*). The Deputy Minister of Public Security delivered a report on behalf of the Minister of Public Security *dangzu* (leading Party group) that promised comprehensive strengthening of public security regulation enforcement and establishment of a better regulated society (*Quanmian jiaqiang zhian guanli gongzuo, wei chuangzao gengjia lianghao de shehui zhixu er fendou*).

More significantly, the Chinese people were becoming worried and the political leaders disturbed.[91] People saw crime as a threat to their traditional way of life. The political leaders feared that runaway crime would jeopardize the nascent reform process. If allowed to persist, the crime problem might cast doubts on the ability of the political leaders and the credibility of the Chinese Communist Party to lead the country. The Minister of Public Security, Tao Siju, made reducing the crime rate one of the top public security priorities of 1994.[92] He blamed the rising crime rate on economic reform, which was bringing about unprecedented social changes. Economic reform had allowed new classes to emerge in society, which led to tension and conflict between groups—for example, the haves and have-nots. The old, comprehensive social control system—public security administration and control, household registration and monitoring, public order regulations and criminal law punishments, labor reform and education—was no longer adequate to address new problems such as mass incidents, but a new system of social regulation and control had yet to be established. Changes in the economic system and in cultural values had affected social morality and individual conduct; for example, there was a lack of consensus over "right" and "wrong." The PSBs were not able to put the new crime situation and social turmoil in a proper, balanced perspective. In the 1950s, security forces dealt with relatively few crimes due to a lack of population mobility and few economic opportunities, but current security forces were not prepared to deal with the new wave of crime and social problems.

Public Security Is Less Concerned with Serving the People in General and More Committed to Meeting the Needs of Economic Development

The overriding mission of public security in the post-Deng reform era is to maintain a stable social and political environment in which economic reform can develop and prosper. This means providing secure and stable social, political, and business environments for investors and entrepreneurs. More importantly, investors and entrepreneurs must be reassured that their property rights and personal safety are truly respected by the people and adequately protected by law. In practice, this requires public security to devote substantial time, energy, and effort to resolve emerging conflicts, prevent new opportunities for crime, and deter potential workplace violence. In concrete terms, this means: (1) resolving conflicts between bosses (business owners and factory managers) and the working people, and (2) protecting enterprises' property and ensuring the safety of their managers. The Ministry of Public Security called for better protection of business bosses and published a circular on taking practical and effective measures to protect the personal safety of enterprise leaders.[93]

The role of public security with regard to enterprise transformation has been characterized as conflict resolution and order maintenance. In the case of the Santai (Sichuan Province) PSB, this meant: (1) dealing with disruptive and destructive acts of disgruntled employees, such as those who have a vested interest in maintaining the old system; (2) dealing with the problems of those who have fallen victim to changes (e.g., have been dismissed, have failed to get hired, are awaiting employment); (3) dealing with internal thefts; and (4) providing protection for factory managers and enterprise property.[94]

Under the leadership of President Jiang and now Hu, both engineers by professional training and bureaucratic administrators by vocation, the MPS has systematically engineered a comprehensive police reform process through a philosophy shift, spiritual education, system overhaul, organizational restructuring, cultural regeneration, technology infusion, law reform, scientific management, and evidence-based policing,

Police Reform History

The reform process for public security in China has happened in stages (1979 to 1985, 1986 to 1995, and 1996 to now). Police reform has been driven by social, political, economic, and cultural forces, punctuated by such drastic events as the Tiananmen incident of June 4, 1989,[95] and dominated by key personalities: Deng[96] ("two hands") vs. Jiang[97] ("Three Represents") vs. Hu[98] ("harmonious society").

First Stage (1979 to 1985)

During this period, public security, as was true for other judicial legal organs (*shifa jiguan*), began to make a comeback after a total breakdown during the Cultural Revolution. There were three primary tasks to reestablish public security as a functional, legitimate, and respected institution. First, public security had to reestablish itself as a legitimate institution and functional agency,[99] both organizationally and operationally. Second, public security had to redefine its role and functions in the new era, both politically and socially. Third, public security had to come to terms with the radical changes in China, both economically and culturally.[100] Modifying the organization and operational styles of the police was necessary to deal with ongoing reform changes.[101] Public security adjusted by doing more, and doing more of the same; for example, it reinstated the age-old, campaign-style mobilization (*yanda*) to fight crime[102] and reinforced traditional police virtues (Lei Feng spirit) to promote police integrity.[103] In doing so, the public security leadership was being more ideological than practical and more reactive than proactive. They were not being reflective, still less critical. There was also a widening gap between police strategy and social reality, public expectations, and police performance.

Second Stage (1986 to 1995)

During this time, public security actively forged a new institutional identity as a service organization and revisited its traditional work style (e.g., as revolutionary vanguards).[104] China was moving away from struggling against class enemies toward building up a market economy, from fighting enemies to regulating economic offenders, with the use of law and by establishing a variety of regulatory systems.[105] In the process, public security reinvented itself "as a force to safeguard and promote," and Deng declared that the "Four Modernizations" (agriculture, industry, defense, and science and technology) would take precedence over class struggle.[106] This movement required radical changes to public security's philosophy, organization, and process.[107]

Third Stage (1996 to Now)

This stage has been marked[108] with promulgation of the PRC Police Law of 1995 on February 28, 1995.[109] The Police Law was intended to institutionalize the organization structure, regularize operational procedures, and legalize enforcement powers of public security, against the backdrop of a maturing socialist legal system. The ultimate objective of the new Police Law was to realize the Chinese Communist Party's explicit policy goal to "govern the police by law" (*yifa zhijing*), with a view toward establishing a modern and professional (competent, qualified, effective, efficient, and accountable) police force able to protect state security, maintain public order, secure social stability, and promote economic development.[110]

The Police Law effectively ended a 38-year quest for a new police law to replace the outdated Police Act of 1957. It became the fundamental law (*jiben fa*) of police reform and was augmented with complementary laws and regulations. First, the "Public Security Organ Inspection Regulations" ("*Gongan jiguan ducha tiaoli*") provided for the internal supervision and inspection of police activities and operations.[111] Second, on July 22, 1995, the Ministry of Public Security promulgated Measures regarding the Reward of Police by Public Security Organs (*Gongan jiguan renmin jingcha jiangli banfa*); these measures allowed individual (*geren*) and collective (*jiti*) commendations (*jiajiang*) to be approved (*shenpi*) by public security organs at the county level or above or by the people's police organ in charge.[112] Third, on January 8, 1996, the PRC State Council adopted the "Regulations of the People's Republic of China Governing the Use of Weapons by the People's Police" ("*Renmin jingcha shiyong jingxie he wuqi tiaoli*"),[113] which for the first time legislated against the abusive use of guns and made provisions for their proper use. The Police Law addressed ongoing concerns, such as police abuse of power, and dealt with such emerging issues as the fiscal integrity of the police.

In 1997, the Ministry of Public Security published "Comments regarding Establishing and Perfecting a Public Security Law and Regulation System" ("*Guanyu jianli ji yuanshan gongan fagui tixi de yijian*"). The comments suggested that, by 1999, a comprehensive system (*situng*) of law (*falu*), regulations (*fagui*), notices (*tonggao*), and decisions (*jueding*), with various degrees of specificity and permanency, would be in place to guide, regulate, and control police work. The police legal system now encompassed constitutional law, state law, administrative rule, departmental regulations, local laws, and regulations.

In terms of police accountability by law, from 1989 to 1999 at least 29 public security offices and bureaus had developed internal legal supervision regulations and case responsibility guidelines. In June 1999, for example, to fortify police accountability, the MPS issued its "Decision regarding Wrongdoing in the Enforcement of Law by Public Security Agencies and Public Security Officers" ("*Gongan jiguan he gongan jiguan renmin jingcha zhifa guo cuo zeren zhuijiu guiding*"). Currently, about half of the national public security organs have established some form of in-house legal organ (*fazhi jikou*) to monitor police legality.

With the reform framework securely in place, this stage has witnessed the consolidation of various public security reform efforts and a deepening of the change process. At the 2001 national conference for public security department heads held in Beijing, the Minister of Public Security, Jia Chunwang, observed: "Concerning public security management work, we launched a number of reform measures. With 'three items of education' as the main focus, we aggressively pushed for public security *institutional* reform (*gongan duiwu jianshe*)." According to political scientist Bruce Dilley, institutionalization reform means:

> So, political institutionalization has both efficacy-enhancing and normatively cohering elements that must obtain in order for a given feature to be institutionalized. By way of negative example, the mass round-ups involved in the Chinese regime's frequent recourse to "Strike Hard" anticrime campaigns have been remarkably "effective" in yielding more convictions, but the violations of due process that the campaigns involve have flatly contradicted the state's commitment to developing the rule of law.[114]

Throughout the reform process, everyone—political leaders, policymakers, and citizens—agreed[115] that the ultimate objective of the police reform was to set up functional and accountable police management and operations to standardize law enforcement (*zhifa zhiqing guifan tixi*). In order to do so, the police needed to establish a comprehensive and dependable legal system with public participation, and they needed to receive adequate resources to perform their jobs. It was agreed that the police should be held strictly accountable to the law and that their powers should be regulated by law and fall under the guidelines of the constitution. Discretion should be clearly guided by rules. Police should be professional and subject to both internal discipline[116] and external supervision.[117] In 2003, newly minted Minister of Public Security Zhou Yongkan issued the "Five Prohibitions" against using guns in violation of regulations, drinking while carrying guns, drunk driving, drinking on duty, and gambling.[118] In 2010, MPS Vice Minister Liu Jinguo implemented strict supervision of police departments at province and city levels.[119]

In February 8, 2009, Li Qiaoming, 24, was beaten to death by three fellow inmates during a game of "hide-and-seek" in southwestern Yunnan Province. In April, the MPS and Supreme People's Procuratorate (SPP) launched a 5-month campaign to ensure proper management of detention centers. On February 26, 2010, the MPS issued further guidelines banning law enforcement personnel from seizing or confiscating detainees' property; protecting detainees against insult, corporal punishment, or maltreatment; and protecting their right to call and meet friends or relatives.[120] From 2005 to June 2009, 1586 police and other government officials were punished by the Supreme People's Procuratorate for abuse of powers, including illegal search, coerced confessions, torture, and abusing detainees.[121]

Reform and Police Functions[122]

Police functions and organization have changed since the days of Mao. Although the police in a communist state still act as an instrument of the state to protect the Party, secure the nation, and suppress the enemies, their primary roles during this period of reform are to protect economic development and to serve the needs of the people. The best way to study how the roles and functions of the Chinese police are changing is to look at how they have changed over time with regard to the central Ministry of Public Security vs. local police posts. The MPS is driven by policy and politics, whereas local police post must adapt to their citizens' needs and public expectations. This doctrine is called *lifa wei gong, zhifa weimin* ("law is made for the public, law enforcement is for the people"). We cannot begin to understand police reform in China without consulting policy from the top and addressing the grassroots reality, with places, people, events, and incidents in the mix.

Changing Ministry of Public Security Functions

All told, we can identify five significant changes to police functions and responsibilities during the first 30 years of reform:

1. In 1982, the MPS assumed all domestic guarding and security functions from the People's Liberation Army (PLA).
2. In 1983, the MPS divested its national security functions, such as counterintelligence, to the Ministry of State Security.
3. In 1983, the MPS transferred its labor reform functions to the Ministry of Justice.
4. In 1987, the MPS assumed national traffic administration functions.
5. In 1995, the MPS relinquished internal security duties to the People's Armed Police, who report directly to the Central Military Commission.

Changing Local Police Post Functions[123]

Throughout history, police posts in China have assumed various roles and functions. On July 7, 1951, the MPS implemented the "Provisional Regulations on Urban Household Management," which were the first managements regulations relating to urban household registration and promised to secure social order and protect the people's safety. On December 31, 1954, the National People's Congress approved regulations regarding the organization of public security police posts. These regulations charged the police posts with a broad range of duties and responsibilities, including protecting the social order; suppressing counterrevolutionaries; preventing crime and deterring criminals; supervising counterrevolutionaries; administering household registration; managing special businesses, such as theaters and hotels, and dangerous goods, such as explosives; securing crime scenes and investigating crimes; and educating citizens so they maintain a high revolutionary spirit, obey the law, follow public regulations, and respect social morality. In essence, the police post became an all-purpose police service unit with a focus on household management. On June 22, 1955, the State Council released "State Council Guidelines regarding Establishment of a Permanent Household Registration System," thereby establishing a nationwide household registration system for both urban and rural citizens.

In 1962, the MPS published regulations pertaining to public security police posts. The regulations empowered the police post to actively engage in counterrevolutionary investigations and social intelligence gathering. For the first time, the police post was given criminal investigation authority and responsibility, but its main duty was still in household management. Deng's reform brought further changes to the roles and functions of the police posts. Soon after the reform began, the MPS issued an opinion on the reform of public security police posts. The published notice pointed out that, "Police post work should be focused on security management, with household management as a foundation. This changes from the past police work focus of having household management as the main function." For the first time, the work of police posts had shifted from household management as an end (e.g., fixed population) to household management as a tool for securing the public order. This changed mission was reinforced in the 1989 MPS opinion regarding questions posed by public security post reform. It specifically provided that, "Maintaining social order within the jurisdictional area, securing peace and order, is the central task of a police post. This includes activities associated with household management in service of the central mission." Henceforth, police posts were granted comprehensive powers to attack, manage, and educate the community to fight crime and maintain order. Increasingly, however, fighting crime became the main focus, at the expense of crime prevention or order maintenance functions.

In 1997, the MPS, observing the weakening of the crime prevention and household management functions, published an essay written by then-Minister of Public Security Tao, "A Discussion on Strengthening of Public Security Police Post Work," pointing out that foundational work, such as household management and crime prevention measures, was still important. Also in 1997, the MPS organized a nationwide public security post meeting in Suzhou. The meeting called for establishing an accountability system focused on establishing lower crime rates, maintaining the social order, and satisfying the public as standards of police post performance review. It aimed to replace the police posts' primary goal of solving crime with the goals of crime prevention and household management. Finally, the MPS also conducted a national criminal investigation work conference in Shijiazhuan City, Hebei Province, in 1997. The conference made it clear that criminal investigation was a special function of the criminal investigation police, not police posts. Based on discussions at these conferences, a clear picture of police post functions emerged: Police posts should be responsible for preventing crime, maintaining order, and providing services by conducting community policing and executing comprehensive management.[124]

The 20th National Public Security Conference held in 2003 articulated the future vision and mission of public security work and put the focus of police reform on building a strong base of policing fundamentals, such as a basic infrastructure, basic skills, and basic attitudes. Improvement of county-level police capacity and services became the spearhead of reform. In time, the Communist Party of China (CPC) "Resolution to Further Strengthen and Improve Public Security Work" (Central Issue [2003] #13) ("*Zhonggong zhongyang guanyu jin yi bu jiaqiang he gaijin gongan gongzuo de jueding*" (*Zhongfa* [2003] 13 *hao*)) established the police post as a comprehensive crime fighting, order maintenance, and social service operational unit. Speaking at the conference, MPS Minster Zhou Yongkan reinforced the idea that police posts had the following functions: (1) provide national security and maintain order through such activities as intelligence gathering to forestall incipient mass incidents; (2) provide emergency response, such as riot control; and (3) perform social service and public welfare duties.

Politics

Politics and Policing

The political nature of law and policing has been long observed by theorists[125] and repeatedly demonstrated with empirical evidence.[126] In China, the symbiotic relationship between Communist political ideology and policing has been unabashedly recognized; police are first and foremost political agents of the ruling class. Mao Tse-tung, the founding father of the PRC, remarked on the eve of its formation: "The state apparatus, including the army, the police, and the courts, is the instrument by which one class oppresses another. It is an instrument for the oppression of antagonistic classes; it is violence and not benevolence."[127] More recently, that the Party and its politics are in control has been openly acknowledged to be a defining and enduring characteristic of PRC police.[128]

In Imperial China, the powers of government emanated from the top, radiating from the center and flowing from the emperor. In the contemporary PRC, citizens are expected to follow Party leadership and embrace the concept of a democratic dictatorship.[129] To study PRC police reform, then, it is important to begin with an examination of the Communist Party of China leadership, especially who they are and what they stand for.[130]

The most important events that have had an impact on police reform and development in China are the 16th National Congress of the Communist Party of China held in 2002 and the 10th National People's Congress in 2003. These meetings (*lian hui*) changed the political leadership and established a new policy agenda for China. Developing an understanding of this leadership change and its implications on police philosophy, policy, and practice is the focus of this section.[131]

The 16th National Congress of the Communist Party of China overhauled China's top leadership, including the Central Committee, the Politburo, the Standing Committee of the Politburo,[132] the secretariat, and the Communist Party's Central Military Commission. This meeting is particularly significant because it gave rise to a whole new generation of CPC leaders and sidelined the remaining old guards.[133] Unlike the old guards, who had earned their right to rule China through armed revolutions and political struggles, these new leaders secured their authority to govern by demonstrating technical competence, professional achievements,[134] Party loyalty, and ideological correctness.[135]

Under the leadership of Hu Jintao, the "fourth generation" of political leadership has set a new course for China.[136] The police have been very much affected; thus, we must examine what the new leadership stood for and determine the likely impact and possible influence on police reform and development.[137] In order to do so, we must ask the following questions: What are the dreams and aspirations of this new leadership—that is, what political philosophy do they espouse and what social policy do they promote? What power base did the new leadership inherit? What social conditions and political issues have confronted these leaders? Put more succinctly, what is their agenda, what is their power base, and what problems do they have to deal with in office?

Background, Vision, and Mission of the "Fourth Generation"

Every Chinese leader (Mao, Deng, Jiang, Hu) has professed to follow the Communist ideology and adhere to the Party line; however, each of them has held a different understanding of what Party ideology entails and portends—from Mao's "continuous revolution" to Deng's "socialism with Chinese characteristics" to Jiang's "Three Represents"[138] to Hu's "scientific development perspective." The way the "fourth generation" of PRC leadership under Hu Jintao governs China is in sharp contrast with the "third generation" PRC leadership under the stewardship of Jiang Zemin.[139] More specifically, Jiang and Hu differ from each other in personal experience and professional background, ideological stance and philosophical outlook, leadership style, and management practice in significant ways.[140] These differences are increasingly demonstrated in the Party line and government policy affecting the police.

Some words of warning about our political analysis before we begin to map out the influences of successive political leadership. It is not suggested here that the personal and philosophical differences between Jiang and Hu would be reflected immediately and completely in the Party line or government policy. Even strong leaders such as Mao and effective politicians such as Deng have had to come to terms with the entrenched cultural matrix, fragile social relationships, and complex Communist political machine before they could translate their personal vision into state action.[141] Studying the political leadership's personal fiefdoms and ideological infighting has been a favorite pasttime of China watchers and makes a respectable subdiscipline of China studies. In terms of fiefdoms, five members of the Standing Committee of the Politburo are clearly Jiang Zemin's protégés. In terms of infighting, in spite of Hu and Wen's impeccable credentials and amicable personalities as defenders of the deprived and oppressed, the left wing members of the Party, old and new, have still clamored for more.[142]

Also, it is difficult to predict with any degree of certainty how the Hu–Wen administration is likely to impact the direction and conduct of public security reform, particularly at the local level and on operational issues.[143] Though theoretically Hu and Wen hold absolute power as President of State/Secretary of the Party and Prime Minister/Head of State Council, their ultimate authority over national policy and local administration in a Communist regime with a factional political ethos and entrenched bureaucratic culture will be tested and can only be speculated upon.[144] Their impact on China Party politics, state policy, and police administration will be determined by a number of factors, including ideological and philosophical resonance, personal leadership (professional experience and achievements), organization skills, Party and military alliances, Jiang's residual influence and opposition, bureaucratic resistance, local autonomy, and public support and dissent. Thus, although Hu and Wen are well liked and have great support within the ranks of the National People's Congress (e.g., Hu was voted in overwhelmingly), the Standing Committee of the Politburo, the State Council, and the Ministries are still manned by many of Jiang's supporters (e.g., Zhou Yongkang, a Standing Committee member of the Political Bureau).

Although Hu is the Party Secretary and leads the Standing Committee of the Politburo, most of the Politburo members (17 out of 25) and most members of its Standing Committee (5 out of 9—Wu Bangguo, Jia Qinglin, Zeng Qinghong, Huang Ju, and Li Changchun) are still Jiang's associates. With the exception of Wen Jiaobao, all of the members of the Standing Committee of the Politburo are engineers. While Hu has good control over the National People's Congress, which is staffed with his provincial and Communist Youth League appointees, who are primarily young and educated, the State Council, especially its Standing Committee, is very much controlled by Jiang. For example, Huang Ju, former Party chief of Shanghai (1994–2002), replaced Li Lanqing as First Vice Premier, and Hua Jianmin, Jiang's protégé, acted as the Secretary General of the State Council. Within the Ministries, Jiang has many die-hard supporters. Zhou Yongkang, the Ministry of Public Security and head of the Party's Central Commission for Political and Legal Affairs, gained Li Peng and Jiang's attention and trust for his crackdown on Falun Gong.

The new "fourth generation" PRC leadership was described by Zong Hairen,[145] a Party insider, as:

> …determined modernizers, intent on integrating China's economy with the world and on maintaining good relations with the United States. They are mostly competent managers, with wide experience in China's complex Party–state bureaucracy, pragmatic technocrats

who are capable of keeping order and promoting development in the world's most populous country. Some of them are willing to allow a degree of political competition with the CCP and to trust the Chinese press and television with more freedom to criticize the performance of low- and mid-level officials.[146]

President Hu rose through the ranks as a dutiful, if compliant, member of the Communist Party. He worked in some of the poorest areas in China (e.g., Guizhou and Tibet) before he came to Beijing. Hu is a prodigious reformer. He works slowly, carefully, methodically, and systematically. He is not a charismatic leaders nor radical ideolog. He is a seasoned politician who knows how to court associations, muster support, and build consensus,[147] and he is an experienced mandarin who knows how to make bureaucracy work.

Premier Wen Jiabao, who has been responsible for running the PRC government since 2003, is a Zhou Enlai type of popular politician.[148] Wen is a consummate politician and experienced administrator. Wen worked as the chief of staff for Hu Yaobang, Zhao Ziyang, and Jiang Zemin. To give some idea of his political skills, he survived the downfall of Zhao and came away from the 1989 Tiananmen incident relatively unscathed. Administratively, he supervised the nation's agricultural affairs and has overseen the reform of the financial and banking systems. One of his defining moments as the premier was his coordination of the anti-flood campaign in 1998, which earned him much praise. The following description of Wen is both revealing and refreshing:

> Wen is a conscientious man with a calm and controlled voice preferring to appear close to the people, particularly those left behind by growth; he is strengthened by his experience of China's poor regions, particularly Gansu; and he is well-liked beyond official circles. But it is significant that he is popular too within these circles! And the vote he won at the NPC at the time of his election as head of government on March 16th tends to demonstrate this; in fact, he registered an even higher level of support than had his predecessor (99.35% as against 98%), whose trenchant and sometimes authoritarian character later attracted much ill-feeling.[149]

Hu–Wen Political Agenda

Both Hu and Wen have an appealing personal style and populist agenda,[150] and the Hu–Wen leadership stands for more balanced (coordinated and integrated) economic,[151] social, and geographic development.[152] In 2003, the Central Committee of the Communist Party of China published a decision on issues regarding the improvement of the socialist market economic system, which called for (1) coordinated development of various regions, (2) development of joint-stock companies and a mixed economy, and (3) standardization and protection of property rights. Particularly, it identified the need to coordinate the development of urban and rural areas, development of different regions, development of the economy and society, harmonious development of man and nature, and domestic development and opening up to the outside world. Hu and Wen have also sought more government accountability with transparency and procedural justice.[153] Above all else, they have stood for achieving stable reform in China by institutionalizing the political and administrative processes through law and with education.

In 2004, the Third Plenary Session of the 16th Central Committee of the Communist Party of China passed a resolution defining the tasks ahead. Of particular interest to police administrators was the call for: (1) narrowing the gap between urban and rural areas, rich and poor; (2) promoting coordinated development of different regions; (3) establishing a mechanism to promote sustainable social and economic development; and (4) active promotion of political system reform. In fact, Wen said that, "Without successful political restructuring, there would be no successful economic reform."[154]

In terms of political reform, the first order of business for the Hu–Wen administration was to establish a scientific and democratic decision-making mechanism, including a group decision-making system and consultations with experts and professionals. The second was to prompt the government to administer the country in line with the law, build a clean and honest government, and pursue the appropriate combination of government power and responsibility. The third goal was to place the government under the scrutiny of every corner of society, including supervision from the National People's Congress and the Chinese People's Political Consultative Conference. Governments must solicit and listen to opinions and views from the general public.[155]

If asked, the Hu–Wen administration would say that it would like to be judged by its performance and achievements in developing the interior; lessening the burden on farmers; making the government accountable through transparency, rule of law, and constitutional supervision; making the government more relevant to the lives of its people; redefining government (e.g., smaller, not as powerful); and reorienting the government's focus (i.e., put people first).[156]

Based on political discourse, initiatives, and signals communicated by the new leaders and their think tanks, Dr. Cheng Li[157] offered six likely future political reforms under the Hu–Wen administration:

1. Intraparty democracy will be more effectively institutionalized.
2. The division between decision making and policy implementation and supervision will be better defined.
3. Provincial governments will have more say in the decision-making process.
4. The law will be more clearly defined and implemented, as some new leaders have received formal training in law and the social sciences.
5. The new leaders will better define the relationships among the state, Party, and military.
6. Both the CCP's legitimacy and transparency will continue to improve.

Inherited Political, Social, and Cultural Problems

The "fourth generation" leadership of Hu and Wen inherited a distinctive set of political, economic, social, and cultural problems to deal with. As observed by noted China watcher Cheng Li:

> China's new leaders have to deal with a long list of daunting economic and socio-political challenges: economic disparity, the negative impact (especially on Chinese farmers) of China's entry into the WTO, urban unemployment, rampant official corruption, ethnic tensions, large-scale industrial accidents and environmental disasters. None of these problems has an easy solution.[158]

In the end, the two biggest challenges to the Hu–Wen administration, after they have consolidated their power, are corruption in high places and inequality at the grassroots.[159]

With regard to policing, the primary problems are political legitimacy[160] and ruling capacity (*zhizheng nengli*). In terms of legitimacy, broad segments of Chinese people are clamoring for political freedom and civil liberties, two things that define a modern society and progressive democracy.[161] With regard to governance, the central government has encountered difficulties in reining in local official corruption, gang collusion, and mass incidents. The common refrain is that, "Policies are coming from the top and responding strategies from the bottom."

Leadership Footprints[162]

A profile of the philosophy and style of the Hu–Wen administration is necessary to studying the PRC police reform agenda, problems, and process.

Harmonious Society

In October of 2006, the Sixth Plenum of the 16th Central Committee of the Communist Party of China passed a resolution that addressed major issues concerning the building of a socialist harmonious society. Harmonious society (*héxié shèhuì*, 和谐社会) is a major policy initiative of President Hu.[163] The initiative shifts the nation's focus from encouraging economic growth to suppressing social ills, including high crime rates, increasing number of divorces, disparity of wealth, and a rising number of mass incidents. Ostensibly, a harmonious society forestalls political instability, social disorder, economic disruption, and personal conflict, promising a more balanced and sustainable development. Its ultimate objective is to return China to a Confucius past where people respect each other and everyone works together for the collective good. To sum up the harmonious society doctrine:

> The building of a "socialist harmonious society" is the rubric under which the Hu Jintao leadership has chosen to advance its particular social, economic, and political vision for China. Observers have suggested that, to a large degree, the drive to build a harmonious society is a response to growing disaffection among Chinese people increasingly frustrated by the inequities that have arisen with rapid GDP growth. The ruling Communist Party of China (CPC) has identified the disparities that gape across region and class as the source of potentially destabilizing civil unrest, which may in turn threaten the nation's continued development and Party control. The harmonious society doctrine aims to diffuse any volatile trends by way of "people-centered reform," whereby the fruits of development are more equitably shared.[164]

Harmonious society doctrine affects Chinese policing in a number of ways, from cleaning up corruption to embracing the rule of law, as highlighted in a number of published articles. Wu Dahu and Wang Fei[165] discussed the issue of applying the harmonious society doctrine to the treatment of criminals and victims. Elsewhere, it has been suggested that a harmonious society as envisioned by President Hu requires "democracy, the rule of law, equity, justice, sincerity, amity, and vitality."[166] In their article, Dahu and Fei addressed when and how we punish in a harmonious society. Harmonious society requires fidelity to the law, but what kind of punishment should the law provide? The answer hinges on the purpose of punishment in a harmonious society: Should punishment fit the crime? Should punishment be forward looking (deterrent) or backward looking (retribution)? Should punishment protect the society or vindicate the victim? Should punishment hinge on protecting the rights of the defendant or the rights of victims? Harmonious society doctrine has radically shifted the paradigm of criminal law, as shown in Table 1.2.

TABLE 1.2 Criminal Paradigm of the Harmonious Society Doctrine

Aspect	Under Deng Xiaoping	Under Hu Jintao
Purpose	Stability for reform	Harmony for sustained development
Philosophy	Reform and deterrence	Vindication and reintegration
Function	Preventive	Remedial
Perspective	Forward looking	Forward looking
Foundation	Public interest	Human rights
Entitlement	Collective (majority)	Individual (minority)
Subject	Criminal	Victim

Meritocracy in Policing

A significant issue of the Hu–Wen administration is meritocracy. Meritocracy in policing calls for an open and transparent recruitment process. Personnel management in the socialist system, particularly the police, is state controlled, government managed, and centrally planned. The reform has transitioned the personnel management system from a central planning dictate by public policy to one that is market driven and based on economic principles. Meritocracy in policing allows open competition for jobs; in other words, let the best candidate win. It is what one knows (competence) and not whom one knows (*guanxi*) that secures a job or a promotion, which represents a break from the past. In 2004, for example, the Shenzhen PSB conducted a nationwide search for experienced and accomplished police officers and recruited them in an open and competitive manner.[167] The Shenzhen PSB recruitment exercise was a departure from the old norm in that the process was conducted nationally, openly,[168] and competitively,[169] and high pay was offered to the successful candidates. Meritocracy in policing calls for the development of knowledgeable officers with the necessary professional skills.[170] In a telephone conference for national public security organs that was organized and chaired by Minister Zhou Yongkang in 2004, the Minister called for all police organs to actively improve police competence through training in three areas: political (*zhengzhi*), professional (*yewu*), and physical (*tineng*).[171]

In addition to developing professional officers, meritocracy in policing also calls for grooming the next generation of police leaders.[172] In practice, this means promoting younger and more educated police officers, including females, to head major provincial administrative or local units. It also means selecting promising young college graduates with specialized skills (e.g., computer or financial) for fast-track development.

Administration by Law (Yifa xingzheng)

Yifa xingzheng is a major policy initiative of the Hu–Wen administration. *Yifa zhiguo* (governing the country by law)[173] is the superordinate mandate for *yifa xingzheng* (administration by law)[174] that demands *yifa zhijing* (governing the police by law).[175] As Premier and head of the State Council, Wen intends to improve the efficiency and effectiveness of the government bureaucracy, including the police, by law in a systematic and comprehensive way.[176] He made clear his intent early on in his administration through a number of high-profile actions, such as championing the Administrative Licensing Law.[177]

In 2008, the role of the Hu–Wen administration was clearly spelled out in a white paper on China's rule of law under a section entitled "Administration by Law and Building a Government under the Rule of Law," summarized here.[178] After promulgating the "Decision of the State Council on Promoting Law-Based Administration in an All-Round Way" in 1999, the Chinese government issued the "Outline for the Implementation of Promoting Law-Based Administration in an All-Round Way" in 2004, which set forth the goals, policy, guidelines, targets, principles, and specific requirements for promoting administration by law over the next decade, including the following:

1. *Establish legal systems for subjects of the administration*, in accordance with the PRC Constitution, Organic Law of the State Council, Organic Law of the Local People's Congresses, and local people's governments.
2. *Establish legal systems for administrative acts.* These would include the administrative licensing system, which must be open, fair, and accessible to the people; a system of administrative expropriation and administrative requisition for use, according to the PRC Constitution and the Property Rights Law;[179] and an administrative penalty system.
3. *Establish legal systems for civil servants.*
4. *Establish legal systems for administrative supervision and remedy.* The Administrative Review Law[180] provides for administrative penalties only in accordance with clear and precise laws, and administrative order violators should be allowed to challenge administrative decisions through appeal, litigation, and compensation.

Three kinds of administrative review laws have been established. First, the Administrative Review Law, Article 6, provides citizens with the right to challenge administrative decision making under any of the following circumstances:[181]

1. Refusing to accept an administrative sanction, such as warning, fine, confiscation of illegal gains or property, order to suspend production or business, suspension or recission of license or permit, administrative attachment, and so on;
2. Refusing to accept a compulsory administrative measure, such as restriction of personal freedom or the sealing up, seizing, or freezing of property, and so on;
3. Refusing to accept an administrative decision of altering, suspending, or discharging certificates, such as a license, permit, credit certificate, credential, and so on;
4. Refusing to accept an administrative decision of confirming ownership or right to use of natural resources such as land, mineral resources, rivers, forests, mountains, grasslands, unreclaimed land, beaches, maritime waters, and so on;
5. Holding that the administrative organ has infringed upon its managerial decision-making power; …

Second, the Administrative Procedure Law of the People's Republic of China, passed in 1989,[182] provides remedies in court for administrative violations of rights. Article 2 reads: "If a citizen, a legal person, or any other organization considers that his or its lawful rights and interests have been infringed upon by a specific administrative act of an administrative organ or its personnel, he or it shall have the right to bring a suit before a people's court in accordance with this Law."

Finally, the Law of the People's Republic of China on Administrative Supervision, passed in 1997,[183] provides citizens with rights to check on government functions and activities. Article 6 states:

Supervision shall be enforced by relying on the general public. Supervisory organs shall institute an informing system, under which all citizens shall have the right to bring to supervisory organs accusations or expositions against any administrative organs or public servants of the State or any persons appointed by State administrative organs that violate laws or are derelict in their duties.

Opposition to Institutionalized Corruption

On December 23, 2003, General Secretary Hu Jintao presided over a meeting of the Political Bureau of the Communist Party of China Central Committee that discussed the need to improve the Party's work style and fight against corruption.[184] Those at the meeting observed that, although great achievements had been made in the fight against corruption, the causes and conditions of corruption were not yet under control. The meeting concluded that an anti-corruption drive was important for the legitimacy of the Party and the stability of the state, and the committee promised to carry on the fight with renewed vigor.[185]

In 2006, the Hu–Wen administration once again sounded the alarm against corruption of historical proportions and unimaginable consequences. An article in the *New York Times* observed the following:

> President Hu Jintao and Prime Minister Wen Jiabao have warned that corruption threatens the credibility and legitimacy of Communist Party rule and have vowed to stamp it out. But many experts say that truly stamping out corruption would involve the type of broad political reform and a full embrace of the rule of law that the Party has long resisted. The current corruption sweep authorized by Mr. Hu in Shanghai and other cities is widely viewed as more of a purge of allies linked to his predecessor, President Jiang Zemin, than an unfettered crackdown.[186]

Whether Hu and Wen are using every means at their disposal to fight corruption or are hedging their bets in the face of political infighting, time will tell. But, few can deny that corruption is weighing heavy on the leaders, and drastic action is necessary to appease the people, stabilize the country, and secure the Party. Wen frankly admitted recently that:

> The Chinese people attach so much importance to the anti-corruption cause when we are coping with the financial meltdown, and why? Because in my opinion, economic development, social justice, and a clean government are the three pillars of social stability.[187]

The Hu–Wen administration has sought to rein in police corruption on a number of fronts: First, the administration has adopted a systematic and scientific national plan to fight corruption.[188] In 2008, the CPC Central Committee formulated a comprehensive, multiagency, multiyear, national plan to fight corruption called the "2008–2012 Work Plan for Establishing and Improving the System of Punishment and Prevention of Corruption" (or "Work Plan"). The guiding principle for fighting corruption in China is to "adhere to the principle of tackling the issue from both its root causes and symptoms, in a comprehensive way, combining punishment and prevention with an emphasis on the latter." The Work Plan consists of six actionable steps:

1. Establish a coordinated anti-corruption platform.
2. Promote pilot projects to explore new ways to prevent corruption. Pilot projects were launched in Hebei, Shanghai, Sichuan, Fujian, Hunan, and Gansu. The Heibei Provincial Commission for Discipline Inspection formulated four implementation

measures: Measures of Urging and Inspecting the Work of Punishment and Prevention System Construction, Measures of Regularly Reporting the Work of Punishment and Prevention System Construction, Measures of Appraising and Assessing the Work of Punishment and Prevention System Construction, and Measures of Responsible Investigation in the Work of Punishment and Prevention System Construction, which calls for the establishment of inspection, reporting, assessment, and accountability of government funded projects.

3. Improve publicity regarding government activities in order to make government work more open and transparent to the public and thus easier to be supervised and held accountable. In 2008, the National Bureau of Corruption Prevention (NBCP) held its first National Experience-Sharing Conference on Deepening Government Affairs Publicity with the Jiangsu Provincial People's Government, Fujian Provincial People's Government, State Administration for Industry and Commerce, Government of Shanghai Pudong New Area, Handan Government of Hebei Province, and Hubei Department of Finance to share their experiences in making the government administration and operations more open and transparent.

4. Expand inspections and research. The NBCP sent personnel to more than 20 provinces, municipalities, ministries, and commissions to learn first-hand how people from different walks of life dealt with corruption. It also entrusted 16 provinces, municipalities, ministries, and commissions to conduct inspections and research on corruption prevention.

5. Cut back on unnecessary and wasteful overseas travel. In 2008, the Central Commission of Discipline Inspection, Ministry of Foreign Affairs, Organization and International Departments of the CPC Central Committee, Foreign Affairs Office of the CPC Central Committee, Ministry of Supervision, Ministry of Finance, National Audit Office, NBCP, and State Administration of Foreign Experts Affairs held a joint conference, which issued circulars regarding the restraint of overseas travel on public funds and governmental cadres and provided for stringent auditing of overseas travel.

6. Promote cooperation and international exchanges, such as sharing experiences with the United Nations Convention against Corruption and learning best practices from the Hong Kong Independent Commission Against Corruption (ICAC).

Second, the administration has established a specialized anti-corruption bureau to coordinate, organize, and execute anti-corruption activities.[189] To that end, the NBCP was established in 2007.[190] Reporting to the State Council, the NBCP is headed by Ma Wen, Minister of Supervision, and works closely with the Central Commission for Discipline Inspection (CCDI) of the Communist Party of China. The mission of the NBCP is to attack the nation's corruption at its roots, systematically and comprehensively, through education, prevention, and deterrence. According to the NBCP:

> The outline points out that in 2010, NBCP should further strengthen construction of corruption prevention systems, mechanisms, and institutions; expand the work arenas of corruption prevention; and deepen international cooperation in corruption prevention. Efforts should be made to explore measures and ways of corruption prevention, focusing on preventing power abuse, standardizing power operation, and avoiding interest conflicts, so as to achieve the work goals of effectively preventing corruption.

The NBCP does not work alone. It works with 13 organizations that have some kind of anti-corruption authority and responsibilities. The first session of the Joint Conference of Corruption Prevention was held in 2008, and the participants included the Central Commission for Discipline Inspection of the CPC, Organization Department of the CPC Central Committee, Legislative Affairs Commission of the NPC Standing Committee, Supreme People's Court, Supreme People's Procuratorate, National Development and Reform Commission, Ministry of Supervision, Ministry of Finance, People's Bank of China, National Audit Office, State-Owned Asset Supervision and Administration Commission of the State Council, and Legislative Affairs Office of the State Council.

Third, the administration has adopted stringent anti-corruption laws, regulations, and measures to prevent corruption and punish corrupted officials. Fourth, the administration has imposed draconian penalties (including death) for corrupt police officials.[191] On August 20, 2010, Yu Bing, the former Internet Supervisory Department head of the Beijing City Public Security Bureau, was sentenced to death (with two years' suspension) for accepting 10 million yuan in bribes in 2005 to help Internet companies seeking to obtain Computer Information System Safety Product Sales Permits for antivirus software. In 2009, Wen Qiang, 53, former director of the Chongqing Municipal Judicial Bureau (2008–2009) and vice director of Chongqing Municipal Public Security Bureau (1992–2008) was arrested for accepting bribes amounting to more than 14.6 million yuan.[192] On July 5, 2010, Wen was executed after losing his appeal with the Chongqing People's Higher Court.[193] He was sentenced to death to set an example for others and to pacify the anger of the people,[194] notwithstanding the fact that the amount of bribes he accepted was not among the largest for similar crimes committed across the country in recent years.

Fifth, the administration has attacked corruption at the highest levels of government, in this case within the senior ranks of the MPS. Hu and Wen orchestrated the removal of Ma Zhenchuan, Director of the Beijing Public Security Bureau, and Wu Yuhua, Director of the Bureau of Justice in Beijing, at the 16th Session of the 13th National People's Congress held on February 26, 2010. Since 2009, the Hu–Wen administration began investigating and arresting high-ranking officials in the MPS, the Supreme Court, and throughout the legal system, including Zheng Shaodong, Assistant Secretary of the MPS and Bureau Chief of the Financial Crime Investigation Bureau; Xiang Huaizhu, Deputy Bureau Chief of the Financial Crime Investigation Bureau; and Yu Bing, Director of the Internet Monitoring Department of Beijing Public Security Bureau. The arrests sent shock waves throughout the nation's public security system, and the Shanghai Public Security Bureau, Beijing Public Security Bureau, Guangdong Provincial Public Security Bureau, and Liaoning Provincial Public Security Bureau were all implicated. This effort achieved the purpose of the "kill one, deter many" objective.[195]

Rights Consciousness

In January 1, 2004, the *Beijing Review* reprinted an op-ed column from the *Beijing Times* calling for an effort to protect patients' privacy. The column approved the steps taken by the Ministry of Health to prevent medical workers from releasing confidential information, intentionally or inadvertently: "All patients have the right to protect their privacy, yet before the Ministry of Health issued the protective document there was no legal means for them to help themselves protect their privacy."[196]

On June 18, 2004, the Chief Justice of the People's Supreme Court, Shao Yang, openly called for respecting human rights and safeguarding the constitutional rights of criminal defendants, without harming the safety, security, and welfare of the people.[197] In so doing, the Chief Justice made clear that the state should do whatever it can to punish the criminals so as not "to return the tiger to the mountain" (*fanghu guishan*) and that it should remember that "neglecting a carbuncle will cause trouble" (*yang yong wei huan*). But, the Chief Justice also used the phrase *ke sha er bu ke ru* ("a gentleman can be killed but cannot be humiliated") to call for respecting the rights of the defendants.[198]

These phrases have deep cultural roots, wide public identification, and visceral personal resonance. When used in a major policy statement, the phrases deserve deeper reflection and further study in a historical and cultural context to fully grasp Hu–Wen's approach to human rights protection and its unintended consequences on the psychic well-being of the people. If one were to do so, one cannot help but be perplexed. The challenge lies in making sense of a new Chinese criminal law policy within a traditional social and cultural context. At first glance, the phrases do not seem to fit with the Chinese cultural understanding of crime and punishment.

In Chinese folklore, *hu* ("tiger") conjures up images of a violent animal that is intimidating in appearance, fierce in temperament, wild in nature, and destructive by instinct, uncontrolled and uncontrollable. It is menacing to humans and must be exterminated. Likewise, in Chinese culture, *yong* is a pus-forming ulcer that is most harmful to the body and disagreeable in every way. It corrodes healthy tissues and fouls up the surrounding air and must be eradicated at all costs. It is best to treat it earlier rather than later.

In conventional usage, both terms are used to describe imminent threats to the social order that require quick and resolute action to contain and remove, with very little extraneous considerations of any kind (i.e., no mercy for killing the tiger nor hesitation in removing the carbuncle). It is thus puzzling that the Chief Justice would use these two common sayings to remind the public that there are countervailing interests in affording rights to criminal defendants. Perhaps the Chief Justice wanted to inform the public that the Party has not gone soft on crime and remind them that they should always be vigilant against criminals.

Now let us turn to the more perplexing and controversial (in use) phrase *ke sha er bu ke ru*. The saying actually stands for *shi ke sha er bu ke ru*, or "gentleman can only be killed but cannot be humiliated." In a historical context, *shi*, as a "gentleman (*junzi*), is to be treated gently, with dignity and respect. Such a moral imperative implores people to respect the dignity of those (honorable cultured persons) who are defeated by a variety of life circumstances and personal misfortunes. For example, in Imperial China, when officials (gentlemen) committed a wrong against the emperor, they were given an opportunity to own up to their misconduct through self-infliction of punishment, such as suicide. It is important to note that such respect was not given to everyone, but only to those who are found to be deserving, and certainly not to common criminals as *xiao ren* (debased people).

The use of such a phrase to promote human rights for criminals is inappropriate at the very least and wrong headed at worst. First, criminals are not honorable people. Second, crimes are harmful to society. Treating dishonorable persons and harmful acts "gently" is never the Chinese way. China treats crimes and deviances as diseases and evils to be detested by all. Are criminals now to be treated as people of high honor? If so, why? Whatever the true intent or real purpose, the use of this and similar phrases sent mixed and confusing messages to the public—criminals should be punished lest they return vs. the rights of criminals should be respected even if it means they must be set free. They recall the unsettled and unsettling debate between substantive vs. procedural justice in PRC criminal jurisprudence. In whatever way this jurisprudential issue is eventually resolved in China, the unfortunate use of phrases such as *fang fu gui shan* and *yang yong wei huan* is likely to defeat the original intent of the policy statement; instead of promoting respect for the rights of defendants, it is likely to remind the public, police, prosecutors, and courts that defendants have rights granted by the constitution, but their existence is subject to the security needs of the people, first and last. Viewed in this light, a defendant's right is less an absolute entitlement that gives rise to duty legally imposed than contingent privileges that result from respect voluntarily given.

Finally, the Hu–Wen administration's attitude toward and policy for the promotion of human rights in China are clearly spelled out in the 2009–2010 National Human Rights Action Plan of China, published by the Information Office of the State Council on April 14, 2009. In the Action Plan, the Hu–Wen administration made clear its concept of human rights and their importance in Chinese society, and more importantly how the administration plans to promote human rights in China:

> The plan was framed on the following fundamental principles: First, in pursuit of the basic principles prescribed in the Constitution of China, and the essentials of the Universal Declaration of Human Rights and International Covenant on Civil and Political Rights, the plan is aimed at improving laws and regulations upholding human rights and advancing the cause of China's human rights in accordance with the law; second, adhering to the principle that all kinds of human rights are interdependent and inseparable, the plan encourages the coordinated development of economic, social, and cultural rights as well as civil and political rights, and the balanced development of individual and collective rights; third, in the light of practicality and China's reality, the plan ensures the feasibility of the proposed goals and measures and scientifically promotes the development of the cause of human rights in China.[199]

Protecting Police Authority

Increasingly, people are taking to the streets to protest or confront the police with violence in the exercise of their authority.[200] According to MPS statistics in Hangzhou, there were 32 cases of assaulting a police officer (*xijing*) over a 10-day period in 2004, resulting in a death and 95 injuries. On one day alone there were five cases. In the first half of 2004, there were about 200 cases of resisting law enforcement (*kuanfa*), 50% related to traffic enforcement. On the afternoon of March 4, 2004, officers from the Kang Qiao Traffic Dispatch were detaining two vehicles without licenses when two people approached and attacked the officers with steel bars and knives. On March 28, 2004, police officer Pan Jiang stopped a minivan for a driving violation but the driver sped up and dragged the officer for 200 feet; he sustained serious injuries.[201] There are many reasons for such violent confrontations, most of them attributable to the reform process. Serious crime and violent criminals are increasing. People are becoming more self-centered, and offenders have less respect for the law or the police. China lacks a well-developed legal culture, and people tend to perceive law enforcement as being discriminatory. The police do not have a good image with regard to their professional or legal conduct; they appear weak and not resolute in the eyes of the public as they try to be civilized (*wenming*) and considerate. Finally, the police try to avoid problematic encounters and troublesome offenders, which encourages strong-headed offenders and emboldens recalcitrant violators.[202]

The Zhejiang Police Department and Hangzhou Municipal Police Bureau launched a public education and deterrent campaign against obstructing or resisting police officers in the exercise of their duty.[203] The campaign started on March 29, 2004, and 18 offenders were arrested or detained for violence against the police. The Party committee of the Zhejiang Provincial Police Department also passed regulations for Zhejiang provincial police organs that protected the rights of the people's police in enforcing the law (*Zhejiang sheng gongan jiguan weihu minjing jifa quanyi rugan guiding*). These regulations called for setting up *ad hoc* committees to protect police officers enforcing the law and to take action against violence police resisters.[204]

The violence against police has led to local self-help efforts to safeguard their rights, protect their interests, and promote their welfare. The Qin Huang Dao Municipality Public Security Bureau recently established a Police Rights Protection Committee (*Jingcha weiquan weiyuanhui*) to deal with violence against police cases. The PSB promulgated "Regulations Protecting the Rights of the People's Police in the Proper Enforcement of Law" ("*Weihu renmin jingcha zhengdang zhifa quanyi guize*"); these regulations authorized the Police Rights Protection Committee to handle all cases and issues arising from or as a result of police officers and their families being obstructed, insulted, threatened, harassed, intimidated, or assaulted in the line of duty.[205]

Violence against police, resisting arrest, and obstructing justice have precipitated calls for national legislations to protect the police in the execution of their duty. Until then there had been no specific criminal charges for either obstruction of justice or assaulting police officers in the exercise of duty. The push to pass national legislation regarding these issues was first begun in 2003, led by Wang Wuding and 35 NPC members. The initiative was addressed in 2004 at the Second Session of the Tenth National People's Congress, and a legislative proposal was submitted by the NPC representative from the Zhanjiang municipality police post, police officer Xin Jiejun.[206]

Issues

As the PRC police reform moves forward, it has been confronted with many old problems, such as corruption and abuse of powers, and it is faced with still more new challenges, such as forging a new identity. The most fundamental problems include how to reconfigure traditional Communist policing to fit new social conditions and political reality,[207] how to change the police organizational culture, how to upgrade the professional knowledge of the police,[208] and how to make the police more proactive than reactive (*bidong yingzhan*).[209,210]

Redefining the Roles and Functions of the Police

One of the many challenges facing PRC political leaders, police administrators, and policing scholars (domestic and foreign) is how to redefine the roles and functions of the police in an economically transformed and politically reforming China.[211] Are the police still a political instrument of the state that can be used to suppress class enemies or are they a social institution of the people to service the economy? Should the police obey local leadership[212] and serve local economic needs[213] or follow central command and promote the rule of law?[214]

Conventional wisdom says that the police are an instrument of the proletarian state used to exercise democratic dictatorship over class enemies and counterrevolutionaries. This perception of the role of police still holds true within certain circles (e.g., radical left)[215] and most certainly under particular circumstances (e.g., Falun Gong);[216] however, growing evidence suggests a rethinking of this model. First, Article 2 of the 1995 PRC Police Law[217] provides that, "Tasks of the people's police are to safeguard State security, maintain public order, protect citizen's personal safety and freedom and their legal property, protect public property, and prevent, stop, and punish illegal and criminal activities." More particularly, Chapter II, Article 6, outlines the functions of the police as follows: "The people's police-men of public security organs shall, in accordance with the division of responsibilities, perform the following duties according to law:

1. to prevent, stop, and investigate illegal and criminal activities;
2. to maintain public order and stop acts that endanger public order;
3. to ensure traffic safety, maintain traffic order, and deal with traffic accidents;
4. to organize and carry out fire prevention and control and supervise routine fire protection;
5. to control firearms and ammunition, and keep under surveillance knives, inflammables, explosives, deadly poisons, radioactive materials, and other dangerous articles;
6. to administer special trades and professions as provided by laws and regulations;
7. to serve as bodyguards for persons specially designated by the State and protect important places and installations;
8. to keep under control assemblies, processions, and demonstrations;
9. to administer affairs of household registration, citizens' nationality, and entry into and exit from the territory, and handle matters concerning aliens' residence and travel within the territory of China;
10. to maintain public order along the border (frontier) areas;
11. to execute criminal punishment with respect to criminals sentenced to public surveillance, criminal detention, or deprived of political rights and criminals serving sentences outside prison, and to exercise supervision over and inspection of criminals who are granted suspension of execution or parole;
12. to supervise and administer the work of protecting the computer information system;
13. to guide and supervise the work of security in State organs, public organizations, enterprises, institutions, and major construction projects, and guide mass organizations such as public security committees in their work of maintaining public order and preventing crime; and
14. other duties as stipulated by laws and regulations."[218]

Second, in a 2003 survey of the Jiangsu Police Officer College student body, 37% of the respondents thought that the police were an instrument of the state dictatorship (*guojia zhuanzheng gongju*); 54% thought that they were an instrument of the people's democracy (*renmin minzhu gongju*), and 9% thought that it was a special force to maintain order.[219]

Third, Professor Li from the People's Public Security University tried to address the fundamental question related to the roles and functions of police in the reform era; that is, what are the origin, nature, and functions of the police?[220] *In terms of origin*, Li agreed with Marx that police first originated with the division of property, division of labor, and the discovery of the state.[221] *In terms of nature*, Li also agreed that the police, as an "armed administrative force" (*wuzhuang xingzheng liliang*), were an instrument of the state used to suppress class enemies.[222] *In terms of function*, Li suggested that the police have two kinds of functions: a basic political function and a general social function. The basic function of the police in any nation is to suppress political enemies, whereas the general function of the police is to provide for the welfare of the people. In making this critical distinction between political vs. social functions of the police, Li was able to liberate the police from the narrow ideological confines of Marxism and Maoism by allowing the police to come to terms with their new-found identity and mission during the reform.

Fourth, Hu Dacheng, a professor of political science at the Jiangsu Police Officer College, argued that the nature and role of police had changed with the reform,[223] from a more political and militant role to a more social and service one (law enforcement, crime control, and order maintenance). Hu's analysis raises more questions than answers. First, the objective of communism is to get rid of the state, police included, once and for all, not to transform police roles and functions, much less to make it serve as a market promoter. Second, Hu's police role analysis is not based on any theory nor supported by any published evidence. Third, Hu did not provide an ideological or theoretical foundation for what the future police roles and functions should be. In the end, Hu's analysis serves simply to raise debate rather than settle issues. The debate over the nature and role of police is here to stay.

Preparing the Police to Deal with Criminality in the Reform Era

A significant challenge is preparing the police to deal with a wide variety of crimes: financial crimes,[224] organized crime,[225] gangs, drug use,[226] computer crimes,[227] international drug trafficking,[228] cross-border crimes,[229] and transnational crimes.[230] For example, the export of drugs from the "golden triangle" (Thailand, Laos, and Myanmar) to the United States, Europe, and Southeast Asia declined from 1999 to 2001, but the importation to China increased. Between January and April 2001 alone, 3.2 tons of heroin and 0.2 ton of crack were seized, 95% of which came from the "golden triangle." China has worked closely with Thailand, Myanmar, Vietnam, Cambodia, and Laos to curb the cultivation, production, and trafficking of drugs. China also has memoranda of understanding (MOUs) with Burma, Cambodia, Laos, Thailand, Vietnam, and the United Nations (UN) Drug Control Program. China was a party to the 1988 UN Drug Convention, the 1961 UN Single Convention on Narcotic Drugs as amended by the 1972 Protocol, and the 1971 UN Convention on Psychotropic Substances. China is a member of INTERPOL and has been a member of the UN International Narcotics Control Board (INCB) since 1984. Still, nothing seems to work.[231]

Pornography on the net is affecting millions of young people in China. The growing use of computers, the global reach of the Internet, online anonymity, the ease of posting and downloading, and difficult enforcement make effective control of pornography on the Internet a most difficult, if not altogether impossible, task.[232]

Globalization means that crimes are crossing national boundaries; such crimes include drug trafficking, terrorism, religious cults, money laundering, illegal arms trade, and illegal cultural relics smuggling. Fighting transnational crime requires international cooperation that has yet to be realized.[233] Cross-border cooperation between the Hong Kong police and the Guangdong police suffers from limitations imposed by court procedures, conflicting laws, overlapping jurisdictions, lack of police expertise, and, more generally, China's "one country, two systems" basic law doctrine.[234]

Impact

A recurrent issue addressed in this book is the impact of police reform on people's lives. More specifically, how successful have the police been in meeting people's expectations, the public and police alike? We need to examine how happy the people are with the police and how the reform has affected the working conditions of the police, from pay to play. These issues are explored later in the book and should help us to gauge the success and failure of the ongoing police reform. In this section, we will first take up the issue of the impact of reform on police by sharing the results of a public relations survey in Hangzhou and reprinting a web essay on the impact on police working conditions from a frontline perspective.

Impact on Police–Public Relationship[235]

How does the public view the police 30 years into the reform? How are the police doing? Are they doing their job? What is the relationship between the police and the public like? How can the police adapt to meet the expectations of the public? Answers to such questions are necessary to put this study of police reform in context. According to Chinese police leaders, past (Mao, Deng) or present (Hu, Wen), the single most important reason for maintaining or reforming the police is to protect the public and serve the masses. Any difference between public expectation and police performance needs to be explained.

1999 Hangzhou Police–Public Relationship Survey

In 1999, the Hunan Province People's Police College (*Hunan Sheng Renmin Jingcha Xuexiao*) conducted a survey on the police–public relationship in an unidentified police district in Hangzhou. The research solicited citizens' views on various police–public relationship issues by asking 23 (Likert-scale) questions that addressed the police–public relationship, familiarity between the public and the police, public satisfaction, public assistance, police conduct, and police law enforcement. See Table 1.3 for a summary of survey respondents.

Overall Assessment of Police–Public Relationship

Overall, a majority of the respondents (89.7%) expressed satisfaction ("very good," "relatively good," or "all right") with the existing police–public relationship (see Table 1.4). Opinions at the extremes ranged from 8.8% ("very good") to 2.6% ("very bad"); however, those who felt that the police–public relationship was relatively good vs. relatively bad exhibited a marked difference, with the "relatively good" exceeding the "relatively bad" by a wide margin (27.3% vs. 7.7%). Most of the people (53.6%) were neither favorably nor unfavorably disposed. This is disturbing for several reasons. Although we have no comparative historical data on satisfaction with the police–public relationship in the past, it can safely be assumed that the people's relationship with the police was much better in the past than now. Also, depending on how one sets the benchmark, an "all right" description of the police–public relationship should not be taken as satisfactory, especially in China, where expectations are set very high

TABLE 1.3 Sample Profile

Sample population = 4000.
Sample size = 200.
Number of respondents = 194 (97%).

	Number	Percent (%) of Sample
Male	101	52.1
Female	93	47.9
Age		
Under 18 years of age	9	4.6
19–35 years	139	71.6
36–55 years	28	14.4
Over 56 years	18	9.4
Occupation		
Government servant	40	20.6
Worker	33	17.5
Peasant worker	12	6.2
Peasant	14	7.2
Private business	63	32.5
Student	32	16.0
Education		
Junior high	16	8.2
High school	61	31.4
College and above	56	28.9

Source: Adapted from Xiangqun, X., *Public Security Studies*, 65, 43–46, 1999.

for official conduct. To most people, "all right" means "so so," a failing grade. There is a distinct possibility that, in the context of the Chinese culture, referring to something as "all right" is a not too subtle way of expressing that something is below their expectations. In China, people generally do not speak their mind when it might be hurtful to another's feelings. Instead, they try to express their feelings in rather circuitous ways. Given the political and police leaders' high expectations for and commitment to a good police–relationship, an "all right" response is a failing grade.

Public Assessment of Police Performance

The respondents were asked to assess police work performance, both generally and specifically, with regard to familiarity, crime fighting, crime prevention, and serving society (see Tables 1.5 and 1.6). Most of the respondents were basically satisfied with the police overall (52.6% responded "all right"); however, those who believed that the police were doing a good job ("very good" or "relatively good") amounted to only 33.5%, not as high as one might expect. Still, 86.1% of the respondents found police performance to be within an acceptable range ("very good," "relatively good," or "all right"). People who thought that overall police

TABLE 1.4 Overall Satisfaction with Police–Public Relationship

	Very Good	Relatively Good	All Right	Relatively Bad	Very Bad
Responses	8.8%	27.3%	53.6%	7.7%	2.6%

TABLE 1.5 Public Assessment of Familiarity with the Police

	Very Familiar	Somewhat Familiar	All Right	Relatively Unfamiliar	Not Familiar
Responses	3.1%	12.4%	19.6%	21.1%	43.8%

work performance was subpar—"relatively bad" (11.3%) and "very bad" (2.1%)—were in the minority. Tellingly, more people held a very good opinion of police work (7.2%) than a very low opinion of police work (2.1%). Thus, unlike what foreigners might think, police performance in China is far from being unacceptable, at least at the city level. By the same token, the data certainly raise the question of whether Chinese leaders are being too critical in suggesting that the police have a low image in the eyes of the public.

Turning to specific areas of performance, overall public satisfaction with police performance in various areas ranked as follows: (1) crime fighting ("very good" and "relatively good," 49.5%); (2) social service ("very good" and "relatively good," 37.6%); and (3) crime prevention ("very good" and "relatively good," 33.5%). Specifically, the police were rated "very good" for preventing crime by 10.3%, for fighting crime by 8.8%, and for social service by 6.6%. Due to the small sample size, these differences fell within the margin of error (2 responses account for 1%). The public thought that the police performance was "very bad" or "relatively bad" in the following order: (1) social service (18.6%), (2) crime prevention (15%), and (3) crime fighting (13.9%). Finally, for the "all right" (average) responses, social service received the most responses, followed by crime prevention, and then crime fighting. See Table 1.7. Because we do not know how the questions were phrased, framed, or asked, we do not know how to interpret the results, beyond viewing them as a rough measure of the public perception of police performance. The one clear conclusion we can draw is that most people are happy with police performance, or at least not unhappy (86.1% overall). Beyond that, again, at least half of the people think that the police are doing a good job of fighting crime (49.5%). As to why people think that the police are better at crime fighting than crime prevention or social service, it is possibly because the Party and MPS have made it clear, by repeated pronouncements and dramatic actions (*yanda*), that crime is not tolerated.

TABLE 1.6 Public Opinion of Police Performance with Regard to Crime Fighting, Crime Prevention, and Social Service

	Very Good (%)	Relatively Good (%)	All Right (%)	Relatively Bad (%)	Very Bad (%)	No Answer (%)
Crime fighting	8.8	40.7	36.1	11.3	2.6	0.5
Crime prevention	10.3	23.2	47.5	14.5	0.5	—
Social service	6.7	30.9	43.8	14.4	4.2	—
Overall	7.2	26.3	52.6	11.3	2.1	0.5

TABLE 1.7 Ranking Police Functions

	Very Good and Relatively Good	All Right	Very Bad and Relatively Bad
Crime fighting	1 (49.5%)	3 (35.5%)	2 (15.0%)
Social service	2 (37.6%)	1 (56.2%)	1 (18.6%)
Crime prevention	3 (33.5%)	2 (52.6%)	3 (13.9%)

Impact on Police Working Conditions[236]

In China, public security consumes only about 1% of the total national expenditure, as compared with developed nations (3 to 5%) and developing nations (9%). Such a serious shortfall of operational funding has resulted in reduced police operations and services and affects the welfare and morale of police staff.

Salary

Police salaries are disproportionate to the demands and complexity of police work. In late 2000, at the Hangzhou PSB, the average salary was 3500 yuan/month (approximately $512). This was fairly high compared to other professions, and it had improved substantially over the past decade; however, police work involves irregular hours, substantial overtime, and potential harm. Taking police working conditions into account, the hourly police wage begins to shrink. Also, compared with other disciplinary services, such as the military, police salaries lag far, far behind. Military pay generally is 5% higher than police, but the salary gap between police and military is widening. Military salaries have been adjusted several times over the past decade or so, but public security personnel have received no such increases. The incomes of entry-level police officers in foreign countries are generally very good; in the United States, new police recruits can expect to earn about $40,000 a year, and up to $60,000 or higher with 8 years of service. Also, after 5 years, U.S. police can take promotion exams; successful candidates can expect to receive a salary of about $75,000.

Pensions

Pensions vary widely. In 2008, the pension at the Hangzhou PSB was about 400 yuan, whereas the pension at the Zhejiang Provincial PSB was about 750 yuan. This is a significant difference.

Rank and Salary

Police schools provide the necessary training for promoted police officers, but with each promotion a police officer can expect to earn only a few dollars more.

Holidays

Frontline officers work an average of 11 to 15 hours a day, with 1 day of rest every 2 weeks. In the United States, however, police are required by law to have 137 days off each year with 20 days of paid leave. One can retire after working 20 years, with 55% retirement pay. Also, police can carry a gun and moonlight after work. In China, insufficient police staffing has led to officers being overworked and enjoying little rest. Such conditions can result in sickness and injury, perhaps accounting for the high rate of police injury in the line duty. Due to their high rate of injury, police cannot obtain insurance for personal injury.

Work Environment
Work Pressure

The ratio of police to the population is about 12/10,000, about a quarter to a third of the rate for the West. Due to rapid economic development and accelerated staff turnover, among other reasons, the public order environment is deteriorating while the crime rate is constantly increasing. Police shortages have led to increased work pressure, resulting in officer illness, injuries, and death. Although the police have set duty hours, in actuality they are on call 24/7 and must always be available. Also, the police are subject to paramilitary discipline, with strict rules for their uniforms and appearance. Any slight imperfections will be noted and disciplined. Police injuries in the line of duty are increasing every year. At least 9000 officers have been killed in the line of duty and tens of thousands of officers injured. In the last 20 years alone, 6000 officers have been killed and thousands injured: "Bleeding every minute, sacrificing every day." According to experts, police injuries have failed to abate because of the inadequate police force and large workload. China's death and injury rates for police officers is higher than those for other nations. In 2001, about 450 officers were killed in the line of duty in China, but in Japan only 2 officers were killed and 3 injured.

As the population has become more mobile, the crime rate has grown rapidly and criminals are becoming more violent and vicious. Hangzhou is a famous tourist city situated in an economically developed area. Many people are coming and going at all hours of the day and night. This creates an extra burden for Hangzhou police. Overnight duty is very common for officers. Each police officer has to work two 24-hour shifts each week. In most cases, after a 24-hour shift, the officer can only sleep 3 to 4 hours before having to report back to work again. In 1999, the Chinese Health Association conducted a physical examination of police officers. Of those who were examined, 15,887 were police officers from Beijing and Liaoning. The examination revealed a sickness rate upward of 86%. Those who were under 45 years of age were in particularly bad health and getting worse each year. According to an analysis of the examinations, factors contributing to such poor health conditions included police officers having high expectations of themselves at work and enduring a very high stress level. After a long period of time without break, stress and exhaustion set in, leading to deterioration of officers' health.

Working Conditions and Working Environment

The police are the nation's public order administrative force. They are the protectors of society. When they are viewed as being weak, it has a significant impact on society, from emboldening criminals to raising questions about the ability of the police to protect the public, maintain social order, and fight crime.

Organization of This Book

This book investigates police reform in the PRC since 2000. The main focus is on how the police have reinvented themselves to be a professional force.[237] The book is organized into seven chapters. After the brief introduction here in Chapter 1, Chapter 2 ("Obstacles to Understanding Chinese Policing") discusses the difficulties encountered when trying to understand China policing, such as a dated image, misinformation, cultural ignorance, ideological hegemony, denial of feelings, and problems with paternalism. It makes recommendations about studying China from a local perspective, informed by local research and data. It suggests that understanding China requires thinking and feeling in Chinese ways.

Chapter 3 ("Taking Stock") provides an overview of police reform in China from 1999 to 2009 by summarizing and reporting selected policy papers from *Gongan Yanjiu*, the leading national policy journal published by the MPS. The chapter observes fundamental changes in policing in China after three decade of reform in terms of research, ideology, agenda, paradigm, leadership, and culture in China.

Chapter 4 ("Legitimacy Crisis") addresses the emergence of a police legitimacy crisis as evidenced by deterioration of the public image, resisting police power, mass rebellions against police authority, mass incidents and Falun Gong, police cynicism, police officers as spouses, and young people's perceptions of policing. The chapter makes the case that the MPS ideology and ethos of old (the spirit of Lei Feng) are increasingly running up against the values and lifestyles of a new mentality.

Chapter 5 ("Reform Measures") discusses steps that can be taken to restore the police ideology. The chapter suggests that the police adopt a more scientific approach to improve their professionalism, abandon static household control in favor of establishing a rapid response system, and maintain some of the Lei Feng spirit.

Chapter 6 ("Reform to Police Accountability") investigates problems and issues associated with controlling police powers. The chapter begins with a discussion of the abuse of discretion and then moves on to provide an overview of the police powers regulatory regime (e.g., constitutional, legal, and media supervision). The chapter ends with a case study into controlling the police use of firearms to illustrate how a variety of control measures can be brought to bear to control one of the most serious forms of abuse in policing.

Chapter 7 ("Reflections") reflects on what we have learned about Chinese police reform since the author published his last work on police reform in China in 2002. The chapter observes that the study of police reform in China is the study of people, culture, values, and interests; that is, it is more suitable for cultural anthropologists than social scientists. In closing, the author invites readers to free their minds, liberate their spirits, and open their hearts to discovering and embracing policing with Chinese characteristics.

Notes

1. (a) Liu Jinsong, "Henan Police Reform: 18 Cities to Close Down Public Security Bureaus," *Economic Observer*, November 10, 2010 (http://www.eeo.com.cn/ens/homepage/briefs/2010/11/10/185428.shtml). "After the reform, local police stations and public security sub-bureaus will be merged into one department, which will be directly controlled by municipal public security bureaus. Traffic police, special patrolmen, security police, and Interpol police will all be under the unified supervision of their local police stations. The duties as well as the resources of the different police forces will also become more integrated. Henan's flurry of police reforms has already resulted in some reconsideration of the nationwide public security system. Sources in the Ministry of Public Security say that a smooth transition is essential." (b) Zhou Le, "Reform Sees Armed Police Stripped of Car Privileges," *Global Times*, December 21, 2010. "PAP official will receive transportation subsidies of around 1600 yuan ($239) a month....Wuhan is the first city to abolish the use of government cars for PAP officials. The move highlights the growing problems concerning government cars that have long created resentment due to their high costs and special privileges." (c) "Police Universities Stop Recruiting Undergraduates," *China Economic Review*, January 2, 2008 (http://www.chinaeconomicreview.com/china-eye/2008_01_09/police-universities-stop-recruiting-undergraduates.html). Article reports that the Ministry of Public Security was planning to abolish the undergraduate police degree at the Public Security University. Students at regular university were considered to be more suited to police work, being more competent and broad minded. The municipalities of Beijing and Shanghai have experimented with the idea; both stopped offering academic lessons in their police academies in 2007 and 2003, respectively. (d) "Deaths in Detention Lead to China Reform Calls," *Reuters*, March 24, 2009 (http://in.reuters.com/article/2009/03/24/idINIndia-38669720090324). Chinese media reported five deaths in detention since mid-February

2009 in the nation's 2400 detention centers. The Communist Party of China promised reform. (e) "China to Reform Police's Detention Centers," *People's Daily*, June 29, 2000 (http://english. peopledaily.com.cn/english/200006/29/eng20000629 44269.html). In 1999, 759 cases involving 1116 officers were cited for abuses. At a police detention national conference in Guiyang, the capital of southwestern Guizhou Province, participants called for reform.

2. Harry Harding, *China's Second Revolution: Reform after Mao*, Brookings Institution Press, Washington, DC, 1987.

3. Nicholas R. Lardy, *China's Unfinished Economic Revolution*, Brookings Institution Press, Washington, DC, 1998. See Chapter 1, "China's Economic Reform Strategy," pp. 1–20.

4. Jianming Mei and Mu Wang, "Social Change, Crime, and Criminology in China," *Crime & Justice International*, 23(97), 14–21, 2007.

5. Hsiao Kung-chuan, *Rural China: Imperial Control in the Nineteenth Century*, University of Washington Press, Seattle, 1960.

6. Jianhong Liu, "Social Transition and Crime in China: An Economic Motivation Thesis," *Australian and New Zealand Journal of Criminology*, 37, 122–138, 2004.

7. Michael R. Dutton, *Policing and Punishment in China: From Patriarchy to the People*, Cambridge University Press, New York, 1992.

8. William Theodore De Bary, Wing-tsit Chan, and Burton Watson, *Sources of Chinese Tradition*, Vol. I, Columbia University Press, New York, 1960, pp. 28, 115.

9. Kam C. Wong, "The Philosophy of Community Policing in China," *Police Quarterly*, 4(2), 186–214, 2001.

10. Jianhong Liu, "Crime Patterns during the Market Transition in China," *British Journal of Criminology*, 45, 613–633, 2005.

11. Kam C. Wong, "Policing Cross-Border Crimes between China and Hong Kong: A Preliminary Assessment," *Asian Policing*, 1(2), 1–30, 2004.

12. Sonny Shiu-Hing Lo, *The Politics of Cross-Border Crime in Greater China: Case Studies of Mainland China, Hong Kong, and Macao*, M.E. Sharpe, Armonk, NY, 2009.

13. Sonny Lo, "Globalization, State Autonomy and the Fight against Cross-Border Crime: Greater China's Cooperation with the World," *Asian Journal of Political Science*, 7(3), 299–322, 2009.

14. Kam C. Wong, "Police Powers and Control in the PRC: A Case Study of *Shouron Shencha*," *Columbia Journal of Asian Law*, 10(3), 367–390, 1996.

15. Harold M. Tanner, *Strike Hard: Anti-Crime Campaigns and Chinese Criminal Justice, 1979–1985*, No. 104, Cornell East Asia Series, Cornell University East Asia Program, Ithaca, NY, 1999. The subject of continued debate is the necessary existence of a relationship between economic development and criminality. Japan, for example, is not afflicted with high crime rates notwithstanding its economic success. See also "Chinese Police Studies Association Invite Famous Experts to Discuss and Analyze Society's Public Order Situation" ["*Zhongguo jingcha xuehui yaoqing shehui zhiming zhuanjia zuotan fenxi shehui zhian qingkuang*"], *Public Security Studies*, 6(38), 1994.

16. Wang Zhimin, *Research on Current Mobile Population Criminality in China* [*Dangqiang Zhongguo liudong renkou fanzui yanjiu*], Zhongguo renmin gong'an daxue chubanshe, Beijing, 2002.

17. Kang Shuhua, *Criminology: History, Status, and Future* [*Fanzui xue—Lishi, xianxiang, weilai*], Qunzhong Chubanshe, Beijing, 1998. See Chapter 17, "History, Current Situation, and Future Trend of Juvenile Delinquencies" ["*Qing shaonian fanzui lishi, xianxiang yu fazhan qushi*"], pp. 580–717.

18. Ye Gaofeng and Liu Defa, *Policy Research on Organized Crime* [*Jituan fanzui duice yanjiu*], Zhongguo jiancha chubanshe, Beijing, 2002.

19. Ibid., Chapter 10, "Special Organized Crime Prevention and Treatment of Secret Society" ["*Teshu de jituan fanzui Heishehui sheng zhuji fanzui de fangzhi*"], pp. 432–460.

20. Ibid., Chapter 16, "New Features of Crimes under the Current Market Conditions in China" ["*Zhongguo xian jieduan shichang jingji tiaojian xia fanzui de xin tedian*"], pp. 419–579.

21. (a) Jiang Ping, *Computer Crime Problem Research* [*Jisuanji fanzui wenti yanjiu*], Shangwu yinshu guan, Beijing, 2000. (b) Kam C. Wong, *Cyberspace Governance in China*, Nova Science Publishers, Hauppauge NY, 2011.

22. Kam C. Wong, "Policing in China: Terrorism and Mandate from Heaven," in John Eterno and Dilip Das (Eds.), *Police Practices in Global Perspective* (pp. 71–103). Rowman & Littlefield, Lanham, MD, 2009.

23. Kam C. Wong, "The Criminalization of Falun Gong in China: A Preliminary Report," *Wisconsin Political Scientist*, VIII(2), 5–7, 2002.

24. Kam C. Wong, "Policing Cross-Border Crimes between China and Hong Kong: A Preliminary Assessment," *Asian Policing*, 1(2), 2–20, 2004.

25. Chris Buckley, "Girl's Death Sparks Rioting in China," *Reuters*, June 28, 2008 (http://uk.reuters.com/article/2008/06/28/uk-china-riot-idUKPEK27256220080628?sp=true).

26. Zhou Xinyao, "Pondering on Preventing and Dealing with Group Conflicts Events," *Journal of Zhejiang Police College Public Security Science*, 97, 64–69, 2007.

27. Murray Scot Tanner, "China Rethinks Unrest," *Washington Quarterly*, 27(3), 137–156, 2004.

28. Jianhong Liu, "Social Transition and Crime in China: An Economic Motivation Thesis," *Australian and New Zealand Journal of Criminology*, 37, 122–138, 2004.

29. (a) Ni He and Ineke H. Marshall, "Social Production of Crime Data: A Critical Examination of Chinese Crime Statistics," *International Criminal Justice Review*, 7(1), 46–64, 1997. Official crime statistics, especially in China, are subject to intentional manipulation and inadvertent distortion. (b) Olivia Yu and Lening Zhang, "The Under-Recording of Crime by Police in China: A Case Study," *Policing: An International Journal of Police Strategies & Management*, 22(3), 252–264, 1999. An internal survey of the Chinese police in the late 1980s and early 1990s showed that the police grossly underreported crimes.

30. He Bingsong, "Crime and Control in China," in Hans-Günther Heiland, Louise I. Shelley, and Hisao Katoh (Eds.), *Crime and Control in Comparative Perspectives* (pp. 241–258), Walter de Gruyter, Berlin, 1992.

31. Børge Bakken, "Comparative Perspectives on Crime in China." In Børge Bakken (Ed.), *Crime, Punishment, and Policing in China* (pp. 64–100), Rowman & Littlefield, Lanham, MD, 2004.

32. "Youth Crime in China Explodes as Social Values Decline: Report," *Sino Daily*, December 5, 2007 (http://www.sinodaily.com/reports/Youth_crime_in_China_explodes_as_social_values_decline_report_999.html). The rise in juvenile crime has resulted from the decline of social values and increase in broken families.

33. Mauro Marescialli, "Crime in China: Some Statistics," *Danwei*, August 11, 2005 (http://www.danwei.org/ip_and_law/crime_in_china_some_statistics.php).

34. Ibid.

35. Kang Shuhua, *Youth Crime and Management/Control* [*Qingshaonian Fanzui yu Zhili*], Zhongguo renmin gong'an daxue chubanshe, Beijing, 2000. Especially see "Basic Circumstances of Development and Changes in Youth Crime in Our Country in the Last 50 years" ["*Wushi nian lai woguo qingshaonian fanzui fazhan bianhua de jiben qingkuang*"], pp. 37–51.

36. (a) Wang Zhimin, *Research into Contemporary Criminality of Migrant Population* [*Dangqian Zhongguo Liudong Renkou Fanzui Yanjiu*], Zhongguo renmin gong'an daxue chubanshe, Beijing, 2002. Especially see Chapter 2, "Description of Migrant Population Criminality in Static Terms" ["*Liudong renkou fanzui qingtai miaoshu*"], pp. 31–52. (b) Guoan Ma, "Population Migration and Crime in Beijing, China," in Jianhong Liu, Lening Zhang, and Steven Messner (Eds.), *Crime and Social Control in Changing China* (pp. 65–72), Greenwood Press, Santa Barbara, CA, 2001. (c) Daniel J. Curran, "Economic Reform, the Floating Population, and Crime: The Transformation of Social Control in China," *Journal of Contemporary Criminal Justice*, 14(3), 262–280, 1998. Much of the crime in the reform era is caused by the "floating population." The current administrative strategy (such as household registration) and penal measures (such as labor reform) are not effective in addressing the economic problem. (d) Kam C. Wong, *Sheltering for Examination: Law, Policy, and Practice*, Occasional Papers/Reprints Series in Contemporary Asian Studies, University of Maryland, School of Law, College Park, 1997, p. 53.

37. An Chen, "Secret Societies and Organized Crime in Contemporary China," *Modern Asian Studies*, 39, 77–107, 2005. Unemployment, impoverishment, economic inequality, relative deprivation, and political corruption created disadvantaged and marginalized social groups, leading to organized gangs.

38. (a) Keith Forster, "The 1982 Campaign against Economic Crime in China," *Australian Journal of Chinese Affairs*, 14, 1–19, 1985. In 1982, the Central Committee of the Communist Party of China (CCCPC) was alarmed at the pervasiveness and severity of economic crime especially perpetrated by Party cadres and state officials. (b) Jiang Zhuqing, "Economic Crimes Rise, Disturb Social Order," *China Daily*, May 28, 2004. Chen Anfu, director of the Department of Economic Crime Investigation, Department of the Ministry of Public Security (MPS), reported that, since 2000, Chinese police had investigated 277,000 cases of economic crimes, arrested 262,000 suspects, and retrieved 67 billion yuan (US$8.1 billion).

39. "Zhongguo fazui yanjiu hui yufang zhiwu fanzui zhuanye," in *Zhongguo zhiwu fanzui yufang tioacha baogao* [*Investigation Report on Chinese Official Crime*], Zhongguo minzhu fazhi chubanshe, Beijing, 2004.

40. Kam C. Wong, "Law and Order in Cyberspace: A Case Study of Cyberspace Governance and Internet Regulations in China," in Roderic G. Broadhurst and Peter Grabosky (Eds.), *Cyber-Crime: The Challenge in Asia* (pp. 56–77), University of Hong Kong Press, Hong Kong, 2005.

41. Mark Cowling, "Would Communism Eliminate Crime?" paper presented at the Fourth Manchester Workshops in Political Theory, September 3–5, 2007. A central claim of much Marxist criminological theory is that Communism would eliminate or greatly reduce crime.

42. Li Liangdong et al., *Stability* [*Wending*], Zhonggong zhongyang dangxiao chubanshe, Beijing, 1999. Especially see "Unstable Factors," pp. 74–111. The Communist Party of China (CPC) identified five major kinds of instabilities: (1) foreign (Western capitalistic) infiltration and destruction, (2) succession efforts (Taiwan), (3) cult activities (Falun Gong), (4) mass incidents (internal contradictions), and (5) crime and disorder.

43. Wen Mucao, "An Important Ideological Weapon for Struggle against Felonious Criminals: Notes on Studying the 'Selected Works of Deng Xiaoping,'" *Journal of Chinese Political–Legal University* (*Zhongguo Zhenfa Daxue Xue Bao*), 2, 40–45, 1983.

44. (a) Murray Scot Tanner, "State Coercion and the Balance of Awe: The 1983–1986 'Stern Blows' Anticrime Campaign," *The China Journal*, 44, 93–125, 2000. (b) Susan Trevaskes, "*Yanda* 2001: Form and Strategy in a Chinese Anti-Crime Campaign," *Australian and New Zealand Journal of Criminology*, 36, 272–292, 2003.

45. "China Begins a Nationwide 'Strike Hard' Campaign Focusing the Attack on Three Crime Categories" ["*Zhongguo Zai Quanguo Fanweinei Kaizhan Yanda Zhengzhi Douzheng Zhongdian Daji San Zhong Fanzui*"], *Xinhua*, April 3, 2001.

46. "*Yanda*: The Four Main Mistakes" ["*Yanda: zouchu sige wuqu*"], *Renmin ribao* (*RMRB*), August 8, 2001, p. 10. "*Yanda* is a vicious cycle; it's a treadmill that we can't get off....The more we attack the busier we get, the harder it is to keep up with the attacks, the harder it is to prevent further crimes from occurring."

47. Børge Bakken, "Crime, Juvenile Delinquency, and Deterrence Policy in China," *The Australian Journal of Chinese Affairs*, 30, 29–58, 1993.

48. Yingyi Situ and Weizheng Liu, "Restoring the Neighborhood, Fighting against Crime: A Case Study in Guangzhou City, PRC," *International Criminal Justice Review*, 6(1), 89–102, 1996. Market reform and social changes posed serious challenges to traditional informal social control system at the grassroots. The introduction of a comprehensive treatment of the social order has helped to breach the gap but has not been altogether successful at keeping criminality at bay.

49. Wan-Ning Bao, Ain Haas, and Yijun Pi, "Life Strain, Negative Emotions, and Delinquency: An Empirical Test of General Strain Theory in the People's Republic of China," *International Journal of Offender Therapy and Comparative Criminology*, 48(3), 281–297, 2004. Agnew's general strain theory was tested on a sample of 615 middle school and high school students from rural and urban areas of China. The findings are consistent with those obtained in the United States.

50. Hu Zhangluan, Qian Wenlu, and Chen Anxing, "Reflecting on Wenzhou Economic Structure and Public Security Work Reform" ["*Wenzhou jingji ju geju you gongan gongzuo de sigao*"], *Public Security Studies*, 5, 1989.

51. (a) Liqun Cao, "Returning to Normality: Anomie and Crime in China," *International Journal of Offender Therapy and Comparative Criminology*, 51(1), 40–51, 2007. (b) Linda Shuo Zhao, "Anomie Theory and Crime in a Transitional China (1978–)," *International Criminal Justice Review*, 18(2), 137–157, 2008.

52. Zhou Lu, "On the Relation between Crimes and Material or Cultural Life," *Studies in Law* (*Faxue Yanjiu*), 19, 1–5, 1982.

53. "More Juveniles Involved in Crimes in China," *People's Daily Online*, August 16, 2005 (http://english.people.com.cn/200508/16/eng20050816202601.html). Juvenile crimes are going up because of a lack of family education.

54. Xiaogang Deng and Ann Cordilia, "To Get Rich Is Glorious: Rising Expectations, Declining Control, and Escalating Crime in Contemporary China," *International Journal of Offender Therapy and Comparative Criminology*, 43, 211–229, 1999.

55. Michael Dutton, "The Basic Character of Crime in Contemporary China," *The China Quarterly*, 149, 160–177, 1997. A commodity economy induces crime.

56. Jianhung Liu, "Social Transition and Crime in China: An Economic Motivation Thesis," *Australian and New Zealand Journal of Criminology*, 37(Suppl.), 122–138, 2004.

57. Murray Scot Tanner, "State Coercion and the Balance of Awe: The 1983–1986 'Stern Blows' Anticrime Campaign," *The China Journal*, 44, 93–125, 2000. *Yanda*, or "Strike Hard," campaigns were organized to arrest spiritual pollution and intellectual liberalism, seen as compromising effective state control.

58. Wan-Ning Bao, Ain Haas, and Yijun Pi, "Life Strain, Negative Emotions, and Delinquency: An Empirical Test of General Strain Theory in the People's Republic of China," *International Journal of Offender Therapy and Comparative Criminology*, 48(3), 281–297, 2004.

59. (a) Liqun Cao, "Returning to Normality: Anomie and Crime in China." *International Journal of Offender Therapy and Comparative Criminology*, 51(1), 40–51, 2007. The study investigates the relationship between anomie and crime in China. It found that "employment, having children, and satisfaction in life were significantly related to anomie; however, the effect of education was related to anomie in the direction that was inconsistent with what was known in the Western literature. Age had no significant effect on anomie." (b) Paul Friday, "Crime and Crime Prevention in China: A Challenge to the Development–Crime Nexus," *Journal of Contemporary Criminal Justice*, 14(3), 296–314, 1998. This article explains the linkage between increases in both crime and development in China utilizing Western theories: Durkheimian modernization, Marxism, and victimology. It reaffirms the need for traditional Chinese crime-prevention policies and practices in the midst of unprecedented social changes.

60. Zhang Chunli, "The Influence of Globalization in Crime," *Journal of Chinese People's Public Security University* (*PSU Journal*), 95, 22, 2002.

61. Ibid., p. 23.

62. Ibid., p. 24.

63. Ibid., p. 25.

64. Ibid., p. 27.

65. Ministry of Public Security, "Our Nation's Public Feeling of Safety Level Has Increased—Second National Public Safety Random Survey Conditions Analysis" ["*Woguo gongzhong anquan gan shuiping yousuo tigao–quanguo de er ci gongzhong anquan gan chouyang diaocha qingkuang fengxi*"], Ministry of Public Security, Beijing, 1991.

66. Hong Lu and Lening Zhang, "Death Penalty in China: The Law and the Practice," *Journal of Criminal Justice*, 33(4), 367–376, 2005.

67. Ben Blanchard, "China Launches 'Strike Hard' Crackdown in Restive West," *Reuters*, November 2, 2009 (http://www.reuters.com/article/2009/11/03/idUSPEK154707).

68. "Society 'Strike Hard' Campaign Targets Violent Crimes," *China Daily*, June 14, 2010.

69. Sue Trevaskes, "Swift and Severe Justice in China," *British Journal of Criminology*, 47(1), 23–24, 2007.
70. (a) Kang Shuhua, *Criminology: History, Present Situation, the Future* [*Fanzui xue–Lishi, xianxiang, weilai*], Qunzhong Chubanshe, Beijing, 1998. Especially see Chapter 14, "Rational Reflection on the Development and Change of New China Criminality" ["*Xin Zhongguo de fanzui fazhan bianhua yu lisheng sixiang*"], pp. 385–419. (b) For a popular media account, see Laurel Mittenthal, "China's Efforts against Crime Ineffective," *China News Digest*, December 28, 2001 (http://www.cnd.org/Global/01/12/28/011228-3.html).
71. Liu Fuzhi, "*Yanda* as a Form of People's Democratic Dictatorship: A Record of Deng Xiaoping's Strategic Policy of the Strike Hard Campaign" ["*Yanda Jiu Shi Zhuanzheng: Ji Deng Xiaoping Tongzhi Dui Yanda De Zhan Lue Juece*"], *China Procuratorial Daily* (*Zhongguo Jianchabao*), January 13, 1992.
72. Ibid., pp. 1–3.
73. During the Cultural Revolution (1966–1976), the legal and judicial apparatus of the nation, including the police, was completely destroyed.
74. Kang Daiwei, *Treatise on Broad Public Security Concept* [*Guangyi gongan lun*], Qunzhong Chubanshe, Beijing, 2001, pp. 28–49. As a theoretical proposition, police roles and functions are contingent on social conditions.
75. (a) Yisheng Dai, "New Directions of Chinese Policing in the Reform Era," in Jianhong Liu, Lening Zhang, and Steven F. Messner (Eds.), *Crime and Social Control in a Changing China* (pp. 151–156), Greenwood Press, Westport, CT, 2001. In 1978, the Communist Party Central Committee (CPCC) officially declared that class struggle was no longer a major contradiction in China, and in 1982 the People's Republic of China Constitution confirmed that class exploitation had been abolished. The police roles and functions shifted from fighting enemies of the class to protecting economic interests. In the process, Western-style policing was adopted (e.g., foot and mobile patrols), but Chinese policing still relies on the community and private citizens to help with crime prevention and control. (b) Allan Y. Jiao, "Traditions and Changes of Police Culture: Organization, Operation, and Behavior of the Chinese Police," in Jianhong Liu, Lening Zhang, and Steven F. Messner (Eds.), *Crime and Social Control in a Changing China* (pp. 159–177), Greenwood Press, Westport, CT, 2001.
76. Michael Dutton and Lee Tianfu, "Missing the Target? Policing Strategies in the Period of Economic Reform," *Crime & Delinquency*, 39(3), 316–336, 1993. In the 1980s, the Chinese government resorted to mass mobilization campaign to suppress crime, but to no avail. In the 1990s, the police adopted more selective and focused measures, such as striking at hot spots and surveillance of at-risk populations, and met with some success. Crime suppression gave way to administration and supervision; however, extralegal forms of control were never abandoned, and substantive justice still prevails over procedural due process.
77. Li Wenxi, "Understanding and Pondering over Building Up "Grand Stability" under the Concept of 'Maintaining Stability,'" *Public Security Studies*, 182, 5–10, 2009.
78. Ren Yinxun, "20 Years of Persistent Search and Development in Public Security Work Enterprise," *Public Security Studies*, 63, 16–19, 1999.
79. The Chinese word for "crisis" (simplified Chinese, 危机; traditional Chinese, 危機; pinyin, wēijī; Wade-Giles, *wei-chi*).
80. (a) Wu Zhong, "Corruption Taints China's Police Heroes," *Asia Times*, April 30, 2009. (b) Kam C. Wong, "A Reflection on Police Abuse of Power in the People's Republic of China," *Justice Quarterly*, 1(2), 87–112, 1998.
81. Jeffery Hays, *Facts and Details: Fighting Corruption in China*, 2010 (http://factsanddetails.com/china.php?itemid=303&catid=8&subcatid=49).
82. (a) Kam C. Wong, "Studying China Policing: Some Personal Reflections," *International Journal of Sociology of Law*, 35(3), 1–20, 2007. (b) Kam C. Wong, *Chinese Policing: History and Reform*, Peter Lang, New York, 2009, pp. 1–30.

83. Lu Zhuo, "The Seven Challenges Confronting the Chinese Police in New Century," *Public Security Studies*, 77, 9–15, 2001.

84. Kam C. Wong, "Policing in PRC: Road to Reform in the 1990s," *British Journal of Criminology*, 42, 281–236, 2002.

85. In the People's Republic of China, "public security" is referred to as *gongan* or *jingcha*, and both terms will be used throughout this text.

86. "Ministry of Public Security," in Jin Mingyuan (Ed.), *The Directory of Chinese Government Organs, 1989–1990* (p. 48), New China News, Hong Kong, 1990.

87. The "People's Republic of China Regulations" ("*Zhonghua renmin gongheguo renmin jingcha tiaoli*"), referred to as the Police Act of 1957, were passed at the 76th meeting of the Standing Committee of the First National People's Congress on June 25, 1957. For an English translation, see *Compendium of Laws and Regulations of the People's Republic of China* [*Chung-hua jen-min kung-ho-kuo fa-kuei hui-pien*], Zhongguo Minzhu Falü Chubanshe, Beijing, 1994, pp. 113–116. The Police Act was nullified during the Cultural Revolution but was revived without amendment in 1980. In 1957, when the Police Act was first promulgated, Mao and the Party were still concerned with counterrevolutionaries and spies.

88. "Shanghai 110 Police Report Service Station" ["*Shanghai 110 baojing fuwuti*"], *People's Public Security Daily* (*Renmin Gongan Bao*), July 10, 1993, p. 1.

89. Ibid.

90. *New China Legal System Construction: Overview of 40 Years of Significant Events: 1949–1988* [*Xin Zhongguo Zhiji Jianshe Shixi Lian Yao Nan: 1949–1988*], Qunzhong Chubanshe, Beijing, 1990, p. 409. The concern with crime led to successive nationwide anticrime campaigns, the most famous one being the *yanda* ("Strike Hard") anticrime movement sponsored by Deng and conducted in three waves from 1983 to 1987.

91. On August 26, 1980, Vice-Justice Minister Xie Bangzhi officially declared to the world for the first time that China, too, has a crime problem (at the Sixth United Nations Congress on Crime Prevention and Criminal Justice).

92. "Tao Siju Discusses Social Security Situation and Public Security Force Organization" ["*Tao Siju tan shehui zhian he gongan duiwu jianshe*"], *People's Public Security Daily* (*Renmin Gongan Bao*), March 27, 1993, p. 1. The pledge to fight crime has by now become an annual ritual.

93. "Work Hard to Protect Transformation of Enterprise" ["*Wei baohu qiye gaige jinli*"], *People's Public Security Daily* (*Renmin Gongan Bao*), March 18, 1993, p. 3. Public security should protect enterprises undergoing transformation. Public security's new role has been institutionalized by "*Jiguan qiye danwei anquan baowei gongzuo guiding*" ("Regulations for the Protection of Organ and Enterprise Units") and "*Hu chang dui zhangcheng*" ("Factory Guard Team Rules").

94. "Support and protect enterprises in the change process" ["*Zhichi he baowei qiye zhuanbian jizhi*"], *People's Public Security Daily* (*Renmin Gongan Bao*), March 6, 1993, p. 1. The Hebei public security organs at various levels pledged support and protection for public enterprises undergoing transformation in the economic reform process. Changes in organization structure, processes, and routines can cause instability. They threaten vested interests, challenge established power arrangements, and destroy existing beneficial relationships. In particular, public security has to see how changes might affect the welfare of the working people and anticipate their likely reactions. It has to be sensitive to latent tensions and inchoate conflicts. It has to be prepared to diffuse the problem by addressing the underlying concerns and resolving the root contradictions. In cases where the conflicts cannot be resolved, public security has to be prepared to provide speedy, responsive, and adequate protection for an enterprise's management.

95. Judy Polumbaum, "Review: Making Sense of June 4, 1989: Analyses of the Tiananmen Tragedy," *Australian Journal of Chinese Affairs*, 26, 177–186, 1991.

96. John Wong and Zheng Yongnian, *The Nanxun Legacy and China's Development in the Post-Deng Era*, World Scientific, Singapore, 2001, p. 12. One hand liberally promotes reform, and one hand strictly maintains order.

97. In 2000, when Jiang Zemin was on an inspection tour of Guangdong Province, he delivered his "Three Represents" theory. As a party, the Communist Party of China (CPC) "unswervingly represents the development trend of advanced productive forces, the orientation of advanced culture, and the fundamental interests of the overwhelming majority of the people in China." For its application to policing, see "The Three Represents Studies," *Public Security Studies*, 72, 8–14, 2000.

98. Lyman Miller, "Overlapping Transitions in China's Leadership," *SAIS Review*, 16(2), 21–42, 1996.

99. To establish legitimacy, the Ministry of Public Security (MPS) ordered the rehabilitation of thousands of political prisoners jailed during the Gang of Four era.

100. (a) Mu Xinsheng, "Preliminary Discussion of the Role and Functions of Public Security Organs during the Primary Stage of Socialism" ["*Shilun shehui zhuyi chuji jieduan renmin gongan jiguan de zhineng*"], *Public Security Studies*, 1, 1–3, 1988. In the inaugural issue of *Public Security Studies*, Mu Xinsheng, the deputy director of the Social Security Bureau, Ministry of Public Security, made clear that there would be no turning back on the reform process. (b) Zhao Ziyang, *Advance by Following the Road of Socialism with China Characteristics* [*Yuan zhe you zhongguo teshi de shehui zhuyi daolu qianjin*], paper presented during the Thirteenth National Congress of the Chinese Communist Party, Beijing, October 25 to November 1, 1987. The author suggested that the success of Chinese reform depends on understanding the doctrinal and theoretical underpinning of the reform. In this regard, the Marxist–Leninist theory is inadequate to explain the economic reform and market opening in China.

101. Daniel Katz and Robert L. Kahn, *Organizations and the System Concept*, John Wiley & Sons, New York, 1966, pp. 14–29. System theorists have long observed that bureaucracies as open systems have to adjust to the changing environment to preserve the basic characteristics of the system.

102. Susan Trevaskes, "Severe and Swift Justice in China," *The British Journal of Criminology*, 47, 23–41, 2007.

103. (a) David Holley, "The Foolish Old Man and Other Heroes: Although Some Sneer at the Stories, All Chinese Are Fed an Endless Diet of Role Models," *Los Angeles Times*, May 8, 1990, Part H, p. 4. The Chinese Communist Party uses heroes and models to inspire and motivate people in service of communism. An old Chinese fable about a foolish old man who moved a mountain was used to demonstrate the power of perseverance in fighting imperialism, and Yue Fei, a popular Song dynasty hero, was used to instill patriotism in generations of schoolchildren. (b) Refer also to the Lei Feng Memorial (*Jingsheng neihan*), http://www.leifeng.org.cn/1043.asp.

104. Zhou Wei, "Preliminary Discussion of Community Policing," *Journal of Chinese People's Public Security University* (*PSU Journal*), 9(1), 11–14, 1993. Community policing and comprehensive social security control will help prevent crime and maintain order.

105. Duan Xue and Xiao Youzhi, "Characteristics of Public Security Work at the Early Stage" ["*Cuoji jieduan gongan gongzuo de tezheng*"], *Public Security Studies*, 1, 13, 1988.

106. (a) "Public Security Reform Should Fit Post WTO Situations and Objective Requirements" ["*Gongan yao shiying rushi hou xingshi fazhang de kekuan yaojiu*"], *CPD.com*, December 20, 2001 (www.cpd.com.cn/xxlr.asp?menulb=039%C8%CB%C3%F1%B9%AB%B0%B2%B1%A8&id=9097). Public security reform in the service of economic development should allow the private sector to take over many of the administrative functions. (b) "Comments on Implementation of Administrative Review System Reform Work Call for Delegation of Prior Public Security Administration Activities to the Market Forces" ["*Guanyu xingzheng shenpi zhidu gaige gongzuo shishi yijian*"], 2001. The Ministry of Public Security (MPS), for example, allowed certain properly certified "middleman agencies" (*zhongjie jikou*) to process exit visa applications for business visits and migrations. By December 20, 2001, the MPS had approved 219 middleman agencies in nine provinces and municipalities, including Shantung, Anhui, Heilongjiang, Zhejiang, Sichuan, Zhongxing, Hubei, and Tianjin. (c) "To Exist the Country Must Find Authorized Mediating

Organizations" ["*Chuguo qingzhao hege zhongjie*"]. In June 2001, the MPS promulgated management measures for private control of border exit and entry (*Yinsi churur jing zhongjie guanli banfa*); see http://www.mps.gov.cn/n16/n1282/n3493/n3823/n441902/449949.html.

107. Warren Bennis, "Organizations of the Future," *Personnel Administration*, September–October, 1967. The Weberian model of bureaucracy is vulnerable in the twentieth century due to radical changes in the political economy.

108. "A Milestone in Police Legal System Building" ["*Renmin jingcha fazhi jianche de lichengbei*"], *People's Public Security Daily* (*Renmin Gongan Bao*), March 2, 1995, pp. 1–2.

109. Decree No. 40 by the President of the People's Republic of China, Law on People's Police of the People's Republic of China, was adopted by the 12th Session of the Eighth National People's Congress (NPC) Standing Committee of the PRC on February 28, 1995, and published in the *Gazette of the State Council of the People's Republic of China* (*Zhonghua renmin gongheguo guowuyuan gongbao*) on April 10, 1995.

110. Feng Luo, *Explanation of the PRC People's Police Law* [*Zhonghua renmin gongheguo renmin jingcha fa shiyi*], Qunzhong Chubanshe, Beijing, 1995.

111. The "Public Security Organs Inspection Regulations" ("*Gongan jiguan ducha tiaoli*") were promulgated by the State Council on June 4, 1997.

112. *People's Public Security Daily* (*Renmin Gongan Bao*), July 22, 1995, p. 1.

113. "Regulations of the People's Republic of China Governing the Use of Weapons by the People's Police" ("*Renmin jingcha shiyong jingxie he wuqi tiaoli*") were passed on January 8, 1996, at the 41st Meeting of the State Council; promulgated on January 16, 1996, by Premier Li Peng by Decree No. 191 of the State Council of the PRC; and published in the *Gazette of the State Council of the People's Republic of China* (*Zhonghua remin gongheguo guowuyuan gongbao*) on January 29, 1996.

114. Bruce Gilley, "The Limits of Authoritarian Resilience," *Journal of Democracy*, 14(1), 18–26, 2003.

115. Shi Tianjian, "Village Committee Elections in China: Institutionalist Tactics for Democracy," *World Politics*, 51(3), 385–412, 1999. In all successful reform movements, no less in China, the support of the various interested parties is essential.

116. "China Suspends 1739 Police from Duty for Discipline Violation in 2009," *People's Daily*, February 23, 2010 (http://english.peopledaily.com.cn/90001/90776/90882/6886316.html).

117. Lee Hong Yung, *From Revolutionary Cadres to Party Technocrats in Socialist China*, University of California Press, Berkeley, 1991.

118. Fu Hualing, "Zhou Yongkang and the Recent Police Reform in China," *Australian and New Zealand Journal of Criminology*, 38(2), 241–253, 2005.

119. "China Issues Detention Center Guideline after Detention Center Death," *People's Daily*, February 26, 2010 (http://english.peopledaily.com.cn/90001/90776/90882/6903885.html).

120. Ibid.

121. "China Suspends 1739 Police from Duty for Discipline Violation in 2009," *People's Daily*, February 23, 2010 (http://english.peopledaily.com.cn/90001/90776/90882/6886316.html). Another 1482 police were placed in confinement for discipline violations, 488 people were transferred to discipline inspection departments, and 50 were referred to judicial departments.

122. Zhao Wei, "The History and Future of Police Reform," *Public Security Studies*, 136, 31–34, 2006.

123. Li Xiaoqiang, "The Function and Evaluation of Local Police State," *Journal of Jiangxi Public Security College*, 84, 79–81, 2004.

124. Gao Zhitian, "Practices in Carrying Out and Deepening Police Station Reform in Yangcheng City," *Public Security Studies*, 63, 83–85, 1999.

125. (a) In Frederick Engels' *The Origin of the Family, Private Property, and the State* (1884), the author observed that there was no state (bureaucracy, law, and police) in communal society. The state resulted from economic development to protect the interests of the capitalistic ruling class.

When the communist revolution was complete, the workers could do away with the repressive state and its police. (b) See also Paul Dorn, "Two Months of Red Splendor: The Paris Commune and Marx' Theory of Revolution," 2005 (www.runmuki.com/paul/writing/marx.html).

126. (a) Louise Shelly, *Policing Soviet Society: The Evolution of State Control*, Routledge, New York, 1996. (b) Robert Reiner, *The Politics of the Police*, Oxford University Press, Oxford, 2000. (c) Stuart Scheingold, *The Politics of Law and Order: Street Crime and Public Policy*, Longman, New York, 1984. (d) Jean-Paul Brodeur, "High Policing and Low Policing: Remarks about the Policing of Political Activities," *Social Problems*, 30(5), 507–520, 1983.

127. Mao Tse-tung, "On the Dictatorship of the People's Democracy," speech given June 30, 1949, in commemoration of the Chinese Communist Party's 28th anniversary.

128. "The Political Nature of Chinese Public Security," in *Research of Public Security with Chinese Characteristics* [*Zhongguo tese gongan zhi yanjiu*] (pp. 16–35), Qunzhong Chubanshe, Beijing, 1996.

129. The influence of political cults started with Mao Tse-tung and ended with Deng Xiaoping, and certainly with the retirement of the old guards Li Peng and Chen Yun. Both Mao and Deng are towering figures in their own right. Mao was a charismatic leader, and Deng was an effective, tireless reformer. Both were visionaries who changed China, and both set out to recreate China in their own image. Without personal charisma, revolutionary experience, and political achievements, Jiang Zemin stayed in power through coalition building and political compromise.

130. Cheng Li exemplifies this trend to focus on elite leadership at the central and provincial levels. See his "China's Leadership Succession and Its Implications: Trends and Paradoxes," written testimony prepared for the U.S.–China Security Review Commission's public hearing held on September 23, 2002. Li is a Senior Fellow of the Brookings Institution and Professor of Government at Hamilton College, New York. See also David M. Finkelstein and Maryanne Kivlehan (Eds.), *China's Leadership in the 21st Century*, M.E. Sharpe, Armonk, NY, 2003.

131. (a) Joseph Fewsmith, "Studying the Three Represents," *China Leadership Monitor*, 8(Fall), 2003. (b) H. Lyman Miller, "The Hu–Wen Leadership at Six Months," *China Leadership Monitor*, 8(Fall), 2003. (c) Barry Naughton, "An Economic Bubble? Chinese Policy Adapts to Rapidly Changing Conditions," *China Leadership Monitor*, 9(Winter), 2004. (d) Joseph Fewsmith, "The Third Plenary Session of the 16th Central Committee," *China Leadership Monitor*, 9(Winter), 2004. (e) H. Lyman Miller, "Hu Jintao and the Party Politburo," *China Leadership Monitor*, 9(Winter), 2004. (f) Li Cheng, "China's Northeast: From Largest Rust Belt to Fourth Economic Engine," *China Leadership Monitor*, 9(Winter), 2004. (g) Joseph Fewsmith, "Continuing Pressures on Social Order," *China Leadership Monitor*, 10(Spring), 2004. (h) H. Lyman Miller, "Where Have All the Elders Gone?" *China Leadership Monitor*, 10(Spring), 2004. (i) Li Cheng, "Hu's New Deal and the New Provincial Chiefs," *China Leadership Monitor*, 10(Spring), 2004.

132. Jiang Zemin, Chairman of the CPC Central Military Commission; Hu Jintao, General Secretary of the 16th CPC Central Committee; Politburo Standing Central Committee Members of the CPC Central Committee, including Wu Bangguo, Wen Jiabao, Jia Qinglin, Zeng Qinghong, Huang Ju, Wu Guanzheng, Li Changchun, and Luo Gan; Cao Gangchuan and Guo Boxiong, Politburo members of the CPC Central Committee.

133. H. Lyman Miller, "Where Have All the Elders Gone?" *China Leadership Monitor*, 10, 1–7, 2004.

134. Deng Xiaoping set the course for meritorious promotion, requiring future leaders to be "revolutionary, younger, more knowledgeable, and more specialized."

135. Shiping Zheng, "Leadership Change, Legitimacy, and Party Transition in China," *Journal of Chinese Political Science*, 8(1/2), 56, 2003. The Communist Party of China (CPC) Organization Department rated candidates for their fitness to hold top CPC leadership posts based on ideological purity, Party loyalty, work attitude, and leadership ability. The CCP has transitioned from a revolutionary party to a reform party to an institutionalization party.

136. Shiping Zheng, "Leadership Change, Legitimacy, and Party Transition in China," *Journal of Chinese Political Science*, 8(1/2), 47–64, 2003. The First Plenary Session of the 16th Central Committee will select the General Committee (Politburo, Standing Committee, CMC), revise

the CCP charter, report on past achievements, and pinpoint/resolve outstanding theoretical issues. There are increasing signs that the "fourth generation" will chart a new course for China policy and politics; for example, socially it championed "building a Party for the interest of the public, governing for people" (*lidang weigong, zhizheng weimin*) and politically it embraced intra-party democracy.

137. (a) Kerry Brown, "The Power Struggle among China's Elite," *Foreign Policy*, October 10, 2010. (b) Jonanthan Fenby, "Xi Jinping: The Man Who'll Lead China into a New Age," *Guardian*, November 7, 2010. As this book goes to print, China will be ready for another generation of leaders, such as Xi Jingping and Li Keqiang. What their policy on crime, law, and justice will be is anyone's guess.

138. The "Three Represents" are advanced productive forces, advanced culture, and the broad masses of the people, each of which should be a central concern of national policy. The "Three Represents" were made part of the Constitution of the Communist Party of China in 2002.

139. David M. Lampton, The Johns Hopkins University, School of Advanced International Studies, presented "China's Domestic Political Scene" at the Council on Foreign Relations conference China's Transition at a Turning Point, September 24, 2003 (www.cfr.org/publication. php?id=6441). Hu and Wen established a distinctive leadership identity different from that of Jiang.

140. (a) H. Lyman Miller, "The Hu–Wen Leadership at Six Months," *China Leadership Monitor*, 8(Fall), 2003. (b) Joseph Fewsmith, "The Third Plenary Session of the 16th Central Committee," *China Leadership Monitor*, 9(Winter), 2004. (c) H. Lyman Miller, "Hu Jintao and the Party Politburo," *China Leadership Monitor*, 9(Winter), 2004. (d) H. Lyman Miller, "Where Have All the Elders Gone?" *China Leadership Monitor*, 10(Spring), 2004. (e) Li Cheng, "Hu's New Deal and the New Provincial Chiefs," *China Leadership Monitor*, 10(Spring), 2004.

141. Joseph, Khan, "Political Moves in China: The More Things Change," *New York Times*, October 23, 2007, p. A3. "Hu knows how he wants to nudge the system forward," said Kenneth Lieberthal, a professor of politics and business administration at the University of Michigan. "But it is not clear that he intends to get tough. He is content to identify the broad elements and leave the implementation to others."

142. Tony Saich, "Social Development in 2006: Focus on Social Development," *Asian Survey*, 47(1), 32–43, 2007.

143. When Zhou Yongkang was the Minister of Public Security, he tried to put his imprint on police reform with campaign-style mobilization efforts, such as nationwide inspection and consultation.

144. Li Yuanhan, "The Removal of Beijing Public Security Bureau Leaders Deals a Heavy Blow to Zhou Yongkang," *KanZhongGuo*, August 3, 2010. "The Chinese Communist Party's system of Public Security, Procuratorate, and Courts is under the control of the Communist Party's Central Political and Legal Committee, hence controlled by Luo Gan and Zhou Yongkang, two major agents of Jiang Zemin. It is almost a separate kingdom, the darkest of the dark in the Communist Party. Some netizens have said, 'Premier Wen Jiabao can handle the financial crisis but is helpless in front of the police abusing their power.'" Allegedly, Hu–Wen sought to rein in Zhou's power by orchestrating the removal of Ma Zhenchuan, Director of the Beijing Public Security Bureau, and Wu Yuhua, Director of the Bureau of Justice in Beijing, at the 13th National People's Congress held on February 26, 2010, in addition to investigating many senior public security officials for corruption. In 2009, Hu–Wen began to investigate the high-ranking officials in the Ministry of Public Security (MPS), the Supreme Court, and other officials in the legal system, such as Zheng Shaodong, the Assistant Secretary of the MPS and the Bureau Chief of the Financial Crime Investigation Bureau; Xiang Huaizhu, Deputy Bureau Chief of the Financial Crime Investigation Bureau; and Yu Bing, Director of the Internet Monitoring Department of the Beijing Public Security Bureau.

145. Zong Hairen is the pseudonym of a Party insider who wrote *The Fourth Generation* [*Disidai*], Mirror Books, Carle Place, NY, 2001.

146. Andrew J. Nathan and Bruce Gilley, "China's New Rulers: The Path to Power," *The New York Review of Books*, September 16, 2002.

147. Increasingly, politics in China is driven by cliques or political networking; for example, Jiang's "Shanghai Gang," Zeng's "Princelings' Party" (*taizidang*), Hu's "Chinese Communist Youth League (CCYL) Officials," Zhu's "Qinghua Clique," and others such as the "Fellow Provincials" (*tongxiang*) and "Personal Secretary Clusters" (*mishuqun*). In addition, some new political groups, such as the "Returnees from Study Overseas" (*haiguipai*), have also emerged as distinct elite groups within the central leadership. See Cheng Li's "China's Leadership Succession and Its Implications: Trends and Paradoxes," written testimony prepared for the U.S.–China Security Review Commission's public hearing held on September 23, 2002. Li is a Senior Fellow of the Brookings Institution and Professor of Government at Hamilton College, New York. He wrote: "Hu [Jintao] is a prominent member of the so-called 'Qinghua University clique,' he headed the Chinese Communist Youth League in the early 1980s, and he has served as president of the Central Party School since 1993."

148. For the work style and achievements of Zhou, see Yongyi Song, "The Role of Zhou Enlai in the Cultural Revolution: A Contradictory Image from Diverse Sources," *Issues & Studies*, 37(2), 1–28, 2001.

149. Jean-Pierre Cabestan, "The 10th National People's Congress and After: Moving towards a New Authoritarianism, Both Elitist and Consultative?" *China Perspectives*, 47(May/June), 4–20, 2003.

150. "Getting Ahead by Telling the Truth," *Beijing Review*, 46(52), 3, 2003. Premier Wen Jiabao went to a village in Chongqing to help Xiong Deming, a commoner, to collect back pay due from a local contractor. The article observed that the premier "is deeply concerned with the interests of the common people." The same page features a photo with the caption: "President cares. Chinese President Hu Jintao shakes hands with rural farmers in a village in Dongming County, Shandong Province. Hu made an inspection tour to Shandong and Henan, two of the country's major grain-producing areas, in mid-December and stressed the need to increase farmers' income."

151. "Viewpoint: Implementing Structural Reform," *Beijing Review*, 47(2), 18, 2004.

152. Hu–Wen sought balanced growth in China, in contrast to Jiang's hope for fast growth. The article, "A Friend of Nature," *Beijing Review*, 46(52), 3, 2003, introduced Professor Liang Congjie, a professor of history at the Academy for Chinese Culture and an editor of China's encyclopedia, who founded Friends of Nature (FON) in 1994.

153. "Supreme Court: Need to Respect and Protect the Entitled Rights of the Accused" ["*Zui gao fa yuan: yao zunzhong he baozheng xingshi beigao ren yingyou de renquan*"], *China Police Net*, June 18, 2004 (www.cpd.com.cn/gb/szyl/2004-06/18/content 307752.htm).

154. "China's Top 10 News Events in 2003: 1. Historical Party Conference," *Beijing Review*, 46(52), 24, 2003.

155. "Chinese Premier Meets Press," March 14, 2004, Embassy of the People's Republic of China in the Kingdom of Sweden (http://www.chinaembassy.se/eng/62933.html).

156. Issue symbol vs. substance, theory vs. practice, intention vs. reality, start vs. finish.

157. Cheng Li, "Does a New Generation of Chinese Leaders Mean New Policy?" luncheon discussion, October 23, 2002, Nixon Center, Washington, DC (http://www.nixoncenter.org/Program%20 Briefs/vol8no19.htm).

158. See Cheng Li's "China's Leadership Succession and Its Implications: Trends and Paradoxes," written testimony prepared for the U.S.–China Security Review Commission's public hearing held on September 23, 2002. Li is a Senior Fellow of the Brookings Institution and Professor of Government at Hamilton College, New York.

159. Tony Saich, "Social Development in 2006: Focus on Social Development," *Asian Survey*, 47(1), 32–43, 2007.

160. Shiping Zheng, "Leadership Change, Legitimacy, and Party Transition in China," *Journal of Chinese Political Science*, 8(1/2), 47–64, 2003; especially see "Challenges to Legitimacy" on p. 51.

161. Whether Western-style democracy is necessary for successful China reform and transition to a modern society is still very much in debate, particularly within the peasants' rank. For the peasants, a secure and prosperous regime is preferable to disorder and an impoverished regime. Deng, as the head of the Peasants Party, insisted on order and security over rights and democracy. Alternatively, there has been debate over people's livelihood (*min sheng*) vs. people's democracy (*min zhu*). China since antiquity has been more focused on the first concern; that is, with regard to rulers, the litmus test for legitimacy is good governance, not popularity.

162. Baogang Guo, "Political Legitimacy and China's Transition," *Journal of Chinese Political Science*, 8(1/2), 1–25, 2003; especially see "Era of Hu Jintao," pp. 16–19.

163. Maureen Fan, "China's Party Leadership Declares New Priority: 'Harmonious Society'; Doctrine Proposed by President Hu Formally Endorsed," *Washington Post*, October 12, 2006 (http://www.washingtonpost.com/wp-dyn/content/article/2006/10/11/AR2006101101610.html).

164. Matthew Boswell, "Harmonious Society," *China Elections and Governance*, July 23, 2007. (http://en.chinaelections.org/newsinfo.asp?newsid=9752). The "harmonious society" evolved through time. Jiang Zemin's report to the 16th Party Congress (November 8, 2002) mentions "social harmony." In 2004, during the Fourth Plenum of 16th Central Committee of the Communist Party of China, the goal to create a "socialist harmonious society" appeared in a resolution designed to improve Party governance. On February 19, 2005, during a speech to the Central Party School, Hu set down specific elements of building a "socialist harmonious society." On March 4, 2006, Hu specified the eight honors and eight disgraces (as a harmonious society platform) in a speech to delegates of the Chinese People's Political Consultative Conference (CPPCC). In 2006, during a politburo meeting, top officials decided to draft a resolution toward building a harmonious society; in October, during the Sixth Plenum of the 16th Central Committee of the Communist Party of China, the draft resolution was adopted, and it specifically addressed major issues concerning the building of a socialist harmonious society.

165. Wu Dahu and Wang Fei, "Legitimation of Criminal Punishment and Reconstruction of a Harmonious Society: An Approach to the Protection of Human Rights of Criminals in the Process of Measuring Punishment," *Journal of Chinese People's Public Security University* (*PSU Journal*), 125, 1–7, 2007.

166. "Premier Wen Stresses Building of Harmonious Society," *News Guangdong*, March 5, 2005 (http://www.newsgd.com/news/China1/200503050017.htm).

167. Shenzhen is the first Special Economic Zone granted wide powers from the central government to experiment with economic matters.

168. Shenzhen has conducted two other open recruitments for police. In December 2003 Shenzhen openly recruited 600 officers from the People's Liberation Army, and in March 2004 it openly recruited 800 recent graduates.

169. The officers from other agencies still need to seek permission from public security officials at the next level before applying to Shenzhen. Not all police agencies are as progressive as Yi Chang. Some agencies require police to resign before applying to Shenzhen (e.g., Jing Zhou).

170. See also "Training for War" ["*Lian wei zhan*"], *People's Police*, 10, 2004 (http://www.cpd.com.cn/gb/newspaper/2004-06/07/content 303832.htm).

171. "Sound the Trumpet for Complete Training of All Police" ["*Chuixiang quanjing da lianbing dehojiao*"], *People's Police*, 10, 2004 (http://www.cpd.com.cn/gb/newspaper/2004-06/07/content 303832.htm).

172. John L. Thornton, "China's Leadership Gap," *Foreign Affairs*, 85(6), 133–141, 2006. Chinese young people, especially those who are talented and well educated, are not joining the government. Unlike in the past when the best and brightest took the rigorous imperial examination and became mandarins, today the most talented students are more attracted by lucrative offers from multinationals than by the high call of public service.

173. Albert Chen's "Toward a Legal Enlightenment: Discussion in Contemporary China on the Rule of Law" was originally presented at a seminar on the rule of law organized by the Mansfield Center for Pacific Affairs in Hong Kong on December 6, 1999. It was subsequently published in *UCLA Pacific Basin Law Journal*, 17(2/3), 125–165, 2000.

174. (a) Randall Peerenboom, *Are China's Legal Reform Stalled?* The Foundation for Law, Justice and Society, Oxford, U.K., 2007. (b) "Establishing Our Country under the Rule of Law," *People's Daily*, September 15, 2009.

175. Kam C. Wong, "Govern Police by Law (*Yifa Zhijing*) in China," *Australian and New Zealand Journal of Criminology*, 37, 90, 2004.

176. Ministry of Public Security, "Outline for Promoting the Comprehensive Implementation of Administration in Accordance with the Law" ["*Quanmian tuijin yifa xingzheng shishi gangyao*"], *Xinhua*, March 22, 2004 (http://news.xinhuanet.com/zhengfu/2004-04/21/content 1431232.htm).

177. Zhao Yuhong, "Public Participation in China's EIA Regime: Rhetoric or Reality?" *Law Journal*, 22(1), 89–123, 2010.

178. Information Office of the State Council of the People's Republic of China, "White Paper: China's Efforts and Achievements in Promoting the Rule of Law," *Xinhua*, February 28, 2008 (http://news.xinhuanet.com/english/2008-02/28/content 7687418.htm).

179. Property Law of the People's Republic of China, adopted at the Fifth Session of the Tenth National People's Congress of the People's Republic of China on March 16, 2007, went into effect on October 1, 2007.

180. Law of the People's Republic of China on Administrative Penalty, adopted at the Fourth Session of the Eighth National People's Congress of the People's Republic of China on March 17, 1996, went into effect on March 17, 1996.

181. Administrative Review Law of the People's Republic of China, adopted at the Ninth Session of the Ninth National People's Congress of the People's Republic of China on April 29, 1999, went into effect on October 1, 1999.

182. Administrative Procedure Law of the People's Republic of China, adopted at the Second Session of the Seventh National People's Congress of the People's Republic of China on April 4, 1989, went into effect on April 4, 1989.

183. Law of the People's Republic of China on Administrative Supervision, adopted at the 25th Meeting of the Standing Committee of the Eighth National People's Congress of the People's Republic of China on May 9, 1997, went into effect on May 9, 1997.

184. (a) "Chinese Premier Vows to Fight Corruption of Gov't Officials," *Xinhua*, March 25, 2008. (b) "China Flexes Muscles to Combat Corruption," *Xinhua*, March 12, 2010. Prosecutor-General Cao Jianming in his Work Report revealed that the nation's procurator's officers investigated 2670 officials above the county level in the last year for corruption charges; eight were at the provincial or ministerial level, including Huang Songyou, former vice president of the Supreme People's Court, and Wang Yi, former vice president of the state-run China Development Bank.

185. "Crush Corruption," *Beijing Review*, 47(1), 3, 2004.

186. Jim Yardley, "The Chinese Go after Corruption, Corruptly," *New York Times*, October 22, 2006.

187. "Chinese Lawmakers Urge Amplified Anti-Corruption Efforts to Maintain Social Stability," *People's Daily*, March 10, 2010.

188. Cheng Wenhao, *Measuring Corruption and Increasing Corruption Awareness in China: An Index to Measure Public Sector Corruption and Case Studies of Important Corruption Investigations*, Center for Strategic & International Studies, Washington, DC, 2009.

189. "2010 Work Outline of National Bureau of Corruption Prevention Printed and Issued," National Bureau of Corruption Prevention of China, February 24, 2010 (http://www.nbcp.gov.cn/article/English/RecentWork/201002/20100200006090.shtml).

190. "China Establishes National Bureau of Corruption Prevention," *People's Daily*, September 13, 2007 (http://english.peopledaily.com.cn/90001/90776/90785/6261846.html).

191. "Death Sentence Given to Ex-Police Internet Supervisory Department Head," *Beijing News*, August 1, 2010 (http://news.qq.com/a/20100821/000065.htm).

192. Wang Huazhong and Ma Wei, "Corrupt Police Officers Racked Up Fortune," *China Daily*, September 29, 2009.

193. "Ex-Justice Wen Qiang Executed in Chongqing," *Xinhua*, July 7, 2010.

194. "Convicted Ex-Top Cop Asks for Leniency," *China Daily*, May 14, 2010.
195. Li Yuanhan, "The Removal of Beijing Public Security Bureau Leaders Deals a Heavy Blow to Zhou Yongkang," *KanZhongGuo*, August 3, 2010.
196. "Protect Patients' Privacy," *Beijing Review*, 47(1), 3, 2004.
197. "Supreme Court: Need to Respect and Protect the Entitled Rights of the Accused" ["*Zui gao fa yuan: yao zunzhong he baozheng xingshi beigao ren yingyou de renquan*"], *China Police Net* (*Zhongguo jingcha wang*), June 18, 2004 (http://www.cpd.com.cn/gb/szyl/2004-06/18/content 307752.htm).
198. In historical context, *ke sha er bu ke ru* actually stands for *shi ke sha er bu ke ru*, or "a gentleman can be killed but he cannot be humiliated." It is a moral imperative, imploring people to respect the dignity of those who are defeated. In Imperial China, for example, officials were given an opportunity to own up to their misconduct through self-infliction of punishment, such as suicide. Note that such respect is not given to everyone (e.g., common criminals) but only to those who are found to be deserving.
199. Information Office of the State Council of the People's Republic of China, "National Human Rights Action Plan of China (2009–2010)," *Xinhua*, April 13, 2009 (http://news.xinhuanet.com/english/2009-04/13/content 11177126.htm).
200. "Violent Protest against the Law Attracted 'Assault against Police Crime' Debate" ["*Buli kang fa yin chu 'xijing zui' zi zheng*"], *China Police Net* (*Zhongguo jingcha wan*), May 21, 2004 (http://www.cpd.com.cn/gb/newspaper/2004-05/21/content 298410.htm).
201. Ibid.
202. Ibid.
203. For a map of Zhejiang and the location of Hangzhou, see http://www.maps-of-china.com/zhejiang-s-ow.shtml.
204. "Violent Protest against the Law Attracted 'Assault against Police Crime' Debate" ["*Buli kang fa yin chu 'xijing zui' zi zheng*"], *China Police Net* (*Zhongguo jingcha wan*), May 21, 2004 (http://www.cpd.com.cn/gb/newspaper/2004-05/21/content 298410.htm).
205. "Qin Huang Dao Established Police Rights Protection Committee" ["*Qin Huang Dao chengli jingcha weiquan weiyuanhui debate*"], *China Police Net* (*Zhongguo jingcha wang*), October 10, 2003 (http://www.cpd.com.cn/gb/newspaper/2003-10/31/content 231425.htm).
206. "Violent Protest against the Law Attracted 'Assault against Police Crime' Debate" ["*Buli kang fa yin chu 'xijing zui' zi zheng*"], *China Police Net* (*Zhongguo jingcha wan*), May 21, 2004 (http://www.cpd.com.cn/gb/newspaper/2004-05/21/content 298410.htm).
207. Wang Shaopeng, "Pondering over Improving the Credibility of Law Enforcement by Public Security Agencies in the New Eras," *Public Security Studies*, 188, 51–54, 2009.
208. Wen Xinhua and Tong Yongzheng, "Variously Enhancing the Police Professional Construction Is an Important Aspect to Improving Policing Performance," *Journal of Shanghai Public Security Academy*, 9(6), 16–17, 1999.
209. Ibid., p. 18.
210. Lu Zhuo, "The Seven Challenges Confronting the Chinese Police in New Century," *Public Security Studies*, 77, 9–15, 2001.
211. Li Tulai et al., "To Bring the Functions of Police Forces into Full Play and Create a Stable and Suitable Environment for Economic Development," *Public Security Studies*, 93, 51–56, 2002. The functions of the police after WTO include: (1) secure political stability, (2) maintain the social order, (3) establish an effective public order control system, (4) improve the public security administrative system to support economic development, and (5) build a high-quality public security organization.
212. Wan Shengzhi, Li Zhenyu, Zhan Caigui, and Zhang Jincun, "The Issue about the Police Participating in Non-Policing Activities," *Public Security Studies*, 69, 21–25, 2000. Local county and village police participated in extralegal and nonpolice activities, such as collecting taxes and fees, enforcing birth control, assisting in demolition and construction, and intervening in commercial disputes. They felt obligated to do so because they feared antagonizing the local political leadership and receiving less financial support.

213. Zhang Zhaoping, "The Way out for Solving the Problem of Unreliable Statistics of Criminal Cases Reported," *Journal of Chinese People's Public Security University* (*PSU Journal*), 66, 105–106, 1997. There are pressures from the Ministry of Public Security and provincial Public Security Bureaus (PSBs) to keep local *paichusuo* crime data stable and low, especially during the *yanda* period.

214. Li Dawen, "Enhancing and Improving Public Security Work and Constructing a Good Investment Environment," *Public Security Studies*, 77, 55–58, 2001. Public security has to create a good investment climate for business, including not regulating business too tightly (*yi dao ce*, literally "cut with one slice," meaning zero tolerance of irregularities), punishing arbitrarily (*luan fa*), and investigating indiscriminately (*luan cha*). Favorable treatment of business attracts justifiable criticism; for example, exercising discretion might be interpreted as corruption and leniency might be construed as favoritism.

215. Examples include Deng Xiaoping's *yanda* ("Strike Hard" campaign) and Hu's New Leftist.

216. Kam C. Wong, "Law of Assembly in the People's Republic of China," *Journal of Civil Rights and Social Justice*, 12(2), 151–181, 2006.

217. Standing Committee of the National People's Congress, People's Police Law of the People's Republic of China, adopted at the 12th Meeting of the Standing Committee of the Eighth National People's Congress on February 28, 1995, effective February 28, 1995.

218. Ibid.

219. Hu Dacheng, "The Nature of Police: Dominated by the Nation's Political Power," *Journal of Jiangsu Police Officer College*, 157–163, 2003.

220. Li Kunsheng, "Discussion on the Concept of Police" ["*Lun jingcha e gailian*"], *Journal of Chinese People's Public Security University* (*PSU Journal*), 55, 9–17, 1995.

221. Ibid., p. 11.

222. Ibid., p. 12.

223. Hu Dacheng, "The Nature of Police: Dominated by the Nation's Political Power," *Journal of Jiangsu Police Officer College*, 161, 2003.

224. Qi Honghan and Peng Yunjun, "The Challenges Confronting the Investigators of Economic Crimes after China Joined WTO and the Possible Solution," *Public Security Studies*, 77, 60–62, 2001.

225. Li Dongtai, "Pondering over Measures against Organized Crime with the Character of Black Society," *Public Security Studies*, 76, 23–27, 2001.

226. Zhou Zhengxin, "Discussion on Drug Abuse and Possible Countermeasures," *Public Security Studies*, 77, 68–71, 2001.

227. Jiagn Zhangqing, "Measures against Pornography on Personal Computers," *Journal of Chinese People's Public Security University* (*PSU Journal*), 66, 69–74, 1997.

228. Yang Fengrui, "The Situation of Illicit Drugs and International Cooperation against the Drugs in China," *Public Security Studies*, 77, 13–18, 2001.

229. Huang Wenya, "Delving into the Legal Issues of Enhancing the Coordination between Hong Kong Police and Guangdong Police," *Public Security Studies*, 73, 80–84, 2000.

230. "Impact of Transnational Crime upon National Security and Countermeasures against Such Crime," *Public Security Studies*, 74, 24–28, 2000.

231. Yang Fengrui, "The Situation of Illicit Drugs and International Cooperation against the Drugs in China," *Public Security Studies*, 77, 13–18, 2001.

232. Zhou Zhengxin, "Discussion on Drug Abuse and Possible Countermeasures," *Public Security Studies*, 77, 68–71, 2001.

233. "Impact of Transnational Crime upon National Security and Countermeasures against Such Crime," *Public Security Studies*, 74, 24–28, 2000.

234. (a) Huang Wenya, "Delving into the Legal Issues of Enhancing the Coordination between Hong Kong Police and Guangdong Police," *Public Security Studies*, 73, 80–84, 2000. (b) "Policing Cross-Border Crimes between China and Hong Kong: A Preliminary Assessment," *Asian Policing*, 1(2), 1–30, 2004.

235. Xu Xiangqun, "Situation, Problems, and Countermeasures: An Initial Inquiry into the Police–Public Relationship," *Public Security Studies*, 65, 43–46, 1999.

236. "Investigative Report regarding Police Welfare" ["*Guanyu jingcha fuli daiyou de tiaoyan baogao*"], August 8, 2008 (http://blog.tianya.cn/blogger/post show.asp?idWriter=0&Key=0&BlogID=16396&PostID=14842684). The investigation targeted selected Hongzhou serving police officers. A variety of research methods were used, including surveys and field interviews, to gather a substantial amount of first-hand data. The policy research and analysis were primarily based on documents from provincial bureaus and municipal departments.

237. Kam C. Wong, "Policing in the People's Republic of China: Road to Reform in the 1990s," *British Journal of Criminology*, 42, 281–236, 2002.

Obstacles to Understanding Chinese Policing[1]

2

Too many Westerners, including those urging trade sanctions over the yuan, assume that they are dealing with a self-confident, rational power that has come of age. Think instead of a paranoid, introspective imperial court, already struggling to keep up with its subjects and now embarking on a slightly awkward succession—and you may be less disappointed.

The Economist (October 21, 2010)[2]

How should we judge whether a youth is a revolutionary? How can we tell? There can only be one criterion, namely, whether or not he is willing to integrate himself with the broad masses of workers and peasants and does so in practice.

Mao Tse-tung (1939)[3]

Let Chinese thinking be Chinese, not Western.

Wu Kuang Ming (2010)[4]

The Problem

Since 1979, the police in China have been undergoing a continuous process of incremental but transformational change in philosophy and ideology, vision and mission, role and function, organization and culture, process and operations, and, ultimately, identity and ethos. The Chinese police today bear little resemblance to the police of yesteryear in outlook, output, or appearance.

Surprisingly, outside of China, few attempts have been made to study Chinese legal, criminal justice, and police reform on her own terms.[5] Instead, most foreign observers have adopted a negative view toward China's political, legal, and criminal justice system to the point of being dismissive (e.g., "uncivilized") and contemptuous (e.g., "barbaric," "punitive," "arbitrary," "capricious").[6] As Edward Said made clear, in the minds of Westerners the Oriental culture and way of life are both inferior and inaccessible:

> The stereotypes assigned to Oriental cultures and "Orientals" as individuals are pretty specific: Orientals are despotic and clannish. They are despotic when placed in positions of power, and sly and obsequious when in subservient positions. Orientals, so the stereotype goes, are impossible to trust. They are capable of sophisticated abstractions, but not of concrete, practical organization or rigorous, detail-oriented analysis. Their men are sexually incontinent, while their women are locked up behind bars. Orientals are, by definition, strange. The best summary of the Orientalist mindset would probably be: "East is east and west is west, and never the twain shall meet" (Rudyard Kipling).[7]

Such negativism toward Chinese ways has not always been the case. Up through the Qing dynasty, China had been well respected by friends and feared by foes.[8] The origin of such negative views on China and their impact on police studies need to be explored, and it

51

is possible that fundamental changes must occur before any true understanding of Chinese policing can be achieved.[9] In the following pages, I address the various obstacles to understanding the police in China: (1) fossilized image, (2) misinformation, (3) cultural ignorance, (4) ideological hegemony, and (5) denial of feelings. I then discuss the problem with paternalism and propose a remedial approach to better understanding of Chinese policing.

Obstacle 1: Fossilized Image

Regrettably, many China observers, especially righteous intellectuals,[10] zealous activists,[11] sensational journalists,[12] and partisan policy wonks,[13] still hold onto a fossilized image of Chinese police. In their minds, China is still very much a backward country,[14] populated by paternalistic mandarins[15] of the emperor who impose on the people for their own good ("paternalism")[16] or who serve as revolutionary guards of the Communist Party, dictating to the people in their own name ("mass line").[17] A Western blogger had this to say about China's speech policy:

> Despite an extraordinary array of media publications and new voices in the Chinese public sphere, the public is still not allowed access to an unfettered range of views and debates on a range of subjects—whether it be the case of Liu Xiaobo, or local governance, or questions related to corruption or Copenhagen, the continuing situation in Tibetan China or the unrest in Xinjiang. Such guided and paternalistic policing of opinion and discussion continues to foster a kind of state demagoguery, and popular zealotry, that already has and will continue to have baleful consequences for China as a global presence.[18]

This is a gross misconception and distortion of Chinese politics and policy, police and policing.[19] Indeed, many people's perceptions of police problems in China are based on how they think the Chinese police operate[20] and should behave, rather than on how the police really do behave.[21] For example,

> The CCP's rule is the darkest and the most ridiculous page in Chinese history. Among its unending list of crimes, the vilest must be its persecution of Falun Gong. In persecuting "Truthfulness, Compassion, Tolerance," Jiang Zemin has driven the last nail into the CCP's coffin. *The Epoch Times* believes that by understanding the true history of the CCP we can help prevent such tragedies from ever recurring.[22]

This misperception, misconception, and misunderstanding regarding the Chinese police must change before true understanding can begin.[23] Instead of pressing China to change, the Western world should reflect on whether it might instead need to change its mindset to accommodate a modern China coming of age in her own image and by her own rights:

> Is there not some possibility that instead of China's "peaceful evolution" it can participate in a "harmonious evolution" into the international order to take a leading role in global affairs not underpinned by outbursts of aggrieved nationalism or slighted dignity, but on the basis of a greater assuredness? Some would argue that the dark anniversaries that linger in the shadows whenever the clamour celebrating state-ordained triumphs offer a guilty reminder of what has been suppressed, forgotten by fiat and negated. They also remind us of the other stories that are part of the complex of narratives informing the history of modern China. Perhaps at some far remove they will again fire the imagination of that country.[24]

Obstacle 2: Misinformation

Misunderstanding Chinese policing is caused by both misinformation and a lack of information. This is exemplified by the work of Martin I. Wayne[25] in *China's War on Terrorism: Counter-Insurgency, Politics and Internal Security* ("*China's War*").[26] The book tells the story of how China was successful in fighting insurgency and terrorism in Xinjiang with ruthless determination: "China acted early and forcefully, and although brutal, their efforts represent one of the few successes in the global struggle against Islamic terrorism." Specifically, the author offers up the following lessons supposedly learned from the Chinese counterinsurgency program in Xinjiang. First, the government must focus on neutralizing support for insurgents, both domestic and foreign. Second, the government must act early, forcefully, and comprehensively, employing a new mix of security forces and political tools. Third, the government must provide the people with meaningful security with overwhelming force, smartly deployed so as to reduce collateral damage to the public. Fourth, the government must fight insurgents from the bottom up, with the use of society-centric warfare. Finally, China's priorities of security and stability (i.e., political will) are necessary to fight terrorism, resolutely and unrelentingly. Challenges to authority and stability must be dealt with speedily and harshly.

I have few things to add to Wayne's list of cogent and trenchant recommendations, many of them adapted from Western counterterrorism and counterinsurgency doctrines, theories, and practices, purported to find expression in China. However, as a scholarly work on and about China, *China's War* raises a number of troublesome issues that undermine its authority as a policy reference, chief of which is a thesis in search of factual support. *China's War* is neither well documented nor properly referenced; for example, Wayne wrote: "In China there is no presumption of innocence....Young men are routinely brought back to the station and roughed up by police over petty theft, and spreading your thoughts on what the state would rather keep secret..." (p. 3). This statement exaggerates police abuses in China and offers no supporting documentation or evidence. The point here is not whether the Chinese police are or are not abusive or whether the citizens are or are not afforded the presumption of innocence, issues that are worthy of frank discussion and honest debate. No, the point here is that Wayne *assumed* that they are so without direct substantiation or circumstantial support. In at least two ways, *China's War* is not a balanced account of how police operate in China:

1. It is a Western-centric book. It looks at China through a Western lens. Few Chinese concepts (including terrorism), theories, strategies, or policies regarding counterterrorism were presented and discussed. In broader terms, there is no investigation into Chinese "thinking" and "feeling" on crime, punishment, order, and social control, either historical or contemporary, to contextualize the study, to anchor the interpretation, or to illuminate the findings.
2. The book is written without the benefit of Chinese scholarship or data. The source materials for the book are mainly in English, most of them having little to do with Chinese counterterrorism. Little Chinese literature was used.

Wayne suggested that Chinese data are mostly unavailable and of dubious quality. He is not alone in this critique, as many other scholars have raised the same concerns. In truth, Chinese data do offer very real challenges with regard to accessibility (availability) and quality (reliability); however, such obstacles to research are not as pronounced, serious, or intractable as they once were (e.g., in the 1960s). Furthermore, any counterterrorism data (from China or, for example, the United States after 9/11) may be more or less inaccessible, unreliable, or invalid but never completely useless. In essence, all data sources are informative in their own way, if exhaustively vetted, judiciously analyzed, and carefully deployed. Wayne's lack of diligence in collecting local data and his evaluation of Chinese scholarship recall Colin Mackerras' critique of foreign Xinjiang research in 2004: "For me, sorely missed are the perspectives of the Han Chinese and the Uighurs themselves."[27] Wayne adopted a problematic Western interpretative framework to analyze what data he did have that ignores entirely Mao's "mass line" theory underscoring the need for mass immersion in fighting terrorism. Wayne also failed to apply Mao's doctrinal thinking on fighting counterrevolutionaries and enemies of the state, to wit: "On the Correct Handling of Contradictions among the People" (1957), which has influenced the thinking of all Chinese leaders since then. Unfortunately, Wayne's haphazard study of China is not an aberration. Meaningful investigation and true understanding of Chinese policing await more grounded research of the most basic kind, as well as neutral and prolonged observation.

Obstacle 3: Cultural Ignorance[28]

Many foreign investigations into Chinese policing suffer from acute cultural ignorance due to the lack of language facility, cultural awareness, and personal curiosity of the investigators.[29] Collaboration with overseas Chinese scholars improves upon individual cultural ignorance but is not capable of entirely alleviating institutionalized cultural ignorance concerns; funding decisions and the peer review process are still governed by concepts, theories, and methods more suited to the study of Western policing than Chinese policing.[30] For example, it is now common for foreign observers to observe that China has failed to embrace the "rule of law" as a philosophy of government and principle of jurisprudence. On its face, such an observation is valid; however, such rush to judgment represents a failure to understand the meaning, functions, and operations of "law" within China's historical and cultural context.

In traditional China, the Confucians proposed to govern people with *li* ("rites")[31] and by means of *ren* ("benevolence").[32] The legalists wanted to govern the people with *fa* ("law") and with the use of *xing* ("punishment").[33] Confucianization of the law integrated these two schools of contending philosophical thoughts, Confucian (*rujia*) vs. legalist (*fajia*), in search of a better way to govern China.[34] By merging these two schools of thought, Confucianization of the law proposed that the law should adopt Confucian ethical values and principles and that Confucian ethical rules should be enforced by the law.[35] Though the Confucianization of law has been variously observed and confirmed as a dominant principle of Chinese law,[36] the impact and effect of Confucianization of the law in reformed China have rarely been studied, theoretically or empirically.[37] The wholesale transportation of the "rule of law" to China is likely to fail without first understanding the meaning, role, and function of Confucianization of the law and its implications in modern China.

If Confucianization of the law teaches us anything, it teaches that the law does not guarantee justice as stand-alone rules of dos and don'ts. Justice can only be had if we consider law alongside with and in the context of *qing, li, fa*, taking a totality of circumstances and multifactorial approach. *Qing, li, fa* (情理法) (hereinafter *QLF*) or *renqing* ("human nature," "compassion") vs. *tian li* ("heavenly principles") or *qing li* ("accepted code of conduct") or *lun li* ("ethical principles") vs. *guo fa* ("state law") are dominant ideals behind the general Chinese legal culture.

As early as 653 AD, imperial courts have pursued *QLF* as a legislative goal. The preface to *Tanglu Shuyi* ("Tang Code") observed that: "Law is established at Tang, but it should represent the essence of human nature [*tongji renqing*] and the dynamics of legal reasoning [*fali zi bian*]." Since then, *QLF* has been adopted as an adjudication norm by courts and as a dispute resolution standard by the people.

From antiquity, Chinese mediators, including judicial officers, have adopted *QLF* as the *de facto* dispute-resolution standard, with *qing* representing *anqing* ("facts of a case") or *zhenqing* ("truth of a case"). In order to decide a case correctly, judicial officers must ascertain *all* of the facts and circumstances of each case, with an eye toward establishing *zhenqing*, or truth. To satisfactorily resolve a dispute once and for all, the magistrate must uncover all of the pertinent facts: the immediate cause, the ultimate cause, all contributing factors and every mitigating and aggravating circumstance. This necessarily involves consideration of *QLF*: *anqing* ("facts of the case") , *daoli* ("reason"), and *guofa* ("law of the land").

During deliberation, *anqing* calls for consideration of *renqing*, which refers to human feelings of the common heart (*ping fan zhi xin*). To have knowledge about *renqing* allows us to determine what others would think and do in like circumstances. *Anqing* also requires an understanding of *qing yi*, or good relationships between people, and *qing mian*, or consideration for others' feelings (i.e., *renqing*). *Qing yi* is the most basic of Confucius' moral principles. Finally, *anqing* calls for embracing the moral principles (*lun li*) of *renqing*, including worldly wisdom (*renqing shigu*), local conditions and customs (*defang fengtu renqing*), and customs and habits (*fengsu xiguan*). As a result, *renqing* carries with it a significant Confucius influence. In some cases, *qing li* refers to logical deduction (*luoji tuili*) or principled reasoning (*guilu sheng de daoli*).

What, then, is *li*? *Li* can be translated as *dao li*, meaning "reason," or a justification for doing something, or as *you dao li* ("possessing reason"). Justifications for actions taken or things done is informed by culture and follow bounded rationality. It goes without saying that what is reasonable in one place, with one person, at one moment, within one community, for one culture may or may not be reasonable for another. *Li*, or reason, in this regard is not the same concept as logic in the West, but instead pertains to the overall experience of life. *Li* can also be expressed as *qing li*, or what we can expect from a person given his or her life circumstances and situational factors. This recalls the "reasonable man" standard in tort law. *Qing li* can refer to: (1) what people would or would not do under like circumstances, or what comes naturally; or (2) the collective feelings of a group regarding a particular issue. Also, *tian li* refers to the natural laws regarding how and why things work the way that they do.

Fa represents law as punishment in China. In traditional China, *fa* was equated with and amounted to *xing*, or punishment, ranging from the aggressions of war and associated enslavement to torture to imprisonment. Because punishment can be inflicted by the Emperor (by and through his officials) or by the family (from the head of family to the chief of the clan), *fa* refers to coercive punishment imposed by *guofa* (state law) and *jiagui* (family rules), incorporating *tianli* (heavenly norms, as reflecting natural/moral rules and as required by Confucius' teachings) and *qing li* (from earth below, as reflected in customary rules and as required by family expectations). Thus understood, *fa* encompasses rules (Tang Code, *jiagui*) as well as informal norms (Emperor's decree, parental expectations), morals (Confucianism), and customs.

This brief excursion into *QLF* demonstrates that traditionally and culturally the Chinese do not understand law as stand-alone rules, still less as categorical imperatives that trump nonlegal or extralegal considerations in settling disputes. Rather, law encompasses and integrates natural justice (*tian li*) and moral principles (Confucianization of the law), to be deciphered with reference to *QLF* and within the context of particular and nuanced situations. Thus, what is observed as a total disregard of the law might just be a case of people putting *fa* alongside *qing* and *li* to determine what situational and particularized justice is required.

Obstacle 4: Ideological Hegemony[38]

By far the biggest obstacle to understanding Chinese policing is seeing, thinking, feeling, and judging Chinese policing through a foreign cultural lens.[39] Jerome Cohen, a preeminent Chinese legal scholar, had this to say about the "human rights" conditions in China:

> Mr. Gao's case is about far more than the tragedy of one man and his family. It is about the rule of law in China. If the government can act with impunity toward a lawyer as prominent as Gao Zhisheng, then just as the police threatened Feng Zhenghu, other dissidents will continue to be "disappeared," as have many protesters unknown to the outside world. As the lavish World Expo continues in Shanghai, we hope that the international community will look beyond the Communist Party's carefully constructed image of China and see the reality of the oppression that sustains it.[40]

Cohen, as a learned Chinese law scholar, has a right to be critical of China's legal regime, and he should be. But, if such a critique is based solely on the "rule of law" or "human rights" principles known only to or as interpreted by the West,[41] then it risks attracting charges of ideological hegemony and cultural imperialism.[42]

In order to understand China as it truly is, there is a dire need to debunk the myth that foreign jurisprudential principles, such as rule of law, human rights, and due process, are universal in theory and absolute in application.[43] The issue I wish to address here is whether foreign ideas of rights, freedom, and democracy are applicable, appropriate, and useful in analyzing and evaluating Chinese police action.[44] Human rights activists and champions of democracy promote the principles of human rights, freedom, and democracy as being universal and fundamentally moral.[45] Many more people from around the world, however, including Lee Kuan Yew of Singapore (who emphasized the special nature of Asian values and defended authoritarianism) and Deng Xiaoping of China (who championed socialism and policing with Chinese characteristics), would beg to differ.[46]

To begin the debate, we need to observe that there are many values worthy of human pursuit,[47] such as freedom from starvation, personal integrity, filial piety, social responsibilities, and loyalty to one's country.[48] In this regard, four observations can be made. First, it is obviously true that not all values are created equal; for example, values related to the acquisition of material goods pale beside moral and spiritual ones. Second, it is also clear that no single value, moral principles included, is so fundamental as to absolutely overshadow others at all times, in all places, and in all situations; even the taking of innocent human lives can at times be justified in the name of stopping a greater evil. Third, judging values in context goes well beyond merely determining which moral principles should apply in a given decision-making frame. Many values are involved, and most of them are in conflict, so priorities must be set. The challenge, given a set of ranked values, national priorities, and limited resources, is in prioritizing them.[49] Fourth, the ranking of values in the abstract is so loaded with conditions and disclaimers as to be of little use when applied to real-life situations. Indeed, they might create problems even in a theoretical multivalue matrix decision-making set—for example, should one kill a few to save the lives of many or possibly to improve the welfare of all?[50] Here, China promotes collective interests over individual rights and the survival needs of many over the personal rights of a few. The complexities and difficulties involved in arriving at agreed-upon values can best be described as follows:

> Second: there is no shared set of value priorities. We make much of the fact that we share values and we frequently say that, well, basically humans want the same things so we ought to be able to work things out. Perhaps, at a survival level, but beyond that, and even then, there is not a shared set of priorities with regard to values. Instead, priorities change with circumstance, time, and group. Here are some examples where value priorities differ depending on the group and circumstance. Short term expedience versus long term prudent behavior and vice versa. Group identity versus individual identity. Individual responsibility versus societal responsibility. Freedom versus equality. Local claims versus larger claims for commitment. Universal rights versus local rights (that can repudiate universal rights; fundamentalisms, for example.) Human rights versus national interests (e.g., economic competition or nationalist terrorism). Public interest versus privacy (the encryption conflict, health information, whether private or not). First amendment limits (pornography, etc.). Seeking new knowledge and its potential benefits versus its potential costs. Who sets the rules of the game and who decides? These are all issues where the priority of values are in contention. There is no reliable set of priorities in place that can be used to choose decisively among actions toward the larger issues.[51]

As examples, Marx's critique of the capitalistic intellectual order—that the consciousness of the mass is conditioned, controlled, and dominated by ideas emanating from the economic base[52]—is flawed, less so because it is an overbroad observation than because it is not carried far enough. Marx failed to explain convincingly why he could liberate himself from such an all-embracing ideological confine to lead the charge against capitalism, while others could not. Rawls' theory of justice[53] suffered from a similar cultural straightjacket, in that the just society behind the "veil of ignorance" envisioned by Rawls looked more like 20th-century Boston than traditional Indonesia or contemporary Japan.

Ultimately, it appears that the successful spread of values, from democracy to gay rights, reflects more upon a country's economic strength and concomitant cultural domination than on any inherent appeal and demonstrated goodness of certain moral principles. Cultural domination, albeit in subtle form, is here to stay. Singapore's senior statesman was right when he said that Asian values are worthy of respect—because those values tell Asians who they are.[54]

The pitfalls of universalization of Western values was captured by a recent online debate. On September 20, 2010, *The Economist* published a report online entitled "The Debate Over Universal Values." In it, *The Economist* asserted that, since dissidents signed Charter 08, a manifesto in support of universal values, in 2008, China has finally begun to confront the "universal value" (*pushi jiazhi*) debate head on. In predicting a breakthrough in favor of more political liberalization in China, the article cited Premier Wen, who had written in 2007 that "science, democracy, rule of law, freedom and human rights are not unique to capitalism, but are values commonly pursued by mankind over a long period of history," suggesting that China might be ready to embrace the more progressive "universal values" of the West.[55] This article attracted 535 comments over the next 15 days (see Table 2.1). The comments succinctly expressed many of the above arguments against "universal values" and more. Here, I will only report upon a few of those from the "Readers Most Recommended" archive, beginning with one of the most read and recommended:

> What values are "universal"? Is the right to bear arms one of them? How about the entitlement to jobs? health care? death penalty? privacy? Are democracy in the US, in Japan, in the UK the same? Should the US bring back a queen or a king, who is above everyone else simply because a lucky sperm finds the correct target? Is this "universal" enough? And who can claim that the Western model is the best and it would do well in the rest of the world? What is a good testimony to that? The economic crisis or the failing state of Afghanistan? Values are the children of a culture. China needs to absorb Western values. But it needs to do it on its unique cultural foundation. Cloning the "Western model" is not the answer, not when the "universal" Western model doesn't even exist. Values are universal only when they are abstract. Nobody in China is arguing against "life, liberty, and the pursuit of happiness," but rather where the boundary of "the pursuit of happiness" is in real life. This boundary is not universal at all. Japan has the most restrictive gun laws and limits the top speed of cars to 112 mph, none of which are acceptable in the US. Even in the US, the 2nd amendment stops people from bearing nukes and the 1st amendment stops people from inciting riots. When an individual's pursuit brings suffering to the others, it should stop, or be stopped. This article reflects the typical mindset of a proselytic culture, which itself is Western and not universal.[56]

The commentator here raised some of the most fundamental issues in the "universal values" debate, namely: What values are "universal"? How can we validate the claim? Who is to judge? Are "universal values" an abstraction incapable of being securely anchored? This commentary and the comments in Table 2.1 bear witness to the diversity of views and intensity of feeling regarding any "universal values" proposition. They reflect pent-up frustration against a spent ideology seeking to hold onto its own values as long as it can, at the expense of others' autonomy, dignity, and self-worth. Huntington was prescient in his observation that future global conflicts will not be fought over geography or nationality but civilization and culture.[57] The cultural war being fought over the intellectual domain is here to stay.

Obstacle 5: Denial of Feelings

People, as individuals and collectively, have strong emotions toward things; an appreciation for good, justice, and beauty comes to mind right away. Thoughts (rationality) and feelings (emotions) are interdependent, objective/subjective experiences that together drive action, give meaning to life, and ultimately define our identity, our existence as persons, a community, a people, a nation. In the words of Damasio, who reflected and expounded on the relationship between feeling and thinking as functions of mind vs. body: "Nature appears to have built the apparatus of rationality not just on top of the apparatus of biological regulation, but also *from* it and *with* it" (emphasis in original).[58] In so doing, Damasio rejected Descartes' bold assertion that "I think, therefore I am" in arguing for the prominence of

TABLE 2.1   Commentary on "The Debate over Universal Values" (*The Economist*, September 30, 2010)

Contributor	Comment
simon says September 30, 2010 Recommended: 85	The government's first white paper on democracy in China, in 2005, began: "Democracy is an outcome of the development of political civilisation of mankind. It is also the common desire of people all over the world." A drafter says he now believes those words were "inappropriate."
Simon K. September 30, 2010 Recommended: 120	So, China should not have a debate whether there are universal values or not because there are some universal values and at the same time there are some values where culture plays an important role….China can build a hybrid system of governance that can accommodate some universal values and China's history and culture. For example, free press.
Kwin September 30, 2010 Recommended: 335	What values are "universal"?…And who can claim that the Western model is the best…? What is a good testimony to that?…Values are the children of a culture. China needs to absorb Western values…on its unique cultural foundation….Values are universal only when they are abstract.
cyberwriter September 30, 2010 Recommended: 220	China's primary value appears to be stability….If and when democracy becomes a better way to maintain stability, as appears to be happening with an increasing critical mass of wealthy, educated and mobile people, then it seems likely that China will embrace more democracy.
TheBornLoser September 30, 2010 Recommended: 231	[The Chinese] are very well aware of democracy and its weaknesses. They are very well aware that democracy has a poor track record. They are very well aware that democracy appointed a George W Bush to the White House in the US, a Tony Blair to Downing Street in the UK, and democracy may very well yet appoint a Sarah Palin as President of the United States in 2012.
StudentOfEconomy October 1, 2010 Recommended: 45	Democracy, freedom, etc. are less important universal values; the most vital universal values are peace, no war, no nuke, good governance or anarchy, equality and prosperity, etc.
politico-economist October 1, 2010 Recommended: 46	As China's economy grows stronger and the West's gets relatively weaker, the values "debate" will progressively turn in China's favour, too. It will then stand a much better chance of reforming politically on its own terms.
BrainWarrior October 1, 2010 Recommended: 60	Let us take a quick look at China's recent history: the collapse of imperial dynasties, internal chaos among all sorts of warlords, invasion and subjugation by Japan, civil war, Mao's cruel dictatorship, the man-made famine that killed millions, oppression and humiliation of the peaceful Tibetans, and the 1989 repression at Tiananmen Square. Let's face it: China has a lot of ground to cover before it comes even close to what we conventionally regard as "universal values."
huaren200 October 1, 2010 Recommended: 69	The Chinese modern history is one of exploitation and invasion by foreigners due to a weak central government. The Western experience is one of distrust of governments. They are polar opposites….The idea that value can be "universal" is generally an offensive Western concept to meddle.
Earthly Goods October 2, 2010 Recommended: 43	Is there a scientific formula for universal values? Or is just another form of religious belief? :-)
politico-economist October 2, 2010 Recommended: 48	"The oldest continuing democracies in the world" only became fully democratic fairly recently, after growing hideously rich from capitalist exploitation of their own through slavery and sweatshops…and colonialism.
Botnet October 2, 2010 Recommended: 57	Democracy has been tried before many times in the past and it has always ended up bankrupt due to overspending. Now some of you are going to bring up the fact that the USA + Europe are the most powerful countries on earth and they are democracies. These great powers did not become great powers due to good governance; these countries became great powers due to Imperialism and World Wars. They became great by destroying the economies of others.

mind over matter. Instead, Damasio astutely observed and later scientifically demonstrated that,[59] "In the beginning it was being, and only later was it thinking....We are, and then we think, and we think only inasmuch as we are, since thinking is indeed caused by the structures and operations of being." Damasio suggested[60] that, in order for people to see and do justice, one must first picture and feel justice, a theory that he referred to as the "somatic marker hypothesis,"

> which I believe is relevant to the understanding of processes of human reasoning and decision making. The ventromedial sector of the prefrontal cortices is critical to the operations postulated here, but the hypothesis does not necessarily apply to prefrontal cortex as a whole and should not be seen as an attempt to unify frontal lobe functions under a single mechanism. The key idea in the hypothesis is that "marker" signals influence the processes of response to stimuli, at multiple levels of operation, some of which occur overtly (consciously, "in mind") and some of which occur covertly (non-consciously, in a non-minded manner). The marker signals arise in bioregulatory processes, including those which express themselves in emotions and feelings, but are not necessarily confined to those alone. This is the reason why the markers are termed somatic: they relate to body-state structure and regulation even when they do not arise in the body proper but rather in the brain's representation of the body. Examples of the covert action of "marker" signals are the undeliberated inhibition of a response learned previously; the introduction of a bias in the selection of an aversive or appetitive mode of behaviour, or in the otherwise deliberate evaluation of varied option–outcome scenarios. Examples of overt action include the conscious "qualifying" of certain option-outcome scenarios as dangerous or advantageous. The hypothesis rejects attempts to limit human reasoning and decision making to mechanisms relying, in an exclusive and unrelated manner, on either conditioning alone or cognition alone.[61]

Oriental thinkers, with Confucius in the lead, have long considered the holistic and integrated nature of the body, soul, and mind with regard to decision making. As such, the Chinese are situational feeler–thinkers who think in a contextual, concrete, and, above all, intuitive (emotional) way, as distinguished from Westerners, who tend to be dispositional (and disproportionate[62]) rationalistic thinkers and whose thinking can be individualistic, general, abstract, or, most significantly for our purposes, logical. The observation here is that who we are as a people and how we think or feel as individuals affect the process, content, and outcome of our decision making or, more generally, our life choices. As observed by Nisbett:

> Each of these orientations—the Western and the Eastern—is a self-reinforcing, homeostatic system. The social practices promote the worldviews; the worldviews dictate the appropriate thought processes; and the thought processes both justify the world views and support the social practices. Understanding these homeostatic systems has implications for grasping the fundamental nature of the mind, for beliefs about how we ought ideally to reason, and for appropriate education strategies for different peoples.[63]

Such an understanding of the Chinese feeling–thinking process and style influenced Chinese jurisprudential thought in material and discernible ways. In traditional China, emotions and feelings matter in justice administration.[64] Doctrinally, *qing* and *li* were found to be as important, if not more so, than law in settling disputes. After an in-depth review of a court case in imperial (*qing*) China, Eugenia Lean concluded that "the moral authenticity of emotions has been a powerful motivating force" in justice administration.[65]

When foreigners study Chinese policing, of necessity (inaccessibility of the culture) and by choice (facility with rationality and being drawn to utility), there is a tendency to substitute Western "thinking" for Chinese "feeling"[66] when considering crime, social control, and justice. It has been suggested that, in time and with sufficient indoctrination, the Chinese will voluntarily sublimate their feelings to Western thinking, making it their own—such is the fate of a culturally colonized people. Not surprisingly, in order for cultural imperialism[67] to work, it is necessary for Westerners to condemn the Chinese justice system as barbaric and capricious, punitive and arbitrary, without considering the context of and feelings for Chinese historical circumstances and conditions giving rise to their existence today.

There are a number of reasons for the West to prefer *thinking* about China than developing a *feeling* for Chinese. First, philosophically, Western thinkers, from Plato to René Descartes, have chosen to separate the mind from the body; they are two distinct and independent domains. The mind thinks and is thus viewed as being autonomous; the body only feels and acts and hence is considered to be an extension of and instrument for the mind. Descartes famously declared, "I think, therefore I am" (*cogito, ergo sum*), insisting that the mind (or "soul") motivated (literally, "caused to move") and ruled the machine of the body. Second, pragmatically,[68] Western civilization, since the 18th century and with the arrival of the Industrial Revolution, has promoted the idea of rationalism as the sole engine of industrial progress and bulkhead against arbitrary governance. During the Age of Enlightenment, rationality was established as a *de facto* state ideology, with the legitimacy and authority to match. Rationality is useful and should be harnessed. Emotion is dysfunctional and must be constrained. Third, intellectually, academic disciplines (e.g., law, economics, political science), as understood, practiced, and promoted in the West, are all exclusively devoted to rationality as a process of discovery and enterprises of learning. Intellectuals prefer reasoning over intuition as a process and are more comfortable with and attuned to using logic than sentiment as an analytical tool.

Finally, experientially, *rationality* (how to reason) can be taught, but *sentimentality* (what one feels) must be lived. The former is transferable as ideas; the latter is inaccessible as feelings. Seeking to transfer (export, import, implant) something that is not transferable, through imagination or the replication or approximation of sentiments with no shared experience or common roots, makes things worse. One's empathetic feelings for others, imported by standing in the shoes of others and exported by following the "golden rule,"[69] for example, are no doubt sincere and real to the empathizer. However, there is no assurance that the nature (e.g., sad vs. mad), degree (e.g., like vs. love), scope (e.g., focused vs. diffused), depth (e.g., superficial vs. embedded), duration (e.g., fleeing vs. lasting), impact (e.g., psychological vs. physiological), or reaction (e.g., resignation vs. revolution) of empathetic feelings projected onto another corresponds to that which was experienced. More often than not, people blinded by lofty goals to help are tempted to act on such empathy-generated chivalrous feelings, without due regard to whether such feelings and in turn actions are warranted; paternalism prevails.

A denial of feelings has dire consequences and lasting impact on the people having their feelings denied. First, feelings, emotions, and sentiments are powerful cultural markers. They define one's way of thinking, acting, and, most importantly, of being. A denial of feelings is a denial of the autonomy, centrality, and importance of self in its totality, resulting in alienation, drift, and ultimately anomie, escape, or rebellion. Second, a denial of feelings subjugates individual will and uproots national spirit. It speaks to the colonization of a people, contamination or surrendering of a culture, and sublimation or transformation of a national identity. In this regard, denying the feelings of people is similar to depriving a wild tiger of his freedom. The colonization of a people, as with the domestication of a tiger, destroys the very essence and spirit of the people, who must cater to their captor and the expectations of observers, aloft and afar. Third, denial of feelings, together with legitimizing reason, can generate cognitive dissonance[70] in the affected people, who must reconcile their natural feelings (e.g., substantive justice in China) with what is being imposed on them (e.g., the procedural justice of the United States), resulting in anxiety, anger, and frustration.

Finally, a denial of feeling privileges the intellectuals' cognitive view of the world and discriminates against the general public, who experience life through sensations. Zhou Guangquan, a member of the Legal Committee of the National People's Congress and Tsinghua University professor, had this to say about the elitist, anti-democratic, counter-majoritarian tendency of thinking vs. feeling:

> There will always be a gap between popular thinking [lit., "intuition"] and the judgment of legislators when it comes to capital punishment—this is true throughout the world. In some European countries where the death penalty has been abolished, opinion polls show that nearly 80 percent of people oppose abolition. Legislative choices cannot entirely follow popular thinking; in the end, some decisions must be made that go against popular thinking.[71]

Evidence of clashes regarding thinking (West) vs. feelings (China) is everywhere evident. In the case of capital punishment, China has been condemned by the foreign media[72] and human rights groups for carrying out the most executions worldwide, and in an apparently arbitrary and capricious way.[73] The Chinese government has also been accused of tolerating wrongful convictions and harvesting organs after executions.[74] John Kamm, Executive Director of the Dui Dua Foundation, has openly called for a more humane approach to justice administration in China:

> China's active use of the death penalty has long sparked international discomfort, particularly as evidence has mounted that the threat of capital punishment does little to deter crime. The official position is that someday China will abolish the death penalty but that "conditions aren't right" to do so now. Yet as long ago as 1984, the Chinese government forbade the public parading of prisoners who were about to be executed. Such spectacles remained commonplace, however, especially in the countryside, prompting Beijing to issue regulations against public executions in 1986. Rumors of executions in sports stadiums plagued China's bid for the 2000 Olympics, and when bidding for the 2008 Games, Beijing made clear that public executions were not permitted....Ten years ago, China was executing more than 10,000 prisoners a year. The human rights group I direct estimates the annual rate to be less than 5,000 now, a reduction due in part to President Hu Jintao's effort to develop a "harmonious society"—and in part to withering criticism at the United Nations and in the human rights dialogue with Europe. China still executes more people every year than the rest of the world combined. Today, executions generally take place in specialized chambers or vans, away from public view. Lethal injections, as opposed to gunshots, are increasingly used.[75]

What is the attitude (feeling) of Chinese citizens toward capital punishment? Survey after survey has shown that the Chinese public is overwhelmingly in support of capital punishment. For example, in 1995, the Law Institute of Chinese Social Science (CASS) and the National Bureau of Statistics of China conducted a survey of three provinces to try to identify a relationship between demographics and attitudes about the death penalty.[76] The study found that 95% of those answering the question "What is your attitude toward the death penalty?" supported the death penalty.[77] In 2005, another opinion survey was conducted at a university in Northwest China among a non-random sample of 1873 students, most of them law students (87%). In this case, 93.8% supported the death penalty.[78]

If these and other opinion surveys (which are admittedly notoriously inexact and arguably invalid in some instances) are to be believed, it appears that the majority of the Chinese for a variety of reasons (from deterrence to incapacitation to just deserts) think (feel) that the death penalty should stay on the books, at least for the most heinous crimes (murder, rape, corruption). This immediately raises the issue of whether or not the West is talking down to (and dressing down) the Chinese when it has been suggested, sometimes in very strong words, that the Chinese, in approving the death penalty, are somehow less civilized and humane than the West. Because support of the death penalty, with only marginal differences, is equally strong in China as in Western societies (e.g., Great Britain, United States, Germany), one wonders whether such a criticism of China is reasonable and if it results from a sort of racial animus. Finally, it is one thing to have differences of opinion on the death penalty, but it is quite another to summarily dismiss China's public opinions as irrelevant and irrational, arbitrary, and capricious. This is a denial of the Chinese people's feelings.

People who take the time to analyze the way Chinese people think and feel about the death penalty will find that their opinions are mixed, nuanced, and sophisticated. Not everyone supports the death penalty in the same way; most support the death penalty in some cases but not others. The necessary conclusion one can draw from such an exercise is that the Chinese people make up their minds on the death penalty based on reasoning and feelings that are different from those of the West, as they have been shaped and influenced by a particular set of historical, cultural, social, and material circumstances. Such being the case, their collective voice should be seriously considered, genuinely respected, and gracefully deferred to. Any attempt to superimpose Western thinking (and feelings) over Chinese feelings (and thinking) is a denial of the right of China to be herself as a people and culture. Chinese feelings and thinking are not necessarily right or wrong. It is just that the Chinese people are entitled to their own, and it is not for the West to judge or, worse, condemn.

Problems with Paternalism

Foreign observers often justify their criticisms of China as being constructive; for example, China needs help to become a better/greater nation, more humane (e.g., death penalty debate), more free (e.g., speech debate), more enlightened (e.g., privacy debate), and more accountable (e.g., corruption debate).[79] In the end, the overriding drive and justification to make China better can be identified as paternalism:

> Paternalism is the interference of a state or an individual with another person, against their will, and defended or motivated by a claim that the person interfered with will be better off or protected from harm. The issue of paternalism arises with respect to restrictions by the law such as anti-drug legislation, the compulsory wearing of seatbelts, and in medical contexts by the withholding of relevant information concerning a patient's condition by physicians. At the theoretical level it raises questions of how persons should be treated when they are less than fully rational.[80]

There are a number of objections to paternalistic offers of help. First, paternalism is a noble and chivalry enterprise; however, such a noble instinct is not without its corrupting tendencies and destructive impact. The impetus to help, arising as it must from a sense of superiority and well being, will easily lead to an arrogance derived from the helper's power (intellectual, spiritual, physical, emotional, or economical). Dependency creates subordination in the helped and in time breeds contempt in the helper.[81] This is manifested in a relationship marked not so much by the actual needs of the one being helped but by the one who ventures the help. Such a tendency seems to grow directly in proportion to the intensity of the willingness to help and is conversely correlated with the helplessness exhibited by the deprived. In the end, the one being helped may be no better off; for example, he may not get what he wants (only what others think he wants). He may even end up worse off than before; he may get more than what he bargained for, such as a loss of self-respect, his own autonomy, and his freedom. Such has always been the pitfall of a paternalistic relationship!

Second, the paternalistic motivation to help is never selfless.[82] There is a certain kind of hypocrisy in all chivalry gestures. No one is totally selfless. By venturing out to help others, we are motivated by a need to gratify ourselves—that is, an instinct to do good by *our* standards, not those of the person apparently in need of help. We should not for a moment think that the interest of the helper and the helped are one and the same. No assumption can be more wrong or more dangerous. A servant cannot be trusted to serve two masters. This is not so much an indictment against the integrity of the servant as it is a realistic assessment of such relationships. The annals of trust law are replete with cautions against such divided allegiance. Our experience with others point unmistakably to that conclusion.

Better Understanding of Chinese Policing

To meaningfully study and truly understand police reform in China, we need to discern how the Chinese people (including the police) see, think, and feel about and evaluate their police. What we see or do not see is governed by our perceptions, mediated by perspective and framework. How we think is governed by a cognitive map,[83] populated by definitions, classifications, and connections of things, or, more simply, by an idea or conception of where everything belongs. What we feel is governed by our reception of things, people, events, and ideas, controlled by values, philosophy, and ideology of an intuitive kind (i.e., what make for good, beauty, and meaning in life). Studying policing in China requires asking three questions: (1) From whose perspective are we looking at police reform (e.g., from an insider's vs. an outsider's perspective, from a top-down vs. bottom-up perspective)? (2) How are ideas conceived and things ordered in the Chinese (police) culture (e.g., duty to collective interests vs. rights of individuals)? (3) How do the Chinese intuitively feel about what is good, just, and beautiful? To such a daunting challenge we now turn.

Notes

1. Alternatively, the chapter could be entitled "Revolutionizing Chinese Police Studies," although the quote from *The Economist* that follows provides evidence for the current title. Mao's quote provides for the remedy, a revolutionary approach to changing the paradigm, assumptions, and methods of studying China.

2. "The Next Emperor: A Crown Prince Is Anointed in a Vast Kingdom Facing Vaster Stresses. China Is in a Fragile State," *The Economist*, October 21, 2010 (http://www.economist.com/node/17308123). This article captures the heart of this chapter—the wide and widening gap of (mis)understanding between China and the West, as evidenced by one of most recommended comments (422 to date) to the article made by a reader: "So what we really shouldn't read in an Economist headline is *juvenile caricatures* like what we have here. Nor do we need *simplistic calls* for China to behave politically in a *more Western* fashion. Note that a democratically elected Chinese government might want the Yuan to be even weaker. And it might want to spend even more on defense. A democratic, populist China might resemble, well, America at its worst. *China's problems are unique*, and Eastern, as are her resources for addressing them. I suggest the Economist hire some journalists who *understand* this." I have italicized the operative terms and phrases that shape and preview the discursive discourse to follow: caricature, simplistic, more Western, unique, understand.

3. Mao Tse-tung, "The Orientation of the Youth Movement," in *The Selected Works of Mao Tse-tung*, Vol. II (p. 246), Foreign Language Press, Peking, 1967.

4. Wu Kuang Ming, "Let Chinese Thinking Be Chinese, Not Western: *Sine Qua Non* to Globalization," *Dao: A Journal of Comparative Philosophy*, 9(2), 193–209, 2010.

5. There are exceptions. See (a) Murray Scot Tanner and Eric Green, "Principals and Secret Agents: Central versus Local Control over Policing and Obstacles to 'Rule of Law' in China," *China Quarterly*, 191, 590–612, 2007. (b) Fu Hualing, "Zhou Yongkang and Recent Police Reform in China," *Australian and New Zealand Journal of Criminology*, 241, 243–244, 2005. (c) Lena Zhong and Peter Grabosky, "The Pluralization of Policing and the Rise of Private Policing in China," *Crime, Law and Social Change*, 52(5), 433–455, 2009.

6. William Jones, "Trying to Understand the Current Chinese Legal System," in Stephen Hsu (Ed.), *Understanding China's Legal System: Essays in Honor of Jerome A. Cohen* (p. 11), New York University, New York, 2003. The Chinese legal system must be understood on its own terms.

7. Amardeep Singh, *An Introduction to Edward Said, Orientalism, and Postcolonial Literary Studies*, September 4, 2004 (http://www.lehigh.edu/~amsp/2004/09/introduction-to-edward-said.html).

8. Jonathan D. Spence, *The Chan's Great Continent: China in Western Minds*, W.W. Norton & Company, New York, 1999.

9. Kishore Mahbubani, "Western Slant on China Skews Shape of Things to Come," *National Times*, May 19, 2010 (http://www.theage.com.au/opinion/politics/western-slant-on-china-skews-shape-of-things-to-come-20100518-vc1q.html).

10. "German Scholar: End of Serfdom in Tibet 'Victory for Human Rights," *Xinhua*, March 27, 2009 (http://www.china embassy.org/eng/zt/mgryzdzg/t555215.htm).

11. (a) *August 2006: Setback for the Rule of Law—Lawyers under Attack in China*, Human Rights in China (HRIC), New York, 2008 (http://www.hrichina.org/public/contents/article?revision_id=36024&item_id=30425); (b) Rosemary Foot, *Rights Beyond Borders: The Global Community and the Struggle over Human Rights in China*, Oxford University Press, Oxford, 2000.

12. "FM Spokesman: 'Anti-CNN' Website Reflects Chinese People's Condemnation," *Xinhua*, March 27, 2008 (http://news.xinhuanet.com/english/2008-03/27/content_7871585.htm).

13. (a) "Walter Lohman on Human Rights in China: Heritage in Focus [podcast]," August 23, 2010. (b) Geremie R. Barmé, "Anniversaries in the Light, and in the Dark," *China Heritage Quarterly*, No. 17, March, 2009.

14. Julia Lovell, "China's Conscience," *The Guardian*, June 12, 2010, p. 20 (http://www.guardian.co.uk/books/2010/jun/12/rereading-julia-lovell-lu-xun): "With the PRC now in its swaggering 60s, I would prescribe—to counter the excesses of Beijing bombast—a stiff dose of Lu Xun for his intensely crafted, sympathetic insights into the blackness of modern China and as a biographical lesson in the Communist party's energetic, though unsuccessful, efforts, to neutralise the country's critical conscience."

15. Julia Strauss, "Paternalist Terror: The Campaign to Suppress Counterrevolutionaries and Regime Consolidation in the People's Republic of China, 1950–1953," *Comparative Studies in Society and History*, 44, 80–105, 2002.

16. (a) "Uyghur Historian Kahar Barat Discusses Xinjiang History," *The New Dominion*, July 26, 2010 (http://www.thenewdominion.net/category/history/). (b) "Kahar Barat on Xinjiang History: The History of the Han in Xinjiang," *The New Dominion*, August 17, 2010 (http://www.thenewdominion.net/1947/uyghur-historian-kahar-barat-2/).

17. "CNN: What's Wrong with You?" *China Daily*, April 2, 2008 (http://www.chinadaily.com.cn/china/2008-04/02/content_6587120.htm).

18. Geremie R. Barmé, "China's Promise," *The China Beat*, January 20, 2010 (http://www.thechinabeat.org/?p=1374).

19. In China, the study of ordering society requires the studying of "police" (law administration, public administration) and "policing" (comprehensive social control), more so the latter than the former. The police are an institution involved with political, and now social, ordering. Policing is a social and moral ordering function that can be achieved through a combination of penal, administrative, social, and other means (e.g., ideology, education). Chinese police studies, in theory as well as in practice, reject the Western approach to understanding the police, as police conduct policing and policing is only done by the police. Specifically, Chinese police scholars reject Western assumptions that: (1) police are the most important social control agency, and (2) police are apolitical, legal agents. Instead, the Chinese have observed since antiquity that social control is everybody's business, starting with the self (cultivation) and ending with the family, clan, or community (control). Police are an instrument of the state to create and maintain political order (of late mediated by law).

20. *Congressional–Executive Commission on China 2006 Annual Report*, U.S. Government Printing Office, Washington, DC, 2006 (http://www.cecc.gov). Executive Summary: "China has an authoritarian political system controlled by the Communist Party....The absence of popular and legal constraints to check the behavior of Party officials has led to widespread corruption and citizen anger. The Party has strengthened the role of internal responsibility systems to moderate official behavior, but these systems have provided some local Party officials with new incentives to conceal information and abuse their power. In 2005, the central leadership called for strengthened controls over society to address mounting social unrest and to suppress dissent."

21. Stanley Lubman, "Citizen Rights and Police Conduct," *Wall Street Journal China Real Time Report*, August 16, 2010. Chinese police should function like American police, starting with respect for individual rights.

22. "Nine Commentaries on the Chinese Communist Party," *The Epoch Times*, December 1, 2004.

23. Lee Kuan Yew, "Two Images of China," *Forbes*, June 16, 2008. In the image game, China cannot win: "It's sad to see the gulf in understanding between Chinese and Westerners. Chinese frustration is captured by Howard French in the *International Herald Tribune*'s Apr. 24 'Letter from China' column, 'The need for unanimity in China exacts a hidden price.' In it French quotes a Chinese student writing to his Western professor: 'How can Chinese people and Chinese media make the foreign world understand the real China?' He also quotes a Chinese person's Internet posting: 'What do you want from us? When we were labeled the sick man of Asia, we were called a peril. When we are billed to be the next superpower, we're called the threat.'"

24. Geremie R. Barmé, "Anniversaries in the Light, and in the Dark," *China Heritage Quarterly*, No. 17, March, 2009.

25. In selecting Dr. Wayne's work to critique, I am not suggesting that he is the worse offender. I am using Wayne's work to make the point that many studies of law and criminal justice in China suffer from misinformation or a lack of information.

26. Martin Wayne, *China's War on Terrorism: Counter-Insurgency, Politics and Internal Security*, Routledge, New York, 2008.

27. Colin Mackerras, "Dissecting China's Far West: *Xinjiang: China's Muslim Borderland (Studies of Central Asia and Caucasus)*, edited by S. Frederick Starr [book review]," *Asia Times*, October 2, 2004 (http://www.atimes.com/atimes/China/FJ02Ad01.html).

28. Jonathan D. Spence, *The Chan's Great Continent: China in Western Minds*, W.W. Norton, New York, 1999.

29. Philip C.C. Huang, "Biculturality in Modern China and in Chinese Studies," *Modern China*, 26(1), 3–31, 2000.

30. Mao Tse-tung, "The Chinese Revolution and the Chinese Communist Party," in *The Selected Works of Mao Tse-tung*, Vol. II (p. 322), Foreign Language Press, Peking, 1967. Western-trained Chinese intellectuals, when discussing and understanding China with Westerners, albeit reflectively and transcendentally (at times apologetically), might do no better in helping our understanding of China than China itself. Here, Mao reminded us: "The intellectuals often tend to be subjective and individualistic, impractical in their thinking and irresolute in action until they have thrown themselves heart and soul into mass revolutionary struggles, or made up their minds to serve the interests of the masses and become one with them. Hence, although the mass of revolutionary intellectuals in China can play a vanguard role or serve as a link with the masses, not all of them will remain revolutionaries to the end." For the plight of Chinese intellectuals, in a postmodern era, see Chapter 1 in Chen Xiaomei, *Occidentalism: A Theory of Counter-Discourse in Post-Mao China*, Rowman & Littlefield Publishers, Lanham, MD, 2002.

31. For Confucius, the term *li* ("rites") embraces all of the traditional forms that provided an objective standard of conduct. Thus, although *li* may in some instances refer to rites, ceremonies, or rules of conduct, it has the general meaning of "good form" or "decorum." See Wm. Theodore De Bary, Wing-tsit Chan, and Burton Watson, *Sources of Chinese Tradition*, Vol. I, Columbia University Press, New York, 1960, p. 28.

32. *Ren* is commonly translated as "benevolence," "kindheartedness," or "humanity." *Ren* is what a person should seek in life; it is perfect virtue. See Confucius, *The Analects*, XV.8 (c. 500 CE).

33. "The Meaning of 'Law' in Han Fei's Thinking" ["*Fa' zai Han Fei sixiang zhong de yiyi*"], in Wang Yaopo, *Compendium on Confucians and Legalists Thought* [*Rufa xixiang lunji*] (pp. 168–186), Shibao chubanshe, Taipei, 1983.

34. For a historical account of the debate between *fajia* (Legalists) and *rujia* (Confucianists), resulting in their ultimate union beginning with the Han dynasty (206 BC–220 AD), see Qu Tongzhu, *Zhongguo falu yu zhongguo shehui*, Zhonghua shuju, Beijing, 1981, pp. 328–346.

35. See "The Legal Thought of Sun Kuan" ["*Sun Kuan de falu sixiang*"] in Liu Hai-nian and Yang Yi-fang, *Knowledge of Ancient Chinese Legal History* [*Zhongguo gudai falu-shi zhishi*], Heilongjiang renmin chubanshe, Heilongjiang, 1984, pp. 69–75.

36. For literature on the Confucianization of the law, see (a) "Research into the Origin of the Characteristics of the Chinese Legal System" ["*Zhonghua faxi tedian tanyuan*"], in Zhang Jinfan, *Discourse on Chinese Legal History* [*Zhongguo falu shi lun*], Falu chubanshe, Beijing, 1983, pp. 11–25. (b) "The Formation and Characteristics of the Chinese Legal System" ["*Zhonghua faxi de chengchang ji qi tedian*"], in Liu Hai-nian and Yang Yi-fang, *Knowledge of Ancient Chinese Legal History* [*Zhongguo gudai falu-shi zhishi*], Heilongjiang renmin chubanshe, Heilongjiang, 1984, pp. 6–24. (c) Chen Gu-yuan, *Chinese Legal System History* [*Zhongguo fazhi shi*], Zhongguo shuju, Beijing, 1988, pp. 53–61. (d) Qian Daqun and Xia Jinwen, *A Comparative Study of Tang Lu and the Current Criminal Law in China* [*Tang lu yu Zhongguo xianxing xingfa bijiao lun*], Jiangsu renmin chubanshe, Nanjing, 1990, pp. 31–42.

37. Ch'u Tung-tsu, *Law and Society in Traditional China*, Mouton, Paris, 1961. Ch'u provided the first systematic study in the English language of classical materials regarding the Confucianization of the law.

38. Qin Yaqing, "A Response to Yong Deng: Power, Perception, and the Cultural Lens," *Asian Affairs: An American Review*, 28(3), 155–159, 2001.

39. John Brenkman, *Culture and Domination*, Cornell University Press, Ithaca, NY, 1989. Pierre Bourdieu coined the phrase "symbolic violence," which defines what counts as legitimate knowledge, what social relations are valuable, and what symbols confer prestige and social honor. It rationalizes and normalizes behavior, sanctioned by violence. See Pierre Bourdieu, *Language and Symbolic Power*, Harvard University Press, Cambridge, MA, 1991.
40. Jerome A. Cohen, "The Silencing of Gao Zhisheng," *Wall Street Journal*, May 31, 2010.
41. Ge Fang, Fu-xi Fang, Monika Keller, Wolfgang Edelstein, Thomas J. Kehle, and Melissa A. Bray, "Social Moral Reasoning in Chinese Children: A Developmental Study," *Psychology in the Schools*, 40(1), 125–138, 2003. Chinese social and moral decision making is less rule bound and rights based than relationship based and duty bound.
42. I know of no case where U.S. police actions have been judged by Chinese or Asian legal (*qing, li, fa*) or moral (Confucius) standards. Does this mean that the Western world is the sole originator and guardian of a global, ideological morality and legal regime?
43. Orlando Patterson, *Freedom in the Making of Western Culture*, Basic Books, New York, 1991. The idea and ideal of freedom are not naturally derived but socially constructed. The existence and perpetuation of freedom in the West, therefore, require explanation, not the lack thereof in non-Western countries.
44. "The Debate over Universal Values," *The Economist* September 30, 2010. The debate over universal values (*pushi jiazhi*) vs. normative Western values vs. normative Chinese values (*Zhongguo tese*) is real and ongoing in China.
45. Joanne R. Bauer and Daniel A. Bell (Eds.), *Human Rights and Asian Values: The Limits of Universalism*, Cambridge, UK: Cambridge University Press, 1999.
46. Chen Shiqiu, "Progress on Human Rights," *China Daily*, October 18, 2010. This article touted the development of economic, social, and cultural rights alongside human rights. China championed negative rights (e.g., right to be free of hunger and exploitation), while Singapore promoted Asian values.
47. William Alford, "Exporting the Pursuit of Happiness," in Stephen Hsu (Ed.), *Understanding China's Legal System: Essays in Honor of Jerome A. Cohen* (pp. 46–122), New York University Press, New York, 2003.
48. Basil Mitchell, "The Value of Human Life," in Peter Byrne (Ed.), *Medicine, Medical Ethics and the Value of Life* (pp. 34–47), John Wiley & Sons, Chichester, 1990. "Not so [respect for life is universal]. In the classical Chinese tradition in which I was brought up, we are taught respect for parents, respect for teachers, respect for ancestors and for duly constituted authority, but the concept of respect due to individual human beings as such does not exist in that culture."
49. Kevin Wm. Wildes, "Sanctity of Life: A Study in Ambiguity and Confusion," in Kazumasa Hoshino (Ed.), *Japanese and Western Bioethics* (pp. 89–101), Springer, New York, 1997. In Buddhist thought, the principle of respect for life must be understood within the context of other aspects of Buddhism teaching as well as other precepts. Various traditions within Buddhism balance the concern for respect for life with concern for doing the "most compassionate action."
50. Lon Fuller, "The Case of the Speluncean Explorers," *Harvard Law Review*, 62(4), 616–645, 1949.
51. Donald N. Michael, *Point: Observations regarding a Missing Elephant*, International Society for Panetics, College Park, MD, 1998 (http://www.panetics.org/DisplayOneEvent.cfm?i=127).
52. Raymond Williams, "Base and Superstructure in Marxist Cultural Theory," in Chandra Mukerji and Michael Schudson (Eds.), *Rethinking Popular Culture: Contemporary Perspectives* (pp. 407–423, University of California Press, Berkeley, 1991.
53. John Rawls, *A Theory of Justice*, Harvard University Press, Cambridge, MA, 1971.
54. Anthony Milner, *What's Happened to Asian Values?* Australian National University, Canberra, 2002 (http://dspace.anu.edu.au/html/1885/41912/values.html).
55. "The Debate over Universal Values," *The Economist* September 30, 2010.
56. Ibid.

57. Samuel P. Huntington, *The Clash of Civilizations and the Remaking of World Order*, Touchstone, New York, 1996.

58. (a) Antonio Damasio, *Descartes' Error: Emotion, Reason, and the Human Brain*, Harper Perennial, New York, 1995. (b) Corinne Zimmerman, "Damasio's Proposition: A Review of *Descartes' Error: Emotion, Reason and the Human Brain*," *Canadian Journal of Experimental Psychology*, 50, 330–332, 1996.

59. See Chapter 1 to Damasio's *Descartes' Error: Emotion, Reason, and the Human Brain*.

60. Antonio Damasio, "The Somatic Marker Hypothesis and the Possible Functions of the Prefrontal Cortex," *Philosophical Transactions of the Royal Society of London, Series B, Biological Sciences*, 351(1346), 1413–1420, 1996.

61. Ibid., abstract.

62. Disproportionate in two senses: (1) Westerners are more inclined to use their brain (cognition) than their heart (sentiments) in processing information and making decisions, and (2) Westerners prefer certain value over others, categorically and absolutely.

63. Richard Nisbett, *The Geography of Thought: How Asians and Westerners Think Differently...and Why*, The Free Press, New York, 2003.

64. (a) Michael Slote, "Comments on Bryan Van Norden's Virtue Ethics and Consequentialism in Early Chinese Philosophy," *Dao: A Journal of Comparative Philosophy*, 9(3), 303–307, 2010. (b) Michael Slote, "The Mandate of Empathy," *Dao: A Journal of Comparative Philosophy*, 9(3), 303–307, 2010.

65. Eugenia Lean, *Public Passions: The Trial of Shi Jianqiao and the Rise of Popular Sympathy in Republican China*, University of California Press, Berkeley, 2008.

66. Jeffrey Kinkley, *Chinese Justice, the Fiction: Law and Literature in Modern China*, Stanford University Press, Stanford, 2000.

67. John Tomlinson, *Cultural Imperialism: A Critical Introduction*, Johns Hopkins University Press, Baltimore, MD, 1991, p. 3. The author defined cultural imperialism as "the use of political and economic power to exalt and spread the values and habits of a foreign culture at the expense of a native culture."

68. The earmarks of pragmatism are rationalism, instrumentalism, utility, and economics.

69. Immanuel Kant, *Grounding for the Metaphysics of Morals: On a Supposed Right to Lie because of Philanthropic Concerns*, 3rd ed. (translated by James W. Ellington), Hackett Publishing, Indianapolis, 1785/1993, p. 30. Kant offered this categorical imperative: "Act only according to that maxim whereby you can, at the same time, will that it should become a universal law."

70. Leon Festinger and James M. Carlsmith, "Cognitive Consequences of Forced Compliance," *Journal of Abnormal and Social Psychology*, 58, 203–210, 1959. The authors described the syndrome as "the feeling of psychological discomfort produced by the combined presence of two thoughts that do not follow from one another."

71. (a) "Translation & Commentary: Greater Steps Can Be Taken to Reduce the Death Penalty," *Dui Hua Human Rights Journal*, September 1, 2010 (http://www.duihuahrjournal.org/2010/09/translation-commentary-greater-steps.html).

72. (a) Holly William, "The Harsh Realities of China's Death Penalty," *Guardian*, March 24, 2009. Nie Shubin "was killed by the Chinese state after a closed trial [for rape and murder] that lasted just two hours, and in which the key evidence was his confession to the crime—a confession that is widely believed to have been extracted through torture, which is illegal but routinely practised by police here....Citizens can now be executed for over 60 different crimes—everything from tax evasion to damaging electrical facilities and even killing a panda." In 2006, the Chinese government banned the sale of executed prisoners' organs for transplant, which had routinely been done before widespread media coverage of the practice. (b) Maureen Fan and Ariana Eunjung Cha, "China's Capital Cases Still Secret, Arbitrary," *Washington Post Foreign Service*, December 24, 2010. Death penalty sentences are not handed down equally; high officials and government cadres have been given suspended sentences for embezzling millions while common people have been executed for stealing thousands. (c) Saibal Dasgupta, "No

More Death Penalty in China for Economic Crimes," *The Times of India*, August 23, 2010. Bending to international pressure and making allowances for the rich, China did away with capital punishment for economic crimes. Li Shishi, director of the Commission for Legislative Affairs of the NPC Standing Committee, said, "Considering China's current economic and social development reality, appropriately removing the death penalty from some economy-related non-violent offences will not negatively affect social stability nor public security." In effect, this reduced the number of capital offenses from 68 to 55, and executions were expected to decrease by 19%. (d) Dwyer Arce, "China Not Considering Eliminating Death Penalty for Corruption," *Jurist*, September 29, 2010. "If adopted, the proposed legislation would eliminate death sentences for 13 non-violent economic crimes," including smuggling out of the country prohibited cultural relics, gold, silver, and other precious metals and rare animals and their products; carrying out fraudulent activities with financial bills; and carrying out fraudulent activities with letters of credit.

73. John Kamm, "Is Mercy Coming to China?" *Washington Post*, August 16, 2010.

74. Debarati Mukherjee, "65 pct of China's Organ Transplants Come from Executed Prisoners," *Deutsche Welle-World DE*, September 9, 2009. The Chinese Vice Minister of Health, Huang Jiefu, announced that about 65% of the organs transplanted in Chinese hospitals were coming from convicts put to death for various crimes.

75. Ibid.

76. Hu Yunteng, *Retention or Abolition: A Study of the Basic Theories regarding the Death Penalty* [*Cun yu fei: Sixing jiben lilun yanjiu*], Zhongguo jiancha chubanshe, Beijing, 2000, pp. 341–346.

77. The study suffered from reliability and validity issues.

78. Jia Yu, "An Investigation Report on Views of Death Penalty of Positivist Research" [in Chinese], *Legal Science Review*, 3, 2005.

79. Mei Ying Gechlik, Nancy Yuan, Stanley Lubman et al., "Legal Reform in China: Problems and Prospects," *Carnegie Endowment for International Peace*, April 18, 2005. This article addresses whether China could do better by seeking help and learning from the United States (e.g., professional judges, independent judiciary). There is no discussion about how to reform China's judicial system in the Chinese image. More appropriate would be law reform with Chinese characteristics.

80. *Stanford Encyclopedia of Philosophy* (http://plato.stanford.edu/entries/paternalism/).

81. (a) Richard M. Emerson, "Power Dependence Relations," *American Sociological Review*, 27, 31–40, 1962. Emerson was the first to observe that power is a function of dependency in an exchange relationship. This has come to be known as the "power dependency theory," which postulates that the power of actor A over actor B is a function of B's dependence on A for scarce outcomes, and *vice versa*. Dependence varies in two dimensions: significance of the values sought and availability of alternatives. (b) Samuel B. Bacharach and Edward J. Lawler, *Power and Politics in Organizations*, Jossey-Bass, New York, 1980.

82. Martin Gunderson and David J. Mayo, "Altruism and Physician-Assisted Death," *Journal of Medicine and Philosophy* 18(3), 281–295, 1993. "We note that the rationale for the passage of such a statute would be respect for individual autonomy, the avoidance of suffering, and the possibility of death with dignity. We deal with two moral issues that will arise once such a law is passed. First, we argue that the rationale for passing an assistance in dying law in the first place provides a justification for assisting patients to die who are motivated by altruistic reasons as well as patients who are motivated by reasons of self-interest. Second, we argue that the reasons for passing a physician assisted death law in the first place justify extending the law to cover some nonterminal patients as well as terminal patients."

83. Alexander L. George, "The Operational Code: A Neglected Approach to the Study of Political Leaders and Decision-Making," *International Studies Quarterly*, 13(2), 190–222, 1969. Cognitive maps are not neutral; they are anchored in values and driven by philosophy.

Taking Stock

3

Focus, Data, and Organization

This chapter provides an overview of Chinese police reform—themes, achievements, problems, and issues—over the last decade (1999–2009), by way of a review of Chinese policing literature that covers research, scholarship, education, paradigms, leadership, culture, and more. Because it is standard for Chinese articles to point out problems and issues before rendering recommendations and solutions, this is also an audit (i.e., taking stock) of police reform. My hope is that this chapter will provide the necessary context for people who are new to Chinese policing to understand what is discussed throughout this book.

This overview is based mostly on Chinese indigenous literature supported by local data and has been developed from the Chinese perspective[1] and in their own words.[2] The purpose of this review is not to provide a systematic and comprehensive review of police reform efforts. Given the body of work regarding policing in China, this would be a huge undertaking, beyond the scope of this chapter. Rather, the review is intended to provide a sample of selected literature to jump start our investigation into Chinese police reform, now in full swing. Key authorities have been consulted and representative literature is discussed to discern, illuminate, and demonstrate the Chinese thinking process on critical police reform issues.

Pronouncements of key leaders and experts on police policies and practices are documented because they set the initial direction and tone and later the focus and standards for public policy debate in China. Representative police literature is reported because there is little free and open discussion of ideas in official public security publications.[3] In China, all police publications are screened for appropriateness of content and consistency with the agenda, and police journal articles follow a set presentation style. Most articles selected for review here are from leading police journals, and they capture the relevant range of issues and reflect the tone and texture of debates undertaken here. In the ultimate analysis, Chinese police scholarship subscribes to the view that experts know best and the Communist Party of China (CPC) is the ultimate arbiter of "truth."

The secondary purpose of this review is to familiarize readers with how Chinese police scholars, political leaders, policymakers, and police managers think about police reform, including how they do research. What does police reform mean? What are the more important issues and emerging problems that have captured the nation's attention? How should public policy be examined and analyzed in terms of data consulted, assumptions adopted, logic used, reasons adduced, solutions proposed, and positions advanced? This review is as interested in the process of thinking as what is being said.

To date, very few criminal justice studies[4] have examined how Chinese scholars and practitioners think, feel, talk, and debate about police reform issues, on their own terms, from their own perspectives, with their own logic, and in their own words.[5] This is a first attempt to do so.

This study has been facilitated by an in-depth examination of selected research published between 1999 and 2009 in *Public Security Studies* (*Gongan Yanjiu*), hereafter referred to as *PS*, which is the most prestigious and authoritative national police policy publication in China. First published in 1988, it is an official publication of the Ministry of Public Security and is sponsored by the MPS Fourth Research Institute, a policy research think tank.[6] The charter of *PS* is to promote police research, distribute research findings, inform policy-making, and guide field practices. The journal calls for submissions from police officers, scholars, and researchers nationwide. It publishes research findings, scholarly dissertations, commissioned reports, theoretic propositions, and experiential observations. It is particularly interested in the following kinds of papers: (1) applied and policy research bearing on public security thinking, organization, administration, law, and operations, in both theory and practice; (2) research on problems and issues with police operations and reform; (3) reports on emerging work experiences; (4) case studies for demonstration and instructional purposes; and (5) comparative research, translated materials, and foreign policing theory, practice, and experience.[7] Beginning in 1999, in order to be published papers must meet the following substantive requirements: Papers must be guided by Marxism and Leninism, Mao's thought, and Deng's theory. They must be based on facts and informed by theory, and they must serve the needs of policymakers and frontline officials. Papers must offer personal viewpoints and logical analysis and must be supported by respected sources.[8,9]

While, ostensibly, the formal publication requirements at *PS* have not changed much through the years, in practice the *PS* has changed a great deal in focus, content, method, and style. It is becoming less ideological and more scientific, less political and more scholarly, with less grandstanding and more problem solving. These changes in the focus (problem oriented), content (policy driven), substance (evidence based), and style (analytical) of the publication can be observed by close examination of the content of *PS* through the years, particularly in regard to the variety of views, novelty of ideas, disputation of theses, challenges to authority, sources of support, number and kinds of citations, and types of evidence offered.[10] See Table 3.1.

In terms of focus and organization, this chapter is organized thematically to provide a detailed discussion[11] of selected Chinese policy papers in the following areas of police reform: police research, scholarship, and education; goals; principles; paradigms; leadership; and culture.

Police Research, Scholarship, and Education

Research Trend

An examination of key police journals and public security research output from 1988 to 2008[12] identifies several areas on which police research in the past 20 years has been focused. With regard to the theoretical foundation of police studies, the focus has been on what is required to develop a more mature police studies discipline. Specifically, how far has China come in establishing a distinctive and mature police studies discipline, with its own foundational literature, theories, and concepts?[13] Research has also focused on police management theories and how to conceptualize and actualize policing with Chinese characteristics. In particular, what are the roles and functions of the police during economic reform, as compared to their predecessor's practices? Research into police organizational theory has focused on how to distribute, deploy, coordinate, command, and control police

TABLE 3.1   Changes in Focus and Content in *Public Security Studies*, 1999 and 2009

Focus	1999 (Political Rhetoric)	2009 (Problem Oriented)	Remarks
Number of titles of articles referencing Deng or Marx	Two titles referenced Deng; one title referenced Marx.	No title referenced Deng or Marx; four titles referenced Hu's scientific development perspective (SDP).	1999—19 Commissioner's Statements 2009—16 Commissioner's Statements
References to Deng's ideological vs. Hu's scientific thinking in article contents	29 items referred to Deng or Marx.	18 items referred to Hu.	It is evident that references to Hu's SDP (12/18) were more dominant in 2009 than references to Deng's reform thinking (7/29 references) in 1999. The ideological torch had shifted. Deng's ideology of emancipation of the mind had been replaced by an ideology of scientific discovery of practices.
Political correctness vs. scientific solutions	Deng was referenced to demonstrate political correctness; for example, "During the last 20 years, under the guidance of Deng Xiaoping's theory, the public security organs boldly attempted to liberate the thought, hold fast to seek truth from facts…"[a]	Hu's SDP was referred to as a process to create solutions to problems; for example, "Livelihood policing is…a work system based on protecting and serving people's livelihood, reflecting the demand of Party policy and scientific development on police work."[b]	Deng's ideology of reform is one born of the heart that steers the soul of the people. It was designed to motivate and mobilize. In contrast, Hu's SDP has been used to solve problems and create solutions. It is found in the head and appeals to reason. It was designed to provoke thinking and facilitate discourse.

[a] *Public Security Studies*, 63, 16, 1999.
[b] *Public Security Studies*, 171, 13, 2009.

resources vertically (central vs. local; headquarters vs. police post) and horizontally (varieties of police functions) in the most efficient and effective manner. Research efforts are moving to bridge the gap between philosophical discourse vs. practical debate, theoretical vs. applied research, and classical analysis vs. empirical investigation. The overall trend is toward the promotion of applied empirical research that is theory driven to inform policy and instruct operations, avoiding philosophical, ideological, and moralistic debates.[14]

Development of Public Security Studies[15]

In 2003, when the interim findings of a major MPS research initiative, "Public Security Academic Discipline System Research" ("*Gongan xueke tixi yanjiu*"),[16] were released, President Wang of the Chinese People's Public Security University (PSU) commented upon the nature, structure, and content of police studies as an emerging academic discipline in China. According to President Wang, police studies as an academic discipline has developed to fulfill three fundamental public security educational and operational needs:

1. *Scientific research needs*—Many fundamental issues in policing have not been scientifically studied or thoroughly investigated.[17] Most of the important public security policy choices or operational decisions are based on personal experience.[18]
2. *Education and training needs*—Research studies are needed to gather data, findings, literature, and materials necessary for police graduate programs.[19]
3. *Police construction and reform needs*—The CPC has called for *kejiao qiang jing* ("strengthening the police through scientific education").[20]

Over time, such perceived needs came to define the public security research agenda, such as investigating the impact of economic reform on criminality and policing, and to shape the approach taken to police research, such as applied studies vs. pure research as an academic exercise. President Wang further observed that with the establishment of police studies as an academic discipline and research field, it was now necessary to set forth certain principles to guide its development: First, police research and instruction must be based on Chinese conditions and characteristics; any uncritical transplantation of foreign ideas to Chinese soil should be avoided.[21] Second, police research must follow basic scientific protocols and must be theoretically sound, conceptually clear, data driven, and empirically validated.[22] Third, police research and education must promote the free discovery, discussion, and communication of ideas,[23] which requires having an open mind and respect for ideas.[24] Fourth, research and education must address the needs and concerns of the police system, operating as an integrated whole; personal research agendas and piecemeal studies should be avoided.[25]

Research Output, Quality, and Utility

In 1995, the MPS Fourth Research Institute organized an expert conference on "Promotion of Public Security Theory Research Development" at the Public Security University in Beijing. The conference focused on issues pertaining to public security theoretical research, specifically its status, problems, and potential improvement. The conference was well attended, including MPS Vice Minister Jiang Xianjin, Fourth Research Institute Director Xu Xiuyi, PSU Party Secretary Liu Liuchuan, PSU Vice President Zhi Qilu, Beijing People's Police College Vice President Liu Zhenxiang, *Gongan Yanjiu* Editor in Chief Zhang Shaojun, and PSU Professor Kang Dan, among others. Participants observed that public security (especially theoretical) research was growing quickly as a distinctive field of academic and professional inquiry. The field boasted many achieved researchers and much noteworthy research output. Still, the field was beset with many problems.[26] Some of the major concerns are summarized here.[27]

Police research was lacking in practical relevancy and operational utility. Public security research had failed to address police policy and operational needs, such as defining the mission and role of the police in the reform era and determining the impact of the "Strike Hard" (*yanda*) campaign on crime and society. As a crime control strategy, was comprehensive control (*zhong he zhili*) effective in controlling transient communities or regulating the jobless? How could Hu's "harmonious society" policy imperative be translated into actionable and results-oriented community policing programs?

Most police research findings are detached from objective reality and based on subjective opinion. At its core, public security research is applied research. Public security theory should be constructed inductively from empirical data. The ultimate test of public security research is applicability, feasibility, practicality, and utility. The consumers of police research are political leaders, policymakers, and police officers in the field. As such, policing researchers should be working closely with field officers to identity problems, address concerns, and develop solutions. This has not been done. Instead, police researchers and police officers live in two different worlds, where the former investigate police problems and the latter work on them.[28] There is little communication and still less collaboration between the two in integrating police research with policing practice.

Strategic thinking and planning are lacking. There is a lack of organization, planning, and coordination of research activities.[29] Police researchers are conducting research without a central focus sufficient to form a core to attract a following. There have been few attempts to conduct cross-disciplinary research. Very few research exercises are built upon the established work of others. Most research findings are guided by Party policy or support government agenda.

Research methods are poor. Research output is neither informed by theory nor supported by empirical data. Little effort has been directed toward learning from others, building upon existing knowledge and research findings, or testing existing police theories. Few attempts have been made to interpret data and analyze problems in new ways. Many articles still maintain that in the early days of reform, in the 1990s, police were found to be corrupt and abusive because they labored under feudalism or otherwise were corrupted by capitalism. This standard explanation for police deviance represents a lack of political education. Police behavioral problems of all kinds, ranging from dereliction of duty to being disrespectful to citizens, are considered to be an individual and unusual problem, not a structural or normative one. Most articles follow the same old organization and presentation style of identifying the problem, reporting on agreed-upon facts, regurgitating known causes, and making recommendations featuring checklists of dos and don'ts.

President Wang's observations on problems with public security policy research, while pertinent, must be contextualized and given meaning. As compared with the past (1980s), police research in the 2000s, as an academic exercise or policy enterprise, has broadened its scope,[30] enriched its content, diversified its approach,[31] and expanded its horizons.[32] There has also been much noted improvement on research method,[33] theory application, data support, and critical analysis.

Still, the call for relevant and quality police research never ceases.[34] It still is observed that research processes and output are still far from serving practical needs at the policy or operational level.[35] Police research still suffers from validity, reliability, and integrity problems[36] and still does not meet commonly accepted scientific standards or scholarly expectations, domestically or internationally.[37]

Improving Police Research and Scholarship

The MPS Fourth Research Institute conference discussed above was a call to arms to improve police research and scholarship in China. It was answered with a survey conducted by a major regional police journal (*Journal of Jiangsu Police Officer College*) regarding its publication output and pattern since the journal was launched. In order to promote police research, Li Kun-sheng, editor of the *PSU Journal*, wrote a series of four articles on how to conduct research, write articles, and get published. These two endeavors should give us a good understanding of the state of police research and scholarship in China to date.

Police Journal Output: A Case Study

Study Design

In 2003, Ji Weiwei, a Jiangsu Police College librarian, compiled statistics regarding 16 years of output for the *Journal of Jiangsu Police Officer College* (*JJPOC*) from 1986 to 2002.[38] The *JJPOC* was first published in 1986 as the *Jiangsu Public Security College Journal*, but took on its current name in 2002. For the first three years (January 1986 to January 1989), it was an internally circulated journal. Between February 1989 and April 1998, it was a provincially circulated journal. In May 1998, the *JJPOC* became a national and international journal open to public subscription. Before 1997, the *JJPOC* was not a well-organized publication; for example, articles included no abstracts (Chinese or English), keywords, authors' biographies, or uniform citation style. In 1998, the *JJPOC* was included in the Chinese Academic Journals archive. In 2002, it was awarded the Jiangsu provincial first-class journal award. In the same year, it was recognized as one of the excellent national social sciences journals. Over a span of 16 years (1986 to 2002), the *JJPOC* published 1929 articles in 82 issues for a total of 8613 pages. From a content analysis of the *JJPOC*, we can make the following observations.

Publication Output: Quantity and Length

Research output grew significantly during the reform period. The number of articles published in the *JJPOC* doubled between 1986 and 1987 (from 36 to 70), stabilized between 1988 (65) and 1989 (63), and took off again, doubling from 1990 (77) to 1996 (146) (Table 3.2). Finally, between 1996 and 2001, the number of articles published increased by another 22.7%, from 146 to 189. The articles published also got longer; for example, the length of an average article grew from 2.7 pages in 1986/1987, to 3.9 pages in 1996, to 6 pages in 2002. This represents a 222% increase in 16 years (Table 3.2) and suggests that the articles are getting more scholarly, providing more detail and in-depth analysis. The increases in the number of publications and the length of articles occurred at a time when other public security and university journals were also expanding (e.g., *PSU Journal*).[39] The output of publications is policy driven, nationwide, as the MPS is promoting evidence-based policing with scientific research.

Delays in Reviewing Articles

The time required to review articles for publication showed a marked increase from 2.5 months in 1997 to 5.1 months in 2001, an increase of 100%. In 1997, about 20% of the articles published were reviewed in less than a month. In 2001, only six were reviewed in less than a month, or 3.2% of all articles published that year (Table 3.3). This suggests that the editorial office encountered difficulty in keeping up with articles submitted for review. Alternatively, it could mean that the editorial office was spending more time with each article because: (1) there were more submissions per publication; (2) the length of published papers doubled between 1987 to 1996 from 2.7 to 6 pages, and it took more time to read the longer papers; (3) the quality of the papers was improving and they provided more sophisticated arguments with more references, thus requiring more time to read, compare, and select; and (4) editors were reading them more closely to improve the quality of the journal. In any event, for whatever reasons, it can be said that the editing and publication process at *JJPOC* had changed for the better.

TABLE 3.2 Annual Article Output of the *Journal of Jiangsu Police Officer College*

Year	Issues	Number of Articles	Average Number of Articles/Issue	Pages	Average Number of Pages/Issue	Average Number of Pages/Article	Provincial Funded Research Articles
1986	2	36	13.0	96	48.0	2.7	—
1987	4	70	17.5	192	48.0	2.7	—
1988	4	65	16.3	226	56.5	3.5	—
1989	4	68	17.0	288	59.5	3.5	—
1990	4	77	19.3	234	58.5	3.0	—
1991	4	81	20.3	236	59.0	2.9	—
1992	4	96	24.0	288	72.0	3.0	—
1993	4	105	26.3	292	73.0	2.8	—
1994	6	124	20.7	456	76.0	3.7	1
1995	6	129	21.5	504	84.0	3.9	—
1996	6	146	24.3	683	113.8	4.7	—
1997	6	155	25.8	722	120.3	4.7	—
1998	6	139	23.2	736	122.7	5.3	—
1999	6	150	25.0	796	132.7	5.3	1
2000	6	166	27.7	960	160.0	5.8	2
2001	6	189	31.5	1104	184.0	5.8	7
2002	4	133	33.3	800	200.0	6.0	—
Total	82	1929	—	8613	—	—	11

Source: Adapted from Weiwei, J., *Journal of Jiangsu Police Officer College*, 18(1), 175, 2003.

TABLE 3.3 Delays in *Journal of Jiangsu Police Officer College* Article Publication

Months	1997	1998	1999	2000	2001	2002
0	32	25	10	7	6	1
1	34	30	43	10	11	15
2	31	22	24	38	33	39
3	20	19	19	23	23	30
4	12	13	10	28	25	11
5	9	11	10	30	17	11
6	5	6	11	8	12	5
7	2	4	6	7	20	3
8	3	1	2	5	6	4
9	1	—	3	2	9	1
10	1	1	2	3	4	2
11	2	—	1	—	4	2
12	1	2	1	1	3	2
13	1	1	1	1	7	1
14	—	1	3	2	—	—
15	—	—	—	—	1	3
16	—	—	—	—	—	1
21	—	—	—	—	—	1
Average delay	2.5	2.7	3.3	4.0	5.1	3.8

Source: Adapted from Weiwei, J., *Journal of Jiangsu Police Officer College*, 18(1), 176, 2003.

Focus More on Law and Operations Rather than on Political Thoughts

Based on this review, in terms of research focus and publication content the top three most published areas were police legal studies (17.9%), public order studies (14.8%), and criminal investigation studies (13.8%) (Table 3.4). Articles reflecting political thoughts represented 6% of the articles and ranked 9th out of the 11 categories of articles. To the extent that publication policy is driven by Party policy, the publication priority is in promoting the rule of law over and above political thoughts, a departure from past practices during the Mao era. The mission of the *JJPOC*, and other police journals across the nation, is changing. It is clear that the *JJPOC* has undergone and continues to be undergoing radical changes in terms of publication policy; it is becoming less ideological and more focused on legal and operational issues (Table 3.5). The watershed year was 1992. Before 1992, political thought articles (PTAs) and police legal study articles (PLSAs) competed for an audience, with PTAs pulling ahead for 4 years (1989, 1990, 1991, 1992) and PLSAs taking the lead for 3 years (1987, 1988, 1992); 1986 was a draw. Except for 1988 and 1989,[40] the margin of difference was not too big, never more than 2.5%. After 1993, PLSAs clearly dominated, sometimes as much as 31.3% PLSAs vs. 1.2% PTAs (2000) (Table 3.5). The difference in publication rates for PTAs and PLSAs is not an accident. More likely than not, it resulted from editorial policy choices (i.e., law over politics) handed down from Beijing.[41]

A Regional Journal with a National Flavor

In its earlier years (1986 to 1992), the *JJPOC* was very much a local journal. In 1986, its first year of publication, it accepted no outside submissions. In 1989, there was only one (Shanghai). Of the 575 articles published between 1986 and 1993, only 20 (3.5%) were outside submissions (Beijing, 3; Shanghai, 2; Hubei, 3; Sichuan, 2; Shandong, 3; Zhejiang, 1; Jiangxi, 3; Fujian, 1; Hunan, 1; Helungjiang, 1). In 2001, 55 articles (30.2%) came from outside of Jiangsu (Table 3.6). For the 16 years under review, the three top locations contributing published articles were Beijing (111, or 6%), Shanghai (38, or 2.1%), and Hubei (33, or 1.8%). Altogether, they accounted for 182 articles originating outside of Jiangsu, or 9.9%. Articles from these three locations alone represented 50% of all articles originating outside of Jiangsu.

More Diverse Authorship and Ideas

From 1986 to 1995, 761 of the *JJPOC* authors (97.6%) came from within the police system (237 from police agencies and 524 from police colleges). The remaining 19 came from outside the police system (9 from colleges, 6 from justice organs, and 4 others). By 2002, the authorship pattern had changed to be more inclusive and diversified. Of the 132 authors that year, 19 (14.4%) were from police agencies, 59 (44.7%) from police colleges, 7 (5.3%) from research institutes, 41 (31%) from other colleges, 3 (2.3%) from justice organs, and 3 (2.3%) others. The *JJPOC* is no longer a bastion of monolithic police voices, representing one school of thought.

How to Do Research in China

Professor Li Kun-sheng, the editor of the *PSU Journal*, has held that position for 20 years. The *PSU Journal* is the leading police journal in China and is read by all police college students, police professionals, and the nation's justice leaders. In 2004, in the *Journal of Hubei Public Security College*,[42] Professor Li offered advice on how to conduct research, write articles, and get published in the field of police studies. He also observed that researchers:

TABLE 3.4 Subject Matter Distribution in *Journal of Jiangsu Police Officer College*, 1986 to 2002

Year	Political Thought	Police Legal Studies	Criminology	Police Management Studies	Police Education Studies	Public Order Studies	Criminal Investigation Studies	Police Technical Skills	Traffic Management Studies	Police Physical Skills	Language, Literature, Writing
1986	4	4	6	1	3	7	4	1	0	0	6
1987	7	8	6	5	8	4	16	6	0	1	9
1988	5	9	3	4	10	4	13	8	0	0	8
1989	12	4	4	5	17	7	6	5	0	0	7
1990	10	8	8	12	11	7	11	4	0	4	2
1991	7	6	3	8	9	22	9	5	0	1	11
1992	11	9	8	12	9	11	10	15	2	1	8
1993	8	22	10	13	9	16	15	8	1	4	2
1994	9	17	8	11	18	20	21	12	1	0	7
1995	6	17	5	12	7	30	17	24	4	1	6
1996	3	24	8	22	13	24	21	19	1	7	5
1997	10	24	6	20	8	33	28	18	2	6	5
1998	3	29	20	14	6	21	18	15	2	7	3
1999	4	28	16	11	16	23	16	20	4	5	7
2000	2	52	32	16	8	19	18	11	1	3	4
2001	4	52	22	21	6	28	24	19	8	2	3
2002	11	34	16	18	3	11	25	15	5	2	0
Total	116	347	181	205	161	287	267	205	31	34	93
Percentage (%)	6.0	17.9	9.3	10.6	8.3	14.8	13.8	10.6	1.6	2.3	4.8

Source: Adapted from Weiwei, L., *Journal of Jiangsu Police Officer College*, 18(1), 176, 2003.

TABLE 3.5   Political Thought and Police Legal Studies Articles in *Journal of Jiangsu Police Officer College*, 1986 to 2002

Year	Total Articles	Political Thought Articles		Police Legal Studies Articles	
		Number of Articles	Percentage of Total Articles (%)	Number of Articles	Percentage of Total Articles (%)
1986	36	4	13.30	4	13.30
1987	70	7	10.00	8	11.43
1988	65	5	7.69	9	13.85
1989	68	12	17.64	4	5.88
1990	77	10	12.98	8	10.39
1991	81	7	8.64	6	7.41
1992	96	11	11.45	9	9.37
1993	105	8	7.62	22	20.95
1994	124	9	7.26	17	13.71
1995	129	6	4.65	17	13.18
1996	146	3	2.05	24	16.44
1997	155	10	6.45	24	15.48
1998	139	3	2.16	29	20.86
1999	150	4	2.67	28	18.67
2000	166	2	1.20	52	31.32
2001	189	4	2.12	52	27.51
2002	133	11	8.27	34	25.56
Total	1926	116	6.00	347	17.90

Source: Adapted from Weiwei, J., *Journal of Jiangsu Police Officer College*, 18(1), 176, 2003.

(1) are ignorant of format and style; (2) fail to grasp the fundamentals of writings; (3) confuse academic research writing with investigative reporting; and (4) are not familiar with research literature, thus wasting everyone's time and effort.

Among the pointers provided by Professor Li were the following suggestions. The first requirement for conducting police research leading to publication is to know the field and its developments (past and present) through a detailed and methodical review of the literature. When conducting such a review of Chinese police research, it can be problematic to define the field and the discipline. Public security studies (PSS) represents a very new discipline. The study of policing in China originated as PSS and later took on the name of police studies (PS). Because Chinese academic disciplines are organized by the state, they are very structured and well defined. What constitutes an academic discipline is specifically provided for by rules and regulations; for example, it must have distinguished scholars, recognized scholarship, a corpus of publications, and research institutes. PSS, being a latecomer, falls under the rubric of law and has become a subdiscipline of law. (This recalls the disciplinary debate regarding criminology in Europe vs. the United States. In Europe, criminology is a branch of law; in the United States, the study of the nature of, prevalence of, causation of, and remedies to crime is a stand-alone discipline known as criminology, or it can be a part of a larger discipline referred to as criminal justice.)

The classification of PSS as part and parcel of law studies requires a historical explanation. Before Deng's reform, and under Mao, law programs were not professional schools for the training of lawyers (as in the West). Rather, law was taught in political–legal institutes, the reason being that in the Communist state there is no law but rather politics and policies.

TABLE 3.6 Origin of Articles in *Journal of Jiangsu Police Officer College*, 1986 to 2002

	1986	1987	1988	1989	1990	1991	1992	1993	1994	1995	1996	1997	1998	1999	2000	2001	2002	Total (%)
Jiangsu	36	69	54	63	74	78	82	99	105	78	128	118	90	114	93	127	78	1436 (80.3)
Beijing	—	—	3	—	—	—	—	—	—	—	2	19	15	12	22	25	22	111 (6.2)
Shanghai	—	1	—	1	—	—	—	—	—	—	—	3	6	2	6	5	10	30 (2.1)
Hubei	—	—	1	1	—	—	—	—	4	—	1	—	4	4	5	6	7	33 (2.1)
Sichuan	—	—	—	—	—	—	—	2	1	2	7	6	4	—	3	—	1	26 (1.4)
Shandong	—	—	1	—	—	—	—	1	—	1	—	2	2	3	7	4	2	24 (1.3)
Zhejiang	—	—	—	—	—	—	1	—	2	2	—	1	4	2	5	2	2	20 (1.1)
Jiangxi	—	—	2	1	—	—	—	—	1	—	2	—	1	2	1	2	—	12 (0.6)
Fujian	—	—	—	—	1	—	—	—	4	—	—	—	1	3	—	2	1	12 (0.6)
Chongqing	—	—	—	—	—	—	—	—	—	—	2	3	—	2	2	1	2	12 (0.6)
Liaoning	—	—	—	—	—	—	—	—	—	—	—	—	1	2	4	2	3	12 (0.6)
Henan	—	—	—	—	—	—	—	—	—	—	2	2	1	—	3	—	1	9 (0.5)
Guangdong	—	—	—	—	—	—	—	—	—	1	1	1	—	1	2	1	—	7 (0.4)
Hunan	—	—	—	—	1	—	—	—	—	—	—	—	—	4	—	1	—	6 (0.3)
Anhui	—	—	—	—	—	—	—	—	—	—	—	—	3	1	—	1	—	5 (0.3)
Heilongjiang	—	—	—	—	1	—	—	—	—	—	—	2	2	—	—	—	—	5 (0.3)
Xiangxi	—	—	—	—	—	—	—	—	—	—	—	—	—	1	1	1	3	6 (0.3)
Jianxu	—	—	—	—	—	—	—	—	—	—	1	2	—	—	1	—	—	4 (0.3)
Guizhou	—	—	—	—	—	—	—	—	—	—	—	2	1	1	—	—	—	4 (0.2)
Jilin	—	—	—	—	—	—	—	—	—	—	—	—	—	1	1	2	—	4 (0.2)
Tianjin	—	—	—	—	—	—	—	—	—	—	—	—	1	—	2	—	—	3 (0.2)
Macau	—	—	—	—	—	—	—	—	—	—	—	—	1	—	1	—	2	3 (0.2)
Hebei	—	—	—	—	—	—	—	—	1	—	—	—	1	—	1	—	2	4 (0.2)
Ningxia	—	—	—	—	—	—	—	—	—	—	—	—	—	—	—	—	—	—
Hainan	—	—	—	—	—	—	—	—	—	—	—	1	—	—	1	—	—	2 (0.1)
Hong Kong	—	—	—	—	—	—	—	—	—	—	—	1	—	—	—	—	—	1 (0.1)
Yunnan	—	—	—	—	—	—	—	—	—	—	—	1	—	—	—	—	—	1 (0.1)
Total	36	70	61	66	77	79	88	103	118	87	146	155	138	151	166	182	132	1850 (100.0)

Source: Adapted from Weiwei, J., *Journal of Jiangsu Police Officer College*, 18(1), 176, 2003.

Law and the police exist to serve the interests of the ruling class. Because the discipline of PSS, like law, is an instrument of the state for political purposes (e.g., suppression of class enemies), law and public security are blood brothers that cannot be easily separated, if at all. After the reform, public security work took on social and economic functions in the form of police services, which led to a need to create a police studies discipline with its own paradigms, theories, research, methods, findings, and protocols.

Another complication with researching police studies rests with its immature development. As an academic field, PS is further divided into two subdisciplines: (1) PS–social science, and (2) PS–science and technology. Many different areas of concentrations or studies can be found under each subdiscipline, such as armed police study (*wujing xue*), public order study (*zhian jingcha xue*), prison administration study (*yuzheng xue*), police history study (*jingcha shi xue*), comparative police study (*beijiao jingcha xue*), police legal study (*jingcha fa xue*), police management study (*jingcha guanli xue*), police psychology (*jingcha xinli xue*), police sociology (*jingcha shehui xue*), police public relation study (*jingcha gonggong guanxi xue*), and police education study (*jingcha jiaoyu xue*). Falling under these areas of study are various other types of study; for example, public order study includes household policing study and public order intelligence study. Because most of these subdisciplines are not well defined and developed, research into the field has been handicapped by a lack of expertise and research output. This makes mastery of the field by anyone nearly impossible. Without clearly defined boundaries and subject matter research literature, it is difficult to conduct meaningful research.

Yet another problem with police research is that, when it comes to developing a research agenda, Chinese researchers have failed to master the fundamentals of the research process: (1) it must have a research focus (*lun dian*), (2) it must provide supporting arguments (*lunju*), and (3) it must gather supportive evidence (*lunzheng*). This has resulted in research output that is unfocused, duplicative, and opinioned. Having mastered the research process, a researcher still must know what requirements they must meet before their work will be considered for publication; that is, they must be guided by political theory or thinking (i.e., *zhengzhi sheng*, guided by Marx, Mao, and Deng, or the "Three Represents"); conform to legal rules and principles (i.e., *falu sheng*, following the Constitution and law); possess professional and expert knowledge (i.e., *kexue sheng*, following scientific principles); and offer new viewpoints (i.e., *chuangzao sheng*).

When conducting academic research, competent researchers must approach the work of pertinent authorities, evidence, and supporting materials in a judicious way. A research article is not an opinion piece, still less a political statement. What counts for evidence and support is ultimately determined by the research focus and attending arguments. Evidence and supportive materials used must be relevant, truthful, reliable, authoritative, lively, and compelling. When conducting police research, it is necessary to consider the following kinds of information: crime data (e.g., murder rate), police work data (e.g., rate of police injuries on duty), social statistics (e.g., poverty rate), state political data (e.g., MPS annual reports), Party policy and guidelines (e.g., Party decisions on corruption), police laws and administrative regulations (e.g., Police Law of 1995), relevant treatises and journals (e.g., *PSU Journal* or *Beijing Law Journal*), classical materials (e.g., Mao Tse-tung's *Red Book*), and dictionaries (e.g., *Chi Hai*).

Finally, manuscripts should be organized into three parts: introduction, discussion, and conclusion. In the introduction, the author must address the following issues: (1) the main theme (*zhu zhi*), such as the focus of or reason for the research, and methods;

(2) reasons for selecting that particular topic (*xuanti*), such as a gap in the existing literature, the feasibility of research, or the availability of data; and (3) theoretical support, as revealed by research findings in the field. In the discussion part, the author should state the research focus, define the issues, muster the evidence, and render the proof. In the conclusion, the author should summarize the arguments, state the findings, and sincerely and humbly discuss the shortcomings or limitations of the paper, offering some suggestions of what lies ahead for future research.

Early Police (Empirical) Research

In terms of scientific, empirical police research, there are some bright spots. Although not often reported, the MPS has conducted large-scale polls regarding public opinions of police–public relations since as early as 1988.[43] One of the earliest MPS nationwide surveys was on public fear of crime, first conducted in 1988 and again in 1991.[44]

Public Safety Survey

In 1991, the MPS Public Safety Research Institute's "Public Safety Feelings Benchmark Research and Assessment" ("*Gongzhong anquan gan zhibiao yanjiu yu pingjia*") project conducted its second national survey.[45] Both the 1988 and 1991 surveys covered 15 provinces, autonomous districts, and cities (Beijing, Shanghai, Tianjin, Liaoning, Hebei, Shandong, Jiangsu, Zhejiang, Jiangxi, Hubei, Guangdong, Guizhou, Sichuan, Shanxi, and Xinjiang); 150 city-districts; 75 counties; 375 streets (townships); and 750 residential committees. They surveyed a total of 15,000 randomly selected respondents who were over 16 years old and residents of the particular area under study. A total of 14,951 survey instruments were returned (a rate of 99.67%); of these, 14,860 were usable (99.39%). The survey defined the public feeling of safety (*gongzhong anquan gan*) as the "people's subjective feelings, expectations, attitudes, and evaluations of social safety conditions."

First, respondents were asked, "With the current public safety condition, what is your personal feeling of safety?" Responses were "safe," 1085 (7%); "relatively safe," 6500 (44%); "average safe," 2660 (18%); "not very safe," 3412 (23%); and "not safe," 1111 (8%). The assessment scoring for feeling of safety was as follows: "safe," 1 point; "relatively safe," 0.75 point; "average safe," 0.5 point; "relatively not safe," 0.25 point; and "not safe," 0 point. The statistical aggregated average safety score was 0.550; compared with the 1988 survey result of 0.473, this represented a slight increase of 0.077 point, or about 14%.

Second, respondents were asked, "What is your assessment of current public safety conditions in the society?" Responses were "very good," 788 (5%); "relatively good," 4755 (32%); "average," 6188 (42%); "relatively bad," 2543 (17%); and "very bad," 52 (4%). The assessment scoring for safety conditions was as follows: "good," 1 point; "relatively good," 0.75 point; "average," 0.5 point; "relatively not good," 0.25 point; and "not good," 0 point. The statistical aggregated average safety conditions score was 0.545; compared with the 1988 survey result of 0.484, this represented a slight increase of 0.061 point, or about 11%.

Overall, 14 out of the 15 provinces (99.3%) reported an increase in feelings of public safety. For the 1988 survey, the average highest and lowest safety feeling scores were 0.623 and 0.326 points, respectively. In the 1991 survey, they were 0.693 and 0.423 points. The average highest feeling of safety score increased by 0.073, or 11.7%. The average lowest feeling of safety score increased by 0.100, or 30.5%. On average, then, notwithstanding a majority of provinces feeling more safe, the number of people feeling unsafe was growing.

TABLE 3.7   Comparing Responses to "Dare to Travel at Night"

Response	1988 Survey		1991 Survey		
	Number of Reponses	Percent of Total (%)	Number of Responses	Percent of Total (%)	Percent (%) Change
Dare	10,217	68.7	7467	50.4	−36.3
Not dare	4514	30.4	7280	49.1	+38.1
No answer	129	0.9	75	0.5	—
Total responses	14,869	—	14,822	—	—

This perhaps has something to do with the fact there is more room for downward than upward adjustment between fear and safety. It is also easier to feel unsafe than to feel safe. Of the 75 districts surveyed, 69 reported increased feelings of safety, 2 were the same, and 6 reported a decline.

Finally, when respondents were asked about their response to not feeling safe ("dare to travel at night") vs. feeling safe (*anquan gan*) (Table 3.7), people were less willing to walk the street at night in 1991 ("dare," 50.4%; "not dare," 30.4%) than in 1988 ("dare," 68.7%; "not dare," 49.4%), a significant decrease. It is clear that the respondents' general feeling of safety was not necessarily reflected in their actions. One way to explain this apparent anomaly is to observe that the different survey questions tapped into different dimensions of security vs. fear. In essence, people generally felt safe overall but were still very much mindful of walking the street at night. Another interpretation could be that actions speak louder than feelings.

Police–Public Relations Survey

In 1992, Zhou Wai and Li Quan published results of a survey entitled, "Police and Citizen Cooperation: The Focal Point of Police Work—Reflection on Shandong Province, Jining City, Public Security Bureau: Dongmen Police Post Survey."[46] The survey was conducted by the MPS Fourth Police Research Institute and Shandong Province, Jining City, Public Security Bureau to evaluate the relationships between the police and citizens at the Dongmen Police Post in the center of Jining City.[47] In 1993, Wang Dai, Jie Jidong, and Zhou Wai published a report entitled, "Building Chinese Community Police: Research Report of Shandong, Jining City, Community Police Work."[48] This research was conducted in Shandong by the MPS Fourth Research Institute to investigate community police developments, especially how its practice has impacted the police and public. The research method included field observations, literature reviews, social visits, expert opinions, and surveys. Over the span of 3 months, 97 researchers spread out over 7 counties and interviewed 2500 people. Most of the people (70.6%) respected the police, but a sizable minority considered police performance to be less than satisfactory; that is, 47% thought the police were doing a very good or relatively good job, 38% thought that they were doing an all right job, and 15% thought they were doing a relatively bad or very bad job. As to social order and public safety, 49% thought that it was very good or relatively good, and 13% thought it was relatively bad or very bad.

Recent Police Surveys

"Career Achievement of Public Security Service and Supply Model Relating to Policemen and People Relations in the Reform Period," *Public Security Science Journal—Journal of Zhejiang Police College*, 103, 12–24, 2007, reported on a survey of police and public relationships at the Yiwu City, Zhejiang Province, Public Security Bureau. Earlier, Wang Yan's "Survey on Occupational Value of College Students in Public Security College," *Journal of Jiangsu Police Officer College*, 99, 195–198, 2005, reported on a survey of the occupational values of 380 students at the Jiangsu Police College.

Ongoing PSU Baseline Surveys

Since 2006, the editorial office of *Police Station Work* (*Paichusuo gongzuo*) magazine, published by the Chinese People's Public Security University Press, has conducted a series of surveys on police work, from promotional prospects to pay schedules to working conditions to police–community relations. The survey data can be used as baseline data to evaluate the impact of police reform on frontline officers. By the end of 2010, the results of 35 studies had been published, addressing such issues as overtime,[49] police–public relations,[50] personal health,[51] police post housing,[52] and extremist militants.[53] Many of the surveys do not disclose the methodology used (e.g., sample population, sampling method, sample profile), which makes independent assessment of the reliability, validity, and generalizability of the findings impossible. The data can be used, however, in collaboration with other more reliable sources to paint a picture of what police and policing are like in the reform era. It can also be used to bolster other qualitative data, such as police stories and commentaries found online. Finally, it is most useful as a window of opportunity to understanding the working conditions and personal lifestyle of officers working on the frontline.[54]

A Sample Survey

To understand the *Police Station Work* survey database and how it was compiled and organized, we can take a look at a survey on overtime published in 2007.[55] This survey was chosen because it is one of the most recent ones posted online. It also addresses one of the most important issues of concern to rank-and-file police officers. If one were to track police web discussion through the years, one would find that most of the debates and discussions are about working conditions, welfare and benefits, social status, and management problems. The one subject that always come up is how hard police officers have to work and what pressures they are under, particularly in big cities (e.g., Beijing, Shanghai) and Special Economic Zones (e.g., Shenzhen).

In 2006, *Police Station Work* magazine conducted a nationwide (over 20 cities) survey on police officers' attitudes toward overtime; it sought to answer the question, "Have you had overtime all night?"[56] The survey subjects consisted of more than 100 local police post (*paichusuo*) officers. The methodology of research, including sampling, was not described; however, the sample gathered was really too small to be of any scientific significance. The male-to-female ratio of the sample was 9 to 2. The average length of service was 7.7 years, with the shortest being 2 months and the longest 26 years. The findings of the survey are summarized below:

- *Officers are overworked.* Overtime (O/T) is the norm. For city police post officers, the average O/T for all was 3.5 hr/day, or 43.5% of a regular 8-hour work shift. The impact of O/T on police health, morale, and effectiveness was a real concern, as it was discussed many times in web postings and commentaries. The health and family problems created by O/T were thought to contribute to officers dying young, long before their peers, or perhaps ending up divorced in mid-career.

TABLE 3.8   Paichusuo City Police Overtime per Month, 2006

	Overtime
By recent month	
Maximum	300 hr/month, or 10.0 hr/day
Minimum	15 hr/month, or 0.5 hr/day
Average	105 hr/month, or 3.5 hr/day
By length of service	
1–10 years of service	60 hr/month, or 2 hr/day/month (average)
10–20 years of service	222 hr/month, or 8 hr/day/month (average)
20–25 years of service	180 hr/month, or 6 hr/day/month (average)
Average	154 hr/month, or 16 hr/day/month (average)

- *The distribution of work is not even.* In a recent month, the range of O/T for officers ranged from 300 hr (maximum) to 15 hr (minimum). Depending on an officer's years of service, O/T could range from 2 hr (junior officer) to 7.7 hr (mid-career officer).
- *Some officers are more burdened than others.* O/T was being performed more by some subsets of officers than others. Those who were most experienced, knowledgeable, motivated, and dependable (i.e., mid-career officers with 10 to 20 years of service) were assuming most of the O/T duties. On average, the mid-career officers were carrying more than three times more O/T hours per month than junior officers: 7.7 hr vs. 2 hr. This perhaps was due to the fact that junior officers (1 to 10 years of experience) are still learning the ropes. Senior officers (20 to 25 years of experience) lagged behind mid-career officers, but only marginally: 7.7 hr vs. 6 hr. This might be due to the fact that seniors are in command positions, work in agencies (i.e., white-collar cops), enjoy seniority privileges, or are on the retirement track. Other factors that are likely to affect O/T load included sex (females being favored), function (criminal investigations being the most demanding), events (festivals requiring more officers), emergencies (mass incidents requiring full deployment), and location (rural areas being less busy). This uneven distribution of workload meant that some officers were carrying a greater workload than others, raising the thorny issues of equality and burnout. See Table 3.8.
- *Officers have little rest.* Officers work a grueling schedule, with little rest in between. They are on night-shift duty three to four times a week, which means that they can enjoy a good night's sleep only three to four times a week. This does not take into account the occasional O/T that can cut into or completely eliminate those few normal sleeping hours. The survey found that, on a regular basis, officers enjoyed only 3 days of rest a month, which deviated substantially from normal expectations of 7 days a month on average, a maximum of 12 days, or a minimum of 4 days. Officers who require more rest days than what they are receiving suffer chronic fatigue, with no end in sight. This was affirmed by the fact that, when asked what they like to do on holiday, most officers (87%) opted for doing nothing but sleep; other activities included visiting parents, reading, watching television, exercising, going out with the family, working on their homes, engaging in training, and surfing the web.

- *Officers have more work than time.* When asked to choose all that applied among multiple-choice options for why they had to work O/T, most officers picked "inability to finish work without O/T" (57%), followed by "need to be on duty" (43%), "emergencies/non-police duties" (39%), and "following the leader" (20%).
- *O/T practice is structural in nature.* Inasmuch as O/T is driven more by need (see above item) than by choice, O/T is a stop-gap measure, and the practical solution is to hire more help.
- *O/T is a stop-gap measure.* A stop-gap measure is a temporary solution to the long-term structural problem of required police work not matching available resources. A majority of the officers performing O/T are compensated in extra pay or rest time. That is to say, the normal duty requirements and financial burden of running a functional police department have been shifted to the police officers working the street, not the government, Party, or people. But, such stop-gap measures are short sighted and self-defeating. The O/T problem cannot be cured by itself, and O/T has an immediate impact on work performance. Police officers reported lower efficiency for both their O/T work performance (not high, 8%; all right, 27%; high, 15%) and their morning-after performance (some impact, 52%; major impact, 48%).[57] Simply put, officers reported working more but achieving less. This downward spiral of inefficiency promises to get worse each day, until people are just going through the motions of working and not getting things done. A tired and disgruntled officer is not only a nonproductive worker but also a liability to the department as far as providing poor services to the people.
- *O/T has an adverse impact on officers.* Most officers do not like O/T (56%). No one expressed liking O/T; instead, 30% expressed disgust, and 26% disliked it. A sizable minority (44%) reported "no feeling." This choice is intriguing, as it is indicative of the officers' mindset. "No feeling" can be interpreted in different ways. First, literally, it would mean that an officer has no opinion, either way. This is hardly likely, as O/T directly impacts their job with regard to the expectations of their supervisors and of themselves, and it indirectly affects their home and social life. Second, the "no feeling" answer does not agree with answers to other questions seeking to gauge the impact of O/T on officers; for example, 99% of the officers felt tired, and 81% felt stressed during O/T. These are real feelings that cannot be dismissed as "no feelings." Third, the "no feeling" answer might mean suppressing one's personal feelings to serve a larger cause, be it the people ("people come first," or *yi ren wei ben*), or the Party, or the military discipline of the MPS. Fourth, the "no feeling" answer might represent a certain amount of cognitive dissonance. Fifth, it could be a short-hand way of saying "no comment" by officers assuming that nothing is going to change and one's career might be hindered by speaking the mind. Sixth, the answer might reflect the fact that the officers had learned to accept reality and were in an advanced stage of burnout. They needed the job but could not improve the work conditions; in other words, "It's just a job, with good days and bad." Finally, the "no feeling" answer offered the best way to avoid the issue altogether, by hiding one's displeasure from the watchful eyes of colleagues and boss. In China, face management is important, so one does not appear weak to one's peers, untrustworthy to one's boss, or a failure to oneself.

- *O/T affects officers physically.* Nearly 100% of the officers felt tired during O/T. They used multiple means to keep themselves awake, including smoking cigarettes (59%), washing their face (30%), using medications (15%), and drinking coffee or tea (11%). Forcing oneself to stay awake night after night is harmful to one's health, especially when stimulants are used routinely and in abundance. The officers surveyed realized this, as 81% of them knew that O/T was bad for their health, but 15% claimed that they could handle it.
- *O/T affects officers psychologically.* Officers said they felt stressed and prone to anger when working O/T.
- *O/T affects officers socially.* In response to the question regarding whether O/T affects officers' personal lives and social relationships, no one offered an opinion of positive impact. In fact, the overwhelming majority (77%) of officers thought that their relationships with family and friends had grown distant, and 19% of the younger officers were worried that their OT work might affect their marital prospects.
- *Officers question the legitimacy of O/T.* When probed further about the O/T issue, 54% of the officers wanted to know whether other police officers were paid for their O/T, 67% wanted to know whether O/T was against the Labor Rights, and 17% wanted to know whether they could refuse O/T.

Research Agenda and Issues (1979–1992)

In 1992, *Gongan Yanjiu* published a list of issues requiring research and debate.[58] The article provided a framework and checklist for measuring, analyzing, and understanding police reform research in China in the formative years (1979 to 1992):

1. Deng Xiaoping's thought on people's dictatorship
    1.1 The content, meaning, and interpretation of Deng's people's dictatorship
    1.2 The theoretical relationship between Deng's thinking and Marxist doctrine
    1.3 The nature, characteristics, target, and function of the people's dictatorship in the reform era
    1.4 The status, relevancy, and utility of the people's dictatorship in police work
2. Policy toward crime attack, prevention, and control
    2.1 The nature, characteristics,[59] causation, and response to crime
    2.2 The current status (incidence and prevalence), pattern (distribution and trend), and change in crime during the reform period
    2.3 The current status, characteristics, and development of organized crime, including gang violence and secret societies
    2.4 The developing trend with "six evils" (*liu hai*)
    2.5 The function of public security in reducing criminogenic conditions
    2.6 The conduct of targeted attack and area control over crime and criminals
    2.7 The relationship between prevention vs. attack vs. control of crime
    2.8 The public order situation, its development in coastal cities, and basic policy
    2.9 Patrol system research
3. Fundamental thinking on police reform during the new era
    3.1 Theory and practice of the "two hands" doctrine (i.e., one hand on reform and one hand on control)
    3.2 Adjusting police work to achieve the goals of deepening reform and speeding up modernization

3.3 Relationship between diverse, divergent, and disparate public security developments in the reform period

3.4 Reforming the public security system to meet realistic needs and emerging challenges during the reform

3.5 Establishing command, control, and supervision systems

3.6 Establishing a highly effective police patrol system

3.7 The purpose, roles, and functions of internal security

3.8 Personnel reform during the reform period

3.9 Assessment of public order and public security work against benchmarks

4. Public security legal system construction

4.1 The roles, functions, and utility of public security legal system work

4.2 The relationship between legal system work and strengthening public security work

4.3 Perfecting public security legal work

4.4 The overall capacity of public security agency in enforcement of the law and mounting operations

4.5 Perfection of public security internal law enforcement supervision system

5. The characteristics and pattern of class struggle

5.1 Change in the nation's class struggle relationship

5.2 Manifestation and patterns of class struggle

5.3 Factors affecting intensification of class struggle and scope

5.4 Public security management strategy and patterns regarding class struggle

5.5 Correct separation between two kinds of contradictions

6. Anti-peaceful transformation strategy

6.1 Lessons from Russia and Eastern Europe

6.2 The strategy, channels, measures, and focus of the enemies' peaceful transformations

6.3 Our nation's basic strategy against peaceful transformation

6.4 The role and functions of public security organs in peaceful transformation struggles

7. Public security nature, mission, and historical lessons

7.1 The nature, roles, and status of public security in the new reform era

7.2 The mission, roles, and functions of public security in the reform era

7.3 The differentiation between public security and other agencies

7.4 The basic direction, policies, and principles of public security work

7.5 Public security work experiences and traditions

Research Agenda and Issues (1995–2010)

Nearly two decades later, we find that the focus of research on crime and punishment, along with the national agenda, has changed (Table 3.9). Ideologically, the administration of General Secretary Hu Jintao and Premier Wen Jiabao (Hu–Wen) has been moving from the political struggles of the past (e.g., Tiananmen Square and Falun Gong) to the scientific development of a "harmonious society" of the future. This means finding ways to remove the root causes of "contradictions" through alleviation of social, economic, and political destabilizing conditions. Examples would include economically adjusting the income distribution to narrow the income gaps between the rich and poor, urban and rural areas (e.g.,

TABLE 3.9 Focus of Police Policy Research in *Public Security Studies*, 1992 vs. 2009

Dimension	1990s	2000s
Ideology	*Deng Xiaoping's thoughts on "people's dictatorship" (PD)* Focus is on two areas: (1) clarifying Deng's thinking (e.g., meaning of PD), and (2) exploring the relationship between Deng's PD in the past (theoretically) and present (practically).	*Hu Jingtao's thinking on the "scientific development perspective" (SDP)* Focus is on the fact that SDP is not a controversial idea, and there is little need to clarify the meaning and explore its utility. SDP is applied in a variety of contexts, settings, and locations, such as dealing with the media, crisis management, and police rights, or, more generally, transforming ideological thinking into scientific (operational) principles.
Crime control	*Policy toward attacking crime and its prevention and control* Focus is on mapping out the nature, prevalence, pattern, trend, distribution, causation, and remedy to crime and disorder, generally (crime trends) and specifically (gang violence), theoretically (criminogenic conditions) and operationally (patrol), nationally or locally. The major concern is with juvenile delinquency, mobile criminality, and cross-border crime. Overall, incident driven and reacting to events.	*Policy toward attacking crime and its prevention and control* Focus shifts from exploring general criminogenic conditions and recurring crime trends (*yanda*) to investigating problems and issues associated with addressing specific kinds of emerging crimes, such as insurance fraud, fake invoices, money laundering, Internet crime, and cross-border crime. There is also a movement to explore new ways of fighting crime, such as private security or contract public order. The major concern is with virtual criminology and mass incidents. Overall, preventive, preemptive, and problem solving.
Police reform	*Fundamental thinking on police reform during the new era* Focus is on "emancipation of the mind" and reflecting upon various kinds of dualistic contradictions in policing thinking of the time, such as Deng's "two hands" doctrine, where one hand is on economic development and the other on crime control, or how to be a stern law enforcer and compassionate people server at the same time.	*Fundamental thinking on police reform during the new era* Focus is on the fact that most of the contradictions in policing thinking have been resolved or accepted; for example, mass incidents should be treated with care and Falun Gong should be suppressed without mercy. The challenge is in mapping out the contour and details of a new set of imperatives, implementing the "Three Represents" (before 2004) or constructing a "harmonious society" (2004 and after).

Legal system construction	*Public security legal system construction* Focus is on perfecting the police legal system with respect to capacity, utility, and supervision.	*Public security legal system refinement* The focus is on perfecting the police legal system through changes in philosophy (e.g., substantive vs. procedural justice, transparency vs. secrecy), framework (e.g., eliminate reform through labor education), and process (e.g., from punitive to restorative justice). Legal construction has moved from building up the legal regime or structure to refining its application and harmonizing its operations—more generally, from structure to process. Legal construction also has to deal with the arrival of citizens' rights (e.g., remain silent) and international human rights (e.g., death penalty).
Class struggle	*Characteristics and pattern of class struggle* Focus is on two areas: (1) investigating the manifestation, patterns, and changes in class struggle during the reform period; and (2) how police should deal with class struggle.	*Demise of class struggle* Focus is on two areas: (1) class struggle is not a major concern, and (2) concern now is with defining and dealing with contradictions among the people (mass incidents) and between the people and the enemy (Falun Gong).
Anti-peaceful transformation	*Anti-peaceful transformation strategy* Focus is on leaders being preoccupied with foreign (Western) attempts to transform China "peacefully" (e.g., corruption of the younger generation).	*Anti-peaceful transformation strategy* Focus is on residual concerns regarding a peaceful transformation strategy; often viewed as an afterthought. The preoccupation is how to integrate with the global community (e.g., World Trade Organization) and deal with problems arising out of, for example, U.N. conventions (e.g., clarifying the China concept of the rule of law or human rights, in theory and practice).
Public security role and mission	*Public security nature, mission, and historical lessons* Focus is on ascertaining what "policing with Chinese characteristics" means, in theoretical and operative terms, especially in the context of history and as an evolving project.	*Public security nature, mission, and historical lessons* Focus is on clarifying the roles and fine-tuning the mission of police in new situations or cases, such as the role of police with regard to migrants or the function of police in taking on violent peasants (the unjustly deprived). Another focus is on observing differences between theory and practice, often by making recommendations for improvement or perfection (e.g., negotiation between competing demands, protecting lawful protests, maintaining necessary order).

Engel's law), and coastal and inland areas (e.g., develop the western region, revitalize the northeast industrial bases, stimulate the central economy), in addition to improving self-governance at the village level, allowing direct suffrage of neighborhood committees, and providing for an aging population (in 2015, 9.5% of the population).[60] That is to say, use soft power to anticipate, preempt, and diffuse "contradictions" rather than the hard power of suppression. In policing, this means moving away from the Lei Feng spirit of old to a new professionalism that seeks to integrate the post-1980s generation into its fold and to promote more educated officers within its ranks. Strategically, this means shifting away from confrontation and suppression and moving toward evidence-based and intelligence-based policing. Operationally, this means pluralization, communalization, commoditization, and privatization of policing. Police research has moved lockstep in these same directions.

In terms of crime prevention and control, research in the 1980s and early 1990s focused on understanding traditional crime patterns and perfecting traditional ways of dealing with crime. This meant mapping (e.g., prevalence, distribution, trends) and controlling (e.g., patrols, *yanda*, household registration) traditional crime (e.g., youth, gang drugs). In the 2000s, the focus has moved toward fighting new types of crime, such as false invoices[61] and multilevel marketing,[62] in new ways. In terms of police reform, research has moved from reforming the old to exploring the new and from reacting to the traditional needs of policing to anticipating future crime, law, and order problems, such as dealing with mass incidents and coping with regulation of the Internet. In terms of updating the legal system, the research has moved beyond institutionalization to systems building; the focus now is on refining, perfecting, and innovating the current organization and practices. The challenge is to develop legal concepts, theories, processes, and culture befitting a harmonious society (e.g., human rights vs. police rights).

Developing an International Police Education at PSU

With the globalization of trade and China's admission to the World Trade Organization,[63] the MPS has had to find ways to internationalize its policing operations, ways, and means. This requires developing an international education program for its officers. Here, the PSU and Zhejiang Police College play a key role. In 2003, the 50th anniversary of the PSU, then-Minister of Public Security Zhou Yongkang called for strengthening the police through scientific education (*kejiao qiangjing*). Earlier still, Deng Xiaoping had promoted enhanced education in service of the nascent Chinese economic reform.[64] In order for the PSU educational program to serve the nation's reform needs, it had to become more modern, global, and future oriented.[65] Thus conceived, internationalization of the PSU is an important part of the reform process. In this regard, global police research and cross-cultural education are necessary to transform PSU into a first-class international university.[66]

Internationalization of the PSU has many benefits. First, it serves to showcase Chinese policing at its best to foreign countries. Specifically, it allows people from all over the world to see how far China has come in achieving efficiency, integrity, and human rights in policing.[67] (Much like the holding of Olympics in Beijing and World Expo in Shanghai to showcase China's achievements.) Second, it gives the next generation of Chinese police officers a more global outlook.[68] Finally, it facilitates the cross-cultural exchange of experiences and learning.[69] In this regard, the PSU has achieved a lot. Since 1984, the PSU has established formal academic exchange relationships with more than 30 foreign universities, including the Scottish Police College,[70] Korean National Police College, and Russia Ministry of

Internal Affairs, among others. Between 2001 and 2004, the PSU has offered 11 police training courses for the Hong Kong Police. In 2003, it began offering senior command courses for Hong Kong Police senior executives. In that same year, the PSU, MPS, and the United Nations Office on Drugs and Crime (UNODC) worked together to offer anti-drug training courses for Chinese officials. Through the years, the PSU has organized a number of international conferences for scholars, professionals, and practitioners,[71] such as the International Symposium on Transnational Crime in 2002 and the International Symposium on Crime, Evaluation, and Countermeasures in 2006.[72]

Despite these efforts, international education and academic exchanges at PSU have not been as successful as hoped. As compared with other leading Chinese national universities (*guojia zhongdian daxue*), it falls way short in effort and outcome; for example, Beijing and Tsinghua Universities can boast hundreds of cooperative research projects, thousands of foreign students, and millions in grants. The PSU is lagging far behind for several reasons.[73]

China has long labored under a centrally planned economy. Cadre initiatives are stifled, which is particularly the case with PSU. The PSU, as a police university, is particularly insulated and isolated from the rest of the world. Police leaders are used to following orders. They have few incentives to innovate and reach out to engage the world; the middle managers are reluctant to learn new things and venture out into the unknown. They are comfortable with established routines and in fear of uncertain failure. Such closed mindedness and conservative attitudes have permeated throughout the police ranks and must be changed before the PSU can become a world-class university.[74] Also, the Chinese police have long suffered from a lack of transparency and accountability. Police leaders usually seek to conceal Chinese policing ways and means from outsiders, especially when they have a world audience. Chinese police conceal information from foreigners out of concern about compromising secrets as well as facing up to criticism. Both have personal, bureaucratic, and political consequences.

The tendency is to showcase China's best and cover up China's blemishes. In the Chinese culture, and within police circles, face matters. This mentality impedes frank communication and honest exchanges.[75] China is a country steeped in civilization and etiquette (*liyi zhibang*). As a result, foreign exchanges have focused more on trying to do things right than learning from others.[76] Many of the international projects undertaken have been "face" projects designed to satisfy superiors or impress visitors. In addition, Chinese civilization preaches humility and learning. Oftentimes, this requires being a passive learner rather than an active participant in the exchange of ideas. The PSU should embrace foreign exchanges of information, learning from them just as their counterparts learn from China.[77]

To internationalize education at the PSU, Professor Li recommended the following:

1. Provide opportunities for younger scholars and beginning teachers to attend international conferences and participate in foreign studies. Exchange opportunities should be based on merit and need, not on seniority and status.[78]
2. Invite more leading scholars and pioneer researchers to China.[79] The focus should be on inviting foreign experts with the expertise to truly address Chinese policing needs and otherwise elevate the PSU to a higher intellectual plain.[80]
3. Seek to broaden and deepen international exchanges in areas of emerging needs, such as investigating technology crimes. The police should establish institutional exchange relationships with leading police universities to promote collaborative research, with the aim of bringing the PSU closer to international scholarly expectations and standards.[81]

4. Encourage the enrollment of foreign students. Since 1996, the PSU has been authorized to accept foreign students, but few have enrolled. Saudi Arabia, Russia, and
Mexico promised to send police students to the PSU for training and education,
but the students have not yet materialized.[82]

5. Organize and sponsor more international conferences in China. These would
provide rare opportunities for PSU teachers and scholars to interact with foreign
scholars and professionals. International conferences also help deepen collaborative relationships with known scholars and prestigious universities, laying the
groundwork for future enduring and productive relationships.[83]

6. Formalize the foreign exchange program to make it part of the PSU's ongoing
operations, not *ad hoc* activities that depend on the interests and enthusiasm of
various leaders.[84]

Goals

Overview[85]

In China, police reform[86] can be defined as "change and readjustment of aspects of police
work system and process which has been found to be incompatible with various social,
political, and cultural developmental factors, in order to increase police efficiency, improve
police role and functions and meeting society's expectations/demands of police."[87] Given
such an understanding, police reform can be viewed as a systematic and comprehensive
planned change process of reacting to or anticipating China's economical and social reform
difficulties. Police reform necessitates changes to police ideology and philosophy, vision
and mission, organization and process, strategies and tactics, and conduct and assessment. There are three major police reform issues to address: (1) how to apply traditional
Marx–Mao–Deng ideology (or, more pertinently, prevailing political thinking, such as the
"Three Represents" vs. "harmonious society") to police reform; (2) how to reform police
organizationally to conform to operational needs (e.g., community policing requires substantial power sharing, Internet policing requires a high degree of autonomy); and (3) how
to reform police operationally (e.g., delegation downward toward the police post level).

The most pressing problem is for the nation as a whole to define the nature and purpose
of police reform; that is, what does police reform mean, entail, and portend? Currently, there
is a lack of consensus on the nature, purpose, and conduct of police reform, in theory and in
practice.[88] The confusion and uncertainty are due to the fact that the reformers have different understandings of what "police reform" is all about,[89] including political leaders (conservative old left vs. 1980s reformers, new left vs. liberals,[90] Beijing vs. Shanghai vs. Guangzhou,
national vs. provincial), police officials (top vs. bottom, young vs. old, judicial vs. regular
police, central vs. local), and the public (intellectuals vs. peasants). "Public security reform"
(*gongan gaige*), for example, can mean any of the following: police work reform (*jingwu
gaige*), police management system reform (*gongan guanli tizhi gaige*), or public security organizational reform (*gongan jiguo gaige*).[91] Needless to say, the focus, scope, priorities, schedul-
ing, and various approaches for police reform have been the subjects of much internal debate
and external discussion. Such differences can easily be discerned from a systematic study of
literature over time and across the nation, region by region, province by province, city by
city, as well as by paying attention to political developments, social phenomena, and cata-
strophic or unfortunate events (e.g., *yanda*, Tiananmen Square, Falun Gong, Sun Zhigang).

The starting point in addressing the question of police reform is to look at how to reorganize police work to address China's pressing and emergent reform needs, including providing political stability (e.g., suppression of Falun Gong), securing social order (e.g., management and control of the transient population), and promoting economic development (e.g., pursuing hackers). The responsibility for gaining support for the police reform agenda and policies falls squarely on the shoulders of political leaders and coalitions (e.g., Jiang vs. Hu, elites vs. populists).[92] Chinese economic reform creates new social and political problems that require the police to rethink their role, mission, organization, and operations. To meet emerging problems, expectations, and demands, the police must reinvent themselves by, for example, encouraging citizens to dial 110 for emergency help, putting patrol units in place to deter and respond to crime, developing community policing to aid troubled communities, and having economic crime experts available to track down white-collar criminals and computer crime officers to confront virtual criminals.

By early 1998, the MPS had developed a systematic plan to restructure the police nationwide.[93] The reform plan called for a speedy response to crime (*kuaisu fanying jizhi*), comprehensive control of order (*zhi-an fangfan jizhi*), "Strike Hard" campaign against criminals (*daji fanzui jizhi*), tightening supervision over law enforcement (*zhifa jiandu jizhi*), rational management of cadres (*gangbu guanli jizhi*), and guaranteed police protection (*jingwu baozhang*). The plan was designed to comprehensively and systematically address problems and issues confronting the MPS during the first decade of reform (1988 to 1998), such as how to fight crime (e.g., computer crime), how to maintain order (e.g., mass incidents), how to promote the rule of law (e.g., *suo qing*, or pleading compassion), how to deliver service (e.g., 110 emergency phone number), and how to organize the police (e.g., central vs. local funding).

To the Chinese reformers, such problems and issues are interrelated and must be dealt with in a systematic and comprehensive, integrated, holistic way. Effective crime prevention, for example, starts with effective household registration. Professional law enforcement depends on secure funding and strict accountability. Satisfactory service depends on paying speedy attention to people's problems. Although a systematic plan had been developed in 1998 to reform the police, it took the MPS another 10 years to put it into place. In the meantime, the problems confronting the police multiplied, evolved, and changed.

Objectives of Reform

Since implementation of China's social market economy, the MPS has successfully spearheaded the following systematic structural reforms:

1. Reform to the social control and management system, including household registration reform,[94] mobile population control reform,[95] and road transportation duty organization reform[96]
2. Reform to the public security operation process, such as comprehensive control of social order or the 110 emergency call system
3. Reform to police management, supervision, and control through adoption of the People's Police Law,[97] People's Police Insignia Regulations,[98] Public Security Inspection Law,[99] and People's Police Professional Ethics Regulations[100] in order to institutionalize, regularize, and standardize police operation and procedure
4. Reform to the police legal system

Principles

Basic Principles in Formulating Policy

According to leading police authorities, police system reform should follow certain basic principles.[101] First, reform should be based on Chinese national conditions (*Zhongguo guo-qing*). This means building up policing with Chinese characteristics and being mindful of Chinese history and culture, social conditions, and political situation. This also means that reformers cannot engage in subjective ideological pursuit, such as seeking human rights for all or blindly adopting other countries' expertise, experience, or practice (e.g., putting liberty before security).[102] The issue here is to clearly define what policing with Chinese characteristics is all about and how to (selectively) learn from the West without being dominated, undermined, or corrupted by such study.

Second, reform should follow the direction of economic development (*jingji fazhan fangxiang*). To promote economic development, the police should have an open mind and enforce the law in a fair, equal, uniform, and independent way, not discriminating against foreign investors nor being moved by economic interests. It also means providing service efficiently and effectively to the market economy, beginning with keeping order and preventing crime.[103] One of the major difficulties here is in protecting the economic interests of foreign investors while at the same time protecting the labor rights of the workers.

Third, reform should follow Deng's imperative to rule the country by law (*yifa zhiguo*).[104] It should not revert back to the rule of man era, before reform.

Fourth, reform should follow the principles of simplicity (*jingjian*), uniformity (*guifan*), and efficacy (*xiaoneng*); for example, police organizations should be based on a functional division of labor and should not be top heavy.[105]

Fifth, reform should follow economic history and development. Thus, when the nation moves from a closed, centrally planned economy to an open-market economy, the police should follow suit (e.g., 110 emergency call system, foot patrols) to meet people's needs.[106]

Sixth, reform should redefine the central vs. local relationship, such as whom should be in control of police funding, operations, administration, staffing, and discipline. The conventional arrangement is *tiao kuai jiehe, yi kuai wei zhu* (integration of vertical and local, with local being dominant). Such an arrangement has a number of adverse consequences: (1) it gives too much power to local Party secretary and government leaders to control the police, resulting in interference with professional policing and strict law enforcement; (2) it contributes to localization of law enforcement and generates provincialism and protectionism; (3) it fosters patronage, manifested as cronyism and nepotism; (4) it detracts from uniform application of the law, in favor of local preference and avoidance of law; (5) it inhibits cross-boundary deployment of police resources and detracts from coordination of police efforts; (6) it results in police resources and support being based on local economic and political conditions, not central planning, coordination, and command; (7) it allows local interests to prevail over national priorities; (8) it makes possible corruption and abuse of powers;[107] (9) it contributes to mixing criminal and administrative powers at the local level; and (10) it means that police work may not be as professional, trained, managed, or equipped at the local level.[108]

Seventh, reform should make clear that criminal and judicial powers should be in the hands of the central government and follow the nation's constitution and laws, rather than being subject to local politics.[109]

Basic Considerations in Formulating Policy

Reform policies[110] must be based on scientific research, not on experience or ideology alone. This means that: (1) policies must reflect public sentiments;[111] (2) policies must take into consideration social reality (e.g., conditions of crime and patterns of disorder);[112] (3) policies must be based on empirical data and scientific research;[113] and (4) policies must include objective indicators for crime control.[114]

In addition, police policies must attend to social realities and actual practice (*shizhan*).[115] The overriding objective of police practice in the reform era is to provide stability through attack (*daji*), prevention (*fangfan*), and control (*kongzhi*). Doing so requires development of:[116]

1. An emergency response system (ERS) (*yingji fanying tixi*) with a centralized command control center—The ERS creates a platform for better coordination and cooperation within and between certain police agencies and units, both nationally and locally.
2. A crime-fighting system (*daji fanzui tixi*)—Criminals are becoming more and more professional, intelligent, organized, and dynamic. The police need to work across geographic boundaries (province vs. local) and functional jurisdictions (CID vs. traffic vs. household) to control criminals and investigate crime.
3. A social crime control system (*shehui zhian fangkong tixi*)—Such a control system should follow the principle of integrating attack (*da*) and prevention (*fang*), with prevention being the more important of the two.

Police should minimize opportunities to commit crimes through four layers of control: (1) penetrate the community to mobilize the community and use community resources to prevent crime;[117] (2) develop a scientific patrol network focusing on time, place, and activities at risk;[118] (3) focus on managing hot spots and at-risk locations through, for example, registration of hotel residents, licensing of second-hand stores;[119] and (4) control key ingress and egress points and set up monitoring posts.[120]

It is also necessary for the police to set up a system to ensure that police duties are being properly carried out.[121] This includes standardizing enforcement of the law and execution of duties (*zhifa zhiqing guifan tixi*).[122] Standardization of police work is required to realize strict (*yange*), fair (*gongzheng*), civilized (*wenming*) law enforcement and to achieve the goal of implementing the law for the people. To do so, the police need to perfect the police legislative system (e.g., public notice, consultation, and deliberation). In implementing the law, each step should be strictly regulated such that there is little room for abuse; that is, discretion should be guided and police searches supported by evidence. Police should be professional and specialized, and they should be held accountable for the processing of cases. An internal supervision system and an external assessment system are both necessary. Police decisions should be justified and administration decisions should be subject to review. Every effort should be made to insulate police from illegal influences and extralegal duties, especially by local authorities. Finally, police should be properly resourced and adequately funded to do their job; for example, police operating funds should be guaranteed by budgets, subject to audit.[123]

Changes in the Policing Paradigm

Demise of Comprehensive Management

The Communist Party of China, State Council, and National People's Congress promulgated the "Decision regarding Strengthening Social Comprehensive Management" ("*Guanyu jiaqiang shehui zhonghe zhili de jueding*") in 1983 to rejuvenate, mobilize, and guide communities in working together to maintain order, control crime, and supervise former offenders. As the reform deepened, the comprehensive control scheme was found not to be functioning as well as hoped, as reflected in rising crime rates, in spite of draconian countermeasures, such as "Strike Hard" campaigns. A number of factors can be cited to account for the derailment, then decline, and now demise of this comprehensive management system:

1. Personal mentality (*xixiang*)—Local people, including leaders, have not devoted the necessary time, effort, and resources to comprehensive management duties. They are too concerned with their own job security and economic activities to participate in community work that promises no direct, tangible economic benefits.
2. Public policy (*zhengce*)—The national policy is to reduce the tax burden on farmers. To do so, the national government had to eliminate the local authority's right to levy fees and apportion charges (*tanpai*) from local government. As a result, local villages and townships can no longer support full-time order maintenance officers (*zhibao lindao*) or compensate joint defense teams (*lianfang dui*), village security personnel (*hu zhuang yuan*), alley security personnel (*hu xiang yuan*), mediation personnel (*tiaojie yuan*), or small area patrol personnel (*xiaoqu xuluo yuan*). Public enterprises have also reduced expenditures by abolishing their security offices.
3. Private security strategy—The reform is moving toward privatization of collective enterprises and the commercialization of public functions. People have shifted from pursuing public service to help others to chasing after self-centered economic returns. Security work has been put in the hands of paid professionals.
4. Social/environmental influences—The society has changed after decades of economic reform. There are a lot more criminals among the unemployed or underemployed ranks. The availability of material goods and a lack of capable guardians have created more criminal opportunities, and temptations are greater as a result of slick marketing and runaway greed. Additional problems include attenuation of social bonds, dilution of social control, and an absence of self-discipline, especially among alienated youths and detached migrant workers. Committing crimes has been facilitated by the ease of crossing borders and by the speed and anonymity of global communications, such as the Internet. This also means that clearing crimes and tracking criminals are much more difficult. Criminals are becoming more organized, mobile, intelligent, and high tech. The Party, government, and public security enjoy less and less control over market enterprises and private businesses, which are becoming more independent and autonomous and less subject to supervision and regulation, as a result of increased economic clout and proliferation of legal rights. Private business enterprises, for example, no longer accept uncompensated public security responsibilities, and public enterprises cannot be asked to assume responsibilities for security breaches (*zhian zeren zhi*). Neither is willing nor able to take responsibility for reforming offenders through labor (*laojiao*) or helping with the rehabilitation of former offenders (*banjiao*).[124]

TABLE 3.10   Comparison of Traditional vs. Rapid-Response System Policing

Attribute	Traditional	Rapid-Response System
Social foundation	Closed community Static population Planned economy	Open society Mobile population Market economy
Focal point of control	Control over person	Control over activities
Nature of police	Political-control agent	Social-service agent
Functions of police	Democratic dictatorship of the people, suppression of counterrevolutionaries	Legal control of crime and disorder, administrative regulation of people and places, provision of social services to people
Mandate	Ideological and political Close ended and restrictive	Constitutional and legal Open ended and expansive
Mobilization	Driven by state	Mobilized by the people
Style of policing	Preventive	Reactive
Operational characteristics	Static	Dynamic
Organization	Household police	Patrol/traffic police

Rapid-Response System (*Kuaisu fanying jizhi*)[125]

The rapid-response system (RRS) is a new way of policing that differs from traditional policing (TP) or comprehensive management (see Table 3.10). TP is designed for closed communities, static populations, and planned economies, such as small towns and close-knit communities, which were common in China before reform. The RRS is geared more toward an open society, a mobile population, and a market economy. TP seeks to control people, whereas the RRS seeks to control activities. The RSS changes the fundamental paradigm of Chinese policing from static administrative regulation to dynamic mobile police control. It also changes the roles and functions of the police, from an instrument of political control to a social service agency. The RSS is built around the 110 emergency call system, with patrol officers and SWAT officers acting as rapid responders to crime, disorder, and emergencies. In their crime-fighting efforts, patrol officers are backed up by other more specialized units, such as traffic, fire, public order, and criminal investigation officers. The system also links patrol officers to other city services, such as medical, electrical, gas, water, and transportation. In this way, the RSS provides city dwellers with 24/7 police and city resources necessary to deal with all kinds of problems. As the 110 promotional slogan attests, the system "will answer all police calls, will attend to every emergency, will solve any difficulty, will respond to any demand" ("*you jing bijie, you zai bi jiu, you nan bi bang, you qui bi ying*").

Emergency Response Systems

In 2004, Zhu Entao, Vice Minister of the MPS and Vice President of the Chinese Police Studies Association, first proposed the establishment of urban emergency response systems (ERSs)[126] designed to deal with emergencies of all kind, from natural disasters to communicable diseases to civil disturbances.[127] At the time, very few such ERSs were in place in the nation, the exceptions being Shanghai (2003) and Guangzhou (1998).

Need for Emergency Response Systems

Looking back in history, China has suffered an abundance of natural disasters and unexpected emergencies, resulting in the huge loss of lives, property, and economic activities. Disasters and emergencies have hit urban centers to the East and along the coast the hardest. Any economic disruption of these urban centers threatens the well-being of the nation as a whole; therefore, China needed a plan for the prevention of, responding to, and recovering from such unexpected crises.[128] The capacity of a nation is best judged during emergencies, specifically with regard to preventing, anticipating, and planning for disasters, as well as responding to and recovering from disasters, avoiding injuries, and reducing harm.[129]

Principles of Emergency Response Systems

Four basic principles can be identified regarding the establishment and operation of an ERS. First, the ERS should be led by Party cadres and supervised by government officials.[130] Second, the ERS should be built upon and integrated with the existing police emergency 110 platform; as such, the ERS should be connected to and work with civil administration, hospitals, utilities, environmental agencies, and commerce departments as part of a coordinated emergency response team.[131] Third, the ERS should provide rapid response to disasters.[132] Fourth, ERS response teams should be based on division of labor and coordination of functions.[133]

History of Emergency Response Systems

Until 2004, the nation as a whole had not set up guidelines for ERSs. Emergencies were dealt with on an *ad hoc* basis by local governments with the help of the national government, such as deployment of the People's Liberation Army (PLA) to provide for province-wide disaster relief. Individual urban centers have experience with their own citywide or regional ERSs. In 1998, Guangzhou took steps to set up an ERS by establishing a Municipality Public Service Task Force Work Group (*Guangzhou shi lianhe xingdong fuwu xiaozu*). The work group was under the leadership of the Guangzhou PSB and built upon the existing 110 emergency-response platform; it was charged with the responsibility to organize and coordinate various city services (fire, medical, water, electricity, commerce, environmental) in case of an emergency. The ERS was put to the test on November 15, 2002, when the holding tank for 3000 tons of petroleum oil exploded.[135] The ERS was found be effective in dealing with that emergency. In 2003, the Shanghai Political Committee and Municipal Government drafted a document, "Preliminary Plan to Set Up Shanghai Municipality Emergency Response Center" ("*Guanyu jianli Shanghai shi yingji liandong zhongxin de chubu fangan*"), that spelled out their intentions to launch an ERS center. This preliminary plan was formalized that same year, and the Shanghai PSB was put in control. The Shanghai model was later adopted by Tianjin and Beijing.[134]

Problems and Issues with Emergency Response Systems

There are a number of problems and issues with ERSs:

1. Party leadership, especially at the local level, cannot agree on the necessity and urgency of ERSs. This is particularly the case when the local government thinks that the occasional risk of emergency does not justify the initial capital investment and continuous funding required for ERSs.[136]
2. Various government agencies, due to organizational interests and resource commitments, are also not in agreement as to the need for such systems or their eventual role in constructing and maintaining it.[137]

3. No state law, Party policy, or administrative guidelines mandate the role, function, structure, or processes of ERSs.[138]
4. It is difficult to coordinate the various agencies involved (e.g., fire, health, police, military) and make them work as a team; for example, a command-and-control system for ERSs has yet to be designed, tested, rehearsed, and perfected.[139]

Leadership: Grooming Police Leadership for a New Era

Political Ideology and Leadership

Consistent with Chinese tradition and culture, the CPC requires police leaders to demonstrate correct political thought, exemplary moral character, and exceptional professional competency before appointment and while in office. More simply, the police are expected to excel in both morality and ability (*de cai jian bi*) as a person first and then as a professional.[140] Therefore, in order to prepare future leaders, Party leaders should "earnestly organize the study of Deng Xiaoping's theory and Party policy in effectively raising Party cadres' political thought and overall quality, and steadfastly maintaining political stance and orientation to elevate the capacity in using Deng Xiaoping's theory in solving concrete problems."[141]

Leadership Thinking and Work Style

In 2001, the Police Commissioner and Party Secretary of Hubei Province, Cheng Xunqui, explored the correct thinking patterns and appropriate work style of a police cadre leader.[142] Chen identified nine thinking patterns and work-style characteristics of a police leader in the reform era:

1. *Police leaders must follow Party discipline.* Police leaders must learn to think and operate in a systems way (*xitung lun*)[143] and should subscribe to the Party organizational principle of democratic centralism.[144] In practice and as applied, this means following Party central policy and guidelines in supporting economic reform. "Every police leader-cadre must at all time be strongly committed to the Party and national work strategy as a whole."[145] This means that the parts must obey the whole and individuals must serve the collective.[146]
2. *Police leaders must be in control at all times.* In fighting crime, police leaders must adopt a control viewpoint (*kongji lun*) focused on both fighting and preventing crime, with crime prevention being dominant. In practice, this means that leaders must learn to control human intelligence and technology interfaces (e.g., computer networks); public opinion (e.g., using public opinion as propaganda); information and intelligence (e.g., early warnings); vertical and local coordination (e.g., for comprehensive crime control); the law enforcement framework (e.g., integration of traffic and patrol police to deter street crime); performance standards (e.g., management by objective); structural formation (e.g., organization staffing); strategic sites (e.g., hot spots); and the process (e.g., dealing with mass incidents preemptively).[147]
3. *Police leaders must stay focused.* Operationally, police leaders must stick to the main focal points (*zhong dian lun*). To be effective, police work must stay focused on important problems and issues (i.e., policing hot spots). In police post reform,

the focus is on eliminating or reducing formalism, superficiality, and paperwork and concentrating instead on what is really happening. In practice, this means moving away from gathering crime data and toward pacifying and reducing the public's fear of crime. During major festivities and events, police should focus on controlling Falun Gong and other cult groups that can be destabilizing forces. Also, the police should focus on leveraging science, technology, and education to improve police capacity and performance. Police leaders must stay focused on solving problems proactively and holistically and avoid dealing with issues reactively, one at a time as they come up.[148]

4. *Police leaders' decisions and actions must be based on facts and experience.* Police leaders must adapt a practical viewpoint (*xijian lun*), and the police should be truthful and practice evidence-based policing. Operationally, this requires strengthening the base by shifting police resources to the grassroots where policing work is done. This also means improving the foundational skills of officers and perfecting routine coordination among police units.[149] In terms of decision making, police leaders should adopt a scientific outlook and avoid subjective opinion. This requires possessing an open mind, being critical, and embracing a wide view.[150]

5. *Police leaders must exercise independent judgment.* Police leaders must adopt a unique viewpoint (*tesi lun*),[151] in addition to practicing policing with Chinese characteristics (i.e., obeying the Party and serving the people).[152]

6. *Police leaders must follow the process.* Police leaders should be mindful of the process viewpoint (*quocheng lun*). In police reform, process matters. Police problems, such as abuse of their power, did not materialize overnight. They have resulted over time due to a change in police culture. Likewise, solving a police problem might require a lengthy, incremental, step-by-step process. As an example, to improve the quality of police personnel, the recruitment process must first be changed (e.g., centralized recruitment, uniform examination, open selection, competitive appointments).[153] The process of police reform and troop building is a lengthy, repetitive, continuous one involving much trial and error, success and failure. It cannot be achieved overnight with stop-gap measures or off-and-on programs.[154]

7. *Police leaders must think and solve problems in a dialectical way.* When selecting and cultivating police leaders, police agencies must be aware of the importance of contradictions (*maodun lun*).[155] This means that when selecting and cultivating police leaders, looking beyond the standard requirements of ideology, capacity, industriousness, and achievements, police agencies must work at understanding the impact of contradictions on police leadership and performance—for example, conflicts between a leader and his deputies.[156] It also means that police leaders should be taught to confront such contradictions head on because they are natural and inevitable and should not be avoided. In solving such problems, police leaders should consider them in dialectical terms (action/reaction) and from various perspectives. For example, police personnel and resource shortages are very real. How to solve such a problem as a contradiction is the challenge. If we were to look at police shortages only in quantitative terms and numerically, we would be ignoring the fact that police shortages in quantitative terms can be resolved with qualitative improvements in enhanced capacity, such as the use of closed-circuit television in lieu of a police presence.[157] Disagreements within the police leadership ranks can also be resolved with this contradiction approach. Police leaders are not all alike in thinking and

acting. They come with different backgrounds, education, and experience, and they each look at policing differently. How to resolve differences regarding key policy issues is a significant challenge. Police leaders' policy differences cannot be resolved through command, discipline, and imposition alone. Policy contradictions within police ranks can best be solved by discussion, debate, and persuasion.[158]

8. *Police leaders must look at matters from the people's point of view.* Police leaders must adopt a "masses" viewpoint (*qunzhong lun*).[159] Police work must be from the mass to the mass. The satisfaction of the people is the ultimate purpose and validation of police work.[160]

9. *Police leaders must consider problems within a developmental perspective.* Police leaders must adopt a developmental viewpoint (*fazhan lun*).[161] They must embrace and welcome development and change. With development comes challenges and opportunities. Without constant development, police performance would deteriorate or fail to catch up with societal changes. Finally, police developmental problems, such as morale, cannot be resolved through ideological education alone. Police morale can only be improved by improving police personnel's sense of security and material well-being.[162]

Culture

Police Professional Values

Professional values are the beliefs and principles that guide one's decisions and actions in their given profession.[163] They affect people's viewpoints, expectations, and performance within a professional organization. In 2001, the Central Committee of the Communist Party launched a research project entitled, "Thorough Implementation of Public Moral Principles" ("*Renmin daode gangyao shishi*"). In conjunction with that, Professors Wang Yan and Zhang Jiangping, from the Jiangsu Police Officer College, and Xia Shufang, head of the Gaochun County PSB, conducted a survey and analysis of the police values at the Gaochun County PSB ("Police Value Study"). The Police Value Study sought to analyze police professional values over five dimensions: (1) social status (*shehui diwei*), including approval, self-respect, and the respect of others; (2) job satisfaction (*gongzuo chengjiu*), including self-actualization and sense of achievement; (3) self-discipline and initiative (*zilu zhudong sheng*), including creativity, responsibility, and transcendence; (4) orientation toward others (*weita zhuyi*), including public service and social morality; and (5) comfort level (*shushi zhongyao sheng*), including work independence, variability, welfare, and working conditions. The sampling method was not disclosed nor the time of the survey. The sample population (148 officers) included all of the police officers serving with the Gaochun County PSB:[164]

- *Sex*—141 male (95%); 7 female (5%)
- *Age range*—21 to 56 years old; 109 (74%) were 30 years old and under
- *Education*—77 (52%), technical college/high school; 71 (48%), college educated
- *Party*—111 (75%), Party members; 37 (25%), non-Party members
- *Seniority*—67 (45%), under 10 years; 37 (25%), 10 to 15 years; 44 (30%), over 15 years
- *Police function*—82 (55%), public order; 34 (23%), criminal investigation; 32 (22%), traffic

TABLE 3.11   A Comparison of Gaochun Police Professional Values

Dimension	(1) Social Status	(2) Job Achievement	(3) Self-Discipline and Initiative	(4) Orientation to Others	(5) Comfort Level
Police type					
Public order	2.9777	2.6341	3.5671	2.8244	2.5671
Criminal investigation	2.9412	2.4698	3.5147	2.5647	2.5441
Traffic	2.9011	2.5625	3.4219	2.6688	2.6797
Police seniority					
Under 10 years	2.8557	2.5224	3.4627	2.6328	2.4590
10–15 years	2.9640	2.5315	3.5811	2.7405	2.6212
More than 15 years	3.0909	2.7945	3.5682	2.8727	2.7500
Age					
Less than 40 years old	2.8823	2.5413	3.5367	2.6917	2.5229
40 years old and above	3.1500	2.6838	3.4872	2.8410	2.7628
Education					
College and above	2.8709	2.4883	3.5845	2.6901	2.5845
High school	3.0281	2.6623	3.4674	2.7688	2.5877
Political status					
Party member	3.0015	2.5796	3.5361	2.7784	2.6126
Not a Party member	2.8063	2.5766	3.4865	2.5892	2.5028

Source: Yan, W. et al., *Journal of Jiangsu Police Officer College*, 85, 152, 2002.

Note: Values represent response scores for various dimensions.

The survey showed that the police officers did not all share the same professional values. They differed along lines of age, education, Party membership, seniority, and type of police service (public order, criminal investigation, traffic).

The data are summarized in Table 3.11. The individual professional values will serve as the focal point of our analysis of the responses of each type of police officer—public order police (POP), criminal investigation division (CID), or traffic police (TP). The latter part of the analysis turns to a discussion of between-group distinctions (e.g., Party members vs. non-members), again based on the various personal value dimensions. Throughout the analysis, we will focus on two questions: (1) What are the differences between groups of respondents regarding the professional values investigated? (2) How can we explain such differences in professional values between groups? It is hoped that this summary and analysis of the Police Value Study will allow us to access the inner core of Chinese police to get a glimpse of what police in China think and feel about their professional values (more generally, work), a topic of much importance in our quest to understand the identity, ethos, and culture of police in China. This kind of data and analysis has never before appeared in print outside of China.

Social Status

With respect to social status, the POP felt that they had the highest social status (2.9775), as compared to the CID (2.9412) and TP (2.9011). This is not difficult to explain. The POP work closely with the public on a daily basis. They are usually on a first-name basis with the residents, especially in smaller communities (*xiao qu*) and rural areas (*nong cun*). Their job consists mostly of helping people and solving problems. Most of the time, the public is appreciative of their help. POP work is the easiest and most satisfying,[165] which is why the POP ranked highest on both Job Achievement (appreciation by others) and Orientation to Others (police as a helping profession).

In contrast, the TP reported the lowest social status; they do not have the opportunity to interact with the public under favorable conditions. The TP are usually involved in traffic code enforcement, and it is never pleasant to be confronted by a traffic cop. The TP also earn the wrath of the people for collecting fines that fund police salaries and operations,[166] and they have been known to set up traps to meet arrest quotas.[167] This is how one officer explained the adverse effect of a quota system:[168]

> I am a policeman from a local police station. I applaud the new policy of the Beijing Municipal Public Security Bureau. My office's job should have been to ensure public safety and to prevent crimes in our precinct; however, because of the quotas we have for making criminal arrests, we focus on meeting the quotas all year round. Also, because the criminals in our precinct already know us well, they are hard to track. We have to go to other precincts to round up the criminals, which makes it impossible for us to focus on crime prevention in our own precinct. My office has a staff of over 40 and we have a quota of arresting 108 criminals a year. I wish we could also abolish the quota system and focus instead on maintaining public safety in our precinct.

On October 14, 2009, Sun Zhongjie, 19 years old, was driving a minivan for the Shanghai Pangyuan Construction Machinery Engineering Company when he was stopped by a man who begged him for a ride because he claimed to be sick. Without being asked, the man left 10 yuan in the car when he was dropped off. The Shanghai Traffic Law Enforcement Team for Pudong New Area immediately arrested Sun for illegally operating a vehicle for hire. To demonstrate his innocence and in protest, Sun cut off his little finger.[169] This police entrapment incident caused a great uproar in Shanghai and around the nation.

The public takes every opportunity to chastise the TP for being incompetent. On June 30, 2009, in Jiangning District, Nanjing City, Jiangsu Province, a driver hit nine people, killing five and injuring four, in addition to damaging six parked cars. Pictures taken at the crime scene showed that the dead bodies, including a pregnant woman, were not covered up. An irate citizen commented online:[170]

> At least use a piece of cloth to cover up the bodies and use a piece of wood to lift up the bodies, how could they just grab their arms and legs and just throw them onto the vehicle, that is too disrespectful to the dead! Imagine if the dead were your guys' own loved ones, would you have treated them the same way? Police officers, your impression in the hearts of the people is already very poor, yet you guys do not even want to slowly bit by bit change how the people see you? Or do you guys believe there is no big deal with how you handled things this way, because after all it is just a routine way of handling problems?

An online survey associated with this story asked the question: "What do you think of how the police handled this situation?" Of those who responded, 204 voted for "They were careless and disrespectful," and only 17 voted for "They did the best they could for the situation."[171] Simply put, the TP are not well liked by many people.

Job Achievement

Generally, all three kinds of police had relatively low Job Achievement scores compared to the other professional values. The POP had a Job Achievement score of 2.6341, lagging far behind Self-Discipline and Initiative (3.5671), Social Status (2.9777), and Orientation to Others (2.8244). It fared better than Comfort Level (2.5671) by only a small margin. The same applied to the CID: Self-Discipline and Initiative (3.5147), Social Status (2.9412), Orientation to Others (2.5647), Comfort Level (2.5441), and Job Achievement (2.4698). Why was it that the police overall expressed such little job satisfaction? Also, why did the POP have a higher Job Achievement score (2.6341) than the TP (2.5625), and why did the TP have a higher Job Achievement score than the CID (2.4698)? As mentioned earlier, the POP were most satisfied because, in most cases, they are able to see that their actions, such as processing a household registration or giving aid to a citizen in need, have made a difference in people's lives, which gives them public validation. Although the actions of the TP are always negative and punitive, these officers can measure achievement based on meeting job-related quotas, which gives them organizational validation.[172] CID officers, on the other hand, are overwhelmed with work and rarely see their work making a difference, such as reducing the crime rate. In spite of their efforts, CID officers see no hope of breaking out of an endless cycle of the world becoming worse by the day, with more and more crimes and worsening criminals.[173] Occasionally, investigators will clear a case and make an arrest, but this is small consolation compared to the backlog of cases waiting to be processed and the constant stream of cases coming in. More often than not, CID officers feel that they cannot do anything about crime because they are not given enough resources to do so. They are also routinely condemned by the public for not doing enough or doing too much or doing it in the wrong way; for example, the police are roundly condemned for using torture (*xingxun*) to obtain confessions to clear cases.

Self-Discipline and Initiative

All three kinds of police scored high on Self-Discipline and Initiative: POP (3.5671), CID (3.5147), and TP (3.4219). This can possibly be attributed to the fact that the police have a lot of discretion in performing (or not performing) their duties. The law is often vague and open ended. The police are often working in the field, making low-visibility decisions with little meaningful supervision. In the United States, one scholar has labeled the police as "street corner politicians"[174] and suggested that police officers could become whatever they want to be—an enforcer here, a professional there—each according to the officer's understanding of the police role. The POP can exercise the most initiative because in China POP work is often open ended, especially in the community-policing era and in local or rural areas. The TP are the most restricted. They have to deal with specific types of incidents (accidents) and take law enforcement action (write tickets), with little choice and a lot of regulation. CID officers are relatively free to do what they want, but their actions are constrained by law and supervised by procuratorates, if cases are to be successfully prosecuted. The CID also has the added pressure of solving cases in a timely fashion. Under such circumstances, these officers are not as free to exercise discretion as their POP peers.

Orientation to Others

With regard to Orientation to Others, the POP ranked highest (2.8244), followed by the TP (2.6688) and CID (2.5647). The POP ranked high on this dimension because they routinely perform service duties, such as taking care of the sick and the old, and solve problems, such as providing marital counseling and mediating disputes. TP officers also consider themselves to be in a helping profession, as they help with car accidents and traffic direction. The CID, in contrast, is not at all a helping or service agency. It is strictly a law enforcement agency responsible for criminal investigations and bringing criminals to justice (i.e., enforcing the law and punishing criminals). Thus, in real terms, CID officers do not see themselves as rendering aid to others. CID officers most closely resemble the early runners (*bu kuai*) at local magistrates whose job it was to catch offenders and deliver them to the magistrate for inquisition. The *bu kuai* most certainly did not have a service role and were hated by the people at that time.[175]

Comfort Level

The TP ranked first (2.6797) in Comfort Level, followed by the POP (2.5671) and CID (2.5441). The scores for the three groups of officers are close and fall within a narrow range (i.e., within statistical error range). Still, the TP appeared to feel more comfortable in their job. Both the POP and CID deal with people and cases over some length of time, which means that they tend to carry their work with them wherever they go. Unlike the TP, the POP and CID work longer hours and have little rest between cases. As to working conditions, those of the TP are arguably the worst (e.g., air and noise pollution, danger), but the POP and CID are not far behind.

Age

It appears that age has a bearing on professional values, as those surveyed who were over 40 years of age expressed more contentment with their work. The one thing that distinguished officers 40 years and older from younger officers was their social status (3.1500 vs. 2.8823). This is consistent with other research findings demonstrating intergenerational differences in attitudes toward work, play, and social status.[176] The 1960s generation, brought up in a different era, had much more respect for policing and was honored to be a part of public security in protecting the nation and servicing the people. Also, this age group had fewer options, and few planned on moving. Most of them were likely to have high school/technical college diplomas or had transferred from the military. Their whole life was bound up in public security, as a career and as a personal identity, right from the start. Generations that came after tend to look at policing as a job providing security, pay, and authority. Thus, although the reputation and status of the police might be deteriorating, it was difficult for the older respondents to recognize this. They might have rationalized that the public knows no better or might genuinely appreciate them when in need. The MPS has helped in this regard by promoting the image that public security is an honorable and respected profession.

In addition, this older generation had joined public security in the 1980s, with high hopes and aspirations. Since then, they had invested over 15 years in an organization they helped build and now helped run as first-line supervisors. They quite rightly felt proud of their work and what they had achieved (2.6838 vs. 2.5413). Furthermore, achievements mean different things to different generations of officers. To those over 40, the sense of achievement being captured here by the survey was perhaps not one that could be measured, such as by a pay raise here or a recommendation there. To them, achievement perhaps referred to their lifetime pursuit of building a better, more secure, and more prosperous China. In essence, the older officers sought internal rewards achieved through self-actualization.

The officers younger than 40 years old who were surveyed perhaps tended to view achievements as immediate, tangible rewards (i.e., commodification and commercialization of achievements). This difference in mentality, which the MPS and leaders refer to as *ren sheng guan* ("view of life"), is what divides the old and the new. At the time of the survey, police officers who were over 40 years old had been indoctrinated by and were steeped in the communist tradition of service to the nation and its people, which was what policing in the 1980s was all about—thinking about others before and at the expense of self-interest (Orientation to Others, 2.8410 vs. 2.6917). This has contributed to police officers in China having the highest rate of work-related health problems, as they figuratively and literally are working themselves to death.[177]

Overall, then, the older officers were happier and more comfortable with the job of being a police officer (Comfort Level, 2.7628 vs. 2.5229). A puzzling finding, though, is that officers under 40 years of age were more self-disciplined and showed more initiative than those over 40 years old (Self-Discipline and Initiative, 3.5367 vs. 3.4872). Perhaps, once again, the two groups of officers defined and perceived self-discipline and initiative differently, with the older officers being brought up to strictly follow Party policy and military order and the younger officers being brought up during the community-policing era when police were encouraged to exercise discretion.

Seniority

Officers with the longest service (15 years or more) were likely to have a higher regard for police work than those with fewer years of service (Social Status, 3.0909 vs. 2.9640 vs. 2.8557). They were also more comfortable with policing (Comfort Level, 2.7500 vs. 2.6212 vs. 2.4590) and scored higher on Orientation to Others (2.8727 vs. 2.7405 vs. 2.6328). Because of the close relationship between seniority and the age of the officers, one would expect that the analysis for age should equally apply to seniority, and it does.

Education

As to education, except for the category of Self-Discipline and Initiative (college graduates, 3.5845; high school graduates, 3.4674), college graduates scored lower on the various dimensions than high school graduates: Social Status (2.8709 vs. 3.0281), Job Achievement (2.4883 vs. 2.6623), Orientation to Others (2.6901 vs. 2.7688), and Comfort Level (2.5845 vs. 2.5877). This was surprising, given that the MPS had been making every effort to recruit and retain university graduates as officers and has continued to do so.[178] Today, just as when the survey was performed, the college-educated police are not as happy with their social status because police jobs are considered a step down for the college educated but a step up for the high school graduates. Once recruited, however, college-educated police officers have more opportunities, receive higher pay, and enjoy greater prospects and more prestige both within and outside of the public security system.[179]

It is when they begin to compare their situation with that of their peers that college-educated police officers begin to wonder whether they have made the right career choice (i.e., the relative deprivation thesis).[180] Their sense of frustration grows as they see that they are lagging farther and farther behind, and their opportunities to leave and begin a new career elsewhere are becoming fewer. As many commentators online have suggested, people join based on their ideals and end up staying because of a lack of choice.[181] Many of the high school graduates might have transferred from the military. Military transfers are indoctrinated to feel proud of both their military work and their police work.

With regard to Orientation to Others and Comfort Level, the margins were too close to call. The college-educated police might have felt slightly less at ease in their job because they might have been shunned by fellow officers, out of jealousy or fear of competition, or both. Of course, how the college-educated police behave and adjust can also make a world of difference, as the following discussion attests.

An online blogger,[182] a master's degree graduate,[183] was hired in 2008 as a police officer after passing the civil service examination. He had been on the job for about a month when he posted a blog entry relating his experiences and expressing his thoughts about policing as an educated cop. He was assigned to a county police bureau as a criminal investigator and was posted to a village police post. The blogger's first impression of his work was one of being bored: "Through this first month, my preliminary understanding of work is that it is very boring."[184] He felt that he was not properly deployed and fully utilized. He further sensed and feared that he had no future within the police. According to him, education qualifications, personal competence, and on-the-job achievements were no substitute for bribery[185] or connections (*guanxi*). As proof, he offered the following:

1. His mentor (training officer) told him that there was no future for people like him in the police.[186] The mentor pointed to many police officers who had worked for years without recognition and promotion.[187]
2. The blogger knew of many master's degree graduates being assigned to special divisions (*ke*) within the administration, instead of on the frontline. They got there not because they were any brighter or more qualified but because they were well connected.[188]
3. The blogger was working alongside officers with only a high school education.[189]
4. His mentor was the recipient of a second-class commendation for solving a difficult criminal case, but he did not get promoted because he was not well connected.[190]

The author came to the following conclusion about his future prospects within the police: "The leaders do not really appreciate high education qualification or good quality work. You just need not to screw up on your work and have a sponsor up top, then you will have a good career prospect."[191] As a result of similar circumstances throughout the public security system, police officers at the frontline are often demoralized and are not motivated to do their best. Instead, they try to do as little as possible at every turn. Summing up, the blogger said:

> In reality, my everyday work consists of watching TV, bantering, reading novels, surfing the net. My unit had a phone originally. But it broke. Everyone is happy. There is no one to repair it. Because if the phone is not working properly, the public could not call the police. We are happy to be left alone. After all, if we do good work, no one would appreciate us.

Lessons for Educated Police[192]
The following five rules are posted to help university graduates to adjust to police work in rural China:

1. *Be humble.* Do not flaunt your qualifications. Be humble, particularly toward old comrades.
2. *Keep quiet.* Say as little as possible. Silence is golden. If you do not say anything, they do not know how good you are. If you reveal too much, people know what you are thinking. You will lose your authority.
3. *Be disciplined.* Learn how to be disciplined and control yourself, no matter what negative comments you hear. Stay cool. Listen to others, right or wrong, good or bad. Do not argue. Do not have conflicts. Do not be confrontational, especially with leaders.
4. *Do not be antagonistic.* Do not fancy to be others' teacher. Do not show that you are smart and know everything. Do not go out of the way to point out others' mistakes.
5. *Do not show off.* Do not be quick to show your achievements. As a budding cadre, the best way to develop a career is not to make mistakes. One mistake will ruin one's career

Party Membership

Compared with non-members, Party members fared better in all areas of professional values, especially Social Status (3.0015 vs. 2.8063) and Comfort Level (2.6126 vs. 2.5028). This can be explained by the fact that Party members enjoy higher social status in society, with all kinds of benefits and opportunities, not to mention authority and connections. Thus, they are more privileged and have greater access to power. Party members edged out non-Party members on Self-Discipline and Initiative (3.5361 vs. 3.4865) and on Orientation to Others (2.7784 vs. 2.5892), because that is what being a Party member is all about. Party members have many opportunities to demonstrate self-discipline and initiative and to make sacrifices for the people. There is never a day that Party members are not reminded of their duty and charge.

The margin for Job Achievement was not large enough to be significant (2.5796 vs. 2.5766). We must wonder, though, why Party members did not express a greater sense of achievement. The reason possibly has to do with Party management and discipline. The Party expects young members to make every effort to perform their duties, selflessly, without tangible and material rewards, on demand, and without complaint. Younger Party members and mid-career police may feel unappreciated and at times taken for granted, especially when asked to perform personal chores, over and beyond the call of duty for senior cadres. When things go wrong, they are the first to be blamed, even if it is not their fault. Many times they are expected to deflect criticism away from their supervisors. Police officers have to learn to accept discipline from demanding supervisors and complaints from irate citizens.

A Case Study of Legal Culture

In 1992, Zhang Daqun from Jiangxi Province, Nanchang City, Public Security Bureau–Legal System Office, published a report on police knowledge of the law.[193] The survey was based on the assumption that, in order to enforce the law, the police must first and foremost know the law. An exam on the law was given to 115 officers (including 25 leaders) at

14 police posts (5 townships, 5 villages, and 4 enterprises). Most officers (63.1%) failed the exam. The average overall score was 52.2%, and the lowest score was 25%. The results are summarized below:

1. *Knowledge of the law*—The police rarely took the time to study the law; for example, the NPS Standing Committee promulgated their "Notice regarding Drug Prohibition" ("*Guanyu jindu de jueding*") in 1990, and it was widely reported in major newspapers at the central, provincial, and local levels. Yet, there was no organized study on the Notice. When asked about how drug addicts were to be treated under the law, 98% responded that they did not know. When asked about the right of administrative appeal by citizens under the Administration Procedure Act passed in 1990, most officers made the wrong assumption that citizens should file a claim in the city's people's court.

2. *Availability of law books*—The police officers had no access to law books. When asked, 38 of the officers said that they did not possess any police law books, such as *Public Order Administration and Punishment Regulations*, and 39 of them did not have the *Police Handbook* issued by the province. Only 37 officers had in their possession some kind of law book, such as the MPS's *Handbook on Law Enforcement* (*Zhifa Shouce*) or the Provincial Judicial Office's *Judicial Handbook* (*Sifa Shouce*). As a result, only 17 public security cases (36%) were upheld on administrative appeal in 1991.

3. *Availability of legal consultation*—The police legal department responsible for law consultation at the basic and city level was not fully functional; for example, no budget nor staff was assigned to the legal department. No officer had been assigned the duty to systematically collect and distribute legal materials. No one was available to provide legal consultation. There was not even a complete set of law books at the City Public Security Bureau–Legal Office.

4. *Distribution of instructional materials*—Officially, there are procedures and systems in place to ensure the timely distribution of public instructional documents, such as notices, decisions, and regulations. In November 1990, the MPS circulated the document "Notice regarding Certain Problems with the Thorough Implementation of Administrative Procedural Law" ("*Guanyu gongan jiguan guanche shishi [Xingzheng Susong Fa] rugan wenti de tongzhi*"). When asked, most of the officers surveyed did not know about the document. Only a few of the county offices had received it. But, according to standard operating procedures, MPS documents of this kind should be dispatched to each and every sub-bureau and county office and immediately put into operation.

5. *In-service training on law*—The police receive very little in-service training with regard to legal and other professional matters. According to another survey, 61 officers out of 193 (31.5%) did not receive job-orientation training of any kind. For those who did receive training, most of them obtained 3 months' training (78, or 40.4%) or over 3 months' training (42, or 21.8%). If police leaders did not receive formal job training, their officers' training opportunities must have been fewer. Most of them learned while doing (*gan zhong xue*). The lack of training has impacted police law enforcement, especially rural and enterprise police. Surveys have shown that policing knowledge among the enterprise police is consistently lower; it was found that some officers did not even know how to record a statement.

6. *Uniform enforcement of the law*—There is no uniform and dutiful enforcement of the law. Police officers appear to engage in selective enforcement based on personal preference or relationships (*guanxi*). For example, in one case, a public order decision was administratively voided but the local police post refused to implement the upper-level administrative order, even after several instructions from the city police bureau.

Developing a Police Culture

Police reform cannot be achieved and will not last without making fundamental changes to the police culture; otherwise, police reform would be compromised by an incompatible or resistant culture.[194] The police culture is an integral part of the larger Chinese culture. It reflects the spirit—philosophy, morality, and ethos—of the time;[195] thus, police attitudes, thinking, sentiments, personalities, and conduct are likely to be byproducts of the police social culture.[196] Chinese reform has drastically changed China's traditional culture from a monolithic one to a diverse one, from a simple one to a complex one, from an exemplary one to a corrosive one, and, finally, from a wholesome one to a corrupted one.[197] Police ideology and culture are facing similar challenges.

At a National Public Security Meeting in 2003,[198] participants called for "serious improvement in public security culture." Although top Party leaders[199] and MPS officials have persistently and repeatedly preached the importance of a police culture, some nebulous issues remain unresolved, hindering the prospect of its robust development; for example: What is the police culture? What is its function and utility? How can the police culture be induced? How can it be maintained and improved?[200]

To begin with, at the policy level, there is a continuous debate over the relative importance of a materialistic vs. moralistic culture in improving the performance of the police.[201] At the local and operational level, there is genuine, if frustrated, acknowledgment that, although the police culture is important in delivering good police work, the police (leaders and officers) do not have the time and money to engage in developing a police culture.[202]

With public pressure mounting for better police conduct, the political leadership and administrative cadres have sought to improve police work styles through cultural enhancement. This has resulted in many divergent approaches to the promotion of a police culture. The differences in approaches are caused by differences in understanding what a police culture entails and how to bring it about. Between these two challenges, the latter is the most perplexing one for police leaders.

The Public Security University has the responsibility for educating the next generation of police leaders, managers, and operatives. Their individual, collective, and institutional vision of what a police culture means and can do is important symbolically for the nation and substantively for the profession. The PSU promotes two kinds of culture: (1) the Chinese historical high culture, or personal character development (nonmaterialistic, not self-centered, spiritual, with a sense of mission and a purpose to serve), and (2) a contemporary, professional, ethical culture achieved through work-related ethical training.[203]

The Jinzhou PSB, in Hebei Province,[204] traditionally and customarily, considers a good police culture to consist of three aspects: (1) a professional culture (*zhongcheng fengxian, guogan zhuhui, weimin zhifa, gang wei ren xian*), which is devoted to service, is resolute and wise, enforces the law for the people, and is not afraid to lead; (2) an artistic culture; and

(3) a social culture. At the Fuzhou PSB, in Fujian Province,[205] the police culture is focused mainly on artistic endeavors, from conducting photographic exhibitions to participating in singing competitions to organizing festivals for the people. At the Shanghai PSB,[206] Baoshan subdivision, the police culture orients around healthy extracurricular activities of all kinds, such as baseball, swimming, gymnastic, and painting.[207]

Besides different understandings of police culture, police leaders and organs have different ways of cultivating a police culture. At the Jinzhou Municipal PSB, Liaoning Province, police leaders have sought to change the police culture in a number of ways. First, the police station was remodeled, inside out. Police station signs outside are no longer the standard black and white, giving off an inhospitable, alien, intimidating look.[208] Once inside the building, there is a "legal system culture wall" (*fazhi wenhua qiang*), tastefully and artistically done. An office hallway features a scenic landscape mural with the gold-laced words "*wei renmin fuwu*" ("in the service of the people"), which reminds officers of their mission of serving the people. The hallway to the dining room, where the officers eat and socialize, is decorated with all kinds of thematic displays, from Newton's inventions to Police Bureau Chief Wang Lijun's presentation at the Japanese Police Research Association to photographs of police around the world. The display reminds the police of the diversity of police work. The dining room walls are decorated with traditional Chinese drawings and memorabilia from various countries.

To cultivate diverse interests and encourage continuous education within the police ranks, Wang Lijung initiated a police culture salon (PCS) (*jingcha wenhua shalong*) that met from 7.30 p.m. to 1:00 a.m. every Monday, Wednesday, and Friday. These meetings involved a variety of special-interest groups and discussion forums on, for example, the English language, technology, and politics. The idea was to offer an opportunity for officers to meet after work and discuss and exchange ideas.[209] It is too early to tell whether police culture can be centrally nurtured and positively induced, but everyone, from political committee members to rank-and-file officers, approached the police culture project with guarded optimism. The official feedback was promising. The Gu To sub-bureau political office chief, Ai Chiping, considered it to be a breakthrough in police cultural management. Zhang Jingxong, a web safety officer, treasured the opportunity to relax and learn at the PCS. Taiping sub-bureau officer Tai Ming used the PCS to discuss books with his colleagues. Wang Weili, a municipal bureau supervision officer, had few opportunities to meet people in his job and treasured the opportunity to improve his English.

In the final analysis, it is clear that this cultural program was successful in offering the officers a time to relax and reflect, away from the hustle and bustle of day-to-day police work, and to learn something new; however, many challenges lie ahead: (1) Can cultural programs be centrally planned and strategically imposed from above? (2) Would police officers continue to support the cultural program, especially after the novelty has worn off or when the officials are not looking? (3) Do the police organization and police officers have the time and resources to devote to cultural activities? (4) Most importantly, how might the cultural oasis be helpful in promoting the police culture when society has no supporting culture for such a venture; that is, can high culture survive in low culture soil?

Ever since the beginning of the nation's reform, the PRC police leadership has had a difficult time maintaining a wholesome police culture against corrupting influences of all kinds. One attempt has been to inculcate police, especially leaders, with the "spirit of public humanity" (*renmin jingshen*), which takes respect for human beings (*yi ren wei ben*) as its basic tenet. As applied, this means showing respect, care, and concern for police interests and welfare and respecting citizens' individual rights and dignity, as victims or defendants.[210] This "spirit of public humanity" has its roots in Jiang's "Three Represents."[211] At the 16th Party Congress, President Jiang introduced the "Three Represents" as a basic Party principle.[212] Since then, the "Three Represents" has been enshrined as a constitutional principle.[213] The MPS has sought to promote the "Three Represents" first as a Party principle and then as a constitutional norm in police work with the slogan "establish police for the public, implement the law for the people" (*"lijing wei gong, zhifa wei min"*). This calls for humanizing implementation of the law. Humanizing policing involves actualization of the humanity (*rendao*)[214] principles embedded within the humanitarianism (*renbenzhuyi*) ideal.[215] It is instrumental to achieving the nation's developmental goal of political civility (*zhengzhi wenming*).[216]

The "spirit of public humanity" in policing reflects the political ideology of humanitarianism and the legal jurisprudence of human rights. The "spirit of public humanity" is based in large part on 18th-century Western liberal thought regarding inherent human rights and dignity, for which Marx was a standard bearer. In promoting the "spirit of public humanity" in policing, China acknowledges the desirability and inevitability of achieving humanitarianism and respecting human rights in advanced society. The question remains, though, as to whether the meaning of humanitarianism in theory and human rights in practice differs materially in China vs. the West and whether it is absolute as an Asian value[217] or a relative one due to China's developmental needs.

Conclusion

This chapter has offered up a review of policing literature and an overview of police reform activities through the eyes and in the hands of the Chinese. It has touched on major themes of research, scholarship, and education; reform agendas, problems, and issues; principles and paradigms; and, finally, leadership and culture. When selecting materials for presentation, parsimony is the rule and representativeness is the yardstick, with revelation as the objective. In this conclusion, it is appropriate to ask what we have learned about Chinese police reform that we did not already know. Some of what we have learned is more revealing than others, but here are a few lessons to reflect on as we plow a new Chinese police studies field outside of China before we sow the seeds; remember, after a long, deep freeze comes spring.

We know painfully little about Chinese policing in general and police reform in particular, from how the police prioritize their agenda to what they think about the issues. We know very little, for example, about the political philosophies or reform agendas of the many variations on national vs. provincial leadership through the years[218] and their impact on MPS policy or frontline operations.[219] How do frontline officers think and feel about police reform?[220] Without understanding the policies of leadership at the top[221] and how line officers think and feel at the bottom,[222] we cannot begin to understand Chinese policing.

What little we know about Chinese policing is incomplete and often distorted. The conventional wisdom is that Chinese police reformers are not interested in conducting police policy research, and they have very few empirical research data to inform their deliberation and choices. There is some truth to this observation, even from an insider's perspective,[223] and this lack of research has been used to suggest that many of the police reform policy choices being made are ill informed or not connected to reality, but this is not entirely the case.[224] Ever since Mao, the CPC has collected substantial survey data and conducted lengthy investigations to support its decision making.

Chinese police researchers outside of China have made gallant efforts to gather empirical evidence (mostly student surveys) on Chinese policing, and many timely and excellent works have been published.[225] Despite this, it is still assumed that Chinese empirical data are either not available or inaccessible,[226] and few attempts have been made to reinterpret Chinese research or survey data.[227,228] The review of Chinese empirical research provided in this chapter tells a different story, though. In keeping with the advice of Mao ("no investigation, no right to speak") and Deng ("seek truth from facts"), many well-conducted empirical studies have been performed and quality data are available. This chapter has discussed only a few of them, with many data sources documented. The lesson learned? Recently discovered evidence-based policing in the West has long been practiced as a "policy science" in China by Mao and later Deng.

A cursory review of existing literature in the West (see Chapter 2) shows that many of our impressions or opinions regarding Chinese policing, past and present, are more often than not groundless and in more than a few cases dead wrong; for example, judging by a Congressional-Executive Commission on China annual report,[229] every Chinese political leader is bent on corruption, and all police officers are equally abusive to the citizens. This is groundless. Furthermore, the assertion that the Party leadership and MPS reformers issue police reform policies and measures without in-depth study or careful deliberation is also wrong.

The whole of this chapter and the remaining part of this book are devoted to showing that the Chinese political leaders and police reformers know what they are doing, more so than we give them credit for. This is not to suggest that, just as in other countries in transition, especially during times of peril and turmoil, Chinese leaders do not falter or are not susceptible to being misled, nor is this is a blanket endorsement of Chinese positions on substantive issues, from how to conduct community policing to what to do to salvage the Lei Feng spirit. It is, however, to observe that, for most of time and on many of the issues during the police reform period, the reform plan has been thoughtfully assembled and its execution has been effectively implemented.

Chinese indigenous policing literature and grounded empirical data are rarely used to inform Chinese policing inside and outside of China. China-bound police researchers (including this author at times) have observed that Chinese policing literature is long on political rhetoric and short on substantive discussion, long on descriptions of the facts and short on analysis of data, long on received wisdom and short on independent thinking, long on shared understanding and short on divergent interpretation, and long on personal opinion and short on empirical findings. Thus observed, Chinese policing literature is, for the most part, sterile in content, monotonous in tone, and unchanging through time. The most damning observation by far is that Chinese police literature, as a form of Party-sanctioned and self-censored publications, are all propaganda materials, not to be relied on in research for any reason. The review of the literature provided in this chapter is generally in agreement with most of these observations; however, general agreement aside, the review has also taken note of the growing exceptions to many of these assumptions. It is these exceptions to the norm that hold promise for serious Chinese police researchers. For example, there are clear and convincing evidence that Chinese policing journals are changing in focus, content, and style (Tables 3.4 and 3.5). Increasingly, and in small steps, policing articles are becoming less political and more scientific (Table 3.1), less descriptive and more analytical,[230] less opinionated and more evidence based,[231] less philosophical and more empirical (Table 3.8). Although Chinese police journals are still officially the mouth-piece of the Party, the Party agenda has changed (Table 3.9), and the editorial policies at individual journals have made a difference.[232] That being the case, a systematic content analysis of various police journals would find that they do not march in lockstep with each other to the cadence of the CPC. In fact, on close inspection, a researcher might notice more differences than similarities between journals, sometimes on the same issue. This line of inquiry holds much promise in deciphering Chinese policing.

Perhaps the biggest revelation from this review is that the Chinese leadership, instead of being secretive and complacent, can be quite forthcoming regarding their shortcomings and critical of their own performance. We have seen a sincere effort being made not only to improve and do better but also to excel and strive to be perfect. Again, there is certainly a case to be made for the disparity between intention and action, words and deeds. Still, it is not fair to ignore clear evidence everywhere we look in the literature; in everyday life, the Chinese are trying, and trying their best, in spite of shortcomings in the system and fallibility of their leaders. This is not the image we might get from reading popular media accounts in China or the pronouncements of policy experts made internationally.

Finally, a research note on where we go from here. The brief excursion into police empirical research reveals that the Chinese police leadership, traditionally and since the days of Mao, is very interested in evidence-based and research-driven policing. In fact, it was Mao who said:

> Everyone engaged in practical work must investigate conditions at the lower levels. Such investigation is especially necessary for those who know theory but do not know the actual conditions, for otherwise they will not be able to link theory with practice. Although my assertion 'no investigation, no right to speak' has been ridiculed as 'narrow empiricism,' to this day I do not regret having made it; far from regretting it, I still insist that without investigation there cannot possibly be any right to speak. There are many people who 'the moment they alight from the official carriage' make a hullabaloo, spout opinions, criticize this and condemn that; but, in fact, ten out of ten of them will meet with failure. For such views or criticisms, which are not based on thorough investigation, is nothing but ignorant twaddle. Countless times our Party suffered at the hands of these 'imperial envoys' that rushed here, there, and everywhere. Stalin rightly says, 'Theory becomes purposeless if it is not connected with revolutionary practice.' And he rightly adds 'practice gropes in the dark if its path is not illumined by revolutionary theory.' Nobody should be labeled a 'narrow empiricist' except the 'practical man' who gropes in the dark and lacks perspective and foresight.[233]

As China-bound police researchers, we can certainly use the survey datasets discussed in this chapter, incomplete and faulty as they necessarily are, to explore in a preliminary way what policing is like in China. The methodological lessons to be learned here are that we should not look at "unscientific" data as being totally useless and irrelevant but as another piece of evidence to help us tell the story of what is going on inside China. In this way, we are acting like an investigator more so than a social scientist. CID officers and investigative journalists would inform us that there are many ways to get to the facts. Perfect truth about China is not what we are after and cannot be had. (In the words of CID officerss, they are not seeking wholesale confession or even admissions, but tidbits of facts to reconstruct the real-ity.) Data points are all that is needed to unlock the closely guarded secret that is Chinese policing. We can learn about China, and understand her through a lifetime of gathering and digesting information, here and there.[234] In the end, all these tidbits of information, individually, cumulatively, and in total, allow us to form an informed opinion of what really is happening, only to be challenged when another bit of information comes our way, with the cycle of knowing, disputing, knowing, disputing,…repeating without end.

To the reconstruction of the Chinese image we now move.

Notes

1. "In their own perspective" means seeing things the Chinese way, not a rendition of what the Chinese see, think, and feel in Western concepts, logic, and sentimentality, the last being most critical. It is easy to change one's mind, but impossible to ignore feelings.

2. "In their own words" refers to how the Chinese present their ideas. At the end of the day, words matter. Alfred H. Bloom, *The Linguistic Shaping of Thought: A Study in the Impact of Language on Thinking in China and the West* (Psychology Press, Hillsdale, NJ, 1981). With the advent of computer translations and word processing functions, the careful crafting of words has become less important, but personal meaning (intent, intimation), not to mention an entire cultural world, can often be lost in translation.

3. (a) There are exceptions; for example, see Chen Peng-zhen and Zuo-Xiu-yang, "Upholding Freedom and Changing Character," *Journal of Jiangxi Public Security College*, 11–15, 2005. The authors, scholars from the People's University School of Law, are supportive of the more humanistic policy of assisting rather than detaining illegal migrants found without proper documentations in cities after the Sun Zhigan incident. The fast change on policy ("Measures for Assisting Vagrants and Beggars with No Means of Support in Cities," effective August 1, 2003) took frontline police officers by surprise and created problems as far as adjusting attitudes and conduct. (b) Wang Wei-bao and Li Peng-zhan, "Situation Analyzing and Countermeasures Considering to the Vagrants and Beggardom on the Present Situation," *Journal of Jiangxi Public Security College*, 5–11, 2004. Wang, a sub-PSB chief, and Li, a police officer, both from Ningbo City, Zhejiang, embrace the wisdom of Premier Wen's policy regarding assistance for migrants ("Measures for Assisting Vagrants and Beggars with No Means of Support in Cities," effective August 1, 2003) but raise issues regarding the feasibility, practicality, and ultimately impact of such a policy on city administrations and police operations (e.g., creating dependency on listless people).

4. Scholars engaged in China studies who have the language capability and cultural facility have done a much better job in deciphering China. The problem here is that China specialists rarely study contemporary policing issues. In fact, very few (if any) Chinese policing scholars consistently publish in this area.

5. Trying to follow Chinese thinking and making sense of the Chinese presentation can be difficult at times. The theories and concepts, logic and reasoning, organization and style, as translated and reported here, are not readily accessible to most Western scholars/readers and take some getting used to.

6. (a) Murray Scot Tanner, "Ideological Struggle over Police Reform, 1988–1993," in Edwin A. Winckler (Ed.), *Transition from Communism in China: Institutional and Comparative Analyses* (pp. 111–128), Lynne Rienner Publishers, Boulder, CO, 1999. (b) Murray Scot Tanner, "Changing Windows on a Changing China: The Evolving 'Think Tank' System and the Case of the Public Security Sector," *The China Quarterly*, 171, 559–574, 2002.

7. "A Call for Papers," *Public Security Studies*, 66, 96, 1999.

8. Ibid.

9. The *Public Security Studies* cumulative index for 1999 shows that a total of 165 articles were published that year. The index also has a special category on statistical data compilation, which had 12 items, making a total of 177 entries. The articles are grouped into various categories,

and the number of articles in each ranges from one (e.g., Book Reviews) to a high of 18 (Commissioners' Forum). The categories and number of articles in each are as follows: Special Articles (7 items); Special Articles from Working Meetings Nationwide against Illicit Drugs (3 items); Commissioners' Forum (18 items); Police Reform (10 items); Theoretical Findings (3 items); Police Administration (6 items); Build-Up of Police Forces (13 items); Police Research (9 items); Legal Construction (10 items); Police Jurisprudence (11 items); Criminology Research (14 items); Policing at the Grass-Roots Level (4 items); Police Post Work (3 items); State Enterprise Reform (5 items); Economic Protection (3 items); Public Order (10 items); Road Traffic Control (3 items); Exit and Entry Administration (2 items); Antidrug Work (2 items); Information and Propaganda (1 item); Science and Technology (3 items); Guarding (1 item); Police Education and Training (2 items); Police Work Guarantee (2 items); Statistical Work (1 item); Comprehensive Treatment of Public Order (2 items); Investigative Findings (3 items); Hong Kong, Macau, and Taiwan (2 items); Foreign Policing (9 items); Police History (1 item); Book Reviews (1 item); and Statistical Data (1 item). The journal had six issues in 1999 (63 to 68), each one more or less 96 pages long. Each of the 165 articles averages 3.25 pages.

10. Zhou Chengshan, "On Basic Feature and Its Embodiment of Editing Thought," *Journal of Chinese People's Public Security University* (*PSU Journal*), 74, 109, 1999. Zhou, from the Editorial Office of the Chinese People's Armed Police Force Academy, Hebei Province, observed that editors play an important role in the creation and distribution of information regarding the police. The selection process is necessarily influenced by the editor's colored lens. To promote better journal publications, editors should adopt a number of views: (1) *agreeable viewpoint*—identify with the author to understand more deeply the author's viewpoint; (2) *critical viewpoint*—challenge the author and engage the author in an exhaustive analysis and debate of all viewpoints; (3) *contrary viewpoint*—embrace a contrary but objective viewpoint (editor vs. author); (4) *multiple viewpoint*—examine arguments from various perspectives; and (5) *comparative viewpoint*—require the editor to compare the author's and the editor's points of views to those of others.

11. One of the many difficulties in studying Chinese police literature is that of becoming familiar with its unique presentation style, specialized concepts, different terminologies, and internal logic. For example, originally the concept of "contradiction" was used by Mao to describe the antagonistic class *struggle* between the capitalistic vs. proletarian classes; however, Mao's original idea of "contradiction" can also be extended to cover non-antagonistic group *conflict* of a more incident nature, namely contradictions within the people. In the reform era, especially after Deng, the terms "contradiction" and "conflict" were used interchangeably to describe conflicts of values and interests of all kinds, such as the state vs. antagonistic groups (subversives, gangs) and the rich vs. the poor. Failure to grasp the many different and nuanced concepts can make translation, analysis, and understanding of the Chinese materials reported here difficult. In this report, I will try to stay close to the Chinese writings with regard to their concepts, logic, and style, at the expense, perhaps, of accessibility. It was Lu Xun (1881–1936), the preeminent Chinese thinker and writer, who famously said: "I'd rather be faithful than smooth" (寧信而不順). See Chen Fukang, *A History of Translation Theory in China*, Shanghai Foreign Language Press, Shanghai, 2000 (http://ishare.iask.sina.com.cn/f/7060023.html).

12. Chen Xiaoji, "A Preliminary Examination of Police Studies Research 1988–2008," *Fujian Tribune*, 2, 71–76, 2009.

13. Kam C. Wong, "The Studying of Policing in China." In Cliff Roberson, Dilip K. Das, and Jennie K. Singer (Eds.), *Police without Borders: The Fading Distinction between Local and Global* (pp. 111–151), Taylor & Francis, Boca Raton, FL, 2010.

14. Lawrence W. Sherman, David P. Farrington, Brandon Welsh, and Doris MacKenzie (Eds.), *Evidence-Based Crime Prevention*, Routledge, London, 2002. This is what we call evidence-based policing.

15. Wang Yanji, "Probe into the Study of the System of Public Security Discipline," *Journal of Chinese People's Public Security University* (*PSU Journal*), 101, 1–5, 2003 (hereafter referred to as Wang).

16. "Public Security Academic Discipline System Research" is a joint research program undertaken by the Ministry of Public Security, Ministry of Judiciary, Ministry of Justice, Armed Police, Forest Police, and other police colleges. The research charter required spending two years looking into the scope, organization, and integration of public studies with other disciplines (e.g., law and criminology).

17. Wang, p. 1.

18. (a) Lawrence W. Sherman and Richard A. Berk, "The Specific Deterrent Effects of Arrest for Domestic Assault," *American Sociological Review*, 49(2), 261–272, 1984. (b) Lawrence W. Sherman, *Evidence-Based Policing*, Police Foundation, Washington, DC, 1998. Notwithstanding the introduction of evidence-based policing to the study of policing, there is still a lack of evidence-based policing in operational policing. (c) Marilyn Peterson, *Intelligence-Led Policing: The New Intelligence Architecture*, Bureau of Justice Assistance, U.S. Department of Justice, Washington, DC, 2005. (d) Willem de Lint, "Intelligence in Policing and Security: Reflections on Scholarship," *Policing & Society*, 16(1), 1–6, 2006. Intelligence-led policing, made famous by William Bratton (NYPD), has been making some inroads into more informed police operations, albeit at the street level and with individual officers, as policing is still very much based on experience and intuition.

19. Wang, p. 1.

20. Wang, p. 2.

21. Wang, p. 2.

22. Wang, pp. 3–4.

23. (a) "A University Student Was Beaten to Death for Having No Temporary Resident Permit," ("大学毕业生因无暂住证被收容并遭毒打致死亡"), *news.sohu.com*, April 25, 2003 (http://news.sohu.com/94/56/news208805694.shtml). Sun Zhigang, a 27-year-old college graduate, was employed by Guangzhou Daqi Garment Company in Wuhan, capital city of Central China's Hubei Province. On March 17, 2003, he was arrested and taken to the Huangcunjie police station for not carrying a resident ID (*jumin shenfen zheng*); he was suspected of being an illegal migrant. The next day, the Huangcunjie police station transferred Sun to the Yisong detention center, and later he was transferred to the detention center's hospital. Sun was found dead on March 19, 2003. The autopsy showed that he had been beaten to death. The case attracted national attention and led to petitions from the public for changes to be made in the outdated and draconian migrant policy. Premier Wen immediately promulgated a policy document, "Measures for Assisting Vagrants and Beggars with No Means of Support in Cities," effective August 1, 2003, that required police to give aid and assistance to beggars and vagrants instead of detention and expatriation (收容遣送). (b) Wang Wei-bao and Li Peng-zhan, "Situation Analyzing and Countermeasures Considering to the Vagrants and Beggardom on the Present Situation," *Journal of Jiangxi Public Security College*, 5–11, 2004.

24. Wang, p. 3.

25. Wang, p. 5.

26. Rui Yang, "Education Policy Research in the People's Republic of China," in Jenny Ozga, Terri Popkewitz, and Thomas Seddon (Eds.), *Education Research and Policy: Steering the Knowledge-Based Economy*, World Yearbook of Education 2006 (pp. 270–284), Routledge, London, 2006. Many of these research problems and issues are not unique to Chinese policing as an academic, professional, or policy field. Rather, they are endemic to Chinese scholarly research enterprises.

27. See also Zhou Changyuan and Wang Yongzhe, "Discussing the Low Stage of Crime Studies in China," *Public Security Studies*, 63, 39–43, 1999.

28. David H. Bayley, "Police Reform: Who Done It?" paper prepared for the Conference on Rank-and-File Participation in Police Reform—Looking Backwards and Forwards, Berkeley, CA, October 12–13, 2006. "Police rank-and-file have not been the source of significant reform ideas....Police organizations themselves have not been the source of significant reform ideas.... In short, significant police reforms have been top-down and outside-inside."

29. In China, coordination of research happens at the national, ministerial level—in this case, the Ministry of Public Security (MPS). The Police Studies Association of China, a quasi-private research center, also has a steering role.

30. For example, moving away from ideological and philosophical debate into policy domain and organizational/operational issues; this is especially so at the provincial and local levels. (a) Cong Mei, "Characteristics and Countermeasures against Crimes Happening in Old Flats [*sic*]," *Journal of Jiangsu Police Officer College*, 108, 13–17, 2006. (b) Kong Xiang-yu and You Su-hua, "On Declining System of Civil Liability," *Journal of Guizhou Police Officer Vocational College*, 52, 26–29, 2002. (c) Li Long and Liu Cheng, "Methodological Thought on the Sources of Law," *Journal of Jiangxi Public Security College*, 87, 5–9, 2004.

31. For example, police journals now welcome contributions from other disciplines offering different perspectives, approaches, and methods with regard to the study of policing.

32. Police studies have expanded beyond domestic issues and include global problems and experiences. See, for example, Marie Ragghianti, "A New Way to Prevent Crimes: American Experience," *Journal of Zhejiang Police College*, 99, 23—39, 2007. Ragghianti was a member of the U.S. Parole Board, as a Clinton appointee. Also, the author of this text (KCW) has been a co-editor of the *Journal of Zhejiang Police College* since 2007.

33. There is less and less concern with being politically correct, with strict adherence to ideological dogma and political doctrine. Instead, more and more citations are being made to foreign data, research, and theories, such as the U.N. International Covenant on Civil and Political Rights (ICCPR), research on fear of crime, and community policing theories.

34. The Communist Party of China designated 2002 as a year of investigation and research. (a) "Forging Ahead with the Times and Bringing New Ideas in Theory," *Public Security Studies*, 2002. (b) "To Further Advance and Enhance the Theoretical Research in Policing Nation Wide," *Public Security Studies*, 2002. (c) "On Further Enhancing the Construction of Theoretical Policing Study," *Public Security Studies*, 2002. (d) "Studying Conscientiously the Spirit of 16th CPC's National Congress and Creating a New Aspect in Police Theoretical Studies," *Public Security Studies*, 2002.

35. (a) Zhang Jinghua, "Researchers Serving the Practice of the Further Development of Police Work with Theoretical Support," *Journal of Zhejiang Police College*, 99, 6–10, 2007. (b) "Academic Corruption Should Be Combated by All [commentary]," *Journal of Zhejiang Police College*, 99, 1, 2007.

36. "Academic Corruption Should Be Combated by All [commentary]," *Journal of Zhejiang Police College*, 99, 1, 2007.

37. Guo Taisheng, "Fifth National Annual Public Security Studies Conference, Public Security Studies Department Heads Summation," *Journal of Chinese People's Public Security University* (*PSU Journal*), 136, 102–105, 2008.

38. Ji Weiwei, "Metrological [*sic*] Analysis of Essays Published by the Jiangsu Public Security College" ["*Jiangsu gongan zhuanke xuexiao xuebao*"], *Journal of Jiangsu Police Officer College*, 18(1), 171–180, 2003.

39. Discussion with *Zhejiang Police College Journal* staff.

40. 1989 could be explained by the June 4 (Tiananmen Square) aftermath. In that year, there were 15 articles coming out of Beijing.

41. Future research should investigate yearly fluctuations between political thought articles (PTAs) vs. police legal studies articles (PLSA), possibly explained by CCPC or MPS mobilization initiatives, such as *yanda* or public agitation for change.

42. Li Kun-sheng, "Basic Knowledge of Composing Police Science Thesis, Parts I–IV," *Journal of Hubei Public Security College*, 2004.

43. Field study of social problems before policy formulation and action is a bedrock CPC principle, made famous by Mao in his *Report on an Investigation of the Peasant Movement in Hunan*, March, 1927. The other principle is expansive and extensive consultation.

44. Ministry of Public Security, "Exploring the Police in China from a New Perspective: A Joint Investigation into the Status of Resources and Support of the Public Security Task Force in Henan and Guangdong" ["*Cong xinde shijue tanjiu woguo gongan ziyuan baozhang de xianzhuang: Gongan ziyuan baozhang tiaojian keti xiaozu zai Henan, Guangdong lian sheng de tiao cha*"], *Public Security Studies*, 15, 1991.

45. Ministry of Public Security, *Our Nation's Public Feeling of Safety Level Has Increased: Second National Public Safety Random Survey Conditions Analysis* [*Woguo gongzhong anquan gan shuiping you suo tigao: quanguo dierci gongzhong anquan gan chouyang tiaocha qingkuang fengxi*]. See Yaru Chang, "Research on Fear of Crime in China," *Police Studies*, 13, 125, 1990.

46. Zhou Wai and Li Quan, "Reflection on Shandong Province Jining City Public Security Bureau: Dongmen Police Post Survey" ["*Shandong sheng Jining city Dongmen paichusuo de tiaocha xikao*"], *Public Security Studies*, 30, 1992.

47. Donmen is one of the oldest police posts, having been established in 1946. Jining city is an old city with good military, police, and citizens relationships. Since 1986, the crime rate has been kept at about 5/10,000 and criminal arrest rate at under 2/10,000.

48. Wang Dai, Jie Jidong, and Zhou Wai, "Building Chinese Community Police: Research Report of Shandong Jining City Community Police Work" ["*Jiangshe zhongguo de shequ jingwu: Shandong Jining shi shequ jingcha gongzuo*"], *Public Security Studies*, 30, 1993.

49. "Survey regarding Overtime from 2005 September to November 2005," *Police Post Work*, 1, 2006 (http://www.phcppsu.com.cn/news/2006/c-1.htm).

50. "Survey of Police and Public Relationships from Police Post Officers' Perspective" ["*Paichusuo minjing yan zhong de jingmin guanxi tiaocha*"], *Police Post Work*, 2, 2006 (http://www.phcppsu.com.cn/news/2006/c-2.htm).

51. "Survey Findings on Police Post Personal Health and Work Conditions," *Police Post Work*, 4, 2006 (http://www.phcppsu.com.cn/news/2006/c-4.htm).

52. "Police Post Police Housing Survey" ["*Paichusuo minjing zhufang qingkuan tiaocha jieguo*"], *Police Post Work*, 6, 2006 (http://www.phcppsu.com.cn/news/2006/c-6.htm).

53. "Survey Findings on Police Post Police Contact with 'Crazy Militants'" ("*Paichusuo minjing jieju 'wu feng zhi' qingkuan tiacha jieguo*"], *Police Post Work*, 8, 2006.

54. (1) "Paichusuo Police Confronted with 'New Four Difficulties' Survey Result," May 18, 2010 (http://www.phcppsu.com.cn/news/show.aspx?showid=2259). (2) Missing (not reported). (3) "Paichusuo Police–Public Relationship Survey Result," January 15, 2010. (4) "Paichusuo Police Current Status of Training Survey Result," December 14, 2009. (5) "Survey into Paichusuo Military Transfer Issues and Status," September 3, 2009. (6) "Paichusuo Police View Auxiliary Police," August 26, 2010. (7) "Paichusuo 'Post 80' Police Current Status of Survey," August 8, 2009. (8) "Survey into How the Police Spend the Night," May 6, 2009. (9) "Survey Results on Female Police in Their Eyes," March 26, 2009. (10) "Paichusuo Police New Year Eve Dinner Survey Result," February 2, 2009. (11) "Paichusuo Police Family Togetherness Survey Result," February 13, 2009. (12) "Paichusuo Police Personal Collection Survey Result," February 11, 2009. (13) "Paichusuo Police and Olympics Survey Result," October 13, 2008. (14) "Regrets of Police Responses of 19 Paichusuo Police," June 26, 2008. (15) "Regarding Paichusuo Police Hobbies Survey Result," December 10, 2007. (16) "Paichusuo Police Heath Status Survey Result," December 10, 2007. (17) "Paichusuo Police Use of Internet Survey Result," December 10, 2007. (18) "Paichusuo Police Rest and Recreation Survey Result," December 10, 2007. (19) "Police Children Education Survey Result," December 10, 2007. (20) "Paichusuo Police Promotion Status Result," December 10, 2007. (21) "Paichusuo Police 'Mobile Phone Life' Survey Result," December 10, 2007. (22) "Paichusuo Police Stress Survey Result," December 10, 2007. (23) "Paichusuo Police Drinking Survey Result," December 10, 2007. (24) "Police Holiday Life Survey Result," December 10, 2007. (25) "Paichusuo Police Use of Vehicle Survey Result," December 10, 2007. (26) "Paichusuo Police Opinion towards Uniform Survey Result," December 7, 2007. (27) "Paichusuo Police Marriage Survey Result," December 7, 2007. (28) "Police Meal

Consumption Status Survey Result," December 7, 2007. (29) "Paichusuo Police Contact with 'Violent Crazies' Survey Result," December 7, 2007. (30) "Paichusuo Police Smoking Status Survey Report," December 7, 2007. (31) "Paichusuo Police Residential Housing Status Survey Report," December 7, 2007. (32) "Paichusuo Reading Status Survey Report," December 7, 2007. (33) "Paichusuo Police Physical Status Survey Report," December 7, 2007. (34) "How Much Do Police Make?" December 7, 2007. (35) "Paichusuo Police View of Police–Public Relationship," December 7, 2007. (36) "Survey regarding Overtime," December 7, 2007.

55. "Survey regarding Overtime," December 7, 2007 (http://www.phcppsu.com.cn/news/2006/c-1.htm).
56. "你有过晚加班" ("*Ni you gou wan jia ban*").
57. The question did not say what kind of impact, positive or negative. From reading the text, a negative impact is suggested.
58. "List of Important Research Issues during the '8–5' Period," *Public Security Studies*, 25, 1992
59. What are some of the more defining characteristics of certain crimes? For example, are gangs becoming more intelligent in planning their crimes, more violent in their execution, and more global in their reach?
60. "Predictions for the Next Five Years," *Beijing Review*, September 16, 2010.
61. Wang Jianxiong and He Feng, "On the Crime of Falsely Making Out an Invoice," *Public Security Studies*, 172, 21–25, 2009.
62. Mei Yan-zhu, "An Analysis of the Cause of College Students' Participating in Multi-Level Marketing and Counter-Measures," *Hubei Jingguan Xuebao*, 79, 93–96, 2004.
63. China was admitted to the World Trade Organization (WTO) on December 11, 2001, as the 144th member.
64. Xiong Yonggen, "Rethinking Education, National Security and Social Stability in China," paper prepared for the Asia-Pacific Center for Security Studies Conference: Security Implications of Economic and Cultural Trends, Honolulu, HI, April 17–19, 2001 (http://www.apcss.org/Publications/Ocasional%20Papers/OPXiong.pdf).
65. Li Chang-chun, "Service for Constructing a First-Class Police University in the World," *Journal of Chinese People's Public Security University* (*PSU Journal*), 108, 2, 2004.
66. Ibid., p. 1.
67. Ibid., pp. 1–2.
68. Ibid., p. 3.
69. Ibid.
70. *Scottish Police College Annual Report 2004/5*, Kincardine, Fife, p. 7 (http://www.martinfrost.ws/htmlfiles/gazette/LawnOrder/Scottish%20Police%20College%20Annual%20rep05.pdf).
71. The author has participated in many such international conferences as an invited foreign policing expert of MPS.
72. Li Chang-chun, "Service for Constructing a First-Class Police University in the World," *Journal of Chinese People's Public Security University* (*PSU Journal*), 108, 1, 2004.
73. Ibid., p. 2.
74. Ibid., p. 3.
75. Ibid.
76. Ibid., pp. 3–4.
77. Ibid.
78. Ibid.
79. In the author's discussion with PSU staff, it is frankly admitted that foreign experts are invited for name recognition more so than their subject matter expertise.
80. Li Chang-chun, "Service for Constructing a First-Class Police University in the World," *Journal of Chinese People's Public Security University* (*PSU Journal*), 108, 4, 2004.
81. Ibid.
82. Ibid., p. 5.
83. Ibid.

84. Ibid.
85. Wei Yongzhong, "Regarding Public Security Organizational Reform Since Open Reform" ["*Gaike kaifang yilai gongan jiguan gugai ji qi qishi*"], *Journal of Chinese People's Public Security University (PSU Journal)*, 136, 7–15, 2008.
86. College Task Team, "Discussion on Target of Policing Reform in Our Province," *Journal of Gansu Police Vocational College*, 6(1), 2008 (http://en.cnki.com.cn/Article_en/CJFDTOTAL-JYLU200801003.htm). This article addresses a 2007 Gangsu Province Public Security Department police reform research progress subject report. The research team leader was Li Suilai.
87. Ibid., p. 1.
88. Policy debate and implementation issues in police reform are real and contentious among regions (coastal vs. inland), provinces ("one country, two systems"), and central vs. local.
89. Jing Huang, *Factionalism in Chinese Communist Politics*, Cambridge Modern China Series, Cambridge University Press, Cambridge, UK, 2000.
90. He Li, "Debating China's Economic Reform: Liberals vs. New Leftists," *Journal of Chinese Political Science*, 15, 1–23, 2010. Many intellectuals are vying for influence. According to the *Social Sciences Frontier Studies in China (2006–2007)* (*Blue Book of Social Science*), other schools of thought include neo-liberalism, democratic socialism, postmodernism, and new cultural conservatism. New leftists (including Hu) want to have a strong state to ensure social justice. Liberals, following Hayek, want a smaller state and advocate for a civil society.
91. Wei Yongzhong, "Regarding Public Security Organizational Reform Since Open Reform" ["*Gaike kaifang yilai gongan jiguan gugai ji qi qishi*"], *Journal of Chinese People's Public Security University (PSU Journal)*, 136, 7, 2008.
92. (a) Lucian W. Pye, *The Dynamics of Factions and Consensus in Chinese Politics: A Model and Some Propositions*, Rand Corporation, Santa Monica, CA, 1980. (b) Cheng Li, "One Party, Two Chinese Bipartisanship in the Making? Chinese Bipartisanship in the Making?" paper presented at the Conference on Chinese Leadership, Politics, and Policy, Carnegie Endowment for International Peace, November 25, 2005. (c) Li Datong, *China's Youth League Faction: Incubus of Power?* OpenDemocracy, October 31, 2007 (http://www.opendemocracy.net/article/democracy_power/china_inside/youth_league).
93. Yang Guangsheng, "Increase Public Security Strength Starts with Establishing Six Big Systems" ["*Yi jianli liu dai jizhi wei pokou, jia dai gongan gaige lidu*"], *Public Security Studies*, 57, 22–25, 1998.
94. *Huji zhidu* (户籍制度).
95. *Liudong renkou guanli* (流动人口管理).
96. *Daolu jiaotong qinwu zhidu* (道路交通勤务制度).
97. *Renmin jincha fa* (人民警察法).
98. *Renmin Jingchu jinghui tiaoli* (人民警察警徽条例).
99. Police Inspection Regulations (*Gongan Jiguan Ducha Tiaoli*).
100. *People's Republic of China Professional Ethics Regulations* [*Renmin Jingcha Jiye Dude Guifan*], Ministry of Public Security, Beijing, 1994. The police professional ethics code includes the following: (1) *Loyalty to the party and the motherland*—stand firm in one's beliefs, listen to command, and defend the constitution. (2) *Serving the people*—love the people, serve as their servant, maintain a clear separation between love and hate, remove the bad, and pacify the good. (3) *Fidelity to the law*—avoid personal favors, be fearless against power, adhere to strict prohibition against torture, and do not unduly impose or avoid guilt. (4) *High integrity and honesty*—struggle hard, discipline oneself to serve the public, watch out for corruption, refuse bribery, and do not be corrupted by others. (5) *Cohesion and cooperation*—be mindful of the whole through cooperation, mutual respect, and mutual support. (6) *Bravery in sacrifice*—be dedicated to one's duties, competent in work skills, enterprising, brave, and unafraid of sacrifice. (7) *Strict discipline*—obey leaders, follow orders, keep faith with the system, and hold onto secrets. (8) *Duties performed in a civilized way*—with care and humility, declining privilege, being polite to people, and maintaining stern police appearance.

101. You Xiaowen, "Thinking Deeply about Reformation of Police System" ["*Guanyu jingcha tizhi kaige de jidia sikao*"], *Journal of Chinese People's Public Security University (PSU Journal)*, 18(2), 97, 2002.
102. Ibid., p. 97.
103. Ibid.
104. Ibid.
105. Ibid., p. 98.
106. Ibid.
107. Ibid.
108. Ibid.
109. Ibid., p. 99.
110. Zhang Jinghua, "An Overall Concept of Exploring and Establishing a Mechanism for Modern Policing," *Public Security Studies*, 120, 11–17, 2004.
111. Ibid., p. 13.
112. Ibid.
113. Ibid., p. 14.
114. Ibid.
115. Ibid., pp. 14–15.
116. Ibid., p. 15.
117. Ibid.
118. Ibid.
119. Ibid.
120. Ibid.
121. Ibid., p. 16
122. Ibid.
123. Ibid.
124. "Causes and Remedies for Factors Affecting Local Comprehensive Management Work" ["*Yingxiang jiceng zhongzhi gongzuode yinsu he duice*"], *China Police Net* [*Zhongguo jingcha wang*], April 10, 2003, p. 6 (http://www.cpd.com.cn/gb/newspaper/2003-04/10/content_1387.htm).
125. Yang Guangsheng, "Increase Public Security Strength Starts with Establishing Six Big Systems" ["*Yi jianli liu dai jizhi wei pokou, jia dai gongan gaige lidu*"], *Public Security Studies*, 57, 22, 1998.
126. Zhu Entao, "Several Considerations over the Establishment and Improvement of Urban Emergency Response System," *Public Security Studies*, 120, 5–10, 2004. Zhu was Vice Minister of the MPS and Vice President of the Chinese Police Studies Association.
127. Ibid., p. 5.
128. Ibid., p. 6.
129. Ibid.
130. Ibid.
131. Ibid., p. 7.
132. Ibid.
133. Ibid.
134. Ibid.
135. Ibid., p. 8.
136. Ibid., p. 9.
137. Ibid.
138. Ibid.
139. Ibid.
140. Liu Qingji, "Issues in Ideological and Political Construction of Leadership within Police Departments in the New Age," *Public Security Studies*, 63, 20–22, 1999.
141. Ibid., p. 20.

142. Chen Xunqiu, "Probing into the Thinking and Working Methods of the Leaders in Police Forces," *Public Security Studies*, 75, 13–19, 2001.

143. Ibid., p. 13.

144. Central Committee of the Communist Party of Russia, *History of the Communist Party of the Soviet Union (Bolsheviks), Short Course*, International Publishers, New York, 1939, p. 198. "The Sixth Party Congress of the Russian Social-Democratic Labour Party (Bolsheviks) held at Petrograd between July 26 and August 3, 1917, defined democratic centralism as follows: (1) That all directing bodies of the Party, from top to bottom, shall be elected; (2) That Party bodies shall give periodical accounts of their activities to their respective Party organizations; (3) That there shall be strict Party discipline and the subordination of the minority to the majority; (4) That all decisions of higher bodies shall be absolutely binding on lower bodies and on all Party members."

145. Chen Xunqiu, "Probing into the Thinking and Working Methods of the Leaders in Police Forces," *Public Security Studies*, 75, 13, 2001.

146. Ibid., p. 13.

147. Ibid., p. 14.

148. Ibid., p. 15.

149. Ibid.

150. Ibid., p. 16.

151. Ibid.

152. Ibid.

153. Ibid., p. 17.

154. Ibid.

155. Ibid.

156. Ibid.

157. Ibid.

158. Ibid., p. 18.

159. Ibid., p. 17.

160. Ibid.

161. Ibid., p. 18.

162. Ibid.

163. Wang Yan, Xia Shufang, and Zhang Jiangping, "Survey and Analysis on the Police Values at Gaochun County," *Journal of Jiangsu Police Officer College*, 85, 150–165, 2002.

164. Gaochun County (Gāochún Xiàn, 高淳县) is administered by Nanjing in Jiangsu. "Gaochun is a county under the jurisdiction of Nanjing, with a driving distance about two hours to the city, the capital of Jiangsu Province. As a satellite city, Gaochun is under the jurisdiction of Nanjing, bordering two neighbors, Lishui and Liyang counties, on the north and east, and Wuhu City of Anhui Province on the southwest. Gaochun does not directly border the Nanjing metropolitan area. Gaochun County has a physical land mass of around 802 square kilometers, in which two thirds plus are the land and the third is water surface. Its population is around half million." (http://www.jiangsu.net/city/city.php?name=gaochun)

165. Ivan Y. Sun, Michael A. Cretacci, Yuning Wu, and Cheng Jin, "Chinese Police Cadets' Attitudes toward Police Role and Work," *Policing: An International Journal of Police Strategies & Management*, 32(4), 758–780, 2009.

166. Mark MacKinnon, "A Police State without TP," *Globe and Mail*, October 18, 2009. "According to the Shanghai Oriental Morning Post, 47.2 per cent of all the new drivers they surveyed paid a bribe (the average price was 502 yuan, or about $75) to get their licenses rather than take the official drivers' test."

167. "Heard on the Web: Beijing Police Abandons 'Quota,'" *China Law and Governance Review*, December, 2006 (http://www.chinareview.info/pages/chat.htm).

168. Ibid.

169. Cao Li, "Driver Cuts Finger to Protest 'Police Trap,'" *China Daily*, October 20, 2009.

170. "Police Criticized in Bloody Nanjing Drunk Driving Accident," *chinaSMACK*, July 4, 2009. "Nanjing Jiangning 6/30 traffic accident, may I ask those police on duty: Could you have given those dead the slightest bit of respect?!" For the original Chinese version and comments, many against the TP, see http://www.tianya.cn/publicforum/content/free/1/1608708.shtml.
171. Ibid.
172. One of the limitations of the research design is that it conceptualizes "job satisfaction" ("*gongzuo chengjiu*") in an open-ended way to capture "self-actualization" and/or a "sense of achievement." Since a person, especially the police, can gain "job satisfaction" in many ways—internal vs. external, material vs. psychological, mission-oriented or job-oriented—it is very difficult to pinpoint the sources of satisfaction, as in traffic police vs. the criminal investigation division.
173. In fact, this is not Chinese criminal police problem but is a general problem with all police worldwide.
174. William K. Muir, Jr., *Streetcorner Politicians*, University of Chicago Press, Chicago, 1977.
175. Bradly W. Reed, *Talons and Teeth: County Clerks and Runners in the Qing Dynasty*, Stanford University Press, Stanford, CT, 2000.
176. Ma Zhenhuan, "Study Identifies Changing Work Priorities of Post-80s in China," *China Daily*, June 23, 2010.
177. "Police Overworked, Bad Health," *China Daily*, March 14, 2005. "A recent health check among 5,907 public security officials in Harbin in northeast China's Heilongjiang Province revealed that more than 65 percent of the city's police officers are not in a good condition. High cholesterol levels, fatty livers, high blood pressure, diabetes and coronary heart disease are the top culprits....[A]nother police officer in the city died, 49-year-old Du Chenghua, deputy head of Chongqing Criminal Police. The local hospital said he passed away from liver failure and a lung infection resulting from overwork."
178. "Chongqing Police Recruited 1250 Police Officers, with Nearly 80% Having Ph.D.s or Master's Degrees," *Chongqing Evening News*, September 18, 2010 (http://news.sohu.com/20100918/n275025868.shtml).
179. See "How Young People Regard Policing," p. 177 in Chapter 4 of this text.
180. Iain Walker and Heather J. Smith, *Relative Deprivation: Specification, Development, and Integration*, Cambridge University Press, Cambridge, UK, 2001.
181. See Table 4.8, p. 191 in Chapter 4 of this text.
182. According to the public record, the blogger was a male born on August 20, 1982, unmarried, from Hebei Provincial, Baoding County.
183. The blogger graduated from a local university with a non-police degree. "I am a graduate of local university. I did not know anything about policing, but I wanted to be a criminal police."
184. Ibid.
185. "Chongqing Hails Death for Biggest Fish," *China Daily*, April 15, 2010. Wen Qiang, former deputy police chief of Southwest China's Chongqing municipality PSB, was sentenced to death for protecting five organized gangs, rape, property scams, and corruption, including accepting bribes for promotions.
186. "On my first day here I asked my mentor: 'Where is the future in this business?' My mentor smiled and said: 'There is no future.'"
187. "He also said that I should resolve to work hard here, at least for ten years! As an example, there are a number of senior police who have worked over ten years here."
188. "Other students who have been appointed, they have the same education background as I do, they were assigned to police bureau, division office, because they were connected."
189. "There were a number of police school graduates who entered with me. Their jobs are the same as mine. That being the case, this job could be filled by high school students. Yet I have to work at this after seven years of master school. Well. No energy (motivation)!"
190. "Our mentor solved a highway robbery case years before, after hiding in the snow for 23 days. He was awarded a second-class honor. But when it comes time for reassignment, he was not listed for promotion."

191. "However high your educational background and top academic qualifications, the leaders basically would not treasure you. If you are not a dummy at work, the boss above has a body count, then they are considered good officials in office, with a bright future."

192. "Five Prohibitions for University Police Officers Working at the Basic Level," *Northern Police* [*Nanguo Jingcha*], October 10, 2010 (http://www.ngjc.com/thread-143942-1-2.html).

193. Zhang Daqqun, "Investigation into Implementation of Law at the Basic Level" ["*Jiceng gongan ganjing jifa zhuankuan de tiaolcha*"], *Gongan Yanjiu*, 24, 1992.

194. Janet Chan, *Changing Police Culture: Policing in a Multicultural Society*, Cambridge University Press, Cambridge, UK, 1997.

195. Cao Feng, "Some Reflection on Construction of Contemporary Police Culture" ["*Dui dangqian gongan wenhua jianshe de ji dian sijkou*"], *Journal of Chinese People's Public Security University* (*PSU Journal*), 108, 149–152, 2004.

196. Ibid., p. 149.

197. Ibid., p. 150.

198. The Twelfth Meeting of the National Police [*Di shier ci quan guo gongan hui yi*] was held on November 20, 2003, in Beijing. The meeting was devoted to implementation of the policies of the Third Plenum of the Plenary Session of the 16th Central Committee of the Communist Party of China, specifically "Decision regarding Progressively Strengthening and Improving Public Security Work" ("*Zhonggong zhongyang guanyu jinyibu jiaqiang he gaijin gongan gongzuo de jueding*"). For a brief summary of the meeting, see "*Jingwu changshi—Lijie gonan huiyi*," *China Police Net* (*Zhongguo jingcha wang*), April 26, 2004 (http://www.cpd.com.cn/gb/jwcs/2004-04/26/content_290932.htm).

199. The Party line for constructing the new police in the reform era is captured by three slogans: (1) constructing police with politics (*zhengzhi jiangjing*), (2) educate police with culture (*wenhua yujing*), and (3) strengthen police with science and technology (*keji qiangjing*).

200. "Put Effort into Creating Civil and Militaristic New People's Police" ["*Zhuoli da zuo wenwu jianbi xinminjing*"], *People's Police*, 11, 2004 (http://www.cpd.com.cn/gb/newspaper/2004-06/22/content_308846.htm). "What is police culture?" ("*Gongan wenhua daodi shi shenmou*?") "What is its utility?" ("*Tade zuoyong zai nanli*?") "How can it be made as effective as it should be?" (*Yinggai zeme cainengyou xiaoying*?")

201. "The strength of culture" ["*Wenhua liang*"], *People's Police*, 11, 2004 (http://www.cpd.com.cn/gb/newspaper/2004-06/22/content_308845.htm). The editor of the *People's Police* questions the wisdom and effectiveness of investing billions of dollars to build a railroad to bring prosperity to economically deprived regions of the country, without at the same time changing the backward culture and poor mentality of the people.

202. "Put Effort into Creating Civil and Militaristic New People's Police" ["*Zhuoli da zuo wenwu jianbi xinminjing*"], *People's Police*, 11, 2004 (http://www.cpd.com.cn/gb/newspaper/2004-06/22/content_308846.htm).

203. "What Is Missing on the College Campus?" ["*Xiao yuan li quexiao shenme*?"], *China Police Net* [*Zhongguo jingcha wang*], May 13, 2004 (http://www.cpd.com.cn/gb/newspaper/2004-05/13/content_295055.htm).

204. For a map of Hebei, see http://www.maps-of-china.com/hubei-s-ow.shtml.

205. For a map of Fujian Province and location of Fuzhou municipality, see http://www.maps-of-china.com/fujian-s-ow.shtml.

206. For a map of Shanghai, see http://www.maps-of-china.com/shanghai-s-ow.shtml.

207. "Put Effort into Creating Civil and Militaristic New People's Police" ["*Zhuoli da zuo wenwu jianbi xinminjing*"], *People's Police*, 11, 2004 (http://www.cpd.com.cn/gb/newspaper/2004-06/22/content_308846.htm).

208. The Chinese public avoids going to the government offices at all costs: "*Sheng bu ru guo men, si bu ru diyu*" ("Do not enter the government office alive nor enter hell after death"). *Guanmen* ("government office"), in imperial China referred to as *yamen* ("magistrate office") at the local level, used criminal law and punishment to compel actions, enforce orders, and settle disputes.

209. "Highbrow Songs Also Find Mass Following" ["*Qugao hezhe ya zhong*"], *China Police Net* [*Zhongguo jingcha wang*], June 14, 2004 (http://www.cpd.com.cn/gb/newspaper/2004-06/15/content_306280.htm). Note: *Qugao hezhe ya zhong* is used here to contrast with conventional wisdom expressed in an adage in China that "highbrow has no mass following" ("*Qu Gao he guo*"). See Jingrong Wu, *The Pinying Chinese-English Dictionary*, The Commercial Press, Hong Kong, 1995.

210. Du Pufeng, "Humanizing Law Enforcement: Improving on Conceptual Transformation and Practice" ["*Renxinghua zhifa: linian zhuangbian yu shijian gaijing*"], *Journal of Chinese People's Public Security University* (*PSU Journal*), 108, 144–148, 2004.

211. Ibid.

212. *Full Text of Jiang Zemin's Report at the 16th Party Congress*. Part II. *Implement the Important Thought of Three Represents in an All-Round Way* (http://www.china.org.cn/english/features/49007.htm). Persistent implementation of the "Three Represents" is the foundation for building our Party, the cornerstone for its governance, and the source of its strength.

213. "China to Put 'Three Represents' into Constitution," *Xinhua News Agency*, December 22, 2003 (http://www.china.org.cn/english/zhuanti/3represents/83062.htm). For discussion of its meaning and significance, see (a) M. Ulric Killion, "The Three Represents and China's Constitution: Presaging Cultural Relativistic Asian Regionalism," *International Trade Law Journal*, 14, 2004. (b) Jia Hepeng, "Three Represents Campaign: Reform the Party or Indoctrinate the Capitalist," *Cato Journal*, 24(3), 261–275, 2004 (http://www.cato.org/pubs/journal/cj24n3/cj24n3-5.pdf).

214. Jingrong Wu, *The Pinying Chinese-English Dictionary*, The Commercial Press, Hong Kong, 1995.

215. Ibid.

216. Du Pufeng, "Humanizing Law Enforcement: Improving on Conceptual Transformation and Practice" ["*Renxinghua zhifa: linian zhuangbian yu shijian gaijing*"], *Journal of Chinese People's Public Security University* (*PSU Journal*), 108, 144, 2004.

217. China has not accepted human rights as absolute, universal, stand-alone rights.

218. The political scientists at the Hoover Institution, Stanford University (*China Leadership Monitor*) have been at the forefront in tracing Chinese political leadership changes and their impact on national policy leadership. In this regard, Cheng Li's work is particularly influential and instructive on methods and findings.

219. (a) See section on "Politics" in Chapter 1 of this book. (b) Fu Hualing, "Zhou Yongkang and Recent Police Reform in China," *Australian and New Zealand Journal of Criminology*, 38(2), 241–253, 2005.

220. See "A Sample Survey," pp. 85–88, and "Culture," pp. 103–112.

221. See section on "Politics" in Chapter 1 of this book.

222. Wang Yan, Xia Shufang, and Zhang Jiangping, "Survey and Analysis on the Police Values at Gaochun County," *Journal of Jiangsu Police Officer College*, 85, 150–165, 2002.

223. See "Development of Public Security Studies," pp. 73–74, and "Research Output, Quality, and Utility," pp. 74–75.

224. See earlier section on "Early Police (Empirical) Research" in this chapter.

225. (a) Lena Y. Zhong, *Communities, Crime and Social Capital in Contemporary China*, Willan Publishing, Devon, U.K., 2009. (b) Mengyan Dai, "Policing in the People's Republic of China: A Review of Recent Literature," *Crime, Law and Social Change*, 50(3), 211–227, 2008.

226. Kam C. Wong, *Chinese Policing: History and Reform*, Peter Lang, New York, 2009, Chapter 1.

227. Olivia Yu and Zhang, Lening, "The Under-Recording of Crime by Police in China: A Case Study," *Policing: An International Journal of Police Strategies & Management*, 22(3), 252–264, 1999.

228. See *Police Post Work Magazine* database (Note 54).

229. "Congressional-Executive Commission on China Releases 2010 Annual Report on Human Rights and the Rule of Law in China," *Congressional-Executive Commission on China Newsletter*, October 15, 2010 (http://www.cecc.gov/pages/annualRpt/annualRpt10/index.php).

230. Ji Weiwei, "Metrological [*sic*] Analysis of Essays Published by the Jiangsu Public Security College" ["*Jiangsu gongan zhuanke xuexiao xuebao*"], *Journal of Jiangsu Police Officer College*, 18(1), 171–180, 2003.

231. Wang Yan, Xia Shufang, and Zhang Jiangping, "Survey and Analysis on the Police Values at Gaochun County," *Journal of Jiangsu Police Officer College*, 85, 150–165, 2002.

232. Zhou Chengshan, "On Basic Feature and Its Embodiment of Editing Thought, *Journal of Chinese People's Public Security University* (*PSU Journal*), 74, 109, 1999.

233. Mao Tse-tung, "23. Investigation and Study," in *Quotations from Mao Tse-tung*, Peking Foreign Languages Press, Peking, 1966 (http://www.marxists.org/reference/archive/mao/works/redbook/ch23.htm).

234. Jeff Ferrell, "Kill Method: A Provocation," *Journal of Theoretical and Philosophical. Criminology*, 1(1), 2009 (http://www.google.com/search?q=Jeff+Ferrell.+Kill+the+Methd&ie=utf-8&oe=utf-8&aq=t&rls=org.mozilla:en-US:official&client=firefox-a).

Legitimacy Crisis

4

Despite their suffering under Mao, many Chinese remembered that era as a time when they could leave their front doors and bicycles unlocked...when officials were honest.

Nathan and Shi (1996)[1]

The social order is chaotic, and there is no longer any faith.

Cao (2000)[2]

There exists no unifying ideology around which the nation can rally. The Communist Party—not to mention communism—is bankrupt in the eyes of many Chinese. It is a corpse...when revolutionary legitimacy disintegrates, power breaks down and factionalizes.

Brick (1989)[3]

The Chinese Communist Party can't do without its forefather, but simply reeling off the fore-father's words all the time won't do either.

Huang (2002)[4]

Introduction[5]

As the People's Republic of China (PRC) police move into the fourth decade of reform (since 1979), they continue to be confronted by many old problems (e.g., corruption, abuse of powers) and still more new challenges (e.g., refurbishing an old image, forging a new identity). One of the most fundamental problems is that of modifying traditional communist policing in light of the quickly changing social conditions and political realities. Ideologically, how can the spirit of Lei Feng be modernized to fit with the youthful aspirations of today?[6] Culturally, how can the police culture be changed to make it more service oriented and market driven?[7] Organizationally, how can the mission, role, and function of police be redefined and realigned to cater to the market economy?[8] Professionally, how can police knowledge be upgraded to meet new challenges?[9] Operationally, how can the police be encouraged to be responsive to local leadership[10] and serve local economic needs[11] while at the same time following directives of the central command and promoting legal objectives?[12] Of all the police reform challenges, sustainability is of the greatest concern and the most difficult to deal with. The task at hand is to secure favorable conditions of sustainable growth amidst permanent social disorganization and radical economic dislocations, within the Ministry of Public Security (MPS) and in the society.[13]

This chapter looks at issues regarding the sustainability of police reform in light of rising public discontent and fading police legitimacy. It discusses the problem of sustainable growth in China, including approaches to dealing with the mismatch between public expectations and Party performance, manifested as social and political discontent. It also addresses police performance in China during the reform which has been stymied by critical bottlenecks in ideas, culture, organization, and thinking. A case study illustrates public thinking and feeling with regard to government corruption; it advances the thesis that it is impossible to understand the police legitimacy crisis without first exploring public perceptions regarding government corruption. Although the public's attitudes toward corruption are rather bleak, they do not suggest the demise of the Party or fall of the government, as some might suggest (or a few wish). The chapter then moves on to define the concepts of police authority and legitimacy and suggests that a looming legitimacy crisis is in the making. The discussion looks for various signs and evidence of a decline in police legitimacy in the reform era. The conclusion suggests another way to look at dissent, resistance, and rebellion against the police—not as loss of legitimacy, but as a mismatch of values between police and various segments of society, such as the post-1980s generations.

Sustainability Problem

In 2007, at the 17th Party Congress, President Hu Jintao sounded the alarm regarding sustainable growth for the nation:

> While recognizing our achievements, we must be well aware that they still fall short of the expectations of the people and that there are still quite a few difficulties and problems on our way forward. The outstanding ones include the following: Our economic growth is realized at an excessively high cost....There are still many problems affecting people's immediate interests in areas such as...administration of justice and public order; and some low-income people lead a rather difficult life. More efforts are needed to promote ideological and ethical progress. The governance capability of the Party falls somewhat short of the need to deal with the new situation and tasks. In-depth investigations and studies have yet to be conducted on some major practical issues related to reform, development, and stability. Some primary Party organizations are weak and lax. A small number of Party cadres are not honest and upright, their formalism and bureaucratism are quite conspicuous, and extravagance, waste, corruption, and other undesirable behavior are still serious problems with them. We must pay close attention to these problems and continue our efforts to solve them.[14]

President Hu addressed the problem of rising expectations of the people and declining performance by the government, brought about by excessive economic growth and gradual erosion of governance capacity. Specifically, with respect to justice administration, President Hu identified the following issues: (1) people were having difficulty with the administration of justice and public order, (2) society was facing the challenges of development and maintaining stability, and (3) the public was displeased with the work style of Party cadres, including their perceived dishonesty, lack of integrity, formalism, bureaucratism, extravagance, waste, and corruption, among other undesirable behaviors. A confidence crisis was looming that could derail the reform and destabilize the nation.

Issues with Police Sustainability

In 2001, the Shanxi Public Security Bureau and others around the nation raised the issue of sustainable police development in the 21st century. They were facing increased disparity between the Chinese police capacity and social developmental needs, including how to reconcile traditional policing with the free market and open society. Sustainability issues arise whenever traditional police structures, processes, cultures, and work styles are incompatible with, and at times resistant to, police reform and social progress such that police operations and development are hindered.[15] As a result, the police in China are encountering a number of bottlenecks, or obstacles.[16]

Command, Control, and Coordination Bottleneck

In theory, the Ministry of Public Security is organized like the military. It has a unified chain of command. Police officers are subject to strict discipline, and they report only to supervisors above. In practice, however, the police are required to answer to two bosses: vertically (professionally) to the MPS and horizontally (politically) to the local Party political–legal committee. In reality, the MPS has little vertical (*tiao*) control over local (*qu*) police operations, particularly with respect to funding, appointments, promotions, and administration. Effectively, this means that no national central command and control system exists. When police are funded by local government and supervised by the grassroots community, provincialism dominates and localism prevails. Such an organizational structure causes disparate police development; for example, the rich coastal cities (e.g., Shenzhen, Hainan) have experienced faster reform than interior cities (e.g., Chengdu, Kunmin), and advanced urban centers (e.g., Beijing, Shanghai) are administered differently than rural areas. The MPS has little control over police operational standards. Furthermore, administratively, police operations are not well integrated with or coordinated horizontally between different police functions and units. Police patrol units do not assist in criminal investigations. Traffic police do not respond to 110 emergency calls. Shenzhen, for example, seldom cooperates with Hong Kong police. Such silo effects impact the efficiency and effectiveness of police operations,[17] a case in point being that a comprehensive crime control network is not feasible if all of the elements of police functions do not cooperate.

Police Quality Bottleneck

There is a mismatch between police capacity (resources, training, competence) and police performance (output, outcome, quality). Police are not well prepared for their jobs. The 21st-century market economy requires specialized knowledge, professional expertise, and technical skills in the fields of finance, accounting, computers, and electronics, but the police are not able to recruit and retain skilled workers who are in great demand elsewhere. Currently, police recruiting and in-service training are not geared toward turning out specialized, technical professionals. Police colleges are designed to train generalists, not professionals or specialists.[18]

Chain-of-Command Bottleneck

Traditionally, the chain of command is tall and centralized. Because the police are a quasi-military organization, officers are trained to obey and execute orders; in fact, many police officers, especially those in high ranks, are retired military personnel. As Party cadres, officers are expected to follow Party policy and guidelines, without protest. Promotions and rewards are based on loyalty to the organization, obedience to superiors, and following instructions. Line officers must deal with many overlapping and conflicting lines of super-vision. The current organizational setup severely restricts efficient and effective police deployment and operations.[19]

Traditional Thinking Bottleneck

Currently, most police work is dependent on traditional modes of thinking and old ways of doing things. Criminal investigation is based on crime scene inspection, case file analysis, and suspect interrogation, with little individualized investigation of suspects, systematic examination of crime scenes, or comprehensive gathering of evidence from crime scenes. Crime control is based on repeated strike campaigns, not consistent crime prevention efforts. Crime campaigns are carried out indiscriminately without regard to special local conditions, rural vs. urban setting, or particular crime characteristics (e.g., white-collar vs. street crime).[20] The solution to such bottleneck problems mentioned above is for police reformers to think and act creatively, integratively, and holistically in a mission-driven, problem-oriented, forward-looking way.[21] Failing that, police capacity and performance are lagging further and further behind economic and social reform needs, generating a confidence crisis in turn.

Audit Storm: Voices of Discontent

Study of the police legitimacy crisis requires an understanding of the larger social context that gives rises to public mistrust and discontent. The single most important reason for public distrust of the Communist Party and Chinese government (including the police) is perhaps the public's perception of the organization's moral bankruptcy. The following study, for the first time, documents how Chinese people think and feel about corruption in China, and in the process it registers the people's discontent and distrust in the govern-ment in their own words.

Background

On June 23, 2004, the China National Audit Office (CNAO)[22] stunned the nation with the submission of "Regarding 2003 Audit Working Report on the Implementation of the 2002 Central Budget and the Revenue and Expenditure of Other Public Funds" (hereinafter referred to as the Audit Report)[23] to the National People's Congress Standing Committee (NPCSC) of the People's Republic of China (PRC). The Audit Report rendered an in-depth accounting of the nation's budgetary health.[24]

The Audit Report uncovered extensive financial improprieties, massive accounting frauds, and egregious budgetary irregularities among 41 of the 55 audited ministries and commissions under the State Council, involving a total of 1.42 billion yuan (US$171.56 million).[25] Implicated organizations included the General Administration of the Sports/Beijing Organizing Committee for the Games of the XXIX Olympiad (BOCOG),[26] State Power Corporation of China,[27] Yangtze Water Resources Commission,[28] Industrial and Commercial Bank of China (ICBC),[29] and the Ministry of Education.[30] At the Ministry of Education, for example, some of the irregularities and improprieties included:

- *Misuse of authority*—From 2001 to 2002, Oriental College Town Development, Inc., illegally signed contracts with five village committees in Langfang, Hebei Province, and in the Tongzhou district in Beijing to lease farmers' collective lands to build five golf courses (5728 acres of cultivated land).
- *Securing of risky loans*—Loans for the construction of college towns were not intended to be made and were unlikely to be repaid. For example, 12 loan projects in the Xianling and Jiangning districts of Nanjing and in the Xinxiao district in Pukou, amounting to 2.7 billion yuan (US$326 million), were in default. The scheduled repayment amount surpassed the annual income of lenders by approximately 40 to 80%.
- *Heavy and growing debt burden*—The audit investigated the secondary education funds of 17 provinces and 50 counties and "discovered that, at the end of 2001, secondary school debts from 50 provinces totaled 2.4 billion yuan (US$289.8 million). By the end of 2002, it had increased 30 percent to 3.1 billion yuan (US$374.3 million). Surprisingly, in just half a year, by the end of June 2003, this number had increased another 25.7 percent, reaching a total of 3.9 billion yuan (US$470.9 million)."
- *Collection of excessive and illegal fees*—This problem was found in 45 of the 50 audited counties. In 2001, 413 million yuan (US$49.9 million) in illegal fees were collected.
- *Diversion of fund to inappropriate use*—Since 1999, the education board had appropriated 13.56 million yuan (US$1.6 million) from textbook funds for their personal expenses. They also took 11.03 million yuan (US$1.3 million) for their personal use and 25.2 million yuan (US$3 million) for entertainment, etc.

With regard to the State Power Corporation of China, the CNAO found irregularities with the disposition of 21.14 billion yuan of state funds, including a loss of 7.84 billion yuan due to unauthorized or irregular decision making. Another 7.8 billion yuan represented deliberate distortion of profits and losses (fraud), a 4.5 billion yuan loss of state-owned assets was revealed, and a 1 billion yuan loss could be attributed to economic crimes by leaders.

The Audit Report outlined five main problem areas:[31]

1. Fraud, embezzlement, and misuse of government funds allocated to disaster relief, education, the Olympics, and treasury bonds by organizations of both the central and local governments
2. Financial irregularities at banks resulting from inadequate supervision
3. Tax irregularities, with some tax bureaus failing to collect taxes or failing to suspend or terminate levies when so ordered
4. Illegal requisitioning of land for development, with some local governments abusing authority in order to obtain profits
5. Misrepresentation and fraud by private enterprises to obtain bank loans

Although the Audit Report did not single out the police as a corrupted institution, in fact many of the problems identified above could not have arisen without the active assistance or passive acquiescence of the police, such as collecting unapproved levies (item 3), acquisition of uncompensated land (item 4), and failure to investigate embezzlement (item 1). The Audit Report attracted immediate attention[32] and gave rise to intense debate among the Chinese media,[33] private citizens,[34] experts,[35] and scholars,[36] as well as critical comments internationally.[37] The controversy has come to be known in China as the "Audit Storm" (*Shenji fengbao*). Auditor-General Li Jinhua became an overnight anti-corruption hero.[38]

The discussion here addresses the thinking and feeling of Chinese Internet users on corruption in China. Specifically, it documents the comments and analyzes the content of online public reactions to three news articles regarding the Audit Storm and its investigation process (how was the CNAO audit conducted?), structure (who should conduct the audit?), and follow-up (what actions should be taken?).

Literature, Focus, and Methods

Research Literature

Research literature into corruption in the PRC is numerous,[39] rich, varied, and multidisciplinary.[40] Technical reports and academic papers have variously looked into the nature and characteristics,[41] incidence and prevalence,[42] distribution and trends,[43] causes and remedies,[44] impact,[45] and implications of corruption.[46] A close examination of the literature shows that one area of corruption studies has not been adequately researched—online public opinion regarding corruption. Public opinion research, to the extent that it exists at all, is generally comprised of attitudinal surveys of how people feel about corruption in global terms, not in their own words or with regard to specific issues, particular contexts, or concrete situations, such as the Audit Storm. No research to date has been conducted that analyzes the reactions of "netizens" to anti-corruption efforts reported in the news.[47] As a result, few data and little knowledge regarding public reactions to corruption issues are available. Today, public discontent toward corruption is often assumed, but not demonstrated or documented. This is a first attempt to fill this vital literature gap.

Research Focus

This discussion is an investigation into the Chinese people's reactions to and reception (i.e., thinking and feeling) of corruption, especially how they view Audit Storm issues. *Reaction* refers to opinion and judgment, and *reception* refers to feeling and understanding. "Feeling and understanding" provide the necessary foundation and point of departure for "opinion and judgment," which are derived from and thus reflect upon the underlying "feeling and understanding." *Feeling* can be defined as an emotional response to certain facts or arguments. Feeling can be observed in the use of such emotionally laden statements as, "Kill the corrupted officials!" *Understanding* can be defined as comprehension with reasoning. Understanding can be observed in the interpretation and analysis of facts and data, with the help of presuppositions; for example, one might ask, "How can a state employee be allowed to misappropriate public money for private use?" *Opinion* and *judgment* can be defined as taking a position on issues based on feeling or reasoning. They can be observed by acceptance or rejection of an argument—for example, "There is hope for China." The data for this research came from a systematic gathering of online comments in 2004, right after the Audit Storm broke. This method of research is one of content analysis for themes and concepts.

Research Methods

To assess the public reception of and reaction to various issues presented by the Audit Storm and related events (e.g., Beijing Audit Report),[48] I familiarized myself with the reach and focus, contour and context, and content and style of Audit Storm online comments by reading all of the 54,540 online comments that have been posted at the website sohu.com[49] regarding various aspects of the PRC government audit at the national and local levels. This provided an overview of the issues and a personal "feel" and "touch" for the data that allowed me to put specific comments into context. This research deals with the reception of and reaction to three newspaper postings regarding the Audit Storm and its investigation process (how was the CNAO audit conducted?), structure (who should conduct the audit?), and follow-up (what actions should be taken?).

When I read the comments, I tried to put myself in the shoes of the commentators, who were generally young, liberal, and educated,[50] and looked for the range of issues raised and kinds of arguments made. In addition to trying to ascertain the tone, texture, style, and manner of the discourse,[51] I also tried to identify the main themes and repeated ideas discussed in this grassroots domain: How diverse and strong were the public's reactions? What was the foundation or basis of the public's reactions? What was the quality of the debate? In the end, I was interested in deciphering the multiple individual attitudes and collective dispositions toward the Audit Storm, as interpreted within historical, political, social, and cultural contexts.[52]

Discourse analysis, as distinguished from linguistic analysis,[53] studies the meaning of discourse "beyond the sentence"—that is, language in context (historical, political, social, and cultural). I was primarily interested in uncovering the discourse framework identifying the political relationships between the people and their government (e.g., offering vs. demanding, solidarity vs. distance, dominance vs. subordination) and the value orientation of the people regarding government corruption policies and actions. This approach allowed me to investigate to what extent and in what ways the people were expressing their discontent with and mistrust of the Party and government.

Research Dataset

The dataset is comprised of the opinions and comments posted on the sohu.com discussion forum (*wangyou pinglun*). The responses were to three news items posted there that originated from other sources. These news items were organized around the theme of the Audit Storm, under the title of "Special Topic: Standing Committee of the NPC Meeting, Ministry of Finance, Audit Office Audit Work Report" ("*Zhuanti: Renda changweihui huiyi, caizhengbu shenjichu gongzuo baogao*"). The "Special Topic" discussion led with the story, "Former National Electricity Company Leaders' Erroneous Policy Decision Led to Serious Losses."[54] This news item reported that the 2003 CNAO Audit Report revealed that the leadership and executives of the State Power Corporation of China had squandered 3.28 billion yuan as a result of erroneous policies (*zhengce shiwu*) and illegal actions, including: (1) acting as a guarantor for the Beijing Wei Ke Rui Company (not a legal entity) between 1994 and 1996, which led to a loss in principle and interest of 1.12 billion yuan; (2) under-reporting profits of 3.2 billion yuan in 2003 and 7.8 billion yuan between 1998 and 2004; and (3) having unaccounted funds amounting to 4.5 billion yuan. In addition, 12 cases of economic crime amounting to 1 billion yuan were identified; these included embezzlement and fraud in the amount of 83 million yuan by the corporation's general manager and his family. This news item captured the essence of the CNAO Audit Report (pervasive corruption and gross abuses of power resulting in huge losses of state capital and assets) and tone (pointed criticism of the wrongdoings). The article attracted voluminous,[55] strong, and diverse comments, with the first saying, "Need to conduct [audit] vigorously," and calling for continued efforts to root out corruption and abuses.[56]

The comments on the Audit Storm were of various lengths. The length of the comments varied, but most were from one to three lines. One line (10 words or less) was the norm, and one or two words was not uncommon. The longer comments (about 10%) ranged from 4 to 8 lines. Few went beyond 12 lines. The style of comments varied, from emotional outbursts to cynical rebukes to enthusiastic support to rational discussion. Most of them were negative and critical, and all of them were in one way or another supportive of the audit, the auditors, and the national leaders. The intensity and length of comments eventually leveled off after June 30, the day that the Audit Storm story was posted on sohu.com, as evidenced by the fact that the number of messages declined, the tone became less visceral, the discourse more reflective, the reactions more nuanced, and the demands less punitive. It was also clear that after about the first 50 to 100 comments, the diversity and richness of the them were beginning to wane. I have thus paid more attention to the first 50 comments.

Online Reactions

This research sought to capture Internet users' reactions to three Audit Storm news stories, their thinking and feeling on the three major issues of process, structure, and outcome.

Audit Process

Auditor-General Li Jinhua submitted a report to the NPC about auditing problems in China. When the China National Audit Office looked into Yangtze River engineering projects in Wuhan, the audit team uncovered a conspiracy to inflate budgets, cut costs, and compromise quality for a key levee project, resulting in a deficiency of 80 million yuan.[57] In a *Zhongguo qingnian bao* report, the audit team was asked to reveal their secrets of success. The team members painstakingly reconstructed their investigation step by step, including, how irregularities in construction were uncovered[58] and how the vice-chairman of the board of directors of the China Electricity Council, Lin Kongxing, was prevented from fleeing the area.[59] The Wuhan auditors also related many of the difficulties encountered during the investigation, including:

- Lack of cooperation with regard to answering questions, producing data, and explaining the work done, in addition to supplying false or misleading information
- Intimidation of audit workers in every way possible and by all kinds of people (e.g., gangs)
- Attempted bribery of the auditors—for example, the team was offered 120,000 yuan to report 1 million yuan less of a loss in the audit report
- Interference with the investigation by corrupt officials through Party leaders, relatives, and friends
- Lack of resources for the CNAO team, such that the Wuhan auditors had to survive on a shoestring budget, augmented by personal outlays for meals and travel

This particular news item was chosen because it provided transparency to the process of investigation. It allowed the readers to react to how the audit was conducted, not just the results achieved. As of July 28, 2004, 351 comments had been posted. The first 100 comments were translated and analyzed.

Outcome of the Audit

One month after release of the Audit Storm, none of the leading Party cadres or senior government officials implicated by the audit had been held officially responsible or had resigned. The question raised and discussed online was, "What is public opinion toward the Audit Storm outcome?" This issue was later addressed in an article published on July 27, 2004. The title of the news item reflected discontentment, "Up Until the Present No Officials Resigned as a Result of Audit Storm: The Press Is Agitating for Four Not Quitting."[60] This article prominently referenced other articles from the *Study Times* (*Xuexi shibao*), published by the CPC Party School, that argued for speedy and resolute follow-up action to the Audit Report findings. Two articles published by the *Study Times* were relevant to the main themes arising out of discussions regarding the original sohu.com article: Fan Dula's "'Audit Storm' Is a Piece of Testing Stone" (hereafter referred to as CPC article 1)[61] and Fan Wei's "What Are People's Expectation after the Storm?" (hereafter referred to as CPC article 2).[62]

In CPC article 1, the author observed the total absence of serious follow-up action and meaningful accountability one month after submission of the Audit Report. Specifically, notwithstanding the shocking Audit Report to the NPC and the strong reaction by the public afterward, there was still no follow-up action, and no senior Party cadres or high government officials had been held responsible. In fact, there were more concerns expressed about the Auditor-General's well-being than the officials audited by him. Many attempts had been made to quibble (*jiaobian*), negotiate (*jiaoshe*), and plea for mercy (*suoqing*), but very little effort had been devoted to confronting the findings of the report and dealing with the issues raised.[63]

In CPC article 2, the author argued for keeping faith with Premier's Wen's "four not quitting" pledges intended to deal with national disasters: (1) not quitting until the cause of the incident has been thoroughly investigated, (2) not quitting until the people responsible have been dealt with properly, (3) not quitting until reform measures have been put into place, and (4) not quitting until lessons have been learned.[64] Fan Wei began by considering what had been achieved by the Audit Storm. He observed, as in CPC article 1, that, in spite of finding of problems and identifying those responsible, no officials had been punished in accordance with the "Regulations of the Communist Party of China on Disciplinary Action,"[65] and none had resigned, in keeping with the "Temporary Regulation on Party Leadership Cadre Resignation."[66] The author suggested that audited departments and officials should correct their mistakes and learn lessons from the audit. They should follow the admonitions of Wen regarding "four not quitting." This item was chosen because it speaks to the remedial actions taken after the Audit Report and the outcome of the Audit Storm. Its posting online allowed the public to address the CPC and government reaction to the Audit Report's procedures and findings of corruption. In essence, it tapped into how people think and feel about the government's response to corruption. To the Chinese, and particularly after Deng, actions can speak louder than words. The first comment to this article was made on July 27, 2004, the last on July 30, 2004. Of the 50 pages of responses the article generated (about 1000 entries), 100 items were randomly analyzed.

Local Audits

After publication of the Audit Report, there were calls for local audits. As proposed by the *Information Times*:

Realistically, the method adopted by the national auditors can set an example for local audit offices. It is more appropriate to say that local audit offices, in carrying out their duties, have made important contributions, but compared with such bold deeds and brave actions, we rarely hear about such large-scale exposure of economic problems at various constitutive government departments at different levels. Is that because there are fewer problems at the local vs. central level? Or is it the case that local audit offices dare not act and are afraid to do so? Looking at the facts of the many problems exposed by the CNAO, many of them involved the local levels. Why is it that the local audit offices have not discovered the same? It looks like local audit offices need to audit themselves, to see how far they have come when compared with CNAO. What should be done next time?[67]

This news item raised an important policy issue: Who has the right, duty, motivation, and capacity to conduct audits at the local level? More importantly, who would be most effective in rooting out local corruption? The debate shifted from being substantive (e.g., how people felt about corruption and countermeasures) to one of how anti-corruption campaigns should be conducted.

Analysis and Discussion of Online Comments

Feeling of Appreciation

The strongest feeling expressed was one of effusive appreciation: "Salutation to all audit workers. Salutation to all people of honesty and integrity." Unreserved admiration was also noted: "You people are really being responsible to history and society and personally." It is important to note that both of these comments spoke to the larger purpose of what the auditors were doing—making history, enriching society, and upholding principles of honesty and integrity. The comments generally reflected the idea that the audit comrades were doing a good job. More specifically, the auditors were appreciated for:

- *Standing up to power*—"Persevere until the end, do not back down in front of the strong, all people under heaven bow in respect, whole nation will remember you! Salutation!"
- *Defending good against evil*—"Comrades, keep on with the good work. The integrity of the country depends on you....Work hard, and do battle with the evil forces."
- *Making a difference*—"You work under extremely difficult situations, and yet you have handled these cases much better than anti-corruption bureaus, courts, and disciplinary commissions."
- *Saving a nation*—"Savior of the Chinese race."

The appreciation came from all quarters, including revolutionaries (e.g., "In the name of revolution, we salute the audit workers."), as well as ordinary citizens (e.g., "The common people support you!!!!").

Rendering of Support

This effusive appreciation was backed up with strong offers of support. These included donating more money for the investigation (e.g., "Whenever there is a need for money, just make an announcement on the web, and I will be first to donate."); demanding higher pay for the auditors (e.g., "The Audit Department should be paid well to instill integrity!!!");

offering political support for the cause (e.g., "Chinese love their country…there is no way to repay. We need to work together, before China can be awakened."); offering emotional support (e.g., "We support you with our lives."); and offering personal support (e.g., "Is the audit office hiring? I want to do it.").

Feeling of Hope

A sense of hope could be observed in such comments as "We have renewed hope!" and "Chinese now really have hope!" At its core, this hope rests on the belief that some officials are still honest and have integrity: "China still has upright people. The Chinese race now has hope." More importantly, the Audit Storm renewed people's hopes for the Party: "We firmly believe that the Party will solve problems involving itself in a proper manner.…We hope that the audit work quickly penetrates different areas, achieves systematic supervision, and uses the weight of the law to punish people who violate the law." In the end, the audit gave the people hope for a better China: "If the current [audit] work is carried out steadily, then our Chinese race will have hope! We might be able to establish an honest, fair, democratic, wealthy, and strong society. If so, our Chinese race will have hope of revival!" These comments clearly show that the Chinese people were sick and tired of corruption practices and policies of old and were yearning for a change. They were looking forward to the day when China would become strong and respected, but that day would not come until and unless the Party and government came clean. Much to the credit of Hu-Wen, the Audit Storm provided a sense of hope that had long eluded the people over the past several decades.

Feeling of Empowerment

With hope, the people also felt empowerment: "In reality, everything cannot escape the watchful eyes of the people." People were now confident that, "Whatever the corrupted officials do, we can all see and feel. They dare not." Justice will be done: "In fact, in this world, all matters are known in heaven, on earth, to you and me. If there is an investigation, no one can escape." Specifically, the people believed that they could clean up China: "Currently, some leaders' children use public funds to do business and earn illegal money. There is corruption. The country must deal with them; otherwise, they will escape to other countries to enjoy themselves! Need to close the door to hit the dog!"

Anxiety

Hope also gave rise to some anxiety. People were anxious that the Audit Storm would not last. Anxiety led naturally to skepticism (e.g., "A lot of empty talk."), and a few comments were critical (e.g., "Do not look at the advertisement, look at the effect."). Others cautioned against a rush to judgment (e.g., "We need to wait and see!!"). In the end, people were afraid that, judging from past experience, the bark might be worse than the bite—in other words, rhetoric over action: "We need to see results; we have witnessed a lot of big thunder and little rain." Many times in the past, Chinese leaders have failed to carry through with their anti-corruption campaigns, especially when senior leaders were implicated. One commenter observed that, "The investigation should go up and up, until it ends. How many times these investigation have ended without reason after discovering the culprits—this is the tragic story of China." As to corruption, people were alarmed by its magnitude (e.g., "Too scary to meet the eyes."), and they expressed hatred for the corrupted officials: "Kill! Kill! Kill!!!" and "Kill—no reason why these kinds of people should escape being killed."

What Needs to Be Done?

The public made a number of constructive comments and concrete suggestions, including the following:

- *More thorough investigations and more of them*—The public wanted the audit to go deeper (e.g., "Should investigate more deeply into the problem"), spread wider and grow stronger (e.g., "Strengthen the audit; this is being responsible to the people and country."), and continue until it was done (e.g., "Preserve until the end, do not back down.").
- *Institutionalization of the audit*—"It is necessary to institutionalize the effort; then and only then can our government live and rule forever."
- *Legalization of the audit*—"Only one Li Jinhua is not enough. Should establish a legal system. Only then can [the audit] be strengthened, deepened, lengthened!!!!"
- *More power to the auditors*—"Recommend that the Audit Department be given the power to arrest, similar to that of Hong Kong ICAC."
- *Greater publicity for the audit*—"Recommend the establishment of a CCTV audit channel."
- *More transparency to the auditing process*—"The more transparent the better."
- *More incentives for auditors*—"Should set up an audit incentive fund; such fund can be taken out of a portion of seized illegal money. The money can be used to reward audit personnel or to pay informers or witnesses and encourage more and more people to participate in this kind of activity and mobilize and speed up our nation's legalization process."
- *Greater supervision over audits*—"Who is to audit the auditors in their execution of audits!?"
- *More restrictions on potential suspects*—"There should be strict investigations into the nationality and foreign travels of sons, daughters, and relatives of high officials! They should openly register all their relatives."
- *Greater accounting for officials*—"Calling for public release of official family property to see whether income and expense are balanced."
- *Investigations into the audit hiring system*—"Why is it that the hiring system is not being audited? That is most fundamental."
- *Prevention over punishment*—"The focus of this line of work should be in prevention, not correction. This way we can stop future problems of this kind from happening. If we audit in the front end, there will not be that many more problems. This way we have achieved the purpose of supervision."
- *Pay attention to systemic small cases*—"When Comrade Jinhua investigates the big and important cases, he should also pay attention to the many small corruption cases that affect collective interests and propose some preventive measures to stop illegal billing. We look forward to reform at the roots."
- *Keep the investigation process secret*—"Is there a need to report on the details of the audit? Reporter comrades should only report the results; otherwise, the tactics and techniques will be revealed."

General Support for Audits
Comments revealed the expected outpouring of jubilation, adulation, and support: "Auditor-General Li Jinhua, you are great! On behalf of the billions of China workers and peasants I salute you! The National Audit office is finally on the right track. Director Li is setting a good example."

General Agreement on Principle
No one argued against public accountability, formal supervision, and an open audit: "All local audit departments should publish their reports; this is being responsible to the people, to the nation."

Necessity of Local Audits
Local audits were deemed necessary to expose and eliminate corruption: "Great! But investigations should get to the bottom of it all! We should learn from painful experiences, change our past painful mistakes. This is the way to make the Chinese civilization great again!" Conversely, national auditing, no matter how vigilant, was not perceived as being able to get to the root of the corruption problem: "China is so big, can we just rely on the National Audit Office? One must understand that basic level audits also represent the image of audit agencies." In fact many commentators argued that local audits were indispensable in the fight against corruption because there was more corruption at the local level: "Local audit is more important, because there are more and larger problems locally." Also, the local level is less open and more conducive to corruption: "I think local places are more dark [corrupt], making the use of more effort necessary." One commenter observed that, "To reduce or eliminate corruption, the National Audit Office must strengthen the leadership of the local audit offices, insist on yearly audits, elevate the powers of the local audit departments, so they are not controlled by local government as a result of dual leadership." Also offered was that, "Local audit organizations should learn from the National Audit Office."

Three Schools of Thought: Idealists, Pragmatists, and Realists
Ultimately, the debate turned on whether a local audit was a preferable or even feasible policy. In this regard, three schools of thoughts emerged: idealists, pragmatists, and realists.

Idealists   The idealists, while conceding difficulties, were of the opinion that local audits should and can be done. For the idealists, the reasons for local audits included the citizens' right to know and official accountability. Their sentiments were best captured by the following comment:

> The National Audit Office openly published financial usage conditions of various departments. This method is very good. The taxpayers and public have a right to know about the financial situation. This is conducive to supervising the work of functional departments. Local governments should also publicize audit reports routinely. Local governments should establish news reporting systems to answer questions of the media and the public.

Following are some more of the idealists' comments:

- *The audit is important for China*—"The National Audit Office methods have great meaning, with a deep and long impact."
- *There is a right to know*—"Local audits should publish annual audit reports that would allow us, the taxpayers, to know that the money paid was used by the people. There should be a right to know. I plea for increased perfection of the legal system."
- *We should do what is right*—"We should do what is required of us; we will not become soft."
- *Where there is a will, there is a way*—"If we have the support of the central government and the coordination of the people, nothing cannot be overcome!"
- *Li Jinhua is a good example*—"An era requires examples, society requires spirit… from their hearts to the central government. We learn about hope for the motherland. There is nothing impossible in this world. Only if we tried to conquer them."
- *China is changing, beginning at the top*—"From the revelation of last year's Audit Storm to this year's audit report, it is evident the nation's top management is becoming more transparent."
- *It is about the balance of power*—"It is all a matter of supervision, a problem with a balance of interests and balance of powers."

To introduce open local audits, the idealists suggested a number of reform measures:

- *Local auditors should report to the NPC*—"Audit should be managed directly by the NPC."
- *Local auditors should report to the State Council*—"Well said, should only report to State Council."
- *Local auditors should report to the Premier*—"Hope that audit offices resemble the Hong Kong ICAC and have more authority. Also, there should be vertical management, so they only obey the command of the Premier, not too many other intervening authorities."
- *Local auditors should report to a central administration*—"Local audits should be vertically led by a central audit office, cannot be controlled by local government."
- *Open local auditing should be required by law*—"Local audit agencies publishing audit report requires revision to the audit law."
- *NPC should strictly enforce the audit law*—"NPC is not only concerned with having law to follow, more importantly law should be obeyed."
- *Audit law must be detailed and sanctioned*—"NPC should immediately legislate that audit departments at every level report directly to the NPC annually about audit results of relevant departments. Failure to report would be considered a dereliction of duty. If the audit findings are not dealt with, officials will be sidelined."
- *Hold auditors responsible and accountable*—"Improve the quality of audit work, hold responsible auditors who become corrupt on audit problems found."
- *Learn from central administration*—"Local audit organization should learn from the National Audit Office."

Pragmatists The pragmatists' problems with local audits included a lack of independence and conflicts of interest:

The reason why the Audit Office dares to do hard battle and reveal so many problems with central ministries and commissions is because it is directly led by the Premier. But local audit agencies are attached to local governments. If the local government heads do not want news of their problems to spread, especially when such problems involve issues of local interests, the heads necessarily will downsize the problem from big to small to none. Local audit agencies are at best local governments' internal [supervision] organs. Their independence is relatively small. It is a difficult situation. There is a need to change the audit management structure.

The pragmatists accused the idealists of ignoring realities: "This fellow is either a dumb book person, or he is speaking blindly with open eyes. What are the conditions with China's audit situation right now, particularly with local audits?" Idealists were also accused of being crazy: "For the local audits to be published like the National Audit Report is a crazy person's dream talk." That did not stop some pragmatists from showing admiration and seeking reconciliation for the idealists' point of view, in spite of differences: "Though not feasible, still admire the person's courage." Specifically, the pragmatists pointed out that local auditors deserve credit in standing by idealistic principles. "To tell the truth, [being ethical] is the most basic requirement of a person, but it is so difficult for the government to achieve this." Also, "There are just too many questions. This is merely the beginning. Most local audits are just passing through. It is difficult to have an anti-corruption effect, but it is all a good thing and should be supported." The idealist should definitely be given credit for trying: "Local audit departments dare not publish annual audit reports! This is too difficult for them, please have mercy for them." The pragmatists pointed out several political, structural, and operational problems associated with local audits:

- *Politics*—"Local audits in the end are a bargain." However, "Local audit departments are protective umbrellas [for people in power] and instruments used to harm others who are against those in power. They should be led vertically by the CNAO and should not be controlled by local governments, otherwise they are just useless."
- *Dual control*—"The hiring and firing of local audit department heads reside in local hands, although business leadership is in the hands of upper-level audit departments, i.e., so called 'dual leadership.' Under this condition of personnel management authority remaining with the local, the idea of dual leadership has no real meaning. Subordinates to audit superiors, how can that be done?"
- *Local financing of operations and control of process*—"How dare the local audit [agencies] expose problems of local governments like the National Audit Office? Local audit offices depend on local financial support to eat!…The local audit only caters to the local government."
- *Administrative control*—"I am a local audit worker. If a local audit is to be published openly, the first thing to do is to have *tiaoguan* [management from above]. It is only after *tiaoguan* that we can strengthen audit independence. Think about it: Can you confront one who can support you and give you your rice bowl?"

Realists   The realists (cynics) viewed the audit process in general and local audits in particular as a big show: "Local audit departments are the ear of a deaf person—for show, only know how to sing songs of compliments!" Or, "For now, local audit departments are decorative vases." Put another way, "It is just a formality, going through the motions; this is the normal official work style of our government officials."

Lack of Follow-Up to the CNAO Audit Report

- *People were disappointed*—The people perceived more words than deeds, more promises than performance: "Loud thunder, noisy wind, heavy clouds, scattered rain." For example, they did not understand why "no responsible people were being held accountable" and wondered "who is protecting the corrupted officials?"
- *People were uncertain about what the future would bring*—"Only thunder strike, with no rain. When the thunder has passed, everything will be back to normal."
- *People were disillusioned and could no longer see any hope*—One dispirited commentator asked, "What happens after resignations or firings? The next lot of officials would be better? If one were to look at what happened to those being fired, I think they would still be corrupted. How many officials have been really punished, except for those who bite each other like a dog?"
- *The public felt misled*—"In reality, it is mild 'wind,' yet it is promoted as a 'storm,' and the Party is putting on a big PR show." Also, "Big thunder, little rain. Engaging in formalism." More pointedly: "If there is no followup with the audit, then it is best not to do it, so the public would not be frustrated. I do not understand why. Is it really the case that punishment stops with high officials?"
- *The public felt betrayed*—"A few days ago there seemed to be hope, but now it is again despair, with no hope. I have to cry."
- *As to coping, some chose to accept reality*—"You can scream and yell until your throat is sore, they do not mind." Others, not knowing what else to do, clung to hope: "It is better to have hope, even though we know that hope is like a building floating in the sky, but the only thing we have is hope."
- *Others found it wise to lower their expectations*—"Forget it, don't have high expectations! Do not know how Li Jinhua feels? We still support the Audit Office, who let us know the truth."

Finally, people became stoic: "Ultimately, all these will disappear into thin air, history tells us so, why be angry?" Others recommended simply to put up with it: "Tolerate."

What Did the People Want?

Regardless of how the public felt, they still had aspirations and dreams, legitimate wants and needs. Unfortunately, "absolute power corrupts," and the stronger the aspiration and grander the dream, the greater the damage done. One commenter noted that, "Firing a batch will make way for another batch. People keep coming, one after another. Should kill it at the roots." Also, "For social order, for the country's development, for the people's trust in the Party—government should act when they must, kill when they need to, cannot be too soft."

The public strongly demanded accountability: "The government has to be more forceful in showing its strength. Do not leave the common people with a bad name to be yelled at for generations to come!!!!" The public demanded accountability as a matter of right and because (according to Mao) the mass (*qunzhong*) knows right from wrong: "The people's eyes are clear sighted, please do not disappoint them!!!"

The people's democratic demands cannot be taken lightly nor avoided easily. They strongly requested the implementation of an accountability system, not simply chanting slogans. Ultimately, the public sought action, not words: "If no one deals with what the audit turned up, it's the same as having no audit." Loud slogans and empty promises were not considered to be harmless: "If we discover audit problems and take no action to resolve the same, it is best not to audit at all because a lot of people will get hurt in the process." Broken promises also challenged the Party's commitment to law: "Need to look at the audit carefully to determine whether the movement is for real, whether we are serious about establishing a rule of law system to hold officials accountable by law." In the process, broken promises threatened to harm the well-being of the people: "Being tolerant of and compassionate with corrupt officials, large and small, is cruelty to the people."

What Were Some of the People's Demands?

- *People wanted the truth*—"What is happening? We need to search for the truth."
- *People wanted quick action*—"Activities that hurt people's interests should be dealt with in a speedy fashion."
- *People wanted resignations*—"Firmly request that they resign."
- *People wanted retribution*—"Should not let bad people off the hook."
- *People wanted a measured and nuanced response*—"Reform is a slow and experimental process, should not take it too fast. Chinese reform is an entirely new exercise. Looking at Russia as an example, the most important things to take care of are maintaining a social stability, promoting a strong nation, creating wealth for the people, and establishing a rule of law for the country and society. Then and only then will China have hope."
- *People wanted solutions*—"Everything can be settled."

Why Did the Officials Not Resign?

- *Officials have privileges*—"Being a Chinese official has a lot of benefits." "It looks like being an official is to obtain benefits for oneself, if not would have resigned early." "Job position is hard to earn, how can one resign that easily?"
- *Officials (cadres) have no shame*—"Are you still behaving like a communist party member? You have done a lot of bad things and still feel no shame. Do you resemble a Chinese? Are you still a human being?" "Should the communist party members not make an example of themselves?"

Why Was There No Official Sanction?

The people identified several areas that posed problems:

- *Leadership*—"If most of the people do not confront the issues head on, and even if we ourselves do the wrong thing there is no shame, why should people resign?"
- *Conflict of interest*—"People will not use a knife to cut up their own kind. In a one-party state, it is natural that there is self-protection and no opportunities given to others. In between money and power, one has lost his self [identity, integrity]. Who can solve this problem?"
- *Rule of man*—The nation cannot function based on personality (Li Jinhua), rule of man (Party leader), or Party discipline (democratic centralism); for example, "Why is it that we need the leader to say something before we punish those illegal people?"
- *Politics*—"Is it true, as foreign scholars said, that contemporary China has regressed to the 20th century, where each force occupies an area, and the central government can do little to rule?"

- *Political culture*—"How far China can be compared with Western countries? This question is not too difficult. Chinese political culture still has a ways to go."
- *History*—"Punishment stops at the doorstep of the officials."
- *Philosophy*—"This is the compassion of our legal system."
- *Morality*—"Conscience is missing."
- *Practicality.* "This is a big country, and there is only one Li Jinhua. Don't set your hopes too high."
- *Work styles*—"Do not confront big ones, dealing with small ones has no meaning!!!"
- *Self-serving reasons*—"How to do deal with it? If one is not careful, one might get another big fish."
- *Prudence*—"If there is an arrest it implicates many; if no arrest is made it is hard to hold anyone accountable. If arrests are made, do not know how many people will be involved."[68]
- *Feasibility*—"Nearly all officials are corrupt; who are you going to audit?"
- *Bureaucracy*—"The audit storm shows that the audit office has done its best!! What problems the audit report revealed that got delayed are the problem of the Supervision Department!" "This society has operated abnormally if everything is turned over to the audit office. What is the use for the discipline commission and the courts?"
- *Supervision*—"Confronted with that much evidence, what did the procuratorate do? Do they not have a problem? If so, who is there to supervise?"

How Can One Be Successful in Fighting Corruption?

Two broad fundamental principles can be identified in the online comments. First, "Without the participation of the people, the anti-corruption struggle will not be won! We have to fight a people's struggle against corruption." More pointedly, "The rise and fall of a nation ultimately rest on the shoulders of each individual. Only the people can move history. The question here is who represents the people." Also, "Only the people's power cannot be resisted; however, who is really standing for the people?" This is where the second principle comes in: "We need to see the conviction of the Party and government leaders!" In terms of strategy and policy, people recommended that the following guidelines be adopted:

- *Earn the people's trust*—"When we cannot take care of obvious problems, how can we obtain the trust of the people? Are we not promoting corruption? What a sorry mess, Li Jinhua trying to get water but turning up empty."
- *Follow the truth*—"This might sound like a slogan, but the only weapon against corruption is truth."
- *Establish legal system*—"Perfect the legal system." "Have rules but do not follow them; implement the law but not strictly. This is the legal system in China."
- *Follow the rule of law*—"Rule the country by law, focus on rule. If rule does not bear fruit, how can we make people obey the law?"
- *Pursue deterrence*—"Drastic action is necessary to set an example to provide for deterrence." "Execute a few by firing squad; otherwise, it is not going to be finished."
- *Set examples*—"If we do not dispose of a few, this kind of thing will last forever."

- *Go after the leaders*—"In small places, in order to arrest the thieves, we must first catch the kingpin."
- *Establish accountability*—"Should let the judicial system investigate the subjects of the audit. If those who are responsible are being suppressed, then it will be easier to deal with later."
- *Instill administrative accountability*—"It should be the case that, once we find out which department has problems, we will hold the department above responsible."

Conclusions to Draw from the Audit Storm

This research has analyzed the thinking and documented the feeling of the Chinese public with regard to the Audit Storm in China. In the process, it found that online comments were overwhelmingly in support of the Audit Storm, especially the auditors and their leader, Li Jinhua. All agreed that the Audit Storm was a move in the right direction: "Great! But the investigation should get to the bottom of it all! We should learn from painful experiences, change our past painful mistakes—this is the way to make China great again!"

Commenters were happy with the audit process but less sanguine with the outcome and most uncertain about the prospect of a clean China: "Loud thunder, noisy wind, heavy clouds, scattered rain." For example, they did not understand why "no responsible people were being held accountable" and wondered "who is protecting the corrupted officials?"

Still, in a moment of hopefulness, they were ready and willing to serve up a fistful of penetrating observations and rendered a bundle of constructive comments intended to make China better: "Need to look at the audit carefully to determine whether the movement is for real, whether we are serious about establishing a rule of law system to hold officials accountable by law." If the country was not serious about fighting corruption, then the people would be the ones who got hurt: "Being tolerant of and compassionate with corrupt officials, large and small, is cruelty to the people."

Not overlooked were the chronic abuse of power and institutionalized corruption, with no efforts to clean them up, thus leading to mistrust of the government, a loss of confidence among the people, and legitimacy deficit: "If there is no followup with the audit, then it is best not to do it, so the public would not be frustrated. I do not understand why. Is it really the case that punishment stops with high officials?" Legitimacy deficits happen when:

- *The government is viewed as untrustworthy*—"It should be the case that, once we find out which department has problems, we will hold the department above responsible." But, that was not happening in the Audit Storm case.
- *The government is viewed as dishonest*—"The investigation should go up and up, until it ends. How many times these investigation have ended without reason after discovering the culprits—this is the tragic story of China." The solution is clear, that the only weapon against corruption is the truth.
- *The government is viewed as incompetent*—"When we cannot take care of obvious problems, how can we obtain the trust of the people? Are we not promoting corruption? What a sorry mess, Li Jinhua trying to get water but turning up empty."
- *The government has failed in maintaining the credibility of one of its major institutions: the rule of law*—"Have rules but do not follow them; implement the law but not strictly. This is the legal system in China." Also, "If rule does not bear fruit, how can we make people obey the law?"

Beyond serving up a declaration of war against corruption, the online voices bared their hearts, minds, and souls. The people revealed themselves: who they are, where they stand, and what they want—totally and completely to all who cared to listen (just as marital arguments are more telling of the relationship than loving hugs and kisses).

The Chinese people do not speak with one voice. They do not all think and feel the same way. They do not, as a rule, march to the same drumbeat of history or culture. The lesson here is that we should move away from looking at China as an integrated whole and pay more attention to its disparate parts. How these people viewed corruption depended on their personal disposition (i.e., idealist vs. pragmatist vs. realist). The lesson here is that in studying China we should look beyond superficial resemblances between people and reach deeper down to draw out differences between individuals and groups. Expanding on this, although everyone might be against corruption, not everyone is against it to the same degree and for similar reasons. When seeking understanding of a people, differences matter more than similarities. Despite substantial agreement on the need to rid China of corruption, there was much less agreement on what it would take to do so, and the difficulties in fighting corruption were considered to be many:

- The *herd instinct* made the acceptance or tolerance of corruption more likely—"If most of the people do not confront the issues head on, then even if we ourselves do the wrong thing there is no shame." The group mentality would suggest that, "Nearly all officials are corrupt; who are you going to audit?"
- The *survival instinct* made anti-corruption efforts that much more difficult—"People will not use a knife to cut up their own kind. In a one-party state, it is natural that there is self-protection and no opportunities given to others. In between money and power, one has lost his self [identity, integrity]. Who can solve this problem?"
- The *political culture* could be used to explain why corruption still existed in spite of repeated attempts to eradicate the same—"Why is it that we need the leader to say something before we punish those illegal people?"
- A *time factor* meant that banishing corruption necessarily had to be an ongoing, intergenerational project, as it was thought that currently "punishment stops at the doorstep of the officials."
- A *lack of morality* contributed to the problem—"Conscience is missing."
- *Practicality* also entered into the issue— "If there is an arrest it implicates many; if no arrest is made, it is hard to hold anyone accountable. If arrests are made, do not know how many people will be involved."[69]

Based on these online observations, it would seem that eliminating corruption in China is less an issue of lack of effort than it is a disagreement over the ways and means to do so, including who is responsible. The lesson here is that many police problems are easier to identify than fix.

When it came to solving the corruption problem, these online commenters were not looking for complete eradication of the problem overnight. What they were looking for was assurance that at the end of the day some honest officials would be willing and able to intervene in individual cases, to punish the wrongdoers, and more importantly to reinforce their sense of justice. This would appear to be the role that must be played by the Party to salvage its reputation. The lesson here is that in cross-cultural research it is important to ask the local people what they want or expect before judging, condemning, or recommending.

Finally, loss of faith in the government prompted many people to contemplate taking matters into their own hands, in line with an old saying: "The rise and fall of a nation ultimately rest on the shoulders of each individual." More explicitly, at the end of the day, "only the people's power cannot be resisted." In this way, the people were making it be known that they, not the Party or government, held the key to China's future. This confidence in the ability of the masses to shape their own destiny, as espoused by Mao, is what keeps people's hope alive. It is also the reason why the public takes to the street and talks back to the government in the most disruptive and violent ways.

Legitimacy

Police Authority and Legitimacy Defined

In Chinese, the term "police authority" is translated to *jingcha quanwei*. The term *quanwei* is itself made up of the two words *quan* and *wei*, where *quan* represents the term *quan li*, meaning "privilege coming with power," and *wei* represents *weiwan*, meaning "deference resulting from respect." Whereas legislation gives police *quan*, only the public can give the police *wei*. More simply, *quan* is given but *wei* is earned. The term *wei* is most closely associated with the English word "legitimacy." People will not concede to and obey the raw exercise of power (*quan*), unless and until compliance is obtained by the legitimate exercise of that power (*wei*). *Wei*, then, is legitimacy in action, or the extent to which power is obeyed. Challenges and disobedience are signs of reduced *wei*, or a lack of legitimacy. One problem with this interpretation of the relationship between legitimacy and *wei* is that the two concepts are not exactly identical. *Wei* can be achieved by the legitimate (normative, legal, reasonable, appropriate) exercise of power (*quan*), but the legitimate exercise of power is only a necessary but not sufficient condition for obtaining *wei*; other necessary conditions are attached. In the context of China, *quan* must be exercised virtuously (*de*), with understanding, compassion, and mercy and in a manner compatible with *qing, li, fa* (sentiment, reason, law). Thus understood, the disobedience of police power in China may not be a function of lack of legitimacy alone but may also be due to a more nuanced lack of *wei*.[70]

Legitimacy Crisis

Of all the challenges and issues confronting the PRC political leaders and police administrators today, the most critical problem is one of widespread complaints about police dereliction of duty,[71] corruption of office,[72] and abuse of powers.[73] The once symbiotic relationship and intimate bond between the police and the masses have been severely tested and found wanting.[74] From the perspective of the public, the police have violated their sacred trust[75] and breached communal expectations.[76] The public expects the police to live the Lei Feng spirit—totally dedicated and completely selfless.[77] Instead, they appear to be corrupt and abusive. From the perspective of the police, the public is not respectful of or helpful to the police. The police expect the public to behave like model communist citizens,[78] who are totally altruistic, completely supportive, and unfailingly respectful.[79] Instead, they appear to be apathetic and antagonistic. Both groups are working from unproven assumptions, unrealistic expectations, and dated relationships. Whatever the reasons, the growing police–public divide has resulted in a huge legitimacy crisis[80] with dire consequences and far-reaching implications for police operations.

The police legitimacy crisis is manifested in many ways. There are mounting negative portrayals in the press, increased violent protests in the street, and widespread criticism on the net. Such media negativism, public violence, and online outbursts are worrisome to the political leaders, as they represent fading communist trust, tenuous public relations, and fragile political stability. The following sections document public discontent with the police. Read in their totality, they suggest growing evidence of a deteriorating police image and decline in police legitimacy and people taking affirmative steps to reject the police—from declining to marry officers to resisting police in their performance of duty to taking up arms in the street.[81]

Deterioration of Public Image[82]

In the 2000s, the police were increasingly portrayed in the PRC public media in a negative light.[83] Research into public opinion (*yulun jiangdu*)[84,85] regarding issues raised on the widely popular CCTV show *Jiaodian Fangtan*[86] organized subjects investigated on the program into a number of functional models (*gongneng moshi*): (1) protecting the rights of the people, (2) protecting the integrity of the legal system, (3) exposés, and (4) value inculcation/orientation (see Table 4.1). These investigations found that the police engaged in all kinds of illegal, abusive, and unprofessional activities, including using power for personal gain (*yi quan mou si*), a disregard for human life (*caojian renming*),[87] committing crimes and doing evil (*weifei-zuodai*),[88] inquisition by torture (*xingxun bigong*),[89] conspiring to cause mischief (*xunban zishi*), perpetrating fraud (*nongxu-zuojia*),[90] having a bad attitude (*taidu elie*), taking advantage of role and status (*wangnong jizhou*), and engaging in a corrupt lifestyle (*shenghu fuhua*).[91] As expected, the reporting of police abuses is appreciated by the public but resented by the police. Some examples of police abuse of authority are provided in the following section.

In the News

On November 13, 2007, Yin Fangming, 43, a doctor and deputy professor at the city's Pearl River hospital, was talking with a friend, Wang Yanwu, in a parked car in the middle of the night when they were approached by two police officers. Yin argued with the police and was shot and killed when he attempted to drive away. Wang, the sole witness, was placed in police custody. The Guangzhou PSB police chief promised a full investigation and public accounting, but the propaganda department of Guangdong Province ordered the media to report only information obtained from official pronouncements. The public was upset. One blogger wrote, "I do not know how many villains and bad people this officer has killed.… This is not only a loss to the nation and the people but seriously infringes the country's legal system. We want to see how this criminal in police uniform will be held responsible."[92]

On April 30, 2002, the *China Police Daily* reported on the abusive use of police cars by Hubei officers. Particularly, police vehicles were used in "four indiscriminate" (*siluan*) ways: (1) indiscriminate use of siren, (2) indiscriminate use of flashing signals, (3) indiscriminate display of police signs, and (4) indiscriminate driving in prohibited areas. This behavior attracted many citizens' complaints. On April 11 and 12, 2002, the Hebei PSB Police Work Supervision Office (*Jingwu ducha chu*) set up a checkpoint to inspect police vehicles. Of the 120 vehicles inspected, they found 31 fake police plates and three illegal police lights. Six police vehicles were impounded.[93]

TABLE 4.1 *Jiaodian Fangtan* Programming Models and Number of Times Aired from April 1, 1994, to December 31, 1998

Model	Number (%)	Content
Protecting people's rights (维护人民权益功能模式)	126 (21.58%)	Misadministration (100): questionable administration activities, policy lapses, actions outside of the law, administrative errors Poor administrative work styles (18): looking down on people, detachment from the public, showing off officialdom, displaying bureaucratism, engaging in authoritarianism, filing false reports Irregular personnel practices (8): appointing people based on favoritism, practicing dictatorship, engaging in bribery or corruption
Protecting legal system integrity (提供制度保障功能模式)	158 (27.5%)	Focus on supervision over legislation, promotion of the law and monitoring over the implementation of the law, with discussion covering what laws should be passed, how laws have been neglected and misused, and when the law mistreats people
"Sunshine" (exposé) function (阳光功能模式)	77 (13.8%)	Focus on corruption in office, abuse of power, and dereliction of duty, particularly corruption in the judiciary (54), education (11), administration (1), and self-rule organizations such as village committees (11)
Values inculcation and orientation (导向功能模式)	68[a] (11.64%)	Focus on how to fight corrupting influences of the capitalistic market economy brought about by Deng's reform, from collectivism to individualism, from idealism to utilitarianism, from spiritualism to materialism, from communitarianism to hedonism Clear values orientation functions: (1) exposing problems of extremely selfish individualism (e.g., conspicuous consumption), and (2) praising examples of socialist morality (e.g., Lei Feng spirit)
Others	155 (26.54%)	No discussion of these cases

Source: Baozhong, S., Media Observer [Chuanmei Guancha], July 7, 2003.

[a] Two figures for this functional model (68 and 70) were reported, with no attempt to reconcile the two. The figure 68 is preferred because this conforms to the sum total of yearly breakdown of programming items.

On December 14, 2000, the *China Daily* reported on cases of police killings in Bazhou, Hebei Province, and Yuzhou, Henan Province. On June 4, 2000, Du Shugui, a policeman in Bazhou, had an argument with a civilian and shot him. On July 3, 2000, Liu Dezhou, a policeman in Yuzhou, killed three people and wounded two with his gun while he was drunk. Both were sentenced to death. The shooting caused widespread agitation among local residents. The MPS further punished the two police chiefs by suspending promotions and stopping their salary raise for a year.[94]

On October 30, 2000, the *China Youth Press* reported that many PRC police officers were lax with firearms discipline. For example, a survey of 987 police officers from Hubei Province uncovered 470 officers unfit to bear arms due to their authoritarianism (*tequan shixiang*), intolerant attitudes, family problems, or financial indebtedness. The MPS reacted with strict regulations regarding the use of weapons for all and outright prohibition for some.[95]

"Police Art" Writings

The police image in popular police writings—"police art" (*jingcha yishu*)—is also very negative.[96] In the 1960s, public security officers were depicted as folk heroes; for example, in 1965, a popular song, *"Yifen qiang"* ("One Cent"), described police–public relations: "I found one cent on the roadside. I picked it up and put it in the hands of the police. Uncle [police] holds onto it and nods at me. I happily said: 'Uncle, goodbye.'" Judging by the content and tone of this song, police officers at that time were well loved by the people and considered to be family members. In more contemporary literature, the police are mostly depicted as law enforcers and rights abusers. In the 1990s, police officers were characterized as abusive and antagonistic;[97] for example, in the fictional police story *Proper Self-Defense* (*Zhengdang fangwei*), the police officer was described as an aggressive and abusive law enforcer: "He was going to raise his hand to rub his face, then realized that he was being handcuffed. He felt pain on his face. He realized that he had been slapped by the police officer."[98]

Police Cause for Concern with the Media

As noted above, the police have a legitimate concern with how the media cover news involving them. From the perspective of the police, the media have been selectively reporting police misconduct and otherwise pandering to the crowd. Li Wufeng, Bureau Chief of the State Council Information Office Internet Affairs Bureau, made these observations in a lecture on media management:

> First, without media hype there will not be popular Internet expression. Second, if the news is reported in an orderly way, then online public opinion will be harmonious and orderly. It is extremely important to safeguard the orderly dissemination of online news. Third, currently, the online republishing of news stories has the following major problems: (1) Republishing articles from small papers and publications, even republishing articles from foreign presses. (2) The online news phenomenon of "news laundering"[99] is still serious. Sometimes standard news sources did not even carry the story [that the republishing source claimed the standard news source published]. (3) Small newspapers and websites republish each other's stories, creating media hype—for example, the Deng Yujiao incident[100] and the Hangzhou street race case.[101] (4) The issues created by these problems are extremely serious…little incidents are hyped into big issues, it breeds a base and vulgar culture, and it seriously influences the direction of public opinion. In response to the above issues, the next step is to vigorously take measures to protect the orderly republication of news stories.[102]

MPS Response

The police have responded to such negative images by blaming the media and insisting that the public does not understand real police work, and the police are viewed unfavorably because they have to enforce the law. Most of the police in China believe that real police work is difficult, and many officers are willing to make sacrifices for the people.[103] A police officer observed that most of the 1.6 million police officers are devoted to doing their duty, often at great personal sacrifice of life, limb, and fortune; corrupt officers are the exception, not the norm. The police point the finger at the media, saying that they make up stories to attract audiences and sell newspapers.[104] The MPS has sought to counter "low-culture" crime and police stories with their own brand of heroic officers and selfless services stories.[105] The Party and the MPS have also launched counteroffensive Internet campaigns waged by paid Internet commentators, and they have created public relations offices at major bureaus (e.g., Shanghai, Beijing, Shenzhen).[106]

Police Internet Campaign

In 2004, the external publicity department of the Changsha Municipality began submitting to the municipal Party committee and municipal leadership's online *Changsha Intelligence Report*. This required recruiting and training Internet commentators (ICs) to manage Internet exchanges online. The ICs are paid a basic salary of 600 yuan per month and 50 cents (*wu mao qian*) for each web posting. Their main duty is to closely monitor Internet opinions, supply opinions, and selectively conduct Internet promotion campaigns. The IC team picks a topic each week designed to promote Changsha Municipality's latest achievements, methods, and experience. The IC comments are distributed on 30 websites, such as renmin.com, minming.com, and sinhua.com. They are also responsible for tracking negative reporting, responding to attacks, and working with web masters to delete Internet materials that are deemed harmful to the municipality. The ultimate objective of the ICs is to promote a positive image of Changsha.[107]

Since this program was initiated, the PRC government has organized in-service courses in "Internet Public Opinion and Promotion of Government" that last from a few days to a few weeks. Taught by university professors and researchers, they train people to be skillful ICs and focus on the impact of the Internet on evaluating government work, crisis management, government administration, and public accountability. Topics include the government's agenda-setting system and public opinion guidance, writing skills necessary to address major incidents, news propaganda and the government image, and mass incident response and crisis management.[108] The ICs are not always well received, and several problems have been identified:

- The qualifications and competence of the various ICs are not all the same; thus, their output and impact differ.
- The ICs are supposed to present facts and articulate viewpoints favorable to the government. At the very least, they are supposed to offer different takes on stories by offering up missing facts, contrary evidence, new perspectives, and different interpretations. At times, this might not be possible without skewing the truth or misrepresenting the facts.
- Sometimes IC entries sound patronizing or contrived. By trying too hard, ICs risk losing the readers' attention and trust of the people, in addition to compromising the creditability of the government. Instead of helping to promote or defend the government, the efforts of the ICs could have the opposite effect of making them appear defensive and causing readers to be cynical.
- The ICs are supposed to mix freely and spontaneously with other netizens on a real-time personal basis, attempting to view things from their perspective and talking like one of them. Trust is necessary if the ICs are to relate to the netizens on their own terms, not court their rejection. This can be difficult to accomplish, especially when the netizens are at odds with the government on a particular issue. Usually, the ICs must first agree with the netizens to disagree; that is, they must acknowledge any wrongdoing upfront before suggesting a better way of doing things.
- The IC's primary job is to promote the government's image, which boils down to promoting and defending the leaders' policies against negative publicity. In practice, the ICs are likely to post comments with the sole purpose of pleasing the boss, which is at odds with the original goal of ICs to promote the image of the government, in a fair and balanced way, even if it means being critical of the leaders.[109]

Police and Media Control

To control the media, some PSBs have resorted to silencing and arresting reporters. In 2010, Qiu Ziming, a reporter at the *Economic Observer*, investigated insider trading at Kan Specialties Material Co., Ltd. As a result, the Suichang PSB, Lishui County, Zhejiang Province, issued a warrant for Qiu's arrest for "injuring the commercial reputation of a company." The *Southern Metropolitan News* first reported the Qui case as the "wanted reporter" case. Journalists and the public were up in arms. Within 36 hours, the Suichang PSB retracted the warrant and apologized to Qiu in Beijing. Meanwhile, to establish a better relationship with the press, Shanghai and Nanjing sponsored a seminar on the relationship between public power and the rights of the media and reporters. All experts attending the meeting agreed that journalists' rights should be protected and that investigative reporting is necessary to check government abuses. Ding Fazhang, Vice Chairman of the Shanghai Journalist Association and Chairman of the Shanghai News Academy, said that the government at all levels should encourage the press to report problems and guide opinions.[110]

In 2008, reporter Zhu Wenna wrote an article for *Faren Magazine* about a businesswoman in Xifeng County, Liaoning Province, whose gas station was demolished to make way for economic development without adequate compensation. The article gave rise to 14,000 angry responses by Chinese netizens. Shortly after, Zhu was arrested for publishing the report.[111] Earlier, in 2007, the police arrested three minor officials in Jishan County in Shanxi Province for writing letters critical of the county Party chief, and in 2006 six farmers in Mengzhou, a county-level city in Henan Province, were arrested for exposing official corruption in a local liquor distillery.[112]

Impact of Poor Image

The negative media portrayals of the police, notwithstanding defense and denials by the police, leave a poor image in the hearts and minds of the people and are telltale signs of an erosion of confidence in the police. This is clearly reflected in the police and media clash over investigative reporter Qui Ziming. Loss of confidence in and respect for the police has planted the seeds of discontentment and resistance. To this subject we now turn.

Resistance to Police Power

Increasingly, people are resisting the police performing their duties.[113] More and more, the police are confronted with threatening crowds and explosive situations, insults, and injuries when exercising their authority. Every year, many police are killed and injured in the line of duty. From 2001 to the first half of 2003, the Beijing PSB reported 2479 cases of obstruction to police performance of duties or creating unnecessary disturbances with Beijing police officers. Police were yelled at or assaulted 10,567 times, resulting in 747 cases of injuries. There were 4197 unproven complaints, 472 of them malicious.[114]

In 2004, the Hangzhou PSB reported 32 cases of assault against a police officer in a short 10-day period, resulting in a death and 95 injuries; on one day alone, there were 5 such cases. In the first half of 2004, they had about 200 cases of resisting law enforcement, half of which were related to traffic enforcement. For example, on March 4, 2004, officers from Kang Qiao Traffic Detachment detained two vehicles that had no licenses. Two people attacked the officers with steel bars and knives, injuring them. On March 28, 2004, police officer Pan Jiang had stopped a minivan for a driving violation when the car sped up, dragging the officer for 200 feet; he sustained serious injuries.[115]

TABLE 4.2   Chinese Police Deaths and Injuries Due to
Assaults in the Line of Duty

Year	Injuries[a]	Deaths
2001	3429	68
2002	3663	75
2003	4000	84
2004	3786	48
2005	1932	27
2006 (January to May)	160	11
2007[b]	—	—
2008	—	486
2009[c]	2871	431

Source: Adapted from "Shadow of Assaulting Police over 'Tragic
Heroes': Why Do They Not Respond When They Should?"
Liaoning Police Web, February 25, 2007 (http://www.jzga.
gov.cn/jywh/Detail.aspx?id=1164).

[a] Three data quality issues should be noted here. First, because the
only data source for police injuries (including deaths) in the line of
duty is the government, certain reliability issues are raised. Second,
because they are not specified, we do not know exactly what kinds
of injuries are included in the police data. Third, because the types
of injuries and causes of death are not defined, we do not know
whether an injury or death resulted from a citizen's assault or
health-related issues; for example, in one case, a police drank himself to death during a police function and received a commendation
posthumously. Also, the MPS death/injury data in this table do not
agree with the police researchers' data shown in Table 3.3
[b] No figures are available, but refer to "2717 Chinese Police Officers
Die in the Line of Duty in Past Six Years," Xinhua, January 12, 2008.
[c] "431 Chinese Police Die on Duty in 2009," Xinhua, April 16, 2010.

Nature and Extent of Problem

According to MPS data, from 2001 to 2005,[116] 200 deaths and 1.4 million injuries to police
officers in the line of duty could be attributed to such resistance (Table 4.2).[117] From 1981 to
2010, 10,414 officers died in the line of duty and 157,000 sustained work-related injuries. In
the last 10 years, 2182 have died in the line of duty and another 15,734 have been injured.
From 2006 to 2010, 1029 officers died as a result of overwork (47% of those who died in
the line of duty) and 790 (37%) died as a result of confrontations with criminals or during
traffic duties (Xinhua, April 4, 2011). As can be seen in Table 4.3, an average of 6660 PRC
police officers were injured or killed each year from 2000 to 2005, 830% of Hong Kong's
average rate of 800. When we compare the rate of injuries and deaths for Chinese police
based on police strength, though, we find that the Chinese police compare quite favorably
with Hong Kong and the United States: 0.41% in China vs. 2.66% in Hong Kong vs. 1.88
in the United States.[118] Furthermore, if we were to express Chinese police officer deaths in
the line of duty as a percentage of population, the rate is still lower: 0.526/100,000 in China
vs. 11.42/100,000 in Hong Kong. Overall, Chinese policing is relatively safe compared to
policing in Hong Kong and the United States.

TABLE 4.3   Chinese Police Injuries, Deaths, and Attacks, 2000–2004

Year	Injuries	Deaths	Deaths as Percentage of Injuries	Number of Attacks	Deaths per Attack
2000	5643	428	7.58%	12,155	1/28
2001	6732	443	6.58%	11,998	1/27
2002	6963	443	6.36%	12,076	1/27
2003	6552	476	7.26%	12,917	1/27
2004	7412	492	6.63%	13,891	1/28
5-year average, China	6660	456	6.85%	12,607	1/28
5-year average, Hong Kong	800	>1	0.075%	6592	1/2564
5-year average, United States	14,487	168	1.02%	57,823	1/344

Source: Adapted from Table 2 in Ming, C.X. et al., *Public Security Studies*, 121, 63–67, 2007.

Why, then, is the alarm being raised about police officers being attacked in the line of duty? It has been observed that, "In Mao's time, attacks on police were virtually unheard of, with an average of just 36 officers dying annually in the line of duty. Since 1990, more than 7000 have died on duty and nearly 1000 were reportedly killed (and 30,000 injured) in deliberate attacks."[119] Assaults on the police continue to rise, whereas in Hong Kong and the United States the situation appears to have stabilized (Table 4.3). Also on the rise are assaults on police officers that cause serious injuries. Citizens who are normally law abiding are beginning to attack the police more often. The public's opinion on assaults of police officers, more often than not, generally reflects apathy for the officers and empathy for the assailants. In the first half of 2006, 23 police officers were killed in the line of duty and 1803 injured due to violent resistance.[120] On February 13, 2006, for example, a Tianjin traffic officer tried to stop a vehicle for making an illegal U-turn, but the driver tried to knock the officer over. The officer hung onto the hood of the speeding vehicle for 2 kilometers before finally being thrown off the car and seriously injured.[121] It turned out that the driver, a recently released car thief, was driving without registration.[122]

On March 8, 2006, a Liaoning man assaulted a female with a knife, and the police were called. Three officers from Heshan County responded. The suspect resisted arrest, attacking one officer with the knife and hitting another officer on the head with a hammer. Police reinforcements arrived, but the suspect refused to surrender and attacked another officer with the hammer. He was given repeated warnings and was finally shot after he rushed toward an officer with his knife.[123] Of note in this case is that the police took a most tolerant approach to the attacker, until their lives were at stake.

On July 1, 2006, Zhang Jianzhong headed out to visit his sister in another village in Hai Nam. He was stopped from entering her village because of local custom, but he finally was able to do so by offering two cartons of cigarettes. Later on, Zhang Richeng was caught entering the village to do business. Zhang's staff was detained and his car impounded by the villagers for a ransom of $4000. Later in the afternoon, another trader, Lie Zhong, was asked to pay thousands of dollars in return for safe passage. These incidents were reported to the police. On July 4, when the police forcibly entered the village, 27 of the 33 officers were injured. Police vehicles were attacked, with damages totaling $380,000. A week later, 50 police officers and 100 armed police officers returned to arrest 35 troublemakers.[124]

One of the most sensational police killings happened in Shanghai in 2007, when Yang Jia, 28, forced his way into Shanghai's Zhabei District Police Post, killing six police officers and injuring four with a knife. Yang reportedly had a grievance against Shanghai police after a lengthy interrogation for riding an unlicensed bicycle in October 2007. He sued the police for 10,000 yuan (US$1464) for psychological injury, but his claim was rejected. Not satisfied, Yang took the law into his own hands and attacked the police. On August 28, 2008, Yang was sentenced to death in the Shanghai No. 2 Intermediate People's Court.[125] Surprisingly, instead of Yang's killing spree being condemned by the public he was treated as a hero. A message left on his MySpace page read, "You have done what most people want to do, but do not have enough courage to do." A blogger, Xiao Bin, wrote, "Because of him, when we go to Shanghai and bike on the street, we don't have to fear policemen beating us."[126] Finally, when reporters interviewed Yang's father, Yang Ming,[127] he said that Yang Jia was a quiet boy who loved to read. He had not gotten into trouble as a child. Many police complained about the favorable reporting of the violent offender, with little attention being paid to the dead and wounded officers. This led to an open debate about the role of media, especially its objectivity toward the police. According to a police blogger, the media have a responsible role to play: "Reporters, first and foremost, should have a moral conscience."[128]

Causes of Obstruction and Resistance

Most of the reasons for such violent confrontations between the police and the public can be attributed to the reform process. China lacks a well-developed legal culture, and the police do not always conduct themselves professionally. The growing number of violent criminals are more inclined to use violence in resisting arrest. People are becoming less civil and less likely to follow police instructions, which leads to the police using force; offenders have very little respect for either the law or the police. People resent the police for carrying out legitimate policing activities, such as traffic code enforcement, but they are quick to take advantage of a police officer who demonstrates tolerance. To the public, the police appear to be weak and irresolute when in fact they are working on being "civilized" (*wenming*). The police try to avoid problematic encounters and troublesome offenders, which only encourages strong-headed offenders and emboldens recalcitrant violators.[129]

In a field study conducted in 2006,[130] it was found that the police were afraid of the people because of the MPS's policy regarding zero tolerance for citizens' complaints. The police had been instructed to "hit without reacting and be yelled at without responding." The police are afraid of citizens' complaints and administrative investigations. Citizens have various channels for registering complaints, such as submitting a *xinfang* (petition) to the national or local government or filing administrative complaints with the responsible police agency (e.g., MPS, police inspection units, political disciplinary committees). Because the number and nature of complaints are used to assess police performance and determine awards of merit and bonuses, there is an incentive to avoid getting into trouble at all costs. Increasingly, the police are willing to pay huge amounts of money to buy aggrieved citizens' silence.[131]

Finally, citizen complaints against the police were often treated lightly; for example, between 2001 and 2006, the Liaoyang Baita substation had a total of 32 cases of police obstruction which were all dealt with administratively (21 received administrative detentions, 2 fines, 4 labor education classes, and 5 no punishment), with no criminal prosecution. In contrast, in 2004 the Shenyang Municipality Police Department reported 40 criminal prosecutions for police obstruction, half of which received criminal sanctions. In

2005, they prosecuted 47 cases with 39 convictions; in the first half of 2006, they reported 35 prosecutions with 28 convictions. The following reasons for challenges to police authority were suggested:[132]

- *Social factors*—The local government or political cadres ask the police to collect excessive taxes and fees to generate revenue or evict lawful residents without compensation. In such cases, the local authorities enlist the police to enforce illegal orders. The aggrieved people turn their frustration and anger with local governments on the police. The citizens have little understanding of the law. They think it is legal to resist and obstruct the police if they do not assault them. The police routinely deal with confrontations with the people in the line of the duty, such as delivering grievance petitions (*xinfang*) or suppressing riots. In such cases, the police become the enemies of the people. The government has promoted the idea of police serving the people, compassionately and legally, but little effort is being made to educate people to respect the police and follow their order.
- *Internal factors*—Some of the police do not act as professionals, giving rise to the people's contempt, lack of cooperation, and resistance. Some police have the wrong attitude that they can boss people around and have failed to serve the people in a legal and compassionate way. The police have failed to protect themselves from potential attacks and violence for fear of escalation or official sanctions; for example, some police agencies have hesitated to equip their officers with arms because they fear that the officers will abuse them. The police tend to approach cases of obstruction, resistance, and attacks gingerly, which only emboldens people wishing to challenge the police.
- *Legal factors*—Laws providing for police use of force and self-defense articulate principles that are too general and inflexible to accommodate the needs of officers working on the street, and officers are hesitant to second-guess these laws. Laws against police obstruction are inconsistently applied by the police, procuratorates, and courts, as there is very little uniform understanding of their meaning and application. Sanctions against obstruction of the police are not adequate; for example, PRC Criminal Law 227 punishes obstruction of public duties with a maximum sentence of 3 years, but no specific provision is made for the seriousness of the incident or its consequences. Article 50(2) of the Public Order Management Punishment Act provides for punishment against obstruction of police with a penalty of only administrative detention of 10 days or a fine of US$500.

Typologies of Police Obstruction and Resistance

A policy paper from the Luoshan County Police Department, Xin Yang Municipality, Henan Province, identified the following types of police obstruction and resistance:[133]

- People challenge police authority because of a sense of adventure and self-importance. This is usually manifested in taunting, tugging, or pushing the police officer.
- People resist the police because of self-interests. This kind of resistance invariably involves violent attacks of police officers with stones, bats, bottles, or knives.
- People do not cooperate with the police when they are drunk and act in an unruly manner.
- People try to aid and abet others to resist the police, especially in a rowdy group situation.

- People are disrespectful of the police. They will yell and scream at or spit on police officers to humiliate or intimidate them.
- Many people passively resist the police as a matter of principle. These people deliberately resist police lawful instruction to air their displeasure or, in some cases, to display their power or show their importance.
- People make a scene on account of their status, such as elderly, female, or handicapped. These people often dare the police to arrest them.

Who Are the Offenders?

People who obstruct police are usually without an education or occupation. Referring to our earlier example of police obstruction cases at the Liaoyang Baita substation between 2001 and 2006, among those involved in the 32 cases, 2 had a college education, 10 had a high-school education, 15 had an elementary-school education, and 5 had a primary-school education.[134] In 2006, in Hainan Island, out of 50 cases of offenses against the police, 31 involved violence against police. The offenders were all between 26 and 35 years old; 46.9% of them were peasants, and 23.1% were without work. In terms of education, 80% of them had less than a high-school education and a limited understanding of the law.[135]

Assault on Police: A Case Study

On June 18, 2008, officer Zhan Zhaolong, from the Lanzhou Hanjiang District Police Post was called to remove a vehicle blocking a driveway. The owner of the car, a Singapore investor, refused to do so. He assaulted Zhan viciously for 18 minutes until Zhan fell unconscious. Zhan was a two-time National Martial Arts runner-up but did not fight back. He was in intensive care for 3 days. When interviewed by the media, Zhan expressed no regret: "It is just a contradiction, a dispute. It is not a public order offense or a criminal violation. At such deployments we usually instruct auxiliary police to persuade and educate the offender….At that time I was equipped with police gears (baton, etc.), and I love to train myself normally. If I started hitting back, it is hard to tell how hard it might be. Therefore, I decided rationally not to do so. Also at that time, the offender might have mistaken me to be on the side of the property owner. This would have deepened the misunderstanding and the situation might get worse. I have been working as a police officer for 20 years. This is just one of those cases where I am having to do my job by trading blood."[136]

Public Reaction   A total of 3640 online comments to this story ran the gamut from being complimentary to cynical to contemptuous. On the whole, the comments were more negative than positive or constructive. The top ten most popular comments are listed here:

1. "Cannot see whether you are a hero or a dog. Since, when you should fight back, you do not." (1699 votes)
2. "Now I know why the Tang Jing case[137] was fully investigated to the rock bottom." (1296 votes)
3. "If you do not hit back you can at least subdue the person. If not, why have the police officers deployed? To serve as a punching bag?" (1213 votes)
4. "Lucky it is a fake foreigner. Otherwise, would have been beat up for nothing." (1007 votes)
5. "If you cannot even protect yourself, how can you protect the people? May as well go home and farm." (998 votes)

6. "If the person said then that I am a Chinese citizen and I am not afraid of JC, I bet he would be rolling on the floor with blood all over." (836 votes)
7. "'I love to train myself normally. If I started hitting back, it is hard to tell how hard it might be.' This statement is very meaningful." (683 votes)
8. "'Lucky it is a fake foreigner.' This comment is the best." (613 votes)
9. "Very fat" (alluding to officer Zhan?) (407 votes)
10. "Comrade Zhan, I was in the same profession. I feel sorry for your assault. Are you not blackening the face of your peers? How can you now promise to protect the life, property and safety of the people?" (0 votes; ranked tenth by website)

Judging by this set of comments, the people were not 100% behind their police in the performance of duty. Instead of admiring the officer for being tolerant, the officer was ridiculed for failing to exercise proper judgment to protect himself, failing in his duty to arrest the culprit, pandering to foreigners, having a double standard against the Chinese, and not being able to protect the people. The comments are as telling as they are clear. The relationship between the police and the public is not very close, the public holds the police in contempt, and the public has lost faith and confidence in the police.

Remedies

The spike in violence against the police has precipitated repeated calls for national legislation to protect the police. Currently, no specific law protects the police in the performance of their duty. In 2003, Wang Wuding and 35 NPC members began to push for the first national legislation regarding assaults on police in the line of duty. The initiative was renewed in 2004 at the Second Session of the Tenth NPC, where a legislative proposal was submitted by an NPC representative from the Zhanjiang municipality police post. The violence against police has also led to local self-help efforts to safeguard the rights, protect the safety, and promote the welfare of the police.

In 2003, in Hebei Province, the Qin Huang Dao PSB established a Police Rights Protection Committee (*Jingcha weiquan weiyuanhui*) to deal with cases involving violence against police officers. As a result, the Qin Huang Dao PSB promulgated the "Regulations Protecting the Rights of the People's Police in the Proper Enforcement of Law" ("*Weihu renmin jingcha zhengdang zhifa quanyi guize*"), which authorized the committee to handle all cases of police officers and their families being insulted, threatened, harassed, intimidated, or assaulted in the line of duty.[138] In 2004, the Zhejiang PSB and Hangzhou PSB[139] launched a public education campaign against obstructing and resisting police officers in the performance of duty. The day the campaign began, 18 offenders were arrested for violence against the police. The Party committee of Zhejiang PSB further promulgated "Certain Regulations of Zhejiang Province Police Organs in Protecting the Rights of People's Police in Enforcing the Law" ("*Zhejiang sheng gongan jiguan weihu minjing zhifa quanyi rugan guiding*"). The regulations call for setting up an *ad hoc* committee to monitor and take actions against those who violently resist the police.[140]

Violence against the police has had grave consequences on relationships between the police and the public. Most police officers feel that they are no longer respected or feared,[141] and they complain about not being able to do their work properly (e.g., enforcing the law in a forthright manner).[142] The police are growing increasingly reluctant to sacrifice their safety for the public,[143] observing that the public does not care about crime and disorder and does not appreciate the police; that is, the public does not know how to show gratitude (*bao en*).

To repair the tenuous and fractured police–public relationship, the police have taken several steps to appease the public:

- The police have been instructed to endure humiliation in order to accomplish the task on hand (*ren ru fu zhong*).
- The police have learned to accept personal affronts as part of their work routine (*jiachang bian fan*[144]).
- The police reluctantly endure personal insults and attacks to avoid complaints and lawsuits; for example, between March 1 and April 20, 2001, a total of 26,065 complaints were filed against the police, but most of them (87%) were not substantiated (*bu shi*).
- The police are cautioned against overreacting to challenges of police authority. A retired public security official from Henan advised the police to stay calm in the face of provocation so as not to antagonize the public or further aggravate the situation, but the police should always stand firm against law and reason. This is easier said than done, though.
- When responding to violence, the police should try to separate the agitators from the followers, punishing the leaders and educating the followers.[145]

An officer from a police post in Shandong Province suggested that the police should earn back the respect of the people by projecting a competent (*zhisu*) and confident (*jing rong*) demeanor and exhibiting an exemplary police work style (*jing feng*). More importantly, the police should develop a close relationship with the people such that they know them intimately. If the police work closely with the people, then the people would support the police and come to their assistance when needed.[146]

Police culture cautions against acting aggressively in the face of challenges to police authority. An online post entitled "32 Classical Police Sayings"[147] instructs police officers on what they should or should not do on the job to make their job less troublesome.[148] An example is the following: "*Do not strike anyone*. When someone says to you: 'If you have the guts you can hit me,' you should stay cool. This type of person is trash. He is waiting for you to act and is playing with you. This kind of person is low life. Our father's generation cautioned against hitting trashy bone kind under any circumstances."[149]

Public resistance to police authority by passive noncooperation (e.g., not reporting crime) or active obstruction (e.g., resisting arrest) provides the clearest evidence yet that the PRC police are losing the respect and support of the people. Without legitimacy, police exercise of authority will likely be increasingly challenged, leaving the police with two equally untenable options: retreat in the face of challenge or confront the attacker with the use of force. Retreating will appease the immediate challengers but invites future trouble. Confrontation will suppress the immediate challengers but risk aggravating the situation further. So far, the MPS has recommended the first alternative, but police officers in the field generally follow the second, with explosive and lasting consequences.

Mass Rebellions against Police Authority

Mass incidents in China are on the rise.[150] In the first quarter of 2009 alone, 58,000 mass incidents were reported in China, a new high.[151] This compared with 120,000 incidents in 2008 and 90,000 in 2006. In 2005, the MPS reported 87,000 mass incidents, up 6.6% from

2004 (74,000) and 50% percent from 2003.[152] Mass incidents grew from 8700 in 1993 to 32,500 in 1997 to 87,000 in 2005, a tenfold increase,[153] although Vice-Minister of Public Security Liu Jinguo reported a temporary decline in mass incidents of 16.5% in 2005.[154]

There is a lingering, unresolved question as to how a mass incident is defined and counted.[155] The Ningxia Autonomous Region Government identified the following types of mass incidents:

1. Charging and laying siege to a county- or higher-level party or government department, political–legal department, military, armed police, news, and other critical departments, thereby causing bad influence; attacking, vandalizing, looting, and committing arson against a town or higher-level Party or government office with serious impact on social stability;
2. Armed clash between groups of people causing injuries and deaths;
3. Terrorist activities, violent incidents, illegal organization and assembly by hostile forces and separatists;
4. Causing the disruption of railroad and state highway traffic, or the blockading of major cities, traffic hubs, and urban transportation;
5. A group petition at the county, city, or autonomous region level with:
   - A likelihood of proceeding to Beijing;
   - More than 100 persons involved;
   - Violent tendency or the possibility of becoming violent;
   - Seriously affecting social stability, sensitive locations, or business operations.[156]

According to Minister of Public Security Zhou Yongkang, mass incidents are increasingly getting worse:[157]

- *The number has obviously increased.* The 10,000+ mass incidents in 1994 and the 74,000+ mass incidents in 2004 represent an increase of more than sevenfold over the span of 10 years. The number of participants increased from 730,000 persons in 1994 to 3,760,000 persons in 2004, more than a fivefold increase.
- *The scope has expanded.* Mass incidents occur in cities, rural villages, enterprises, governments, schools, and a variety of domains and sectors, and they occur in all of the provinces, autonomous regions, and municipalities.
- *The main participants in mass incidents are more diversified.* They include dismissed workers, farmers, urban dwellers, enterprise owners, teachers, and people from various social strata.
- *The methods are more extreme.* They include laying siege to and attacking party and government offices, blockading public roads, and stopping trains.
- *The tendency is toward greater organizing.* Spontaneously rising organizations with identifiable leaders have been observed.

Throughout the late 1990s, the public demonstrations (mass incidents[158]) got bigger, more organized, sophisticated, and belligerent. In June of 1998, cab drivers organized an anti-corruption rally in Beijing. In another case, 1000 gathered to demand a management change.[159] In 1998 alone, there were eight cases of attacks on government property and police officers.[160] For example, in May 1998, a Fengtai county Party cadre was trying to quell a demonstration when he was taken hostage and held for 20 hours. In the ensuing rescue operation, 60 officers were attacked and 28 vehicles were damaged. In 1999, 837 mass public demonstrations with 59,000 participants occurred in Anhui Province, and 948 cases of mass public demonstrations involved 66,000 people in Henan Province.[161] On January 4, 1999, about 100 farmers from Guoyuan village in eastern Jiangsu Province clashed with police over high taxes (over 5% of household income), with 30 injured and 10 arrested. On January 8, 1999, about 10,000 small farmers from the village of Daolin near Changsha, Hunan Province, clashed with hundreds of police, resulting in one dead and hundreds injured. The demonstration was an armed protest against the arrest of the leaders of the Society for Reducing Taxes and Saving the Nation, a local group formed to protest against excessive and arbitrary taxations. On January 11, 1999, about 1000 farmers from Leibei village in Shanxi Province took to the streets to protest against the manipulation of local elections by CPC members. In the process, they clashed with the police and overturned their vehicles. In March 1999, 5000 demonstrated in Henan Province as the result of a busted pyramid sales scheme. People came from four provinces (Sichuan, Henan, Shandong, and Chongxing), and they were very well organized. Civil disturbances and mass demonstrations can be attributed to a number of factors.[162] Most of them have involved economic protests; for example, in 1999 alone 244 of the mass incidents were related to back pay, although many demonstrations resulted from oppressive government officials and corrupted police practices.[163]

The agitations and demonstrations must be viewed in a larger social context. The exploited workers and deprived villagers were aggravated by widening inequalities between the haves and haves-not, especially between the corrupted officials, who exploited their public trust for private gain, and the industrious workers who could not made ends meet.[164] As a result of economic reform, the job market promised to get worse without any signs of revival:

> According to a recent estimate by Ministry of Labour and Social Security researcher Ma Rong, the number of people looking for jobs is expected to reach 30 million this year. These include 11 million school leavers, five million laid-off workers, and 170,000 demobilized soldiers. As a result of the slowing of the Chinese economy, he estimates only 14 million will find work, leaving 16 million urban workers or 11 percent of the urban workforce unemployed. These figures, the highest acknowledged in any official publication, ignore the fate of an estimated 130 million in rural areas who are also unemployed. If they were included the jobless rate would reach 17 percent. The crisis in the countryside is being further compounded by the return of many of the millions who left for work in the Special Economic Zones (SEZs) and coastal cities.[165]

Such incidents do not bode well for the PRC leadership in terms of stability and reform.

Mass Incident Studies

Wang Bin conducted one of the first government-sponsored research projects on mass incidents, "Examination of Village Special Mass Confrontation Incidents and Response Policy" ("*Nongcun qunti chongtu tefa shijian ji duce tantu*").[166] The first MPS book on mass incidents was *Examination of Village Mass Confrontation Incidents and Response Policy* [*Nongcun qunti chongtu shijian de duice tantu*], published in 1995.[167] Around 1997, the frequency and intensity of mass incidents changed drastically and became a threat to social order and stability. Mass incidents have a long history in China, especially among villages and townships and in the countryside. Collective violence (*xie dou*) by families, clans, or villages has been considered a kind of self-help to secure group interests or achieve informal social control (e.g., disputes over land boundaries or burial sites). In urban areas, similar activity is considered gang violence.

In early days of the reform, from the 1980s to the early 1990s, an unreasonable tax burden on peasants and a draconian one-child policy caused mass incidents. Later, when the market economy settled in, inept/corrupt government administration, inadequate social security, exploitative labor practices, poor working conditions, and natural resource disputes were added to the list. These were considered at the time, and still, as reform pain.[168]

Mass incidents rose precipitously in 1997 due to the reorganization of industry (displacement of workers), corruption among local cadres (heavy levies on peasants), and unregulated economic development (expropriation by law without adequate compensation, illegal demolition and removal, fight for natural resources without recourse). In 2002, mass incidents nationwide rose to 47,000, with 2.643 million participating.[169] In 2004, Jiangxi Province had 928 mass incidents with 39,204 participating, a slight decrease over 2003, but the 188 incidents involving over 50 participants represented an increase of 11%. More telling, incidents in Jiangxi that obstructed traffic or blocked highways, mass disturbances, and illegal assemblies rose from 2003 to 2004 by 31.6%, 20%, and 16.7% respectively.[170]

What are the concept, characteristics, causation, constitution, and psychology of mass incidents?[171] *Qunti* ("mass") is a group of people associated by blood (such as clan) or a social organization (such as college students) that share a mutual identity, interests, or rights. *Shijian* are incidents that have an impact on society, such as Tiananmen Square.[172] A *qunti sheng shijian* is a collective of ten or more people engaged in illegal, harmful, or disruptive public activities. It includes grievance petitions, sit-ins, marches, demonstrations, obstruction of traffic, group fights, and attacks on the government. Mass incidents can generally be classified as:[173]

- *Mass incidents by individuals*—Individual incidents that attract people who are curious, sympathetic, or disruptive, resulting in obstruction of traffic; if not handled well, they might turn violent.
- *Mass incidents by group*—Incidents organized by like-minded people with shared ideas or mutual interests who are in pursuit of their own agenda in the public; these incidents can cause social disorder and harm.

Mass incidents can be classified in other ways, depending on who is involved (students, factory workers, peasants), whether it is local or more widespread, the place (public or private property, urban or rural, highway or mall), the cause (government tax policy, unemployment), and the nature of the protest (economic vs. political, emotional vs. instrumental).[174] The groups participating in mass incidents can be divided into three types: (1) tight-knit groups, which have an internal organization and established identity, such as a union or clan; (2) loose-knit groups, which people join voluntarily, or *ad hoc* groups that assemble for a particular occasion, such as a rally for a cause; and (3) spontaneous, or opportune, groups, which people join on the spur of the moment (e.g., street rioters).[175]

Mass incidents are a complex phenomenon related to social issues; they may be collective events or spur-of-the-moment events that can cause social harm.[176] Mass incidents are purposeful, organized, dynamic, and evolving.[177] They are driven by a number of factors, including *political* (e.g., corruption, incompetence),[178] *economic* (e.g., unequal distribution of resources,[179] inequality in income), *regional* (coastal vs. inland), *class* (e.g., migrants vs. residents),[180] *employment* (e.g., unemployment, social security, college graduate placement),[181] *cultural* (e.g., anomie, ideology, change in values),[182] and *ethnic/religious* (e.g., cults, minorities).[183]

With regard to political factors, the central government policies are not always properly executed as intended; local interests (i.e., provincialism) prevail over government administration, and state laws conflict with Party discipline. The Party and government are losing power and influence to the emerging market system and are losing credibility due to corruption, abuses of power, and misadministration.[184] As to economic factors, the restructuring of the economy has created winners and losers and an unequal distribution of opportunities, resources, rights, and benefits.[185]

Since the beginning of the reform, the PRC has been confronted with an unending series of small-scale social protests, with some escalating into large-scale civil disturbances,[186] and the situation is getting worse:

> Police admit to a nationwide increase of 268 percent in mass incidents from 1993 to 1999 (from 8,700 to 32,000...). In not a single year during this period did unrest increase by less than 9 percent. The rate spiked upward by 25 percent and 67 percent, respectively, in the financial crisis years of 1997 and 1998 and grew by another 28 percent in 1999. China witnessed more than 30,000 mass incidents during January–September 2000, a rate that yields an annual projected estimate of more than 40,000 incidents and an increase of 25 percent over 1999, according to Chinese police sources cited in the Hong Kong press.[187]

Protest groups are becoming larger and more organized, violent, frequent, and difficult to deal with. The threats come from many quarters, including those who are ideologically disillusioned (e.g., agitated students), economically deprived (e.g., displaced workers), or spiritually awakened (e.g., Falun Gong practitioners).[188] These disturbances attest to the public's pent-up frustration with the government's economic policies and antagonism toward the illegal, corrupt, and abusive practices of the police.[189] They send a clear signal to the political leaders and police administrators that not all is well in terms of stability and reform.[190] The CPC, PRC government, and MPS are all concerned with securing political stability and maintaining social order during reform;[191] for example, in one case local cadres were strictly held accountable for large-scale demonstrations and violence that resulted in a person's death.[192] In 2006, the 16th Central Committee of the Communist Party of China issued the "Resolution of the CPC Central Committee on Major Issues regarding the Building of a Harmonious Socialist Society," which called for the proper handling of mass incidents in the process of building a harmonious society.[193] A legitimacy crisis is in the making,[194] and the political leadership and police reformers are intent on regaining the people's trust.[195]

Falun Gong

Rapid industrialization and massive urbanization have caused significant social and economic dislocation, resulting in growing crime rates in large urban areas and unrest in rural areas. The breakdown of traditional control mechanisms laid the foundations of these problems. The disappearance of communal support systems has sowed the seeds of discontent and given rise to mass demonstrations.[196] The power and capacity of the police are put to the test daily. Their legal authority and political legitimacy are challenged every day. The ultimate litmus test of sustainability for the country and its police lies in their ability to meet public expectations; failing that, they must contend with discontent of all kinds—spiritual, economical, social, political.

Let us consider the case of Falun Gong. The sudden emergence and swift spread of Falun Gong can be attributed to the aforementioned discontentment and pent-up frustration brought about by years of economic, political, and social upheaval, with no relief in sight.[197] Falun Gong fills the commonly experienced and strongly felt spiritual void within the mass.[198] This is particularly the case with disillusioned communists brought up to believe in communist ideology and to follow the Party. Deng's open-door policy and the introduction of a market economy have made China vulnerable to political, economic, and spiritual corruption everywhere. Communism and spiritualism are being replaced by capitalism and materialism as the *de facto* state ideologies. This is in stark contrast to Mao's puritanical and ideological regimentation. For some, Falun Gong offers an escape from such evils and promises a better tomorrow, a countercultural revolution.[199] For others, it is a nostalgic trip to the past, a soul-searching exercise. It is this otherworldliness that is most attractive to a despairing and despondent Chinese mass caught in a world of change:

> I don't want to get involved in politics. I don't care for it. Governments focus only on the problem at hand, instead of looking at what has caused this problem in the first place. If ordinary people's society does not become more virtuous, any number of problems may occur, and I cannot concern myself with this prospect. I am only responsible to the practitioners of Falun Gong.[200]

Falun Gong stands for wholesomeness and goodness. The motto of Falun Gong—"Truth, Benevolence, Tolerance"—captures the puritanical calling of Confucianism, utopian vision of communism, and basic yearning of the people in a time of turmoil.[201] In the past, Confucianism called for cultivation of the self in the service of one's family. More recently, the "spiritual civilization" campaign has sought self-sacrifice in the service of the state. Both call for the establishment of a more moral and just society through self-striving and serving others. A Falun Gong observer eloquently captured this:

> The Chinese people suffered traumatic treatment in the Cultural Revolution, everything was bad, and everything was unsafe. To join Li's Falun Gong movement is to be told you are good, and that you are safe. Not only are you good, but Falun Gong can change the entire degenerate world (not just the degenerated CCP) into a good world if only everyone would become a Falun Gong practitioner. It's as if the Chinese people are saying they want to be good, they want to be spiritual, and they want the CCP to officially recognize them as such. Their high sensitivity to criticism of Li or his philosophy seems to be based on a strong emotional desire, even a demand, to be recognized as good. Is it possible that the trauma of the Cultural Revolution has come back to haunt the CCP?[202]

Falun Gong offers the promise of self-control and certainty in life through self-help and controlled expectations. Falun Gong allows people who are adrift in the middle of a violent ocean of change, with no stability or security in sight, to feel they have some semblance of order through control of one's life.[203] People can attain an inner peace, notwithstanding outside turbulence. Falun Gong asks practitioners to be self-directed, driven more by internal spiritual satisfaction than external material rewards or politics. In this way, Falun Gong offers the practitioners a peaceful mind, free of the resentment and uncertainty brought about by the fast pace of reform.[204]

Falun Gong also fills unmet social and medical needs caused by the far-reaching changes brought about by economic reform, especially with regard to transformation of the government's role and potential economic downturns. The government's paternalistic role is waning. This is most evident in the provision of social services:

> One aspect of this is the de-linking of cradle-to-grave welfare provision from state work units. At the same time, health and education services have largely shifted to a "user pays" principle, resulting in a marked growth in inequality of access. Investment is heavily concentrated in urban areas, where populations can afford to purchase services, whereas heavily indebted local governments in rural areas often cannot even afford to pay their schoolteachers. In poor rural areas, people can seldom afford to use local health facilities that are caught in a vicious cycle of rising prices and falling quality.[205]

A high rate of economic growth cannot be sustained for long. The 12.4% average economic growth rate recorded from 1990 to 1995, when investment was flooding into China, became but a dim memory. The official growth rate fell from 9% in 1997 to 7.8% in 1998, but the actual decline could have been even greater. Levels of foreign direct investment continued to fall; in the first two months of 1999, investments dropped by 48%. Industries such as garments and plastic products saw orders shrink by over 20% in the first months of 1999. Exports of toys, textiles, and footwear fell by more than 10%, and the machinery and electrical products sector experienced a drop in sales of 1.9%. Manufacturing overcapacity in 1999 was estimated to be as a high as 50%.[206]

The economic slowdown led to a mounting social crisis and growing hardship for tens of millions of workers and peasants. In the countryside, a vast pool of surplus labor produced by the break-up of the commune system in the 1980s was predicted to reach 200 million people by 2000, or 30% of the workforce. Around 90 million rural migrants seeking work flooded into China's cities, and an "urban poor" of more than 20 million people who could not afford even basic food, shelter, and clothing, had developed even before the onset of the economic crisis throughout Asia. Many were workers laid off by state-owned industries. The World Bank estimated that the suicide rate in China was 30.3 per 100,000 deaths, three times the world average; the suicide rate for women was five times the world average. Each day, 500 Chinese women were committing suicide, overwhelmingly in rural areas. Protests and demonstrations grew over a range of issues, including road tolls, school fees, and mistreatment by local police. According to one estimate, over 10,000 separate incidents took place in rural areas in 1999 alone. In China's major industrial cities, protests by unemployed workers or those threatened with layoffs were a daily occurrence.[207]

In the words of Falun Gong practitioners, the economic conditions in China were becoming intolerable:

> Despite the impressive growth of the economy at a national rate of 10% to 11% during this period, an increasing number of people were threatened with unemployment, displacement, and social insecurity such as delayed pension payments and the reduction or lack of medical benefits. City dwellers could no longer rely on government- or work-unit-subsidized medical benefits. Additionally, the population aging problem was not seriously being met...health maintenance surged, with all major pharmaceuticals companies producing international brands, almost eliminating inexpensive domestic products for disease treatments.[208]

Anxiety over health care pushed people to consider the use of alternative medicine.[209]

The Party and government faced a daunting combination of service gaps, expanding demands for services, and severe fiscal constraints, but they seemed to have little appetite for confronting the situation.[210]

Police Cynicism

This section investigates how PRC officers and the public look at various policing issues by drawing upon the comments posted on an online police forum.

On Police Disillusionment

There are constant complaints that the performance and quality of police officers are not up to professional standards. A new probationary officer ("Jianji jingguan21"[211]) openly complained after he did not make rank:

> When I first wore this police uniform I loved it. It fulfilled my desire for a public security career. But now I am disappointed. There is nothing to do the whole day. People are playing dominos all day. No one is wearing the uniform. I cannot afford to stand out like a sore thumb. After all I am nothing but a probationary officer. Now I have to hang up the uniform by the window. I will probably never wear the uniform again. It is not a good idea to enter the public security system now. Another police officer in my unit informed me that in order to enter the public security system it is better to serve in the military for two years rather than come from the police college. At that time I was very much disappointed.[212]

A female police officer ("maggiesum"[213]) shared the same sentiment:

> Dalian patrol officer, what he [Jianji jingguan21] said is correct. It is more beneficial to serve in the military for assignment purposes. There are 40 people who entered the police with me. After counting and recounting there are no more than 10 people who are graduates of police colleges with me. And then there are a number of municipality and department leaders' children, who graduated from health and arts colleges. One of them was not even 18 years old (a juvenile worker!). There are at least 50% officers who are from the military. Usually they are assigned houses after just a short while. For those of us who have finished a few years of college, we still are not deemed qualified. I do not agree with this. But there is nothing I can do. This is the general environment. Public security college graduates do not get good police assignments, those who have connections do, oh well! At this juncture, I feel very gray. I do not want to say anymore. Too complicated [*fuza*]. Too corrupt [*hei an*]!!![214]

The above comments from the perspective of police practitioners reflect what is going on inside the police: nepotism, favoritism, corruption, and dereliction of duties. Military service and personal connections are considered more important than a police college education and professional training. It is obvious that these younger police officers were disillusioned.[215]

On Police Immorality

In reformed China, police officers are considered to have loose morals (e.g., engaging in extramarital sex) and to be engaging in activities that are illegal and immoral. This runs counter to the Lei Feng spirit. One police officer observed that:

There is a rumor that currently there are a few hundred police officers in my municipality who seek lovers outside the marriage [*jiawai zhao qingren*]. I was disturbed when I heard this. This gives the police a bad name about their social life. I am afraid that I might not be able to find a girl friend. Are the police only supposed to be good at their job? They can be irresponsible in their private life? This is not supposed to happen....[216]

A respondent ("lucia"), possibly a civilian, was quick to comment that, "The women's federation in your area should be busy!"[217] This statement suggests that this kind of misconduct is widespread but not tolerated by the public. More revealing, it suggests that such conduct is significant enough that the public is aware of it and should take action against it, such as monitoring by the women's federation (*fu lian*). The police, rather than serving as role models, are quickly becoming objects of ridicule.

A university graduate in public administration from Fujian considered extramarital affairs to be wrong, for both the public and the police.[218] This stance was supported by another Beijing student ("Xonxue"):

Those who are married and seek out lovers are not being faithful to their own marriages, not being responsible to their families, not being considerate of their lovers, and it should not be done.[219]

An unmarried, university-educated police officer from Guangzhou ("jingcha xia tao"[220]) observed:

Police who seek a mistress, second wife, prostitute…should be fired by the police and expelled from the Party. Why are there no regulations?[221]

This suggests that such conduct is considered by some to be serious enough to warrant Party and state disciplinary action. In essence, the CPC and MPS should have standing policies and rules against conduct considered to be immoral and unprofessional. This comment drew a sharp rebuke from "lucia," the civilian who earlier advocated public accountability and civilian control via the women's federation. It is clear that "lucia" did not think that police internal controls would be effective at all: "Have you not heard of *shang you zhengce, xia you duice* ("central policy, local remedy")?"[222] In an attempt to deflect criticism of the police by a civilian, "jingcha xia tao," the police officer from Guangzhou, immediately challenged this comment: "If nothing happens to you, how can you report!"[223] He was asking the civilian to try to understand the police before pronouncing judgment. In real life, people (including the police) do not, as a rule, report wrongdoings, and superiors do not take action against infractions unless something bad happens. In essence, police officers who have mistresses is no one else's business.[224]

The conversation took another turn when a separated police officer (*fen li jingcha*) observed that: "One will get one's feet wet if one walks by the river." This means that that police are exposed to many corrupting influences, including prostitution, while on duty.[225] Those who do not want to get their feet wet should not join the police. In the United States, it is the same as saying, "If you can't stand the heat, get out of the kitchen." This argument about the corrupting influence of police work was quickly countered by "Qifeng":[226]

What are the police supposed to do? The police are supposed to correct themselves before correcting others [*xian zhengji hou zheng ren*].

The exchange raised another issue: Should officials in general and police officers in particular be held to an exemplary standard of conduct, like the Lei Feng spirit, as in the past? A female college student ("ying fa xue yu") from Hubei[227] best summed up the expectations of the public toward the police:

> The following are a few of my viewpoints: (1) It is absolutely not appropriate for the police to find mistresses. (2) It appears that there is a need for much political thought education at your place. (3) A qualified officer must not only be cautious and conscientious at work [*jing jing ye ye*], but also be strict with one's work style [*zuo feng shang ya yao yanjin*]. (4) Police must start with correcting themselves and not only worry about putting down others. Some people have ruined the police image, but you as a police officer can establish an exemplary image, can you not? (5) "Gold would shine everywhere" if only one does not act contrary to the national symbol and police uniform.[228]

The above exchanges speak to police mentality and vulnerability toward on-the-job corrupting influences. A police officer from Shanghai observed:

> As police officers, we should not find mistresses. From the point of view of a man of economic resources, doing so is understandable. As a salary worker with a fixed income, this is a dangerous game.[229]

The message is clear, that having a mistress is an expensive proposition not to be indulged in, particularly on the salary of a police officer (the low salaries of which have been an issue of much contentious debate).[230] Such indulgence in sex will corrupt the soul and lead to corruption on the job. In contrast, "Xia jingcha," an unmarried police officer from Beijing who had a graduate education, reinforced the theme that having mistresses is not a moral issue but a personal one, commenting that, "I think this is a private affair. If it does not affect work, there should not be a problem."[231] There is a wide range of opinions on this issue. Officers from rural areas, for example, are more likely to reject this kind of conduct on moral grounds. A Sichuan officer replied to an earlier post:

> Police definitely cannot seek out mistresses. You are a police officer. This is not appropriate on the surface of it. The police should have both discipline and dignity. Only the morally degenerate seek out mistresses. Where are you from? If I were you I would report it to the proper authority above.[232]

These comments reveal the existence of and extent of tolerance for police extramarital affairs outside work; such affairs are considered to be immoral by both the police and the public. It is less clear whether such conduct should be prohibited legally or condemned morally, but there is also little doubt that such conduct tarnishes the police image in the eyes of the public.

On Public Apathy
Police always complain about public apathy:

> Let me tell you another real case. A young man was beaten to death with poles for twenty minutes. During the whole time, the victim cried in agony and for help. No one in the residential area reported the case. Yes, I do not deny that there is corruption in our justice system, but that is not the reason why the public failed to testify.[233]

People do not report crimes or give testimony for a number of reasons: (1) they are not keen on the rule of law; (2) they do not feel a civic or legal duty to do so; (3) they do not want to testify against friends and relatives; (4) they do not want to take time from work; (5) they are afraid of retaliation; and (6) they are turned off by police lacking in professional courtesy.[234] Simply put, the police and public do not see eye to eye on public participation in crime control. Disagreement on such a basic issue speaks volumes on the state of the police–public relationship.

On Police Dissent

Police reform measures have taken a toll on officers, giving rise to rumors of police strikes, an idea never before raised with police in a totalitarian country.[235] Not many people online have been brave enough to discuss the issue in public for fear of possible repercussions. One person ranted and wanted to know about the professional responsibility of senior officials commanding dissenting police. Another was upset about such outspokenness: "This is bullshit! Police expressing discontent would not leave any evidence, but street protests will surely be asking for death!"[236] These comments provide a rare opportunity to view Chinese policing from an insider's perspective, with some suggesting that the police are lazy, corrupt, immoral, and not beyond taking their grievances to the street. This is a far cry from the Lei Feng spirit that the Party instilled in the police and presented to the public. This disparity between formal exaltation and informal revelation speaks to a growing credibility gap between leaders and followers, police and public.

On Police Officers as Spouses

Although many Chinese people hold a low opinion of the police and consider the police to be corrupt, abusive, incompetent, and of a lower social status, that has not always been the case. During the Mao era, the police were very well respected. Mao described the relationship as "fish [police] in water [people]." During the reform era, public attitudes toward the police are in free fall. The image of the police can best be observed by examining police marriages.

In an online post, a woman said she had been dating a police officer for two years and planned to marry him. When she asked her father for permission, he disapproved for a number of reasons. Her police officer boyfriend was not her equal in education or socioeconomic status. A traditional Chinese saying suggests that a compatible marriage is one that results in "a bamboo door pairing with a bamboo door, a wooden door pairing with a wooden door." In essence, people should not marry beyond their social and economic status.[237] Also, the boyfriend was not a good person (hao ren). Like others, her father thought the police had no good people. They all used their authority to abuse the people. He also thought that the police were of low quality, low culture, bad temperament, and shady character. A traditional saying advises that, "Good boys do not join the police." Finally, the police were perceived as a big melting pot, capable of corrupting anyone working within it (警察系统是个大染缸).

This web entry elicited 36 comments, nearly all agreeing with the father: "When getting married, do not marry police [嫁人莫嫁警察]." "Your father is right [你的父亲都说对了]." "The image of the police is not very good [貌似现在警察的形象都不怎么好啊]." A woman who was married to a police officer agreed that the occupation is a corrupt melting pot: "Listen to your dad. Few can come out clean from the huge dye pot. I used to have a dedicated and honest husband by my side, but he became shameless, unconscionable, and a crook in that environment [听你父亲的话吧,在大染缸里能够出污泥而不染的太少.我身边就有曾经 一个忠 厚老实 的丈夫在这个环境里变成无耻,无赖,无良的流氓]."

Discussion

As compared with the Mao era, the police image in China is at best an unwholesome one and at worst a despicable one. This is routinely demonstrated by repeated transgressions by rogue police officers on and off duty[238] and has been well documented by insiders (e.g., retired police officers), outsiders (e.g., disgruntled citizens),[239] reformers (e.g., Party leaders and police executives), and the media.[240]

The subject of police quality (really, human quality) has been discussed widely online. Police quality (*jingcha sushi*) has been a major problem for the police and of much concern to the public.[241] It has been referred to as both "quality" (*sushi*) and "self-cultivation" (*xiuang*). For most people in the street, *sushi* is the same as *suyang*, which refers to a person's standards and ability to assume certain tasks and the necessary fundamental conditions for completing certain assignments. Thus, the success and failure of police work hinge on police quality.[242] In the eyes of the public, the Chinese police are "licensed crooks" (*you pai lan-zai*) or "wolves in sheep's clothing." Police are to be feared, not respected. In an online forum regarding a news report of a police officer instigating a deadly attack by discharged criminals on a fellow police officer after an altercation, a commenter said:

> From the perspective of a majority of the Chinese people, they do not have a good impression of the police. This is a "cruel" fact. To be sure…there are real heroes with high stature, but they are woefully few. The staff within the Chinese public security system should take time to reflect upon it. Why are you suffering in public opinion today? Could it be that the people do not understand you?

Although the deteriorating image of the police is not in doubt, the cause and cure defy understanding. The official explanation attributes the poor police image to personal deviance and individual malfeasance—the bad apple theory. The grassroots understanding of the problem is that it is more of a systemic, structural, and cultural problem.

Deteriorating Police and Public Relations

In 2006, the MPS conducted a survey to evaluate relationships between the police and the public from the perspective of urban police officers.[243] Proper interpretation of the data requires knowing something about the sampling method, but the sampling method was not made public; however, the survey did reveal that police officers thought that relationships between them and the public were deteriorating. Based on information about the basic characteristics of the officers responding to the survey, 42% of them had served as police officers between 11 and 20 years; that is, they were mid-level and mid-career officers. Those with fewer or more years of service amounted to 29% each. Because most of the frontline officers are entry-level junior officers (1 to 10 years), the findings might be somewhat skewed by their exposure to or relationships with the public, unless the questions were designed to elicit knowledge of police–public interactions and not simply personal experience, past as well as present. Some of the more important findings of this survey include the following:

- *Frequency of conflicts*—When asked whether they had experienced conflicts with the public when enforcing the law, 71% of the officers reported having conflicts ranging from verbal altercations (50%) to physical encounters (21%); 8% reported that such conflicts resulted in injury. In essence, conflicts with the public seemed to be becoming the norm, supporting the basic premise of this discussion that police have not earned the respect of the people so their authority is challenged on every turn. This makes it difficult to establish a good working relationship between the police and the public.

- *Circumstances*—When asked what kind of duties were more likely to lead to confrontations, 34% said "dealing with public disputes," 23% said "dealing with mass incidents," 13% said "making arrests," 12% said "dealing with non-police operations," 10% said "dealing with public order cases," 6% said "rescuing kidnapped women and children," and 2% said "dealing with traffic incidents." These responses lay to rest the idea that conflicts result from reactions to police actions, especially law enforcement activities such as traffic enforcement. In this survey, making arrests accounted for only 13% of the conflicts; in fact, the primary situations leading to conflicts were public disputes and mass incidents (57% of responses).

- *Background of people involved in confrontations*—When asked about the occupational status and characteristics of those involved in confrontations with the police officers, respondents reported that 32% were unemployed, 29% were itinerants, 24% were peasants, 6% were workers, and 3% were traders (6% were not identified). Among these, 30% were drunk. This breakdown of people who have confronted the police is instructive. In most instances, the police rarely had problems with educated, urban, upright citizens; most of the people involved in conflicts with the police appeared to be unemployed, itinerants, or uneducated peasants. In that case, the police seem to be getting a bad rap from having to deal with society's marginal individuals, those who are unemployed or drifters. Because both of these groups are likely to be from out of town and with few roots, the police are less likely to have a permanent relationship with them. This goes against conventional wisdom that only when the police take on the good citizens should the public begin to be concerned.

- *Age of people involved in confrontations*—When asked about the age distribution of people involved in police confrontations, the respondents reported that 4% were between 15 and 20, 35% between 21 and 35, 29% between 36 and 45, and 25% were 45 and above (7% were not identified). This tells us that people protesting police actions are not confined to a certain age group. Aside from juveniles, the confrontations reported appeared to be a fairly universal phenomenon; in fact, a fairly significant percentage of protestors came from the pre-reform generation. People of all ages have their own reasons for challenging police authority. Young people have less respect for the police and are more harassed by them. Middle-aged people tend to have more run-ins with the police, and the older generation faults the police for not living up to their lofty expectations of what a cop should be like.

- *Dealing with confrontations*—When asked how they deal with police and public confrontations, 79% of the respondents reported that they adopted the principle of maintaining a peaceful attitude without sacrificing fundamental principles, 17% chose to be tolerant and smile, and 4% did not know what to do. No officer chose either to stand firm and argue or to walk away.

- *Police–public interactions*—When asked about their interactions with the public, 80% of the officers indicated that they had regular exchanges with the public, 80% said they received regards from the public, 46% routinely assisted the public, and 54% had occasionally assisted the public.

- *Declining legitimacy*—Overall, 50% felt that they had lost legitimacy and authority in the eyes of the public, 21% believed otherwise, and 13% said their image had not changed (16% were not identified).
- *Reasons for decline in respect for police authority*—The respondents readily pointed to negative media reporting, low image of the police, shifting social conditions, heightened public legal knowledge, unstable policy and unclear law, and lack of timely and adequate sanctions for attacks on police officers.
- *Lack of public support*—The loss of police legitimacy is reflected in lack of public support. In this survey, it was reported that, in the majority of confrontations between the police and the public, 55% of the public would stand by and watch, 13% would actively support the police, 7% would support the agitator, and 25% would want to stir up the situation more. This is the clearest evidence yet, from the perspective of the police, that civilians are no longer their friends. Police law enforcement and order maintenance activities are becoming a spectator sport. The battle line between the police and public has clearly been drawn.

Reasons for Joining the Police Force

Research has shown that people the world over join the police force for many reasons, including opportunities to help people and enforce the law, job security, good salary, and exciting work. In the United States, the top reasons why young people are attracted to policing are being able to help people and the excitement of police work.[244] In the two Asian countries of Korea and Taiwan, we find that the reasons for joining differ, in both type and priority.

Korean police cadets reported choosing a police career because of job security and a steady salary, as well as the intrinsic qualities of the job (fighting crime, helping people, excitement) (Table 4.4).[245] They are less attracted by the authority of law enforcement and not influenced by significant others (parents, teachers, friends, siblings). Given a long tradition of neo-Confucius teachings, a surprising finding of this study was that the attraction for job security rated higher than public service, and there was an especially exceptional low regard for parental influence. These unexpected findings can be explained by looking through the eyes of the sampled respondents—young police cadets of lower economic status who decided to join against all odds. These cadets chose to join this profession despite mainstream thinking and parental advise that police officers are not well respected in society. In so doing, they were being somewhat rebellious. When they had started to live their dream at a police university, they had to rationalize and defend their decision. They justified their rebelliousness as the price to pay for autonomy and self-sufficiency. Independency and security are important goals for lower class youth and, once achieved, are taken as signs of success within their peer group. It helps to interpret these findings by drawing a distinction between Confucian culture in books and on the street, in historical times and today. The Confucian high culture of fighting crime and helping others might still be subscribed to in theory, but in day-to-day life pragmatic considerations, such as job security, dominate.

Among the Taiwan police cadets, the top five reasons for joining the police were good salary and fringe benefits, influence of parents, job security, helping people, and fighting crime (Table 4.5). The bottom three reasons were the influence of classmates, giving policing a try until promotions, and no other choice. In Taiwan, the reasons for joining fall

TABLE 4.4   Factor Analysis for Reasons to Choose Policing as a Career in South Korea

Factor	Loading	Mean
Influence from significant others		2.15
Influence of parents	.76	
Influence of relatives	.79	
Influence of teachers	.62	
Influence of siblings	.75	
Job security and steady salary		4.02
Need for steady salary	.80	
Good salary and fringe benefits	.74	
Security of the job	.66	
Authority and law enforcement		3.46
Working with autonomy	.60	
Prestige and status of the occupation	.72	
Enforcement of the law	.68	
Authority and power	.72	
Intrinsic qualities of the job		3.77
Excitement and adventure	.72	
Chance to fight crime	.54	

Source: Moon, B. and Hwang, E.-G., *Journal of Criminal Justice*, 32(3), 223–229, 2004. With permission.

within the range of cultural expectations. Three of the top five reasons are exactly what would be expected of a young person starting out in life in a Confucius society. Obeying one's parents is a family mandate, helping people is a communal obligation, and fighting crime is a moral and social imperative. By Confucius' reckoning, a well-ordered society begins with cultivating oneself, then regulating the families, and finally ordering the States:

Wishing to order well their States, they first regulated their families
Wishing to regulate their families, they first cultivated their persons.
Wishing to cultivate their persons, they first rectified their hearts.
Wishing to rectify their hearts, they first sought to be sincere in their thoughts.
Wishing to be sincere in their thoughts, they first extended to the utmost of their knowledge.
Such extension of knowledge lay in the investigation of things.[246]

The high ranking of seeking a good salary and fringe benefits as well as job security can be explained by what I called the secularization of Confucius' teachings and should not be considered to be a case of inverting Confucius' values. In a modern, materialistic society, in order for one to seek self-cultivation, help others, and fight crime, one must have the material resources and job security to do so. A good way to respect one's parents is to be self-sufficient and able to tend to the parents' needs. Indeed, many young Chinese justify their search for a good job as repaying their parents by honoring their expectations and securing their retirement.

TABLE 4.5   Score and Rank of Reasons for Choosing a Police Career in Taiwan

Reason	Mean	Mode	Median	Rank
Good salary and fringe benefits	1.086	1.0	1.0	1
Influence of parents	1.073	1.0	1.0	2
Job security	0.914	1.0	1.0	3
To help people	0.759	1.0	1.0	4
To fight crime	0.709	1.0	1.0	5
Need for a steady salary	0.659	1.0	1.0	6
Excitement and adventure	0.491	1.0	1.0	7
Law enforcement	0.42	1.0	1.0	8
Early retirement and good pension	0.35	1.0	1.0	9
Influence of other relatives	0.227	1.0	1.0	10
Avoid military service or enter male-dominated occupation	0.191	0.5	1.0	11
Authority and power	0.168	0.0	1.0	12
Influence of siblings	0.132	0.0	1.0	13
Prestige and status	0.023	0.0	1.0	14
Influence of teachers	−0.214	0.0	0.0	15
Work autonomy	−0.218	0.0	−1.0	16
Influence of classmates or friends	−0.306	0.0	−1.0	17
Just try until seeing promotions	−0.5	−1.0	−1.0	18
No other choice	−1.041	−1.0	−1.0	19

Source: Tarng, M.-Y. et al., *Journal of Criminal Justice*, 29(1), 45–46, 2001. With permission.

Note: The survey sample consisted of freshmen at the Central Police University in Taiwan. They had just graduated from high school and passed the entrance examination for the university on July 10, 1998; they did not have any previous academic training or police work experience. The sample included 190 male (86.4%) and 32 female (13.6%) respondents for a total of 222). All but one male were married. Most of them were very young; 93.4% were between 18 and 20.

The lowest ranking choices can be explained by the fact that modern Taiwanese classmates are no longer as close as they once were. Trying out for the police as a job prospect contingent on promotion and otherwise as a backup career when all else fails does not generally apply to the high-achieving, military-age police cadres found in Taiwan today, those who have pursued this profession by choice rather than considering it to be a fallback, last-resort job.

Turning back to China, Wu et al. published a study in 2009 that addressed police cadets' motives for becoming police officers in China.[247] When they surveyed 182 cadets from a prominent police college by asking them 63 close-ended questions, they found that the highest ranking motives for joining included job security and benefits, the opportunity to help people, the desire to enforce the law, and family influence.

How Young People Regard Policing[248]

Looking at the reasons why young people join the police is instructive with regard to the status of the police in society and how they are perceived by the people in the street. From the online discussion below, we can see that the police have lost much of their past admiration. People, especially young people, do not look up to the police as their parents once did.

To many young people, public security is just another job, attractive because of its uniform and potential power and security, not because it is viewed as an honorable profession or prestigious job. This is a total departure from how the Party envisioned the police and how the MPS sees itself. This investigation into such conflicting expectations begins with a look at reasons why people join the police. The web postings below, from the *Tianya* "Police Corner" in 2006 and 2007, will serve as an introduction. If one reads them with care, they sum up quite nicely what the debate is all about (Table 4.6).

When the forum master, "Mature Criminal Police" ("成熟刑警"), invited commenters to post opinions on why they became a cop, he received 121 responses over the next several months. "Mature Criminal Police" started the discussion with his own observations.[249] His basic assumption was that people join the police to put food on the table (当警察是为了吃饭).[250] He suggested that people join the police to make a living, not for ideological reasons, such as serving the people:

> I think we all are secular people. Secular people naturally join the police for secular reasons. When I was young and idealistic, my motive to join the police was full of idealism. Now that I have grown up my motive to join the police naturally involved a lot of secular reasons.[251]

The forum master's proposal of a secular vs. ideological model resonated with many of those who participated in the discussion. He further observed four main reasons, in addition to the secular one, why people join the police:

1. *Wearing a uniform* (穿警服)—This can be considered the egotistical reason. Many people join the police because of the respect the uniform can impart. Some wish to don a uniform to impress others with their police authority, some to make sure that the hawkers do not cheat them, some because small-time hoodlums are afraid of them, and some because pretty girls love it. This is a childish reason to join, and after a while wearing the uniform becomes a burden, but the majority of recruits join for the uniform.
2. *Carrying out justice* (打抱不平)—This can be considered the idealistic reason. When people see others being taken advantage of, they have the urge to right the wrong. Private citizens have neither the power nor weapons to protect themselves, much less help others. But, if one were a police officer, then it would be an entirely different matter. After joining the police, though, people change. Still, this idealistic motive to serve others remains an important reason for joining the police force.
3. *Media influence* (影视剧的影响)—This can be considered the publicity reason. No matter what the police function, even if it is just communications work, people want to join police out of a sense of pride picked up from watching movies and television shows. They think they would be lucky to be a police officer and expect to find the work to be psychologically rewarding.
4. *Being realistic* (现实的想法)—This can be considered the pragmatic reason. Policing is stable work. Working in the cities, one can obtain some income on the side as a result of one's position and authority.

The forum master could not identify a single, pervasive reason for why people wanted to join the police. He did not specifically single out any of the reasons listed here as having more bearing on the decision. He clearly thought, though, that the secular reason was the

TABLE 4.6   Online Comments on Why People Join the Police

No.	Commenter	Comment	Themes
1	kill155	The same as saying to have rice to eat.	Making a living
2	leftcoffee	LZ is crazy…attack anyone on sight.	—
3	iamga	To wear a uniform. TV influence. I joined for these two reasons. I bet 95% of the brothers joined for the same reason.	Attracted to uniform; influenced by television
4	路过秋风	20 years ago, it was my career; 10 years ago, it was my job; now it is for my survival needs.	Change from idealism to making a living
5	追梦人0	In order to live, no other way. With my low qualifications, can only join the police.	Not qualified to do anything else
6	luoningyuxuan	My educational qualifications are not high. I graduated from police college and do not know what I am good at. Only know what I do not know.…It happened that this job was assigned to me at graduation. I dare not go anywhere else. I chose PSB because it is a familiar place. Good or bad I can handle it.	Not qualified to do anything else
7	猫眼瞧人	Want to chat with prisoners.	Get to know criminals
8	书生惆怅英雄梦	My motive is to satisfy my living needs.	Making a living
9	iamga	Forum master should be a bureau chief by now.	—
10	zhihuhark	What would I do if I did not join the police?	Not qualified to do anything else
11	活不明白	When I graduated, I was about to sign an employment contract with Jiu Chuan Satellite Center but I missed the appointment. With no other options on hand, I applied to the provincial PSB.…If asked the real reason, it is because I had no choice. If I had to choose again, I would rather enter the factory or make my first pot of gold.	Force of circumstances
12	laochuo	I believe many people join with aspirations for justice. But as many join for childish reasons. Whatever the reasons, once one joins the police one should try to be a good officer.	Idealism
13	卜小斋	*Internal Affairs* Chinese People's Public Security University version.[a]	Infiltrate police
14	卜小斋	[Incomprehensible]	—
15	海岛浪子23	Realization of self-actualization needs, because police can provide society with the broadest level of service.	Maslow's self-actualization
16	高桥健一	I was following the crowd. The police were recruiting a lot of officers. I scored exceptionally high.	Following the crowd
17	iamga	Adoration of violence.…I suspect this is the reason for many brothers.	Lure of violence
18	zpl8888	Originally it was to remove the bad and secure the good. Now it is to protect oneself.	Change from idealism to making a living
19	lspln123	Get to know a police officer. He will tell you stories about solving crimes.[b]	Interesting work
20	高桥健一	According to my test score with public security, I could qualify for any job in the municipality, including local taxation bureau…really stupid.	Regret

TABLE 4.6 (Continued)   Online Comments on Why People Join the Police

No.	Commenter	Comment	Themes
21	muxiaosad	Too simple minded when signing up. Working as a police to get something to eat.	Making a living
22	mangzu	Graduates of police college can be assigned jobs… simple reason.	Making a living
23	非非舞舞	I overslept and missed the graduate entrance examination. I was too afraid to tell my parents. Luckily, I noticed the police were recruiting.…I signed up to keep my parents off my back.	Force of circumstances
24	titagon	Originally, police is an ideal job. Now, it is to make a living,	Change from idealism to making a living
25	人小妖子	Agree with #18.	Change from idealism to making a living
26	iamga	Agree with #23.	Force of circumstances
27	rencolqq	Attracted to uniform, now regret.	Attracted to uniform
28	好个实在人	There is no alternative but to do so.	Force of circumstances
29	aiweiang	When I joined the police at the bottom level, my father wrote me a letter: "Son, father joined the police at 26. You are also 26 years old. Father and son should eat out of the same bowl."…I worked hard to test for police once again, in order to honor my father and mother. I think it is worth it.	Honor the parents
30	小心我咬死你	I joined for food. I now regret. Police work as a living is difficult to do.	Making a living
31	hugh857	It's all for making a living.	Making a living
32	长白山泡泡	Is there a friend who works in the border, why do you pick this profession?	—
33	blue	Police make a living.	Making a living
34	鹰009	Other jobs are boring. In this job, I have contacts with a lot of people.	Interesting work
35	盛唐狂情	I studied economics and management in college. Right after school, I worked competitively until I became a manager. The money I made then was more than what I make now after 7 years as a cop.…I missed seeing my old mother every day. There was no alternative but to apply for the lowest level of civil service.…After all, once you get used to being a police officer, you will not get used to doing other work.	Take care of parent
36	高桥健一	It is all very boring.	Making a living
37	llnn000	To make a living.	Making a living
38	kffjj	I graduated from a political–legal college. I joined the police by accident. If I had to do it all over again, I would not be a police officer.	Making a living
39	TH211027	I was born to be a police officer. I should maximize my talent.	Idealism
40	苍苍茫茫	Police is my dream.…It is all fate.	Idealism
41	153623648	To make a living.	Making a living

TABLE 4.6 (Continued)   Online Comments on Why People Join the Police

No.	Commenter	Comment	Themes
42	TACteam	To make a living.	Making a living
43	飞花无声	Railroad police is my work, never my profession.	Making a living
44	这名总可以了吧	Grew up in military camp. Father left the military for the police. I fell in love with the uniform. Mother did not want me to leave.	Family legacy
45	默默的梦想	Make a living, no other reason.	Making a living
46	警界一哥	Do not know how to do anything except for policing.	Police college graduate without other job skills
47	淹面王子	Boss. Graduates from police college naturally become police officers, not security guards.	Police college graduate
48	高桥健一	Response to #46: Do you think being a police post head is easy?	—
49	michaelado	I have had this dream since I was a child. I wanted to be a solider. Being a cop is for a hot-blooded man. There is no other choice.	Idealism
50	小马车酷酷	Attracted to uniform and influenced by TV. It is funny. Before I joined the police, I thought about wearing the uniform to show off. During my 4 years of policing, I have worn my uniform only 5 times.	Attracted to uniform; influenced by television
51	marlizq	Once upon a time it was a dream; now it is a way to make a living.	Change from idealism to making a living
52	QQ我来也	Make a living.	Making a living
53	披着狼皮的羊007	Originally I wanted to go to police college and not take a higher education examination. Now it is a way to make a living. Originally a bit of honor came with the job, but now no one respects the police. When they need you, you are treated like a god. When they do not need you, you are not treated as a human being. This is the reality.	Making a living
54	本ID已注销	For 8 eight years I acted as a hero (侠客), now I am just a police officer (捕快).	Change from idealism to making a living
55	caoxiooo	To tell the truth, this few years of being a cop is tragedy enough for eight lifetimes.	Regret
56	当门牙	"Wanted to chat with prisoners"—this guy is joking.	—
57	秋天梧桐	Making a living.	Making a living
58	我要生两个孩子	Joined the police because I do not study well and could not enter university. Police college requires lower entrance grades and I could earn civil servant status. The income is not small, uniform and shoes are issued, agency provides free food.	Making a living
59	花香玖玖	Above, your answer could easily mislead people about the police. Ha, Ha.	—
60	留得话1	In the beginning, I joined the police because of honor. After I joined, a leader asked me to become a criminal investigator because I was young. I joined criminal investigation as instructed. In the beginning, I had the feeling of being a criminal investigator on TV. Later I found out that I got the promotion so I could be a tool of the leaders, because the measure of success here is by clearance, arrest, and prosecution rate. Sub-bureau chiefs try to outperform each other in their numbers.	Change from idealism to making a living

TABLE 4.6 (Continued) Online Comments on Why People Join the Police

No.	Commenter	Comment	Themes
	留得话1 (cont.)	They encourage clearing fake cases and obtaining coerced confessions. If you do not go along you are deemed a coward and incompetent. You will be given restrictive assignments, and they can even make up reasons to fire you and deprive you of your living. Now I feel so conflicted. On the one hand, policing is just a job to put food on the table. On the other hand, we need to live by our principles. I am no longer on why I work as a police officer. It is driving me crazy.	
61	A诺诺	Why do you join the police? To make a living. Whoever joins this discussion is a crazy person.[c]	—
62	不是BT不聚头	Oh, after three years of police college, what can I do besides being a police officer? Lack of awareness….	Police college graduate without other job skills
63	古君王剑	I suffer from carsickness, that is why I want to conquer all cars.	—
64	necnecnec	If I do not join the police, I can only steal and rob to live.	Not qualified to do anything else
65	我要生两个孩子	Response to "Above, your answer could easily mislead people about the police. Ha, Ha."—That is because the police officers around me are all like that.	—
66	叉叉你个圈圈	At that time I looked into civil service recruitment. Everywhere I looked in the small place I lived only the police were recruiting. I thought I'd give it a try, so I applied. After practicing for 6 months, I actually qualified. What is strange is that the police accepted those 0.5 point above recruitment standard. After the interview and physical, and training, I joined.	Desire to be a civil servant
67	lengxue1128	Just a job.	Making a living
68	我要生两个孩子	My ex-boyfriend told me that if he did not join the police he would be a hoodlum.	Making a living
69	未央花	In the beginning, it was for a stable occupation. Also, having a job in hand is better than having no job and waiting to be hired. I do not like the occupation. As to wearing the uniform? After wearing it, it is disgusting. Wearing the uniform is uncomfortable, very restrictive, and troublesome when going out!	Making a living
70	廿八都	Police is an occupation, not a personal career.	Making a living
71	老鼹鼠	Basically, I had no chance to choose my occupation. At the time, my higher education scores only allowed me to enter police college or finance school. But I get a headache whenever I look at figures, thus I joined the police. It took me a minute to fill out my wish list. This one minute decided my life in uniform. Good or bad, there is nothing to complain about. We have only one life to live, and cannot lead two lives. That is why I think the LZ's question is meaningless.	Police college graduate without other job skills
72	议勿使用	Like this occupation. After a year there was some regret. After a few years I fell in love with it. Besides policing I really do not know what else to do.	Likes policing

TABLE 4.6 (Continued)   **Online Comments on Why People Join the Police**

No.	Commenter	Comment	Themes
73	piratemc	In the beginning, I had no job! I applied to be a civil servant. I did not qualify for other jobs. Only the police accepted low entrance scores! I took the test and scored a 4, nearly fainted.	Police college graduate without other job skills
74	bjcn	[Incomprehensible]	—
75	我其实真的是只猫	To be yelled at by others. In reality, because of being lazy, because the police guarantee jobs upon graduation. Its intake decision is made early and no school fees. Because I have watched many movies. Because I want to hold guns, etc. It is complicated. I just went along and became a police officer. After joining the police, I feel especially happy when a case is cleared and I help victims to lose their anger. Many of my colleagues have this kind of feeling.	Complicated
76	68121	Making a living is the main reason for most police officers.	Making a living
77	killall79	Dream since young.	Idealism
78	岸边的虾子	I chose to join the police because, first, my father influenced me. Second, it is a stable job, and a civil service one. I used to feel that this job is glorious. Third, after three years of police college, I do not know what else I can do.	Parental influence; police college graduate without other job skills; making a living
79	maverick_1	Uniform! Actualize a dream! Development! Make a living.	Idealism; making a living
80	岸边的虾子	If you are unemployed you can be a police officer. If you can go to any other department do not be a cop.	Making a living
81	perlute	Don't know the reason.[d]	—
82	巡大街	TMD [Swear by mother], in order not to clean dishes, I applied to the police. Now that I am a police officer, it is to make a living.	Making a living
83	迎风的篱笆	I joined the police college without any urge to do so. Later, I joined the PSB without any expectations. I work and live with a conscience and with an ordinary peace of mind.	Making a living
84	闲敲键盘落烟灰	When we are young, we have dreams. When we grow older, our thinking matures. When I first applied for the police I spoke about the benefits of being a cop: wearing a uniform, carrying a gun, being tough, showing glory. For these reasons, I joined the police. Now that I think about it, police work is a chicken bone.[e] There are no benefits to being a police officer. Let's talk about wearing a uniform. I wore the uniform all right, but the first time, with the old uniform, the green one, recruits had to pay for their uniforms. The second time I had a new uniform. This time I do not what happened with the police recruits, but they are treated differently from older cadres anyway. The finance department sent money for the uniforms to the PSB, which resulted in the police chief using the money to buy cars, and we had to pay for our new uniform. Let's talk about firing guns.	Change from idealism to making a living

TABLE 4.6 (Continued)   Online Comments on Why People Join the Police

No.	Commenter	Comment	Themes
	闲敲键盘落烟灰 (cont.)	Since I joined the police until now I have fired a gun on the range three times and held it twice....I have applied for a gun permit for the Nth time and still am not done. Lets talk about toughness. Now who dares to get tough. If you raise your voice a bit, people might petition against you. Let's talk about achieving glory. I have not achieved the slightest bit of glory.... Finally, bottom line, it is like a chicken bone.	
85		[Not relevant]	—
86		[Not relevant]	—
87	lg930	My dream was to be a football star, but my family cannot support me! Later, I found out that I was not cut out to be a football player. When I applied at universities, my family insisted on police college because of future job stability. I thought to myself, it is great to have stability! Nothing to worry about! Playing every day. It is not only stable for making a living but I have a sumptuous meal every day. This is what a good job is all about. Who cares about whether it is police or not police work?	Making a living
88	放狼的孩子不说谎	Making a living. Making a good living.	Making a living
89	txzhuyec	I became a police officer quite by accident—it is an occupation I did not dream of.	Joined by accident
90	pc9960	Family influence—three generations of police. Yes. All are new China's police officers. Also another reason—eat rice!!!	Family legacy; making a living
91	本溪县	What's so good about being a police officer? Others all think that the police are civil servant service jobs with good work and good pay. But all of us know how much a police officer makes in a month. Police still want face....Being a police officer is arranged by fate....From my perspective, until now, it is for raising a family, more simply for survival.	Making a living
92	朱朱1023	Response to above: Have to consult psychologist often, tiring.	—
93	laifulin	It is said that the salary is high—now I found out that is a rumor. Very few civil service jobs are for generalists; the police is one of the few. Working for a state enterprise for a few years I learned that it is in reality a family business of the leaders.	Making a living
94	hbhrudy	It was a dream of mine to enter police college to be a police officer. In order to be a police officer, I studied hard for the examination, but this is kind of an unspeakable job.	Change from idealism to making a living
95	koolzx	Seeing as one has joined, one should be at peace with it. Let bygones be bygones.	Acceptance
96	jingcha122	Purely attracted by the uniform.	Attracted by uniform
97	两点零二分	I have been cheated.	Revenge

TABLE 4.6 (Continued)   Online Comments on Why People Join the Police

No.	Commenter	Comment	Themes
98	偶尔想说	I chose to enter police college with my higher education examination.…After you have been a police for a few years, when your police age is similar to mine, you will know what I mean.	—
99	田螺姑娘11	Our family has two generations of police. If I am successful in joining the police, it will be the third generation. I respect one of my uncles very much. Rumor has it that he is a very well-respected criminal investigator. I have to catch up with him!	Family legacy
100	see-sea	At the time the university was not recruiting. My higher education examination could only get me into police college. That is how I joined the police.	Police college graduate without other job skills
101	whud	To be frank, at the time I did not give it much thought. Just wanted to change jobs and experience the mystique (that is what I think) of public security work.	Change jobs
102	arniu1234	After graduation I needed to find work to support myself. It so happened I qualified [for the police]. I applied.	Making a living
103	see-sea	I joined the police not knowing what I was doing.	Regret
104	蓝天ZF	Response to # 96: Don't you think the 99 uniform is ugly?	—
105	昨夜纯情	Police work is like a chicken bone. Awhile ago I was considering transferring to the City Committee or other units. I have worked for the police for 15 years. Not only do I have nothing to show for it, but all that is left are a few bitter memories.…Currently, my heart feels lonely and distant…Shenzen is recruiting for police officers and I have been selected, but I feel that the working conditions there might not be as good as I imagine—for example, public order is bad, cost of living is high, and development space limited, etc. Finally, I did not go. Best to find an opportunity to work in small business. Just a bit of happiness is fine, damned tenderness of heart.	Change from idealism to making a living
106	卡菲勒	Purely attracted by uniform, although it is rather naïve. But, really, I joined because of the police uniform.	Attracted by uniform
107	xinbo826	Welcome to those joining the police elite, demonstrate your ability.…	—
108	丽影天使	I objected to the arrangement of my parents	Rebellion
109	iamga	Was seduced.	Idealism
110	西窗夜烛	I studied at a police college. After graduation, I could not go to work anywhere else, nearly fainted and died!	Police college graduate without other job skills
111	xianditianma	I am an easy-going person. I have worked a number of jobs. Legal assistant is boring. As with court and procuratorate. Being a lawyer is too corrupt. Later, after getting a bit older, I felt that the police would be more stable and I joined. The only thing is that I did not think it through too carefully and joined as railroad police…a little troublesome.	Making a living

TABLE 4.6 (Continued)   Online Comments on Why People Join the Police

No.	Commenter	Comment	Themes
112	leiyutian_1011	In the beginning, it was for a dream. Reflecting now, I regret my innocence and naivety....If not for the need to make a living, I would not think about joining the police.	Change from idealism to making a living
113	弟弟1500	For the rise of China.	Idealism
114	basics	Accident and mistake.	Regret
115	徐三疯	Originally, it was to make a living. After graduation from police college, there was nowhere else to go. Now, it is to fight for face. Cannot be a police officer who is looked down upon by black society.	Police college graduate without other job skills; change from making a living to idealism
116	特警也怕人多	While in training I lost weight, trained my body, and got paid. Worthwhile.	Get in shape
117	黑猫警官	Police...will not make you rich, but will not keep your stomach empty.	Making a living
118	超级大头	[Not relevant]	—
119	zcp6803	I didn't give enough thought to becoming a police officer, and I thought about giving it up to do something I am more suited for. Later, I discovered that except for police, it is not possible for me to do other things! Because all my knowledge is job related!	Police college graduate without other job skills
120	Jay518201	Cost of housing is high now. Working as civil servant to obtain housing benefits.	Housing benefits
121	我爱小海鸥	The police have a lot of power, a lot of supplemental income.	Power and extra income

[a] Gang members have been known to infiltrate the police to spy on them. *Internal Affair* is a movie about gangsters infiltrating the Hong Kong Police with police recruits to compromise its operations.

[b] This comment could be in jest, but it might also be sincere in its suggestion to talk to a police officer to better understand their work and their motivation.

[c] We do not know why the commenter thinks it is crazy to join this discussion. Perhaps he is fed up with the negativism.

[d] Perhaps this commenter had multiple reasons, too many to list, or, more likely, perhaps it was difficult to figure out a particular reason for joining.

[e] Police work is like a chicken bone—there is no meat left but it is not yet ready to be thrown away.

most influential, capable of trumping the others. He further suggested that people joined for all sorts of reasons, more than those listed here; for example, one might decide to join for job security but still relish the opportunity to serve people and wear an impressive uniform. In this regard, Maslow's multiple motivations of behavior come to mind:

Within the sphere of motivational determinants any behavior tends to be determined by several or *all* of the basic needs simultaneously rather than by only one of them. The latter would be more an exception than the former. Eating may be partially for the sake of filling the stomach, and partially for the sake of comfort and amelioration of other needs. One may make love not only for pure sexual release, but also to convince one's self of one's masculinity, or to make a conquest, to feel powerful, or to win more basic affection. As an illustration, I may point out that it would be possible (theoretically if not practically) to analyze a single act of an individual and see in it the expression of his physiological needs, his safety needs, his love needs, his esteem needs and self-actualization. This contrasts sharply with the more naive brand of trait psychology in which one trait or one motive accounts for a certain kind of act, i.e., an aggressive act is traced solely to a trait of aggressiveness.[252]

The forum master's understanding of the decision to join the police is supported by research into Chinese thinking styles.[253] Unlike Westerners, the Chinese are not linear, dualistic thinkers (e.g., this/that, either/or, here/there). Chinese are dynamic, multiplex thinkers (e.g., give and take, a bit of this and a bit of that, if not this then that). To make a decision, all kinds of considerations come into play, and many factors play off against each other, individually or collectively, until a well-balanced solution is at hand that recognizes the relative contribution of each factor in a holistic way.[254]

Online Discussion

The forum master's proposed reasons for why people wish to join the police[255] initiated a lively web discussion and laid the foundation for this investigation into people's motivation to join the police (see Table 4.6). The call for comments garnered a total of 121 comments, which have been translated and summarized in no more than 40 words. The first 50 comments have been divided into various categories, from job security to family to attracted by uniform and influenced by TV (Table 4.7). Two questions were posed for this analysis: (1) Why do Chinese youth join the police? (2) How are their reasons for joining similar to or different from two other Asian countries, Korea and Taiwan? Refer back to the earlier discussion on why youths from Korea (see Table 4.4) and Taiwan (see Table 4.5) join the police. Taiwan was chosen for this comparison because it is part of China politically ("one country, two systems"), economically (trade), socially (family roots, marriages), and culturally (language, history, tradition, Confucianism). Korea was chosen because of its deep Confucianism roots, recent economic liberation, and persistent political challenges; that is, it resembles China's reform process.

Analysis of Online Comments

The top two reasons for joining the police were to make a living (22%) and having no other choice (14%). One person joined out of necessity: "I joined for food. I now regret. Police work as a living is difficult to do." Another apparently joined by accident: "I graduated from a political–legal college. I joined the police by accident. If I had to do it all over again, I would not be a police officer." Still another did so because he overslept and was fearful of his mother's admonition: "I overslept and missed the graduate entrance examination. I was too afraid to tell my parents. Luckily, I noticed the police were recruiting....I signed up to keep my parents off my back." All in all, many of the commenters had joined for a very practical reason: security.

Very few (only 2, or 4%) joined for altruistic reasons, such as helping people, saving lives, or fighting crime; however, if we were to combine those who originally joined for idealistic reasons but became jaded later and ended up staying for good pay and job security, these would represent 12% of the sample. As one commenter frankly admitted: "Originally it was to remove the bad and secure the good. Now it is to protect oneself." Separating the reasons for joining between being *pulled* (attracted for perhaps idealistic reasons) vs. being *pushed* (to get a job, no other choice, police college) suggests slightly more push (force of circumstances) than pull (intrinsic appeal of police work).

TABLE 4.7   Reasons Cited in 50 Online Comments for Joining the Chinese Police

Reason	Comment No.	No. of Comments
Make a living	1, 8, 21, 22, 30, 31, 33, 36, 37, 38, 41, 42, 43, 45	14
Force of circumstances	11, 23, 26, 28	4
Change from idealism to making a living	4, 18, 24, 25	4
Idealism	12, 39, 40, 49	4
Parents/family	29, 35, 44	3
Not qualified to do anything else	5, 6, 10	3
Attracted to uniform and/or influenced by television	3, 27, 50	3
Police college graduate	46, 47	2
Interesting work	19, 34	2
Get to know criminals	7	1
Infiltrate police	13	1
Self-actualization	15	1
Following the crowd	16	1
Lure of violence	17	1
Regret	20	1
Reason not clear; irrelevant entry	2, 9, 14, 32, 48	5

Very few people opted for policing because they thought it would be exciting or offer the opportunity to fight crime. Reading through the comments and between the lines, one cannot help but get the feeling that policing is not what it once was in revolutionary China, before the reform and under Mao, an honorable vocation in service of the people, with high respect and real authority, formally and informally. Instead, today's Chinese youth consider policing to be just another job, a way to make a decent living with ample security and good benefits, not to mention a flashy uniform.

What is conspicuously missing is mention of communist ideology, leader's thinking, or the Party line as reasons for joining. It is fair to observe that police candidates who were born after the 1980s have abandoned Mao's ideal and the Lei Feng spirit. It would appear that what they want out of life and from a police career is radically different than that of their communist predecessors. What they want is an easy life—material goods, immediate gratification, and self-satisfaction—without sacrifice. One might wonder, then, what would attract the more materialistic youth of today to policing and how they would carry out their duties under leaders from a different era and laboring under another paradigm. More particularly, would they be able to work under a traditional communist mindset, a mindset that was born of the revolutionary years of oppression, suffering, and struggle? Alternatively, how might the MPS adjust the police philosophy and culture to accommodate this new generation of police without compromising the institutional identity, core values, organizational ethos, and work style of the storied MPS?

Based on recent events and according to Chinese political authorities, the Party line is that post-1980s recruits, when given the opportunity and under correct Party leadership, are capable of rising to the occasion and showing their true Lei Feng credentials of self-sacrifice and public service:

> As a matter of fact, it is not a coincidence that the young generation would bring home the virtues of "great compassion, benevolence, and gallantness," as enlightened in Chinese traditional culture. By fully enjoying the achievement of China's 30 years of reform and opening up, the Post-80s take more advantage over any other previous generation.[256]

Wishful thinking, astute assessment, or putting the best face on a bad situation? Only time will tell. In the meantime, with regard to the conflict between utility and ideology, we need to concede that post-1980s police officers, compared to earlier generations, are relatively more individualistic, egotistical, utilitarian, and self-serving. This is not to say, though, that they are entirely oblivious to the higher calling of their position or lack enthusiasm for the notion of public service, especially in times of crisis and for good causes.

It is necessary to address the reliability of the data presented here. Because these online comments were voluntary, we have no way of telling how representative this self-selected sample is.[257] More importantly, there are some telltale signs of perhaps deliberate omissions;[258] for example, corruption ("gray income"), power, and relationship (*guanxi*), three reasons why people are attracted to government jobs, are not mentioned. It could be, however, that the lack of comments regarding these factors can be attributed to most people taking them for granted.

Comparing Reasons for Joining

Before comparing the reasons for joining among recruits in China, Taiwan, and Korea, it is necessary to mention that the type of research for each country differed; for example, the Korean survey was much better conceptualized, and the survey in Taiwan was much more descriptive, whereas the Chinese survey presented here was entirely exploratory and based on voluntary online comments. The surveys in Korea and Taiwan had clear sampling strategies and relied on structured questionnaires, as compared to the Chinese collection of online comments, which by its nature was a selective sampling. The most obvious observation one can make in all three surveys is that the top reasons why people joined the police was for job security and benefits; that is, material incentives outweighed all other considerations, such as the intrinsic nature of the job. Officers from all three countries considered job security, salary, and benefits to be important reasons to join (see Table 4.8). All three

TABLE 4.8 Ranking of Reasons to Join the Police: China, Taiwan, and Korea

China	Taiwan	Korea
1. Make a living	1. Good salary and fringe benefits	1. Job security and steady salary
2. Force of circumstance	2. Influence of parents	2. Intrinsic value of job
3. Change from idealism to making a living	3. Job security	3. Authority of law enforcement
4. Parents/family	4. To help people	4. Influence of others
5. Not qualified to do anything else	5. To fight crime	
6. Idealism	6. Need for a steady salary	
7. Police college graduate	7. Excitement and adventure	
8. Interesting work	8. Law enforcement	
9. Attracted to uniform and/or influenced by television	9. Early retirement, good pension	
	10. Influence of other relatives	
	11. Avoid military service or enter male-dominated occupation	
	12. Authority and power	
	13. Influence of siblings	
	14. Prestige and status	

studies, however, found that altruistic motives still played an important role; for example, in the Chinese survey, idealism accounted for 26% of the responses, and it ranked relatively high in both Korea and Taiwan. In spite of Confucius' teachings, officers in China and Korea generally did not consider their parents' preferences; only in Taiwan was doing so considered to be important. As we can see from these surveys, people join the police for different reasons. Some join for an ideal—serving their country or fighting crime. Others join to pursue a life-long dream to wear a uniform and hold a gun. Many more join due to individual circumstances—from failing to get into a good university to a desire to obtain a secure civil service job. Whatever the reasons for joining, they are a far cry from what the Party had in mind and what the MPS expects of their officers. This discrepancy in expectations between the Party and the public spells trouble for policing, as it raises issues of legitimacy of the Party and police in the eyes of a new generation.

Conclusion

This chapter tells two stories, one about sustainability and the other legitimacy. More specifically, it investigates the looming legitimacy and sustainability crisis in China. President Hu was the first to refer to the sustainability issue, or what amounts to government performance not keeping up with social developmental needs, real or imagined. The sustainability problem is very real when the police fail in their duties, such as keeping corruption under control, or when they lack the computer experts necessary in an Internet world. Because reform in China is driven by economic development and economic reform is moving faster than police development, sustainability is a significant problem not likely to disappear soon.

Issues with sustainability are exacerbated when public expectations rise faster than the police can realistically hope to meet them. This occurs when the public chases after perfection, after what is possible not necessarily probable. In essence, the people of China are suffering from a severe case of relative deprivation. People's relative expectations are fed by the rhetoric of reform achievements and are always moving ahead of the police performance/capacity curve. For this reason, sustainability is going to be a chronic and enduring problem.

Many factors contribute to the police sustainability problem, chief of which are uncoordinated reform and unbalanced development within and outside of the police, otherwise known as bottlenecks. Uncoordinated reform occurs when there is a lack of a well-thought-out reform plan due to discrepancies between the planning assumptions and grounded reality and to insufficient coordination among various elements of the reform plan. With the best reform plan, a lack of coordination most likely results from failure of execution or deviation from the plan (contingencies). Lack of coordination is a process problem. Unbalanced development refers to lack of fit within or between various aspects of reform and development; for example, ideologically, socialism (with or without Chinese characteristics) stands in sharp contrast to capitalism, and culturally there is a great different between the Lei Feng spirit and post-1980 utilitarian values. Lack of balanced development is a substantive issue.

Both uncoordinated and unbalanced police development can happen within and outside of the police. Within the police, uncoordinated development occurs when central and local leadership cannot agree, and unbalanced development happens when urban and rural policing experience disparate economic development. Development of the police is seldom coordinated with economic reform, as it is assumed that the former is there to serve the latter. From the Party's point of view, coordinated development between the economy and

TABLE 4.9 Sustainability Problem Caused by Unbalanced and Uncoordinated Development

	Within the Police	Outside of the Police
Unbalanced development	Police reform moves at different speeds in various jurisdictions (Beijing vs. Shanghai vs. Guangzhou, central vs. local), legally (rule by law vs. rule of law), organizationally (agency vs. grassroots), geographically (urban vs. rural, coastal vs. inland), economically (developed vs. undeveloped), and functionally (prison vs. patrol vs. detective).	Police reform moves in different directions, at different speeds, and in a different manner compared to economic, social, political, or cultural reform and change.
	Police reform in Shenzhen (e.g., salary) is ahead of the nation, leading to brain drain.	Public expectation moves faster than and always ahead of police development.
	Construction of the police legal system is moving ahead faster than the police legal culture, generating false expectations with the public.	Police performance moves more slowly than and always behind social requirements and public needs.
	Professional police reform (law, bureaucracy, technology) is not compatible with people's policing (mass line principle).	
Uncoordinated development	No central coordinated reform plan for reform has been developed or implemented.	There is no coordination between economic policy and police development.
	The Ministry of Public Security has little control over local policing.	There is no coordination between social policy and police capacity (e.g., migrant policy).
	No mechanism is in place to resolve policy differences among locations, agencies, and functions.	There is no coordination between political ideology and policing reality.

the police is not necessary, as the police are expected to adjust to and provide support for the economic reform. Police reform and development are always contingent on leadership and economics, which are not evenly distributed within organizations or geographically (see Table 4.9).

It is clear that more often than not the police will suffer from a chronic, structural problem in sustaining performance and capacity that defies the best intentions for a quick fix. Working harder to improve capacity or performance does not help. Indeed, the more the police try to meet expectations, the more the people expect.

The situation of runaway expectations is exacerbated by three inconvenient facts about reform in China. First, China is a communist state. In a communist state, the objective of the Party is to achieve a utopian ideal, without compromise. Second, China is a Confucian culture; in a Confucian culture, the ruler rules with a mandate from heaven to pursue benevolence (*ren*) and justice (*yi*), absolutely. Third, both Confucius and Mao believed that, in order to mobilize the people to attain greatness, they should set high standards for themselves and others. Perfection was the gold standard; nothing less would do. Given this propensity for striving to achieve perfect governance, the Party is building unrealistic expectations in the people, leading to frustration and a legitimacy crisis.

This chapter has studied the police legitimacy crisis from a variety of contexts and perspectives in an attempt to determine how the Chinese people perceive the police. The Audit Storm online comments give us the clearest evidence that the people are not happy with the nature and extent of corruption in China, and they are dissatisfied with government performance in this regard. But is that the only story to be told? Could the data be interpreted in another way? On closer inspection, the online comments give us a much more complex and engaging story, as they reveal the people's thinking and feeling about their government—good, bad, functional, dysfunctional. They tell us about the people's hopes and fears, expectations and disappointments, dreams and realities, as lived and experienced; in other words, what it is like to be a Chinese in reform China.

The comments tell us that corruption is not only a legal wrong that needs to be eradicated but also an obstacle to be overcome if China is going to, once again, earn her destined place in history. Frustration aside and despair notwithstanding, as one reads through the comments, one gets the distinct feeling that the people still have faith in the Party and that the government will do the right thing. More importantly, the people retain hope that in time the Chinese people will prevail over all adversities and make China great again. All in all, an unhappy people, yes; a hopeless nation, no.

The challenge to understanding China is accurately capturing the mood of the people and translating the complexities in thinking and richness of feelings into a legitimacy scale or matrix. So far we have erred on the side of simplicity of calculation for the sake of clarity of the message; we are told repeatedly that the Chinese government has a legitimacy crisis looming, but this does not come close to reflecting the reality as lived by the people.

In the eyes of the public, the image of the police is poor. The police no longer live up to the standards set by Mao during the revolutionary era. This unsavory image of the police is partly real (e.g., rogue police) and partly constructed through sensationalism (e.g., the media). Real or constructed, the effect is the same—the people no longer embrace the police as one of their own. The police likewise feel alienated from the people: "The fish [police] are out of the water [people]."

From a policy standpoint, it is necessary to draw a clear distinction between the real police image and a socially constructed one. The former is correctable; the latter is not. A more accurate image of the police can be cultivated through visible police actions and shared experiences. The socially constructed police image, however, is at the mercy of the media (e.g., Internet), and police legitimacy is dependent on marketing and propaganda, not what the police actually do.

Personal resistance and mass rebellions are sure signs of the people's disrespect for, impatience with, and defiance of the law, but the causes and cures for such disrespect, impatience, and defiance are not readily apparent and await further investigation. It is certainly too early to tell whether and to what extent government and police legitimacy is on the line.[259] The proposition that government legitimacy invariably leads to obedience with the law and government illegitimacy necessarily leads to disobedience of the law needs to be revisited in China. This has not been done.

The starting point for discussing the relationship between legitimacy and obedience to the law was the morality of actions, not the legitimacy of the government. In China, old and new, the obedience of its citizens without question is expected. Nevertheless, the aggrieved people have the right and duty to challenge government authority if and when a ruler acts beyond bounds, immorally (*guanbi minfan*); that is, the ruler has drifted away from the mandate from heaven and has deviated from Party doctrine (Marx, Mao, Deng, "Three Represents"). Viewed in this light, many of the people's actions against the police or the law can be considered "contradictions" among the people, not challenges to the authority of the Party or government. In the eyes of Chinese authorities, such "contradictions" are justified and tolerated because they are not challenging the legitimate authority of the Party or government but are only expressions of pent-up frustration with social change.

Specifically, personal assaults on officers and mass incidents in the street, while representing discontent, do not necessarily suggest a challenge to police legitimacy. The decision to join the police is a weighty one that is taken very seriously, particularly because changing jobs or divorcing is not readily accepted in China. Comments made relevant to this issue clearly indicate that policing is not the respected profession it once was.

In China, those born after the 1980s have been brought up in the reform era and have witnessed tremendous changes in values, from collectivism to individualism, spiritualism to materialism, volunteerism to hedonism (ironically as a result of Deng's "successful" pragmatic reform policy). It is reasonable to ask how such changes in values are affecting policing, particularly when what the Party stands for and promotes (Lei Feng spirit) is at odds with the lifestyle of today's young people.[260]

It is clear that people in China have joined the police for reasons similar to those of other young people in Korea and Taiwan—more for secular reasons (security, good pay, authority) than for idealistic motivation (serve people and country). Such a mismatch of values within the ranks of the police spells trouble for organizational control and creates an unintended and unfortunate image of the police.

A police agency that is controlled by rules is not the same as one operating under shared goals and values. Workers operating under the constraint of rules do the minimum that the rules require to earn the greatest return on their investment of time and effort. Workers operating under conditions of shared goals and values do the most they can to create value in the organization and elsewhere. To complicate the matter, the MPS preaches revolutionary values but operates under bureaucratic rules. The police cultural rules found online in "32 Classical Police Sayings" are particularly telling.[261] Below are a few of these "32 Classical Police Sayings":[262]

6. *Do not be too zealous in your work.* Do not chase after cars nonstop, arrest people nonstop. If you are traffic police and a car will not stop on command, you should pretend that you did not see it. It is alright that it drove away, just assume it has rolled over. Do not chase them into the ditch, this will only cause you trouble. It is the same with making arrests. If you cannot arrest, do not worry. There will be other chance and other arrests. It is alright not to make an arrest, but if you arrest the wrong person you will be in trouble.

19. *Do not volunteer.* Do not think that you are a key worker. Otherwise, you will have to be paid a lot, and the result might not be as expected. With many things, others can do them besides you. If there are things only you can do, the leaders will find you, and other people will be critical on the side.

20. *Hard work does not pay.* Do not think that hard work will lead to promotion. Hard work will offend many people. Public surveys are not in your favor. Also, people who do little will for certain have better public opinion surveys than you. Thus, in most instances those who are recommended for promotion are those who do little, those with ability are cut out to do work.

29. *Do not be brave.* Certainly, do not be too bold. During peacetime the focus is on economic construction. Others do not believe that police bravery will bring about peace and order. It is more important to have lesser courage. We cannot rely on hot heads or individual courage.

What the above internal police cultural rules make clear is that one should do the least, not the most, to get by. Be a bureaucrat, not a revolutionary worker.

These sayings obviously go against everything the MPS stands for, both personally and organizationally. The formal requirements of a good officer were summed up online by a police officer:[263] obedience (服从), execution (执行), initiative (主动), industriousness (勤劳), duty (尽职), persistence (坚持), involvement (投入), and cooperation (合作). The original sayings certainly did not include any of these professional police attributes, and it can fairly be said that they represent a sort of counterculture,[264] in direct opposition to the official MPS duty creed.

The mismatch in values between the Party and MPS and young police officers leaves the younger officers confused and perplexed. Anomie sets in, and avoidance, subversion, and escapist behaviors become the norm. Once again, such conduct is reflected in the "32 Classical Police Sayings"—everyone for himself or herself:

5. *Do not expect your leaders to support you.* Do not think that because you acted correctly the leaders will speak in your favor and support you. There are leaders who only know how to put on a big show. They are only concerned with their official position (i.e., career). There might also be a chance that you have offended the friends and relatives of the leaders.[265]
9. *Do not trust the organization's care and concern.* Insist on strengthening your body at all times. This body is yours. If your body fails, no one can help you. Officials will only offer you fake consolation, and you have to face up to the pain and suffering.
24. *Do not expect colleagues to save you.* Do not expect your co-workers to sacrifice their lives to save yours in a critical moment. Only you can save your own life.

In the life of the young officer, the Party and MPS are neither legitimate nor illegitimate, but irrelevant. There is a continuous and at times contentious debate about the relevancy of Lei Feng in policing of today. More specifically, does Lei Feng, who was born to a revolutionary movement fighting a proletarian cause, resonate with young people brought up in an economic reform era consumed by individualism and materialism?[266] Although many young people think that the Lei Feng spirit is out of date,[267] the MPS still insists that Lei Feng lives in the hearts and minds of the people,[268] as reflected in the culture and attitude of the police agency and words and deed of police officers.

Rejection of the Lei Feng spirit by young people today is based on the suggestion that communism is dead in Chinese police reform. There are two versions of this thesis. One observation is that, theoretically, communism is fundamentally flawed. Its understanding of human nature and society's culture is wrong. There is no selfless man and very few altruistic persons. People are made in the image of Hobbes (i.e., predatory), not Mengzhi (i.e., cooperative). The other proposition is that there is nothing wrong with Marxism (later Maoism) as a utopian ideal, but as applied to secular society it will never work.[269] Whatever view one takes of this dispute over values and ideology, it affects policing in major ways.

The proposition proposed here is that people from all walks of life will fight the police less because of abstract theory of legitimacy and more because they do not share the same values, outlook, and approach to life that the police stand for. Such mismatches of values show up in all kinds of places; for example, in an ironic way, the legal, bureaucratic, officious, and professional policing style promoted by the MPS to serve the city crowd is resented by rural residents who are used to a more customary, informal, and down-to-earth style of enforcement.[270]

The most significant aspect of the legitimacy and sustainability crisis that needs to be addressed is the widening gap between what the Party stands for and what society is evolving into, not necessarily, at least not only, that the police are corrupt, abusive, or incompetent.

Notes

1. Andrew J. Nathan and Tianjian Shi, "Left and Right with Chinese Characteristics: Issues and Alignments in Deng Xiaoping's China," *World Politics*, 48(4), 522–550, 1996. Despite their suffering under Mao, many Chinese remembered that era as a time when they could leave their front doors and bicycles unlocked, when prices were stable, when everyone had a job, when officials were honest, and when China was not afraid of war with the West.
2. Cao Jinqing, *China along the Yellow River: A Scholar's Observation and Reflection on Rural Society* [*Huanghebian de Zhongguo: Yige xuezhe dui xiangcun shehui de guancha yu sikao*], Shanghai wenyi chubanshe, Shanghai, 2000, p. 448. The social order is chaotic, and there is no longer any faith. As for the local basic level cadres, they are busy all day implementing tasks assigned to them from above, but inside their minds they feel deeply frustrated. They see no direction. They don't know the meaning of what they are busying themselves with all day. They feel that if things continue in this fashion we may run into big trouble some day.
3. Andrew Brick, "Reform in China after Tiananmen Square," paper presented at Gettysburg College, Gettysburg, PA, June 5, 1989.
4. Jifu Huang, "On the Characteristics of the Legitimacy of CCP Rule" ["*Lun Zhongguo Gongchandang Zhizheng Hefaxing de Tedian*"], *Tanqiu*, 72, 16–17, 2002.
5. Wang Shaopeng, "Pondering over Improving the Credibility of Law Enforcement by Public Security Agencies in the New Eras," *Public Security Studies*, 188, 51–54, 2009.
6. Sun Weiping, *Remarks on the Transformation of Value System in China*, Bureau of International Cooperation, Chinese Academy of Social Sciences, May 27, 2003 (http://bic.cass.cn/english/infoShow/Arcitle_Show_Conference_Show_1.asp?ID=336&Title=The%20Roles%20of%20Values%20and%20Ethics%20in%20Contemporary%20China&strNavigation=Home-%3EForum&BigClassID=4&SmallClassID=9).
7. Wen Xinhua and Yongzheng, "Variously Enhancing the Police Professional Construction Is an Important Aspect to Improving Policing Performance," *Journal of Shanghai Public Security Academy*, 9(6), 16–17, 1999.
8. Li Tulai et al., "To Bring the Functions of Police Forces into Full Play and Create a Stable and Suitable Environment for Economic Development," *Public Security Studies*, 93, 51–56, 2002. The functions of police after WTO are to: (1) secure political stability, (2) maintain social order, (3) establish an effective public order control system, (4) improve the public security administrative system to support economic development, and (5) build a high-quality public security organization.
9. Ibid.
10. Wan Shengzhi, Li Zhenyu, Zhan Caigui, and Zhang Jincun, "The Issue about the Police Participating in Non-Policing Activities," *Public Security Studies*, 69, 21–25, 2000. Local county and village police are required to participate in extralegal and non-police activities, such as collecting taxes and fees, enforcing birth control, assisting in demolition and construction, and intervening in commercial disputes. Police are pressured to participate in non-policing duties for fear of antagonizing local political leadership, resulting in dilution of financial support.
11. Zhang Zhaoping, "The Way out for Solving the Problem of Unreliable Statistics of Criminal Cases Reported," *Public Security Studies*, 65, 105–106, 1997. There are pressures from the MPS and provincial PSBs to keep local police station crime data stable and low, especially during the *yanda* period.

12. Li Dawen, "Enhancing and Improving Public Security Work, and Constructing Good Investment Environment," *Public Security Studies*, 77, 55–58, 2001. Public security has to create a good investment climate for business, including not regulating too tightly (*yi dao ce*, laterally "cut with one slice," or zero tolerance of irregularities), punishing arbitrarily (*luan fa*), and investigating indiscriminately (*luan cha*). Favorable treatment of business attracts justifiable criticism; for example, exercising discretion might be interpreted as corruption, and leniency of treatment might be construed as favoritism.

13. Liu Zhendong, "An Assessment of the Trends of Social Development and Stability in the New Era," *Public Security Studies*, 77, 35–39, 2001.

14. Hu Jintao, *Hold High the Great Banner of Socialism with Chinese Characteristics and Strive for New Victories in Building a Moderately Prosperous Society in All*, report to the 17th National Congress of the Communist Party of China, Beijing, October 15, 2007.

15. Ibid.

16. Lu Zhuo, "The Seven Challenges Confronting the Chinese Police in the New Century," *Public Security Studies*, 77, 9–15, 2001.

17. Chen Yuan Xiao, "Reflection on Sustainability of Public Security Work," *Public Security Studies*, 77, 22–25, 2001.

18. Ibid., pp. 22–23.

19. Ibid., p. 23.

20. Ibid.

21. Ibid., p. 24.

22. For the first 30 years, the People's Republic of China had no national audit agency. The China National Audit Office (CNAO) was first established in 1982 at the Fifth Plenary Session of the Fifth National People's Congress. Article 2 of the Audit Law of the People's Republic of China stipulates that: "The State Council shall establish an audit institution who will take charge of auditing revenues and expenditures of public finance of departments of the State Council and local governments at various levels, revenues and expenditures of state banking institutions, state enterprises and undertakings. The audit institution shall be under the direct leadership of the Premier of the State Council and exercise its power of supervision through auditing independently in accordance with the law and subject to no interference by any administrative organ or public organization or individual. People's governments at and above the county level shall establish corresponding audit institutions. Local audit institutions at various levels shall be accountable and report on their work to the people's governments at the corresponding levels and to audit institutions at the next higher levels." For a brief overview of the history, development, structure, and process of the CNAO, see "Government Auditing in the People's Republic of China" at the CNAO website (http://www.gov.cn/). The Audit Law of the People's Republic of China was adopted at the 9th Meeting of the Standing Committee of the Eighth National People's Congress on August 31, 1994, and amended in accordance with the "Decision on Amending the Audit Law of the People's Republic of China" at the 20th Meeting of the Standing Committee of the Tenth National People's Congress of the People's Republic of China on February 28, 2006.

23. *Guanyu 2003 nian zhongyang yuxuan zhixing he qita caizheng de shenji gongzuo baogao*, report to the Tenth Meeting of the Standing Committee of the Tenth National People's Congress of the People's Republic of China. For a Chinese version, see *Li Jinhua shenjizhang zuo 2003 shenji gongzuo baogao* at http://news.xinhuanet.com/zhengfu/2004-06/24/content_1543949.htm. For a brief discussion of the background and content of the Audit Report, see "Cleaning Up" and "Corruption Levels Astonishing," *Beijing Review*, 27/28, 18–25, 2004.

24. For an overview of the charter, law, structure, and process of the PRC's audit system, see Li Jinhua, "China's Governmental Auditing System," *International Journal of Government Auditing*, April 1999 (http://findarticles.com/p/articles/mi_qa3662/is_199804/ai_n8798793).

25. "China to Audit More State-Funded Institutions to Curb Corruption," *People's Daily Online*, July 7, 2004 (http://english.people.com.cn/200407/07/eng20040707_148713.html).

26. The General Administration of Sports was accused of misappropriating 131 million yuan (US$170 million) earmarked for the Beijing 2008 Olympics Organizing Committee, of which 109 million yuan (US$13.2 million) went for constructing staff quarters. See "Sports Administration Denies Misuse of Funds," *China.org.cn*, July 7, 2004 (http://www.china.org.cn/english/2004/Jul/100537.htm).

27. "China's Audit Storm Involves the Issue of Power Shortage," *China Economic Net*, July 26, 2004.

28. One official from the Yangtze Water Resources Commission, which was accused of collusion with jerry-builders in embankment construction, accused audit offices of trying to score political points by disclosing misconduct that had already been uncovered. See "'Audit Storm' Stirs Furor in Media," *China Daily*, July 5, 2004 (http://www.china.org.cn/english/BAT/100262.htm).

29. (a) "ICBC Lost 1B Yuan in Bad Loans," *China Daily*, June 24, 2004 (http://www.china.org.cn/english/features/audit/102450.htm). China's largest bank, Industrial and Commercial Bank of China (ICBC), lost more than 1 billion yuan (US$121 million) in loans made to a privately owned firm in Guangdong's Nanhai city. (b) "CNAO Reveals Widespread Corruption," *China Daily*, November 3, 2004 (http://www.china.org.cn/english/2004/Nov/111119.htm). After an 8-month inspection of 21 subsidiaries, CNAO found irregularities involving 6.9 billion yuan (US$833.7 million), with problems in its billing, consumer lending, and loans to local governments and private companies. In one case, 110 million yuan were illegally withdrawn. In another, 1 billion yuan in corporate loans ended up in individual savings accounts.

30. Tian Jing, "Rampant Corruption Haunts Education Minister Chen Zhili," *Epoch Times*, July 18, 2004 (http://english.epochtimes.com/news/4-7-18/22515.html).

31. "Reform to Bloom after Audit Storm," *China Business Post*, July 9, 2004 (http://www.china.org.cn/english/2004/Jul/100846.htm).

32. "Audit Report Fallout Stirs Public Interest," *China Daily*, July 26, 2004 (http://english.sohu.com/20040726/n221195895.shtml).

33. (a) "'Audit Storm' Stirs Furors in Media," *China Daily*, July 5, 2004 (http://www.china.org.cn/english/BAT/100262.htm). *Beijing News* described the audit report as "startling," attributing as its source many online comments. The *Beijing Youth Daily* observed that the "audit storm" unleashed by Auditor-General Li Jinhua showed no signs of abating. (b) "State Auditors Reveal Widespread Fiscal Irregularities," *Interfax.com*, June 25, 2004. (c) "Audit Storm Shows Government Determination," *People's Daily*, July 1, 2004. China's Auditor-General Li Jinhua submitted an astonishing auditing report to the Standing Committee of the Tenth National People's Congress on June 23, 2004. (d) "Reform to Bloom after Audit Storm," *China Business Post*, July 9, 2004 (http://www.china.org.cn/english/2004/Jul/100846.htm). (e) "Sports Administration Denies Misuse of Funds," *China.org.cn*, July 7, 2004 (http://www.china.org.cn/english/2004/Jul/100537.htm). (f) "'Audit Storm' Whets Watchdog's Appetite," *China Economic Net*, July 16, 2004 (http://www.china.org.cn/english/BAT/100360.htm). The CNAO had been filing audit reports since 1983 but was not taken seriously until 2004. The "audit storm" grabbed the attention of the media and the Chinese public. (g) "'Audit Storms' Not Best Solution," *China Daily*, July 6, 2004. The rule of law, not a mass, campaign-style "audit storm," should be used to correct government abuse. Mass campaigns, like those of "Cultural Revolution" (1966–1978), are disruptive and should not be repeated.

34. "Experts Discussing the 'Audit Storm'" ["*Zhuanjia tan zhongguo 'shenji fengbao'*"], *dajiyuan.com*, July 16, 2004 (http://www.dajiyuan.com/gb/4/7/16/n597601.htm). The audit was well received by the people but it uncovered only the tip of the iceberg. In order for the audit to be totally effective, it must be done by an independent body, which is why local auditing units are not effective in evaluating local problems and it takes the CNAO to uncover corruption and abuses.

35. School of Public Administration, Anti-Corruption Research Office, "Anti-Corruption Audit: Important Signal in Anti-Corruption Progress" ["*Lianzheng shenji: Fanfu douzheng jincheng zhong de zhongda xinhua*"], *dayoo.com*, July 7, 2004 (http://china.dayoo.com/gb/content/2004-07/07/content_1620156.htm).

36. "'Audit Storm' Stirs Furors in Media," *China Daily*, July 5, 2004 (http://www.china.org.cn/english/BAT/100262.htm). *People's Daily*: The Yangtze Water Resources Commission accused the CNAO of political grandstanding but later retracted their statement. The Industrial and Commercial Bank of China (ICBC) acknowledged failings and disciplined 336 staff members. *Southern Weekend*: The CNAO report exposed funding abuses unprecedented in depth, breadth, and magnitude. *Beijing News*: "Startling" is the word people are using to describe Li's report, and this is not an exaggeration, considering the scope and extent of official misconduct in the use of public money. *Youth Daily*: The "audit storm" unleashed by Auditor-General Li Jinhua on June 25 shows no signs of abating.

37. (a) Chen Wu, "China Airs Some Very Dirty Laundry," *Business Week*, June 28, 2004. http://www.businessweek.com/bwdaily/dnflash/jun2004/nf20040628_1545_db039.htm. (b) "Chinese Officials Misuse $27M of Olympics Funds," *China Daily*, June 25, 2004 (http://newspapers.nl.sg/Digitised/Issue/straitstimes20040625.aspx). (c) "China Audit Report Reveals Widespread Abuse of Public Funds but Marks a Shift Toward Transparency [press release]," Transparency International, Berlin, July 23, 2004. (d) "Organizers of 2008 Beijing Olympics Caught Diverting Millions," Associated Press, June 24, 2004. (e) "Scandal Hits 2008 Beijing Olympics: Officials Diverted Funds Meant to Build Facilities," *NBC Sports*, June 25, 2004 (http://www.msnbc.msn.com/id/5281250/).

38. Yuan Man, "2003 Top 10 Financial Celebrities in China," *Beijing Morning Post*, December 2, 2003. Li Jinhua was selected as the fourth most influential financial person in China in 2003 for publishing the audit report.

39. (a) Feng Chen, "Subsistence Crises, Managerial Corruption and Labour Protests in China," *The China Journal*, 44, 41–63, 2000. (b) Kang Chen, "Fiscal Centralization and the Form of Corruption in China," *European Journal of Political Economy*, 20(4), 1001–109, 2004. (c) Gregory C. Chow, *Corruption and China's Economic Reform in the Early 21st Century*, CEPS Working Paper No. 116, Princeton University, Princeton, NJ, 2005. (d) Chengze Simon Fan and Herschel I. Grossman, "Incentives and Corruption in Chinese Economic Reform," *Journal of Economic Policy Reform*, 4(3), 195–206, 2001. (e) Ting Gong, "Dangerous Collusion: Corruption as a Collective Venture in Contemporary China," *Communist and Post-Communist Studies*, 35(1), 85–103, 2002. (f) "Forms and Characteristics of China's Corruption in the 1990s: Change with Continuity," *Communist and Post-Communist Studies*, 33(3), 277–288, 1997. (g) Yufan Hao, "From Rule of Man to Rule of Law: An Unintended Consequence of Corruption in China in the 1990s," *Journal of Contemporary China*, 8(22), 405–423, 1999. (h) Yufan Hao and Michael Johnston, "Reform at the Crossroads: An Analysis of Chinese Corruption," *Asian Perspective*, 19(1), 117–149, 1995. (i) Zengke He, "Corruption and Anti-Corruption in Reform China," *Communist and Post-Communist Studies*, 33(2), 243–270, 2000. (j) Alan P.L. Liu, "The Politics of Corruption in the People's Republic of China," *The American Political Science Review*, 77(3), 602–623, 1983. (k) Jean C. Oi, "Market Reforms and Corruption in Rural China," *Studies in Comparative Communism*, 22(2–3), 221–233, 1989. (l) Jean-Louis Rocca, "Corruption and Its Shadow: An Anthropological View of Corruption in China," *The China Quarterly*, 130, 402–416, 1992. (m) Hilton Root, "Corruption in China: Has It Become Systemic?" *Asian Survey*, 36(8), 741–757, 1996. (n) Richard Levy, "Corruption, Economic Crime and Social Transformation Since the Reforms: The Debate in China," *Australian Journal of Chinese Affairs*, 33, 1–25, 1995. (o) Xiaobo Lü, *Cadres and Corruption: The Organizational Involution of the Chinese Communist Party*, Stanford University Press, Stanford, CA, 2000. (p) Xiaobo Lu, "Booty Socialism, Bureau-Preneurs, and the State in Transition: Organizational Corruption in China," *Comparative Politics*, 32(3), 273–294, 2000. (q) Barbara N. Sands, "Decentralizing an Economy: The Role of Bureaucratic Corruption in China's Economic Reforms," *Public Choice*, 65(1), 85–91, 1990. (r) Andrew Wederman, "The Intensification of Corruption in China," *The China Quarterly*, 180, 895–921, 2004. (s) Lening Zhang, "White-Collar Crime: Bribery and Corruption in China," in Jianhong Liu, Lening Zhang, and Steven F. Messner (Eds.), *Crime and Social Control in a Changing China* (pp. 23–46), Greenwood Press, New York, 2001. (t) Flora Sapio, *Implementing Anticorruption in the PRC Patterns of Selectivity*, Working Paper No. 10, Centre for East and South-East Asian Studies, Lund University, Sweden, 2005.

40. Ting Gong and Stephen K. Ma (Eds.), "Corruption and Anti-Corruption Reform in and beyond China. Part I. China: A Corruption-Embattled Country," *Crime, Law and Social Change*, 49(1), 1–6, 2008.

41. (a) Xie Baogui, Director, Prosecution Department against Economic Crime of Supreme People's Procuratorate in the PRC, "The Function of the Chinese Procuratorial Organ in the Combat Against Corruption," *Asian Journal of Public Administration*, 10(1), 71–80, 1988; especially see discussion on the characteristics of corruption crimes in China on pp. 73–74. (b) He Qinglian, "The Evolution of Corruption in China. Part 1," *Epoch Times*, August 13, 2004. This article discusses how corruption evolved from individual activities before 1995, to organized behavior until 1998, to being systemic in nature in the 2000s. (c) Hong Lu and Elaine Gunnison, "Power, Corruption, and the Legal Process in China," *International Criminal Justice Review*, 13(1), 28–49, 2003. This article provides an analysis of 1554 criminal court cases, adjudicated between 1986 and 2001, and suggests that corruption offenses differed significantly from non-corruption offenses in both offender and offense characteristics and in key legal decisions.

42. Minxin Pei, "Corruption Threatens China's Future," *Carnegie Endowment for International Peace*, No. 55, October 2007. Corruption penetrates every department of the state. It is "concentrated in sectors with extensive state involvement, such as infrastructure projects, real estate, government procurement, and financial services." Railroad, aviation, telecommunications, and electricity production sectors are particularly vulnerable to corruption.

43. (a) Stephen K. Ma, "Reform Corruption: A Discussion on China's Current Development," *Pacific Affairs*, 62(1), 42–52, 1989. (b) Gong Tin, "Forms and Characteristics of China's Corruption in the 1990s: Change with Continuity," *Communist and Post-Communist Studies*, 30(3), 277–288, 1997. This article focuses on recent patterns of China's corruption to see how new and different, if not more, corruption has occurred despite the gradual shrinking of non-market elements in the economy.

44. Keith Henderson, "The Rule of Law and Judicial Corruption in China: Half-Way over the Great Wall," in Transparency International, *Global Corruption Report 2007* (pp. 151–159), Cambridge University Press, Cambridge, UK, 2007.

45. Angang Hu, "Corruption and Anti-Corruption Strategies in China," *Carnegie Endowment for International Peace*, February 13, 2001 (http://www.carnegieendowment.org/events/?fa=event Detail&id=284). Corruption has been conservatively estimated to represent 13 to 16% of China's GDP.

46. (a) Minxin Pei, "Corruption Threatens China's Future," *Carnegie Endowment for International Peace*, No. 55, October 2007; especially see the discussion on policy implications for the United States and its allies on pp. 6–7. (b) Julia C. Kwong, Richard J. Levy, Randall Peerenboom, and James V. Feinerman, "Corruption: China's Achilles' Heel?" presented at Woodrow Wilson International Center for Scholars, Washington, DC, December 1, 2003.

47. For example, when, after 5 years of research, the Hunan provincial government in 2004 suggested partial amnesty for corrupt officials, public reactions were initially negative; in fact, 80% of Sichuan Internet users opposed the idea, 62% argued that it violated the principle of the rule of law, 20% disliked the idea, and only 16% thought the idea should be tried. *Ming Bao*, June 22, 2004, p. B12.

48. On July 29, 2004, the Director of the Beijing Municipal Audit Bureau, Yang Xiaochao, submitted the bureau's annual audit report: "Audit Work Report regarding Implementation of 2003 Beijing Municipality Budget and Other Government Receipts and Expenditures" ["*Guanyu Beijing shi 2003 nian shiji yuxuan zhixing he qita caizheng shou zhi de shenji gongzuo*"] to the 12th Standing Committee of the Beijing Municipality People's Congress in accordance with the "Temporary Method for Implementation of the Beijing Municipality Budget Audit," Beijing Municipality People's Government Order Number 29 ["*Beijing shi yuxuan zhixing qingkuan shenji jiangdu zanxing banfa*," *Beijing shi renmin zhengfu di 29 hao ling*], November 3, 1995.

49. http://comment.news.sohu.com/comment/topic.jsp?id=220685254.

50. Kam C. Wong, *Cyberspace Governance in China*, Nova Science Publishers, New York, 2011.

51. John Searle, *Speech Act*, Cambridge University Press, Cambridge, UK, 1969. Devices indicating illocutionary force include word order, stress, intonation contour, punctuation, the mood of the verb, and the existence of performative verbs.

52. Jay L. Lemke, "Resources for Attitudinal Meaning: Evaluative Orientations in Text Semantics," *Functions of Language*, 5(1), 33–56, 1998.

53. This contrasts with types of analysis more typical of modern linguistics, which are chiefly concerned with the study of grammar: the study of smaller bits of language, such as sounds (phonetics and phonology); parts of words (morphology); meaning (semantics); and the order of words in sentences (syntax). Discourse analysts study larger chunks of language as they flow together.

54. "Former National Electricity Company Leader's Erroneous Policy Decision Led to Serious Losses" ["*Yuan guojia dianli gongsi lingdao banshi juece shiwu zaocheng zhongda sunshi*"], *news.sohu.com*, June 23, 2003.

55. 2313 comments in one week, between June 23, 2004, and July 2, 2004.

56. *Hen* can describe action or mental state (*The Pinying Chinese-English Dictionary*, The Commercial Press, Hong Kong, 1995). The translation provided expresses a need for vigorous action. The other possible translation is to conduct the audit with a ruthless heart; that is, show no mercy. It is not uncommon to attach two meanings to one word or phrase (e.g., vigorous action vs. ruthless heart). Chinese civilization, as reflected in its literary tradition, prides itself on subtleness of expression, nuance in articulation, and richness in meaning. The conventional saying, "All is in what is not being said" ("*Jinzai buyan zhong*"), informs that what is not said in China is as important, if not more important, than what is being said. This understanding of Chinese civilization and linguistic tradition cautions against a rush to judgment of what is being said online due to potentially uncertain translations or problematic interpretations of the text. It is not clear in context whether "ban" or "deal with" refers to the audit process or audit results. The comment might be directed at the conduct of the audit itself (i.e., need to investigate the case with thoroughness), or it might be directed at the follow-up actions (i.e., need to follow through with the audit findings to hold people responsible), or possibility both.

57. Cong Wanghua, "How Corruption on the Yangtze River Engineering Projects Is Being Investigated," ["*Shenji neimu: Changjiang fang yinbi gongcheng tougong jianliao shi zenme chade*"], *news.sohu.com*, June 30, 2004 (http://news.sohu.com/2004/06/30/71/news220777101.shtml).

58. Ibid. The Wuhan auditors meticulously checked receipts and billings against work done.

59. Ibid. Lin wanted to go back to Henan for a summer break, but the investigators were suspicious that he might flee. The case was reported to Auditor-General Li Jinhua, and Lin and a number of partners were detained at the airport. They were charged with stealing 83 million yuan earmarked for a construction project.

60. "*Shenji fengbao qijinwu guanyuan chizhi, meiti xu 'shige bu fangguo,*'" *news.sohu.com*, July 27, 2004 (http://news.sohu.com/20040727/n221220499.shtml).

61. Fan Dula, "'*Shenji fengbao*' shi yi kuai shijinshi," *studytimes.com*, July 27, 2004 (http://www.chinaelections.org/NewsInfo.asp?NewsID=53813).

62. Fan Wei, "*Fengbao*" zhihou renmin huan qidai shenmo?" *studytimes.com*, July 27, 2004 (http://news.enorth.com.cn/system/2004/07/27/000829518.shtml).

63. Fan Dula, "'*Shenji fengbao*' shi yi kuai shijinshi," *studytimes.com*, July 27, 2004 (http://www.chinaelections.org/NewsInfo.asp?NewsID=53813).

64. The "four not quitting" are *shigu yuanyin bu chaqing bu fangguo* (事故原因不查清不放过), *shigu zeren zhe de budao chuli bu fangguo* (事故责任者得不到处理不放过), *zhongguo cuoshi buluoshi bu fangguo* (整改措施不落实不放过), and *jiaoxun bu xiqu bu fangguo* (教训不吸取不放过).

65. *Zhongguo gongchandang jilu chufeng tiaoli* (中国共产党纪律处分条例).

66. *Dangzheng lingdao ganbu ciji zhanxing guiding* (党政领导干部辞职暂行规定).

67. "Local Government Auditing Should Also Be Reported Daily" ["*Difang shenji ya ying gong-bao niandubao*"), *Information Times*, June 25, 2004 (http://news.sohu.com/2004/06/25/44/news220704463.shtml).

68. Jim Yardley, "The Chinese Go after Corruption, Corruptly," *New York Times*, October 22, 2006 (http://www.nytimes.com/2006/10/22/weekinreview/22yardley.html). "The problem with China today is that if you want to pursue corruption, so many people are tainted," said Minxin Pei, a scholar at the Carnegie Endowment for International Peace in Washington, DC.

69. Ibid.

70. (a) For most purposes, however, the lack of respect for police power can be used as a proxy indicator of lack of legitimacy, without violation of validity assumptions. See the discussion of *quan wei* in Chen Jinsheng, "On the Authority of Police Enforcement," *Public Security Studies*, 76, 66–70, 2001. (b) For a discussion of the relationship between rule by law and government by morality and to develop an understanding of *wei*, see "A Primary Discussion on Running the Country by Moral Integrity [editorial]," *Public Security Studies*, 79, 5–7, 2001.

71. When asked to rank in a survey the "most detestable conduct," 11.9% of the people ranked "neglect of duty" in the top three. See Table 9 in Stanley Rosen, "The Chinese Communist Party and Chinese Society: Popular Attitudes Toward Party Membership and the Party's Image," *Australian Journal of Chinese Affairs*, 24, 51–92, 1990.

72. When asked to rank in a survey the "most detestable conduct," 23.5% of the people ranked "corruption" at the top of the list. See Table 9 in Stanley Rosen, "The Chinese Communist Party and Chinese Society: Popular Attitudes toward Party Membership and the Party's Image," *Australian Journal of Chinese Affairs*, 24, 51–92, 1990.

73. Ibid.

74. Huang Demao and Yang Shuyao, "On New Police–Community Relations," *Public Security Studies*, 66, 35–38, 1997. In the early years of the PRC, the relationship between the police and the public was alternatively described as "flesh and blood" and "water and fish." As provided for in Article 3 of the PRC Police Law of 1995, the police are required to obtain the support of the people and maintain an intimate relationship with the people. The police are supposed to listen to the people, be open to their supervision, and serve their interests.

75. Morality should inform everything the police do. Legality alone does not represent all of the duties and responsibilities of the police. See discussion on *lun gongan dude* in Kong Damin, *Guangyi Gongan Lun*, Qunzhong chubanshe, Beijing, 2001, pp. 146–154.

76. Huang Demao and Yang Shuyao, "On New Police–Community Relations," *Public Security Studies*, 66, 35–38, 1997. The masses are too dependent on the police. They have unrealistic expectations of the police; for example, the police are invincible, can resolve all problems, and solve all crimes. The people are frustrated when such expectations are not met.

77. "The Story Inside Lei Fung Police" ["*Lei Fung paichusuo nei de gushi*"], China Police Net [*Zhongguo jingcha wang*], July 31, 2003 (http://www.cpd.com.cn/gb/newspaper/2004-03/05/content_274243.htm).

78. Stanley Rosen, "The Chinese Communist Party and Chinese Society: Popular Attitudes toward Party Membership and the Party's Image," *Australian Journal of Chinese Affairs*, 24, 51–92, 1990. Most people think highly of teachers (very good, 32.7%; good, 44.6%). Very few people think highly of commercial and industrial administrative personnel (very good, 2.7%; good, 9.8). Public security cadres ranked in the middle (very good, 11.8%; good, 28.5%).

79. Stanley Rosen, "The Chinese Communist Party and Chinese Society: Popular Attitudes toward Party Membership" and the Party's Image," *Australian Journal of Chinese Affairs*, 24, 51–92, 1990. A survey of workers' attitudes toward the Party in 1986 found that 54% believed that few of the Party members were living up to exemplary standards, and 10% believed that they were worse off than the masses. In an earlier survey of peasant youths in 1983, respondents had a negative opinion of the Party, as indicated by these responses: 47.9% said that Party members engaged in "suppression of democracy and retaliation," 36.8% accused them of "corruption and degeneration," and 66.8% accused them of "backdoor practices."

80. (a) Wang Gungwu and Zheng Yongnian, for example, summarized the three sources of legitimacy as development, stability, and national unity. See the Introduction to Gungwu Wang et al. (Eds.), *Reform, Legitimacy, and Dilemmas: China's Politics and Society*, Singapore University Press, Singapore, 2000. (b) Peter Hays Gries and Stanley Rosen (Eds.), *State and Society in 21st Century China: Crisis, Contention, and Legitimation*, Routledge, New York, 2004.

81. Contrary evidence provided by the 2001 World Values Survey (WVS) and the 2002 East Asia Barometer (EAB) suggests that the Chinese people have faith and trust in their government and Party. Those surveyed responded to "Please tell us how much confidence you have in the following institutions" as follows: For the national government, "a great deal of confidence" (WVS, 39%; EAB, 63%) and "quite a bit of confidence" (WVS, 58%; EAB, 35%); for the Party, "a great deal of confidence" (WVS, 30%; EAB, 71%) and "quite a bit of confidence" (WVS, 63%; EAB, 27%). See Table 1 in Wang, Zhengxu, "Explaining Regime Strength in China," *China: An International Journal*, 4(2), 217–237, 2006.

82. "China Prepares \$6.6b to Improve Image in Foreign Media," *World Focus*, January 13, 2009 (http://worldfocus.org/blog/2009/01/13/china-prepares-66b-to-improve-image-in-foreign-media/3589/). Generally, China is mindful of the importance of public image and has spent substantial amounts of time and money to groom its own image.

83. Hugo de Burgh, "Kings without Crowns? The Re-Emergence of Investigative Journalism in China," *Media, Culture and Society*, 25, 801–820, 2003.

84. The research was conducted as a content analysis exercise of *Jiaodian Fangtan* programming between April 1, 1994, and December 31, 1998. All told, 1700 programs were examined, and 584 were subjected to analysis based on two criteria: representativeness (*daibiao*) and impact (*hongdong*). The programs addressed the administration, legal system, economy, culture, people, villages, reform, and feedback. The analyses concentrated on four primary areas: legal system construction (*fazhi jiangshe*), government work (*zhengfu gongzuo*), anti-corruption (*fan fubai*), and value orientation (*jiazhi quxian*).

85. Su Baozhong, "An Analysis of a Functional Model of Development in Opinion Supervision: A Perspective on the "Focus Interview" ["*Yulun jiangdu dui minzhu zhengzhi fazhan de gongneng moshi tanxi: toushi "jiaodian fangtan"*], *Media Observer* [*Chuanmei Guancha*], July 7, 2003.

86. (a) *Jiaodian Fangtan* has been variously translated as "news focus" (*Beijing Online*), "focal point interview" (*Clearwisdom.net*), or "interview focus (*Asiaweek.com*). It is a first of its kind national China Central Television (CCTV) program featuring investigations into government wrongdoing and abuses. Beginning in 1990, *Jiaodian Fangtan* and other similar investigative programs, such as *Xinwen Tiaocha* ("Investigative News"), *Dongfang Shikpong* ("Eastern Horizon"), and *Jianri Suofa* ("Speaking about Law Today"), have proven to be effective in bringing transparency to the political and administrative process, making the Party more responsive and the government more accountable. *Jiaodian Fangtan* is very popular with the Chinese public, according to CCTV surveys, which found that about 1 billion mainland Chinese watched television between 8:00 and 9:00 p.m. every evening, of which 73% watched news programs. Among the news programs, *Xinwen Lianbo* ("National News Broadcasting") was the most favorite followed by *Jiaodian Fangtan* ("News Focus"). Another program featuring investigative reporting, *Dongfang Shikong* ("Oriental Horizon"), attracted 48.3% viewership (as compared with MTV at 51.7%). Data from *Beijing Online*, January, 2000. (b) For a general discussion of *Jiaodian Fangtan* as a CPC policy tool, see "From Propaganda to Hegemony: *Jiaodian Fangtan* and China's Media Policy," *Journal of Contemporary China*, 11(30), 35–51, 2002. (c) For a critique of *Jiaodian Fangtan*, see Yu Jie, "Only Having *Jiaodian Fangtan* Isn't Enough," in Fengtai Qu (Ed.), *Wanquan Shi Jia Yi Hao, Shuo Haishi Bu Shuo* [*To Say or Not to Say*], Wenhua Yishu Chubanshe, Beijing, 1999. The essay suggests that investigative reporting is usurping the role of government supervision through the prosecution and court system.

87. *The Pinying Chinese-English Dictionary*, The Commercial Press, Hong Kong, 1995, p. 66.

88. Ibid., p. 714.

89. Ibid., p. 722.
90. Ibid., p. 502.
91. "Observing Police Style Construction from 'Exposé' of Special Cases" ["*Cong dianxing anli 'baoguang' kan jingfeng jiangshe*"], *Renmin Gongan Banyue Kan*, January 31, 2002.
92. "Chinese Police Launch Probe into Shooting of Neurosurgeon," *Xinhua*, November 14, 2007 (http://www.china.org.cn/english/China/231880.htm).
93. "Hebei Police Work Supervise Police 'Four Abusive' Use of Vehicles" ["*Hebei jingwu ducha zhijing yong cheliang 'siluan'*], *China Police Daily*, April 30, 2002.
94. "Authorities Step Up Fight against Police Crimes," *China Daily*, December 12, 2000.
95. Chan Jieren, "What Are 'Police Not Suitable to Wear Arms' Suitable for?" ["*Bu shihe pei chang de jingcha" shihe shenme?*"], *China Youth Daily* [*Zhongguo qingnian bao*], October 30, 2000; reprinted in *China Police Forum*, April 6, 2001.
96. Jeffrey Kinkley, *Chinese Justice, the Fiction: Law and Literature in Modern China*, Stanford University Press, Stanford, CA, 2000.
97. "What Should Be the Police Image in Police Artistic Writing?" ["*Jingcha yishu xingxiang gai zenyang*"], *China Police Daily*, January 31, 2002.
98. "Police Image in Art" ["*Jingcha de yishu xingxiang*"], *China Police Daily*, January 31, 2002.
99. "News laundering" (*xi gao*) is a term coined to describe a situation in which a news organization is unable or unauthorized to be the first to publish a certain item of news and consequently finds another news organization to first post the news. When the news has been posted by the second news organization, the first news organization will republish the news, citing the second news organization.
100. The Deng Yujiao incident refers to a case in which a young woman claimed that she stabbed a Party official in self-defense after he solicited sex. The Internet was critical in rallying public support that led to her acquittal.
101. The Hangzhou street race case refers to a case in which a wealthy young man, Hu Bin, struck and killed another young man, Tan Zhuo, as Hu was speeding in Hangzhou. He was later convicted after the case aroused a great deal of online discussion about the role of wealth in judicial proceedings.
102. Li Wufeng, "Safeguarding the Orderly Dissemination of Online News," *China Digital Times*, December 16, 2009.
103. "What Should Be the Police Image in Police Artistic Writing?" ["*Jingcha yishu xingxiang gai zenyang*"], *China Police Daily*, January 31, 2002.
104. "Do Not Allow Floating Clouds to Obscure Perceptive Eyes" ["*Mo wai fuyun wanyan*"], *China Police Daily*, January 31, 2002.
105. Jeffrey Kinkley, *Chinese Justice, the Fiction: Law and Literature in Modern China*, Stanford University Press, Stanford, CA, 2000, pp. 313, 317.
106. "Police Seek Kinder, Friendlier Image," *Beijing Times*, August 12, 2010.
107. "Report regarding Nanchang, Changsha, Chengzhu Propaganda Culture Work," http://friendfeed.com/yihuaderen/45787d69/4.
108. http://www.mail-archive.com/gfw-blog@googlegroups.com/msg00336.html.
109. "Dissecting an Internet Monkey," *Southern Metropolitan Weekly*, June 19, 2009 (http://www.nbweekly.com/Print/Article/7956_0.shtml).
110. Yang Meng, "Press, Legal Communities Appeal for Protection of Media Rights," *People's Daily Online*, August 31, 2010.
111. David Bankdusrsky, "Media Decry Return of China's 'Toughest Party Secretary,'" *China Media Project*, November 26, 2008 (http://cmp.hku.hk/2008/11/26/1399/).
112. Mark O'Neill, "China's Bad Comrade Cops," *Asian Sentinel*, November 22, 2007.
113. "Violent Protest against the Law Attracted 'Assault against Police Crime' Debate,'" *China Police Net* [*Zhongguo jingcha wang*], May 21, 2004 (http://www.cpd.com.cn/gb/newspaper/2004-05/21/content_298410.htm).

114. (a) "Beijing Police Were Assaulted and Yelled at over 10,000 Times in the Last Two Years," *Sina.com* (http://news.sina.com.cn/c/2005-01-03/07365406545.shtml). (b) "A Drunken Male Driver Arrested for Assaulting Police," *Shanxi Youth Newspaper*, February, 21, 2010 (http://www.sxqnb.com.cn/2010/0221/81880.html).

115. "Violent Protest against the Law, Attracted 'Assault against Police Crime' Debate,'" *China Police Net* [*Zhongguo jingcha wang*] May 21, 2004 (http://www.cpd.com.cn/gb/newspaper/2004-05/21/content_298410.htm).

116. *Renmin Ribao*, July 24, 2006, p. 10.

117. "MPS Will Soon Draft Regulations on the Obstruction of People's Police in the Carrying Out of Duties," *Enorth Netnews*, July 20, 2006 (http://news.enorth.com.cn/system/2006/07/20/001363275.shtml). Resistance to and obstruction of police duties represent a complex social problem that requires extensive study and comprehensive treatment.

118. Table 1 in Chen Xiao Ming et al., "Investigation into Causes and Remedies to Current Police Deaths and Injuries in the Process of Law Enforcement" ["*Dong qiang Gongan minjing zhifa guocheng zhong shangwang yuanyin zhi duice yanjiu*"], *Public Security Studies*, 121, 63–67, 2007.

119. Murray Scot Tanner, "We the People (of China)," *Wall Street Journal*, February 2, 2006.

120. "The Status, Cause and Response to Obstruction of Police in the Execution of Duties," *Shandong Provincial Legal Network*, August 30, 2007 (http://www.sd-law.gov.cn/sdlaw/site/detail.jsp?id=8967).

121. "Dragged Traffic Police for Two Kilos before Absconding, Jin BT6617 in Big Trouble," *Enorth Netnews*, February 14, 2006 (http://news.enorth.com.cn/system/2006/02/14/001232249.shtml).

122. "Jin BT6617 Driver Who Assaulted Police Caught, Three People Arrested for Harboring a Criminal," *Enorth Netnews*, February 21, 2006 (http://news.enorth.com.cn/system/2006/02/21/001237602.shtml).

123. "Report of Secrets to Shooting of Liaoning Jin Zhou Male Who Indecently Assaulted Female and Attacked Police," *Enorth News*, March 17, 2006 (http://news.enorth.com.cn/system/2006/03/17/001258052.shtml). The police have experienced increased obstruction, attacks, insults, and framing of officers on duty. In 2003, the Liaoning PSB set up a committee to protect the interests of police and help ensure their safety; this committee required clarification of false complaints against the police system and put a system in place for investigating attacks on the police.

124. "Villages Conducting Customary Rituals Cause Incident; 27 Police Attacked while Enforcing the Law," *Enorth News*, July 20, 2006.

125. "Chinese Court Upholds Death Penalty for Police Killer," *Xinhua*, October 20, 2008.

126. Maureen Fan, "Confessed Police Killer Lionized by Thousands in China," *Washington Post*, November 14, 2008.

127. "Shanghai Assault on Police Case," *Jinhua Shi Bao*, July 2, 2008 (http://sh.xinmin.cn/shehui/2008/07/02/1217050.html).

128. "Discerning Media Value from Reporting on Shanghai Police Attack Case," *Tianya*, July 3, 2008 (http://www.tianya.cn/techforum/content/158/547153.shtml).

129. "Violent Protest against the Law Attracted 'Assault against Police Crime' Debate,'" *China Police Net* [*Zhongguo jingcha wang*] May 21, 2004 (http://www.cpd.com.cn/gb/newspaper/2004-05/21/content_298410.htm).

130. "The Status, Cause and Response to Obstruction of Police in the Execution of Duties," *Shandong Provincial Legal Network*, August 30, 2007 (http://www.sd-law.gov.cn/sdlaw/site/detail.jsp?id=8967).

131. "Chinese Police Chief Pays Cash to Settle Hit-and-Run Case," *NTDTV*, November 10, 2010. Deputy Chief Li Gong paid off (US$69,000) victims of a hit-and-run case involving his son Li Qiming, who was arrested for the incident and said: "My father is Li Gong."

132. "The Status, Cause and Response to Obstruction of Police in the Execution of Duties," *Shandong Provincial Legal Network*, August 30, 2007 (http://www.sd-law.gov.cn/sdlaw/site/detail.jsp?id=8967).

133. "Preliminary Analysis of Policy for Prevention and Handling of Problems with Obstruction of Police in the Execution of Duties," *xyszf.gov.cn*, May 9, 2008 (http://www.xyszf.gov.cn/ARTICLE/View.asp?id=3255).

134. "The Status, Cause and Response to Obstruction of Police in the Execution of Duties," *Shandong Provincial Legal Network*, August 30, 2007 (http://www.sd-law.gov.cn/sdlaw/site/detail.jsp?id=8967).

135. "Increase in Assault on Police, NPC Considers Assault on Police Offense in Criminal Law," *Hainan Daily*, March 12, 2007 (http://hicourt.gov.cn/xwztc/show_news.asp?newsid= 2007-3-12-9-16-16).

136. "Man Violently Hit Police for 18 Minutes, Tired of Hitting Said: 'Hit More after Rest,'" *Net East*, June 22 (http://news.163.com/08/0622/03/4F0TNT0L00011229.html).

137. "Three South Koreans Appear to Be Involved; Details about the Case of Tan Jing," *Net East*, April 16, 2008 (http://news.163.com/08/0416/03/49KBP80K00011229.html). Tan Jing was killed on April 4, 2008; his body was found dangling outside the window. Three Koreans were suspected of murdering him.

138. "Qin Huang Dao Established Police Rights Protection Committee" ["*Qin Huang Dao chengli jingcha weiquan weiyuanhui*"], *China Police Net* [*Zhongguo jingcha wang*], October 10, 2003 (http://www.cpd.com.cn/gb/newspaper/2003-10/31/content_231425.htm).

139. For a map of Zhejiang and location of Hangzhou, see http://www.maps-of-china.com/zhejiang-s-ow.shtml.

140. "Violent Protest against the Law Attracted 'Assault against Police Crime' Debate,'" *China Police Net* [*Zhongguo jingcha wang*] May 21, 2004 (http://www.cpd.com.cn/gb/newspaper/2004-05/21/content_298410.htm).

141. "What Do Police Amount To?" ["*Jingcha suan shenme?*"], *People's Daily*, April 4, 2002.

142. "Why Need to Fight a War from the Side," *China Police Daily*, April 4, 2002. "Fight a war from the side" has figurative as well as literal meaning. Literally, fighting a war from the side means that one has to be careful of the enemy, suggesting that the enemy is enjoying the upper hand. Figuratively, to say that the police have to fight a war with the criminal 'on the side' is to observe that the police are no longer a righteous, stand-up force to be reckoned with.

143. PRC Criminal Law, Chapter 1, provides that police are protected by law in the proper execution of their duties. Chapter 5, Article 35, provides that those who resist and obstruct police will be punished administratively and criminally.

144. Literally, like "routine dinner at home," or nothing special.

145. "It Is Important to Talk about Reactive Tactics" ["*Jianggou duice han zhongyao*"], *People's Daily*, April 4, 2002.

146. "Need to Make Oneself Strong" ["*Yao zuo dao zishen ying*"], *China Police Daily*, April 4, 2002.

147. "Regarding 32 Classical Police Sayings," *Tianya*, May 23, 2007 (http://www.tianya.cn/techforum/content/158/1/543736.shtml).

148. For a researcher, especially one who has little access to the inner world of policing in China, this is a gold mine. The "32 Classical Police Sayings" offer China-bound researchers a personal and intimate view of Chinese police culture. Still, a few caveats on the limitations of this dataset are in order: (1) The origination of the "Sayings" is unknown. We do not know who assembled the dataset or when, where, how, or why it was compiled. This makes interpretation of the data difficult and susceptible to erroneous interpretation. If we knew more about the origination of the data, we could better put the "Sayings" in context; for example, an officer who had an axe to grind might have compiled them out of spite, which would certainly affect the objectivity of the "Sayings." (2) Police officers and the police culture are not monolithic. The "Sayings" do not, and cannot be made to, stand for the thinking and feeling of all, or even most, of the police officers in China. China is a big country. Police officers in Beijing, the nation's political capital in the north, do not

face the same problems as those in Shenzhen, a regional commercial city down south. There are many kinds of police. City police deal with problems differently than rural police. Criminal investigators' views regarding suspects' rights differ from those of community police officers. Police officers come from all walks of life, regions, and age groups. Police college graduates are more disciplined, whereas military transfers are more ideologically pure. The 1970s generation was more collective minded, and the post-1980s generations tend to be more self-centered. Differences can also be found among ranks, top leaders, managers, and street cops. Finally, one cannot overlook gender and personality differences. (3) Because the Internet in China is subject to censorship by web masters and government surveillance, it is likely that the "Sayings" were subject to unconscious self-censorship before publication. If that is the case, then the "Sayings" may not be as forthcoming as they could have been; however, although the "Sayings" raise issues of authenticity, validity, and utility as a database for culture audit, they do meet the self-validation test. The observations of the "Sayings" are in agreement with most other web police comments, statements, observations, and debates that the author has read through the years, although the scope, tone, and certitude of such observations can exhibit some differences. Also, the "Sayings" are offered up not as an exact replica of existing cultural code or as a quantitative survey of police cultural beliefs, but rather as an indication of the existence of a specific counterculture. As such, it is a heuristic device that generates debate and further research regarding the police cultural code.

149. (a) "Do not strike back" is an admonition born out of the MPS policy, "Do not hit back, do not yell back." The rationale for the "do not hit back/do not yell back" policy is to allay public concerns about police abuse of power (see http://blog.china.com.cn/whbsuwc/art/3470196.html); however, the "do not hit back/do not yell back" policy is a most unreasonable rule. It is derived from the need to prevent the police from assaulting citizens at will and to realize "civilized law enforcement" ("文明执法"), especially with regard to the violent and abusive enforcement techniques of city administrators (*Chengguna*) which have resulted in scores of citizens being injured. (b) This zero tolerance policy has had a grave impact on line officers. Research in medical facilities has shown that medical and nursing staff suffer various kinds of psychological trauma associated with such a policy. In one study, the psychological reactions of 56 (of out 286) medical staff who had been assaulted (100%) included aggrieved (56), angry (45), tolerant (35), revengeful (9), seeking avoidance (19), rebellious (8), and fearful (42) (see http://journal.shouxi.net/qikan/article.php?id=323113). (c) "Lady Traffic Violator Used Violence to Break Law, Slapped Two Traffic Police 40 times in 15 minutes," *Xinhua*, April 26, 2006. The MPS rule precipitated a nationwide debate as to its reasonableness, impact, and implications, and the "do not hit back/do not yell back" policy has encouraged the public to challenge police activities or otherwise obstruct police in the performance of their duty. In 2006, two traffic police officers, Qu Jiasong and Wang Xingshen, from Dehui City in Jilin Province, stopped a woman driver for a traffic violation and wanted to detain the car. The woman refused and slapped Officer Qu 20 times in front of a large crowd (50 to 60 people) in broad daylight. Neither officer fought back. Qu, the more experienced officer, instructed Wang to back off because it was a woman who was doing the hitting. The officers would not run away because it would not look good for police officers to do so. (d) Police should follow the law but defend themselves if and when appropriate. Ren Zhi said, "In the face of violent assault, the police should fight back; 'police' is not an alternative term for weakness." (e) "Obstructionist Used Violence to Resist Arrest, Chop City Administrator with Knife," *joy.cn*, June 6, 2010 (http://news.joy.cn/video/1634857.htm). Police officers have been repeatedly assaulted and insulted in the line of duty. On June 6, 2010, the Lo Wu city administrator enforcement team sought cooperation from a restaurant keeper with regard to removing a street obstruction but he refused. The man assaulted the officers with a knife, and the officers did not fight back, even though they sustained wounds requiring 25 stitches. (f) "Drunken Man Assaults Traffic Police, Summons Friends to Violently Resist Law," *Sina.com*, September 7, 2010. To avoid getting into trouble, the police have adopted a passive, sometimes apologetic, attitude when being hit or yelled at. As a result, the police consider themselves to be a vulnerable group (弱势群体). In 2010, in Li Shui District, Zhejiang, a vehicle was stopped for suspected DUI. The

driver refused to take the DUI test and summoned his friends to assault the police. The police did not fight back and were awarded a "tolerant" award for proper handling of incident. (g) "Are Police Considered to Be a New Vulnerable Group? Repeated Assaults on Police," *Xu Chang Morning Post*, November 2, 2005 (http://www.police.com.cn/Article/xinwen/jslc/200511/4629. html). (h) "PSB Director Openly Exposed Shortcomings Leading to Heated Debate: Are Police a Vulnerable Group or Fox Appearing as Grandmother?" *CCTV.com*, October 10, 2008.

150. "Statistics of Mass Incidents." *EastSouthWestNorth*, November 15, 2006 (http://www.zonaeuropa.com/20061115_1.htm). There are no reliable statistics on mass incidents, no uniform definition, and substantial underreporting.

151. "58,000 Mass Incidents in China in First Quarter as Unrest Grows to Largest Ever Recorded," *Libcom.org*, May 6, 2009. If this trend continues, then 2009 would break all previous records, with over 230,000 mass incidents, compared to 120,000 in 2008 and 90,000 in 2006.

152. "China Strives to Handle Mass Incidents," *Xinhua*, December 9, 2006 (http://www.chinadaily. com.cn/china/2006-12/09/content_754796.htm).

153. "China: Geopolitical Data," *ChinaBalanceSheet.org* (http://www.chinabalancesheet.org/ Documents/Data_Domestic_Sociopolitical.pdf).

154. "CCMPS Officials Discuss Social Stability Goals for 2007," *Chinese Law and Politics Blog*, January 17, 2007 (http://sinolaw.typepad.com/chinese_law_and_politics_/2007/01/ccmps_officials.html).

155. "Are Mass Incidents Increasing or Decreasing in China?" *Chinese Law and Politics Blog*, January 31, 2007 (http://sinolaw.typepad.com/chinese_law_and_politics_/2007/03/are_mass_incide. htm). Since 2005, official Chinese statements regarding mass incidents have been incomplete and confusing. Some foreign media have (incorrectly) reported that Chinese officials stated that 87,000 mass incidents occurred in China in 2005. This number, however, does not refer to mass incidents; rather, it refers to public order disturbances.

156. "Notice regarding Management of Information Work Methods of Ningxia Shizui Shan Municipality, Weinong District" ["*Guanyu fabao Ningxia Shizui Shan Shi Weinongqu xinxi guanli banfa tongzhi*"], *Ningxia mofcom.gov.cn*, November 11, 2006 (http://ningxia.mofcom. gov.cn/aarticle/sjdixiansw/200611/20061103704074.html).

157. Ta Kung Pao on June 5, 2005. Reprint at "Statistics of Mass Incidents," *EastSouthWestNorth*, November 15, 2006 (http://www.zonaeuropa.com/20061115_1.htm).

158. (a) See section on "Estimated Mass Incidents in China: 1993 to 2005" in "Statistics of Mass Incidents," *EastSouthWestNorth*, November 15, 2006 (http://www.zonaeuropa.com/20061115_1. htm). (b) Chinese police dealt with 17,900 mass incidents from January 2006 to September 2006, a drop of 22.1%. There are some indicators that the numbers are dropping; see "China Says Protests, Riots Down a Fifth This Year," *Reuters*, November 7, 2006.

159. Cu Yedong, "A Few Points of Reflection on How to Handle Crowd Incidents Appropriately," *Gongan Daixue Xuebao*, 88, 19–22, 2000.

160. Han Jiangui, "A Preliminary Discussion of Public Order Incidents and a General Plan to Handle Such Incidents," *Public Security Studies*, 80, 76–81, 2001.

161. Dai Gang, "Thoughts on the Way to Deal with Xin Hua Xi He Massive Accident," *Gongan Daixue Xuebao*, 88, 36, 2000.

162. Han Jiangui, "A Preliminary Discussion of Public Order Incidents and a General Plan to Handle Such Incidents," *Public Security Studies*, 80, 76–81, 2001.

163. Cu Yedong, "A Few Points of Reflection on How to Handle Crowd Incidents Appropriately," *Gongan Daixue Xuebao*, 88, 19–22, 2000.

164. James Conach, "Thousands of Officials Punished in China's Anti-Corruption Purge," *World Socialist Web Site*, February 1, 2000 (http://www.wsws.org/articles/2000/feb2000/chin-f01.shtml).

165. Peter Symonds, "Social Tensions Rise in China," *World Socialist Web Site*, January 2, 1999 (http://www.wsws.org/articles/1999/jan1999/chin-j22.shtml).

166. Zhou Zhongwei, *Managing Mass Incidents* [*Quntisheng Shijian ji Chuzhi*], Jiangxi renmin chubanshe, Nanchang, 2006, p. 1.

167. Ministry of Public Security, *Examination of Village Mass Confrontation Incidents and Response Policy* [*Nongcun qunti chongtu shijian de duice tantu*], Qunzhong chubanshe, Beijing, 1995.
168. Zhou Zhongwei, *Managing Mass Incidents* [*Quntingxing Shijian ji Chuzhi*], Jiangxi renmin chubanshe, Nanchang, 2006, p. 1.
169. Ibid., p. 2.
170. Ibid., p. 3.
171. Ibid., Chapter 1, "Mass Incidents Overview."
172. Ibid., p. 15.
173. Ibid., p. 16.
174. Ibid., p. 18.
175. Ibid., p. 19.
176. Ibid., pp. 20–21.
177. Ibid., p. 23.
178. Ibid., p. 24.
179. Ibid., p. 25.
180. Ibid., p. 26.
181. Ibid., p. 27.
182. Ibid., p. 28.
183. Ibid., p. 29.
184. Ibid., p. 24.
185. Ibid., p. 25
186. "Shenzhen: 1 billion dollars of wealth being returned to the workers" ["*Shenzhen*: 10 *yi yuan caifu huan mingong*"], *China Police Daily*, March 28, 2002.
187. Murray Scot Tanner, "China Rethinks Unrest," *Washington Quarterly*, 27(3), 138, 2004.
188. Wu Jian, "Making Great Efforts to Maintain Public Order in the First Year of the New Century, with Clear Tasks and Future Emphases in Mind," *Public Security Studies*, 76, 6–11, 2001. (Wu Jian was a Public Order Management Bureau Chief for the MPS). The first order of business for the new century is to deal with public order (mass disturbance) events in an effective manner. This requires broadening the collection of intelligence and effective implementation of "Guidelines regarding Public Security Organs' Handling of Mass Public Order Events" ("*Gongan jiguan chuli qunti sheng zhian shijian guiding*"). It also requires strengthening riot troop construction and controlling the Falun Gong.
189. Peter Symonds, "Social Tensions Rise in China," *World Socialist Web Site*, January 2, 1999 (http://www.wsws.org/articles/1999/jan1999/chin-j22.shtml). The *Hunan Economic Daily* reported that there had been more than 60 mass protests in Changsha and 20 road blockages last year, but few demonstrations by workers or farmers are reported in the official press.
190. "Major Problems and the Reasons Thereof Existing in the Contemporary Public Order," *Public Security Studies*, 79, 12–16, 2001. During the "8–5" period (eighth five-year plan) an average of 400 mass disturbances occurred each year, but that number increased to an average of 900 in the "9–5" period (ninth five-year plan). In the year 2000, in Hebei Province, there were 1260 mass disturbance cases involving a total of 60,159 people.
191. MPS Fourth Research Institute, *Collected Research Essays on Mass Incidents* [*Quntisheng Shijian Yanjiu Lunwenji*], Chinese People's Public Security University Press, Beijing, 2001.
192. Marie Edin, "Remaking the Communist Party-State: The Cadre Responsibility System at the Local Level in China," *China: An International Journal*, 1(1), 1–15, 2003.
193. Ibid.
194. Legitimacy can be viewed externally by the public (e.g., lack of progress) or felt internally by regime members (e.g., lack of purpose).
195. (a) Mass disturbances, or "public order events" (*quntisheng shijian*), have received the close attention of the MPS. The MPS Fourth Research Institute launched a research project to study public order events in 2000 and received a total of 386 articles from 30 provinces. Three of these articles were published in *Public Security Studies*: (1) Fujian Provincial Public Security

Department, "On Public Order Incidents and the Treatment Thereof," *Public Security Studies*, 80, 67–71, 2001. (2) Zhou Guanyang, "On Public Order Events," *Public Security Studies*, 80, 71–76, 2001. (3) Han Jiangui, "A Preliminary Discussion of Public Order Incidents and a General Plan to Handle Such Incidents," *Public Security Studies*, 80, 76–81, 2001. (b) See also "Regulations regarding Public Security Organs' Handling of Public Order Events" passed in 2000, and Zhang Shengqian, *Handling Social Order Incidents* [*Shehui Zhian Shijian Chuzhi*], People's Public Security University Press, Beijing, 2001.

196. Ibid.
197. Ernest Tucker, "Chinese Movement Is Quietly Growing Here," *Chicago Sun-Times*, May 3, 1999. According to Marl Allee, a professor of early modern Chinese history at Loyola University in Chicago, "People want to pigeonhole [Buddha law], but it may offer different benefits to different people who participate in it. For some, it may just be about health. For others, it could be spiritual."
198. "Crackdown Shows Communist Party Cracks," *Asia Times*, July 24, 1999. Falun Gong fulfills a spiritual void after the demise of communism and rise of materialism.
199. "China vs. Mass Spiritual Thirst," *Christian Science Monitor*, August 3, 1999. Ma Junshui, a Chinese graduate student, said: "My father's generation was educated to believe in Marxism.... But in our generation we generally don't believe in anything except for money and materialism. There is a spiritual vacuum in China, morals are declining, and many people are now beginning to search for ways to reverse the trend....More and more people are practicing Falun Gong because their spirits are empty."
200. Jonathan S. Landreth and J.S. Greenberg, "Eye of the Storm," *New York Times Magazine*, August 8, 1999 (http://www.nytimes.com/keyword/li-hongzhi).
201. Matt Pottinger, "China Cult Promises Healing, Blasts Immorality," *Reuters*, April 25, 1999.
202. Patsy Rahn, "Criticism of Falun Gong," *Facts of Falun Gong*, September 28, 2010 (http://factsof-falun.wordpress.com/2010/09/). "There's one aspect of the movement I'd like to address, and that is Li Hong Zhi's and the group's strong desire to be 'officially' recognized by the Chinese government as 'good.'"
203. John Leicester, "China: Lost Souls Join Falun Gong," Associated Press, November 4, 1999 (http://www.rickross.com/reference/fa_lun_gong/falun134.html). PRC top government spiritual authorities acknowledged that the banned Falun Gong spiritual movement has attracted people lost amid the unsettling changes.
204. Matt Pottinger, "China Cult Promises Healing, Blasts Immorality, *Reuters*, April 25, 1999. Hou Huilan, a 55-year-old factory worker, said Li's teaching helped her to be a good wife and citizen. It taught her lessons about family values and civic virtues.
205. For a discussion of social crisis and popular discontent generated by economic slowdown, see James Conachy, "Unemployment and Poverty Spirals: Beijing Accelerates Market Reforms as Economic Growth and Investment Slow," *World Socialist Web Site*, May 20, 1999 (http://www.wsws.org/articles/1999/may1999/chin-m20.shtml).
206. Ibid.
207. Ibid.
208. Zixian Deng and Shi-min Fang, "The Two Tales of Falun Gong: Radicalism in a Traditional Form," paper presented to the Annual Conference of the American Family Foundation, Seattle, WA, April 28–29, 2000 (http://www.xys.org/xys/netters/Fang-Zhouzi/religion/2tales.doc).
209. Ibid.
210. Nick Young, "Three 'Cs': Civil Society, Corporate Responsibility, and China," *China Business Review*, Special Report, January 2002 (http://www.chinabusinessreview.com/public/0201/young.html).
211. The background information on this person indicates that he was a male from Xianxi who graduated from Luo Yang Police College and is now unemployed (website unavailable).
212. "Say Goodbye to the Uniform I Love ["*Gaobie wo hai de jingfu*"], *China Police Forum*, February 24, 2002 (website unavailable).

213. Judging from the intimate knowledge she has of Dalian police not readily available to outsiders, she must be a serving police officer, but there is no background information available (website unavailable).

214. "Response: Response: Say Goodbye to the Uniform I Love" ["*Huifu: Huifu: Gaobie wo hai de jingfu*"], *China Police Forum*, February 24, 2002.

215. The comments must be taken with a grain of salt, as there is no validity check. Such statements certainly cannot be trusted to represent all or many of the officers or agencies. The comments, however, do allow us to see how insiders view police and policing problems and issues in China.

216. "Is It Appropriate for the Police to Seek Out Mistresses?" ["*Jingcha zhao qingren daodi ying bu yinggai a?*"], *China Police Forum*, February 18, 2002.

217. "Response: Is It Appropriate for the Police to Seek Out Mistresses?" ["*Huifu: Jingcha zhao qingren daodi ying bu yinggai a?*"], *China Police Forum*, February 18, 2002. No background information is available for this commenter.

218. "Response: Response: Is It Appropriate for the Police to Seek Out Mistresses?" ["*Huifu: Huifu: Jingcha zhao qingren daodi ying bu yinggai a?*"], *China Police Forum*, February 18, 2002 (http://www.ok100.net/read.php?ltype=&BBS_id=policeman&write_ID=1920367).

219. "Response: Is It Appropriate for the Police to Seek Out Mistresses?" ["*Huifu: Jingcha zhao qingren daodi ying bu yinggai a?*"], *China Police Forum*, February 20, 2002.

220. There is no background information on this person other than that he is a male. Three things suggested that he might be a police officer: (1) his online name, (2) his knowledge of what conduct police officers should not be engaging in, and (3) the way he responded to the question posed: "How come you do not have regulations?" (website unavailable).

221. "Response: Is It Appropriate for the Police to Seek Out Mistresses?" ["*Huifu: Jingcha zhao qingren daodi ying bu yinggai a?*"], *China Police Forum*, February 18, 2002.

222. "Response: Response: Is It Appropriate for the Police to Seek Out Mistresses?" ["*Huifu: Huifu: Jingcha zhao qingren daodi ying bu yinggai a?*"], *China Police Forum*, February 18, 2002.

223. It is now common for police to accuse civilians of not understanding police work before they evaluate civilians' critical comments.

224. The police administrator has tried to reach into the private affairs of the police officers, which has raised grave concerns.

225. Contacts with promiscuous females with minimal supervision are part of police work, and sooner or later every police officer will be propositioned. Some women are attracted to the uniform or the aura of the occupation. See Mark Stevens, "Sex on Duty or Off Duty," in *Police Deviance & Ethics*, North Carolina Wesleyan College, Rocky Mount, NC (http://faculty.ncwc.edu/mstevens/205/205lect11.htm).

226. "Response: Is It Appropriate for the Police to Seek Out Mistresses?" ["*Huifu: Jingcha zhao qingren daodi ying bu yinggai a?*"], *China Police Forum*, February 18, 2002.

227. "Response: Is it appropriate for the police to seek out mistresses?" ["*Huifu: Jingcha zhao qingren daodi ying bu yinggai a?*"], *China Police Forum*, February 20, 2002. A female student from Beijing (Shui Liu Yin) pointed out, "Police are also people. They are not god. To find a mistress is not illegal. If this does not harm the society and cause social problem, there is no need for such strict scrutiny."

228. "Should not be done!" ["*Bu yinggai!*"], *China Police Forum*, February 18, 2002.

229. "Response: Is It Appropriate for the Police to Seek Out Mistresses?" ["*Huifu: Jingcha zhao qingren daodi ying bu yinggai a?*"], *China Police Forum*, February 18, 2002.

230. "Response: Response: Is It Appropriate for the Police to Seek Out Mistresses?" ["*Huifu: Huifu: Jingcha zhao qingren daodi ying bu yinggai a?*"], *China Police Forum*, February 18, 2002. Gong Dai Heshehui said, "You do not have enough money for your family, how can you have spare for your mistress to pay debt?"

231. "Response: Is It Appropriate for the Police to Seek Out Mistresses?" ["*Huifu: Jingcha zhao qingren daodi ying bu yinggai a?*"], *China Police Forum*, February 18, 2002.

232. "Response: Is It Appropriate for the Police to Seek Out Mistresses?" ["*Huifu: Jingcha zhao qin-gren daodi ying bu yinggai a?*"], *China Police Forum*, February 18, 2002.

233. "Deep Thinking about Why Public Did Not Like to Testify" ["*Qunzhong bu yuanyi zuozheng de shengxi kou*"], *China Police Forum*, January 4, 2002.

234. "Response: Deep Thinking about Why Public Did Not Like to Testify" ["*Huifu: Qunzhong bu yuanyi zuozheng de shengxi kou*"], *China Police Forum*, January 5, 2002.

235. "*Tingsuo zai Shanghai kao 'ligan peixun' de shihou, Shanghai minjing jiti shang jie youxing,*" *China Police Forum*, April 26, 2001.

236. "I Just Want to Say That If Li Jizhou Bureau Chief Has a Problem, Does It Mean That His Boss…Should Also Be Responsible?" ["*Wo xiang suo Li Jizhou buzhang chuwanti, tade shangsi lingdao…yao bu yao fuze?*"], *China Police Forum*, April 26, 2001.

237. *Wedding Rituals*, LurveStory, Singapore, 2011 (http://www.lurvestory.com/index_files/WeddingRituals.htm).

238. Christopher Carothers, "Outrage as 'Wrong-Beating-Gate' Scandal Breaks," *China Real Time Report*, July 22, 2010 (http://blogs.wsj.com/chinarealtime/2010/07/22/outrage-as-wrong-beat-ing-gate-scandal-breaks/). Six plainclothes police officers beat up Chen Yulian, 58, the wife of a Hubei provincial committee official, for trying to enter the main gate of the Hubei provincial government office buildings in Wuhan. They mistakenly identified her as a prostitute. Chinese news articles, blogs, and forums voiced their disapproval at what became known as "Wrong-Beating-Gate" (*da cuo men*, 打错门). (b) "Police Erroneously Assault the Wife of Hebei Provincial Official," *Southern Metropolitan News*, July 20, 2010. For over 70 blog entries in reply, see http://comment.news.163.com/news3_bbs/6C174N4200014AEE.html.

239. "Poll: Corruption, Public Discontent Most Worrisome," *People's Daily*, July 9, 2010. *People's Daily* interviewed 6575 Chinese citizens and 50 scholars. The citizens thought that the corruption of officials was a major concern.

240. "Former Senior Chinese Police Official Stands Trial for Corruption, Power Abuse," *People's Daily*, July 7, 2010 (http://english.peopledaily.com.cn/90001/90776/90882/7055977.html). Zheng Shaodong, former Assistant Minister of Public Security, stood trial for allegedly accepting bribes and for abuse of power. Zheng, also the former director of the economic criminal investigation bureau under the Ministry of Public Security, was dismissed from the Communist Party of China and his public office in 2009.

241. "Why Do We Feel That Police Quality Is Low?" ["*Wei shenme daijia juede jingcha de suji di*"], *Tianya*, May 23, 2009 (http://www.tianya.cn/techforum/content/158/550173.shtml).

242. That is to say rule of man and not of man.

243. "Survey of Police and Public Relationship from Police Post Officers' Perspective" ["*Paichusuo minjing zhong de jingmin guanxi tiaocha*"], *Police Post Work*, February 2006 (http://www.phcppsu.com.cn/news/2006/c-2.htm).

244. Anthony J. Raganella and Michael D. White, "Race, Gender, and Motivation for Becoming a Police Officer: Implications for Building a Representative Police Department," *Journal of Criminal Justice*, 32(6), 501–513, 2004.

245. Byongook Moon and Eui-Gab Hwang, "The Reasons for Choosing a Career in Policing among South Korean Police Cadets," *Journal of Criminal Justice*, 32(3), 223–229, 2004. The survey was carried out in the summer of 2001 at the auditorium of the academy. The instructors of the police academy made sure that participation in the study was voluntary and anonymous. In the summer of 2001, 558 male and 300 female cadets were trained at the Line Officer Course of the Central Police Academy. A total of 410 completed questionnaires were collected: 199 from males and 211 from females. The overall response rate of cadets was 48% (36% for males and 70% for females).

246. Confucius, *The Great Learning*, 500 BC (http://www.sacred-texts.com/cfu/conf2.htm).

247. Yuning Wu, Ivan Y. Sun, and Michael A. Cretacci, "Study of Cadets' Motivation to Become Police Officers in China," *International Journal of Police Science & Management*, 11(3), 377–392, 2009.

248. After being issued their new uniforms, the police trainees had a party, where they gathered and discussed their reasons for joining the police. "Factso" said that he joined because of police powers and the respect they are given. He used to work in a restaurant; his boss had money but still had to treat the police with respect (e.g., buying them food and drinks, giving them presents). "Su 3" was a Chinese major in college; he joined because there were not enough candidates for Police College, and the department recommended him. "Lao 4" joined because he wanted to see justice done. When he was young, he learned the martial arts so he could defend other students against hoodlums. "Lu Xiao 5" joined because he wanted to protect his fishing community from gangsters. When he was a child, his fishing family has to appease the gangs with portions of their catch, and he was frustrated that he was not able to do anything. "Guizhi 6" joined because he wanted to avenge his father, a traffic police officer, who was killed while on duty. "Beggar" joined because policing was considered a respectable occupation. The lesson here is clear. One cannot fully understand why people join the police without looking at their backgrounds and experiences. These trainees all indicated that their life choices were based on something that happened to them in their lives. To understand the Chinese people's reasons for joining the police, for whatever reason, is to study individual life circumstances, as played out in a larger social, economical, political, and, most importantly, cultural context. See http://www.fanwentiandi.com/a/zongjie/yiyu-angongzuozongjie/2010/0629/14443.html.

249. "Heart to Heart Talk on Why You Became a Cop: Do Not Say Anything That Is Fake, Inflated, or False" [用真心话来谈谈 你为什么当警察？假、大、空的请不必讲], *Tianya*, December 12, 2006 (http://www.tianya.cn/New/TechForum/Content.asp?idWriter=0&Key=0&idItem=158&idArticle=541947).

250. The forum master was quoting Lui Lok, who was a Detective Staff Sergeant in Hong Kong in the 1960s. He was alleged to have made millions of dollars before being charged and convicted in Hong Kong by the Independent Commission Against Corruption (ICAC) for corruption. See T. Wing Lo, "Hong Kong: Minimizing Crime and Corruption," *Trends in Organized Crime*, 4(3), 80–80, 1999. (The author served in the Royal Hong Kong Police as an Inspector of Police during Lui's tenure.)

251. Abraham H. Maslow, "A Theory of Human Motivation," *Psychological Review*, 50, 370–396, 1943. What the forum master observed finds theoretical support in Maslow's theory that physiological needs must be satisfied before self-actualization needs.

252. Ibid.

253. (a) Francesco Sofo and Ting Wang, *East Meets West: Thinking Styles of Chinese Executives*, University of Canberra, 2005. (b) *The Brains behind Your Organization's Success—Understanding Whole Brain® Thinking: What You Don't Know Can Hurt You*, Herrmann International, Lake Lure, NC, 2004 (http://www.hbdi.com/whitepaper-final.pdf). Four quadrants characterize the way people think. The left cerebral hemisphere corresponds to analytical thinking, preferring to focus on logic, analysis, and facts. The right cerebral hemisphere equates to future scenario thinking, preferring to focus on intuition, integration, synthesis, and a holistic view. The left limbic hemisphere corresponds to action thinking, focusing on detail, planning, and sequencing. The right limbic hemisphere represents social thinking, preferring to focus on the interpersonal, social–emotional, and kinesthetic dimensions.

254. Chinese are holistic thinkers (*zhengti guanlian*). See John L. Graham and N. Mark Lam, "The Chinese Negotiation," *Harvard Business Review OnPoint*, October 2003 (www.globalnegotiationbook.com/John-Graham.../negotiation-v1.pdf).

255. "Heart to Heart Talk on Why You Became a Cop: Do Not Say Anything That Is Fake, Inflated, or False" [用真心话来谈谈 你为什么当警察？假、大、空的请不必讲], *Tianya*, December 12, 2006 (http://www.tianya.cn/New/TechForum/Content.asp?idWriter=0&Key=0&idItem=158&idArticle=541947).

256. "Complete New Appraisal of the Post-80's Generation," *People's Daily Online*, June 4, 2008 (http://english.peopledaily.com.cn/90001/90780/91345/6424404.html).

257. The sample is self-selected in a number of ways: First, Internet access is unevenly distributed in China, with urban centers having greater access than rural areas. Second, younger people have greater access than older adults. Third, although use of the Internet is not entirely confined to the educated class, they are more likely to participate in online discourse. Fourth, the comments from which this discussion is drawn have been made primarily by police officers or people who are interested in policing, a major qualifier for the opinions being analyzed here.

258. See introduction to "Heart to Heart Talk on Why You Became a Cop: Do Not Say Anything That Is Fake, Inflated, or False" [用真心话来谈谈 你为什么当警察？假、大、空的请不必讲], *Tianya*, December 12, 2006 (http://www.tianya.cn/New/TechForum/Content.asp?idWriter=0&Key=0&idItem=158&idArticle=541947).

259. Tom R. Tyler (Ed.), *Legitimacy and Criminal Justice: International Perspectives*, Russell Sage Foundation, New York, 2007.

260. Zhang Yuyuan, *Economic System Reform in China*, World Institute for Development Economics Research, Helsinki, Finland, 1989, p. 4. Part of the reason for instituting economic reform in China was the need to find a system of work incentives not based on personal "enthusiasm," which was fast waning. Chinese reform planners have long known about this problem of waning revolutionary spirit.

261. A Google search for "32 Classical Police Sayings" ["警察的32条经典话语"] on November 25, 2010, netted 18,900 entries. I chose to search for "32 Classical Police Sayings" because it is authentic and was written by and intended for police officers. It truly reflects what is going on. "32 Classical Police Sayings" resembles many books in the United States that offer advice for police officers or those who want to be. Such books are usually written by seasoned officers or police retirees who wish to pass along their experiences and professional wisdom gained as a cop. What these kinds of books offer is realistic accounts of what it is like to be a police officer, as well as some dos and don'ts for the job. Their timely advice and insightful lessons are usually well received. With regard to Barry Baker's *Becoming a Police Officer: An Insider's Guide to a Career in Law Enforcement* (Universe, 2006), for example, a police officer observed, "I found the book to be packed with invaluable advice. I've only been a cop for about 6 months now, but I wish I had read the book before I became a cop."

262. To validate the authenticity, relevancy, and utility of "32 Classical Police Sayings," one need go no further than to read the web comments posted in response. Of 54 comments found by the author, several have been translated and listed here. All of them, with few exceptions, in one way or another, thought the sayings were authentic and useful: (1) "I feel this is really classical." (2) "Am in the process of learning." (3) "Too absolute." (4) "Is it really like that?" (5) "Kept this to learn. Thank you." (6) "From new police to senior police. Ho. Ho. Not totally agree, but worth reading." (7) "Well said. Tops." (8) "In most cases, there is no absolute." (9) "Strong… Classic…Learned already." (10) "Maybe some would feel it is too absolute. I felt the same way before. But after I have experienced a few things, I found what it said to be true. Thus, I feel it is a summary of my experience." (11) "Learn one more time!" (12) "Very real and practical." (13) "On account of your ID, it is worth topping you once more. Ho Ho." (14) "Classics." (15) "Tianya! Tianya!! Tianya!!! Too classical!!!" (16) "Better learn it well, be safe and secure." (17) "Revisit one more time." (18) "There is no moon in Jiangnan. There is no justice in the country. Culture is deteriorating, morality is dead." (19) "After I read it line by line, I could not calm down for a long time, too sensational…a most brilliant posting." (20) "Do not learn from hero figures. Heroes are to be respected, but you need not imitate, otherwise you will pay a big price. Treasure your life, on account of your family." (21) "Why is it that police in real life is not what I have imagined?" (22) "In the process of learning! Worth comparing notes." (23) "Worth collecting." (24) "Speak the truth. Tops." (25) "Not bad." (26) "Big brother, I have stored it! How much should I pay you!" (27) "'Do not trust anyone except yourself.'…This saying is correct, that is why always feel lonely." (28) "Correct." (29) "Store and study." (30) "Study anew." (31) "Study it well. Safety and peace every day." (32) "Mark it to remember." (33) "I also have to seriously learn again. This is much stronger than 'three stresses.' They have more practical value."

263. 当一名好警察要具备的八大职业操守; see http://blog.sina.com.cn/s/blog_6233f1190100fedp.html.

264. Peter Foster, "Western Companies Use Rock Music to Tap into China's Youth Market," *Telegraph*, November 20, 2009. As China's youth exercise their newfound wealth and independence, the battle for their business is heating up.

265. There is a growing crisis in confidence between the leaders and the led. The police officers in the field have very little respect for their bosses, particularly those at headquarters. It is clear from a sampling of web entries that there are a gross disconnect and gathering mistrust between the leaders and the led. This lack of trust is due to a number of reasons: (1) Police leaders are not competent. (2) Police leaders have few leadership skills beyond demanding absolute obedience. (3) Police leaders have little understanding of local conditions and very little appreciation of frontline operational needs. (4) Police leaders are not moral; they are not good role models. (5) Police leaders double talk; they do not live up to the high standards set by the Party or expected of them by their followers. (6) Police leaders are not supportive of their staff; they do not defend their subordinates in what they do. (7) Police leaders are more concerned with their own careers than the well-being of their subordinates; they do not take care of their subordinate's welfare.

266. "China's Stressed-Out 1980s Generation 'Slaves' to Their Own Happiness," *China Daily*, February 9, 2010. An Internet survey on people.com.cn, a major Chinese Internet portal, nearly 61.5% of 2384 respondents regarded themselves as "slaves" to their babies. Some complained that they had spent all of their money on their children, and the fees to send their children to kindergarten were "incredibly high." Elsewhere, about 60.7% of 3236 peopled surveyed believed that economic pressures were the main cause of social problems. (b) "1980s Generations Differ Greatly in US, China," *China Daily*, July 6, 2001. (c) "China's Post-1980s Generation Most Enthusiastic about Public Service," *People's Daily Online*, May 10, 2010. On May 4, 2010, southern China's Guangzhou Communist Youth League released an attitude survey on differences among China's post-1970s, post-1980s, and post-1990s generations with regard to family, love, work, and play. The 100 questionnaires had a response rate of 96%. Of the three groups, the post-1980s generation was the most enthusiastic about public service, with 53% having performed public services. In addition, 95% had applied to work as volunteers during the Asian Games. The post-1990s generation also had a high sense of social responsibility, with 99% willing to assume more social responsibilities as adults. The post-1970s generation was less enthusiastic about public service. (d) "Survey: 1980s Generation Faces Highest Pressure," *People's Daily Online*, May 5, 2010. A survey found that the 1980s generation was into securing a good life: 66% spent most of their income on housing and automobiles, and 57% preferred to spend bonus money from work on tourist travel. As a result, the 1980s generation faces the highest pressure to make money and be rich. The 1970s generation was found to be the most industrious. They never said "no" to their bosses, even when overtime was involved. The 1980s generation thought that divorces were worth celebrating as well as weddings. (e) "Survey Reveals Youth Attitudes on Values," *China Daily*, May 5, 2010. In terms of consumer behavior, 65% of the post-1970s generation billed themselves as "bankaholics" who preferred to save money; 70% of the post-1980s generation admitted that they were "month-ending" people, who used up all their salaries or earnings by the end of every month. The post-1990s generation was addicted to online shopping and believed that they could buy anything on the Internet. This survey also found that as many as 67% of the post-1980s generation claimed that they would never work overtime. (f) Qian Yanfeng, "Crimes Climb for 80s Generation," *China Daily*, June 18, 2009. The CPC has conducted an extensive and systematic study of young people's attitudes toward the Party in the later part of the 2000s. Young people in Shanghai have few qualms regarding embezzling money at work. The Shanghai prosecutor's office attributed part of this trend to a lack of responsibility and said that the post-1980s generation tended to "squander money" and was more concerned with "enjoying the present instead of thinking for the future."

267. "China's 'Good Samaritan' Turns Party into a Laughing Stock," *The Observers*, March 25, 2010 (http://observers.france24.com/content/20100325-china-good-samaritan-turns-party-laughing-stock-lei-feng-diary-blog).

268. "Chinese Treasure Spirit of Lei Feng," *Beijing Time*, March 6, 2002.

269. Michael Keane, "Redefining Chinese Citizenship," *Economy and Society*, 30(1), 10–14, 2001.

270. (a) William V. Pelfrey, Jr., "Style of Policing Adopted by Rural Police and Deputies: An Analysis of Job Satisfaction and Community Policing," *Policing: An International Journal of Police Strategies & Management*, 30(4), 620–636, 2007. Arguably, the same mismatch of values is happening in the United States. Police best practices and cutting edge research have focused on professional policing and are based on urban policing, whereas most policing is done in small communities and rural areas. (b) Ivan Sun and Doris Chu, "Urban v. Rural Policing: A Study of Taiwanese Officers' Occupational Attitudes," paper presented at the Annual Meeting of the American Society of Criminology, Los Angeles, CA, November 01, 2006 (http://www.allacademic.com/meta/p126014_index.html). "Abstract: This study compares attitudinal differences between urban and rural police officers in Taiwan. Using survey data collected from more than 870 officers in two urban and one rural Taiwanese police departments, this research compares officers' attitudes toward aggressive patrol, fellow officers, local residents, and career advancement. The results from the multivariate regression indicate that urban officers are more likely to favor aggressive patrol, have fewer friends in work units, have less positive attitudes toward citizens, and view promotion as an important issue in their career. Implications for policy and areas for future research are discussed."

Reform Measures

5

Introduction

Since the Third Plenum of the 11th Communist Party of China (CPC) Central Committee in 1978, the Party has adopted Deng Xiaoping's "liberating the mind" and "seeking truth from facts" principles as keys to successful reform in China. In 2006, at the Sixth Plenum of the 16th CPC Central Committee, the Party has shifted the focus of reform from uninhibited growth of Jiang's era[1] to one of a more balanced development under the leadership of the Hu Jintao and Wen Jiabao administration. Since then, Chinese reform has pursued the twin goals of advancing humanity (putting people first)[2] and achieving a harmonious society (seeking balanced growth),[3] with scientific development as the process to do so.[4] Slowly but surely, President Hu Jintao's new ideology—people, harmony, and science—is replacing the ideology of Marx, Mao, and Deng—class, revolution, and doctrine. Chinese police reform has finally come of age. With regard to police reform goals and strategies, the Ministry of Public Security (MPS) commissioned a study of police work problems, particularly at the grassroots level, with a view toward their eradication in an evidence-based, scientific way:

> In order to inform public security organs at various levels, we need to conduct investigations and research: (1) on major public security issues in order to provide a scientific foundation for policy determination by leaders; (2) on "focal problems" and "difficult issues" to provide for detailed, concrete, feasible solutions and discover innovative breakthroughs; (3) on emerging problems and developing trends in order to avoid arbitrariness and spontaneousness.[5]

This brief MPS policy statement summarized the MPS's thinking on how to accomplish police reform through field investigation and research and refers to the Chinese leadership's desire to carry out police reform in a scientific way (evidence-based policing). Evidence-based policing with Chinese characteristics can be traced to Mao Tse-tung's 1927 trip to Hunan,[6] when Mao proposed using field investigation to aid in solving problems. Later, Deng Xiaoping reconceptualized Mao's approach to investigation and problem solving—"seeking truth from facts" (evidence-based policymaking) and "crossing the river by feeling the stones" (experimentation-based policymaking)—as the preferred way to conduct economic reform. Finally, Hu Jintao consolidated and elevated this investigative approach and fact-based problem solving to a science with his "scientific development perspective,"[7] which has joined "Party ideology" and "leader's thinking" as one of the three key determinants. The Party guides the nation with political doctrine, leaders supply the government with implementation policies, and experts provide the scientific evidence to analyze policies or assess operations:

> We need to closely integrate efforts to establish and implement the scientific outlook on development with efforts to promote a realistic and pragmatic spirit....Being realistic and pragmatic means always taking the actual situation as the starting point, seeking truth from facts, continuously striving to better understand the true nature of things, understanding the laws governing their development and objective truth, and upholding and developing scientific theories. In other words, being realistic and pragmatic means using scientific theories to guide practice and further our work, getting real results, and testing and developing truth through practice.[8]

In calling for investigative policymaking, the MPS had the following ideas in mind. First, policymaking by leaders should have a scientific foundation based on theory and supported by evidence and logic. Without a scientific foundation, all policy choices are speculative ideas, abstract propositions, and subjective opinion, which are to be avoided at all costs. The scientific approach to policymaking fundamentally changes the nature, content, process, and outcome of policy debate. Policy deliberation should no longer be predominantly dependent on self-evident principles (by virtue of political correctness), received wisdom (from experience), or attributed authority (as a result of rank or seniority), but instead should turn on proven theoretical propositions, reliable empirical evidence, and logical reasoning.[9]

Second, police reform measures should adopt a problem-oriented approach, meaning that reform issues should not be dealt with individually but should be dealt with as a larger problem, comprehensively and at its roots. Mass incidents, for example, should not be treated as individual incidents of malcontent to be suppressed but as structural contradictions to be resolved.

Third, problem solving should focus (*zhongdian*) on high-priority problems and difficult issues. Not all problems and issues deserve full or immediate attention. Priorities must be set; for example, work-style problems come before individual corruption cases, because the proper handling of work-style problems would remove many of the structural and cultural causes of corruption.

Fourth, problem solving should seek to provide concrete, detailed, and feasible solutions capable of application, assessment, modification, and replication using the *shidian* ("trial point") approach to reform. This approach tests out new theories and methods of reform with controlled case studies, such that lessons can be learned and damage controlled. The first test of economic liberation, for example, was establishment of a Special Economic Zone (SEZ) in Shenzhen. Lessons learned from the economic liberalization in Shenzhen were later applied, with necessary modifications, to other Chinese cities and zones.[10]

Finally, police reform must be centrally planned but locally implemented at respective levels of government, stepwise to the top, with the Party being the arbiter of the nation's future police development plan. Capricious and impulsive decision making should be replaced with a scientific, research-based approach.

The MPS has launched a number of reform projects to improve the police work style and to address public concerns, including:

- A three-year *san xian jiaoyu* ("three items of education") campaign to cleanse the police ranks of incompetent and abusive officers and at the same time imbue the officers with correct work ethics and professional attitude
- A *jingwu gongkai* ("transparency in policing") initiative to fight formalism and bureaucracy and to reconnect with the people[11]
- A strong police supervision system to check police abuse of power, corruption in office, and incompetence at work[12]
- Upgrading recruitment and training standards to fill the police ranks with competent, responsive, responsible, and reliable officers[13]

The MPS decision to make 2002 a year devoted to investigating and changing work styles revealed the MPS' basic investigative approach to police reform, and their follow-up implementation further clarified the MPS's basic methodology for improving police work—through moral, ideological, and professional education; transparency in police work; internal and external supervision; and recruitment and training. This chapter reports on major MPS efforts at reform since 2000, including their agenda, ideology, ethics, command and control, culture, funding, and operations.

Agenda

During the 2000s, the goal of the MPS was to increase police capacity, improve the quality of their work, and enhance their performance. This required: (1) making the police organization more *rational* (i.e., scientific, rule-bound, and results-oriented); (2) making police personnel more *qualified* (i.e., educated, trained, and specialized); (3) making police services more *professional* (i.e., responsive, responsible, and competent); and (4) making police conduct more *accountable* (i.e., more open and better supervised). The ultimate objective was to make the police more *effective* in the hands of the government ("instrument of the state" theory) and more *legitimate* in the eyes of the public ("mass line principle").[14] This was to be achieved by revolutionizing (*geming hua*), regularizing (*zhenggui hua*), modernizing (*xiandai hua*), and legalizing (*fazhi hua*) the police. *Geming hua* required liberating police thinking from the straightjackets of old, such as treating all criminals as class enemies or every mass incident as an antagonistic confrontation. *Zhenggui hua* required institutionalizing policing by promulgating laws, establishing systems, and laying down processes to rationalize and routinize work,[15] in effect making police work more predictable (for planning purposes) and dependable (in meeting public expectations). *Xiandai hua* required adopting professional standards and progressive policies and following best practices. Finally, *fazhi hua*[16] required governing the police sternly (*congyan zhijing*) with the use of law (*yifa zhijing*) and having rules to follow (*you fa ke yi*); laws must be followed (*you fa bi yi*), and law violators must be held accountable (*wei fa bi gou*).[17] The future direction of police reform will be determined by public opinion, expert proposals, Party agenda, and national policy.

Public Opinion

Public opinion in China in the 1990s clearly pointed to a need for more government reform in three areas: corruption, crime, and bureaucracy (Table 5.1). About half of the respondents to a random survey felt that the government was not paying enough attention to corruption, crime, and bureaucracy. It is instructive to read between the lines to derive the full meaning and subtle implications of this set of data. First, only about a quarter of the people said that they had "no interest" in government (i.e., corruption, 25.3%; crime, 21.4%; bureaucracy, 4.6%), which means that three-quarters of the respondents were interested in such matters. This suggests that such public concerns were quite real and pressing. Public interest in government ranked higher than interest in economics (66.9%), reform (50.6%), and foreign affairs (46.6%). The message was clear: People were keeping a close watch on the government.

People were 8.4% more likely to think that the government had not done enough on government misadministration issues (corruption, crime, and bureaucracy, 51.3%) compared to other government economic and social issues (income distribution, education, and unemployment, 40.8%). This suggests that people were as concerned about the government not paying enough attention to government misadministration as government economic and social policy issues. Both problems are competing for limited government time, attention, and resources, which raises the limited resources/unlimited demand issue typical in

TABLE 5.1   Attitudes toward Government Handling of Issues

Issue	Not Enough Attention (%)	Just Right (%)	Too Much Attention (%)	No Interest (%)
Inflation and other issues				
Price control	55.7	19.7	1.9	22.7
Corruption	53.8	17.9	3.0	25.3
Crime	47.1	28.6	3.0	21.4
Bureacracy	46.8	16.8	1.8	34.6
Economic welfare				
Income distribution	42.5	15.0	1.7	40.8
Education	42.1	35.6	3.8	18.5
Unemployment	37.8	20.6	1.5	40.0
Housing	34.2	29.0	3.0	33.8
Consumer protection	33.6	21.7	1.7	43.1
Environment protection	33.6	30.3	2.6	33.5
Subsidies	27.9	21.7	7.4	43.0
Population control	24.7	50.4	12.8	12.2
Reform				
Anti-bourgeois liberalization	21.2	25.2	5.2	48.4
Private enterprise	18.2	25.4	9.4	47.1
Economic reform	17.9	28.6	4.1	49.4
Political reform	17.6	26.6	2.8	52.9
Foreign policy				
Taiwan	17.0	32.5	4.0	46.5
Opening	12.6	34.4	5.5	47.4
Defense	9.8	33.4	3.2	53.6
Foreign aid	5.7	20.0	8.1	66.1

Source: Nathan, A.J. and Shi, T., *World Politics*, 48(4), 522–550, 1996. With permission.
Note: N = 2896.

a developing state.[18] In conventional jargon, should the government rob Peter to pay Paul? This observation recalls China's human rights vs. collective welfare debate. In the West, human rights, such as equality and free speech, are considered absolute and stand-alone individual entitlement against collective encroachment for the public good. In China, individual human rights (such as reproduction) pale alongside other, more pressing collective rights of survival; developmental needs overshadow individual rights. This line of argument, if embraced, fundamentally changes the nature and course of debate regarding government mismanagement vs. government economic and social policy issues; that is, the benevolent neglect of corruption to maximize public utility is to be applauded, not deplored.[19]

Respondents to this survey were slightly more concerned with economic well-being, particularly "price control," than government misadministration; nearly 9% more people wanted the government to do more about price control (55.7%) than minimizing bureaucracy (46.8%). In fact, as a policy issue, the people would be more interested in their government delivering economic security than improving government efficiency. This is interesting because the topic of price control never comes up when people discuss government malfeasance, such as corruption, so one would think that it is not a major concern of the people.

**TABLE 5.2   Zhejiang Public Opinion
on the Seriousness of Corruption (2000)**

Level of Corruption	Survey Result (%)
Very serious	10.28
Serious	22.48
Somewhat serious	41.90
Not serious	25.32

Source: Adapted from Chinese University of Hong Kong, "Survey Shows Corruption Is the First Factor Affecting Social Stability," *Eastday.com*, January 7, 2001.

The lesson here is that in evaluating public policy what is left out is often as important as what is included. Most people, especially foreign observers, quite rightly point out that corruption, crime, and bureacracy are major social problems for the Chinese people, but most of them also fail to tell the rest of the story—that is, that the Chinese people are also concerned about price control and income distribution.

What are the social implications arising from this analysis? If these findings are to be taken to heart, they go against the conventional wisdom that the government should be setting priorities and focusing all of its precious and limited energy on fighting corruption, crime, and bureacracy. Indeed, if the government is paying more attention to corruption, crime, and bureacracy than price control, for example, then it is not tending to the people's business and might provoke public displeasure. To the Chinese way of thinking, people's livelihood (*minsheng*) is as important, if not more so, as people's rights (*minquan*) or democracy (*minzhu*). More simply, bread over rights.

Although about half of the survey respondents thought that the government was not doing enough to fight corruption, crime, and bureacracy, there was still a sizable minority who thought that the government was doing just right in their fight against corruption, crime, and bureacracy. If we add those who thought the government was doing just right or doing too much to those showing no interest, then it becomes apparent that the other half of the respondents were, for one reason or another, rather satisfied with the *status quo*. This finding reveals that the impression that the government was not doing anything about government malfeasance and that no one in China was happy with the government's efforts in fighting corruption, crime, and bureacracy was not accurate.

It is not the purpose of this analysis to suggest that the Chinese government has no problem maintaining a clean, efficient, and effective government, nor is the purpose to observe that the government has done all it can about corruption, crime, and bureacracy. Obviously it can do more. Instead, this analysis is intended to suggest that the magnitude and urgency of corruption, crime, and bureacracy in China are not as great as perceived by some. The earlier observation that corruption and government misadministration are not the most important, or even the only, problem that the nation has to face in the reform era is supported by other surveys (see Tables 2.2 and 2.3).

In 2001,[20] the Zhejiang Communist Party of China (CPC) Discipline Committee released the findings of a public opinion survey[21] on Party work styles and clean government. It found that a majority of the Zhejiang people (75%) considered corruption in government to be a serious problem (very serious, 10%; serious, 22%; somewhat serious, 42%). The rest thought that it was not serious or had no opinion (25%) (see Table 5.2). Again, the

TABLE 5.3   Top Seven Social Problems in Major Cities in China (1999–2002)

1999 (11 Cities)	2000 (10 Cities)	2001 (10 Cities)	2002 (10 Cities)
Clean government	Environmental protection	Unemployment	Unemployment
Unemployment	Unemployment	Environmental protection	Social security
Public security	Children's education	Social security	Environmental protection
Pension system	Public security	Economic development	Medicare
Housing reformation	Clean government	Housing reformation	Economic development
Environmental protection	Economic development	Clean government	Housing reformation
Inflation	Pension system	Public security	Children's education

Source: How Chinese People View Their Government, Society, and Foreign Countries, Horizon Research, Beijing,
       2003 (www.carnegieendowment.org/files/chinesegames.pdf).

problem of corruption was considered by 10% to be "very serious," by 22% as "serious," and
by 42% as "somewhat serious," but it was considered to be "not serious" by 25%. This again
runs counter to the perception that corruption is uniformly considered by all Chinese to
be the country's most serious problem, one that must be addressed at all costs and above
all things.

When the Zhejiang people were asked, however, to rank the impact of corruption
on social stability, the respondents ranked it as number one. In order of ranking, the
factors affecting stability included: (1) corruption, (2) unemployment, (3) social disorder, (4) uneven income distribution, (5) superstition, and (6) cults.[23] A Horizon Research
Group annual nationwide survey conducted in 2001 found that 95% of the urban residents considered the problem of corruption to be serious or very serious;[22] however, when
the Horizon Research Group asked urban residents to list the seven top social problems,
"clean government" did not show up as the most significant concern in three of the four
years (1999–2002) that the survey was conducted. In fact, "clean government" was picked
as the number one social problem only once, in 1999. The number of people citing the
"clean government" problem declined each year until it dropped out of the results entirely
in 2002. In 1999, the first three social problems cited were "clean government," "unemployment," and "public security." In 2000, they were "environmental protection," "unemployment," and "children's education." In 2001, they were "unemployment," "environmental
protection," and "social security." In 2002, they were "unemployment," "social security,"
and "environmental protection" (see Table 5.3).

Another national public opinion survey was commissioned in 2003 by the Political
Bureau and conducted by the Central Research Center, Chinese Academy of Social
Sciences, Centre for Sociological Research, and the *People's Daily* Social Research Office.
It was conducted in 26 large and medium size cities, where respondents were asked about
their five most urgent expectations of the government. The top two expectations of the
people both involved fighting corruption. The first expectation was for Party cadres and
their family members to release their personal financial data. The second expectation was
for Jiang Zeming to account for his efforts in fighting corruption and explain his failure;
respondents further requested Jiang to open up all government records (investigation files,
hearing records) relevant to corrupt cadres and officials.[24]

In terms of remedies, in 1999, *Xinhua* news reported that a Communist Party of China
(CPC) survey of 121 communist members showed that 65% of the respondents believed that
curbing corruption through strengthening the self-discipline of Party cadres and external

monitoring of government officials was vital to improving their morality and social ethics. Earlier, in 1997, 22.3% of respondents to another CPC survey cited education and propaganda as being the most effective ways for improving government morality.[25]

From these surveys, we can safely conclude that for the nation as a whole corruption was considered a very serious problem nationwide, especially to urban dwellers. Clean government, while of some concern, was not the only issue uppermost in the minds of the Chinese people.[26] These surveys suggest that the respondents wanted a more open, clean, accountable, and efficient government and confirmed what the Party and state leadership already knew from their personal experience—that corruption and bureaucracy were pervasive in government, generating discontent among the people and eroding the legitimacy of the Party. People wanted the Party, government, and police to become more transparent and responsive to the people. The Party and government launched repeated campaigns addressing anticorruption, open government, and work style with little impact but some public recognition. The Party and government also know that, while corruption and clean government are major concerns of the people, other pressing problems also require attention, such as unemployment and disparate distribution of wealth.

Expert Thinking

In light of the nation's political and economic situation, many experts and scholars have proposed police programs to support and facilitate reform. One such proposal was offered by Zhang Jinghua, who recommended seven guiding principles to expedite police reform,[27] many of them reflecting and reinforcing the Party's political agenda and policy directives.[28] According to Zhang, public security modernization had to focus on the follow areas:

1. *Modernization of the concept of law enforcement (zhiifa linian xiandaihua)*[29]—The MPS must continually keep pace with social and economy change in the nation and never lose sight of the overall objective of law enforcement, which is to implement the law for the people (*jifa wei min*). This guideline admonishes police leaders to keep pace with the fast-paced reform and radical changes occurring without being overwhelmed by them, suggesting that many police personnel were set in their old ways because of political conviction or personal habits. Apparently, it was difficult for many police leaders, especially older ones and military transferees, to come to terms with Party directives and police policies calling for enthusiastic support of economic reform without also worrying about crossing the fine line between rendering services to business people and selling out to the capitalists. There was a real concern about becoming corrupted and compromised by commercial interests, such as turning a blind eye to foreign investors who brought jobs and investment to an area or making available police powers to the highest bidder.

2. *Data-driven policing (jingwu xingxihua)*[30]—Information is an important and indispensable resource for policing,[31] particularly in an era of cyber crimes and globalization.[32] This guideline seeks to change traditional ways of policing in China (e.g., formulating policy by fiat, making operational decisions by experience, fighting crime by intuition, clearing crime by coercion).

3. *Integration of strike, prevention, and control of crime strategies (da fang kong yitihua)*[33]—The MPS must adopt a comprehensive (*zhonghe zhili*) crime control strategy that integrates strikes against (*daji*) crime,[34] prevention (*fangfan*) of

crime,[35] and control (*kongzhi*)[36] of crime to fight crime and maintain order. This means that the MPS should not rely solely on national "Strike Hard" (*yanda*) campaigns or local crime case clearance efforts to deter crime. There was a need to fight crime on all fronts, at different levels, and with a variety of measures, including contracting out security functions to private firms or parties and enlisting the help of the community to fight crime proactively, holistically, and interactively.

4. *Standardization of police practices (zhifa zhiqin guifanhua)*[37]—Police work must be institutionalized, rationalized, and regularized by putting standard operating procedures (SOPs) in place. This guideline seeks to address a number of organizational and operational problems ranging from facilitating national command and control to allowing for uniform recruitment and training, from tempering the excess of localism to promoting interagency cooperation, from actualizing the rule of law to making possible effective supervision, from reining in *ad hoc* decision making by leaders to restricting unfettered discretion among street officers.

5. *Standardization of expenditures and equipment (jingfei zhuangbei biaozhunhua)*[38]— In order for the police to operate efficiently and effectively, they must be fully equipped and adequately funded. This guideline addresses the age-old problem of lack of adequate and guaranteed funding for police operations, resulting in local interference with police operations and law enforcement through funding and police commercialization of police powers to earn support.

6. *Regularization of police establishment (duiwu jianshe zhengguihua)*[39]—The police should be properly organized in terms of ideology and thinking, recruitment and training, command and control, and supervision and accountability to make them a politically strong and professionally competent force.

7. *Scientific utility assessment (xiaoyi pinggu kexuehua)*[40]—The MPS must evaluate the utility of police and effectiveness of policing scientifically, or pursue evidence-based policing. This guideline introduces the MPS to evidence-based, intelligence-led, research-driven expert policing. Ultimately, this will transform the MPS into a 21st-century professional police force that is driven by scientific, rational decision making, more so than ideology, personality, or the masses.

To understand police reform in China we need to explore the thinking of relevant policy experts. In the People's Republic of China, the Party and government rely on subject matter experts (academicians and researchers) to help with central planning and market regulation. Most of these policy experts are classically trained in methods of research and reasoning. The impact of such a drive to standardize and professionalize policing is huge, and the implications are many. Chinese policing is moving into uncharted territory. It is moving from a conventional and long-tested form of people's policing developed among the peasants to an untested and unexamined form of professional policing designed to accommodate an urban crowd. This represents a radical shift in the police paradigm.

The debate here is not how to establish a revolutionary force that can assume nation-building duties, as Deng tried to do, nor is it one of old (traditionalists) vs. new (reformists) ways of organizing society, as Jiang would have imagined it. Instead, it represents the resurrection of an old political governance debate, first observed by Mao but never resolved and now turning up with a new twist under Hu. In Mao's era, the debate regarding whether China could best be run by the people (Mao) or by experts (Liu Shaoqi) was real and contentious.[41] The issue was raised during attempts to define the role of the Party. The communist leadership group was viewed as being learned and rehearsed in the Marxist ways, whereas the masses were uneducated and uninterested, lacking in proper political consciousness. How could the people run the government without the Party taking a lead? Mao settled the issue by insisting that the Party *is* the people and a sublimation of the consciousness of the people. When the Party conducts the people's business, it is mindful of its historical role of being the vanguard of communism in that the Party possesses the most advanced thinking in communist ideology. The relationship between Party leadership and the masses is influenced by the *mass line principle* (i.e., "from the mass to the mass"); that is, the people govern themselves with the help of the Party. The Party listens to the people and seeks to understand their problems and concerns. The Party then digests the people's problems to come up with solutions incorporating broader principles and relying upon sophisticated analysis.

Under the Hu–Wen administration, the issue of people vs. experts is a moot one. To borrow a line from Deng—"The cat that catches the rat is a cat"—and put it into engineering terms, all of the people's problems can be solved if we adopt a "scientific development perspective." The issue with Hu–Wen's reformulation of Mao's debate is that it misses the point altogether when it comes to policing. Engineers can solve mechanical problem because physical materials follow scientific rules. Police cannot solve people's problems without their own effort, involvement, and immersion, according to Mao. The challenge of how to synthesize public experience vs. expert knowledge and public sentiment vs. expert detachment still awaits answer. In the meantime, the relationship between the police (experts) and the public (mass) has deteriorated, because the police and the people are not thinking, feeling, and working together as one.

Party Agenda

The Party is most concerned with maintaining proper Party discipline and work style. The term "work style" (*zuo feng*) is difficult to define in English. The closest other terms that come to mind are "work ethics," "occupational culture" (e.g., police culture), or "professionalism." All of these terms speak to work-related attitudes and disposition commonly shared in a profession, but "work style" differs from these in distinct ways. "Work style" encompasses not only norms and values imposed from without but also a certain outlook and way of life emanating from within. "Work style" represents a set of unique values and distinctive principles to live by, as well as a fully integrated and mutually reinforcing system of morals to live with. Also, "work style" is not simply a set of moral or ethical principles but is first and foremost a political ideology. "Work style," as a prescriptive principle, is perhaps best defined as the totality of a police officer's disposition, attitude, and manner toward policing. On occasion, the PRC leaders have referred to it as an outlook on life (*rensheng guan*).

In 2001, the Communist Party of China issued a "Resolution to Strengthen and Improve Party Work Style." This document set forth the basic tenets and fundamental principles for all Party members, including the police, to follow after 2001. In the document, the Party made amply clear that it was very much concerned with the existing work style of its officials, particularly at the local level:

> There are some urgent problems with regard to Party work style that need to be resolved. Mainly, at certain locations, and with certain leaders and departments, there exist dogmatism (*jiaotiao zhuyi*), book worship (*ben ben zhuyi*), formalism (*xingshi zhuyi*), bureaucratism (*guanliao zhuyi*), fraud (*nongxu zuojia*), false reporting and inflated accounting (*xubao fukua*), making arbitrary decisions and taking perfunctory actions (*duduan duxing*), being

weak and slack in discipline (*ruanruo huansan*). In the ultimate analysis, these resulted from a detachment from reality and removal from the people. Their negative effects and consequences should not be underestimated. Both history and facts repeatedly inform us that if, as the Party in power, we are not committed to promoting a wholesome work style and we allow a corruptive work style to erode the Party's body, this would harm the relationship between the Party and the people, contributing to the eventual demise of the political regime and state.[42]

Several guiding principles for improving upon Party work style were stated:

- Insist on "liberating the mind" (*jiefang xixiang*) and "seeking truth from facts" (*shisi jiushi*), in addition to rejecting conservatism and blindly following tradition—To dislodge the past, Deng called for "liberating the mind." To make way for the future, Deng preached "seeking truth from facts." But, what if people were not doing both. What if they were stuck in their own and old ways? Many Party members are still not fully embracing the reform after all these years. The old Party guards (conservatives) and the new Turks (reformers) have been very much at odds, but the Party must come to terms with a new generation of members who are neither for nor against reform. The post-1980s generations just do not care. They think that the Party ideology is dead and has little relevancy in their lives. The Party has an ideological battle on its hands and a political legitimacy problem looming.
- Insist on linking theory with practice; avoid copying ideas and worshiping books (*ben ben zhuyi*)—The Party must deal with another group of members who are neither joiners nor rebels but followers. They go along to get along, without actually putting the Party's teaching to practical use. In this, they have not lived up to Mao's admonition that all Party thinking must be tested in practice before it can be deemed to reflect the truth. Practice is the lifeblood of theory; without it, theory does not exist. Conversely, practice without theory is work without understanding. Mao's thinking and teaching on the relationship between theory and practice recall community engagement and action research, where a theory is applied, tested, and revised all at the same time, gaining more and more realism, validity, precision, and authority with each dialectical interchange, finally fusing theory and practice as one.[43]
- Insist on working closely with the people; fight against formalism (*xingshi zhuyi*) and bureaucracy (*guanliao zhuyi*)—This principle points to the existence of formalism and bureaucracy in the Party's ranks. One of the biggest complaints against the Party is that its members are detached and aloof from the people. Instead of serving the people, they are serving their own interests by playing the bureaucratic game. What is being said and performed has little to do what is being done and achieved. This principle just states what is obvious to most.
- Insist on democratic centralism (*mingzhu jizhong zhi*); fight against arbitrary decision making and taking perfunctory actions (*duduian duxing*)—This principle goes to the heart of Party leadership. According to democratic dictatorship principles, Party policy is arrived at through open and robust debate, but once policy is decided its execution is pursued in a top-down, dictatorial, zero-tolerance fashion. A Party member is to abide by central command, notwithstanding his disagreement; however, because of personal interests (individualism), relationships (*guanxi*) among various groups, and local power (localism), people are sometimes acting as they please, so much so that it has been said, "If there is a policy from above, then there must be a strategy to diffuse it from below."

- Insist on Party discipline; fight against liberalism (*ziyou zhuyi*)—Whereas the first principle calls for the liberation from Maoism, this principle warns against liberalism. The tenets of liberalism celebrate individual interests over the collective welfare and rights over duties.
- Insist on personal integrity and honesty; fight against the abuse of power (*yiquan mousi*) for personal gains, which is totally against Party principles of honesty and integrity—Personal integrity and honesty are constantly being tested by the market economy every day. More often than not, the free-for-all market system is too strong for the Party members to resist.
- Insist on industriousness and perseverance; fight against hedonism (*xiangshou zhuyi*)—How to adopt market principles (e.g., competition, incentives) as reform principles without also encouraging self-serving conduct is one of the most difficult challenges confronting the Party. In real terms, communist members who are driven by external reward are not likely to resist corruption and the abuse of power.
- Insist on meritocracy; fight against incompetence—This principle makes it clear that the Party is a meritorious agency at risk of being run down by mediocrity.

These Party principles are elaborations of President Jiang's "Eight Dos and Don'ts":[44]

1. Emancipate the mind and seek truth from facts; do not stick to old ways and make no progress.
2. Combine theory with practice; do not copy mechanically or worship books.
3. Keep close ties with the people; do not be formalistic or bureaucratic.
4. Adhere to the principle of democratic centralism; do not act arbitrarily or be weak and lax.
5. Abide by Party discipline; do not pursue liberalism.
6. Be honest and upright; do not abuse power for personal gain.
7. Work hard; do not be hedonistic.
8. Appoint people on their merits; do not let personal interests influence personnel decisions.

In 2001, in furtherance of the above resolution, PRC President Jiang instructed CPC police members to pursue the "Three Represents" (*sange daibiao*):[45] (1) developing China's advanced productive forces,[46] (2) developing China's advanced culture,[47] and (3) supporting the fundamental interests of the majority of the people in China.[48] President Jiang introduced the "Three Represents" as basic Party principles to guide political governance for China.[49] Since then, the "Three Represents" have been elevated to constitutional principles.[50] The MPS has sought to promote Party principles and constitutional norms in police work with the slogan, "Establish police for the public, implement the law for the people" ("*Lijing wei gong, zhifa wei min*"). This calls for humanizing implementation of the law. Humanizing the police essentially requires actualization of the humanity (*rendao*) principles as embedded within the humanitarianism (*renbenzhuyi*) ideal. It is required by the philosophy of political civility (*zhengzhi wenming*) and socialist market developmental needs.[51]

The first task to strengthen and improve the Party work style is to keep faith with the people; that is, make the Party the "flesh and blood" of the people. To do so, the police must "liberate their minds" and "seek truth from facts." In practical terms, this means conducting regular and systematic grassroots investigations to find out what the people want and how government policies can better serve them. Party, provincial, and municipal officials should live among the people for a month or two each year to understand their situations, problems, and issues. Such investigations and reports should form the basis of Party policy and government programs.[52]

National Police Reform Policy

The police reform agenda for the 21st century was clearly articulated at the National Public Security Bureau (PSB) Department Heads Conference in Beijing in 2001.[53] Minister Jia Chunwang outlined the plan for police construction and development work in 2002 as follows: (1) full implementation of a community policing strategy; (2) further reform to strengthen local police posts (*paichusuo*) nationwide; (3) establishment of a comprehensive crime prevention system; and (4) enlisting grassroots assistance and support for maintaining social security and public order. To address World Trade Organization issues, the following points were raised:

1. Police reform must be sped up.
2. Public security must be standardized.
3. The public security administrative review system must follow the principles of legality, reasonableness, effectiveness, accountability, and supervision.
4. Police administration and management procedures must be improved to better serve state reform and economic restructuring.
5. The police must be strengthened through technology, including implementation of the Golden Shield Project.
6. It is necessary to push policing into the information age and exploit science and technology to solve crime problems.

Public security reform was supposed to be accomplished within three years. The implementation of police reform was focused on: "One major theme (*yitiao zhuxian*), two focal points (*liange zhongdian*), one point of entry (*yige qieru*)."[54] The one major theme referred to in the slogan is to improve upon police work styles, such as holding them accountable to the people (*qunzhong luxiang*) and in accordance with the law (*fazhi*). The two focal points are (1) reforming the cadre personnel system while establishing a functional appraisal and incentive system for public security, and (2) implementing public security police security organ training regulations (*gongan jiguan renmin jingcha xunlian tiaoli*) to promote overall qualifications. The one point of entry is to strengthen political ideology work.

The police reform agenda for the 2000s established at the National PSB Department Heads Conference was further elaborated upon at a National Public Security Post Work Conference held in Zhejiang in 2002.[55] The conference identified the problems, established the objectives, and outlined the work plan for public security post reform in the coming years. In so doing, it established concrete plans to achieve the priorities laid down by National PSB Department Heads Conference the previous year; that is, continue to improve upon the current public security structure, process, and operations to make it more professional (i.e., establish higher standards), effective (i.e., control crime and criminals), efficient (i.e., streamline operations through privatization), responsive (i.e., implement community policing), and accountable to the people (e.g., open police work to public).

The National Public Security Post Work Conference decided to move in two major directions: (1) improve upon guiding political ideology (*zhidao xixian*), and (2) set higher standards for public security leadership, officers, and their work. Particularly, the conference set several strategic goals (*san dai zhanlue*) for the coming year. The first was to further strengthen basic (*jichu*) police work by improving upon population registration and household management (*renkou guanli*). The second was to work hard at completing implementation of the community policing strategy (*shequ jingwu zhanlue*) by 2004. To do so, it was necessary to establish a community policing office with full accountability to engage in a comprehensive reorganization of the local police responsibility district (*minjing zerenqu*); to clearly delineate the focus and reach of community police work and establish a corresponding support system; to utilize community resources to prevent and control criminal networks; and to improve police dealings with mass incidents.

Another goal was to establish a regulatory system (*baozhang guifan tixi*) for public security post operations within three years. To do so required standardization (*guifanhua*) and regularization (*zhenggui hua*) of public security posts, which in turn entailed setting objective standards and seeking impartial inspections at all levels in eight areas of police work: population control (*renkou guanli*), public security management (*zhian guanli*), safety prevention (*anquan fang fan*), law enforcement (*zhifa ban an*), public service (*fuwu renqun*), troop construction (*duiwu jianshe*), internal administration (*neiwu guanli*), and logistics support (*houqin baozhang*), as specifically required by public security local police post evaluation methods (*gongan paichusuo dangji pingding banfa*).

Public security posts were expected to improve their quality of service by adopting and implementing standards mandated by the regulations regarding inspection and assessment of the quantity and quality of public security organs law enforcement work[56] and standards for public security post enforcement of laws and execution of duty.[57] The level of resources and equipment supplied to public security posts should, as much as possible, be uniform and in accordance with local needs and functional requirements. Furthermore, it was necessary to establish a system of coordination among public security posts and other government organs working closely with the police.

To address these initiatives, the MPS issued the "2004–2008 National Public Security Troop Regularization Construction Outline" ("2004–2008 *Quanguo gongan duiwu zhenggui hua jianshe gangyao*").[58] Also, the CPC issued its "Decision regarding Progressively Strengthening and Improving Public Security Work."[59] In its introductory paragraph, the Decision stated that it was a policy directive implementing the strategic planning of the 16th Chinese Communist Party Congress to enhance stability and to achieve an affluent society (*xiaokang shehui*). The Decision, coming from the Central Committee of the Communist Party of China, which is responsible for strategic planning for the nation, is as revealing as it is important. The Decision made known the Central Committee's major concerns for the future (e.g., instability, such as mass incidents) and detailed its aspiration for the long term (e.g., professionalization of the police). The headlines and fine print of the Decision provide a glimpse of where police reform has been and is going. In order of importance, the Decision made nine policy pronouncements:

1. *Fully recognize the importance of the status and functions of public security work (during the reform era).* In this directive, the Decision reiterated these points: Public security organs are instruments of a democratic dictatorship to suppress the enemy, to protect the people, to punish the criminals, to service the people, to safeguard national security, and to maintain social order. In the early part of the 21st century, the nation has been confronted with all kinds of destabilizing and disabling challenges, from both within (e.g., mass incidents, crime) and without

(e.g., foreign infiltration, agitation). Also, the public security organization is responsible for securing the Communist Party as the ruling Party from all kinds of encroachment and attacks, large and small.

2. *Use every effort in performing stability work.* The Decision made it clear that, in the coming years, maintaining political, social, and economic stability would be the most important job for the Party as a whole, at every level and among all government agencies. Stability threats can come from all quarters, including foreign infiltration, cult manipulation, mass incidents, secessionist violence, terrorists, and extremists. With regard to mass incidents, the preferred strategy should be to predict, prevent, and resolve "people's contradictions" before they blossom into a full-fledged confrontation requiring forceful suppression. To control the manifestation and address the impact of mass incidents, the Decision cautioned against using force and promoted the use of education (persuasion).

3. *Effectively strengthen social order work.* The Decision, taking a page out of the 1980s, called for striking hard at serious crimes, proactively, pointedly, heavily, and speedily. This was to be supplemented with comprehensive crime control with the full participation of the people and communities, who must realize that they have to work together to prevent crime before crime can be controlled and reduced. This is especially the case with white-collar and economic crime, such as financial irregularities, tax evasion, and smuggling.

4. *Firmly establish the idea of enforcing the law for the people.* The idea of enforcing the law for the people pertains to serving the people's needs and defending the people's rights by applying the law in a fair, open, and objective manner. It is also about holding the police accountable to the law. To improve working relationships with the people, the police should operate as a professional/expert agency but should also follow the mass line principle and be dependent on the people and support the people. Also, the people must obey the law voluntarily.

5. *Strengthen basic public security work.* Strengthening basic public security work is at the heart of Chinese policing reform. It means that the MPS will focus on strengthening grassroots police capacity and efforts in whatever way it can, be it policy, systems, organization, benefits, or equipment. The strategy is to effectively improve the capacity and performance of local police agencies.

6. *Aggressively pursue modernization of the police.* To conduct policing properly, one must pay attention to troop construction, establishing standards, setting forth procedures, abiding by laws, and adopting scientific principles in policing. Ideologically, this can be achieved by strengthening political work, a concept represented in Deng Xiaoping's thinking and guided by the "Three Represents."

7. *Comprehensively implement the strategy of strengthening the police through science and technology.* To achieve modernization of police work, it is necessary to pursue strengthening the police through science and technology. Technology should be used liberally and extensively in police work to fight crime and serve the people. The Golden Shield Project was important in offering a nationwide platform for police to collect, organize, and share information.

8. *Build up an ideal public security protection system.* This means that police work should be well financed with an adequate budget guaranteed by central and local government, and it requires enhanced support for county-level police and extra help for central and western police departments. All expenditure items should be

appropriately itemized, systematized, and centralized. Province government and the MPS must carefully examine any extraordinary outlay before submission to the central government for consideration. The police should be paid a salary and receive benefits that exceed the local levels. Depending on economic conditions, the police should receive supplemental income and benefits. People who do police duty should be adequately compensated.

9. *Further strengthen Party leadership of public security work.* This can be achieved by holding police leaders responsible for their actions and improving the system in place for appointing leaders; for example, have all leaders approved by the MPS above and by the Party Committee of the same level.

Ideology

Introduction

Throughout the reform effort, Chinese police reformers have tried unrelentingly to make the police ideologically pure. Of late, the effort has shifted to making the police more professional—that is, being more scientific, rational, rule bound, and humane. In China, police ideology and professionalism speak the same language (i.e., loyalty, integrity, dedication, fairness, self-sacrifice, and service). The goal is to infuse the police with a new ethos in keeping with its reformed role, changed functions, and transformed identity, much fractured by the reform process. The hope is to return the police to their glorious past. How successful the communist leadership has been in creating an ideology capable of reenergizing the police and appeasing the skeptics is the focus of this discussion. It is important to make a few important observations about police ideology in China before we begin.

The relative scope and reach, impact, and influence of communist ideology on Chinese society have been hotly debated and critically challenged during the reform era by various segments of society, including partisan cadres,[60] competing reformers,[61] disenchanted intellectuals,[62] disgruntled administrators,[63] disillusioned students,[64] disenfranchised peasants,[65] and disengaged youth,[66] but the dominance and importance of ideology in Chinese politics and policing have never been in doubt.[67] China as a nation and people has never lived without a utopian ideal, from Confucianism to Marxism to Maoism. Although not all leaders are as capable as Mao in exciting the imagination, stirring the passion, and mobilizing the Chinese, each and every Chinese citizen is more than willing to embrace a larger cause and live a transcending dream.

Depending on sources and context, policing with Chinese characteristics means different things to different people. Many people consider corruption and abuses to be characteristics of Chinese policing.[68] Others consider traditionalism and feudalism to be distinctively Chinese. For CPC political leaders or MPS policymakers, policing with Chinese characteristics, while capable of changing over time and for various applications, does have one constant meaning—whatever the CPC, the vanguard of communism, says it is.

Definitions

Harold Walsby defined *ideology* simply as "mental attitudes to life" and "world outlook."[69] Claude Destutt de Tracy, who first invented the term, referred to it as the "science of ideas."[70] *The American Heritage Dictionary* defines *ideology* as the "body of ideas reflecting the social needs and aspirations of an individual, group, class, or culture" and as "a set of doctrines or beliefs that form the basis of a political, economic, or other system."[71] Coming back to China, Karl Marx observed that ideology is a social construct, ideas and ideals created by the ruling class to justify its domination and exploitation. It refers to a range of things related to the social production of people's ideas (e.g., beliefs, expectations, ideals). Specifically, Marx considered ideology to be part of the superstructure of a society generated by an economic base. Friedrich Engels suggested that ideology creates a "false consciousness" in people, obscuring the truth as it rationalizes the exploitation relationship behind it.[72] Finally, John McMurtry, author of *The Structure of Marx's World-View*, listed five defining criteria of ideology in accordance with Marxism: (1) ideology is constituted of formulated ideas; (2) it refers to human matters or affairs; (3) its content is materially unproductive; (4) it obtains in a public mode; and (5) it is subject to state control.[73]

Roles and Functions of Ideology in PRC Political Economy

The significance and importance of ideology in defining, shaping, and distinguishing the PRC police from other nations cannot be fully grasped without first understanding the role and functions of communist ideology in Chinese politics.[74] Ideology is the lifeblood of the CPC.[75] Ideology provides an identity for the Communist Party. It gives purpose to its members. It supplies consciousness for the masses. It bonds people and holds organizations together. It separates friends and foes. It controls thoughts and guides actions. It inspires the cadres to revolutionary feats and mobilizes the masses for communist causes. It provides vision, sets agendas, establishes missions, informs policies, and guides actions. Last, but not least, it gives the Party and state the moral authority and political legitimacy[76] to govern and rule.[77] In communist China, ideology penetrates the collective consciousness and pierces individual souls. It permeates every interstice of society, in time and space. Nothing is spared, not even art.[78] Communist ideology is an all-embracing theory for individual actions and a master blueprint for social engineering. As Thomas Metzger observed about the nature and functions of contemporary Chinese political theory:

> The leading contemporary Chinese schools of thought…all examine the problem of traditional values by trying to set up a full-scale philosophical system somewhat like Hegel's. Thus, they seek a system that solves all epistemological, ontological, and cosmological problems and establishes teleological principles of historical development defining both necessary historical stages and the moral mission of the heroic or enlightened individual in the present.…Evaluated according to perfectionist criteria, China's current condition is perceived as a predicament, and progress is regarded as depending on the ability of "intellectuals" to propagate the correct understanding of the world.[79]

Mandate for Ideology

The mandate for communist ideology is enshrined in the PRC Constitution:

> China is currently in the primary stage of socialism. The basic task of the nation is to concentrate its effort on socialist modernization in accordance with the theory of building socialism with Chinese characteristics. Under the leadership of the Communist Party of China and the guidance of Marxism–Leninism and Mao Zedong thought, the Chinese people of all nationalities will continue to adhere to the people's democratic dictatorship, follow the socialist

road, persist in reform and opening up, steadily improve socialist institutions, develop socialist democracy, improve the socialist legal system and work hard and self-reliantly to modernize industry, agriculture, national defense, and science and technology step by step to turn China into a powerful and prosperous socialist country with a high level of culture and democracy.[80]

Interpretation and Application

The communist ideology has been variously interpreted and differentially applied by successive generations of Party leaders according to the shifting priorities of the country and changing sociopolitical circumstances of the time. Interpretations and applications are further mediated by personal philosophies and political factionalism of the moment.[81] In this regard, generations of PRC leaders purported to govern the society with reference to utopian principles under a central command, but they were actually ruling the people in accordance with popular sentiments (morality).[82] The clearest case is that of Mao, who wanted to keep the revolution spirit alive by mounting a cultural revolution, with the people in charge.

Viewed in this way, the ideological clashes in China today are not necessarily communism vs. capitalism or conservatism vs. liberalism; instead, they are between the dominant mass sentiments and various group interests (capitalists, industrialists, urbanites)[83] and intellectual entitlement.[84] In real terms, these clashes represent populism vs. elitism, collectivism vs. individualism, substantive justice vs. procedural justice, and duty-bound community vs. rights-based society.

The battle over ideology is a clash of civilizations of the first order, within the Party (Liu vs. Mao, Hua vs. Deng) and outside the Party (intellectuals vs. old guards, left vs. right), with elites defining the political agenda, setting the ideological tone, and establishing policy objectives. In this way, the interests and powers of the silent majority of the masses are captured and controlled by the Party and intellectual elites, who, while championing for a better China in the name of the masses, are actually doing so at the masses' expense. The best example of this is the "Three Represents," which claim to represent the collective interests of the people while promoting the rights of the business class and intellectual elites.

The CPC justified their actions with the mass line principle ("from the people, to the people"), claiming transcendence of vision and purity of purpose as the vanguards of a revolutionary movement. Subjugation of the masses is deemed necessary to liberate them from a self-induced false consciousness. The masses are not able to find their way in the midst of the forest and should trust the CPC to lead them to utopia.

The intellectual elites (zhishi fenzi) have a long history of acting as the conscience of the nation.[85] The elites' claim of political foresight is based on class enlightenment earned as a result of education, contemplation, and discipline, as traditionally defined ("superior man," or junzi) and contemporarily understood ("enlightenment scholars," or qimeng xuezhe). The ignorant masses, living in feudalism (fengjian) (e.g., attached to a rigid family structure) and suffering from dogmatism (e.g., subscribing to superstition, or mixin), are not able to and should not be allowed to set critical policy for the state without the tutorage of the Party. To further illustrate the dissonance between the people and elite political culture, one need look no further than the fact that the peasants have little cognitive understanding of or emotive resonance with progressive and enlightened political concepts, such as privacy, procedural justice, freedom of speech, or civil society.[86]

In the early days of the Republic and during the socialist construction period (before 1954), the ideological conflict was between Mao Tse-tung, who insisted on a purely ideological, revolutionary approach, and Liu Shaoqi, who preferred a more conciliatory, pragmatic, organizational approach; in other words, it was a struggle between the masses (Mao) and the experts (Liu).[87] This conflict fermented and spilled over into the Cultural Revolution (1967 to 1976), ending with an ideological struggle between the rightists (capitalists) and the leftists (communists).

With reform, Deng has chosen pragmatism over communism by introducing his theory of "socialism with Chinese characteristics." The capitalistic orientation of Deng's political stance is summed up in the following proposition: "We should let some people get rich first, both in the countryside and in the urban areas. To get rich by hard work is glorious." Deng's pragmatic approach to economic and social reform is best captured by the following quotation: "It doesn't matter if a cat is black or white as long as it catches mice."

Deng's pragmatism is not without its principles. Deng insisted that "socialism with Chinese characteristics" is be achieved by following: (1) the socialist road, (2) the leadership of the Communist Party of China, (3) the dictatorship of the proletariat, and (4) Marx–Leninism and Mao Tse-tung's thought. The theory and practice of public security with Chinese characteristics is ultimately derived from and traceable to these "Four Principles."[88] More recently, Jiang Zemin was successful in getting his ideological principles, the "Three Represents,"[89] incorporated into the Constitution alongside the thoughts of Lenin, Mao, and Deng. Hu sought to establish his political identity with the scientific development perspective now firmly entrenched in the Party Constitution.

Police Ideology of Old

In the past, a good police officer must first and foremost be a good communist. Both are expected to devote oneself to the revolutionary cause, to sacrifice for the collective good, and to serve the masses, nation, and Party wholeheartedly. Liu Shaoqi, one of PRC's founding fathers, wrote in *How to Be a Good Communist* that communists must be ideologically pure. They must be good students of Marxism and Leninism.[90] Communists are not born but self-made. Good communists engage in constant self-cultivation, continue the class struggle,[91] and must keep studying[92] and practicing communism:

> [N]o communist should rest contented with being a Party member who merely fulfills the minimum requirements; as laid down in the Party Constitution, he should strive to make progress ceaselessly raise the level of his political consciousness and diligently study Marxism–Leninism, as manifested throughout their lives.[93]

Self-cultivation is a full-time engagement and life-long pursuit:

> We must engage in self-cultivation in the Marxist–Leninist theory; self-cultivation in applying the Marxist–Leninist stand, viewpoint, and method to the study and handling of all problems; self-cultivation in proletarian ideology and morality; self-cultivation in upholding unity in the Party, practicing criticism and self-criticism and observing discipline; self-cultivation in developing the style of hard work and persistent struggle; self-cultivation in building close ties with the masses; self-cultivation in various branches of scientific knowledge, etc. We are all members of the Communist Party and therefore we must all without exception carry on self-cultivation in these respects.[94]

Furthermore, communists come from all walks of life. They gain class consciousness at various times in their development, depending on their social origin, life experience, and political exposure.[95] In essence, no set path and time exist for attaining the communist creed.

Police officers in China are vanguards of CPC ideology and foot soldiers of class struggles. As such, they are expected to exemplify and personify Party ideology. They are expected to live the life of a good communist, in private as well as in public, in thoughts as well as in deeds. In this regard, communist ideology is more like a religion, demanding that those who believe must follow a strict code of uncompromising standards. Liu made this last point amply clear:

> As you know, a man's words and actions are guided by his ideology. And a man's ideology is inseparable from his world outlook. The only world outlook for members of the Communist Party is the communist world outlook. This world outlook is the philosophical system of the proletariat and also our communist methodology. All of this has been abundantly discussed in Marxist–Leninist literature, and especially in the philosophical works of the founders.[96]

The communist ideology of perfection corresponds closely (in nature, substance, and operation) with that of puritanical ethics, especially in a military setting:

> Puritanism tells us to follow not only the ethical path, then, but to follow strictly a path that is straight and narrow. Thus, our first reason why many ethicists develop a streak of Puritanism is that the very nature of ethics encourages a tendency toward that way of thinking. More often than not those who become puritanical will have additional reasons or causes working on them before they succumb to this way of thinking. But, for some, this reason is enough to lead them down the path of Puritanism.[97]

Communism also resonates well with another faith-based belief system, Calvinism, upon which puritanical ethics was based. Calvinism demanded self-cultivation, self-discipline, and self-sacrifice in the service of God. Likewise, the U.S. military ethics and honors code demands integrity,[98] service before self,[99] and excellence in all we do.[100] Communist ideology is reflected in and reinforced by every aspect of PRC police work, from recruitment to training to assessment.

Ideology in Policing

A candidate's political–ideological orientation is an important consideration in the recruitment and development of a communist police office. In the Mao era, only people with the correct status (*chengfen*) or from a good background were allowed to join public security. Police candidates were expected to be ideologically pure and politically correct to be worthy of trust by the Party and deserving of respect from the public. During Deng's reform era, ideological purity took a back seat. In reform China and since Deng, anyone who identifies with Party ideology and follows CPC leadership is welcome to join.[101]

The MPS recruitment guidelines state that police candidates must firmly uphold the "Four Principles" (*jiben yuanze*);[102] support the Party line (*luxian*), directives (*fangzhen*), and policy (*zhengce*); and love the Chinese Communist Party, socialism, and the people.[103] The guidelines preclude considering candidates who are "backward in political ideology and exhibit dissatisfaction with the Party and socialism system in words and deeds."[104] The MPS is much concerned with infesting the police ranks with political impurities by hiring less than ideologically pure people as part-time or contract police officers to meet economic development needs.[105] The MPS proposed three measures to maintain the purity of the police ranks. First, actively work to prevent impure people from becoming contract police; this can be achieved by conducting vigorous political vetting (*zhengzhi shencha*).[106] Second, educate part-time contract police to abide by the police disciplinary code.[107] Third, closely supervise and inspect contract police work to ensure good discipline and a healthy work style ("Public Security Personnel—Eight Important Disciplines; Ten Things to Pay Attention to," *Gongan renyuan ba dai jilu, shi xiang zhuyi*).[108]

The MPS leadership cadres (*ganbu*) are expected to uphold the "Four Principles." They should adopt a dialectical materialism worldview and a "seek truth from facts" mentality. They must possess a reform spirit and not be afraid of hard work nor be fearful of death. They must be fair, objective, and committed to serving the people wholeheartedly.[109]

Police education and training are comprised of ideology indoctrination, and thought education. In 1988, the MPS issued a memo asking police universities and colleges to improve upon their political, moral, and ideological education.[110] In 2001, students sitting for the national higher education certification examinations were expected to pass tests covering Mao Tse-tung thought, Deng Xiaoping theory, and Marxism political philosophy.[111]

"Public security policy (*gongan zhengce*) is the product of our practice when we, as a nation and Party, use Marxism and Mao Tse-tung thought to solve Chinese state security and social order problems."[112] Police policymakers[113] are supposed to integrate ideological considerations into their decision-making efforts;[114] for example, they should be thinking about the Party line and policies from above and understand the mood, thinking, and demands of the police officers below. They should be thinking about the old in light of the new and the new in the context of the old. They should adopt an internal as well as external perspective.

Every police unit has a political department to provide ideological education and political supervision. The MPS (*gongan bu*) Political Department (*zhengzhi gongzuo jiguan*) was first established in 1953. Its major mission is to provide political, strategic, policy, and discipline education. It is responsible for ensuring that the Party line and policy guidelines are properly executed. It is also responsible for maintaining police discipline and ideology purity among the ranks.

Public security political work (*gongan zhengzhi gongzuo*) keeps police work in line with ideology. The purpose of public security political work is to ensure that the Party line, guidelines, and policies are followed and that the nation's laws and regulations are complied with. Specifically, such work includes: (1) perfect thought education for the police; (2) perfect selection, training, assessment, supervision, and management of police; (3) inspections and discipline, pointing out deficiencies and honoring exemplary work; and (4) helping police officers solve their work, study, and thought problems.[115]

The specific roles, functions, duties, and responsibilities of a police political instructor (*zhengzhi zhidao yuan*) are more specifically provided in "Regulations for People's Police Basic Unit Political Instructors" ("*Renmin jingcha jiceng danwei zhengzhi zhidao yuan gongzuo tiaoli*"), promulgated by the MPS in 1984.[116] The role of the political instructor at basic police posts is to promote Party ideology and thought work (*zhengzhi xixiang gongzuo*). The political instructor and the ranking police officer at a post share in leadership of that unit. The political instructor is responsible for ideological control and political discipline; the ranking police officer is responsible for dealing with professional problems and operations issues. The specific functions of the political instruction officers include the following:

1. Promote the Party line, principles, and policy. Educate the people's police to maintain political uniformity with Party central. Supervise and ensure that the orders and directions from above are thoroughly executed.
2. Guide the people's police in the serious study of Marxist–Leninism, Mao Tse-tung thought, and the Party line, principles, and policies.
3. Educate the people's police on communism, patriotism, and collectivism, as well as on the revolutionary tradition and the anticorruption struggle; raise their consciousness to wholeheartedly serve the people.
4. Follow the Party charter, offer criticism and debate, and enhance Party members' understanding of the Party.
5. Educate and manage the people's police, implement the PRC people's police internal regulations (*Zhonghua renmin gongheguo renmin neiwu tiaoli*) and other regulations, maintain discipline, and reform police work styles.
6. Implement a police post responsibility system, develop meritorious and exemplary activities, set up an assessment and examination system, and discover and cultivate progressive examples.

The PRC police are rewarded for the proper display of ideological commitment and political consciousness. The "People's Police Reward and Punishment Regulations" ("*Renmin jingcha zhangcheng tiaoli*") make clear that the purpose of reward is to arouse the positive revolutionary spirit of the general police population and to enhance patriotism, communism, and revolutionary heroism.[117] Specifically, it provides rewards for acts that demonstrate upholding the "Four Principles,"[118] including adherence to the Party line, guidelines, and policies. Rewards are also offered for exemplary execution of state law and public security work. The regulations also provide for the punishment of officers who violate Party policy and the Constitution. When the PRC was first established, police assignments[119] and advancements in rank[120] were made contingent on an officer's political orientation, professional qualifications, and job performance. In 1950, the Central government instructed provincial and administrative areas to formulate their own standards for the assignment of rank based on political attitude (*zhengzhi tidu*), work achievements, public relations, and technical skills. Political orientation was considered more important than work achievements or functional skills.[121] Today, promotions are primarily based on both moral and academic performance (*decai biaoxian*).[122] The CPC ideology (Table 5.4) finds expression in *jingcha zhixu* ("police character"), *jing feng* ("police culture"), and *jingji* ("police discipline") as embodied in the Party line, police laws and regulations, departmental policies, and professional codes of conduct.

Thought Work

To promote ideological purity and political correctness, police leaders and MPS and Party officials have to engage in ideological and political work (*sixiang zhengzhi gongzuo*), more commonly known as "thought work."[123] The purpose of thought work is to ensure proper execution of the Party line to fulfill the objectives of the CPC. Specifically, thought work is intended to: (1) guarantee implementation of the Party line and policies, (2) maintain Party oversight of public security work, (3) ensure achievement of public security objectives, and (4) ensure achievement of the objectives of democratic dictatorship and socialist modernization and construction.

TABLE 5.4 Formalization of CPC Ideology in Aspects of PRC Policing

Aspects of PRC Policing	Formalization of CPC Ideology
Police cadre background	
Mao Tse-tung	Proper class background (people over experts)
Liu Shaoqi	Proper political orientation (commitment to communism)
Deng Xiaoping	Proper professional background (experts over people)
Jiang Zemin	All people contributing to PRC reform and development, including entrepreneurs and capitalists
Hu Jintao	Professionals with scientific outlook
Police attributes	
Police model	Lei Feng
Police (regular) recruitment standards	Ideologically pure[a]
Police (part-time/contract) basic requirements	Ideologically pure[b]

[a] Firmly uphold "Four Principles" (*jiben yuanze*); support the Party line (*luxian*), principles (*fangzhen*), and policy (*zhengce*); and love the CPC, socialism, and the people.

[b] For the regular police, it is a "select in" process. This means that an affirmative case must be made that the candidate possesses the correct ideological orientation; failing that, the candidate must be rejected. With regard to part-time/contract police, it is a "select out" process. This means that candidates will be accepted *unless* some ideological impurity is discovered.

Major tasks of thought work include educating police officers on the proper Marxist–Lenin worldview and methods of thinking; making them realize that they have the power to change the world by changing themselves; helping them resolve any ideological conflicts; facilitating relationships among the cadres, police, and public; improving upon police political ideology, work discipline, and professional ethics; and investigating the patterns and principles of ideological work. Political ideological education consists of five types of education: (1) the Party line regarding socialism ("one central point, two focal points," or "*yige zhongxin dian, liang ge jiben dian*"); (2) Marxist–Leninism and Mao's thoughts; (3) the Party line and policies; (4) socialist legality, professional discipline, and personal morality; and (5) wholeheartedly working for the people.[124]

Political ideology education is customized, individualized, and personalized using reasoning and persuasion rather than coercion.[125] It requires varying approaches and methods, depending on the situation, to resolve differences of ideas; in particular, it involves education through persuasion (*shuofu*) by clarifying principles and analyzing facts. It can be based on theory and logic (*lilun jiaoyu*), such as convincing people through the use of reason (*yili furen*), or it can appeal to human emotions by way of images and examples (*xingxiang jiaoyu*). Such education can be preventative (*yufang jiaoyu*) or remedial (*lianzheng jiaoyu*). In addition to education based on persuasion (*shuofu jiaoyu fa*), practical education (*zhidao shijian jiaoyu fa*) corrects mistakes by pointing them out. To be effective, this type of education involves enlightening with reason (*xiao zhi yi li*), moving with emotions (*dong zhi yi qing*), arousing with ideas (*lian zhi yi yi*), and guiding by actions (*dao zhi yi xing*). Police officers can also be self-educated (*zhi wo jiaoyu fa*), which involves critical introspection and independent learning initiative, as well as group activities and consulting with others.

Police leadership regularly mounts campaigns to purify the thoughts or ratify the work styles of the police; for example, Mao launched the *san fan* ("three anti") campaign and Jiang spearheaded the "Three Represents." Some of these thought-work campaigns are driven by events (e.g., Falun Gong), others by social trends (e.g., corruption and abuse of power).[126]

Deng: A Police Ideology for All Seasons

Leadership of the PRC is ideologically anchored, centrally planned, and personality driven.[127] Reform in China has effectively destroyed communist ideology,[128] eroded Party leadership,[129] and upended the *status quo*.[130] The ideology and leadership void has been filled by Deng Xiaoping's thoughts,[131] which provided: (1) *direction*, such as setting the goal of the police to be securing the people's democratic dictatorship (*renmin minzhu zhuanzheng*);[132] (2) *inspiration*, such as achieving police reform by liberating the mind (*jiefang sixiang*");[133] (3) *doctrine*, such as police reconstruction through progressive policy decision making (*jian jin juece*);[134] and (4) *methods*, such as holding the police accountable to the masses (*qunzhong luxian*).[135] Specifically, Deng advocated building socialism with Chinese characteristics by following the "Four Principles" of socialism: follow the socialist road, proletarian dictatorship, Communist Party leadership, and Marxism–Leninism–Mao thought.[136] Other relevant Deng doctrines guiding police reform include "liberating the mind" and "seeking truth from facts,"[137] which promise to liberate China from the old ideology while it searches for new ideas of all kinds—for example, a democratic dictatorship to put class enemies in check; "crossing the river by feeling the stones" as a call for incremental and experimental reform; and "black cat, white cat, it's a good cat if it catches the mouse" as a reflection of conducting reform with pragmatism (i.e., by result).

In pursuing reform, Deng sought radical departures from old ways of thinking and doing and preached bold new approaches to established ways and means. Deng's thoughts on reform in China were succinctly summed up in a book released by the Central Committee of the Communist Party of China (CCCPC) in memory of Deng's passing in 1999[138] which documents and elaborates on Deng's thoughts.[139] Except for insisting on democratic dictatorship over the enemies of the state and maintaining political stability and social order at all costs, Deng provided little guidance for police reform. The interpretation and application of Deng's reform philosophy and thinking to Chinese policing were comprehensively reported in a book published by the China Police Studies Society.[140] Again, Deng offered no concrete ideas for how to reform the police, other than in the most general of ways. Finally, the basic framework of PRC police reform, with Deng's footprint, was ably captured in a book on how to create a 21st-century police force with Chinese characteristics.[141] This framework was put into practice through a variety of National People's Congress (NPC) laws, Party notices, Administrative Council regulations, and MPS policies.

Conceptualizing Policing with Chinese Characteristics

To the public and in everyday practice, the Chinese police have a lot of things in common with other police forces around the world, as their primary function is to serve and protect; however, the Chinese police are unique because they are an instrument of the state to impose democratic dictatorship on enemies of the state. Chinese political leaders from Mao to Deng to Hu preached that in conducting police reform China must learn from others without sacrificing its own identity and uniqueness. Learning from abroad does not mean wholesale importation of foreign ways and means or ideology and values. Foreign lessons must be first digested and made to fit China's social circumstances before importation,[142] because the characteristics of China public security work are determined by the conditions of China.[143]

To observe that policing with Chinese characteristics is a unique form of policing is to suggest that China is different from other countries. It also presupposes that there is something special about the Chinese people that leads to particular expectations of the police and requiring different treatment by police.[144] A basic theoretical definition of policing with Chinese characteristics is as follows:

> The characteristics of Chinese public security work are determined by China's condition [*guoqing*]. It is a necessary byproduct of the Chinese social system [*shehui zhidu*], historical tradition [*lishi quantong*], ethnic character [*minzhu tedian*], and geographic features [*diyuan huanjin*]. It is a comprehensive reflection of our current political, economic, and cultural characteristics. It is a realization of public security work in practice under the leadership of the China Communist Party.[145]

The above definition makes Chinese police work contingent on the national conditions (*guoqing*) of China; thus, the police and *guoqing* are interdependent and mutually reinforcing.[146] The definition goes on to suggest that the characteristics of Chinese policing are a product of the environment—social, historical, ethnic, and geographical—but this situation is not unique to China. Police actions around the world are all subject to the same considerations. With regard to social influences, communist policing is obviously organized differently than capitalistic policing.[147] With regard to historical development, traditional police departments, such as those found in Philadelphia or Cincinnati, operate differently than professional agencies such as the Federal Bureau of Investigation.[148] With regard to ethnic considerations, the Japanese police treat their citizens differently than the police in the United States or Great Britain.[149] Finally, with regard to geographical considerations, urban and rural police everywhere are organized and function differently.[150] As to the notion that the police reflect the country's politics, economy, and culture, this is also true of other societies. Police characteristics are shaped and defined by the underlying society's ideology, values, and culture, which are translated into a vision and mission for police policies and practices.[151]

With reform in China, the question of how Chinese society can influence the police in ideology and philosophy, role and functions, organization and process has yet to be clearly specified systematically and comprehensively. This is causing policy problems at the leadership level and implementation problems at the operational level. The following text attempts to map out the principles and practices of policing with Chinese characteristics.

Some Fundamental Principles of Policing with Chinese Characteristics

Policing with Chinese characteristics is an integral part and manifestation of the idea of socialism with Chinese characteristics.[152] This means that police ideology, values, and ethics reflect those of socialism with Chinese characteristics. This also means that policing in the reform era is devoted to the building of socialism with Chinese characteristics, not to obstructing it.[153] In this context, then, the PRC police are a liberating force. PRC police work should be guided by the basic tenets of socialism, and the PRC police will accept and defend the socialist market as an integral part of Chinese socialism. The PRC police will follow Party leadership in achieving a socialist democracy and upholding the rule of law. The PRC police will promote economic reform without sacrificing spiritual progress and should aim toward achieving the "Three Represents." Finally, the PRC police should recognize that police reform in China takes time and must be conducted incrementally.

Chinese Characteristics and Politics

The Chinese police have many defining and distinctive characteristics, with politics (*zhengzhi shenzhi*) being paramount. In communist China, political ideology dictates police ideology and philosophy, their vision and mission, their roles and functions.[154] Communist societies and capitalist societies have different perspectives on the nature of the police and in turn their mission, roles, and functions. In capitalistic societies, the police are supposed to be nonpolitical; that is, they are supposed to be legal and social agents fighting crime and serving people. In communist China, the political nature of police work is explicit; the police are an instrument of the state to impose a democratic dictatorship and effectuate proletarian class rule.[155] In practice, this means that the police treat the people differently than they do enemies of the state. As to defining who are people and who are enemies of the state, that changes with political development and exigencies of the times; for example, during the war with Japan, the CPC joined hands with the Kumintang (KMT) to fight the Japanese, temporarily becoming comrades in arms. In the formative year of the PRC, the people consisted mainly of communists, and KMT sympathizers were purged. Today, in the reform era, the people include capitalists who are loyal to and support the Party.

In Mao's time, enemies of the state were counterrevolutionaries and spies. During the Cultural Revolution, the enemy label was extended to include anyone who was not ideologically pure, including revisionists and capitalists. During Deng's reform, enemies of the state included anyone who disrupted economic reform (e.g., criminals) and attempted to destroy the socialist political economy (e.g., Falun Gong). Finally, the Jiang administration has sought to accept capitalists within traditional communist ranks.

In promoting a people's democratic dictatorship, the police should make a distinction between Western (capitalist) democracy and Chinese (socialist) democracy. Chinese socialist democracy is a class-based proletarian democracy, in which the values and interests of the proletariate are to be secured and promoted at the expense of the capitalistic (property) class.[156] Proletarian democracy is majority rule, where the collective subsumes the individuals, and the majority trumps the minority;[157] it is intended to be a nondiscriminatory and non-exploitative, true democracy with equality for all.[158] Proletarian democracy presupposes the necessity of a dictatorship to fight class and state enemies.[159]

The Chinese police also perform vital social functions, such as securing socialist economic relationships, promoting the socialist culture, and protecting socialist means of production.[160] Another mission of the police is to oversee integration of ethnic races and unification of the nation.[161]

Chinese Characteristics and Stability above All

Deng insisted on "security above all." To him, without stability there can be no reform and nothing can be achieved. This insistence on stability was driven by the fear that China will suffer the fate of the Cultural Revolution and Russia's disintegration. Intellectually, it is informed by the "new authoritarianism" of the 1980s and the "neo-conservatism" of the 1990s.[162] In 1989, Deng said in a CPC Central Committee meeting,

> The key to our success in modernization, reform, and opening to the outside is stability....
> We must counter any forces that threaten stability, not yielding to them or even making any
> concessions. We must send out a signal that China will tolerate no disturbances.[163]

That same year, Deng told President Bush that, "In China, the overriding need is for stability. Without a stable environment, we can accomplish nothing and may even lose what we have gained....China is now in a period when it must concentrate on economic development."[164] Deng reiterated the point with CPC General Secretary Zhao Ziyang and Chinese President Yang Shangkun: "I've said over and over that we need stability if we're going to develop."[165] This concern was shared by President Jiang Zemin, who, in 1998, said:

> Stability is the basic premise for reform and development. Without stability, nothing can be achieved....In the process of carrying out reform, opening-up, and developing a socialist market economy, contradictions among the people may notably increase, and some may even become increasingly prominent....We need to nip those factors that undermine social stability in the bud, no matter where they come from.[166]

Maintaining stability was the reason most often cited by Chinese leaders to justify taking repressive actions against the students at Tiananmen Square on June 4, 1989.[167] Today, the stability issue pertains to how to deal with antagonistic vs. non-antagonistic forces of disorder, such as Falun Gong and mass incidents. Although both kinds of disabling forces must be put under control, antagonist forces must be mercilessly suppressed and non-antagonistic forces must be masterfully defused.

Chinese Characteristics and Pragmatism

Deng was a doer, not thinker. He was a consummate politician, not a romantic ideologue. He was a practitioner, not a theoretician.[168] Deng articulated a number of ideas on how to reform China, but offered no comprehensive theory or master plan to achieve them. In this, Deng was a pragmatist not an ideologue. Except for insisting on stability and dictatorship, Deng's theory of reform was otherwise open to all kinds of ideas and featured a willingness to experiment with anything[169] that might work.[170] Deng's lack of ideological interest and his attachment to the pragmatic left the police in the dark with regard to reform.[171] They wondered, for example, what the roles and functions of the police should be in the reform era. How should the police relate to the people vs. class enemies?[172] This ideological confusion was aptly observed by Minister of Public Security Wang Fang in 1988:

> Currently, there are many issues urgently requiring research and answers within public security theory. For example, what are the nature [*benzhi*], mission [*renwu*], and function [*zuoyong*] of public security organs at this stage of reform? How do we establish a people police system that is uniform, efficient, responsive, and adaptable to protecting modernization construction needs? How can public security work adjust to reform, follow reform, serve reform, and promote reform? How can we understand crimes generated by today's society, as well their roots, patterns, attacks, and prevention? How can we implement comprehensive administration and social management policies under these new conditions? How can we give full play to the advantages of our nation's public security work and continue to develop the fine tradition of the mass line?[173]

Deng's reform policy, justified on pragmatic grounds, is not properly anchored ideologically or clearly explained theoretically.[174] It is difficult to comprehend, much less apply in practice: "In the case of contemporary China, the regime's ideology is bankrupt. The transition from a socialist to a quasi market economy has created a great deal of social unrest. And the regime relies heavily on coercion to repress political and religious dissent."[175]

What counts for policing with Chinese characteristics few people know.[176] There is no conceptual definition of what these Chinese characteristics are all about.[177] The phrase, much like "community-oriented policing" in the United States, can mean different things to different people. Thus, one of the more challenging problems confronting and confounding Chinese police reformers is defining exactly what policing with Chinese characteristics means, in theory and practice. This has created problems in planning, implementing, researching, validating, explaining, understanding, assessing, and improving Chinese police reform.[178]

Since the beginning of the reform, public security has been forced to operate in a new environment, caught between old traditions and new opportunities, such as a static vs. dynamic society, closed vs. open borders, planned vs. market economy, and individual vs. collective culture. As a result, there is a substantial amount of anomie in the MPS; for example, in Mao's era, public security was responsible for stamping out speculative conduct (e.g., hoarding goods) and exploitative behavior (e.g., enslavement of workers). In the reform era, however, public security protects and promotes such activities. In Mao's era, police officers were asked to make sacrifices to serve the masses; today, they provide services for a fee.

All in all, Deng as a thinker and leader failed to supply the nation and equip the police with a well thought out, coherent, and all-embracing ideology to weather reform changes. In his defense and to his credit, Deng did attempt to fill the void with his insistence on a democratic dictatorship, national security, and stability at all costs.

Hu: Discovery of a New Professional Police Ethos

Problem with Ideology[179]

Between 1978 and 2010, the MPS and provincial security officials were struggling to meet newly emerged operational challenges, from juvenile crime to a mobile population, and the MPS was searching for a new identity, including redefining[180] police roles and functions during the reform era. One of the major debates has been the relevancy of communist ideology in a newly established capitalistic political economy (socialist market economy with Chinese characteristics). With the demise of the counterrevolutionaries as a class problem, questions are being raised about the meaning and necessity of a people's democratic dictatorship. What are the roles and functions of the police in a socialist market economy?[181] There are more questions than answers: What should the police do as an instrument of the state that is against the enemy and for the masses? Who exactly are the enemies of the state? What types of people belong to the masses? How should reformed China deal with the masses vs. enemies of the state?[182] Foreign observations, referring to domestic sources, have identified three competing domestic schools of thoughts: public security reformers, mainstream Leninists, and Neo-Marxists.[183]

Representing public security reformers, the MPS objects to treating criminals as enemies of the state. They want to deal with crimes more rationally and scientifically.[184] For example, it has been observed that China is entering into a new era of economical, social, and political reconstruction wherein class struggle is no longer the main focus of public security work. As a result, public security should be democratized to serve the interests of the people and the needs of reform (e.g., economic development).[185] As a first step, the police should be separated from the Party and follow the Constitution. The mainstream Leninists consider criminals of all kinds to be class enemies and they must be fought.

Leninists believe that the *yanda* campaign was an anti-rights campaign, resembling similar campaigns in earlier years.[186] The basic principles that Leninists espouse include: (1) the police should be controlled and led by the CPC; (2) although not all crime is political in nature, crimes are capable of being political; (3) class struggle against crime should be more sophisticated, and the Cultural Revolution era should not be repeated;[187] and (4) the Party and the MPS seriously neglected class enemies in the 1980s, and the Party must be on guard against the emergence of new or transformed class enemies (e.g., Falun Gong).[188] The Neo-Marxists observe that, because the old exploitative class has been destroyed, the class struggle of old is not necessary. Still, they think that the threat is there for people (foreigners and domestics) to conspire and destabilized the state. The following sections explore in some depth how political ideology has changed for the police since 1999.

Dominance of Political Ideology

In 1999, political leadership of the nation (at all levels of government) was very much troubled by the short-term impact and long-term implications of economic reform on the legitimacy of the Party, integrity of the police, and stability of the country.[189] Of particular concern was how economic, social, and political development in the country over the last 20 years had come to dilute the appeal of CPC ideology and compromise the commitment of the police to Party discipline.[190] In response, Party leaders called for the unquestionable following of Deng's theories on reform,[191] such as "liberating the mind," "seeking truth from facts," maintaining stability above all, striking hard at crime, closing ranks with the people, and supporting economic reform.[192] The Party and police leaders have spent much time and effort to clarify the meaning, articulate the relevancy, and amplify the importance of Deng's principles of reform to police theory and practice.[193]

Centrality of Deng's Thinking in Police Reform[194]

It is clear that Party ideology played a central role in the guiding and ordering of police reform.[195] In 1998, on the tenth anniversary of *Public Security Studies*, the Editorial Board affirmed the necessity and utility of integrating ideology with practice in conducting police reform: "Marxism maintains that theory devoid of practice is abstract and sterile. Action without theoretical guidance is blind action."[196] In the same editorial, Marx's ideology, Mao's thought, and Deng's theory[197] were considered to be the guiding principles for police research, action, and reform.[198] Also in 1998, the MPS Institute of Public Safety (IPS) held a conference celebrating the twentieth anniversary of the Third Plenary Session of the 11th Party Central Committee.[199] The conference emphasized the relevancy, utility, and importance of political ideology in police operations, such as adopting Marx methods and viewpoints to resolve new reform problems.[200] Particularly, it reaffirmed the need to stay close to Deng's thinking of "practice is the sole criterion for testing truth," "liberating the mind," "seeking truth from facts," and uniting to face the future as the keys to police reform and development.[201] In 1999, the Editorial Board of *Public Security Studies* once again impressed upon readers the centrality of Deng's theory on police reform: "In the last year, public security organs at every level seriously studied Deng Xiaoping's theory and insisted on using Deng's Xiaoping's theory as a guide to integrate the reality of social order and public security work. The capacity to use theory to resolve real problems is increasing."[202]

Centrality with Little Content and No Relevancy

Party mandate aside, the challenge today is how to correctly apply and creatively adapt[203] Deng's thinking to address a whole host of emerging problems never before anticipated.[204] How can China improve police work with respect to catching up with or adapting to the fast-changing pace of economic reform?[205] How can the public order be maintained in the reform era?[206] How about the social order?[207] How can conflicts among the people be resolved?[208] How can the mass line principle be reinvented to adjust to changing conditions in China?[209] How can relationships among the Party, state, police, and the people be redefined?[210] What is the role of the police with regard to promoting economic development?[211]

Consider the challenge of fighting economic crime without unnecessarily and unduly disrupting economic reform. Deng was committed to fighting economic crime as the first order of business in the reform era;[212] however, Deng also realized that Chinese reform could not be achieved without a solid foundation brought about by economic reform. But, economic reform brings with it new types of crime, such as financial fraud, official corruption, social disorder, and mass incidents.[213] The police role must be to keep economic crimes, social discontent, and political disorder at bay while protecting the legal interests of foreign investors and social welfare of domestic workers.[214] This is easier said than done. Again, communist ideology and Deng's thinking fail to provide sufficient guidance for police actions.

Many of the situations, problems, and issues requiring police attention during the reform were never anticipated by Deng or addressed by the Communist Manifesto. In fact they cannot easily be resolved, if at all, with reference to political ideology alone. As Deng put it, "practice is the sole criterion of truth," and there is a lot of "crossing the river by feeling the stones" (experimentation) to be had. In such cases, the invocation of political ideology or leaders' thinking contributes little to resolve the problems at hand. It appears that, as a general rule, as issues become more concrete, political ideology becomes less and less relevant and useful. Such is the case with the pressing reform issues of police incentives,[215] population migration,[216] fast response mechanisms,[217] the 110 emergency call system,[218] and traffic control.[219] In seeking to apply political thinking and ideology principles to such cases, the political leaders and police officials often appear to be insincere, disinguuous, and inept, stretching logic and straining credibility, resulting in wholesale disaffections among the troops.

Shift in Political Ideology

In 2008, a National Conference of PSB Commissioners was held at Nanjing.[220] There, the MPS Party Committee discussed the importance and implementation of three key points (*san xiang zhongdian jianshe*) to realize the scientific development concept (SDC) nationwide.[221] The SDC was first discussed in 2003.[222] It was formally launched and incorporated in the CPC Constitution in 2004. Premier Wen described SDC as follows:

> The scientific development concept focuses on integrating humanism with overall, coordinated and sustainable economic and social development, while pushing forward the reform and development drive to coordinate development in both urban and rural areas and in different regions, achieve harmonious development between man and nature, coordinate domestic development and open up to the outside world.[223]

In 2006, President Hu had this to say about SDC before a Yale faculty and students audience:

> In order to prepare China for the 21st century, China needs a new concept of development in line with its national conditions and the requirements of the time…to pursue a scientific outlook on development that makes economic and social development people oriented, comprehensive, balanced, and sustainable.…We will work to strike a proper balance between urban and rural development, development among regions, economic and social development, development of man and nature, and domestic development and opening wider to the outside world.…We will bring about coordinated economic, political, cultural, and social development.[224]

The Editorial Board of *Public Security Studies* characterized the work done in 2008 as seeking liberation from traditional concepts, customary methods, and constraints that were deemed to be at odds with the scientific development viewpoint,[225] while relying upon Deng Xiaoping's theory and Jiang's "Three Represents" as important guidance.[226] This observation, appearing in the nation's leading policy journal, signaled a change of course with reform thinking in China, from following ideology (from the heart) to adhering to science (from the head), suggesting that the Chinese police were finally moving away from its pre-reform revolutionary (effusive) *modus operandi* to a post-reform bureaucratic (calculating) one. The *Public Security Studies* message raised the fundamental political–ideological question of how to reconcile Hu's scientific development viewpoint with Deng's pragmatic theory as it applied to police reform, without appearing to downgrade Deng's theoretical contribution or importance to future reform work. Another consideration was how might the scientific development perspective come to affect traditional police theory, doctrine, and operations?[227] More simply, was it possible for Deng and Hu to coexist? Was Hu's idea an extension of Deng's? A renewal? A supplement? A refinement? A revision? The critical question to ask today is whether or not Hu's scientific development viewpoint has successfully eclipsed the traditional concepts, customary methods, and established constraints of Deng's era. The answer appears to be "not yet."

Deng's theory of reform, as with Hegel–Marx ideology, is a scientific theory of dialectical changes. Marx observed that the development of communism was driven by historical and social changes in economic conditions (means of production) and social relationships (relations of production). Deng has insisted all along that reform in China must take into account Chinese characteristics, being mindful of her historical circumstances and social conditions. If that should be the case, change in China will necessitate corresponding changes in political ideology. In this regard, Hu is no more changing Deng's thinking than laboring in his shadow; refer to Deng's "black cat, white cat, it's a good cat if it catches the mouse."

The question remains whether Deng's theory ("stability above all") or Jiang's thinking ("Three Represents") may one day be found to be defunct or otherwise eclipsed by Hu's "harmonious society" doctrine. This very likely could happen. The reasoning here is that change is constant, and the content and substance of ideas and thinking reflect the conditions of the society and expectations of the people at any one point in time. At the beginning of reform, China required "stability above all," but later sustainable harmonious development was necessary.

In the ultimate analysis, Hu's scientific development theory, as with Deng's pragmatic reform theory, must be robust enough to accommodate continual changes in the political economy, appealing enough to command the loyalty of a variety of economic interests, and strong enough to stand up to the challenges of political factions.[228]

In 2012, as the old revolutionary guard dies off or otherwise fades into the background, China will be led by a whole new generation of leaders who have no experience with revolutionary China and are much more at ease with reformed China.[229] These new leaders will have the opportunity to reconstruct China in their own image, shedding the ideological baggage of the past. Toward this end, Hu has been laying the necessary groundwork with the science of institutionalized evolutionary changes.[230]

It is clear that Deng's reform theory, while still influential as a set of reform ideas, has run its course; for example, the proposition that the police are an instrument of the state on guard against or at war with enemies of the state does not fit well with the new orientation of the police as service providers and the protectors of rights.

From Political Ideology to Professional Best Practice[231]

What does political ideology look like? In 2004, Wen Tai Yuan, a Police Commissioner from Hebei Province, following the leadership of MPS Minister Zhou Yongkang, called for the proper development of a police law enforcement ideology. He suggested six don'ts (eliminate) and dos (replace)[232] in policing:[233]

1. Completely eliminate the rule of man (*renzhi*) and replace it with the rule of law (*fazhi*). This is known as the *legality principle*.
2. Completely eliminate special privileges and replace them with judicious use of police powers, which are a public trust to be used for the public good.[234] This is the *accountability principle*.
3. Completely eliminate disregard and disrespect for the masses and promote the idea that the masses come first.[235] This is the *mass line (democratic policing) principle*.[236]
4. Completely eliminate police abuses and strengthen human rights. Human rights are not only a Western idea; in fact, China has its own concepts of human rights (e.g., right of survival comes before the right to free speech).[237] This is the *human rights principle*.
5. Completely eliminate cases for payment and promote the impartial enforcement of law. In spite of a shortage of resources, the police should enforce the law fairly and avoid relationship (*guanxi*) cases, personal (*renqing*) cases, and money (*jinqian*) cases.[238] This is the *integrity principle*.
6. Completely eliminate the idea of "five emphases, five lights"[239] and establish law enforcement for the people. Police law enforcement has traditionally been guided by the "five emphases, five lights" principle—emphasis on dictatorial functions, light on human rights protection;[240] emphasis on crime fighting, light on public service;[241] emphasis on striking, light on prevention;[242] emphasis on substantive justice, light on procedural justice;[243] and emphasis on quick case clearance, light on legal handling of cases.[244] All of these emphasis vs. light practices must be totally eliminated. This is the principle of *service* of public, *protection* of rights, *prevention* of crime, following *due process*, and abiding by the rule of *law*.

This proposed police law enforcement ideology, reduced to working principles of dos and don'ts, recalls police professional rules and best practices in other modern, progressive police agencies anywhere in the world.[245] Stephen D. Mastrofski's 1999 "Policing for People" article in the journal *Ideas in American Policing* set forth certain basic principles of democratic policing (policing for the people). Mastrofski made the case that democratic policing in action means being attentive, reliable, competent, responsive, fair, and well mannered. Following the lead of Mastrofski, it is more appropriate to refer to the Chinese newly discovered law enforcement ideology as good and professional police practices. Viewed in this light, police reformers in China are fast embracing global best practices and in the process are seeking integration with worldwide professional policing practices founded upon Western ideological, bureaucratic, professional, and legalistic principles.

If that is the case, it is legitimate and appropriate to ask the following questions, which have long perplexed China observers and at present are hotly debated among Chinese reformers: How can China reconcile modern professional policing theory and practice with traditional communist political philosophy? How is community policing different from mass line policing? In practice, how should mass incidents that have taken on a civil disturbance character and class struggle mentality be dealt with? What remains of policing with Chinese characteristics beyond the fact that the police still remain loyal to the Party, function as an instrument of the state, and act in the best interests of the of the masses? How can professional policing, which calls for legal, bureaucratic, and expert policing, be reconciled with mass line policing, which features informal and self-help social control? The list of questions goes on and on.[246]

Finally, changes in law enforcement ideology tell us about where the Chinese police are headed, their vision and mission, their roles and functions, and their manner and conduct, from class struggle to order maintenance, from rule of man to rule of law, from substantive justice to procedural justice, from crime fighting to providing service, from being Party directed to people driven. In essence, the Chinese police are radically changing from the political policing of old to the professional policing of new, with roles, relations, ways, and means that have yet to be clearly defined and worked out. The open discussion of police dos and don'ts also suggests that gaps exist between expectations and performance, implying a certain amount of disconnect between the rhetoric and reality of reform and most certainly disagreement over goals and process between leaders and among the people.

From Speedy Reform to Sustained Development

Reflecting on the year 1999, the *Public Security Studies* Editorial Department[247] uncharacteristically did not note any spectacular development or major breakthrough in police reform. It only noted that the MPS had been doing a good job in keeping pace with the nation's reform plan. Specifically, the MPS had successfully changed the nation's traditional police structure, process, and mentality to address new challenges and emerging problems. Looking ahead to 2000, the editorial did not foresee any new initiatives or drastic measures, except perhaps those dealing with stability issues. The journal staff dutifully revisited its mantra, in an obligatory and well-rehearsed way:

> Clarifying the situation, strengthening construction, enhancing overall quality and capacity; increasing political legitimacy, promoting benchmarks in struggles with the enemy; strengthening capacity in attacking crimes, preventing criminals, maintaining social order;

strengthening legal system ethos and public service mentality, achieving stern, fair and civilized law enforcement, in warmly serving the people and diligently working for a stable environment to facilitate reform and establishment of modern socialism.[248]

From the vantage point of the Editorial Department at *Public Security Studies*, 1999 was an uneventful year and 2000 promised more of the same. In the words of the Commissioner of Police from the Beijing Police Bureau, the focal point of the capitol's public security work in the year 2000 would be to "secure stability, focus on reform, strengthen foundation, promote science and technology, and improve quality."[249]

As it turned out, 2000 was very much a year devoted to strengthening the base. Public security reform, under the leadership of Jiang, entered a consolidation phase, a deepening of reform (*shenhua gaige*). For the first time, Chinese police reformers had to come to terms with sustaining police reform and development.[250] The concern with sustainable development of the economy and now policing was real and palpable. Under Deng and later Jiang, economic reform meant seizing the moment and maximizing opportunities. In the economic arena, this meant being focused on the growth of economic output[251] and personal income while disregarding the impact on the environment and on crime in the community. In policing, this meant keeping crime rates low (*yanda*) to maintain order (e.g., fighting crime was job one) and keep dissenters at bay (e.g., Tiananmen Square). Security came above all else, at whatever cost, with neither concern for wrongful convictions (e.g., as the result of coerced confessions) nor a genuine appreciation for constructive feedback (*xinfang*). Other sustainability issues at the time included concerns about the hidden costs of police reform, such as encroachment on people's rights, wrongful convictions, and falsification of statistics, all of which could contribute to the ultimate decline and denial of police legitimacy.

Hu and Wen are champions for balanced development, to be achieved via the scientific development perspective,[252] with a harmonious society as the goal. As social engineers, Hu and Wen understand that growth cannot happen, or will be slowed, if all the parts are not working together as a system. With the introduction of harmonious growth, Hu made clear his intent to pursue a balanced growth and measured reform strategy. In policing, as with other social policies, this approach is being touted as putting people first (*yi ren wei beng*). In practice, police leaders are urged to think about the implications of police policies, strategies, and tactics with regard to the common people, such as taking care of migrants and reducing capital punishment.

Reform to Police Ethics: Rejuvenating the Police Work Style

The first initiative the MPS took to win back the trust of the people in the 2000s was to improve on the police work style. The MPS did so with a renewed call for political–ideological education.[253] The MPS launched a "three items of education" campaign, which was designed to educate public security on the principles of serving the people, on the need to seek truth from the facts (*shisi jiushi*), and on the importance of consolidation of the legal system. They also initiated an ambitious "thought education" (*sixiang jiaoyu*) program to purify police thought and enhance police performance in the areas of police accountability, public relations, and professional competence. The "three items of education" campaign sought to promote professional conduct and induce greater ideological zeal among the police ranks,[254] in addition to purging public security agencies of unproductive, corrupt, and abusive police officials.[255] The campaign's ultimate aim was to reinvigorate public security agencies and reform police officials all over the nation. The "three items of education" campaign involved four stages: testing police offices to ascertain whether they were fit for duty (*testing and assessment*); examination of troubled cases to determine appropriate sanctions, including termination (*screening and evaluation*); assigning those who failed to measure up to further targeted training (*isolation and training*); and making recommendations to improve upon the work style of the system (*program assessment and reform*).

Implementation of the "Three Items of Education" Campaign

Implementation of the "three items of education" campaign began in 1999. That December, the MPS reported to the Ninth National People's Congress on the current status of PRC police construction. A three-year plan to conduct a "three items of education" campaign nationwide was proposed, and it was launched shortly after that. In February 2000, the MPS held a National Public Security Agencies Three Items of Education Experimental Site Discussion Meeting. A week later a press release announced the official launch of the "three items of education" campaign with twelve police improvement and construction measures. Following is an outline of what occurred:

- April 19–20, May 20–21, July 5–6, August 10–12, 2000—The "National Public Security Agency 'Three Items of Education' Experimental Site Work Report" was submitted and discussed at Hefei, Anhui Province; Suzhou, Anhui Province; Changchun, Jilin Province; and Weihai, Shandong Province.
- October 12, 2000—A national public security agency "three items of education" teleconference was held in Beijing.
- October 19–27, 2000—Public security agencies cooperated with the MPS Police Work Supervision Bureau to send six undercover investigation teams to investigate conditions in 13 provinces, autonomous regions, and municipalities directly under the Central Government.
- November 2000—The MPS Party Committee conducted three separate "three items of education" discussion meetings for public security agencies.
- December 25–27, 2000—The MPS discussed the main guidelines of the "three items of education" campaign at the Hubei National Public Security Bureau chiefs meeting.
- January 7–15, 2001—Six undercover teams were sent to 12 provincial public security organs (Jilin, Hebei, Anhui, Zhejiang, Hunan, Jiangsu, Guizhou, Sichuan, Fujian, Hainan, Ningxia, Qinghai).
- January 9, 2001—MPS Deputy Minister Bai Jingfu reported to the National People's Congress on the progress of the "three items of education" campaign and status of the public security construction initiative.
- February 20–21, 2001—The first batch of "three items of education" candidates graduated. The planning meeting for a second "three items of education" campaign began in Beijing.
- April–October, 2001—The MPS conducted a nationwide public security agency "three items of education" public speaking competition; 6000 police officers and their families participated.
- April–November, 2001—The MPS conducted a nationwide public security agency "three items of education" essay competition.

- June 5–6, 2001—A National Public Security Troop Management Permanent Structure Construction Meeting was held in Hebei.
- June–July, 2001—The MPS conducted a nationwide public security agency "three items of education" knowledge competition; 830,000 police, public security, and military officers participated.
- February 20–21, 2001—The second batch of "three items of education" candidates graduated. A planning meeting for a third batch was held in Jiangsu.
- June 5–6, 2001—A National Public Security Troop Management Permanent Structure Construction Meeting was held in Shantung.
- November 16–30, 2001—The MPS conducted a comprehensive assessment of the "three items of education" campaign at 100 county-level public security organs.
- February 26, 2002—A nationwide public security agency "three items of education" awards teleconference was held in Beijing. Awards were given to 100 progressive units, 200 progressive collectives, and 300 collective individuals.[256]

Three Examples

A closer look at three provinces—Henan, Qinghai, Zhejiang—reveals how the "three items of education" campaign was conducted at the grassroots level.

Henan Province[257]

The Henan PSB conducted a "three items of education" campaign from October to December of 2001. The purpose of the campaign was to educate officers on serving people wholeheartedly (*quanxin quanyi wei renmin fuwu*), adopting an attitude of seeking truth from facts (*shishi quishi de sixiang*), and carrying out strict, fair, and civilized law enforcement systematically (*yange, gongping, gaiming zhifa*). The campaign was divided into three stages. First, police were mobilized to study the nature and expectations of the campaign. Second, problems requiring attention were investigated and analyzed before a "three items of education" action plan was set up. Finally, the "three items of education" campaign was implemented to identify and correct officers who lacked political enthusiasm, had a poor service attitude, demonstrated subpar professional ability, or engaged in corruption and abuses.

Qinghai Province[258]

In 1999, Qinghai Province adopted a "three items of education" implementation plan for public security organs all across the province. To establish priorities for the "three items of education" campaign, the public security organs sent out 60,000 suggestions forms, set up 183 suggestions boxes, and established a reporting hotline to solicit public feedback. A total of 3031 surveys were returned. Based on these, 15 county-level public security organs and 147 public security units were singled out for focused treatment. This resulted in 1349 revisions or new management regulations, and 367 police officers received mandatory in-service training. The PSB paid special attention to 110 officers found to be lacking in enthusiasm or delivering poor-quality service. Local problems such as failing to respond in a timely fashion to calls for service and abusive charges of fees also received attention. As a result, the province opened 15 case files on 30 police officers for legal violations and breaches of discipline. A total of 29 officers were disciplined. Over the course of a year, the province gave in-service examinations to 1000 officers assigned to commercial, drugs, and criminal investigations; these officers achieved an 85% passing rate.

Zhejiang Province[259]

Zhejiang Province's "three items of education" program coincided with the National People's Congress appraisal of public security organs. The Zhejiang PSB took advantage of the opportunity to visit National People's Congress members at the national and provincial level to explain their "three items of education" campaign. They distributed 63,000 public comment forms, including to all county-level National People's Congress and Chinese People's Political Consultative Conference members. To subject the police to public scrutiny and feedback, the PSB launched a program for "public security assessment by thousands of families and households" (*qianjia wenhu ping gongan*). The PSB also conducted random inspections of every 1 out of every 1000 of their cases and thorough investigations of 1 out of every 100 cases, thus exposing the bureau's performance to National People's Congress scrutiny and appraisal. The PSB picked out three county public security organs and 233 public security sections for special corrective treatment (*zhengzhi*). This resulted in 2150 police being relieved of duty to engage in educational training. A total of 47 basic-level and 126 middle-level cadres were removed from their posts.

Success of the "Three Items of Education" Campaign

The "three items of education" campaign was declared a success,[260] although no overall assessment of its impact was made. Anecdotal accounts suggest that, notwithstanding the official praise, the "three items of education" campaign might have been less than successful. Many officers did not understand the concept and application of the work style reform (*zheng feng*). As espoused by the leadership, *zheng feng* involved reforming police officers' thinking pattern (from being dogmatic to having an open mind), reasoning process (thinking deductively rather than inductively), and learning style (learning from experience rather than from books). Each of the *zheng feng* dimensions was subject to different interpretations and endless debate. As a result the standard applied and outcome obtained were subject to manipulation. Many officers did not identify with the purpose of the *zheng feng* campaign. To many police managers and officers, it was more important to engage in police work (e.g., arresting criminals) than to participate in "make work" (e.g., off-site education and filling out reports for the campaign). Many officers refused to change. They held onto traditional police principles and continued policing based on their past experiences, without engaging in critical reflection and creative thinking. The "three items of education" campaign had a tendency to encourage blindly following guidelines and instructions rather than achieving the objectives of the *zheng feng* campaign; that is, many participants preferred form over substance. Many officers were still beholden to bureaucracy; although they thought that bureaucracy was a problem, it was not their concern. The high-ranking officials would take care of any problems. Finally, the culture of formalism, from selective reporting of news to under-recording of crime, was firmly entrenched and could not be easily dislodged.

Reform to Command and Control: Perfecting Control of Local Police[261]

One of the recurring management problems confronting PRC political leadership and police managers is how central and local governments should share control of the police.[262] Specifically, should the police report vertically to the central government (MPS) or should they answer horizontally to the local Party leadership? Central command ensures uniformity and efficiency, but local control achieves responsiveness and accountability. In the reform era, the debate over central vs. local command and control has become more acute. Professionalization and legalization call for central control. Democratization and community policing call for decentralize control.

Local Control Problems

One of the major concerns with PRC police is that they engaged in extralegal duties at the behest of local authorities, county government, or the Party secretary.[263] From 1999 to 2000, the Gansu Province PSB mounted an investigation into the nature and extent of police engaging in extracurricular activities in four local areas (Dingxi City, Longxi County, Jinchang City, Linxia Prefecture). The investigation confirmed that the practice of police engaging in extralegal activities was very prevalent:

1. The police were used to gather levies (*cu lian*), demand money owed (*yao kuan*), collect taxes (*shou shui*), and solicit donations (*wu juan*). The peasants at the village level had a poor concept of taxation and were resistant to the collection of levies or fees of any kind. More often than not, local taxes and levies far exceeded a peasant's ability to pay.[264] The local tax/commerce departments and county/village cadres enlisted the police to collect overdue taxes, especially at the end of the year.[265]
2. The police were used to enforce the state birth-control policy and implement Party birth-control directives. Beginning in 1997 and for the next 3 years, the Longxi County PSB was asked to deploy 93 officers to participate in birth-control enforcement actions. In Linxia, a county-level PSB pledged to enforce birth-control rules in 17 villages, and the PSB chief was fined 400 yuan for failure to achieve enforcement goals. In 1996, the Wudu County PSB instructed the Sancong police post chief and another police officer to enforce birth-control rules. The police were instructed to beat two offenders and parade them on top of a vehicle. One of them died. The responsible officials were punished.[266]
3. The police were used to enforce reconstruction in towns and villages. In Longxi County, the PSB chief was instructed to remove residents from a house that was to be demolished to make way for reconstruction. The residents were not compensated or given a new home by the government. In 1995, a county removal and reconstruction operation was stopped by hundreds of agitated people. The police were called, and a public security official (*jiaodao yuan*) was pushed into the river.[267]
4. The police were used to implement or enforce agriculture technology enhancement projects. Such projects sometimes were conducted to make the local leadership look good. At other times, the projects were required for local development and approved by the peasants. The police were instructed to enforce Party policies or government directives, even in the face of objections by the local citizens; for example, in 1997, when a villager was not able to implement agricultural enhancement projects, the police illegally handcuffed him.[268]
5. The police were used to resolve commercial disputes; they were often used to collect contractual debts and business delinquencies, in addition to settling commercial disputes.[269]

There are many reasons why police officers engage in extralegal activities:[270]

1. Public security officials, particularly at the rural, village, and township level, are ignorant as to the social role, professional responsibility, and legal authority of the police. They are overly concerned with coordinating police work at their level at the expense of following central policy directives.[271]
2. Local public security officials fail to follow existing laws and regulations. Local PSB officers participate in extralegal assignments because local Party leaders control their appointment, employment, or promotion. They are afraid of ruining their relationship with local village and township leaders, thereby making their work more difficult. They also worry about being held responsible for not supporting extralegal assignments.[272]
3. Systematic preventive measures guarding against abuses of authority are lacking.[273]
4. Public security suffers from inadequate financing. According to historical data, local counties and townships are only able to provide partial funding (about 1/5 to 3/5) of police expenditures. In many cases, public security officials are required to support themselves through fines. Failure to do so might result in a drastic reduction in police operations or cuts in staff salaries. In some cases, the county government might pay only for salaries, not daily expenses (e.g., rent, phone, utilities). In such cases, the local police must follow the directions and instructions of the local village or township officials or risk having their offices closed or utilities turned off.[274]

Remedies to police extralegal activities include improving the education of police officers so they respect the laws and protect the rights of the people; this is particularly applicable to Party leadership at the local village and township level who tend to use the police for illegal purposes. Another approach is to establish meaningful checks and balances to forestall the illegal deployment of police and the abusive use of police authority for illegal or inappropriate purposes; an example would be institutionalizing a formal and mandatory application and approval process before police are deployed. Local Party leadership should be held strictly accountable for unauthorized or illegal deployment.[275] Finally, and most importantly, the funding and command structure of the police must be modified. Public security should be adequately funded such that local PSBs do not need to resort to the illegal collection of fines or otherwise earn the support of local officials by doing their bidding. Local police should be commanded and controlled by the county and township Party and government, one level up the chain of command.[276]

Central vs. Local Control of Police

The problem of central (professional) vs. local (political) control of the police has been dealt with by police organizations worldwide.[277] In the United States, police services are organized and funded locally. In China, police command and control can best be summed up by the following slogan: *"Danwei lindao, fenji fuze, tiao kuai jiehe, yikuai waizhu."* ("Led by Party committee, responsible at each level, top line and bottom level combine, the bottom being more important.") *Tiao* means one straight line, and *kuai* means basic or root, or local government. This statement reflects dual control, where the MPS manages the police organizationally and professionally, and local Party and government officials control personnel and funding.

Before the current reform, the PRC police adopted the Russian model, where the police are commanded and controlled centrally, not locally. In theory and practice, the police are an instrument of the state. MPS ranks are filled with Party cadres who are expected to follow Party policy and are subject to Party discipline. For all intents and purposes, the Party and the MPS chain of command are one and the same.

During the reform era, as a result of the demise of central planning and the emergence of a market economy, the notions of federalism and localism resurfaced. With newfound wealth, local governments began to assert themselves to protect and advance their interests. There arose many *de facto* political centers of power, struggling for influence.[278] Thus, in day-to-day operations, public security offices are commanded by two masters—the next-level-up public security office and the same-level Party committee and government officials, the latter being the more important and dominant of the two. The local police, then, report to managers above professionally and administratively but are held accountable to local Party and government officials in financial and personnel matters,[279] such as recruitment and complaints.[280]

The coexistence of professional and administrative control from above vs. financial and personnel control from below led to predictable confusion regarding jurisdictions and conflicts of interest that resulted in disputes of authority and responsibility, lapses in performance, and avoidance of accountability. One way to diffuse the tension was to decentralize personnel management but still maintain control by leadership cadres:

> Three pairs of parallel developments are highlighted here. The first pair is the decentralization of personnel management of ordinary cadres and the delegation of evaluation and monitoring functions to the community. This is in combination with the strengthening of Party organization control over its leading cadres. The second concerns the replacement of old mandatory targets with guidance targets. How cadres implement guidance targets is linked to the bonuses they receive. At the same time, the goal is to ensure that local leaders carry out its priorities and policies, and the implementation of priority targets is linked to promotion and demotion decisions. The final pair is the increasing autonomy given to localities generally but higher levels also increase their control over selected counties. In a way, this is similar to the approach used to control strategically important leaders.[281]

A survey of the Gan Shi Kiu police post and senior police officers from the Jinan PSB showed that the officers favored central/professional/administration control over local/political/economic control (see Tables 5.5 and 5.6), despite the fact that they were financed predominantly by the local government (73.7% local vs. 1.6% central). This finding indicates that police in China prefer to act professionally without undue political and economic influence from the local government. The officers gave the following reasons for their displeasure over local or dual management: (1) central administration facilitates command and control; (2) central administration helps remove local political and economic influences from professional law enforcement; (3) central administration prevents corruption and promotes objective and fair disposition of cases; and (4) central administration improves management skills, professional development, and promotional process of officers.

The MPS is moving toward professional policing, which requires more centralized administration to improve the accountability and integration of functions to promote efficiency and effectiveness. Article 43 of the PRC Police Law supports this reform direction: "The people's police organ at a higher level shall exercise supervision over law enforcement of the police organs at the lower levels."

TABLE 5.5   Survey of Jinan Police Officers' Views on Top-Down Leadership vs. Bottom-Up Organization

Survey Items	Beat Officers	Superior Officers
Change to central uniform control	58 (78.4%)	62 (76.5%)
Maintain double leadership	14 (18.9%)	16 (19.8%)
Change to local government control	0	2 (2.5%)
Other	2 (2.7%)	1 (1.2%)
Total	74 (100%)	81 (100%)

The central vs. local relationship is further spelled out in Article 3 of the "Regulations on the Management and Organization of Public Security Organs": "The MPS under the guidance of the State Council, controls all public security work in the nation. It is the leading organ for all public security work in the nation. Public security organs under local people's governments above the county level shall be led by the people's government at that same level and are responsible for the public security work of the administrative region."[282]

Reform to Organizational Culture: Fighting Formalism and Bureacracy[283]

Another initiative taken by the MPS to win back the trust of the people was to declare war on formalism and bureaucracy, both entrenched organizational culture problems. Ever since the founding of the PRC, formalism and bureaucracy together with corruption of powers and abuse of office have been considered cardinal sins by the CPC.[284] During yet another round of PRC government reform, Premier Zhu Rongji again[285] identified formalism and bureaucracy as the twin vices of the Party and government: "Formalism and bureaucracy run rife, and deception, extravagance, and waste are serious in some localities and with many government departments and some leading cadres."[286]

In 2007, President Hu, in his Work Report, found it necessary to remind the people that formalism and bureaucracy, while under control, were still rife in some quarters:[287]

Some primary Party organizations are weak and lax. A small number of Party cadres are not honest and upright, their formalism and bureaucracy are quite conspicuous, and extravagance, waste, corruption, and other undesirable behaviors are still serious problems with them. We must pay close attention to these problems and continue our efforts to solve them.[287]

TABLE 5.6   Source of Funding for Gan Shi Kiu Police Post

Source of Income	Amount	Percentage (%)
Local	450,000 yuan[a]	73.77
Ministry of Public Security	10,000 yuan[b]	1.64
Self-raised	150,000 yuan[c]	24.59
Total	610,000 yuan	100.00

[a] Local tax, mainly for salaries.

[b] Public security internal office administrative expenditures.

[c] From joint security fees, penalties, temporary resident permits, and parking fees.

Formalism Defined

Formalism is conducting government business by the book, dogmatically, unreflectively, and inflexibly. In so doing, *form* is made to stand for *substance* (i.e., looking good rather than doing well) and *process* is equated with *outcome* (e.g., following the letter, not the spirit, of the law). Formalism involves not only doing things by the book, but also "cooking the books" to make one look better.[288] A *Xinhua* commentary observed in April of 2000:

> For a long time, some localities have favored formalism, that is, cooking official accounts and exaggerating their working performances....These officials often hope that through boasting and exaggerating their performances they can impress their superiors and thereby gain promotion to higher positions. Formalism has gravely undermined the relationship between the Party and the people, and between the government and the masses, sullying the image of the Party and the government.[289]

Bureaucracy Defined

Bureaucracy is conducting people's business arrogantly and officiously (i.e., not being responsive to and being out of touch with the people). The police, instead of serving the interests of the people, are serving their own organizational interests. In the end, bureaucracy alienates the people.

Seek Truth from Facts

Both formalism and bureaucracy run afoul of the CPC political and scientific principle of "seeking truth from facts" (*shishi jiushi*). According to CPC doctrine, formalism and bureaucracy undermine the truth, allowing the subjective to override the objective, ideology to supersede reality, a closed mind to rule over an open mind, blind faith to overshadow dialectical materialism, and conservatism taking precedence over change.[290] "Seeking truth from reality" can be defined as follows:

> Seeking truth from facts is the core of the spirit of scientific innovation. Innovation means a breakthrough to old thinking and old concepts. Innovation requires readjusting, improving and reforming the system, mechanisms and related ideologies and concepts inconsistent with the objective reality, so that they can conform to the objective reality. To uphold the principle of seeking truth from facts, it is necessary to engage in innovation; to adhere to innovation, it is necessary to persist in seeking truth from facts. Innovation is essentially identical with the principle of seeking truth from facts.[291]

In layman's terms, "seeking truth from facts" means getting back to the basics—being close to the people and attending to reality. The solution is to "emancipate the mind":

> In fact, the current debate about whether practice is the sole criterion for testing truth is also a debate about whether people's minds need to be emancipated....When...everything has to be done by the book, when thinking turns rigid and blind faith is the fashion, it is impossible for a party or a nation to make progress....Seeking truth from facts is the basis of the proletarian world outlook as well as the ideological basis of Marxism.[292]

The CPC implemented a number of measures in the 2000s to attack the problems of formalism and bureaucracy with the hope of reconnecting with the people and reestablishing the legitimacy of the police.

Breach the Gap between the Police and the Public

Formalism and bureaucracy isolate the police from the people and alienate the people they serve. The isolation is a result of public security's perceived cold attitude toward the people, and the alienation is demonstrated by the public not seeking help from the police.[293] The estrangement between the police and the people is deemed ideologically objectionable (in violation of the mass line principle) and practically dysfunctional (being deprived of citizen help and support). Formalism and bureaucracy have organizational as well as social causes. Police reform initiatives (i.e., professionalization, legalization, regularization, standardization, and bureaucratization) have put distance between the police and the public. The police are instructed to obey professional and legal rules not in line with the personal and collective wishes of the people. This is a far cry from the policy in place during the Mao era, when what the mass wanted the mass got.[294] According to Mao, the masses are clear sighted; they can tell right from wrong. Police reform has not met the public's expectations for change (e.g., the police being conscious of legal and human rights). More significantly, the more the police open up to the people, the less dissatisfied the people have become. To reduce the distance between the police and the people, the MPS has returned to their Lei Feng roots. Police are asked to be at one with the people, living, listening, identifying, and serving the people—in essence, making the people their political masters, friends, and crime fighting partners.

The police should live, eat, and work with the people. The MPS has asked the police to return to the basics and to be one with the people (*dacheng yipian*),[295] which requires identifying with the people and looking at issues from their perspectives.[296] In 2002, Nanping, Fujian Province, promulgated an implementation plan for Nanping public security organs to develop activities in recognition of the "change work style" year (*Nanping shi gongan jiguan gaizhan "gaibian zuofeng nian" huodong shishi fangan*). The police (151 police posts) were required to engage the public in three ways (*san tong*[297]): living with the people (*tongzhu*), eating with the people (*tongqi*), and working with the people (*tong laodong*).[298] The *san tong* initiative was designed to make the police a part of the community capable of understanding local problems and sharing people's concerns, both personally and emotionally. Particularly, the police were instructed to reach out to those who were deprived and marginalized (*ruoshi qunti*). The *san tong* initiative worked at two levels: (1) the police got to know the people in the community, and (2) they established close bonds with the local community and personalities:

> The municipality regulations require that during the period of examining and experiencing people's conditions, the police should eat, live, and work alongside the people; [this allows] full comprehension of local social order conditions, understanding the public's dissatisfaction with public security, assisting problems that cannot be solved by the local people, finishing an investigation report that focuses on social security and rural village economic development.[299]

The *san tong* initiative was effective in changing the attitudes of the police and the behavior of the people. In the past, rural people had very little formal contact and few informal associations with the police. The only time they came into contact with the police was if they were victims, offenders, or witnesses. Because such encounters are usually unpleasant, the people were left with a negative opinion of the police. The *san tong* campaign changed the social dynamics between the police and the public and allowed the parties to get to know each other. The people learned about the roles, functions, and availability of the police, and the police helped the people get organized and resolve some of their problems.[300]

Police business is to be open and accessible to the public.[301] The MPS launched an initiative to open police work to the public (*jingwu gongkai*[302]) as part of a program to improve government transparency. The intent was to allow people to learn about their police—who they are, what they do, how they work, why they act. The *jingwu gongkai* initiative revealed police policies, rules, and practices to the public, making police work more transparent and the police more accessible in the following areas:[303]

- *Mission and role*—The nature, characteristics, vision, mission, roles, and functions of police organs, as well as the duties and authority of police officers, must be clearly articulated.
- *Criminal jurisdiction*—The criminal jurisdictions and standards for taking and establishing cases must be established; the legal rights of suspects and professional responsibility of lawyers must be maintained.
- *Administrative process*—Administrative jurisdictions, powers, standards, and processes must be clear (e.g., household registration, business licenses).
- *Police accountability*—Police work must be opened up to public supervision, including spelling out which disciplinary rules apply to various types of police actions (e.g., use of deadly force). The public must know how to file complaints against police misconduct and abuse of rights.
- *Police operations*—Law enforcement operations must be made public. The community should be informed, for example, about traffic enforcement campaigns and the numbers of arrests.

The *jingwu gongkai* initiative has improved police work in many ways:

1. *Jingwu gongkai* has increased transparency and the release of information into the public domain. Transparency reveals illegal and irregular police activities. The release of information allows the public to supervise the police. Both promote understanding and reduce misperceptions of police work. Transparency also prevents *renqing an* ("cases based on sympathy"), *guanxi an* ("cases based on relations"), and *yousui an* ("cases based on benefits").
2. *Jingwu gongkai* has improved police efficiency and helped with the timely processing of cases, thus reducing citizens' complaints (*xinfang*) and avoiding unnecessary case reviews (*fuyi*).
3. *Jingwu gongkai* has helped to cultivate a police sense of duty and responsibility, and thus pride. Transparency has encouraged the police to follow the rule of law.
4. *Jingwu gongkai* has helped improve the image of the police and their relationship with the people. The police are now more likely to conduct their business by following the rule of law, by the book. The citizens now understand more about how the police work and can set their expectations of the police accordingly.

The *jingwu gongkai* initiative has taken many forms:

- *Police museums*—The MPS and regional PSBs established police museums to educate the public about the history and development of the police. For example, the Beijing Constable Museum, which opened in 2001, features 7000 items tracing Chinese policing back to the Qin Dynasty (206 BC to AD 220).[304] Another example is the Kunming Police Museum.[305]
- *Police open days*—The PRC police organs have begun to organize open days for the police to see how police work. The first one was held in Guangzhou, Guangdong Province, in 2001. The second was held at the Xicheng police station in Beijing. Police open days usually include a display of crime campaign exhibits, police vehicles and equipment, and athletic and marksmanship demonstrations. According to Qiang Wei, director of the Beijing Municipal Public Security Bureau at the time, the major purpose of open days is to enhance the public's understanding of police work, such as how criminal investigations are conducted.[306]
- *MPS website*—A cost-effective way to communicate with the public is on the Internet. The MPS launched its website in 2001. The MPS website serves two specific purposes: transparency and accountability. The MPS uses the website to help the public understand the roles, functions, structure, and processes of the police (e.g., jurisdictions, law enforcement policies, public assistance announcements). It was hoped that making more information available would allow citizens to better monitor police activities. Minister of Public Security Jia Chun-wang specifically instructed the police to be prompt and thorough in their handling of public inquiries and citizen complaints.[307] In 2010, the Beijing PSB initiated various blogs and podcasts to better communicate with the public. Fu Zhenghua, head of the PSB, explained that, "With the aid of modern technology, we hope to communicate with residents and vulnerable groups with frankness and sincerity, as well as promote social justice."[308]

Despite these efforts, relationships between the police and the public have not improved greatly. The public still complains about disrespectful, detached, aloof, unresponsive, irresponsible, abusive, and unaccountable police. Although the scope and magnitude of citizens' concerns about the police have never been comprehensively studied or openly reported,[309] their existence is an open secret. Without receiving satisfactory solutions (or in anticipation thereof), citizens have begun to take matters into their own hands, from insulting, assaulting, or obstructing police in the line of duty to taking their grievances (*xinfang*; "letters and calls" petitions) to Beijing and organizing mass incidents in the street. In such cases, instead of seeking to address the people's concerns, the local police have attempted to cover up the problem (e.g., jailing petitioners), appease the complainants (e.g., by bribing them), or suppress their voices (e.g., arresting reporters). All such measures are not commensurate with the MPS's efforts to build a close, warm, and trusting bond between the police and the people. The impression from the people's perspective is that the police are saying one thing ("we love the people") and doing another (controlling the people with a heavy hand).[310]

Funding Reform: A Budget System for Police

Police, especially at the local level and in less developed areas, are inadequately funded, in some cases not at all. Basically, there is no amount budgeted for police operations; for example, in the 1970s and 1980s, police funding accounted for only 2.8% of the gross domestic product (GDP) in China, as compared to 9% in other developing countries. In China, the police are funded primarily by local governments. The unstable and local nature of police funding has affected police performance in measurable ways; for example, it has contributed to localism and corruption in law enforcement.[311] The police endure poor living and working conditions, and some public security organs have to work with outdated, old, and broken equipment. Many police organs have to work without budgeted salaries or administrative and operational funds. They have to find money on their own initiative, such as through the use of fines.[312]

In the 1990s, a National People's Congress representative, a specially appointed inspector (*jiangdu yuan*), called for rationalizing police funding by making it a guaranteed budget item. To remedy the situation, he proposed a resolution to adequately provide for the operational expenditures of public security organs (*gongan jiguan de jingfei ying yu qieshi baozhang*), which was endorsed by other NPC members.[313] In 2002, Premier Zhu Rongji openly acknowledged the existence of persistent police problems:

> Local governments in those places that owe salaries to cadres, procurators, judicial and public security officers and teachers must take effective measures to solve this problem as soon as possible. Local financial departments should first of all ensure that wages and salaries are paid. Wages and salaries that are in arrears must be paid as soon as possible. We need to ensure that wages and salaries are paid on time and in full even if new construction projects have to be cancelled and things that are not urgent have to be given up or reduced in scale. On the basis of strict determination of the number of personnel, the central financial authorities will subsidize these outlays through transfer payments to those provinces, autonomous regions and municipalities directly under the Central Government that cannot meet their obligations. Provincial financial departments will also subsidize those cities and counties in financial straits through transfer payments.[314]

Specifically, Zhu called for setting up an institutionalized mechanism to guarantee funds to the police:

> Under the principle of combining action with prevention while putting prevention first, we must implement measures for the all-round improvement of social order, and we must actively establish a prevention and control system for public security and a mechanism that guarantees that funds are available for operations of procuratorial, judicial, and public security organs.[315]

At the Fifth Session of the Ninth National Committee of the Chinese People's Political Consultative Conference (CPPCC), held in 2002, a CPPCC member and CPCC Deputy Party Chairman made several observations about the problem of police funding. Police organs suffered from a significant lack of operational funds. Delays in and nonpayment of staff salaries, benefits, and medical expenses were chronic. In Shanxi Province, at the end of 2001, police officers at 29 of the 119 police organs at the county, municipal, and local level were not being paid on time. A total of 1.35 million yuan was owed to 5032 officers. In 2002, 50 of the police organs at the county level did not budget any money for administrative and operational expenditures, only staff costs. The police officers had to pay for their own medical expenses to the tune of 1.688 million yuan. Criminal investigations, too, were lacking in funding. The police did not even have money for telephones or cars. Sometimes police officers had to use their own money, and police organs had to borrow money to investigate cases. The police did not have the money necessary to purchase basic police tools, such as uniforms and body armor. The police had to work out of rented or borrowed premises; some even worked and lived in broken-down, decrepit houses.

The lack of police funding was attributed to poor local government, as the police are required to come up with some or all of their administrative and operational funds. This has led to punishment by quota and abuse of power for organizational gain. An NPC member observed that, in some places, over 50% of the police had to come up with their own means of living, which has led to corruption and excessive punishment. The Yunnan Province PSB chief, himself a NPC member, suggested several ways to tackle the police funding shortfall:

1. An itemized public security annual budget must be established to provide for staff salaries and benefits, administrative and operational expenditures, and equipment and capital costs.
2. A two-tiered funding system should be established for the central government and provincial government. The central government should be responsible for capital, facility, and equipment costs. The provincial government should be responsible for staff, administration, and operational expenditures.
3. Funding for the western and interior regions, due to a lack of economic development and financial resources, should be the sole responsibility of the central government.
4. The accounting of funds from punishment accounts and for expenditure accounts should be separated. Money from punishment accounts should be collected and remitted to the central or provincial government for disposition. Funds from punishment accounts should not be mixed with funds for expenditure.

Policing in China suffers from inadequate funding and lack of an established budget. The former exposes the police to local politics; the latter invites corruption. Both detract from professional policing in accordance with the rule of law.

Funding Debate[316]

Ever since establishment of the PRC, the funding of public security administration and operations has been a recurring problem that escapes satisfactory treatment. As emphasized earlier, the debate is over who should pay for public security services: central government or local government. From 1949 to 1954, public security expenditures were centrally budgeted. The Central Military Commission of the Ministry of Public Security (*Zhongyang Junwei Gonganbu*) was first established in 1949. Soon after, the Central Military Commission issued a preliminary plan for how to handle the Central Military Commission financial system (*Zhongyang Junwei Gonganbu caizheng zhidu zhangwu fanwei chubu fangan*). Beginning that September, all public security expenditures were provided by the Financial Office of Northern China (*Huabei Caizhengbu*). At that time, money for public security came out of the national defense budget.[317] Within a year, a uniform public security system was formally established, and the funding of public security work became a major issue for the Central Military Commission as well as the Central Treasury (*Zhongyang Caizhengbu*).

In 1951, the Central Military Commission and Central Treasury issued "Regulations regarding Limits of and a System for Special Public Security Expenditures" ("*Guanyu Gongan tefei kaizhi fanwei ji guanli zhidu de guiding*").[318] These regulations provided that public security expenditures were to be centrally budgeted by the MPS but distributed locally at the different levels. Later the budget for public security was required to be approved by the finance bureaus of local administrative districts. At the very beginning, though, the Minister of Public Security made it clear that the Central Treasury could not provide all necessary local funding. Local public security expenditures would have to be provided for locally, with a budget submitted to central approval.

From 1955 to 1958, the nation's expenditures for public security organs were still operating under the Public Security Party Committee. In 1953, in order to maintain smooth operations and operational secrecy, the Public Security Party Committee proposed that public security be funded by means of military budget; however, due to administrative difficulties at that time, the Public Security Party Committee agreed to have public security business expenditure paid locally, with budget approval conducted centrally.[320]

Starting in January of 1954, the State Council instructed that all administrative organ fees must be budgeted and paid for by the State Council's Business Bureau. The MPS found this funding process inappropriate and took over the financing of public security operations with funding from the State Council. The MPS was responsible for the entire funding process, from budgeting to dispensation. The Central Military Commission was required to report to the Central Ministry of Finance once a year. In order to institutionalize this arrangement, on January 1, 1955, the Public Security Party Committee, the Central Military Commission, and the Central Ministry of Finance jointly issued temporary regulations putting into place a system and limits for public security special expenditures (*Gongan tefei kaizhi fanwei ji zhidu zhanxing guiding*).[321]

No sooner had this centralized funding and budget system been established than it was discovered that local governments had used centrally budgeted public security funds to conduct their own business. This directly affected local public security work and operations. In 1956, the MPS proposed that public security expenditures again should be paid locally. There were three reasons for this new funding arrangement. First, local governments had a more intimate knowledge of local conditions and needs, thus they were in the best position to develop a realistic budget that provided for pressing problems and emerging needs. Second, due to their knowledge, the governments were in the best position to separate *ad hoc* special-expenditure items from routine administrative fees. Third, the local finance offices were more effective at funds distribution, accounting, and auditing.[322]

In 1958, after much consultation, the MPS and Ministry of Finance promulgated the following notice: "Joint Notice regarding Delegating Public Security Business Expenditures to the Management of the Provinces and Municipalities." The notice provided that, effective in 1959, the financial management of public security expenditures would be delegated to the provinces, autonomous regions, and municipalities directly under the central government. How public security funding was budgeted, managed, and audited would be the sole responsibility of the public security organs and local finance departments, which had to report to Party committees for approval and supervision. During the Cultural Revolution (1966 to 1976), the public security funding system was destroyed. Specifically, on November 11, 1966, the MPS and Ministry of Finance jointly issued a notice instructing that local areas must decide how to fund public security, to be approved by provincial and municipal Party committees.[323]

China economic reform began at the end of 1970s. The reform called into question once again how to fund police expenditures. Without guaranteed funding, public security suffered from low morale, dated equipment, and inadequately funded operations. In 1981, as a result of public security reform, special police budgetary items began to make their way back into the nation's central budget; for example, in 1980 the People's Border Police Force was established and funded by the central administrative financial system. This was followed in 1982 by the People's Armed Police and the Guard Police.[324]

The MPS routinely submitted special consultation reports to the Ministry of Finance. The Ministry of Finance studied these reports and accepted, in principle, their findings and recommendations. The MPS and Ministry of Finance agreed in principle that, once the nation's economic conditions improved, a major portion of the public security budget would be guaranteed and managed by central authority. This was never put into effect, however. In the meantime, certain well-off provinces took the initiative to budget for their own public security needs.

In 1988, the Ministry of Finance issued the following opinion: "Certain Opinions regarding Political–Legal Organs Not Being Allowed to Engage in Commercial Activities and Implementation of a Guarantee of Operation Funds after the Two Lines of Income and Expenditure Are Taken into Account" ("*Guanyu zhengfa jiguan buzai congshi shangye huodong he shixing shouzhi liangxian guanli hou caizheng jingfei baozhang de rugang yijian*"). This notice affirmed the role of provinces in the management of public security operational funds, especially as it outlawed commercial activities by the police. In 1996, the MPS and Ministry of Finance worked together to establish a framework for centralized control and management of public security funding and expenditures. As a result, two laws were passed to guarantee public security funding.[325]

In 1994, Article 2 of the Budget Law[326] established the basic funding principle of budgeting in China: "The State shall establish budgets at each level of the government, namely, at five levels: the Central Government; the provinces, autonomous regions, and municipalities directly under the Central Government; the cities divided into districts and autonomous prefectures; the counties, autonomous counties, cities not divided into districts, and municipal districts; the townships, nationality townships, and towns." Article 37 of the People's Police Law[327] further provided that, "The State must ensure the supply of funds needed by the people's police. The funds shall be incorporated respectively into the central and local financial budgets according to the principles of division of labor."

Increasingly, the PRC has been moving away from a purely central taxation and expenditure model. It is moving toward a rational income and expenditure system. Under such a system, financial obligations rest on the different levels of government authority and are contingent on the varying financial capacities and functional needs. Under this new thinking, the central government would be responsible for national security and provincial governments would be responsible for criminal justice, including policing. Local public security budgets would be supplemented by the central government on an as-needed basis.[328]

Currently, the public security funding and budgeting process is still in limbo. As a result, police operations at the local level, especially in poorer parts of the country or in less developed provinces, are severely underfunded. The police must take matters into their own hands by engaging in corruption or collection of illegal fees.

Reform to Operations: Making Police More Effective in Fighting Crime

Police reform in China dates back to 1979, when Chinese leadership took radical measures to reform and modernize the police organization and institution. Policing in China before the reform was founded on passive (*dongtai*) administrative control, as exemplified by the household registration system (*hukou guanli zhidu*). The system, following the long-established *baojia* system established by Wang Anshi of the Song Dynasty (960–1279), required the registration of every resident in a city or rural area. The *hukou* registration, monitoring, and control system was established to regulate internal migration of people, mainly from rural areas to the cities. It was backed up by two administrative measures: (1) the commune system, which bound peasants to the land in rural areas,[329] and (2) workplace organizations (*danwei*), which tied workers to their workplace in urban areas.[330]

Economic reform changed China. The household registration system, which was built upon a closed society and a land-based agricultural community, is not well suited to serving an open society and market economy with a global reach. Increasingly, the household registration system has failed as a measure of mutual surveillance and administrative control. People are moving in record numbers; as a result, population tracking has become impractical,[331] social bonding is reduced, the communal spirit is marginalized, customary moral sentiments are diluted, and collective support is disappearing.[332] Crime rates have skyrocketed. The Chinese government has changed its social control and crime fighting strategy from being passive (*jingtai*) to active (*dongati*). The watershed event was the "Strike Hard" campaign from 1983 to 1987,[333] which was followed later by the rapid-response system and emergency call system.

Foot Patrols

The first police patrol officers can be traced back to the Qin dynasty (221–207 BC).[334] During that time, *ting*, a kind of local security organ, was established to prevent crime. *Ting* served two purposes: (1) crime prevention through patrol, and (2) criminal detection through surveillance. While on patrol, a *ting* official was armed with a stick to subdue criminals and a rope to restrain them. During the Sung dynasty, the emperor established patrol inspectors (*xun jian guan*) to lead soldiers on patrol. In 1029, Sung Renzhong decreed that patrol officials could not stay in any town for more than 2 to 3 days, and they were required to record and report their arrival and departure.

Modern policing was introduced to China in 1898 with the establishment of *Hunan Baowei Ju*,[335] under the leadership of Huang Zunxian (1848–1905).[336] As the Qing envoy to Japan (1877–1881),[337] Huang had the opportunity to observe the Japanese police up close, including how they were organized and deployed. As stated in the Hunan Public Security Office Charter (*Hunan Baowei Ju Zhangcheng*), the role of the police was to "remove public harm, protect public welfare, prosecute offences, to detect crime" ("*qu min hai, wei min sheng, jin fei wei, suo fan zui*"). These functions were to be performed by patrol officers—inspectors, or *xuncha yuan* (*xun* means "to patrol," *cha* means "to investigate")—who patrolled day and night. Patrol officers were organized in six patrol shifts of 4 hours each, with 12 noon to 4 p.m. being the first shift. While on patrol, the officers removed public dangers, prevented street crimes, and arrested offenders (e.g., prostitutes, gamblers).[338]

In 1898, Li Nengshi provided the first assessment of police patrols in his book, *Qingji Hunan de weixin yundong* (*Reform Movement in Hunan during Qing Time*). Li observed that, "Both inside and outside the city there were people on patrol day and night. Unsavory characters are no longer in sight. The city was peaceful. Commercial people all feel safe."

In 1902, Governor Yuan Shikai set up the first patrol office in Tianjin and promulgated regulations regarding the Tianjin South Sector Patrol Headquarters (*Tianjin nanduian xunjing zhongju xianxing zhangching*). By 1905, foot patrols had become a fixture in cities and towns.[339]

In 1984, at the MPS National Public Security Basic Level Meeting (*Quanguo gongan jiceng huiyi*), it was decided to put more police in the street. In 1988, the MPS issued an "Opinion on Certain Issues regarding the Reform of City Public Security Post Work" ("*Guanyu gaige chengshi gongan paichusuo gongzuo rugan wenti yijian*"), which formally adopted the concept of active (*dongti*) public security work. This strategy was more compatible with policing in an urban environment and dealing with a mobile workforce. A few cities and localities were picked as test cases (*shidian*).[340]

Foot patrols gained legal status when regulations regarding city people's police patrols (*Chengshi renmin jingcha xunluo guiding*) were promulgated. These regulations charged police patrols with the following responsibilities:[341]

- Maintain public order and security within the police district.
- Prevent and deter conduct in violation of public order administration.
- Prevent and deter criminal acts.
- Maintain order and direct people during emergency public order incidents.
- Deal with illegal assemblies, processions, and demonstrations.
- Deal with natural disasters, maintain order, and preserve property.
- Direct traffic.
- Prevent obstructions to official duties.
- Receive police reports.
- Mediate and prevent public conflicts and disturbances.
- Subdue drunk or mentally ill people.
- Give people directions and assist with injuries, sickness, crises, or difficulties confronting the handicapped, old, or young.
- Take care of lost and found property.
- Educate residents on crime prevention and risk reduction.
- Inspect and improve police appearance.
- Enforce the law.

In 1994, the Shanghai PSB promulgated "Regulations regarding the Shanghai Public Security Bureau Patrol Police Work and Duty Inspection and Assessment" ("*Shanghai shi gongan ju xunjing qinwu jiancha kaohe banfa*"), referred to here as the Patrol Regulations, to establish a police patrol performance system.[342] Article 1 states that the Patrol Regulations were established to perfect the patrol system with regard to maintaining the police image and improving patrol efficacy. The Patrol Regulations consist of five chapters: Preamble (Articles 1 to 2); Inspection (*Jiancha*) (Articles 3 to 9); Assessment (*Kaohe*) (Articles 10 to 24); Standards for Demerits (*Kou fen biaozhun*) (Articles 15 to 26); and Supplemental Regulations (Articles 27 to 28).

The Inspection chapter of the Police Regulations provides for daily patrols and monthly inspections. Inspections can be conducted openly or in secret. They can be universal or random, general or focused. Inspection reports regarding status, commendations, or discipline must be filed in writing. The Assessment chapter provides for a grading system with points awarded in the areas of police discipline (30 points), duty system (30 points), and patrol responsibility (40 points). The Standards for Demerits chapter makes provisions for deducting points for improper uniforms, missing equipment, unprofessional conduct, violating the duty system and report process, violating the rest and dinner system, violating the duty station rules, violating methods of patrol, failure to carry out patrol duty, failure to enforce the law, and lack of patrol discipline.

Of interest to our investigation into police patrols are Articles 23, 24, and 25. Article 23 informs us that police patrols are conducted on designated beats with fixed police posts. Patrols are conducted in pairs and on foot, not bicycle. Patrols should move along without staying too long in one place (more than 10 minutes) when making rounds. Article 24 penalizes patrol officers for failure to attend to or inadequately dealing with public disorder and mass incidents, natural disasters, labor strikes, traffic accidents, road congestion, 110 calls, conflicts and disturbances, mentally ill or drunk people, and people who are sick, old, young, or needy. Article 25 penalizes patrol officers for failure to take actions against public obstructions, nuisances, or disorder, including loiterers and beggars, bicycles on a pedestrian way, businesses extending into public areas, businesses selling in public places, things being stored in a public place, signs and lights in public not being properly secured, hanging clothes to dry in public, keeping areas in front of residences and shops clean, and construction sites not being secured.

By 1991, at the 18th National Public Security Conference, the value of foot patrols was formally acknowledged. Two systems of patrolling competed for dominance: the *Tianjin model* and the *Shanghai model*. With the Tianjin model, police patrols are an integral part of the police organization. There is no special patrol command. Police patrol is a function to be staffed by police post personnel, municipal PSB emergency/riot police, and the Chinese People's Armed Police Force. The municipal PSB is in charge of patrolling the municipality as a whole. The police district organizes patrols through the local police substations and posts. The 110 police communication center is responsible for coordinating police deployment. To properly staff local police station patrol beats, the Tianjin PSB has augmented the police post in three ways: (1) new replacements for retired police are sent to the local post, (2) new graduates from police colleges are deployed to local stations, and (3) the workload of police posts has been reduced.[343]

The Shanghai PSB[344] has claimed the following benefits of its foot patrols:

- Foot patrols can better serve the people through faster response times and proactive problem solving.
- Foot patrols facilitate exchanges and improve communication between the police and citizens. According to a survey that asked the public how they would like to improve relationships between the public and the police,[345] 65% wanted faster responses, 33% wanted a greater police presence, and 2% wanted to see police at the station.[346]
- Foot patrols reduce the fear of crime and enhance the feeling of security.
- Foot patrols prevent, suppress, and detect crime.

- Foot patrols increase police knowledge of local conditions, making them more effective in maintaining order and controlling crime; for example, a mobile population leads to the demise of traditional neighborhoods. The survey referred to above showed that only 22% of the community had basic knowledge and information about their community. Foot patrol officers can help keep a close watch over who is coming and going and what is happening.[347]

Between 1993 and 1994, Shanghai patrols reported handling 4.44 million cases, including 40,000 public order cases, 3.38 million traffic cases, 739,000 public nuisance cases, and 280,000 commercial cases. During this period, the police arrested 22,000 offenders and educated or punished 4.43 million people with fines amounting to 34.6 millions yuan. This led to a decline in *laojiao* ("reform by labor") cases of 18% and public order cases by 50%.[348]

Urban Police Patrol

In 2001, Shanghai PSB Huang Pu Sub-bureau Chief Zhang Jiang proposed a more dynamic way of organizing and controlling Shanghai patrol services.[349] Zhang's proposal encompassed demonstrated needs and justifications,[350] theoretical support,[351] and plans and assessment.[352] Zhang pointed to fundamental changes brought about by a more open economy as justification for his proposal. The free movement of people, materials, technology, and information had caused fundamental changes in the number and nature of the crimes being committed. The traditional static crime control model (i.e., household registration and community surveillance) no longer sufficed nor was it effective. With the introduction of the 110 emergency call system, a more dynamic model of police mobilization and crime control emerged.[353] The urbanization and modernization of Shanghai as an international city required a drastic change in policing strategy, from stationary administration regulations to dynamic control, from surveillance of the masses to organized mobile patrol.[354] In a big city, relationships among people and the police are weakened, which can create a sense of isolation, fear, and helplessness in the face of crime and problems. The establishment of a 24/7 patrol system can help alleviate people's fear of crime by expanding the police presence and providing timely services.[355] With regard to theoretical support, Zhang suggested that by analyzing the cause of crime (offenders, opportunities, guardianship) a case could be made for improving control through the systematic and focused patrol of vulnerable targets (hot spots) and at-risk people. Using rational choice theory and adopting economic analyses, the police as a resource can be better deployed as mobile patrols to reduce incentives to commit crime. Also, the establishment of 110 call centers in Shanghai in 1993 further supported police patrols in the street. Finally, according to modern management and organizational theory, police activities must be planned, organized, coordinated, supervised, and evaluated in order to achieve planned organizational goals and operational objectives. Police patrols should be organized to prevent crime, deter criminals, and secure public safety through centralized deployment and community supervision.[356]

Police Patrols and ID Checks[357]

In 2001, two Hunan officers, Tang Taxuan and Peng Jinsong, discussed the need for,[358] status of,[359] and improvements in[360] police patrol street ID checks and interrogations. Tang and Peng observed that random ID checks and interrogations during street patrols (vehicle or on foot) were necessary to deter crime and to discover criminals on the run in a systematic, proactive, and cost-effective way. They also serve as effective population management tools to rein in mobile populations and transients who lack identification, are unregistered, and have no job (*san wu*). They are difficult to track, prone to crime, and impossible to catch.[361] Chang Sha started a street patrol in 1995 in conjunction with a 110 call center. At that time, it did not have a police patrol team dedicated to checking IDs. In 2000, the police patrol uncovered 101 crimes, cleared 404 crimes, arrested 98 fugitives, confiscated 25 guns, and saved 96 lives.[362] ID checks and interrogations, however, have been used only on a case-by-case basis to check the IDs of suspicious persons, not to systematically investigate crime or gather evidence, and they have not moved beyond the street level and so provide few clues for further follow-up investigation.

110 Call System

The 110 call system has a long and illustrious history in China. In the early 1950s, the PSB offices in urban cities all had phone lines dedicated to reporting enemy sightings, from KMT spies to counterrevolutionary landlords to religious cult members. The system at that time was called 110 *feijing* ("110 banditry police line"). Later, from the 1960s to 1970s, the country turned its attention from fighting class enemies to promoting social order. The major social problem at that time was thefts, thus the 110 *feijing* system was changed to 110 *dao jing* ("110 thief police line"). In the 1980s, the nation started the *yanda* or "Strike Hard" campaign against criminals of all kinds, and the 110 call system was then dedicated to serving the people who had emergencies. In 1984, the forward-thinking Guangzhou PSB implemented a command and coordinated communication system. The first national 110 police emergency service system came into service in 1986. In June of 1987, after successful experimentation with the 110 system, the MPS issued a notice regarding the establishment of 110 police service stations in PSBs in all large and medium cities (*Guanyu zai dai zhong chengshi gonganju pupian jianli 110 baojing fuwu ta de tongzhi*). Since then, 110 call systems have spread across China.[363]

The service ideals of the 110 call system can be captured in four phrases: (1) *youjing biejie* ("receive all police reports"), (2) *younan bie ban* ("help with all difficulties"), (3) *youzai bie jiu* ("rescue from crisis in every instance"), and (4) *youqiu beiying* ("respond to all calls for assistance").[364] The service ideals of the 110 call system were first proposed in 1990 by a public security patrol team leader, Guo Shaochang. Instead of its being used as an emergency phone for reporting crime in the criminal investigation office, Guo turned it into an active tool to reach out to the people. He encouraged people to use the 110 call system not only to report crime but also to call the police if they had problems and needed help. He put up signs everywhere that said: "If you have any matter you want help with, please call police patrol." Later, the promotional campaign was carried one step further with newspaper and television ads (e.g., "Your trouble is my trouble, and 110 is willing to solve any and all of your problems"). It was at this juncture that the four phrases (*youjing biejie, younan bie ban, youzai bie jiu,* and *youqiu beiying*) were officially adopted and established as operational standards and expectations of the police.[365]

The PRC police categorize 110 calls as *baojing* ("report to the police"), *jiejing* ("response by the police"), or *chujing* ("deal with by the police"). Successful resolution of a call depends on a timely report, speedy reception, and responsive action. According to Japanese data, timely calling of the police was key to successful resolution of a case.

In Japan, crimes reported within 3 minutes were successfully resolved 30% of the time. Within 3 to 5 minutes the rate dropped to 24%, and within 5 to 10 minutes the rate dropped still more to 18%.[366]

The public in China does not always report crimes in a timely fashion, or ever, despite the fact that citizens in China have a moral and political obligation and legal and constitutional duty to report crimes to the police. People do not report crime to the police for a number of reasons. First, they consider it to be useless and a waste of time and effort, as the crime is not going to be solved anyway; they prefer to absorb the loss and limit any further outlay of resources. Second, the public has a negative view of the police and believe that the police do not care, or they lack confidence in the police. Third, it is too difficult and complicated to file a report; for example, the police post may not be well marked, it may be out of the way, or the person does not know whom to contact. Fourth, some do not understand how reporting to the police works and may be under the impression that reporting requires the payment of a fee. Fifth, people may refuse to report due to concerns about confidentiality and privacy (e.g., shame associated with prostitution, loss of good will associated with bank embezzlement, exposure of trade secrets due to hacking). Finally, some people fear revenge.[367] Essentially, people do not report simply because they do not want to deal with the police, do not care as citizens, or are worried about retaliation or revenge.

A constant problem facing police reformers is the "one size fits all" reform mentality. The "one size fits all" syndromes derives from the fact that the reform is directed by one central (CPC) authority and managed as a mass campaign with one best way of doing things. A centrally directed campaign ignores local differences and glosses over individual context and particular circumstances. The "one best way" approach ignores diversity, other alternatives, contingencies, and emergencies; for example, a centrally managed 110 call system may not function effectively, if at all, in a small city, township, or county. In fact, classical centrally organized and deployed 110 call systems look good on paper but are of little use in most rural cities, towns, and villages.

The Jiangchuan County PSB was one of the first police organs to observe that 110 call systems may serve big urban city needs but do not address the needs of smaller, rural area.[368] The Jiangchuan County PSB established its 110 call system in 1997 (see Table 5.7) but found that the system, which was designed for larger cities, was not well suited to their situation, as they had limited capacity and needs, especially in terms of managerial (*guanli*) costs and operational (*yunzuo*) requirements. The PSB found that it wasted police manpower and resources; maintaining a 24-hour, rapid-deployment police emergency team of 23 officers required a substantial investment of resources. The few calls received did not

TABLE 5.7   110 Calls from January 1 to October 30, 2001, in Jiangchuan County, Yunnan Province

Nature of Cases	Number	Percentage (%)
Criminal and public order	384	20.22
Traffic	7	0.37
Natural disasters	244	12.85
Public assistance and services	546	28.75
Locating people	46	2.42
Dispute resolution	672	35.39
Total	1899	100.00

justify the outlay, especially given the limited resources available and potential alternative uses of the officers. Under normal circumstances, the 110 dispatcher would refer cases to the responsible beat patrol or community police officer; however, because the quality of such officers was not particularly high, these referrals often fell on deaf ears. Also, police officers responding to 110 calls usually were not able to reach remote areas in sufficient time or with the necessary reinforcements to be of help in emergencies. Finally, the communication channels were confusing, as calling 110 might not be the most appropriate way to reach the police; such calls resulted in delays and duplication of effort.

The Jiangchuan County PSB decided to take a number of steps to remedy the situation. The designated 110 police response team was reduced from 23 to 6. The 110 command center assumed total control over coordinating responses to calls. It was given direct command authority and trumps any local police post. Calls are referred to the local criminal unit (*xingjing*), public order unit (*zhian jingcha*), or street patrol (*xunjing*) for action. These officers are closest to the community and understand the local situations best. This arrangement saves time, eliminates the middleman, and enhances public satisfaction. Because most of the 110 calls in rural areas are concerned with personal disputes,[369] it is best to refer these disputes to local community leadership, such as a village committee (*cunwei*), rather than to the police, for investigation, mediation, and disposition. It is not necessary to have the police involved.

The PRC State Council has designated 110 as the "People's 110" ("*Renmin* 110"). The Zhangzhou PSB established its 110 call system in 1990 and since then it has become a role model for the entire nation. From 1998 to 2000, its 110 call system received 50,386 calls for police services that led to the detection of 8363 crimes and the arrest of 13,070 people. The program has received over 192 citations and 10 provincial-level commendations.[370]

The MPS awarded the Nanjing PSB second place as a national public security system model for its 110 organization and services (*Quanguo jingshen wenmin chuangjiang huodong shifan dian*). Under normal circumstances, the police can be expected to arrive 5 minutes after a 110 call. From 2000 to 2001 the 110 call system received a total of 780,000 calls, including 10,196 criminal calls, 32,206 public order calls, and 11,264 traffic accident and disaster calls. The police detected 5201 criminal cases and arrested 4763 people. The public called 110 for assistance and help 414,615 times, with cases involving the mediation of disputes (77,861), solving problems (81,439), saving and rescuing people (5176), and generally assisting the public (3019).[371]

The Jilin PSB 110 call system was established in 1996. Over the next several years, the 110 call system received 565,357 calls for service and responded to 265,493 public inquiries. The police were dispatched 78,990 times, leading to the detection of 3472 crimes and 1259 arrests. It has helped people to resolve their problems 18,007 times and assisted the public another 16,057 times.[372] The Shandong PSB 110 call system has also been in place since 1996. Over the first 5 years, 5.2 million calls for police assistance were received, of which 4.8 million were actually handled by the police. This led to the disposition of 150,000 criminal cases and 70,000 public security cases and the arrest of 370,000 suspects.[373] Established that same year, the Anshan PSB 110 call system was staffed with 300 patrol officers and riot officers. To deal with whatever crises or emergencies might arise, each response team vehicle carried bulletproof vests, steel helmets, safety ropes and harnesses, lights, life jackets, life buoys, and first-aid kids. Over the next 5 years, the 110 call system handled 38,755 calls—3420 criminal cases and 35,335 public order cases. These calls led to the arrest of 667 criminal suspects, settlement of 4704 civil disputes, and providing assistance to the public in 6780 cases.[374] The Liuzhou PSB also established its 110 call system in 1996. The system met with considerable success in attacking crimes and serving the public. It received 317,800 calls in its first 5 years which led to the deployment of 471,600 police officers.[375]

Since the introduction of the 110 call system nationwide, a number of steps have been taken to improve it, including reducing the workload of the system by anticipating problems and preventing crimes from happening. At the Zhao Dong PSB, there was an immediate decline in 110 calls after a new program was put into place that called for 24-hour police patrols and further prevention work (*Zhao Dong shi gongan ju chengqu xuluo fankong gongzuo banfa*). The decline of 110 calls in 2001 was remarkable: from 482 calls in July to 242 calls in September and finally to an average of 100 calls each month since then.[376] The use of patrols 24/7 in troubled areas was found to be especially effective. In Lanzhou's Dongkou District, a busy town center, calls for police services declined by 40% after initiating aggressive patrolling compared with the previous year. These patrols were conducted by general patrol teams (*xunjing dui*), district patrols (*qu xun jing*), and the military police (*wujing*).[377] The municipality deploys 300 officers in 100 patrol teams between the hours of 8 p.m. and 2 a.m., the most troublesome hours. Another way to improve upon 110 call systems is to enlist other government agencies to help deal with the public's calls.

Issues and Problems

The 110 call system has often been abused. It has been used as an all-purpose solution for all types of problems. People call for all kinds of reasons, from the trivial to the absurd—family feuds, noisy neighbors, household needs (e.g., replacement of gas canisters), and personal problems (e.g., being locked out). In some cases, the officers are utilized to provide basic social welfare services, such as transporting the elderly to hospitals.

In 2001 in Nanchang, the 110 call center recorded an average of 3500 calls for police services a day, of which only about 80 (or 2.3%) were legitimate. Among the non-emergency calls were calls to test out new mobile phones for sound clarity. Such abuses led to a comprehensive study that revealed that most of the prank calls (about 50%) were made by youngsters. Most surprising, university and college students accounted for another 30% of the prank calls. Remedial steps were taken (e.g., school authorities were informed), but to no avail.[378] During the Chinese New Year's celebration in 2002, 80% of the 110 calls for emergency assistance received at the Cixi call center were nuisance or prank calls. Only 394 out of the 4850 calls were valid. On a normal day, the municipality handled about 500 to 600 calls for services.[379] The Huzhou municipality received 196,815 calls in 2001, and prank calls accounted for 129,185 of these.

Such calls delay the delivery of services and strain manpower. The public should be taught the proper use of the 110 call system; it should not be used to seek revenge or air grievances against the government.[380] The reasons for inappropriate and abusive use of the 110 call system are many. The MPS has been too successful in promoting permissive, rather than restrictive, use of the system; in particular, the slogan "*You kunnan, zhao jingcha*" ("have difficulties, call the police") has been construed by the public as an open invitation to call for any kind of services.

Proper use of the 110 call system must be understood within the context of the proper roles and functions of the police, as promoted by the MPS and as understood by the public. The MPS has, for ideological reasons, promoted the police as "blood family members" to the people; that is, they are intimately bound to and closely associated with the people.[381]

This image of the police–public relationship gives rise to the expectation that the police, as family members, would and should solve any and all problems, whatever the costs and whatever the means. The people in turn are encouraged to turn to the police whenever they have difficulties and problems, often as a first alternative rather than as a last resort. After all, in the traditional Chinese family, all members are expected to take good care of each other's welfare and best interests. In contemporary China, the Communist Party preaches that they will take care of the people, with much enthusiasm and with few reservations. This Confucius ideal and communitarian vision of the police run counter to the increasingly professionalized and bureaucratized police that speak in terms of cost–benefit analysis and marginal utilities.

A 110 Case Study

In 2001, the Fujian PSB studied the problems and issues they were having with their 110 call system.[382] Most of the 110 calls were initially responded to by patrol officers and followed up by other police units, such as criminal investigation, or by various government agencies. Interviews with the patrol officers revealed that they had to rush from call to call nonstop all day, every day. The officers were worn out, both physically and mentally. Some of the officers did not take 110 calls seriously. They either failed to respond or they responded late, thus creating a negative image for the police. Patrol officers reported that, as first responders to a scene, they could not get other police units or government agencies to follow up on the case to its final resolution in a timely, responsible, and satisfactory fashion. This further delayed their responses to subsequent calls and led to frustration among the public and the police. The PSB determined that one way to improve the 110 call system would be to let the officer assigned to a call deal with the case from beginning to end. This would improve response times and allow more efficient handling of the cases. When the Fujian PSB examined their 110 call records, they identified 11 major types (e.g., criminal offenses, public order cases, social disorder issues, traffic violations, traffic control). For many of the 110 calls, the police were not able to help.

Conclusion

This chapter has discussed police reform efforts over the last decade, including the reform agenda, ideology, ethics, command and control, culture, funding, and operations. The CPC and MPS have made Herculean efforts to adjust traditional police ideology (democratic centralism), theory (mass line), organization (dual control), practices (*yanda*), and processes (procedural justice) to address new issues (e.g., urban policing, migrants, conflicts among the people). They have met with a modicum of success, but not without major difficulties. The reform strategy is to move in the direction of creating a police force that is more transparent (*jingwu gongkai*), professional, legal (*yifa zhijing*), disciplined, scientific (*kexue qiangjing*), and technocratic (e.g., Golden Shield Project). The Hu–Wen administration has injected a scientific development perspective in the guise of harmonious society.

As discussed in this chapter and elsewhere, police reform has encountered many difficulties. There is a lack of consensus over police reform goals and means; as a result, the traditional democratic centralism has been maintained, with latitude for differential interpretations of Party policies and the discretionary application of laws. Top-down police reform runs counter to the people's expectations,[383] which has slowed its development, dissipated its impact, and compromised its efficacy. In theory, professional policing (formalized, standardized, legalized, bureaucratized) is at odds with mass line policing, which is responsive and accountable to the people. The people apparently do not want a standard system of universal justice but would prefer individualized, personal justice. This is best illustrated by a 2006 web discussion[384] on the police and procedural vs. substantive justice.[385]

The forum master observed that the debate over whether police should be pursuing substantive justice could not be properly resolved without first investigating why substantive justice was being practiced, culturally, organizationally, environmentally, practically, and emotionally.

Culturally, Chinese is given to the pursuit of substantive justice (*shiti zhengyi*) as an ultimate good.[386] This is manifested in the traditional notion and conventional saying: "Murder must be repaid with life, debt must be repaid with money" ("*Sharen changing, qiangzhai huanqian*"). This recalls Kant's theory of retributive justice, which is non-negotiable. Chinese police, who share the same cultural universe as the people are inevitably affected by it, notwithstanding their mandate, roles, and education. In the reform era and with the professionalization movement, the issue to be considered is whether the police should follow a different rule of justice (procedural) than what the public desires (substantive justice).

Organizationally, the Chinese police, under the leadership of the CPC, function as an instrument of the state to maintain the democratic dictatorship and defeat enemies of the state. The mission of the police is to serve the needs and protect the interests of the people. This means that the majority interest or collective welfare of the people takes precedence over the rights of criminals; thus, criminals should not be able to hide behind procedural rules to avoid punishment.

The nation, law (administrative and criminal), and police are recognizing the necessity and importance of procedural justice. Procedural law holds the police accountable, but it has not changed their zealous pursuit of substantive justice. This can be attributed to the fact that Party leadership promotes procedural justice without relinquishing mass line policing. Mass line policing under Mao subscribed to the view that the masses are clear minded and able to tell right from wrong. The people, not the Party, much less legal institutions and administrative bureaucracy, should be in control of rendering judgment and imposing punishment on criminals. In the final analysis, the administration of justice must abide by two rules: (1) what the people want, the people get; and (2) disposition of cases should reflect the desires of the people.

In practice, police administration has only paid lip service to procedural justice while still pursuing substantive justice. While the legal professional is zealously pushing for the right to remain silent, the MPS remains adamant in its defense of substantive justice over procedural justice. The police have used administrative powers under "education through labor" (*laojiao zhidu*) to pursue substantive justice; for example, in cases where the court or the procuratorate refuse to intervene, the police have resorted to using their administrative powers to deliver substantive justice, summarily. To improve administrative efficiency, the police have liberally used their administrative powers to sanction offenders or supervise their behavior without ever going through the necessary and cumbersome procedures to mount a criminal prosecution. Some police laws have created procedural opportunities for the police to deny and defy procedural justice at will; for example, the PRC Criminal Law did not make clear whether live witness testimony is required in court, which has allowed the police to use written statements in court without concern for procedural regularity. The media have been promoting themselves as champions of progressive legal development, but they have also been guilty of promoting, or at least subscribing to, substantive justice at every turn. In case after case, the media have applauded the elimination of violent gangsters and other criminals, and each report has ended with the phrase *dai kuai ren* ("happiness to all"). If the *de facto* and unspoken rule in judging the criminal justice system is *dai kuai ren*, then it is little wonder that the police, prosecutors, and courts do not embrace procedural justice. Time and again, the public has demonstrated that it is not above using their voices in the media or on the Internet to influence, and in some cases dictate and derail, the course of justice,[387] as in the 2003 case of gang member Liu Yong, where the people forced the courts to change their sentencing of Liu from imprisonment to death.[388]

Emotionally, the police are bound to substantive justice. Taking away substantive justice from the police is akin to stealing a child's innocence. In teaching children the ways of society, however, it is necessary to destroy their innocence; similarly, to make the police respect procedural justice it is necessary to sever their emotional bonds to substantive justice, which is easier said than done.

Finally, what if the police are not pursuing substantive justice and not determining right or wrong? Do people have faith in the police to do the right thing and to protect them? To meet our desire for procedural justice, are we not asking the police to forgo substantive justice? Would this not turn the police into a legal machine?

To achieve substantive justice within a procedural justice framework may just be a naïve dream. If we use dialectical methods to understand the relationship between substantive justice and procedural justice, we should be able to derive a satisfactory logical relationship; otherwise, we can only engage in endless discussion. Most proponents of procedural justice think that substantive justice is all relative, and procedural justice can be achieved without unduly sacrificing substantive justice; that is, procedural rules can be set up to achieve substantive justice. In reality, though, legal procedures are never perfect, try as we might, and substantive justice cannot be achieved without bending the rules.

In light of the fact that the law can never keep up with changing reality, judicial workers are required to choose between procedural justice and substantive justice. At such times, the personal orientation of the judicial officer and institutional culture of the justice institution will dictate the outcome of a case. If the police were allowed to choose, they would most likely choose substantive justice. In some cases, the tension between procedural justice and substantive justice is not very significant. If we deviate from procedural justice slightly to realize substantive justice, this might not be a bad thing; however, if we were to insist on following procedural justice with zero tolerance, we run the risk of doing away with substantive justice altogether. Do we want to ignore that end altogether and insist on advancing the means? This is a worthy issue to reflect upon. The Chinese police did, and overwhelmingly decided for substantive justice, much to the surprise of foreign observers.

Notes

1. CCTB, *Introduction to the Scientific Outlook on Development*, Bureau central des compilations et traductions, Chine, Fondation Gabriel Péri, Pantin, France (http://www.gabrielperi.fr/Introduction-to-the-scientific?lang=fr). "However, single-minded pursuit of economic growth while overlooking social progress and fairness and neglecting environmental protection and energy and resource conservation in some countries has resulted in unbalanced economic structure, poor social development, growing shortages of energy and resources, and drastic

ecological and environmental degradation, as well as greater division between haves and have-nots, increased unemployment, corruption and political unrest, and other problems that can arise with a high growth rate. In these countries, economic growth did not bring tangible benefits to the people, the growth was not sustainable and development was not true development."

2. Ibid. "Putting people first means taking their all-round personal development as our goal, planning and promoting development on the basis of their fundamental interests, meeting their ever-growing material and cultural needs, protecting their economic, political and cultural rights and interests, and ensuring that development benefits everyone."

3. Ibid. "Balanced development is development that balances urban and rural development, development among regions, economic and social development, development of man and nature, and domestic development and opening to the outside world, and promotes balance between the productive forces and the relations of production, between the economic base and the superstructure, and among all links and aspects of economic, political, cultural and social development."

4. For a full treatment of the scientific development perspective, see: (a) *Chinese Communist Party Central Committee's Resolution on Major Issues of Building a Socialist Harmonious Society* [*Zhonggong zhongyang guanyu guojia shehuizhuyi hexieshehui ruogan zhongdawenti de jueding*], Renminwang/Shizheng/Zonghe baodao, October 18, 2006. (b) Ai Guo Han, "Building a Harmonious Society and Achieving Individual Harmony," in Sujiang Guo and Baogang Guo (Eds.), *China in Search of a Harmonious Society*, Lexington Books, Lanham, MD, 2008.

5. "Ministry of Public Security Decided the Year of 2002: Change of Work Style Year" ["*Gonganbu jueding 2002 nian: gaibian zuofeng nian*"], *China Police Daily*, February 9, 2002.

6. Mao Tse-tung, *Report on an Investigation of the Peasant Movement in Hunan*, March 1927 (http://www.marxists.org/reference/archive/mao/selected-works/volume-1/mswv1_2.htm).

7. There are two sides to this coin. Substantively, the "scientific development outlook" is about achieving sustainable and balanced development, with people at the center. Procedurally, the "scientific development outlook" is about seeking truth from facts and linking theory with practice.

8. CCTB, *Introduction to the Scientific Outlook on Development*, Bureau central des compilations et traductions, Chine, Fondation Gabriel Péri, Pantin, France (http://www.gabrielperi.fr/Introduction-to-the-scientific?lang=fr).

9. The scientific policymaking process cannot be used to defeat Marxism as an ideology, since Marx's theory of class conflict is built upon a scientific foundation of historical materialism. The debate between science and ideology recalls the debate between science and religion. According to defenders of religious order, the assertion that the theory of evolution rejects and defeats God's creationism is incorrect. Science can never be used to prove or disprove the existence of God.

10. Tatsuyuki Ota, "The Role of Special Economic Zones in China's Economic Development as Compared with Asian Export Processing Zones: 1979–1995," *Asia in Extenso*, March 2003 (http://www.iae.univ-poitiers.fr/EURO-ASIE/Docs/Asia-in-Extenso-Ota-mars2003.pdf).

11. (a) Lucy Hornby, "China Praises Its Growing Transparency in Rights Report," *Reuters*, September 26, 2010 (http://www.reuters.com/article/2010/09/26/us-china-rights-idUSTRE68 P0MD20100926). (b) "Beijing Police Launch Blogs, Podcast to Boost Transparency," *Xinhua*, August 2, 2010 (http://www.chinadaily.com.cn/china/2010-08/02/content_11080178.htm).

12. (a) "China's Press Administration Voices Support for Media Supervision after Journalist Listed as Wanted," *Xinhua*, August 2, 2010 (http://english.peopledaily.com.cn/90001/90776/90882/7088466.html). China's General Administration of Press and Publication (GAPP) supported journalists' rights to watch over the police: "News organizations have the right to know, interview, cover, criticize, and monitor events regarding national and public interests. Journalistic activities by news organizations and their reporters are protected by law." (b) Jin Jianyu, "Hubei Police Hire Private Investigators to Supervise Staff," *Global Times*, November 9, 2010 (http://en.huanqiu.com/china/news/2010-11/590707.html). (c) Liu Hanqing, "The Process and the Plight of Supervision by Public Opinion on the Internet: From the 'Lin Jiaxiang Take Indecent Acts to 11-Year-Old Girl' Case," *Journal of International Relations*, June 27, 2010 (http://www.focusire.com/archives/427.html).

13. "Chongqing Police Recruited 1250 Police Officers with Nearly 80% Having PhDs or Masters Degrees," *Chongqing Evening News*, September 18, 2010 (http://news.sohu.com/20100918/n275025868.shtml). It was reported that 79% of the 1250 new police recruits had graduate degrees, 40 of them their doctorates.

14. Wang Zhengxu, "Explaining Regime Strength in China," *China: An International Journal*, 4(2), 217–237, 2006. The Party believes that the best way to maintain legitimacy and secure support is through economic performance. For the police, this translates to providing a secure, stable, and supportive business environment.

15. (a) Administrative Punishment Law of the People's Republic of China, adopted at the Fourth Session of the Eighth National People's Congress of the People's Republic of China on March 17, 1996. (b) "Regulations of the People's Republic of China on Administrative Penalties for Public Security," adopted at the 17th Meeting of the Standing Committee of the Sixth National People's Congress of the People's Republic of China on September 5, 1986; promulgated by Order No. 43 of the President of the People's Republic of China on September 5, 1986; amended in accordance with the "Decision on Amending the Regulations of the People's Republic of China on Administrative Penalties for Public Security," adopted at the Seventh Meeting of the Standing Committee of the Eighth National People's Congress of the People's Republic of China on May 12, 1994. (c) "Regulations of the People's Republic of China Concerning Resident Identity Cards," adopted at the 12th Meeting of the Standing Committee of the Sixth National People's Congress of the People's Republic of China; promulgated for implementation by Order No. 29 of the President of the People's Republic of China on September 6, 1985; effective as of September 6, 1985.

16. *Fazhi hua*, establishing a system of law to empower and control police activities, is not the same as *falu hua*, establishing a rule of law that holds police accountable to the letter as well as spirit of the law. The former adopts an instrumental view of law to make the police serve the Party and with it the state; the latter adopts a cultural view of law to make the police, Party, and state subject to an independent and autonomous law empire.

17. MPS, *Public Security Troop Construction in 2000* [*2000 nian gongan duiwu jiangshe*], Ministry of Public Security, Beijing, China, 2000.

18. "Limited Resources vs. Unlimited Demand: HASLink Interviews Dr. William Ho on the Challenges Faced as Chief Executive of the Hospital Authority," *HASLink*, 2011 (http://www.ha.org.hk/ho/haslink/00-76/english/sp2.htm).

19. One such example is Deng's strategic decision to allow some to get wealthy quickly to lift the living standards for all. An example is Shenzhen; with help from the government, it became a shining example of economic success under communist rule. The same can be said of Hong Kong. Here, Deng's "one country, two systems" has allowed the colony of Hong Kong to return to China as a Special Administrative Region with a high degree of autonomy. In both instances, China traded the sound principles of equitable development and national sovereignty, to speed up economic development (Shenzhen) and achieve political reunion (Hong Kong).

20. Potential misinformation and misinterpretation always make it dangerous to work with incomplete, unsubstantiated, and second-hand official survey data reported in the news. Such data are subject to agenda setting and gatekeeping; they lack focus, scope, depth, and context; their reliability and validity are in doubt; and they are subject to selection and perspective issues. This is particularly the case with Communist Party of China (CPC) research and People's Republic of China (PRC) press accounts, which tend to lean toward propaganda. A number of methodological and analytical issues must be considered when analyzing these data: How was the survey item "corruption" conceptualized and operationalized? How was the survey conducted? Why was there a 100% respond rate? How might CPC-sponsored research affect the integrity of the research, in terms of conduct (e.g., biased researchers) and responses? This is particularly problematic in rural settings where the people are relatively uneducated, unsophisticated, and not familiar with research matters. Party, clan, and family members are also prone to "group speak"—to give only socially correct responses. Some of the same considerations afflict the

democratic election process; for example, rural people in China rarely speak their minds; when they do, they do not voice individual concerns but collective ideas. Research problems and electoral issues due to Chinese characteristics should be a subject of study.

21. Chinese University of Hong Kong, "Survey Shows Corruption Is the First Factor Affecting Social Stability," *Eastday.com*, January 7, 2001. This was a province-wide survey involving 11 municipalities and 25 cities and prefectures. The 2500 questionnaires distributed had a 100% response rate. The random sample consisted of Party members, league members, democratic members, enterprise workers, peasants, political cadres, intellectuals, students, unemployed workers, retirees, and others.

22. For further official (CPC and government) empirical data validating that corruption was the top concern among the Chinese people from 1996 to 2002, see note 6 in Sun Liping, "Mechanisms and Logic: Research regarding China's Social Stability," in Minxin Pei and Michael Swaine (Eds.), *Assessing the 16th Party Congress and China's New Leadership*, Carnegie Endowment for International Peace, Washington, DC, 2002.

23. The difference between Zhejiang (74.66%) and Horizon (94.6%) is substantial but not surprising. The Horizon survey was conducted in cities where corruption is considered to be more rampant and crude, thus more serious. The Zhejiang survey covered cities as well as counties, with the latter being more represented.

24. "Two Items of Public Opinion Made Jiang Zemin Fearful," *Renmin Bao*, January 7, 2003. The other three requests were that Jiang should have breached the gap between the rich and the poor and provided a social net for the less fortunate, Jiang should have sought political reform and protected the rights of the people, and Jiang should have established the rule of law, with equality to all and privileges to none. When asked about their opinion of the Party and the new leadership, a full 72% had no confidence with the CPC leadership. Only 17% expressed confidence or very much confidence. Still, most of the respondents (68%) were full of confidence or had confidence about the nation's future. The approval ratings of Hu and Wen were over 80%. Wen was not considered to be corrupt, and Hu was viewed as being careful. Jiang's rating was 0%.

25. "Senior Heads Roll as Fears of Social Unrest Mount," *Associated Press*, January 15, 1999.

26. The respondents also thought that the government had taken the necessary and aggressive steps to address corruption issues. Thus, between 1999 and 2000, 7.8% more people thought that corruption was under control and 10.93% more people were satisfied or very satisfied with the Party's clean government and anticorruption efforts. Finally, the most encouraging survey finding was that 44.68% of the people thought that government organs had used great or very great effort in dealing with leading Party cadres' disciplinary and legal violations. This represented an increase of 7.36% from 1999 and 9.76% from 1998. See Victor Yuan's PowerPoint presentation, "How Chinese People View Their Government, Society and Foreign Countries," presented at Taking the Pulse of the Chinese Public, Carnegie Endowment for International Peace, Friday, April 25, 2003 (www.carnegieendowment.org/files/chinesegames.pdf).

27. (a) *Xiandai* means "modern," *jingwu* means "police work," and *jizhi* means "mechanism." (b) Zhang Jinghua, "An Overall Concept of Exploring and Establishing a Mechanism for Modern Policing," *Public Security Studies*, 120, 11–17, 2004. Modern police work (*jizhi*) can be contrasted with traditional centrally planned household management system.

28. Unlike in the West, China has very few independent scholars and experts; generally, they work for the government to provide policy justifications and detailed plans for executing policy.

29. Zhang Jinghua, "An Overall Concept of Exploring and Establishing a Mechanism for Modern Policing," *Public Security Studies*, 120, 11–17, 2004.

30. Ibid.

31. Information is important for police work. Conversely, without adequate and reliable information, police cannot work efficiently, much less effectively, in controlling people and catching criminals. The Tiananmen Square incident in 1989 is a reminder of how far governments will go to obtain information to stay in control.

32. "Research, Data, and Policy Supplement" ["*Tiaoyan, xinxi yu fuzhu juece bian*"], in Zhen Yuegang and Guan Shuguan (Eds.), *Handbook on Public Security Internal Administration Work* [*Gongan neiqin gongzuo shouce*] (pp. 1–41), Jingguan Jiaoyu Chubanshe, Beijing, 1993. Communist security agents and PRC public security officials, then as now, are keen on collecting and analyzing data to inform policy, guide operations and evaluate practices. This is partly due to Marx's insistence that Marxism is a scientific theory of society. Mao has since interpreted "scientific" Marxism as requiring testing political theory with social practice. In the reform era Deng has called for "seeking truth from facts" to break the gridlock of Mao's ideological hold on the people.

33. Zhang Jinghua, "An Overall Concept of Exploring and Establishing a Mechanism for Modern Policing," *Public Security Studies*, 120, 11–17, 2004.

34. *Da* or *daji* means "to attack." It refers to the police taking assertive measures (e.g., arrest, detention, investigation, prosecution, imprisonment) to deter or incapacitate criminals, as in the case of *yanda* (1983–1984, 1991–1992, 2003–2004, 2010).

35. *Fang* or *fang fan* means "to guard and prevent." It refers to the police and community working together to keep the community safe through preventive patrols and community crime watches.

36. *Kong* or *kongzhi* means "to control." It refers to administrative control of crime-prone populations through supervision and regulation (e.g., registration of mobile population).

37. Zhang Jinghua, "An Overall Concept of Exploring and Establishing a Mechanism for Modern Policing," *Public Security Studies*, 120, 11–17, 2004.

38. Ibid.

39. Ibid.

40. Ibid.

41. "China: Reds Versus 'Experts' in the 1950s and 1960s," *Library of Congress Country Studies*, July 1987 (http://rs6.loc.gov/cgi-bin/query/r?frd/cstdy:@field%28DOCID+cn0258%29).

42. "Resolution to Strengthen and Improve Party Work Style" ("*Zhonggong zhongyang guanyu jiaqiang he gaijin dan de zuofeng jianshe de jueding*"), passed during the Sixth Plenum of the 15th Central Committee of the Communist Party of China, September 26, 2001.

43. (a) D.A. Schon, "The New Scholarship Requires a New Epistemology," *Change*, 27(6), 26–34, 1995. Action research is "a cycle of posing questions, gathering data, reflection, and deciding on a course of action." (b) Eileen Ferrance, *Themes in Action Research*, Northeast and Islands Regional Educational Laboratory at Brown University, Providence, RI, 2000, pp. 2–3. Action research is not about problem-solving but is more of a continuous process of improvement through on-the-job research and study.

44. "Jiang Zemin's Report at the 16th Party Congress," *People's Daily Online*, December 10, 2002 (http://english.peopledaily.com.cn/200211/18/eng20021118_106983.shtml).

45. "Retired Guangzhou Public Security Cadre Seriously Learned about 7-1 Speech," *Guangzhou Jindun Wang*, November 13, 2001.

46. *Dangyuan minjing yao zai gongan gongzuo zhong daibiao xianjin shengchang li de fazhan yaojiu* (党员民警要在公安工作中代表先进生产力的发展要求).

47. *Dangyuan mingjing yao zai gongan gongzuo zhong daibiao xianjin wenhua de qianjin fangxian* (党员民警要在公安工作中代表先进文化的前进方向).

48. *Dangyuan minjing yao zai gongan gongzuo zhong daibiao zui guangfan renmin de jiben liyi* (党员民警要在公安工作中代表最广泛人民的根本利益).

49. "Jiang Zemin's Report at the 16th Party Congress," *People's Daily Online*, December 10, 2002 (http://english.peopledaily.com.cn/200211/18/eng20021118_106983.shtml). "Persistent implementation of the 'Three Represents' is the foundation for building our Party, the cornerstone for its governance, and the source of its strength."

50. For a discussion of the meaning and significance of the "Three Represents," see: (a) "China to Put 'Three Represents' into Constitution," *Xinhua*, December 22, 2003 (http://www.china.org.cn/english/zhuanti/3represents/83062.htm). (b) M. Ulric Killion, "The Three Represents and

China's Constitution: Presaging Cultural Relativistic Asian Regionalism," *International Trade Law Journal*, 14, 2004 (http://papers.ssrn.com/sol3/papers.cfm?abstract_id=490722). (c) Jia Heping, "Three Represents Campaign: Reform the Party or Indoctrinate the Capitalist," *Cato Journal*, 24(3), 243–275, 2004 (http://www.cato.org/pubs/journal/cj24n3/cj24n3-5.pdf).

51. Du Pufeng, "Humanizing Law Enforcement: Improving on Conceptual Transformation and Practice" ["*Renxinghua zhifa: linian zhuangbian yu shijian gaijin*"], *Journal of Chinese People's Public University* (*PSU Journal*), 108, 144–148, 2004.

52. "Communiqué of CCP Central Committee Plenum," *People's Daily Online*, September 27, 2002 (http://english.peopledaily.com.cn/200109/26/eng20010926_81115.html).

53. "National PSB Department Heads Conference" ["*Quanguo gongan ting juzhang huiyi zai jing kaimu*"], *China Police Daily*, December 20, 2001. At the National PSB Department Heads Conference, the Minister of Public Security, Jia Chunwang, reflected on the past and planned for the future.

54. The CPC is fond of slogans that are meant to capture the essence of certain policy initiatives.

55. "National Public Security Post Work Conference Opens" ["*Quanguo gongan paichusuo gongzuo huiyi zhaokai*"], *China Police Daily*, March 20, 2002. The conference was well attended by MPS as well as CPC leaders, including the Deputy Minister of Public Security, the MPS Disciplinary Committee Secretary, the Zhejiang Provincial Political Commissar Secretary, and the Zhejiang Political–Legal Committee Secretary.

56. *Gongan jiguan zhifa zhiliang kaohe pingyi guiding* (公安机 关执法 质 量 考核评议规定). According to MPS data, between 2003 and 2009, the approval rates for public security administrative appeals and administrative litigation increased by 6.3% and 9.4%, respectively, whereas their dismissal rates dropped 9.7% and 4.7%, respectively. Law implementation assessment rates of pass and excellent rose 9.9% to 98.5%.

57. *Gongan paichusuo zhifa zhiiqin gonguo guifan* (公安派出所执法执勤工作规范).

58. Yu Chang-an, "The Problems to Be Settled for Putting into Effect the Compendium" ["*Guanshe luoshi gangyao xuyao jiejue jige wenti*"], *Public Security Studies*, 137, 59–64, 2006.

59. CPC Central Committee, "Decision regarding Strengthening and Improving Public Security Work" ("*Guanyu jin yi bu jiaqiang gaijin gongan gongzuo de jueding*"), November 18, 2003.

60. Andrew J. Nathan and Perry Link (Eds.), *The Tiananmen Papers*, Public Affairs, New York, 2001, pp. 191–193. The Standing Committee of the CPC Politburo was split over the decision to use force against the protesting students on June 4, 1989. Zhao Ziyang and Hu Qili opposed martial law, Li Peng and Yao Yilin were in favor, and Qiao Shi abstained from voting. Deng, as a senior Party elder, ruled in favor of the crackdown championed by Li Peng.

61. Joseph Fewsmith, "Is Political Reform Ahead? Beijing Confronts Problems Facing Society—and the CCP," *China Leadership Monitor*, Issue 1, 2002. Jiang Zeming's called for admitting private entrepreneurs into the Party and reformulation of Marxist's theory on surplus labor attracted widespread resentment from "leftist" Party members who preferred less, not more, political liberation.

62. (a) Wei Jingsheng, "The Fifth Modernization," http://www.rjgeib.com/thoughts/china/jingshen. html. Deng's Four Modernizations would come to naught if there were no Fifth Modernization, political reform through democratization. To accomplish modernization, Chinese people could first practice democracy and modernize China's social system. (b) Mark O'Neil, "Hu Jintao Takes Personal Charge of Fight against Charter 08," *Asian Sentinel*, January 7, 2009. On December 10, 2008, on the eve of 60th anniversary of the Universal Declaration of Human Rights, 350 prominent Chinese intellectuals and human rights activists, including now-jailed Nobel Peace Prize recipient Liu Xiapo, issued "Charter 08," which called for political reform in China: "All kinds of social conflicts have built up and feelings of discontent intensified.... The current system has become backward to the point that change cannot be avoided. China remains the only large world power to still retain an authoritarian system that infringes on human rights. The situation must change. Political democratic reforms cannot be delayed any longer....After experiencing a long period of human rights disasters and a tortuous struggle

and resistance, Chinese citizens are increasingly recognizing that freedom, equality, and human rights are universal common values and that democracy, a republic, and constitutionalism are the basic framework of modern governance."

63. Barry Naughton, "Zhu Rongji: The Twilight of a Brilliant Career," *China Leadership Monitor*, Issue 1, 2002 (http://www.hoover.org/publications/china-leadership-monitor/article/7874). Zhu Rongji was strongly committed to the ideal of the upright official (*qingguan*); however, the privatization of state-owned enterprises that he sought created opportunities for corruption among those in a position to sell government assets, power, or influence for gain.

64. Jeffrey T. Richelson and Michael L. Evans, *Tiananmen Square, 1989: The Declassified History*, National Security Archive Electronic Briefing Book No. 16, George Washington University, Washington, DC. Students protested in 1985 and again in 1986 for "Law, Not Authoritarianism" and "Long Live Democracy." The disillusioned students finally protested at Tiananmen Square on June 4, 1989, resulting in violent suppression by the People's Liberation Army.

65. Joseph Fewsmith, "Continuing Pressures on Social Order," *China Leadership Monitor*, Issue 10, 2004.

66. James Farrer, *Opening Up: Youth Sex Culture and Market Reform in Shanghai*, University of Chicago Press, Chicago, 2002. In Shanghai in the 1980s and 1990s, the urban youth were opening up more to Westernization and foreign influences; for example, they were adopting more individualistic lifestyles and their value systems were changing.

67. Joseph Fewsmith, "The Third Plenary Session of the 16th Central Committee," *China Leadership Monitor*, Issue 9, 2004. There are conflicts within the Politburo over political reform and at the top (Jiang vs. Hu) over ideology (elitist vs. populist, technocratic vs. humanistic, pro-business vs. pro-peasants), but all agreed that the CPC must change to harness more support from the people to improve "state capacity" (*zhizheng nengli*).

68. "Tip of an Iceberg in China," *Shanghai Star*, December 8, 2000. Every official in China expects *xiaofei* ("tips"). Tips are considered to be a characteristic of Chinese society, including the police. Those who refuse to accept tips are exceptional and newsworthy.

69. See the Foreword in Harold Walsby, *The Domain of Ideologies: A Study of the Development and Structure of Ideologies*, Social Science Association, Thwickenham, Middlesex, 1946 (download at http://gwiep.net/wp/?tag=domain-of-ideologies&paged=7).

70. Antoine Destutt de Tracy, *Eléments d'idéologie*, Parts I–V, 1801–1815.

71. http://www.postcolonialweb.org/poldiscourse/ideology.html.

72. Karl Marx, *The German Ideology*, 1845.

73. Liu Kang, *Aesthetics and Marxism: Chinese Aesthetic Marxists and Their Western Contemporaries*, Duke University Press, Durham, NC, 2000, p. xi.

74. Kalpana Misra, *From Post-Maoism to Post-Marxism: The Erosion of Official Ideology in Deng's China*, Rutledge University Press, Piscataway, NJ, 1998. The way to clearly understand the undercurrents of Chinese politics in communist China was through ideology.

75. (a) Franz Schurmann, *Ideology and Organization in Communist China*, University of California Press, Berkeley, 1968. (b) Tao Jiang, "Intimate Authority: The Rule of Ritual in Classical Confucian Political Discourse," in Peter D. Hershock and Roger T. Ames (Eds.), *Confucian Cultures of Authority*, SUNY Press, New York, 2006. Observers new to China studies have condemned such ideological imposition and manipulation as excessive and overbearing, but a moment's reflection on Chinese history informs us that China has labored under state-sponsored ideological orthodoxy of one form or another since the Zhou dynasty (1046–221 BC), the most prevalent of which is none other than Confucianism with its central tenets of *ren* and system of *Li*.

76. (a) Legitimacy is whether or not people accept the validity of a law or ruling or the validity of a governing regime (http://www.wordiq.com/definition/Legitimacy). The right to and acceptance of rule can derive from many sources, ranging from spiritual endowment (Pope in Rome) to moral superiority (Sage in China). (b) The three basic types of legitimate rule are traditional, charismatic, and legal; see Max Weber, *Politics as a Vocation*, 1919. (c) "The Mandate of Heaven, Selections from the *Shu Jing*" ["The Classic of History"], in James Legge, trans., *The Sacred Books*

of China: The Texts of Confucianism, Clarendon, Oxford, 1879–1910 (http://acc6.its.brooklyn.cuny.edu/~phalsall/texts/shu-jing.html). In the PRC, as with imperial China, no distinction is drawn between the moral and political realms when it comes to earning the legitimacy to rule. The imperial rulers governed by a "mandate from heaven" (*tianming*). Such a mandate can only be attained and maintained with virtuous rule, or *renzhi*: "He [Yi Yin] said, 'Oh! of old the former kings of Xia cultivated earnestly their virtue, and then there were no calamities from Heaven.…But their descendant did not follow their example, and great Heaven sent down calamities, employing the agency of our ruler, who was in possession of its favoring appointment. The attack on Xia may be traced to the orgies in Ming Tiao.'"

77. The PRC communist ideology, if followed closely, legitimizes the Party rule. There are many similarities between contemporary communist ideology and traditional Confucian ethics. They both define good (virtue) and bad (evil). They are spiritual tenets, philosophical principles, moral codes, and conduct norms all wrapped into one. They both seek to create perfect individuals on the way to realizing utopian society (family, community, Party, state). They both speak to the ultimate moral truth in things in the image of Kantian's categorical imperatives. They are both monolith and universal principles. They both consist of inflexible and non-negotiable rules. They are both "discovered" rules. Confucian ethical rules emanate from nature and reside in the person, and Marx ideological principles are derived from historical and material forces. They both govern one's thoughts as well as actions. They both demand introspection and require self-cultivation. They both require active effort to apply and realize in action. They both draw a distinction between classes; for Confucianism, it is *junzi* (noble) vs. *xiaoren* (debased), and for Marxism it is proletarian vs. capitalist.

78. Mao's revolutionary cultural theory requires artists to support the communist quest and to keep their artistic endeavors more in line with workers' tastes and better reflect their points of view. (a) Julie F. Andrews, *Painters and Politics in the People's Republic of China, 1949–1979*, University of California Press, Berkeley, 1994. (b) Bonnie S. McDougall, *Mao Zedong's "Talks at the Yan'an Conference on Literature and Art": A Translation of the 1943 Text with Commentary*, Michigan Papers in Chinese Studies No. 39, University of Michigan Center for Chinese Studies, Ann Arbor, 1980.

79. Cited in John Flower, Portraits of Belief: Constructions of Chinese Cultural Identity in the Two Worlds of City and Countryside in Modern Sichuan Province, unpublished dissertation, University of Virginia, Charlottesville, 1997 (http://www.virginia.edu/history/graduate/placement/history).

80. Preamble, Paragraph 7, Constitution of the People's Republic of China, adopted at the Fifth Session of the Fifth National People's Congress and promulgated for implementation by the Proclamation of the National People's Congress on December 4, 1982. The 1982 Constitution has been amended four times. For latest amendment proposal, see "People to Get More Rights," *Beijing Review*, February 26, 2004 (http://www.china.org.cn/english/10th/88511.htm).

81. For centuries, political legitimacy and the right to rule in China have been based on the ancient principle of "perfection with virtue" (*dude zhishan*). (a) Zeng Dexiong, "The Basis of Legitimacy: Morality or Rights," *Modern China Studies*, Vol. 1, 2004. (b) Yan Sun, *The Chinese Reassessment of Socialism, 1976–1992*, Princeton University Press, Princeton, NJ, 1995.

82. "Populist Politics in China: Why Grandpa Wen Has to Care," *The Economist*, June 12, 2008 (http://www.economist.com/node/11541327).

83. Although China's authoritarian party-state centralizes all power and streamlines its policy-making process, multiple interest groups have managed to emerge and exert extensive influence: institutional interest groups, corporate interest groups, associational interest groups, and anomic interest groups. Powerful corporate interest groups and their government protectors were able to delay passage of the Anti-Monopoly Law for 13 years. Guangbin Yang, *Interest Groups in China's Politics and Governance*, EAI Background Brief No. 361, East Asian Institute, Singapore, 2007 (www.eai.nus.edu.sg/BB361.pdf).

84. Zhiyue Bo, *China's Elite Politics: Political Transition and Power Balancing*, World Scientific, Singapore, 2007.

85. Congressional–Executive Commission on China Issues Roundtable, "Public Intellectuals in China," March 10, 2005.

86. (a) See section on "The Language of Political Discourse in China" by Hemant Adlakha, "Toward an Understanding of Socialism with Chinese Characteristics," in Tan Chung (Ed.), *Across the Himalayan Gap: An Indian Quest for Understanding China*, Gyan Publishing House, New Delhi, 1998. (b) The term "civil society" first appeared in China's intellectual and political discourse in 1986 in an article by Shen Yue, who interpreted "civil society" to mean "towns-people's right" (*shimin quanli*), which, according to Marx, is an economic concept referring to people who participated in towncenter activities. The article later appeared again in the *People's Daily Online* on November 24, 1986. This interpretation of "civil society" was far from what the concept meant originally, and it gave rise to further interpretations among China's intellectual circles. "Civil society" in contemporary Chinese literature has been translated into: (1) *shimin shehui*, or "society of city people," (2) *chengshi shehui*, or "society of the cities," (3) *gongmin shehui*, or "society of the citizens of the country" (a dissident Chinese perspective), (4) "*minjian shehui*, or "society not associated with the government" (a Taiwanese perspective), (5) *qunzhong shehui*, or "society of the masses" (as a precursor to civil society), (6) *pingmin shehui*, or "society for ordinary people" (used to describe issues of Eastern Europe), and (7) *shehuizhuyi shimin shehui*, or "socialist society of urban people." All represent different connotations, denotations, and moods.

87. Jing Huang, *Factionalism in Chinese Communist Politics*, Cambridge University Press, Cambridge, UK, 2000.

88. Deng never made clear how pragmatism, a teleological theory of action, could be reconciled with the "Four Principles," an ontological framework of belief.

89. Jiang Zemin's theory of "Three Represents" focuses on the future role of the CPC as "a faithful representative of the requirements in the development of advanced productive forces in China, the orientation of the advanced culture in China, and the fundamental interests of the broadest masses of the people in China" (http://chineseposters.net/themes/ideological-foundations. php).

90. As of Liu Shaoqi's writing (1931), the work of Mao was mentioned but only as an interpretation, not as classic communist doctrine.

91. See "Part IV. The Unity of Theoretical Study and Ideological Self-Cultivation," in Liu Shaoqi, *How to Be a Good Communist*, Vol. I, Foreign Languages Press, Beijing, 1939.

92. In Part II of his *How to Be a Good Communist*, Liu Shaoqi cited Confucius as a supporting authority: "At fifteen, my mind was bent on learning. At thirty, I could think for myself. At forty, I was no longer perplexed. At fifty, I knew the decree of Heaven. At sixty, my ear was attuned to the truth. At seventy, I can follow my heart's desire without transgressing what is right."

93. "Part I. Why Communists Must Undertake Self-Cultivation," in Liu Shaoqi, *How to Be a Good Communist*, Vol. I, Foreign Languages Press, Beijing, 1939.

94. "Part III. The Self-Cultivation of Communists and the Revolutionary Practice of the Masses," in Liu Shaoqi, *How to Be a Good Communist*, Vol. I, Foreign Languages Press, Beijing, 1939.

95. "Part II. Be Worthy Pupils of Marx and Lenin," in Liu Shaoqi, *How to Be a Good Communist*, Vol. I, Foreign Languages Press, Beijing, 1939.

96. "Part V. The Cause of Communism Is the Greatest and Most Arduous Undertaking in Human History," in Liu Shaoqi, *How to Be a Good Communist*, Vol. I, Foreign Languages Press, Beijing, 1939.

97. Nicholas Fotion, "Puritanism in Ethics: Or Some Speculations on How Not to Teach Ethics to the Military," paper presented at JSCOPE 98 (XX), Ethics and Leadership during Organizational Change, Washington, DC, January 1998 (http://isme.tamu.edu/JSCOPE98/FOTION98. HTM).

98. Integrity consists of a number of personal traits: courage, honesty, responsibility, accountability, justice, openness, self-respect, and humility. "Integrity is a character trait. It is the willingness to do what is right even when no one is looking. It is the 'moral compass'—the inner voice; the voice of self-control." *United States Air Force Core Values* [*Blue Book*], Department of the Air Force, Washington, DC, 1997 (www.e-publishing.af.mil/shared/media/document/AFD-070906-003.pdf).

99. Ibid. "Service before self tells us that professional duties take precedence over personal desires." The types of service defined in the *Blue Book* are rule following, respect for others, discipline, and self-control.

100. Ibid. "Excellence in all we do directs us to develop a sustained passion for continuous improvement and innovation that will propel the Air Force into a long-term, upward spiral of accomplishment and performance." Various types of excellence are defined in the *Blue Book*: product/service excellence, personal excellence, community excellence, resources excellence, and operations excellence.

101. The debate as to who qualifies to be a communist police officer harks back to the early days of the CPC. With regard to CPC membership, can a person without the necessary class credentials (e.g., exploited rural peasants) be allowed to march alongside the proletarians (e.g., oppressed industrial laborers)? Alternatively, can people with little political class consciousness of the proletarian kind (e.g., capitalists and intellectuals) be allowed to join the ranks of the CPC? Finally, and more controversially, can people who have different ideological orientations (some even contradictory with the CPC) but share common causes with the CPC (e.g., united front against Japanese in 1930s) be co-opted into the CPC ranks? The CPC's position of who can be a communist fluctuates with prevailing circumstances (e.g., Second United Front from 1939 to 1939 vs. Cultural Revolution from 1966 to 1976), and it changes from one generation to the next (e.g., Mao vs. Jiang). Opinions on the matter also differ among political leaders and factions within the Politburo.

102. The "Four Principles" are upholding the socialist road, the people's democratic dictatorship (i.e., dictatorship of the proletariat), the leadership of the Communist Party, and Marxism–Leninism and Mao Tse-tung thought (http://www.marxists.org/subject/china/documents/cpc/history/01.htm).

103. Section 2(1) of MPS Labor and Personnel Office, "Guidelines on Recruitment of Police" ("*Guanyu xishou renmin jingcha de guiding*"), August 15, 1984. See *Compendium of PRC Public Security Laws* [*Zhonghua renmin gongheguo gongan falu quanshu*], Jilin renmin chubanshe, Jilin, 1995.

104. Section 3(1) of MPS Labor and Personnel Office, "Guidelines on Recruitment of Police" ("*Guanyu xishou renmin jingcha de guiding*"), August 15, 1984. See *Compendium of PRC Public Security Laws* [*Zhonghua renmin gongheguo gongan falu quanshu*], Jilin renmin chubanshe, Jilin, 1995.

105. MPS Political Department, "Notice regarding Certain Issues to Pay Attention to in Recruiting Contract People's Police" ("*Guanyu xishou minjing yinggai zhuyi jige wenti de tongzi*"), May 25, 1985. See *Compendium of PRC Public Security Laws* [*Zhonghua renmin gongheguo gongan falu quanshu*], Jilin renmin chubanshe, Jilin, 1995.

106. Section I of MPS Labor and Personnel Office, "Guidelines on Recruitment of Police" ("*Guanyu xishou renmin jingcha de guiding*"), August 15, 1984. See *Compendium of PRC Public Security Laws* [*Zhonghua renmin gongheguo gongan falu quanshu*], Jilin renmin chubanshe, Jilin, 1995.

107. Section II of MPS Labor and Personnel Office, "Guidelines on Recruitment of Police" ("*Guanyu xishou renmin jingcha de guiding*"), August 15, 1984. See *Compendium of PRC Public Security Laws* [*Zhonghua renmin gongheguo gongan falu quanshu*], Jilin renmin chubanshe, Jilin, 1995.

108. Ibid.

109. "Quality of Public Security Organ Leadership" ["*Gongan jiguan lingdao de suzhi*"], *China Public Security Encyclopedia* [*Zhongguo Gongan baike quanshu*], Jilin renmin chubanshe, Jilin, 1989.

110. "Opinion regarding Improving and Strengthening Political Thought Work in Colleges," ("*Gonganbu jiaoyubu guanyu gaijin he jia qiang gongan yuanxiao sixiang zhengzhi gongzuo de yijian*"). See *China Public Security Encyclopedia* [*Zhongguo Gongan baike quanshu*], Jilin renmin chubanshe, Jilin, 1989.

111. Students were also expected to pass classes in Chinese, English, law and morality, constitutional law, criminal law, criminal procedural law, public security foundational theory, public security secretary work, public security management, public order management, security, preliminary hearings, criminal investigations, police theory, public security administrative procedure, public security policy, criminal intelligence, public security information, criminal evidence, criminology, and foreign police work. See "2001 Subject and Education Materials for Higher Education Independent [Police] Students," *Public Security Education* [*Gongan Jiaoyu*], 71, 45, 2001.

112. *China Public Security Encyclopedia* [*Zhongguo Gongan baike quanshu*], Jilin renmin chubanshe, Jilin, 1989.

113. "Required Qualities of Public Security Policy Makers" ["*Gongan juecezhe ying jubei de suzhi*"], *China Public Security Encyclopedia* [*Zhongguo Gongan baike quanshu*], Jilin renmin chubanshe, Jilin, 1989.

114. "Three-Dimensional Thinking of Public Security Organ Leaders" ["*Gongan jiguan lingdao de liti siwei fangshi*"], *China Public Security Encyclopedia* [*Zhongguo Gongan baike quanshu*], Jilin renmin chubanshe, Jilin, 1989.

115. "Public Security Political Work" ["*Gongan zhengzhi gongzuo*"], *China Public Security Encyclopedia* [*Zhongguo Gongan baike quanshu*], Jilin renmin chubanshe, Jilin, 1989.

116. MPS Labor and Personnel Office, "Regulations for People's Police Basic Unit Political Instructors" ("*Renmin jingcha jiceng danwei zhengzhi zhidao yuan gongzuo tiaoli*"), May 5, 1984. The Fifth Public Security National Political Work Conference passed these regulations, which replaced the earlier 1962 MPS regulations regarding "Interim Detail Rules on Public Security Post Political Instructor Interim Work" ("*Gongan paichusuo zhengzhi zhidaoyuan zhanxing xize*"). See *China Public Security Encyclopedia* [*Zhongguo Gongan baike quanshu*], Jilin renmin chubanshe, Jilin, 1989.

117. "People's Police Reward and Punishment Regulations" ("*Renmin jingcha zhangcheng tiaoli*"). See *China Public Security Encyclopedia* [*Zhongguo Gongan baike quanshu*], Jilin renmin chubanshe, Jilin, 1989.

118. Ibid.

119. MPS Policy and Law Research Office, *Compilation of Public Security Laws and Regulations: 1950–1979* [*Gongan fagui huibian: 1950–1979*], Qunzhong chubanshe, Beijing, 1980, p. 440.

120. People's Central Government, Ministry of Finance, People's Central Government, MPS, "Regulations regarding Standards for the Classification of Ranks, Uniform, Collar Insignia, Cap Badge and Other Remunerations" ["*Zhongyang renmin zhengfu caizhengbu, Zhongyang renmin zhengfu gonganbu, "Guanyu renmin jingcha de dangji huafen, fuzhuang, lingzhang, maohui ji qi gongji daiyu biaozhun de guiding*"], in MPS Policy and Law Research Office, *Compilation of Public Security Laws and Regulations: 1950–1979* [*Gongan fagui huibian: 1950–1979*], Qunzhong chubanshe, Beijing, 1980, pp. 438–439.

121. "Basic Principles on Awarding Police Rank" ["*Shouyu jingxian de jiben yuanze*"], in *Public Security Internal Work Manual* [*Gongan Neiqing Gongzuo Shouce*], Jingguan jiaoyu chubanshe, Beijing, 1997, p. 471.

122. The "Four Principles" are upholding the socialist road, the people's democratic dictatorship (i.e., dictatorship of the proletariat), the leadership of the Communist Party, and Marxism-Leninism and Mao Tse-tung thought (http://www.marxists.org/subject/china/documents/cpc/history/01.htm).

123. "Public Security Political Thought Work" ["*Gongan sixiang zhengzhi gongzuo*"], in MPS Policy and Law Research Office, *Compilation of Public Security Laws and Regulations: 1950–1979* [*Gongan fagui huibian: 1950–1979*], Qunzhong chubanshe, Beijing, 1980, p. 333.

124. Ibid.
125. Ibid.
126. (a) "Methods of Public Security Political Thought Work" ["*Gongan sixiang zhengzhi gongzuo de fangfa*"], in MPS Policy and Law Research Office, *Compilation of Public Security Laws and Regulations: 1950-1979* [*Gongan fagui huibian: 1950-1979*], Qunzhong chubanshe, Beijing, 1980, pp. 333-334. (b) "Principles of Public Security Political Thought Work" ["*Gongan sixiang zhengzhi gongzuo de yuanze*"], in MPS Policy and Law Research Office, *Compilation of Public Security Laws and Regulations: 1950-1979* [*Gongan fagui huibian: 1950-1979*], Qunzhong chubanshe, Beijing, 1980, pp. 334-335.
127. In China, the great man makes this history thesis still hold. See Jing Huang, *Factionalism in Chinese Communist Politics*, Cambridge University Press, Cambridge, UK, 2000.
128. (a) Wang Xiaoming, "China on the Verge of a 'Momentous Era,'" *East Asia Cultures Critique*, 11(3), 585-611, 2003. With the demise of Mao's ideology, the nation's spiritual platform became empty. (b) Liu Junning, "Classical Liberalism Catches on in China," *Journal of Democracy*, 11(3), 48-57, 2000. With the demise of the old communist ideology, new liberal ideas are vying for influence.
129. Christine Wong, "Rebuilding Government for the 21st Century: Can China Incrementally Reform the Public Sector?" *China Quarterly*, 200, 929-952, 2009.
130. Zhiyue Bo, "Hu Jintao and the CPC's Ideology: A Historical Perspective," *Journal of Chinese Political Science*, 9(2), 27-45, 2003. Deng, having lived through the Cultural Revolution, wanted to liberate the country from Mao's personality cult by insisting on "liberating the mind" and "seeking truth from facts."
131. Liu Junning, "Classical Liberalism Catches on in China," *Journal of Democracy*, 11(3), 48-57, 2000.
132. Public security must secure the people's democratic dictatorship against capitalistic attacks, foreign encroachments, and domestic destabilizing elements during the reform era. See Huang Yong, "Tentative Discussion of the Guiding Impact of Deng Xiaoping's Democratic Dictatorship on Public Security Work" ["*Shilun Deng Xiaoping renmin minzhu zhuanzheng sixiang dui gongan gongzuo shijian de zhidao yiyi*"], in China Police Studies Society, Police Scientific Management Professional Committee (*Zhongguo jingcha xuehui jingcha guanli kexue zhuanye weiyuanhui*), and China Public Administration Studies Society, Public Security Administration Research Affiliated Society (*Zhongguo xingzheng guanli xuehui, gongan guanli yanjiu fenhui*) (Eds.), *Comprehensive Discussion on Police Management* [*Jingwu guanli zonglun*], Zhongguo renmin gongan daxue chubanshe, Beijing, 1998, pp. 3-16.
133. "Discussion on Liberating the Mind and Public Security Work" [*Jiefang sixiang*], Ibid., pp. 35-44. Deng admonished Chinese leadership to liberate their thought (*jie fang sixing*) in pursuing reform, to be objective and not subjective (*zhuguan yu keguan shuang fu*), to unite thought with reality (*sixiang yu shiji shuangfu*), and to seek truth from facts (*shishi jiushi*).
134. (a) "Strengthen the Theoretical Research on Deng Xiaoping's Thoughts on 'Progressive Policy Making,' Raising the Macro Strategic Policymaking Standard of Public Security" ["*Jiaqiang Deng Xiaoping 'jian jin juece' sixiang de lilun yanjiu, tigao gongan hongguan zhanlue juece shuiping*"]. Ibid., pp. 16-22. (b) For how such policy decision-making works in economic reform, see Staya Gabriel, "Economic Liberalization in Post-Mao China: Crossing the River by Feeling for Stones," *China Essay Series*, October, 1998 (http://www.mtholyoke.edu/courses/sgabriel/economics/china-essays/7.html).
135. Public security as professional organs should work with the masses in providing for law and order; that is, the police should depend and rely on the masses (*yikao qunzhong*) when mediating disputes, maintaining order, securing premises, and investigating crime. See "Basic Understanding of Public Security Work with Chinese Characteristics" ["*You zhongguo deshi de gongan gongzuo luxing qianshi*"], in China Police Studies Society, Police Scientific Management Professional Committee (*Zhongguo jingcha xuehui jingcha guanli kexue zhuanye weiyuanhui*), and China Public Administration Studies Society, Public Security Administration Research

Affiliated Society (*Zhongguo xingzheng guanli xuehui, gongan guanli yanjiu fenhui*) (Eds.), *Comprehensive Discussion on Police Management* [*Jingwu guanli zonglun*], Zhongguo renmin gongan daxue chubanshe, Beijing, 1998, pp. 23–34.

136. Andrew J. Nathan and Tianjian Shi, "Left and Right with Chinese Characteristics: Issues and Alignments in Deng Xiaoping's China," *World Politics*, 48(4), 522–550, 1996.

137. CCCPC Literature Research Office, *Memories of Deng Xiaoping* [*Huiyi Deng Xiaoping*], Zhongyang Dangxiao, Beijing, 1999.

138. "Practice is the sole criterion of truth."

139. Deng Xiaoping, *Selected Works of Deng Xiaoping (1975–1982)* [*Deng Xiaoping Wenxuan (1975–1982)*], Renmin chubanshe, Beijing, 1983.

140. China Police Studies Society, Police Scientific Management Professional Committee (*Zhongguo jingcha xuehui jingcha guanli kexue zhuanye weiyuanhui*), and China Public Administration Studies Society, Public Security Administration Research Affiliated Society (*Zhongguo xingzheng guanli xuehui, gongan guanli yanjiu fenhui*) (Eds.), *Comprehensive Discussion on Police Management* [*Jingwu guanli zonglun*], Zhongguo renmin gongan daxue chubanshe, Beijing, 1998.

141. (a) Deng Xiaoping, "Build Socialism with Chinese Characteristics," excerpt from a talk with the Japanese delegation to the Second Session of the Council of Sino–Japanese Non-Governmental Persons, June 30, 1984 (http://www.wellesley.edu/Polisci/wj/China/Deng/Building.htm). (b) Shaun Breslin, *Capitalism with Chinese Characteristics: The Public, the Private and the International*, Working Paper No. 104, Asia Research Centre, Murdoch University, Perth, Western Australia, 2004 (http://wwwarc.murdoch.edu.au/wp/wp104.pdf). (c) Police Studies Society, Public Security Fundamental Theory Professional Committee, and Research Group on China Public Security Characteristics (Eds.), *Research on Public Security with Chinese Characteristics* [*Zhongguo gongan tese zhi yanjiu*], Qunzhong chubanshe, Beijing, 1996.

142. Police Studies Society, Public Security Fundamental Theory Professional Committee, and Research Group on China Public Security Characteristics (Eds.), *Research on Public Security with Chinese Characteristics* [*Zhongguo gongan tese zhi yanjiu*], Qunzhong chubanshe, Beijing, 1996, p. 1.

143. Ibid., p. 3.

144. James Q. Wilson, *Varieties of Police Behavior*, Harvard University Press, Cambridge, MA, 1968.

145. Police Studies Society, Public Security Fundamental Theory Professional Committee, and Research Group on China Public Security Characteristics (Eds.), *Research on Public Security with Chinese Characteristics* [*Zhongguo gongan tese zhi yanjiu*], Qunzhong chubanshe, Beijing, 1996, p. 3.

146. Sir Robert Peel's classic observation is, "The public are the police and the police are the public."

147. Kam C. Wong, "The Philosophy of Community Policing in China," *Police Quarterly*, 4(2), 186–214, 2001.

148. David Bayley, *Patterns of Policing: A Comparative International Analysis*, Rutgers University Press, Piscataway, NJ, 1986.

149. Lord Grocott, "Police: England and Wales," *Parliamentary Business*, 692(97), June 7, 2007 (http://www.parliament.the-stationery-office.co.uk/pa/ld200607/ldhansrd/text/70607-0002.htm).

150. National Institute of Justice, *Crime and Policing in Rural and Small-Town America: An Overview of the Issues*, National Institute of Justice, Washington, DC, 1995 (http://www.nij.gov/pubs-sum/154354.htm).

151. James Q. Wilson, *Varieties of Police Behavior: The Management of Law and Order in Eight Communities*, Harvard University Press, Cambridge, MA, 1968.

152. Police Studies Society, Public Security Fundamental Theory Professional Committee, and Research Group on China Public Security Characteristics (Eds.), *Research on Public Security with Chinese Characteristics* [*Zhongguo gongan tese zhi yanjiu*], Qunzhong chubanshe, Beijing, 1996, pp. 3–7.

153. John Chan, "As Chinese Premier Urges 'Respect' for Workers, Police Prepare Crackdown," *World Socialist Web Site*, June 18, 2010 (http://www.wsws.org/articles/2010/jun2010/chin-j18.shtml).

154. Police Studies Society, Public Security Fundamental Theory Professional Committee, and Research Group on China Public Security Characteristics (Eds.), *Research on Public Security with Chinese Characteristics* [*Zhongguo gongan tese zhi yanjiu*], Qunzhong chubanshe, Beijing, 1996, p. 16.

155. See discussion on Chinese public security organs being an important tool of the people's democratic dictatorship (*Zhongguo gongan jiguan shi renmin minzhu zhuanzheng de zhong yao gongju*) in Police Studies Society, Public Security Fundamental Theory Professional Committee, and Research Group on China Public Security Characteristics (Eds.), *Research on Public Security with Chinese Characteristics* [*Zhongguo gongan tese zhi yanjiu*], Qunzhong chubanshe, Beijing, 1996, pp. 16–22.

156. Ibid., pp. 29–31.

157. Ibid., p. 30.

158. Ibid., p. 31.

159. Ibid., p. 32.

160. Ibid., pp. 23–24.

161. Ibid., p. 33.

162. Joseph Fewsmith, *China since Tiananmen: The Politics of Transition*, Cambridge University Press, Cambridge, UK, 2001, pp. 75–101.

163. Deng Xiaoping, *Selected Works of Deng Xiaoping (1982–1992)* [*Deng Xiaoping Wenxuan (1982–1992)*], Vol. 3, Foreign Language Press, Beijing, 1983.

164. Deng Xiaoping, *Selected Works of Deng Xiaoping (1982–1992)* [*Deng Xiaoping Wenxuan (1982–1992)*], Vol. 3, Foreign Language Press, Beijing, 1994, p. 277 (translated by the Central Compilation and Translation Bureau).

165. Liang Zhang, Andrew J. Nathan, and Perry Link (Eds.), *The Tiananmen Papers*, Public Affairs, New York, 2001, p. 148.

166. *Chinese President's Speech to Mark 20 Years of Reform*, Third and Final Part, British Broadcasting Corporation, December 18, 1998.

167. Erik Eckholm, "Clinton in China: News Analysis," *New York Times*, June 28, 1998, p. 1. President Jiang debated President Bill Clinton on June 27, 1998, in Beijing.

168. Benjamin Yang, *Deng: A Political Biography*, M.E. Sharpe, London, 1998. Deng was able to transform China because of his political skills and astuteness, not as a result of his ideology.

169. Deng: "We must cross the river by feeling the stones with our feet."

170. Deng: "Black cat, white cat, it's a good cat if it catches the mouse."

171. It has been suggested that the ideological crisis in China during the reform period is due to a lack of a core ideology and the existence of competing schools of thoughts. Kalpana Misra, *From Post-Maoism to Post-Marxism: The Erosion of Official Ideology in Deng's China*, Rutledge University Press, Piscataway, NJ, 1998.

172. According to standard communist doctrine as understood by Chinese political leadership, the existence, roles, and functions of the police changed with development of the communist state. The police should handle mass disturbance incidents with care; they should anticipate conflicts with intelligent citizens and resolve conflicts through education. "Properly Handling Mass Incidents, Correct Way to Handle Internal Contradictions with the People," *Public Security Studies*, 15(1), 61–64, 2000.

173. Wang Fang, "Strengthen Public Security Social Science Theory Research, Open Up New Phase of Public Security Work" [*"Jiaqiang gongan shehui kexue lilun yanjiu, gaituo gongan gongzuo xin jumian]," Public Security Studies*, 1, 1988 (available on PSU CD).

174. Wang Jingron, "Strengthening Public Security Theoretical Research Is an Urgent Task Confronting Us" [*Jiaqiang gongan lilun yanjiu shi women mianlin de yixiang zhongyao er jinji de renwu*], *Public Security Studies*, 1, 1988 (available on PSU CD).

175. Andrew J. Nathan, "Authoritarian Resilience," *Journal of Democracy*, 14(1), 6–17, 2003.

176. Sam Crane, "Chinese Characteristics," *The Useless Tree: Ancient Chinese Thought in Modern American Life*, November 17, 2007 (http://uselesstree.typepad.com/useless_tree/2006/11/chinese_charact.html). "Thus the 'China' v. 'us' distinction does not really hold up. China is not as Chinese as we might think, and the West is not at Western as we might want."

177. (a) Deng Xiaoping, "Build Socialism with Chinese Characteristics," excerpt from a talk with the Japanese delegation to the second session of the Council of Sino–Japanese Non-Governmental Persons, June 30, 1984 (http://www.wellesley.edu/Polisci/wj/China/Deng/Building.htm). (b) Shaun Breslin, *Capitalism with Chinese Characteristics: The Public, the Private and the International*, Working Paper No. 104, Asia Research Centre, Murdoch University, Perth, Western Australia, 2004 (http://wwwarc.murdoch.edu.au/wp/wp104.pdf).

178. Wang Lihua, "China Needs Critical Thinkers," *The China Lawyer Blog*, September 25th, 2007. Learning how to do business in China requires trying to learn how Chinese people think.

179. Murray Scot Tanner, "Ideological Struggle over Police Reform, 1988–1993," in Edwin A. Winckler (Ed.), *Transition from Communism in China: Institutional and Comparative Analyses* (pp. 111–128), Lynne Rienner Publishers, London, 1999. This article draws upon original essays published in *Public Security Studies*, a journal sponsored by the MPS.

180. I use "redefined" or "being redefined" and not "to define" in order to make clear that there is a difference between MPS's assertive effort to "redefine" (reinvent) itself in light of ideology and "being redefined" due to force of circumstances (i.e., reacting to events). There is still the other issue of how police are being "redefined" by the public or key constituents, such as human rights activists, foreigners, and businessmen. In "redefining" the police, the Chinese leadership, as advocates of scientific Marxism, claim to follow a historical trajectory (historical materialism) when forecasting the future (CPC as vanguard of utopianism) by negotiating the present (dialectics), incrementally and experimentally ("crossing the river by feeling the stones").

181. Murray Scot Tanner, "Ideological Struggle over Police Reform, 1988–1993," in Edwin A. Winckler (Ed.), *Transition from Communism in China: Institutional and Comparative Analyses* (pp. 111–128), Lynne Rienner Publishers, London, 1999. This article draws upon original essays published in *Public Security Studies*, a journal sponsored by the MPS.

182. Sarah Biddulph, *Legal Reform and Administrative Detention Powers in China*, Cambridge University Press, Cambridge, UK, 2007.

183. Murray Scot Tanner, "Ideological Struggle over Police Reform, 1988–1993," in Edwin A. Winckler (Ed.), *Transition from Communism in China: Institutional and Comparative Analyses* (pp. 111–128), Lynne Rienner Publishers, London, 1999. This article draws upon original essays published in *Public Security Studies*, a journal sponsored by the MPS.

184. Ibid., p. 115.

185. Ibid., p. 119.

186. Ibid., p. 118.

187. Ibid., p. 121.

188. Ibid., p. 124.

189. Guoguang Wu, "Legitimacy Crisis, Political Economy, and the Fifteenth Party Congress," in Andrew J. Nathan, Zhaohui Hong, and Steven R. Smith (Eds.), *Dilemmas of Reform in Jiang Zemin's China* (pp. 13–32), Lynne Rienner Publishers, London, 1999.

190. "CPC Pledges to Focus on Party Building for Advancement of Ruling Capacity," *News of CPC*, September 24, 2004 (http://english.cpc.people.com.cn/66097/66185/4480039.html).

191. Deng Xiaoping, "Excerpts from Talks Given in Wuchang, Shenzhen, Zhuhai, and Shanghai, January 18 to February 21, 1992," in *Selected Works of Deng Xiaoping (1982–1992)* [*Deng Xiaoping Wenxuan (1982–1992)*], Vol. 3, Foreign Language Press, Beijing, 1994, p. 277 (translated by the Central Compilation and Translation Bureau).

192. Li Qingyu, "Studying Deng Xiaoping's Theory and Improving the Police Ability to Control Public Order," *Public Security Studies*, 63, 6–7, 1999.

193. "Senior Chinese Leader Calls for Enhanced Research on Marxism," *News of CPC*, January 17, 2006 (http://english.cpc.people.com.cn/66106/4479842.html).

194. "Staff in IPS of MPS Are Celebrating the Twentieth Anniversary of the Third Plenary Session of the 11th Party Central Committee," *Public Security Studies*, 68, 95–96, 1999.
195. The Editorial Office, "To Enhance the Research of Public Security Theories and Guide the Practice of Public Security Work," *Public Security Studies*, 72, 6–7, 2000.
196. Editorial Board, "Reflection and Prospecting," *Public Security Studies*, 57, 1–17, 1998.
197. It is often difficult to decide the meaning and import of such recitations of leaders' thinking. Are they obligatory mentions or do they have real significance? Obligatory or not, the frequent mentions of Deng speak to his appeal to an entire generation of police reformers. Many of Deng's ideas are still in vogue, such as emancipation of the mind and stability above all.
198. Editorial Board, "Reflection and Prospecting," *Public Security Studies*, 57, 1–17, 1998.
199. "Staff in IPS of MPS Are Celebrating the Twentieth Anniversary of the Third Plenary Session of the 11th Party Central Committee," *Public Security Studies*, 68, 95–96, 1999.
200. Li Qingyu, "Mastering the Marxist Stand, Viewpoint and Method to Improve Our Competence in Analyzing and Solving Problems," *Public Security Studies*, 66, 6–8, 1999.
201. Ding Jinfa, "Handling the Six Relationships Properly to Promote the Coordinated Development in Policing," *Public Security Studies*, 63, 11–14, 1999.
202. Editorial Board, "Making Great Efforts in Editing PS: New Year Message," *Public Security Studies*, 57, 5, 1999.
203. Figuring out how to revise fundamental political thinking and doctrine in China without offending key constituents or being politically incorrect (or, worse, inept) is difficult. The strategy of reformers is not to be labeled as "revisionist" or "revolutionary," as both terms suggest that current ideology and its promoters are wrongheaded.
204. Jiang Zemin delivered a report at the 16th National Congress of the Communist Party of China on November 8, 2002, entitled "Build a Well-Off Society in an All-Round Way and Create a New Situation in Building Socialism with Chinese Characteristics" (http://xibu.tjfsu.edu.cn/elearning/lk/16en.htm).
205. Wei Zhenzhong, "Deepening the Campaign of Trying to Be the Best in Work and Promoting Policing," *Public Security Studies*, 66, 9–10, 1999.
206. Li Qingyu, "Studying Deng Xiaoping's Theory and Improving the Police Ability to Control Public Order," *Public Security Studies*, 63, 6–7, 1999.
207. Zhao Zhengyong, "Shouldering the Responsibility Conscientiously to Ensure Social Stability," *Public Security Studies*, 66, 11–13, 1999.
208. Wang Yingjie, "A Discussion of General Planning to Deal with Public Order Incidents," *Public Security Studies*, 64, 12–14, 1999.
209. (a) Yu Guoxing, "Public Security Organs Must Stick to the Principle of Being Responsible to Law and Satisfaction of the People," *Public Security Studies*, 65, 1–4, 1999. (b) Lu Yuming, "Make People Satisfied with Our Police Force," *Public Security Studies*, 65, 5–7, 1999.
210. Li Shuntao, "Pondering over the "Masses Supervision over Public Security Organs," *Public Security Studies*, 67, 21–23, 1999.
211. Lu Zhuo, "Enhancing Policing in Rural Areas to Promote a Stable Economic Development," *Public Security Studies*, 63, 8–10, 1999.
212. "Combating Economic Crime and Carrying Out International Cooperation: Role of the State in Combating Economic and Financial Crimes," statement made by Jia Chunwang, Minister of Public Security of People's Republic of China, at the Monaco World Summit on Governments and Private Sector Fighting Economic Crime, October, 24, 2002 (http://www.china-un.ch/eng/gjhyfy/qqwt/t85743.htm).
213. "On Deng Xiaoping's Thinking of the Comprehensive Management of the Anti-Corruption," *Free Papers*, June 8, 2009 (http://www.hi138.com/e/?i74574).
214. Zhang Tao, "On Deng Xiaoping's Ideology against Economic Crimes," *Public Security Studies*, 63, 14–19, 1999.
215. Li Shuntao, "Discussion on Establishing and the Practice of Incentives for Reward and Punishment within Public Security Organs," *Public Security Studies*, 64, 1–3, 1999.

216. Yang Wenzhong, "Thought and Measures regarding the Administration of Incoming Populations in Terms of a Sustainable Development Strategy for Cities," *Public Security Studies*, 64, 8–11, 1999.

217. Lu Shimin, "Practice and Thoughts on Setting Up a Fast Response Mechanism to Improve Capability to Maintain Public Order," *Public Security Studies*, 64, 4–7, 1999.

218. Guo Yusheng, "Try Hard to Keep the Promise of 'Four-Have' and 'Four-Must,' and Strongly Support the Establishment of '110,'" *Public Security Studies*, 65, 11–13, 1999.

219. Sun Jianguo, "Enhancing the Four Kinds of Consciousness to Promote the Level of Public Traffic Administration," *Public Security Studies*, 66, 14–16, 1999.

220. Han Baozhong, Wang Xin, and He Yinghua, "Survey of and Pondering over the Situation of Building Up a Harmonious Relationship between the Police and Public" ["*Guanyu gouhian hexie jingmin guanxi qingkuang de tiaocha yu xikao*"], *Public Security Studies*, 172, 79–86, 2009.

221. Joseph Fewsmith, "Promoting the Scientific Development Concept," *China Leadership Monitor*, 11, 1–11, 2004 (http://www.hoover.org/publications/china-leadership-monitor/article/6226). Alternatively, "scientific development perspective" or "viewpoint."

222. (a) "China to Adhere to Scientific Development Philosophy," *Xinhua*, November 7, 2003 (http://www.chinadaily.com.cn/en/doc/2003-11/07/content_279693.htm). The SDC championed the concepts of *balanced development*, thus the idea of people as the foundation (*yi ren wei ben*); *coordinated development*, thus the idea of constructing a harmonious society (*hexie shehui jian-she*); and *sustainable development*. (b) "China Embraces New Scientific Development Concept: Hu," *People's Daily Online*, April 29, 2006 (http://english.peopledaily.com.cn/200604/22/eng20060422_260256.html).

223. "Premier Wen Highlights Scientific Development Concept," *People's Daily Online*, February 22, 2004 (http://english.peopledaily.com.cn/200402/22/eng20040222_135467.shtml).

224. "China Embraces New Scientific Development Concept: Hu," *People's Daily Online*, April 29, 2006 (http://english.peopledaily.com.cn/200604/22/eng20060422_260256.html).

225. "Put into Effect a Scientific Viewpoint of Development in an All-Round Way," December 14, 2004 (http://english.cpc.people.com.cn/65547/65573/4480400.html).

226. Editorial Board, "New Year's Message," *Public Security Studies*, 171, 5–7, 2009.

227. Zeng Shenquan, "Advance Good and Fast Development of the Cause of Public Security Guided by the Concept of Scientific Development," *Public Security Studies*, 171, 8–12, 2009.

228. Ibid.

229. Dexter Roberts and Chi-Chu Tschang, "China's Rising Leaders," *Businessweek*, October 1, 2007.

230. Alice Miller, "The 18th Central Committee Politburo: A Quixotic, Foolhardy, Rashly Speculative, but Nonetheless Ruthlessly Reasoned Projection," *Chinese Leadership Monitor*, June 28, 2010.

231. Willy Lam, "CPC Campaign for a New Generation of 'Red and Expert' Officials," *China Brief*, 9, 13, 2009.

232. Pairing "eliminate" and "replace" is consistent with Chinese admonitions to get rid of the bad and replace it with the good.

233. Wen Taoyuan, "Knowledge of the 'Six Points of Elimination' and 'Six Points of Establishment' Is a Must in Making a Revolution of Law Enforcement Ideology," *Public Security Studies*, 116, 59–61, 2004.

234. Ibid., p. 60.

235. Ibid.

236. Sir Robert Peele, "The people are the police, and the police are the people."

237. Wen Taoyuan, "Knowledge of the 'Six Points of Elimination' and 'Six Points of Establishment' Is a Must in Making a Revolution of Law Enforcement Ideology," *Public Security Studies*, 116, 59–61, 2004.

238. Ibid.

239. This means that the police are focusing on ("emphasis") certain police missions and functions and neglecting others ("light").

240. This means that the police are more concerned with national security and social stability, at the expense of protecting human rights (e.g., "Strike Hard" campaign of 1983). The focus was entirely on striking hard and fast with little regard for defendants' rights.

241. This means that the police are focusing on the crime fighting function, not the service delivery function. This also means that the police are not service oriented; for example, they treat all law violators as class enemies.

242. This means that the police are only interested in crime fighting (e.g., "Strike Hard" campaign), not crime prevention (e.g., community education).

243. This means that the police are seeking substantive justice and ignoring procedural justice, such as with regard to tortured confessions.

244. This means that the police are clearing cases with little regard for the law. See Wen Taoyuan, "Knowledge of the 'Six Points of Elimination' and 'Six Points of Establishment' Is a Must in Making a Revolution of Law Enforcement Ideology," *Public Security Studies*, 116, 59–61, 2004.

245. Senior Police Adviser to the OSCE Secretary General, *Guidebook on Democratic Policing*, Organization for Security and Cooperation in Europe (OSCE), Vienna, 2008, pp. 9–10 (polis.osce.org/library/view?item_id=2658&attach_id=2639).

246. Kam C. Wong, *Policing in China: History and Reform*, Peter Lang, Bern, Switzerland, 2009, Chapter 9.

247. Editorial Department, "Greetings at the Beginning of the Year," *Public Security Studies*, 69, 1, 2000.

248. Ibid.

249. Qiang Wei, "Carrying Forward and Forging into the Future, Making Great Effort to Meet the New Century," *Public Security Studies*, 69, 4–7, 2000.

250. Chen Yuanxiao, "Pondering over the Sustained Development and Improvement of Policing," *Public Security Studies*, 78, 22–25, 2001.

251. Kui-Wai Li, "The Two Decades of China's Economic Reform Compared," *World Economy and China*, 9(2), 55–60, 2001. Economic overheating in the past was caused by industrial bottlenecks and a lack of complementary development in infrastructure, such as energy and transport.

252. "Profile: Hu Jintao—Chinese President, Chairman of Central Military Commission," *China Daily*, March 16, 2008 (http://english.peopledaily.com.cn/90002/93244/93297/6374356.html). The "scientific development perspective" was written into the Party Constitution at the 17th CPC National Congress, becoming a guiding principle for the country's efforts to build "socialism with Chinese characteristics."

253. Shi Yuanliang, "Public Security Political Thought Education under Conditions of Socialist Market Economic Conditions" ["*Shilun shehui zhuyi sichang jingji tiaojian xia de gongan sixing zhengzhi gongzuo*"], *Public Security Studies*, 55, 24–29, 1995. Political–ideological education is a favored measure for improving police performance in China.

254. The "three items of education" campaign focused on "idea education" (*sixiang jiaoyu*) and was based on self-education. See items 1 and 2 on p. 28 in Zheng Xingjun, "Pondering over the Campaign of 'Enforcing Education in Three Respects,'" *Public Security Studies*, 77, 28–32, 2001.

255. The "three items of education" campaign called for resolute actions to investigate and dispose of police misconduct and illegality. Police who do not love the profession and perform to standards must be fired without mercy. See item 2 on p. 32 in Zheng Xingjun, "Pondering over the Campaign of 'Enforcing Education in Three Respects,'" *Public Security Studies*, 77, 28–32, 2001.

256. "Major Events of 'Three Kinds of Education,'" *Police Daily Online*, February 26, 2002.

257. "Henan Principal Started 'Three Items of Education,'" *China Police Report*, October 24, 2001.

258. "Qinghai Province's Stern Handling of Troops Achieves Great Improvements," *China Police Report*, January 17, 2002.

259. "Zhejiang Public Security's 'Three Items of Education' Opportunistically Merged with People's Congress's Appraisal" ["*Zhejiang gongan zhang 'sanxian jiaoyu' yu rendai pingyi you ji jiehe*"], *China Police Daily*, December 21, 2001.

260. Zheng Xingjun, "Pondering over the Campaign of 'Enforcing Education in Three Respects,'" *Public Security Studies*, 77, 28–31, 2001. The "three items of education" campaign allowed participating police agencies and officers to engage in subjective, critical self-examination and objective constructive assessment, and it allowed the public to criticize police performance.

261. Murray Scot Tanner and Eric Green, "Principals and Secret Agents: Central Versus Local Control over Policing and Obstacles to 'Rule of Law' in China," *China Quarterly*, 94, 644–670, 2007.

262. Xue Chun-Bo, "A Brief Comment on the Significance of Sticking with the Current Leading System of Public Security Organ," *Journal of Quizhou Police Officer Vocational College*, 14(2), 75–78, 2002. The MPS should continue with the current dual central vs. local management over the police.

263. Wan Shenzi, Li Zhenyu, Zhang Caigui, and Zhang Lincun, "The Issue regarding Police Participating in Non-Policing Activities" ["*Guanyu gongan minjing canyu fei jingwu huodong de tiaocha*"], *Public Security Studies*, 69, 21–24, 2000.

264. Claude Aubert and Xiande Li, "Peasant Burden: Taxes and Levies Imposed on Chinese Farmers," in *Agricultural Policies in China after WTO Accession*, Organization for Economic Cooperation and Development (OECD), Paris, 2002, pp. 160–179.

265. Wan Shenzi, Li Zhenyu, Zhang Caigui, and Zhang Lincun, "The Issue regarding Police Participating in Non-Policing Activities" ["*Guanyu gongan minjing canyu fei jingwu huodong de tiaocha*"], *Public Security Studies*, 69, 21–24, 2000.

266. Ibid.

267. Ibid.

268. Ibid.

269. Ibid.

270. Ibid., pp. 22–23

271. Ibid., p. 22

272. Ibid.

273. Ibid., p. 23

274. Ibid.

275. Ibid., p. 24

276. Ibid.

277. Ma Yaxiong, "Competence in Police Administration Systems Combining Centralization and Decentralization in Britain and Japan" ["*Ying Ri jingcha tiao kuai jiehe guanli tizhi zhong de quan xian hua feng*"], *Public Security Studies*, 97(11), 91–94, 2002.

278. Zheng Yongnian, "Institutional Economics and Central/Local Relations in China: Evolving Research," *China: An International Journal*, 3(2), 240–269, 2005.

279. Wang Dawei, "From Gan Shi Qiao Model to the Trend of World Policing Reform—Comparative Study on the Police Reform of China and the West," *Public Security Studies*, 88, 21–28, 2000.

280. Kevin J. O'Brien and Li Lianjiang, "The Politics of Lodging Complaints in Rural China," *China Quarterly*, 143, 756–783, 1995.

281. Maria Edin, "Remaking the Communist Party-State: The Cadre Responsibility System at the Local Level in China," *China: An International Journal*, 1(1), 1–15, 2003.

282. "Regulations on the Management and Organization of Public Security Organs," promulgated by the State Council on November 13, 2006, at its 154th Meeting; implemented January 1, 2007, by State Council Order 154.

283. "Premier Zhu Reports on Government Work (III)," *People's Daily Online*, March 5, 2002 (http://english.peopledaily.com.cn/200203/05/eng20020305_91440.shtml). The CPC has long been concerned with the problem of bureaucracy, an ill they are trying to eradicate. Anti-bureaucracy is a constant rallying cry for large-scale rectification campaigns. Zhu Ronzhi has called for getting rid of the formalism and bureaucracy that harmed both the country and the people.

284. In 1952, the CPC launched the *san fan* ("three anti") and *wu fan* ("five anti") campaigns. The former was directed against the evils of "corruption, waste, and bureaucracy." Its main goal was to eliminate corrupt, abusive, irresponsible, and incompetent public officials. The *wu fan* movement was aimed at eliminating "tax evasion, bribery, cheating in government contracts, thefts of economic intelligence, and stealing of state assets." More generally, the two movements were initiated to purify the Party and clean up Chinese society.

285. Condemning formalism and bureaucracy has now become a daily ritual of the PRC government and CPC.

286. "Premier Zhu Reports on Government Work (I)," *People's Daily Online*, March 5, 2002 (http://english.peopledaily.com.cn/200203/05/eng20020305_91416.shtml).

287. "Hu Jintao's Report at the 17th Party Congress," *China Daily*, October 25, 2007 (http://www.china-embassy.org/eng/zt/768675/t375502.htm).

288. Olivia Yu and Lening Zhang, "The Underrecording of Crime by Police in China: A Case Study," *Policing: An International Journal of Police Strategy & Management*, 22, 252–263, 1999.

289. "Xinhua Commentary Criticizes Formalism," *People's Daily Online*, April 12, 2000 (http://english.peopledaily.com.cn/200004/12/eng20000412_38767.html).

290. Gong Zhengrong, "Making Efforts to Create a New Prospect in Policing in Buildup of Police Force," *Public Security Studies*, 75, 37–41, 2001. Developing and constructing police work requires a "seeking truth from facts" mentality.

291. Ren Zhongping, "Opinion: Fundamental Ideological Weapon for Great Advance toward New Century," *People's Daily Online*, October 31, 2000 (http://english.peopledaily.com.cn/200010/31/eng20001031_53965.html).

292. "Emancipate the Mind, Seek Truth from Facts and Unite as One in Looking to the Future," *People's Daily Online*, December 13, 1978 (http://english.peopledaily.com.cn/dengxp/vol2/text/b1260.html). This speech was presented at the closing session of the Central Working Conference that made preparations for the Third Plenary Session of the Eleventh Central Committee of the Chinese Communist Party that immediately followed. In essence, this speech served as the keynote address for the Third Plenary Session.

293. Research Group Project, "Career Achievement of Public Security Service and Supply Mode Relating to the Policeman and People Relations in the Reform Period," *Public Security Science Journal*, 103, 12–32, 2007. A standard item of police–public relations research in China is whether citizens would seek help from the police when in need.

294. "Decision of the Central Committee of the Chinese Communist Party concerning the Great Proletarian Cultural Revolution, adopted on August 8, 1966," *Peking Review*, 9(33), 6–11, 1966.

295. The campaign to go back to basics recalls earlier attempts by Chairman Mao to have cadres return to villages to experience firsthand what it is like to be a peasant.

296. "Returning to the Basics: Lessons from Fujian Province, Nanping Municipality, in Developing 'Three Mutual' Police and Peasant Activities" ["*Huigui benshi zhilu: Fujian sheng Nanping shi, kaizhan minjing yu nongmin 'san tong' huodong qishi lu*"], *China Police Daily*, March 29, 2002.

297. Literally, *san* is "three" and *tong* is "mutuality" or "link." Together, they mean that the police should be bonded with the people in three ways.

298. David W. Murphy and John L. Worrall, "Residency Requirements and Public Perceptions of the Police in Large Municipalities," *Policing*, 22(3), 327–342, 1999. This is not unlike American police's requirement that police officers must reside in the community where they are employed, although studies suggest that residency requirements have a negative impact on citizens' confidence in the ability of the police to protect them.

299. "Returning to the Basics: Lessons from Fujian Province, Nanping Municipality, in Developing 'Three Mutual' Police and Peasants Activities" ["*Huigui benshi zhilu: Fujian sheng Nanping shi, kaizhan minjing yu nongmin 'san tong' huodong qishi lu*"], *China Police Daily*, March 29, 2002.

300. "Lan Xi Police Bring Their Own Mats and Covers into Farmers' Homes" ["*Lan xi minjing zi dai pugai jing nonghu*"], *China Police Daily*, April 4, 2002.

301. "Shanghai Improves Transparency in Administration, Lawmaking," *People's Daily Online*, October 8, 2001 (http://english.peopledaily.com.cn/200110/08/eng20011008_81777.html). *Jingwu kongai* is part of a larger government transparency program launched by the central government to make government more open and accessible to the public.

302. *Jing* is short for *jingcha*, or "police," and *wu* means "work"; thus, *jingwu* means "police work." *Gong* means "public" and *kai* means "open"; thus, *gongkai* means "open to "public." *Jingwu gongkai* literally means "opening police work to the public."

303. "Laizhou's Practical Experience in Opening Up Police Work" ["*Cong Laizhou shihian kan jingwu gongkai*"], *China Police Daily*, August 18, 2001.

304. "Beijing Constable Museum Opens," *People's Daily Online*, August 3, 2001.

305. "Kunming to Build Police Museum," *People's Daily Online*, August 3, 2001.

306. "Beijing Police Hold First Open Activity for Public," *People's Daily Online*, August 5, 2001.

307. "A Letter to Web Readers" ["*Ji wanwen de yi feng xin*"], November 1, 2001.

308. "Beijing Police Launch Blogs, Podcasts to Boost Transparency," *People's Daily Online*, August 2, 2010.

309. With the exception of the MPS survey on public opinion regarding the police; see Chapter 3 in this text.

310. John Chan, "As Chinese Premier Urges 'Respect' for Workers, Police Prepare Crackdown," *World Socialist Web Site*, June 18, 2010 (http://www.wsws.org/articles/2010/jun2010/chin-j18.shtml).

311. S.T. Chen, "A Brief Discussion of the Current State of Public Security Manpower and Response" ["*Qiantan danqian gongan jingli xianzhuang yu duice*"], in Tian Jiacai (Ed.), *Construction of Public Security* [*Lun gongan duiwu jianshe*], Guangdong renmin chubanshe, Guangdong, 1995.

312. "Shortage of Funds Perplexes Public Security Organs" ["*Jingfei duanque kunrao gongan jiguan*"], *China Police Daily*, March 15, 2002.

313. "Editorial," *People's Daily Online*, March 15, 2002. A shortage of funds in an expanding economy is not a problem affecting only the police; it has been a problem for other government organs, too. Beijing Middle School principal Wu Changxun, for example, observed that, of the more than 20 places he traveled to and observed throughout the country, most of them failed to pay their teachers in full or on time. In Hebei Province, as of April 2001, eight of the Chengde counties, including Xinglung, were voted the "best relatively well-off," due to their middle and high school teachers' salaries and benefits totaling $17,023,000.

314. "Full Text of Premier Zhu's Government Work Report (2)," delivered by Premier Zhu Rongji at the Fifth Session of the Ninth National People's Congress on March 5, 2002 (http://english.peopledaily.com.cn/200203/16/eng20020316_92212.shtml).

315. "Full Text of Premier Zhu's Government Work Report (3)," delivered by Premier Zhu Rongji at the Fifth Session of the Ninth National People's Congress on March 5, 2002 (http://english.peopledaily.com.cn/200203/16/eng20020316_92213.shtml).

316. Liu Jiying, "Development of Preservative System for Police Fees" ["*Gongan yewufei baozhang tizhi de yuange yu qizhi*"], *Public Security Studies*, 95, 97–102, 2002. Perhaps a more suitable translation of the title is "Development and Revelation of the Public Security Operational Fees Guarantee System." The article traces the development of the police funding process; the author, an accountant, is the head of the Equipment and Finance Bureau of the MPS.

317. Ibid., p. 97.

318. Ibid.

319. Ibid.

320. Ibid., p. 98.

321. Ibid.

322. Ibid.

323. Ibid., p. 99.

324. Ibid.

325. Ibid., p. 100.

326. Budget Law of the People's Republic of China, adopted at the Second Session of the Eighth National People's Congress on March 22, 1994; promulgated by Order No. 21 of the President of the People's Republic of China on March 22, 1994; and effective as of January 1, 1995.

327. People's Police Law of the People's Republic of China, adopted at the 12th Meeting of the Standing Committee of the Eighth National People's Congress on February 28, 1995; promulgated by Order No. 40 of the President of the People's Republic of China on February 28, 1995; and effective as of the date of promulgation.

328. Liu Jiying, "Development of Preservative System for Police Fees" ["*Gongan yewufei baozhang tizhi de yuange yu qizhi*"], *Public Security Studies*, 95, 97–102, 2002.

329. William L. Parish and Martin King Whyte, *Village and Family in Contemporary China*, University of Chicago Press, Chicago, 1978, pp. 30–43.

330. Yanjie Bian, *Work and Inequality in Urban China*, State University of New York Press, Albany, 1984.

331. Wang Dazhong et al., "Gonguan Phenomenon: Certified Right of Existence as a New Right Belongs to Mobile Population," *Journal of Chinese People's Public University* (*PSU Journal*), 124, 110–120, 2006.

332. Wang Zhimin (Ed.), *Research on Contemporary Chinese Mobile Population Criminal Activities* ["*Dangqiang Zhongguo liudong renkou fanzui yanjiu*"], Zhongguo renmin gongan daxue chubanshe, Beijing, 2002.

333. The "Strike Hard" campaign marked an effort of the police to go on the offensive at the expense of prevention (*zhong daji, qing fafeng* means "focus on attack, neglect prevention"). Harold M. Tanner, *Strike Hard: Anti-Crime Campaigns and Chinese Criminal Justice, 1979–1985*, East Asia Program, Ithaca, NY, 1999.

334. Wang Yong and Li Jianhe, "Police Patrol: Origin, Development, Status, and Function" ["*Jingcha xunluo de youlai, xianzhuang ji zuoyong*"], *Journal of Chinese People's Public University* (*PSU Journal*), 47, 1–7, 1994.

335. Yuan Xiaohong, "*Huang Zunxian Jingzheng Sixiang Shulue*," *Journal of Chinese People's Public University* (*PSU Journal*), 1, 95–96, 1999.

336. Wang Yong and Li Jianhe, "Police Patrol: Origin, Development, Status, and Function" ["*Jingcha xunluo de youlai, xianzhuang ji zuoyong*"], *Journal of Chinese People's Public University* (*PSU Journal*), 47, 1–7, 1994.

337. Noriko Kamachi, *Reform in China: Huang Tsun-Hsien and the Japanese Model*, Council on East Asian Studies, Cambridge, MA, 1981.

338. Wang Yong, *Police Patrol Work Teaching Manual* [*Jingcha Xunluo Qinwu Jiaocheng*], Zhongguo gongan daxue Chubanshe, Beijing, 2000, p. 27.

339. Wang Yong and Li Jianhe, "Police Patrol: Origin, Development, Status, and Function" ["*Jingcha xunluo de youlai, xianzhuang ji zuoyong*"], *Journal of Chinese People's Public University* (*PSU Journal*), 47, 1–7, 1994.

340. For a short history, see He Wai, "A Cursory Review of the Need for Foot Patrol Services in Community Policing" ["*Shitan shequ jingwu xuyao xunluo qinwu*"], *Shanghai Public Security Academy Journal*, 7(6), 23–26, 1998.

341. Wang Yong, *Police Patrol Work Teaching Manual* [*Jingcha Xunluo Qinwu Jiaocheng*], Zhongguo gongan daxue Chubanshe, Beijing, 2000, p. 27.

342. Ibid., p. 89.

343. Ibid.

344. Cheng Lianming, "A Survey Report on the Situation of Shanghai Police Patrol Work" ["*Shanghai xunjing gongzuo qingkuang chouyang tiaocha baogao*"], *Theory and Practice of Public Security* (*Gongan Lilun Yu Sijian*), 9(1), 1–5, 2001.

345. The survey was conducted in an 8-year-old *anquan xiaoqu* (small secure area) with 120 survey instruments. The usable response rate was 50%. For a brief review of the methodology, see He Wai, "A Cursory Review of the Need for Foot Patrol Services in Community Policing" ["*Shitan shequ jingwu xuyao xunluo qinwu*"], *Shanghai Public Security Academy Journal*, 7(6), 23–26, 1998.

346. Ibid., p. 25.
347. Ibid., p. 26.
348. Wang Yong, *Police Patrol Work Teaching Manual* [*Jingcha Xunluo Qinwu Jiaocheng*], Zhongguo gongan daxue Chubanshe, Beijing, 2000, p. 47.
349. Zhang Jian, "Exploring and Pondering on the Establishment of Street Patrol Mechanism for Dynamic Management," *Public Security Studies*, 77, 52–56, 2001.
350. Ibid., p. 52.
351. Ibid., pp. 53–54.
352. Ibid., pp. 54–56.
353. Ibid., p. 52.
354. Ibid., pp. 52–53.
355. Ibid., p. 52.
356. Ibid., p. 53.
357. Tang Taxuan and Peng Jinsong, "Pondering the Practice of Patrol Police's Interrogation and Checking of Identity Cards," *Public Security Studies*, 78, 29–32, 2001.
358. Ibid., pp. 29–30.
359. Ibid., pp. 30–31.
360. Ibid., pp. 31–32.
361. Ibid., p. 30.
362. Ibid.
363. Tan Yingjiang, *110 Control and Service Guidebook* [*110 kongzhi yu fuwu zhinan*], Jingguan jiaoyu chubanshe, Beijing, 1998, pp. 6–8.
364. Ibid., pp. 168–169. These four service principles of 110 as practiced all over China today were first developed in Zhangzhou in Fujian Province.
365. Ibid., pp. 169. The program was judged a success. From August 1998 to June of 1998, the Zhangzhou 110 program responded to 36,818 calls for police services, handled 11,574 cases, resolved 9180 cases, arrested 14,697 offenders, and did 6.13 million good deeds for the people.
366. Ibid., pp. 168–169.
367. Ibid., p. 165.
368. "Jiangchuan County: Small City and Township with New 110 System" ["*Jiangchuan xian xiao chengzhen 110 jizhi xin*"], *China Police Daily Online*, December 27, 2001 (http://www.cpd.com.cn/xxlr.asp?menulb=039%C8%CB%C3%F1%B9%AB%B0%B2%B1%A8&id=9354).
369. From January to October 2001, the Jiangchuan County Public Security 110 center received and recorded 384 criminal and public order cases. It handled 7 natural disasters and 244 accident cases. It provided assistance and service to 546 citizens, helped to locate 46 people, and resolved 672 disputes.
370. "Zhangzhou 110 Sidelights" ["*Zhangzhou 110 ceji*"], *China Police Daily Online*, July 20, 2001.
371. "Nanjing City PSB Communication Center: 110 Deep in the Heart of the People" ["*Nanjingshi gonganju zhihui zhongxin: 110 shenru renxin*"], *China Police Daily Online*. September 30, 2001.
372. "Jilin Municipality Institutionalized 110 Rapid Response System" ["*Jilin shi qianghua 110 kuaisu fanying jizhi*"], *China Police Daily Online*, September 21, 2001.
373. "January Tenth: 110 Appeared on the Street" [*Yi yue si hao*: 110 *jiu shang jietou*"], *China Police Daily Online*, January 11, 2002.
374. "Anshan Patrol Police Provide 110 Reporting Service by Internet" ["*Anshan xunjing wanshang 110 baojing fuwu*"], *China Police Daily Online*, January 26, 2002.
375. "Liuzhou 110 Handled 310,000 Police Calls in Five Years" ["*Liuzhou 110 wu nian chujing 31 wan*"], *China Police Daily Online*, January 4, 2002.
376. "There Is a Lack of Enthusiasm for 110" ["110 *jingyuan he xiao*"], *China Police Daily Online*, February 1, 2002.
377. "*Lanzhou chuan jie 110*," *China Police Daily Online*, February 22, 2002.

378. "Everyday Nanchang Received 3500 Calls for Police, Only 80 Were Valid Calls" ["*Nanchang meitian jiejing* 3500, *youxiao jiejing zhi* 80"], *China Police Daily Online*, February 1, 2002.

379. "80% Are Nuisance Calls, Cixi 110 Cannot Sustain the Heavy Burden" ["*Bacheng diahuo shi saorao Cixi* 110 *buzhna zhongfu*"], *China Police Daily Online*, March 1, 2002.

380. "Do Not Tell the Story of 'The Wolf Is Coming' to 110" ["*Bie ba 'langlailiao' de gushi jiangei* 110"] *China Police Daily Online*, January 24, 2002.

381. "Anhua People's Police Help Mountain Village People Remove Heartfelt Problems" ["*Anhua minjing wei shancun qunzhong chu "xinbing"*], *China Police Daily Online*, April 12, 2002. In rural areas, the police as members of the village and servants of the people are jacks of all trades with amorphous roles and ill-defined functions: part law enforcer, part mediator, part order maintainer, and last, but not least, mostly odd-jobman (*qinwuyuan*). When the village people have "problems" (*kunnan*), they are supposed to seek out the police for advice, support, and assistance.

382. Yang Xiaohua, Gao Hui, Xu Juan, and Hoou Shitan, "Exploring and Analyzing the Prominent Conflicts in Operation of 110," *Public Security Studies*, 78, 33–36, 2001.

383. I call this "expectation policing." In the consumer arena, the customer is always right, and "we are here to please" is company policy. By "expectation policing," I mean that the police should do everything in their power to meet people's reasonable expectations under the law.

384. http://www.tianya.cn/techforum/content/158/531022.shtml.

385. (a) "Formal Justice and Procedural Justice," *Journal of Zhejiang University*, 5, 1999. The debate regarding procedural justice vs. substantive justice can also be considered to be one of formal justice vs. substantive justice and abstract justice vs. substantive justice. (b) Gao Min, "The Reality and Lack of Procedural Justice in China: Revelation of the Yu Chang and Liu Chong Case," *Journal of Hangzhou Dianzi University*, 2, 2006. Substantive justice cannot be obtained without proper procedural justice. China needs to learn from the West.

386. Dang Guohua, "Jurisprudence Explanation of Yuan Drama Doueyuan: On the Surreal and Substantive Notion of Justice of Ancient Chinese Crowd," *Journal of Inner Mongolia University*, 31(20), 2005.

387. Zuo Jianwei, "The Influence of Public Opinion on Application of the Death Penalty," *Chinese Sociology & Anthropology*, 41(4), 80–88, 2009. Public opinion plays a key role in the administration of Chinese justice.

388. "Shenyang Gang Leader Liu Yong Gets Death Penalty," *People's Daily Online*, December 22, 2003 (http://english.peopledaily.com.cn/200312/22/eng20031222_130952.shtml). China's Supreme People's Court (SPC), for the first time, retried an ordinary criminal case and overturned the previous ruling of the second-instance trial.

Reform to Police Accountability

6

Power without supervision will lead to abuses of power for personal gains, destruction of state laws and even corruption. So, to strengthen the supervision system is a sound guarantee for political democracy and social justice.

Chen Miaozhen, National People's Congress Deputy (2001)[1]

Introduction

The People's Republic of China (PRC) police have been given wide-ranging responsibilities and extensive powers over China's social, economic, and political life.[2] The police have enforcement and administrative jurisdiction over four criminal and 42 security administrative laws, regulations, and decisions.[3] They are charged with no less than 19 official functions, including maintaining order, investigating crime, supervising prisoners, administrating household registrations, directing traffic, fighting fires, regulating the border, and more.[4] They have comprehensive control over every citizen's life, from cradle to grave, on the land, in the water,[5] in the air,[6] and at the border.[7] People cannot give birth,[8] live, work, move,[9] visit with relatives, migrate,[10] demonstrate,[11] engage in business,[12] drive,[13] travel abroad,[14] or indeed die without the police being involved in the process. The police are vested with extensive authority in the execution of their legal duties. They have the power to examine a citizen's resident card.[15] They are authorized to use force, including deadly force, to maintain law and order.[16] They are equipped with lethal weapons, including firearms,[17] and they can interfere with a citizen's freedom and property rights at will.

This chapter studies the regulation of police powers in China. It begins by detailing problems with expansive police powers and supervising police exercise of discretion in China. The next section follows up with case studies on extended detention that suggest that extended detention is the norm, not the exception. The research study discussed in this section suffers from insurmountable methodological flaws but nevertheless offers up a unique opportunity for outsiders to size up the nature, prevalence, pattern, and causation of this abuse of power in reform China. Also discussed is the case of the "Big Spender," Cheung Tse-keung, which will help the reader to understand extended detention and what the Chinese authorities have done about it. The next sections address the constitutional foundation and legal mandate for supervision of police and various forms of police supervision, including constitutional supervision, legal supervision, and media supervision. Finally, this chapter concludes with a case study on controlling the police use of firearms that demonstrates how far Chinese police reformers have come in regulating the abusive use of firearms and, by extension, other police abuses and negligence by applying a variety of legal, administrative, and disciplinary measures.

The Problem with Expansive Police Powers

A major issue in police reform is how to control the police exercise of powers—that is, the proper use of discretion.[18] In theory, the Chinese police are supposed to follow the law strictly (*you fa bi yi*) and to implement the law sternly (*zhifa bi yan*). In practice, the police exercise a substantial amount of discretion, with little meaningful supervision and still less real accountability. For example, the Chinese police have nearly unlimited power to fine people for minor public order offenses (*zhian anjian*). This has led Biddulph, a student of Chinese administrative law, to observe:

> Despite these efforts, legislation has not entirely displaced pre-reform modes of administrative regulation, either in defining the powers of the public security organs, or in the manner of their exercise. An examination of these detention powers reveals that instructions issued through both Party and administrative channels remain the dominant source of regulatory norms. Because these detention powers are defined at the highest levels of generality, public security personnel possess almost unfettered discretion in their enforcement. Due to their legal form, these instruments also escape the legislatively imposed procedural limitations on the exercise of power and legal mechanisms for accountability.[19]

Discretion in *Zhian* Cases

In *zhian* (public order) cases, the Chinese police are authorized to levy fines in accordance with "Regulations of the People's Republic of China on Administrative Penalties for Public Security" ("*Zhonghua renmin gongheguo zhian guanli chufa tiaoli*")[20] and as supplemented by the Law of the People's Republic of China on Administrative Penalty (*Zhonghua renmin gongheguo xingzheng chufa fa*).[21] Administrative penalty procedures and fine structures under the Administrative Penalty Regulations have been incorporated by reference into a multitude of laws; for example, Section 41 of the Mineral Resources Law of the People's Republic of China states:

> If a person steals or plunders mineral products or other property of mining enterprises or exploration units, damages mining or exploration facilities, or disrupts order in production and other work in mining areas or areas under exploration, he shall be investigated for criminal responsibility in accordance with relevant provisions of the Criminal Law; if the case is obviously minor, he shall be punished in accordance with relevant provisions of the Regulations on Administrative Penalties for Public Security.[22]

Article 47 of the Water Law of the People's Republic of China states:

> Whoever commits any of the following acts in violation of this law shall be ordered by the water administrative departments or other concerned competent departments of the local people's governments at or above the county level to stop the illegal acts, compensate for the losses incurred, take remedial measures, and may be concurrently fined; when public security administrative punishment is merited, the punishment shall be given in accordance with the Regulations on Administrative Penalties for Public Security; when a crime has been committed, it shall be investigated for criminal responsibilities in accordance with the Criminal Law.[23]

Article 19 of the Law of the People's Republic of China on the National Flag states:

Whoever desecrates the National Flag of the People's Republic of China by publicly and willfully burning, mutilating, scrawling on, defiling or trampling upon it shall be investigated for criminal responsibilities according to law; where the offence is relatively minor, he shall be detained for not more than 15 days by the public security organ in reference to the provisions of the Regulations on Administrative Penalties for Public Security.[24]

The interpretation and application of Administrative Penalty Regulations are provided for by Ministry of Public Security (MPS) administrative decrees: (1) notices (*tongzhi*), such as the "Notice regarding Investigating and Dealing with Public Order Offenses"; or (2) interpretations (*jieshi*), such as the "Interpretation of Certain Issues regarding Implementation of Administrative Penalty Regulations."

A careful study of the Administrative Penalty Regulations reveals that they provide for a wide range of penalties and offer only vague application criteria; they also establish an unsupervised administrative process to guide uniform enforcement and determine appropriate punishment.[25] Article 6 of the Administrative Penalty Regulations states that, "Penalties for acts violating the administration of public security are divided into three types as follows: (1) warning; (2) fine, ranging from a minimum of one yuan to a maximum of two hundred yuan…; or (3) detention."[26] There is little guidance as to how and in what amount administrative fines are to be imposed, within the permissible range of penalty.[27] This lack of guidelines invites abuse of discretion,[28] and the lack of uniformity ensures disparate treatment of offenders from place to place,[29] officer to officer, agency to agency, problem to problem, situation to situation.[30]

Article 16 of the Administrative Penalty Regulations states that, "Penalties for acts violating the administration public security shall be mitigated or exempted under any of the following circumstances: (1) the adverse effects are extremely minor; (2) when those responsible voluntarily admit their mistakes and correct them in time; (3) when those responsible were coerced or induced by others." In Article 16, the term "extremely minor" is not defined. The provision that those responsible who voluntarily admit their mistakes will be treated more lightly invariably raises troubling questions as to how remorseful or cooperative people have to be before they can enjoy exemption or mitigation under the law. More damningly, the provision invites subjective evaluation of attitudes that is likely to be disproportionately applied to marginal groups, uncooperative offenders, or disrespectful people.

Article 17 of the Administrative Penalty Regulations states that, "Heavier penalties shall be given for acts violating the administration of public security under any of the following circumstances: (1) when acts have caused relatively serious consequences; (2) when those responsible coerce or induce others or instigate persons under the age of eighteen to violate the administration of public security; (3) when those responsible take revenge on the informants or witnesses; (4) when those responsible have been repeatedly punished and refuse to amend."[31] Article 17 is as vague and open ended as the provisions in Article 16. What exactly is meant by acts that have caused relatively serious consequences? How incorrigible must one be to deserve an assessment of being repeatedly punished but refusing to amend?

Article 33 of the Administrative Penalty Regulations states that, "Penalties for acts violating the administration of public security shall be ruled on by the city or county Public Security Bureaus or sub-bureaus or public security organs equivalent to the county level. Warnings and fines of a maximum of fifty yuan can be ruled on by local police stations; in rural areas where there is no local police station, the people's government of a township or town can be entrusted with the ruling."[32] Article 33 allows fines of 50 yuan (one week's pay in some of the less developed areas) to be ruled on locally, without guidelines and supervision. The only meaningful guideline on public security administration of fines is provided by the MPS's "Notice regarding Investigating and Dealing with Public Order Offenses" ("*Guanyu chapo he chuli zhian anjian de tongzhi*"). The appendix to this notice is entitled "Standard for Filing Public Order Cases."[33]

Looking at penalty dispensations in the Administrative Penalty Regulations, it is clear that a lot of discretion is given to PSB officers to administer the law. There are no national or central rules (in the guise of sentencing guidelines[34]) on how punishment (e.g., fines) should be imposed by individual police officers or between public security organs, especially for minor public security offenses. As observed, the Administrative Penalty Regulations only provide for optimal ranges and ill-defined general considerations. The control of discretion ultimately rests with local police chiefs, who are charged with the legal responsibility to control such exercise of discretion. But, in most cases, local police chiefs are swayed by local politics, personal relationships, pervasive organizational culture, peer pressure, pervasive corruption, and undue influences. It appears that the MPS is keenly aware of the twin issues of unfettered discretion[35] and disparate penalty guidelines[36] but has not yet been able to control discretion.

Discretion and Abuses

The police have a tendency to take liberties with their discretion because the police often make the law fit the situation or particular people instead of the other way around. Also, police decisions are based on police culture (e.g., solidarity, defensiveness, cover-ups), not necessarily on law or facts, and the police often obey Party leadership or policy rather than law.[37] As to why the police in China are able to abuse their discretion, there are many reasons. First, the Chinese legal system is still developing and is far from perfect. Laws are often poorly drafted and are intentionally vague and open ended.[38] Second, it is neither wise nor practical for any legal system, no matter how mature or sophisticated, to provide for every possible situation circumstance and contingency.[39] Thus, many laws authorize the police to exercise discretion based on the seriousness of the situation and attitude of the offender—in other words, seeking individual justice grounded on local circumstances and individual situations. Third, the police have limited resources to deal with the many problems that require attention; the police must prioritize, improvise, and at times negotiate and compromise to get the job done. Fourth, the police are frequently confronted with many minor, technical violations of the law; in these cases, they avoid invoking the law each time to save time and effort.[40] Finally, from imperial China to Mao's regime, the overall approach was to settle disputes and resolve problems personally and informally, at their roots, instead of relying on prosecution, bureaucracy, and formalism to suppress the symptoms and manifestations of "contradictions" begging for an audience.[41]

Research in China has shown that: (1) the police often exercise discretion to avoid invoking the law (and thus making work for themselves); (2) the exercise of discretion by the police is affected by the nature of the crime and seriousness of the consequences (e.g., greater discretion in administrative cases than in criminal cases); (3) the exercise of discretion by the police is affected by the prevailing circumstances (e.g., how discretion might deter or prevent crime); and (4) the exercise of discretion by the police represents situational justice rather than universal justice, holistic justice rather than rule-based justice. With regard to how best to control the exercise of discretion, some of the recommendations include enhancing the ability of the police to exercise discretion properly through thought and moral education. Police should be taught to exercise authority in accordance with the spirit of the law and expectations of the people. Police should be trained to achieve the purpose and spirit of the law in a balanced and reasonable manner and not to apply the law discriminately or indiscriminately for self-serving reasons, such as meeting administrative quotas.[42]

Problems with Extended Detention

A Case Study of Extended Detention in a Mid-China Province[43]

In November of 2006, Professor Zhang Chao, of Wuhan Law School, conducted an empirical study of criminal investigative extended detention (ED) (*chaoqi juliu*) in a central China city.[44] ED becomes a criminal case when the police detain a suspect for investigation beyond the time limit set by the PRC Criminal Procedure Law. This research is one of the very few scholarly studies performed anywhere that investigates the subject matter of ED. In China, those researching police misconduct encounter three problems: (1) accessibility to research sites,[45] (2) reliability of data,[46] and (3) sensitivity of the subject matter. Zhang Chao was able to gain access to police pretrial activities, including detention, and to data not available to other researchers. This was a significant accomplishment that spelled a new beginning for Chinese criminal justice research.[47] The study found clear and compelling evidence of substantial ED that demonstrated a consistent pattern of police noncompliance with procuratorate supervision and the rule of law.[48] What follows is a discussion of the original research report. This study observed Chinese policing from the bottom up, inside and out.[49] This study breaks new ground in Chinese policing scholarship.[50]

Research Focus

The focus of the ED research was to determine the incidents, prevalence, and causation of extended criminal investigative detention by police during the investigative phase of policing. Particularly, the study focused on the following:

1. The incidence and prevalence of detention vs. no detention cases[51]
2. The incidence and prevalence of regular vs. extended detention cases[52]
3. The duration and distribution of detention cases[53]
4. The duration and distribution of extended detention cases[54]
5. The incidence of legal vs. illegal supervisory inspection cases[55]
6. Whether and to what extent there were applications for approval in extended detention cases[56]
7. Applications for arrest after detention and illegal applications[57]
8. Duration and cases of untimely approval of extended detention[58]
9. Procuratorate opinions with regard to approving arrest vs. not approving[59]
10. Duration of immediate vs. delayed release by police after procuratorate opinion disapproving arrest[60]

Source of Data

The research is based on criminal investigative case files submitted by a provincial city public security bureau (PSB) to a middle China province for an annual legal audit, as required by the "2006 Annual Law Enforcement Quality Assessment" ("2006 *Zifa Zhiliang Kohe Pingyi*"), referred to here as the Legal Assessment. The Legal Assessment data filed with the province consisted of 720 investigative case files (*taiocha an juan*) involving 951 criminals. The Legal Assessment case files came from the following police operational units: criminal and economic crime investigation units (57 files), five city district sub-Public Security Bureaus (396 files), and three county-level PSBs (267 files). The original Legal Assessment case files were selected and prepared by 10 separate police agencies. The published report provides no documentation or discussion of how the audited agencies were selected, which more than likely affects the representativeness of the study and generalizability of its findings. Also, there is no indication that these agencies were representative of the population, areas (rural vs. urban), or agencies under study. It is also possible that there was some conflict of interest on the part of the data file compilers. In the province studied, police agencies must submit to the Legal Assessment process each year. The Office of Law Implementation Supervision Committee at each police agency is required to *self-select* a number of cases[61] to send to the provincial city public security bureau Law Implementation Supervision Committee Office for inspection. According to PSB annual audit rules, the Legal Assessment can award a maximum of 100 total points; 0.2 point is deducted for each deficiency. Extended detention items are worth 1 point each. The outcome of the Legal Assessment impacts the job performance and career prospects of the police officers involved. The case file selection process raises a significant question of bias, which likely affected the completeness and validity of the data; thus, the utility of the dataset is limited and in doubt, as noted by the researcher Professor Zhang:

> The assessment of these case files has a direct impact on case processing agencies' and police officers' self-interest. It is easy for people to see that the case files have been "selected" for submission and exposed to serious charges of fabrication....They do not reflect the reality....It is the opinion of this author, since the analysis of the case files has revealed that there are many obvious problems with ED, the issue of selection bias need not be of concern.[62]

In essence, notwithstanding bias and interpreting the data in the PSB's favor, ED is still found to be a substantial problem. Alternatively, if we were to factor in near certain data manipulation, as Zhang intimated, ED abuse could be much worse than that being reported here.

Data Preparation

To collect data for analysis, the case files were mined for data bearing on various aspects of investigative detention and extended detention, including the nature of the case, number of suspects, number of detainees, and length of detention. ED-related data, including actual detention time, approved detention time, approved extended detention time, and actual extended detention time, can be obtained from the following documents: "Report for Application of Detention" ("*Chengqing juliu baogao shu*"), "Detention Certification" ("*Juliu zheng*"), "Notice of Detention" ("*Jiuliu tongzhiszhu*"), "Report for Application for Extension of Detention" ("*Chengqing yanchang juliu qixian baogao shu*"), and "Extension of Detention Notice" ("*Yanchang juliu qixian tongzhi shu*").[63]

The kinds of cases analyzed included: (1) 27 incidents of endangering public security (Chapter 2, PRC Criminal Law); (2) 30 incidents of undermining the order of the socialist market economy (Chapter 3); (3) 279 incidents of infringing upon the rights of the person and the democratic rights of citizens (Chapter 4); (4) 291 incidents of encroaching on property (Chapter 5); and (5) 99 incidents of disrupting the order of social administration (Chapter 6).[64] Six cases overlapped two classification of criminal charges. Again, no information was provided regarding how various types of cases were chosen, particularly with respect to the usual distribution of cases in the field and among the respective agencies. There is a distinct possibility that some kinds of cases might result in more detention and more prolonged detention than others, such as commercial cases with foreign residents (who might flee the country) or violent criminals from outside of the province (who may be difficult to identify). As a result of these methodological flaws, the findings of this research should be considered exploratory, suggestive, and demonstrative, rather than definitive, conclusive, reliable, and generally applicable. Simply, read and interpret these findings with care.

Data Analysis

Criminal investigative detention cases and persons are regulated by the PRC Criminal Procedure Law, Article 69:

> A public security organ that finds it necessary to arrest a person already detained shall, within three days after the detention, submit a request to the people's procuratorate for approval. Under a special circumstance, the time limit for submitting the request for approval may be extended by one to four days.[65]

An examination of the legislative history, intent, language, and spirit of the PRC Criminal Procedure Law makes it clear that investigative detention is temporary, for emergency purposes, and it should be imposed sparingly and selectively based on necessity and for the shortest duration possible.[66] Article 12, for example, provides that a person is innocent until proven guilty by the court: "No person shall be found guilty without being judged as such by a People's Court according to law." When first promulgated, the "Regulations on Arrest and Detention of the People's Republic of China" (1954) only allowed for 24 hours of investigative detention. The 24-hour period was extended in 1979 to the current 3-day detention with a possible 4-day extension (a total of 7 days). In 1998, the Ministry of Public Security, due to concerns raised regarding the investigation of wandering migrants, issued the "Regulations on the Public Security Process for Handling Criminal Cases." Article 112 of these regulations provided for prolonged (30-day) detention for suspects who refused to reveal their name, address, or background to investigators. The time for initiating such an extended detention begins with ascertaining the suspect's name, address, and background, so, in effect, the MPS regulations allow for unlimited detention of uncooperative suspects. Article 112 was justified as being a necessary and exceptional measure and was later incorporated into Article 16 of the PRC Criminal Procedure Law: "With regard to major suspects committing crimes from one place to another, repeatedly committing crimes or committing gang crime, the time limit for submitting requests for approval may be extended to 30 days." This brief excursion into the history of investigative detention suggests that investigative detention is to be selective employed and only under the most exceptional circumstances. Routine detention is never the goal.

Finding 1. Police Investigative Detention Is the Norm, Not the Exception

A key finding of the research is that investigative detention is standard operating procedure. The data provided in Table 6.1 indicate that investigative detention was preferred in 90.42% of the cases, or 88.64% of the suspects. Only in a small minority of cases were the suspects

TABLE 6.1   Investigative Detention by Public Security Agencies

Detention	No. of Cases (% of Total)	No. of Persons (% of Total)
No detention	69 (9.58%)	108 (11.36%)
Detention	651 (90.42%)	843 (88.64%)
Total	720 (100.00%)	951 (100.00%)

Source: Chao, Z., *Journal of China Lawyer and Jurist*, 25, 4, 2007, Table 1.

TABLE 6.2   Extended Investigative Detention by Public Security Agencies

Detention	No. of Cases (% of Total)	No. of Persons Detained (% of Total)
No extended detention	381 (58.53%)	468 (55.52%)
Extended detention	270 (41.47%)	375 (44.48%)
Total	651 (100.00%)	843 (100.00%)

Source: Chao, Z., *Journal of China Lawyer and Jurist*, 25, 4, 2007, Table 2.

allowed to be free while under investigation (9.58%).[67] Thus, the first major finding from this study is that investigative detention, contrary to the letter and spirit of the PRC Criminal Procedure Law, is the norm, not the exception. Such routine detention does not appear to be justified by legitimate investigation needs and more likely serves to ease demand on police resources or some other illegal purpose, such as detention as punishment without due process or detention as a coercive means to leverage a commercial settlement of some type.[68]

Finding 2. Police Practice Extended Detention as Often as Regular Detention

The second most controversial finding is that ED is practiced as frequently as routine investigative detention. Because ED is prohibited by law (Article 69 of the PRC Criminal Procedure Law), one would expect it to occur rarely, but this is not the case. Table 6.2 shows that, at the time of this research (2006), the police violated Article 69 41.47% of time, which was nearly as frequent as legal detention in accordance with the law (58.3%) and within the legal limits. This suggests that ED might be necessary to facilitate the investigation of cases by the police. These cases appear to involve more suspects per case compared to non-ED cases. Regular detention cases averaged 1.23 suspects per case, while extended detention cases averaged 1.39 per case. More suspects mean more work for the police. More suspects also mean more complex investigations; these suspects are more likely to be organized gang members and uncooperative. It would be helpful if future research would clearly distinguish among structural (investigation-related) ED, organizational culture ED, and personal animus ED. Although the physical impact is the same (i.e., illegal deprivation of freedom), the psychological impact of the various types of ED might not be the same. Extended detention due to necessity is a far cry from ED caused by organizational culture or personal animus. Repeatedly, Chinese practitioners have complained that ED is necessary because of a lack of resources.

Finding 3. Most Criminal Investigations Cannot Be Completed in Three Days, as Envisioned by Article 69

Table 6.3 answers an interesting question: How many days does it take to process a criminal investigation while the suspect is detained? More specifically, can a case be investigated in 1 to 3 days, or even 4 to 8 days, under normal circumstances? For detention

TABLE 6.3 Length of Investigative Detention by Public Security Agencies

Duration of Detention	No. of Detention Cases (% of Total)	No. of Persons Detained (% of Total)
≤3 days	201 (30.88%)	216 (25.62%)
4 to 7 days	225 (34.56%)	276 (32.74%)
8 to 30 days	198 (30.41%)	324 (38.44%)
≥31 days	27 (4.15%)	27 (3.20%)
Total	651 (100.00%)	843 (100.00%)

Source: Chao, Z., *Journal of China Lawyer and Jurist*, 25, 5, 2007, Table 3.

Note: A minor discrepancy in the original table for the number of cases of detention lasting from 8 to 30 days has been corrected here.

policy purposes, the question is a significant one. If most criminal investigation cases cannot be completed in 3 days or less (as envisioned by law), due to the complexity of the cases, inadequacy of resources, or lack of cooperation of the suspect, then police leaders need to realistically think about changing the assumption upon which Article 69 is based. As it stands, Table 6.3 clearly suggests that only a small number of the investigative detention cases studied were disposed of in the first 3 days, as provided by law (30.88%). In fact, the majority of investigative detention cases were cleared between 4 and 30 days (66.36%). It was also rare that it took more than 31 days to investigate a case (4.15%). The use of detention duration as an indication of the time required to process criminal cases makes sense; however, such data are subject to the following distortive or confounding factors of police work.

First, in most police agencies around the world, criminal cases are only actively investigated for the first 24 to 48 hours; after that, they are moved to cold case status, to be followed up occasionally or as new leads appear. The fact is that the police do not have the resources to handle every case the same. Police are always playing a catch-up game, but one might argue that most cases could be cleared in 1 to 3 days if enough resources were available. Second, the speed at which cases are cleared and in turn the duration of detention are contingent on many factors, chief of which are the complexity of the case and availability of resources. Clearance of cases, though, is also dependent on the perceived sense of urgency, particularly with regard to the legal framework, administrative priority, organizational culture (internal), and nature of the case its seriousness, dangerousness, urgency, publicity, and supervision (external). In terms of the legal framework, it is clear that a 30-day time frame would be adequate for closure in most of the cases, as few cases in this study ever went beyond 31 days. The abrupt drop of cases requiring from 8 to 30 days to clear to 31 days or more cannot be adequately accounted for, except perhaps by legal time limits being strictly enforced. As to the nature of cases being a determinant, one would expect to find (not reported here) a marked difference between how nondetention vs. detention cases are handled, with the former being less urgent and therefore being given more time to clear. Before ascertaining the optimal time required to clear criminal investigative cases, however, one must consider that nondetention cases are likely to be more minor or less complicated cases, which would certainly affect the investigative period. It is apparent that we need to learn more about normal investigative times for a variety of cases before we can offer up a reasonable policy regarding optimal investigative detention.

TABLE 6.4 Extended Detentions

Duration of Detention	No. of Extended Detention Cases (% of Total)	Percentage of 651 Total Detentions	No. of Persons Receiving Extended Detention (% of Total/% of Detained)
4 to 7 days	201 (74.44%)	30.88%	276 (73.60%/32.74%)
8 to 30 days	51 (18.89%)	7.83%	81 (21.60%/9.61%)
≥31 days	18 (6.67%)	2.76%	18 (4.80%/2.14%)
Total	270 (100.00%)	41.47%	375 (100.00%/44.49%)

Source: Chao, Z., *Journal of China Lawyer and Jurist*, 25, 5, 2007, Table 4.

Table 6.3 shows that the number of cases exceeding 31 days of investigative detention dropped off precipitously, which indicates that the legal framework in place was working. Alternatively, notwithstanding routine police standard operating procedures, the police had the sense to limit such detention to no more than 30 days, thus making it a *de facto* standard of investigative detention, beyond which the law would not tolerate.[69]

Finding 4. The Extended Detention Problem Is Significant but Tolerable

Table 6.4 provides further data on extended detention. Interpreting the results in the most favorable light for the police (using a set of data prepared by the police), we can come to several conclusions: This study uncovered a significant problem with ED, as more than a third of the investigative detainees were given extended detention. Most of the ED cases lasted no more than 4 to 7 days, but a sizable number of cases received prolonged ED of over 31 days. The research also reported a case of ED that lasted for 3 years and 155 days.[70] Overall, however, this set of data shows that ED is a serious but tolerable problem with proper procuratorial oversight. For publicity and policy considerations, the real concern is not with ED *per se* but with the length of ED. In this regard, 4 to 7 days of detention does not appear to be too harsh in the eyes of the public.

Finding 5. A Quarter of the Extended Detention Cases Had No Legal Application for Approval

Table 6.5 addresses the issue of proper supervision by and approval from procuratorates over the police with regard to extended detention. Most of the detention cases in the study received timely and proper approval, under Article 69 (i.e., within 3 days), but a rather significant number of cases did not receive such approval.[71] In fact, 10% of the cases were given approval for detention of 31 to 37 days, which is not allowed by law. Another 24% of the cases received approval of extended detention *automatically* for 30 days, not contingent on demonstrating individual need or special circumstances.[72]

Finding 6. Most of the Detention Cases Received Applications for Arrest

Table 6.1 and Table 6.2 address the issue of police responsiveness in applying for authorization for arrest in detention cases. Here, we see that 48 cases (Table 6.6) involving 69 persons (Table 6.7) failed to obtain approval for arrest. If were to look at ED cases in Table 6.6, we would find that for under 7 days the failure rate was approximately 56%, for 8 to 30 days it was 25%, and for 31 or more days it was almost 19%. The message is clear that the police are not in the habit of asking for approvals for arrest. In fact, many of the ED cases were already substantially delinquent when approval was applied for.[73]

TABLE 6.5   Legality of Detention Approval

Legality	No. of Detention Cases (% of Total)	No. of Persons Detained (% of Total)
Legal approval	498 (76.50%)	615 (72.95%)
Illegal approval	153 (23.50%)	228 (27.05%)
Total	651 (100.00%)	843 (100.00%)

Source: Chao, Z., *Journal of China Lawyer and Jurist*, 25, 5, 2007, Table 5.

TABLE 6.6   Extended Detentions Resulting in No Application for Approval for Arrest (Cases)

Duration of Detention	No. of Detention Cases Resulting in No Approvals for Arrest (% of Total)	Percentage of Detention Cases with No Application for Approval for Arrest	Percentage of 270 Total Extended Detentions
4 to 7 days	27 (56.25%)	11.39%	10.00%
8 to 30 days	12 (25.00%)	5.06%	4.44%
≥31 days	9 (18.75%)	3.80%	3.33%
Total	48 (100.00%)	20.25%	17.77%

Source: Chao, Z., *Journal of China Lawyer and Jurist*, 25, 6, 2007, Table 6.1.

TABLE 6.7   Extended Detentions Resulting in No Application for Approval for Arrest (Persons)

Duration of Detention	No. of Persons Not Given Approvals for Arrest (% of Total)	Percentage of Detained Persons with No Application for Arrests	Percentage of Persons Receiving Extended Detention
4 to 7 days	42 (60.87%)	14.29%	11.20%
8 to 30 days	18 (26.09%)	6.12%	4.80%
≥31 days	9 (13.04%)	3.06%	2.40%
Total	69 (100.00%)	23.47%	18.40%

Source: Chao, Z., *Journal of China Lawyer and Jurist*, 25, 6, 2007, Table 6.2.

Finding 7. Approvals for Arrest Were Granted for Less than Half of the Cases within Three Days of Detention

Tables 6.8, 6.9, and 6.10 address the issue of the timing of applications for approval in detention cases. Table 6.8 reports that approval was applied for within 3 days in almost 39% of the detention cases, within 4 to 7 days in 30% of the cases, within 8 to 30 days in 27% of the cases, and within 31 days or more for nearly 4% of the cases. Table 6.8 clearly shows that applications for approval during the first three days are unusual, and applications for approval after 30 days still exist.

Finding 8. Procuratorates Contributed to Extended Detention in a Quarter of the Cases

Table 6.11 and Table 6.12 now shift our inquiry to the procuratorate office. Specifically, how did the procuratorate office contribute to extended detention or otherwise aggravate the adverse consequences of illegal ED? Extended detention is not exclusively a result of police actions. It can occur when procuratorates do not act on approval for arrest applications in a timely fashion. Such tardiness has a number of adverse consequences. The lack of timely approval turns police legal detention into illegal detention. From the

TABLE 6.8   Applications for Arrest Approval and Detention Time

Time Required to Obtain an Application for Arrest Approval after Detention	No. of Cases (% of Total)	No. of Persons (% of Total)
Within 3 days	162 (38.85%)	174 (31.69%)
4 to 7 days	126 (30.22%)	165 (30.05%)
8 to 30 days	114 (27.34%)	195 (35.53%)
≥31 days	15 (3.59%)	15 (2.73%)
Total	417 (100.00%)	549 (100.00%)

Source: Chao, Z., *Journal of China Lawyer and Jurist*, 25, 7, 2007, Table 7-1.

TABLE 6.9   Extended Detentions and Untimely Approvals for Arrest (Cases)

Time Taken to Initiate an Application for Arrest Approval after Detention	No. of Cases (% of Total)	No. of Cases as Percentage of 417 Total Detention Cases	No. of Cases as Percentage of 270 Total Extended Detention Cases
Within 7 days	30 (47.62%)	7.25%	11.11%
8 to 30 days	30 (47.62%)	7.25%	11.11%
≥31 days	3 (4.76%)	0.72%	1.11%
Total	63 (100.00%)	15.22%	23.33%

Source: Chao, Z., *Journal of China Lawyer and Jurist*, 25, 7, 2007, Table 7-2(1).

TABLE 6.10   Extended Detentions and Untimely Approvals for Arrest (Persons)

Time Taken to Initiate an Application for Arrest Approval after Detention	No. of Persons (% of Total)	No. of Persons as Percentage of 549 Persons Detained	No. of Persons as Percentage of 375 Persons Receiving Extended Detention
Within 7 days	30 (40%)	5.46%	8.00%
8 to 30 days	42 (56%)	7.65%	11.20%
31 days	3 (4%)	0.55%	0.80%
Total	75 (100%)	13.66%	20.00%

Source: Chao, Z., *Journal of China Lawyer and Jurist*, 25, 7, 2007, Table 7-2(2).

perspective of the person being detained, it does not really matter who is at fault. Because the police are on the front line and directly in contact with the citizens, they represent the system and are always blamed. Repeated or unexpected delays in approval can jeopardize the already fragile working relationship between the police and procuratorates. Throughout history, the police have not appreciated procuratorate supervision and at times question their competency and judgment; further souring of this relationship would make cooperation between these two agencies all but impossible. A dysfunctional working relationship between the police and procuratorates invites the police to work around procuratorates on investigative detention issues.[74] Most of the delayed approvals occur within the first 7 days, and procuratorate delays affected nearly a quarter of the extended detention cases.

TABLE 6.11   Extended Detention and Time Taken for Approval by Procurator (Cases)

Approvals for Arrest by Procurator Beyond Legal Limits	No. of Cases (% of Total)	No. of Cases as Percentage of 417 Total Detention Cases	No. of Cases as Percentage of 270 Total Extended Detention Cases
Within 7 days	51 (85.00%)	12.23%	18.89%
8 to 30 days	3 (5.00%)	0.72%	1.11%
≥31 days	6 (10.00%)	1.44%	2.22%
Total	60 (100.00%)	14.39%	22.22%

Source: Chao, Z., *Journal of China Lawyer and Jurist*, 25, 8, 2007, Table 8-1.

TABLE 6.12   Extended Detention and Time Taken for Approval by Procurator (Persons)

Approvals for Arrest by Procurator Beyond Legal Limits	No. of Persons (% of Total)	No. of Persons as Percentage of 549 Persons Detained	No. of Persons as Percentage of 375 Persons Receiving Extended Detention
Within 7 days	69 (85.20%)	12.57%	18.40%
8 – 30 days	6 (7.40%)	1.09%	1.60%
≥31 days	6 (7.40%)	1.09%	1.60%
Total	81 (100.00%)	14.75%	21.60%

Source: Chao, Z., *Journal of China Lawyer and Jurist*, 25, 8, 2007, Table 8-2.

Finding 9. Procuratorates Play a Significant Role in Approving Police Arrests

The PRC Criminal Procedure Law envisioned a checks-and-balances system for criminal case processing. Specifically, Article 3 of the PRC Criminal Procedure Law provides for divided responsibility among public security, procuratorates, and the court:

> The public security organs shall be responsible for investigation, detention, execution of arrests, and preliminary inquiry in criminal cases. The people's procuratorates shall be responsible for procuratorial work, authorizing approval of arrests, conducting investigations, and initiating public prosecution of cases directly accepted by the procuratorial organs. The people's courts shall be responsible for adjudication. Except as otherwise provided by law, no other organs, organizations or individuals shall have the authority to exercise such powers.

The respective justice agencies are to be regulated by law:

> In conducting criminal proceedings, the people's courts, the people's procuratorates, and the public security organs must strictly observe this Law and any relevant stipulations of other laws.

Finally, the checks-and-balances principle is further stipulated in Article 7 of the PRC Criminal Procedure Law:

> In conducting criminal proceedings, the people's courts, the people's procuratorates, and the public security organs shall divide responsibilities, coordinate their efforts, and check each other to ensure the correct and effective enforcement of law.

TABLE 6.13   Procuratorate Opinions on Applications for Arrest

Procuratorate Opinion	No. of Cases (% of Total)	No. of Persons (% of Total)
Arrest	159 (38.41%)	207 (37.70%)
No arrest	204 (49.28%)	273 (49.73%)
No legal documentation	51 (12.32%)	69 (12.57%)
Total	414 (100.00%)	549 (100.00%)

Source: Chao, Z., *Journal of China Lawyer and Jurist*, 25, 8, 2007, Table 9.

TABLE 6.14   Procuratorate Arrest Disapprovals and Police Release Actions

Procuratorate Opinion	No. of Cases (% of Total)	No. of Persons Released (% of Total)
Immediate release	90 (88.24%)	123 (91.11%)
Deemed immediate release (1 day)	12 (11.76%)	12 (8.89%)
Total	102 (100.00%)	135 (100.00%)

Source: Chao, Z., *Journal of China Lawyer and Jurist*, 25, 8, 2007, Table 10.

Mindful of the above checks-and-balances framework, Table 6.13 addresses whether the procuratorates in this study were performing their legal role in checking the police in investigative detention cases. The data in Table 6.13 suggest that the procuratorates were performing their assigned role with due diligence and some success. The procuratorates rejected about half of all applications for arrest approval. From this set of data, we can discern that the Chinese checks-and-balances system is not a "paper tiger" (all bark and no bite), as some conspiracy theorists claim. Some are of the opinion that public security works in collusion with procuratorates and the courts to predetermine guilt and otherwise railroad innocent people to jail without due process.

Finding 10. Police Are Subject to Effective Procuratorate Supervision
Table 6.14, Table 6.15, and Table 6.16 further examine the relationship between procuratorates and the police. For the first time, we have some empirical evidence addressing this issue. The data show that, for those people whose police detention was not approved by procuratorates, about half were released immediately and the other half within 7 days. This shows that the police were adhering to procuratorate opinions enforced by the local political legal committee. It also means that the system of checks-and-balances seems to be working.

What We Learned
This study of extended detention in a mid-size Chinese city offers a unique opportunity to look at how the Chinese criminal justice system functions. In so doing, it allows us to address issues not possible before, such as whether the police are effectively under the control of procuratorates. We have learned a mixed bag of lessons about Chinese policing, some of them myth shattering. We learned, for example, that investigative detention is a norm, not the exception. Extended detention is a very real and serious problem, but the magnitude of the problem is not as great as initially perceived, as most ED in the study terminated during the allowable 30-day period. The legal framework regulating ED appears to be working, as very few ED cases in the study lasted beyond 31 days. Systematic and rule-bound supervision is apparently effective. Procuratorates are providing meaningful supervision of the police, as reflected by their rejection of 50% of the applications for arrest approval, and the police are willing to release the detainees when required by procuratorates in a timely fashion.

TABLE 6.15   Delayed Releases and No-Arrest Opinions (Cases)

Duration of Delayed Release	No. of Cases (% of Total)	No. of Cases as Percentage of 204 No-Arrest Opinions	No. of Cases as Percentage of 270 Extended Detention Cases
Within 7 days	93 (91.18%)	45.59%	34.44%
8 to 30 days	9 (8.82%)	4.41%	3.33%
Total	102 (100.00%)	50.00%	37.38%

Source: Chao, Z., *Journal of China Lawyer and Jurist*, 25, 9, 2007, Table 11-1.

TABLE 6.16   Delayed Releases and No-Arrest Opinions (Persons)

Duration of Delayed Release	No. of Persons (% of Total)	No. of Persons as Percentage of 273 No-Arrest Opinions	No. of Persons as Percentage of 375 Extended Detention Persons
Within 7 days	123 (89.13%)	45.05%	32.80%
8 to 30 days	15 (10.87%)	5.49%	4.00%
Total	138 (100.00%)	50.55%	36.80%

Source: Chao, Z., *Journal of China Lawyer and Jurist*, 25, 9, 2007, Table 11-2.

Reasons for Prolonged Detention

Police officers are still holding onto an outdated legal culture; that is, they prefer substantive justice (*shiti zhengyi*) over procedural justice and focus on attacking criminals more than on the protection of rights. The most important responsibilities of the police are to investigate facts, discover truth, and seek justice. Thus, the accepted norm for police investigations should be completing their investigations within 30 days before charging and arresting a suspect. The justification is that, if the person is guilty, it hardly matters whether he spends a few more days in jail. If the suspect is not responsible for the crime, a few more days of detention is not such a big thing; it is more important that he has been cleared of all wrongdoing.[75]

The language of Article 69 is not entirely clear. Recall that Article 69 allows for extending investigative detention from 1 to 4 days if and when necessary, as well as providing for prolonged detention of up to 30 days, upon special circumstances. The specific meanings of "necessary" conditions and "special circumstances" justifying such extensions were not defined. The police routinely apply Article 69 to out-of-town criminals, repeat offenders, or criminal gangs as they consider them to be deserving of prolonged detention. Article 69 can be considered, then, an open invitation to impose prolonged detention based on internal police needs of all kinds.[76]

A Case Study of ED: The Cheung Tse-keung Case

On October 20, 1998, Cheung Tse-keung, also known as the "Big Spender,"[77] and 35 accomplices went on trial in China for a host of criminal charges[78] ranging from murder to kidnapping to smuggling of explosives in Hong Kong and China[79] from 1991 to 1997. The 36 defendants in this case included (see also Table 6.17):[80]

- Cheung Tse-keung, 43, Hong Kong; kidnapping, illegal trading of explosives, smuggling of arms and ammunition
- Chan Chi Ho, 36, Hong Kong; kidnapping, illegal trading of explosives, smuggling of arms and ammunition, murder, and robbery
- Ma Shan-chung, 33, Hong Kong; illegal trading of explosives, smuggling of arms and ammunition, murder, and robbery
- Liang Fei, 32, Mainland; kidnapping, illegal trading of explosives, smuggling of arms and ammunition, murder, and robbery
- Qian Han-shou, 42, Mainland; illegal trading of explosives
- Chu Yuk-sing, 42, Hong Kong; robbery, kidnapping, smuggling of arms and ammunition
- Li Wan, 41, Hong Kong; robbery, kidnapping, smuggling of arms and ammunition
- Lau Ding-fun, 47, Hong Kong; illegal trading and transport of explosives
- Ye Xinyu, 29, Shantou; robbery
- Wong Wah-sang, 36, Hong Kong; robbery
- Or Yin-ting, 47, Hong Kong; kidnapping
- Luo Ji-ping, 30, Xiaoguan, kidnapping and smuggling of arms and ammunition
- Zhang Huan-qun, 23, Haifeng; kidnapping and smuggling of arms and ammunition
- Wu Chai-shu, 47, Hong Kong; kidnapping
- Wang Ying-de, 52, Heifei; illegal trading of ammunition
- Kam Wing-keung, 47, Hong Kong; kidnapping
- Tang Lai-hin, 47, Hong Kong; kidnapping
- Ho Chi-cheung, 54, Hong Kong; kidnapping
- Yu Chuan, 46, Shantou; illegal trading of explosives
- Jiang Yongchang, 46, Shantou; illegal trading of explosives
- Jiang Chai-gu, 20, Shantou; illegal trading of explosives
- Wang Wenxiong, 27, Shantou; illegal trading of explosives
- Lau Kwok-wah, 29, Hong Kong; illegal trading of explosives
- Yu Hong-jian, 33, Lufeng; robbery
- Wang Yi, 26, Hunan; robbery
- Chan Shue-hon, 47, Hong Kong; kidnapping
- Chen Hui-guang, 28, Shantou; illegal transport and hiding of arms and ammunition
- Luo Yue-ying, 26, Xiaoquan; illegal transport and storing of arms and ammunition
- Chen Lixin, 30, Shantou; illegal trading of arms and ammunition
- Liu Ganyong, 27, Haifeng; hiding arms and ammunition
- Yip Kai-chung, 30, Haifeng; hiding stolen property
- Yi Kai-yuk, 30, Hong Kong; hiding stolen property
- Chin Hon-yip, 43, Hong Kong; illegal transport of explosives (might be Qian Han-ye in Table 6.17)
- Cai Zhijie, 34, Mainland; robbery
- Cheung Chi-fung 53, Hong Kong; kidnapping
- Hon Fa, 24, Hong Kong; illegal trading and transport of arms and ammunition, smuggling weapons and ammunition

TABLE 6.17   PRC Public Security Investigative Detention of "Big Spender" Defendants

Defendant	Detained	Arrest Approval	Approved Arrested	Time Detained
Cheung Tse-keung	Jan. 26, 1998	July 21, 1998	July 22, 1998	5 months, 25 days
Chan Chi Ho	April 27, 1998	July 21, 1998	July 22, 1998	2 months, 24 days
Ma Shan-chung	Imprisoned for other offense	Imprisoned for other offense	Imprisoned for other offense	Imprisoned for other offense
Liang Fei	June 19, 1998	July 21, 1998	July 22, 1998	1 month, 10 days
Qian Han-shou	July 6, 1998	July 21, 1998	July 22, 1998	15 days
Chu Yuk-sing	May 2, 1998	July 21, 1998	July 22, 1998	2 months, 19 days
Li Wan	May 7, 1998	July 21, 1998	July 21, 1998	2 months, 14 days
Lau Ding-fun	April 11, 1998	July 21, 1998	July 21, 1998	3 months, 10 days
Ye Xin-yu	June 26, 1998	July 28, 1998	July 30, 1998	1 month, 2 days
Wong Wah-sang	May 1, 1998	July 28, 1998	July 29, 1998	2 months, 27 days
Qian Han-ye	May 3, 1998	July 21, 1998	July 22, 1998	2 months, 20 days
Or Ying-ting	May 29, 1998	July 21, 1998	July 22, 1998	1 months, 23 days
Luo Ji-ping	June 2, 1998	July 21, 1998	July 22, 1998	1 month, 19 days
Zhang Huan-qun	June 17, 1998	July 21, 1998	July 22, 1998	1 month, 4 days
Wu Chai-shu	Jan. 26, 1998	July 21, 1998	July 22, 1998	5 months, 25 days
Wang Ying-de	July 21, 1998	July 29, 1998	July 29, 1998	8 days
Kam Wing-keung	May 9, 1998	July 21, 1998	July 22, 1998	2 months, 20 days
Tang Lai-hin	May 10, 1998	July 21, 1998	July 22, 1998	2 months, 19 days
Ho Chi-cheung	June 6, 1998	July 21, 1998	July 22, 1998	1 month, 15 days
Yu Chuan	July 14, 1998	July 28, 1998	July 29, 1998	1 month, 14 days
Jiang Yongchang	July 10, 1998	July 28, 1998	July 29, 1998	18 days
Jiang Chai-gu	July 10, 1998	July 28, 1998	July 29, 1998	18 days
Wang Wenxiong	August 20, 1998	August 22, 1998	August 26, 1998	2 days
Lau Kwok-wah	April 10, 1998	July 21, 1998	July 21, 1998	3 months, 11 days
Yu Hong-jian	July 14, 1998	July 28, 1998	July 29, 1998	14 days
Wang Yi	July 9, 1998	July 28, 1998	July 29, 1998	19 days
Chan Shue-hon	April 12, 1998	July 21, 1998	July 22, 1998	3 months, 9 days
Chen Hui-guang	May 4, 1998	July 28, 1998	July 30, 1998	2 months, 24 days
Luo Yue-ying	June 2, 1998	July 28, 1998	July 29, 1998	1 month, 26 days
Chen Lixin	June 25, 1998	July 28, 1998	July 30, 1998	1 month, 3 days
Liu Ganyong	May 30, 1998	July 28, 1998	July 30, 1998	2 months, 29 days
Yip Kai-chung	June 24, 1998	July 28, 1998	July 30, 1998	1 month, 4 days
Yi Kai-yuk	May 1, 1998	July 28, 1998	July 29, 1998	2 months, 27 days
Average				2 months, 6 days

Source: Extracted from the Bill of Prosecution, pp. 1 to 9.

Note: Three defendants, Cai Zhijie, Cheung Chi-fung, and Hon Fa are not included in this table. Qian Han-ye might be the same person as Chin Hon-yip, due to various translations of Chinese names.

A detailed examination of the court papers reveals that the police did not handle the criminal defendants in the "Big Spender" case in accordance with established criminal procedures; in other words, substantive justice prevailed over procedural rules. Specifically, all of the defendants were detained illegally and extensively. Article 69 of the PRC Criminal Procedure Law, referred to earlier, provides that:

If the public security organ deems it necessary to arrest a detainee, it shall, within three days after the detention, submit a request to the people's procuratorate for examination and approval. Under special circumstances, the time limit for submitting a request for examination and approval may be extended by one to four days. As to the arrest of a major suspect involved in crimes committed from one place to another, repeatedly, or in a gang, the time limit for submitting a request for examination and approval may be extended to 30 days. The people's procuratorate shall decide either to approve or disapprove the arrest within seven days from the date of receiving the written request for approval submitted by a public security organ.

It is also not clear from the court records why Cheung was first detained on January 26, 1998, but the approval for his formal arrest was only sought belatedly, some 5 months and 25 days later (on July 21, 1998).[81] The prolonged detention far exceeded the legal limit of 30 days within which arrest approval must be sought from procuratorates. PRC officials explained that a plausible explanation for such an overly extended detention was that Cheung tried to disguise his true identity, claiming himself to be "Chen Xing-wei" upon arrest.[82] Article 126 of the PRC Criminal Procedure Law[83] allows for exceptionally long detention (2 months) with the approval of a procuratorate of the province. Furthermore, Article 128 allows for "indefinite" investigative detention of a suspect if that suspect's true identity cannot be ascertained: "If the criminal suspect refuses to disclose his true name, address, and identity, the period under which he can be held in custody starts from the date the identity is clarified."[84]

If this explains the extended detention, then we must consider the relevancy and propriety of applying these rules to this case. Was Article 128 applicable to the facts and circumstances in this case? By all accounts, the PRC police knew, very early on the investigation, that the person they arrested ("Chen Xing-wei") was in fact Cheung Tse-keung, notwithstanding his denial. In reality, the PRC police were just waiting for Cheung to confess to the details of his crime.[85] Even if the PRC police did not know the true identity of Cheung when they arrested him, they could have ascertained his identity in a very short period of time through DNA or fingerprint matching[86] or by eyewitness identification.[87] This was not a case where the PRC police had no clue as to the suspect's identity, nor would they have been fooled by Cheung's fake identity. Also, even if Article 128 applied, the question remains as to why Cheung was not formally approved for arrest until the end of July when he had confessed to his true identity in the middle of June.

Cheung Tse-keung was not the only one detained beyond the legal limit. In fact, almost all of the criminal defendants in the "Big Spender" case were detained beyond the statutory limits. Keeping in mind that one month is the optimal period for investigative detention before an approval must be sought, 26 out of the 36 defendants were detained for over 30 days without approvals for arrest. The average detention time for all of them was 2 months and 9 days, ranging from a maximum of 5 months and 25 days to a minimum of only 2 days.

Extended Detention Reform

The prolonged detention of criminal suspects in the Cheung case reflects and is consistent with a national trend. According to PRC official data, overly long extended investigative detention is the norm, not exception. Illegal extended detention is not new, nor is it a small problem in China. For example, in 1986 Chinese official data showed that of the many thousands of "detention for investigation" cases nationwide only 36.3% met all legal requirements, with some provinces falling below 10%. The illegal detention problem is more prominent in the southern part of China than in the north; for example, official self-reported data showed that in 1990 5.7% of all arrests in Beijing involved illegal extended detention, whereas 23.8% of arrests in Guangdong were illegal. Illegal arrest and detention have variously been used as retribution (*yiquan dai fa*), summary punishment (*dai xing*), as an aid to investigation (*dai cha*), and in the settlement of commercial disputes.[88]

The National People's Congress Standing Committee for Internal and Judicial Affairs sent six teams to Tianjin, Inner Mongolia, Heilongjiang, Zhejiang, Shaanxi, and Hubei in 2001 to look into how the PRC Criminal Procedure Law was being implemented. Their report shows that 3 years after the new Criminal Procedure Law was implemented,[89] extended detentions of criminal suspects and forced confessions were still a problem in many parts of China.[90] Lawyers in these areas complained of difficulties in meeting their clients, problems with accessing court files, and routine denial of legal petitions.

In 2003, the Supreme People's Procuratorate, under the leadership of Jia Chunwang, engaged in an "overextended detention" clearance (*qingli*) campaign. Specifically, Jia required that all courts, procuratorates, and police in China must clear their detention centers of cases of "overextended detention" or be held personally accountable.[91] The campaign to clear up the nation's extended detention was launched with the Supreme People's Court's "Notice regarding Clearing Up of Extended Detention Cases," which called for a national effort to control ED by 2004:

> All higher level People's Courts should provide a comprehensive and detailed account of extended detention in their respective jurisdictions, seriously analyze it for the causes of extended detention, immediately take effective clean-up actions, and report to the Supreme People's Court by August 20, 2003.…Especially for those extended detentions lasting for 3 years and over, they should be cleared up by end of 2003; for those extended detention lasting for 1 year, they should be cleared up by September 2004.

Later that year, the People's Procuratorate and the Ministry of Public Security jointly issued a "Notice on Stern Execution of Criminal Procedure Law to Thoroughly Correct and Prevent Overextended Detention Problems" ("*Guanyu yange zixing xingshi xusong fa, cheshi jiuzheng chaoqi kouya de tongzi*") to prevent the problem of illegal or overly long extended detention from happening again. This notice was followed by the Supreme People's Procuratorate's "Certain Regulations of the Supreme People's Procuratorate regarding the Prevention and Correction of Overextended Detention in Procurator Work" ("*Zuigao renmin jianchayuan guanyu zai jiancha gongzuo zhong fangzhi he jiuzheng caoqi kouya de ruogan guiding*").

From May through December, 2003, the procuratorate organs cleared 530 cases of extended detention, the police cleared 14,270 cases (with 10 cases remaining), and the court system cleared 7454 cases (with 1919 cases remaining).[92] In 2004, the Supreme People's Procuratorate reported that 4700 persons were being subjected to extended detention nationwide, on top of the 2187 persons not yet cleared in 2003, making for a total national count of 6887 to be dealt with. Justice agencies at different levels and parts of the country corrected 95% of the cases, involving 6775 people. Essentially, today there is no more extended detention beyond 3 years.[93]

The central government's concerted effort to control ED appears to be working. The 2008 Supreme People's Procuratorate Work Report showed that persons subjected to extended detention dropped from 24,921 in 2003 to 85 in 2007.[94] As the extended detention saga comes to a close, another problem with illegal imprisonment of those with grievances, "letters and calls" petitioners (*xinfang*), has arisen,[95] but this is an issue for another study.

Foundation for Supervision

Constitutional Foundation for Law Supervision

The People's Republic of China police are subjected to political as well as legal supervision by the people. Four articles in the PRC Constitution of 1982 (as amended and hereinafter referred to as the PRC Constitution) provide the constitutional foundation for holding the PRC police accountable to the law and people. Article 2 of the PRC Constitution makes it clear that:

> All power in the People's Republic of China belongs to the people."[96] This expressly affirms that the police derive their power from the people and, by extension, are subject to the people's supervision. Article 5 of the PRC Constitution provides that: "All state organs, the armed forces, all political parties and public organizations and all enterprises and undertakings must abide by the Constitution and the law. All acts in violation of the Constitution and the law must be investigated. No organization or individual may enjoy the privilege of being above the Constitution and the law.

This article makes it clear that the police are to carry out their duties in accordance with and being held accountable to the Constitution and the law. Finally, Article 27 and Article 41 empower the people to supervise the police. Article 27 provides that: "All state organs and functionaries must rely on the support of the people, keep in close touch with them, heed their opinions and suggestions, accept their supervision, and work hard to serve them." This article makes the police accountable to the people. Article 41 gives the people the right to criticize and file complaints against irregular, illegal, or abusive police conduct: "Citizens have the right to make to relevant state organs complaints and charges against, or exposures of, violation of the law or dereliction of duty by any state organ or functionary; but fabrication or distortion of facts with the intention of libel or frame-up is prohibited."

Party Plan on Government of Law

In 2001, the Fifth Plenum of the 15th Central Committee of the Communist Party of China approved a 5-Year Plan (2001–2005) for national economic and social development.[97] The plan laid down 16 priority items of development for the whole of China over the next 5 years.[98] "Strengthening construction of the socialist democracy and legal system" was one of the items on the agenda.[99] The plan asserted that legal system development was important to facilitate market development and associated economic activities. It espoused the following ideal of legal supervision:

> Government work should operate in line with statutory laws while improving the public servant system, with government functionaries being held responsible for their conduct and their performance regularly checked. The need for legal system development is especially acute in the rural area and countryside, where social relations and local influences are strong and dominant.[100]

National Policy Directive on Fidelity to Law

When Premier Zhu Rongji delivered the Report on the Work of the Government at the Fifth Session of the Ninth National People's Congress on March 5, 2002, he specifically pointed out the need for clean government:

> The Sixth Plenary Session of the Fifteenth Party Central Committee adopted an important decision on strengthening and improving the Party's style of work....Efforts were intensified to build a clean and honest government and fight corruption, yielding notable results....Local protectionism remains a problem despite repeated orders to ban it, and the order of the market economy is yet to be fully rectified. In some localities and government departments and among some leading cadres, formalism and bureaucracy are rife; deception, extravagance, and waste are serious problems; and corruption is relatively conspicuous. There are cases of work units misappropriating budgetary funds or special funds in disregard of the relevant rules and regulations.[101]

In 2010, Premier Wen Jiabao promoted the rule of law as a way to establish a fair and just society:

> "To create a world ruled by law" indicates that law is more powerful than the world....To specify the spirit, I want to say five points. First of all, the dignity of the constitution as well as laws transcends all; second, all people are equal before the law; third, all organizations and institutions shall undertake activities within the scope of the constitution and laws; fourth, laws shall be made in a democratic manner and be publicized and popularized among the masses; last but not least, see to it that there are laws to go by, the laws are observed and strictly enforced, and law-breakers are prosecuted. A Chinese saying goes that, "The difficulty lies not in legislation, but in implementation." If laws are not fully observed, why should we have them?
>
> ...
>
> Fairness of law is crucial to our country. It is easy to understand when you could always find a balance displayed in the courts. Just now when I mentioned equity and impartiality, I mean equitable legislation and impartial implementation of the law. Fairness and justice are most important for a law, whose opposite is abuse of law and practice of favoritism. If we are to build a society that is fair and just, we should follow the principle of fairness and justice.[102]

Premier Wen further expounded on his observations about problems with the rule of law in China at the National Work Conference for Legal Administration:

> In a time of peace and development, the greatest danger to a ruling party is corruption. And the root of corruption is a lack of supervision and restriction of power. If these issues are not sufficiently resolved, the nature of the political power itself can change, leading to a situation where the whole undertaking comes to a stop because the leading figure ceases to exist.[103]

In not so many words, two Premiers, years apart, set down the ultimate challenge for good governance, intended to usher in a clean government that does not abuse its power and violate the rights of the people, one that promotes the fair, equitable, and, most importantly, full implementation of the rule of law—an accountable government.

PRC Police Law and the Supervision of Police

The PRC Police Law of 1995[104] set forth a legal framework for the regulation and supervision of police law enforcement powers. Specifically, Article 3 of the Police Law provides that the police are accountable to and come under the supervision of the people: "People's policemen must rely on the masses, keep close ties to them, listen attentively to their comments and suggestions, accept their supervision, safeguard their interests, and serve them whole-heartedly." The accountability system and supervision framework are laid out in more detail under Chapter VI, "Supervision over Law Enforcement," which is made up of five articles (Articles 42 to 47); for example, Article 42 provides that, in performing their duties, the police are supervised by the Supreme People's Procuratorate and administrative supervisory organs.[105]

Constitutional Supervision

No constitutional body other than the National People's Congress enforces the Constitution. Article 62 of the Constitution gives the National People's Congress this power.[106] Like power is also given to the Standing Committee,[107] the alter ego of the National People's Congress.[108] Specifically, the National People's Congress and its Standing Committee have supervisory responsibility and authority over all state agencies. Article 3(2) of the Constitution states that, "All administrative, judicial, and procurator organs of the state are created by the people's congresses to which they are responsible and by which they are supervised." The constitutional grant of power to the National People's Congress is not realized in practice. The National People's Congress only meets once a year, and the Standing Committee has no special executive committee charged with the responsibility of inspection and supervision over law enforcement; it is otherwise preoccupied with other legislative concerns and activities. Neither the National People's Congress nor the Standing Committee has the necessary time, expertise, or resources to effectively supervise enforcement of the constitution and execution of the laws. In fact, before 1993, the National People's Congress and Standing Committee's legal supervision existed only on paper.[109]

Supervision Regulations and Regime

In 1993, the Standing Committee adopted "Certain Regulations on Reinforcing Inspection and Supervision over Actual Implementation of the Law" to institutionalize (*zhidu hua*), standardize (*guifan hua*), and proceduralize (*chengxu hua*) law enforcement inspection and supervision activities.[110] The Standing Committee[111] wanted to make law implementation as important as law making, thus closing the gap between laws on the book and laws in the street.[112] The regulations provide that (see Table 6.18):

- Article 1—The Standing Committee or a special committee of the National People's Congress[113] is responsible for checking and supervising the implementation (*guanche shishi de qingkuan*) of laws and associated resolutions and decisions of the National People's Congress and the Standing Committee. The main focus is on important problems associated with economic reform and socialist modernization and those reflecting the masses' most important concerns.

TABLE 6.18 Law Enforcement Inspection and Supervision by the National People's Congress or Standing Committee

Legislative purpose	Standardize, systematize, and proceduralize law enforcement inspection and supervision
Constitutional authority	Article 62 (NPC), Article 67 (Standing Committee)
Inspection targets	Organs responsible for law enforcement—departments under State Council, Supreme People's Procuratorate, Supreme People's Courts
Inspecting agent	Legal enforcement inspecting team (*zhifa jiancha zu*) from the Standing Committee and Special Committee
Inspection team	A team leader and a few members—regular members from the Standing Committee, optional members from local representatives of the organs under inspection, and, as required, experts
Inspection planning	Inspection plan to address substance, organization, time, place, and method
Inspection procedure	Prepared by the Standing Committee, submitted and approved 1 month after
Inspection methods	Reports, conferences, interviews, surveys, onsite inspections
Inspection report	State and conditions of law enforcement; problems and causes; recommendations and proposals for action and correction; required legal reform and change (e.g., amendment, supplement, clarification)
Report procedure	Submit to Standing Committee for deliberation; responsible person from inspected organs explains and answers questions of Standing Committee
Remedial actions	Standing Committee to examine written recommendations for actions and corrections; forward to the inspected organ any remedial actions rquired; report corrections within 6 months

- Article 2—Inspection and supervision are conducted at the respective organs responsible for law enforcement, various departments under the State Council, Supreme People's Court, and Supreme People's Procuratorate. The inspecting unit (*jianchazu*) will not be involved with the direct handling of noted problems or irregularities.
- Article 3—The inspection plan (its substance, organization, time, place, and method) will be decided in advance and approved by the Standing Committee one month after the meeting.
- Article 4—The Standing Committee law enforcement inspection team (*zhifa jianchazu*) will be small but capable; it will be made up of a team leader and several members chosen from the Standing Committee, supplemented by specialists, local people's congress members, and representatives from the responsible organization being inspected as required or deemed necessary.
- Article 6—Inspections will take on a variety of forms, including reaching down to the grassroots, touching base with reality, mixing with the masses, listening to reports, organizing discussions, initiating individual interviews, conducting sample surveys, and inspecting sites.
- Article 7—The inspection team leader will file a comprehensive report, which includes: (1) the state of law enforcement, (2) problems with law enforcement and their causes, (3) recommendations on reform and corrections, and (4) proposals on law amendment, supplement, and clarification.
- Article 8—The inspection report will be submitted to the Standing Committee by the team leader for its deliberation and consideration. The responsible person of the inspected organization should also attend and answer questions.

- Article 9—Inspection reports that have been reviewed by the Standing Committee will be forwarded to the inspected organs responsible for law enforcement, with recommendations for action or correction. The organization will take appropriate remedial actions and report on the effort and results to the Standing Committee within 6 months.

The Constitutional authority and responsibility given to the National People's Congress with regard to policing were rarely exercised before 2000. Zeng Xiaozhen, a National People's Congress deputy and vice chairman of the Standing Committee of the Jilin Provincial People's Congress, confessed that, "I had almost no sense of exercising the right of supervision 18 years ago when I first came to Beijing as a National People's Congress deputy attending the annual session; instead, I had only two things in mind: participating in meetings attentively and retelling what I had learned about the central government's policies to people back home."[114]

Mandate for National People's Congress Police Supervision

On March 10, 2000, National People's Congress Chairman Li Peng admonished the Ninth National People's Congress members about their constitutional duty to supervise the Supreme People's Court, the Supreme People's Procuratorate, and the Ministry of Public Security in enforcing the law. Specifically, the National People's Congress was told to shift from a "support instead of supervision" role to a strict supervisory capacity. Since then, the National People's Congress Standing Committee has passed a number of resolutions to improve upon supervision of police performance.

In 2007, the National People's Congress passed a law providing for local congressional supervision of law enforcement, the Supervision Law of Standing Committees of People's Congresses at Various Levels.[115] The law requires that local congressional members ensure that the nation's laws (national, provincial, city, local, administrative regulations) are being properly enforced. In 2010, there were renewed calls for National People's Congress supervision of implementation of the law.[116] China has more than 230 effective laws, over 700 administrative regulations issued by the State Council, and about 9000 local ordinances issued or approved by provincial-level legislatures. To strengthen the supervisory authority of the National People's Congress, it passed a number of laws in 2010, including the following:[117]

- An amendment to the Electoral Law grants equal representation in legislative bodies to rural and urban people. The amendment requires "both rural and urban areas to adopt the same ratio of deputies to the represented population in elections of people's congress deputies," which was an effort to close the urban–rural gap and promote equal rights.
- A revision to the Law on Guarding State Secrets narrowed the definition of "state secrets," boosting transparency and ensuring the people's right to know.
- An amendment to the State Compensation Law gives citizens a better chance of obtaining compensation when their rights have been violated by the state. The amendment also codified compensation for psychological injuries, for which the state may be liable for the first time.

- A decision to amend the Administrative Supervision Law was aimed at strengthening the supervision of public servants; it gives rural people more say in deciding village affairs and improves protection for whistleblowers who report corruption by officials.
- An amendment to the PRC Criminal Procedure Law proposed that fewer crimes be subject to the death penalty. It also proposed harsher punishments for crimes endangering public security—such as organized crime, drunk driving, and street racing—to better protect human rights. The draft also proposed tougher penalties for the crime of forcing others to work.
- A Social Insurance Law prevents the improper use of social security funds and grants all citizens the right to access and enjoy five forms of social insurance.
- The Organic Law of Villagers' Committees was revised, and an amendment was drafted to the Law on Deputies to the National People's Congress and Local People's Congresses at Various Levels.

Also in 2010, the National People's Congress passed a new Administrative Supervision Law to replace that of 1997.[118] The law gives the State Council authority to supervise various administrative functions and staff appointments.[119] Article 16 of the 1997 Administrative Supervision Law defined the jurisdiction of the State Council:

> State Council supervisory organs exercise supervision over the following organs and personnel: (1) the State Council's various departments and its government functionaries; (2) other personnel appointed by the State Council and by the State Council's various departments; (3) provincial, autonomous regional, and municipal people's governments and their leading personnel.

Article 16 provides similar authority to local people's government supervisory organs at respective levels of government. The duties and responsibilities of supervisory organs at respective levels of government include: (1) "check on problems" with implementation of the laws (decisions, regulations, orders) (Article 18(1)); (2) "accept the handling of charges" against administrative disciplinary violations and irregularities (Article 18(2)); (3) "investigate and handle acts of administrative discipline violations" (Article 18(3)); (4) "accept appeals against decisions of administrative punishments imposed by competent administrative organs" (Article 18 (4)); and (5) any other duties as required by law (Article 18(5)). Upon receiving a complaint, the supervisory organs should "conduct investigations of and handle the behavior in violation of administrative discipline" (Article 30), including conducting preliminary examinations to determine whether further investigation is required (Article 30(1)). They should organize an investigation to collect evidence (Article 30(2)), examine the evidence for violations (Article (3)), and "make a decision or recommendation of supervision" (Article 30(4)).

The supervisory organs may recommend supervision based on the following findings of irregularities: "refusal to enforce laws and regulations, or violation of laws and regulations" (Article 23(1)); "decisions, orders, and directions" that need to be corrected (Article 23(2)); "infringements upon state and collective interests and legitimate interests of citizens" that need to be ratified (Article 23(3)); inappropriate "employment, appointments, removals, awards, and punishments" (Article 23(4)); and any other administrative law violations (Article 23(5)).

National People's Congress supervision of the police is not the only supervisory system in China; others include the media and public supervision. Statistics show that the masses provide 80% of the evidence leading to the prosecution of officials at all levels. Despite this, supervision of the government, including the police, falls far short of expectations. There are still too many "power-for-money" exchanges.

Implementation of National People's Congress Police Supervision

In 1999, the National People's Congress Subcommittee for Internal and Judicial Committee sent inspection groups to investigate how the PRC Criminal Procedure Law was carried out in the Tianjin Municipality, the Inner Mongolia Autonomous Region, and the provinces of Heilongjiang, Zhejiang, Hubei, and Shaanxi. It was the first investigation ever conducted on such a large scale and in such a manner.[120] The report found that the PRC Criminal Procedure Law was not being properly implemented; examples included extended detentions, coerced confessions, and interference with lawyers, issues that are still relevant today in many parts of China. Hou Zongbin, chairman of the Committee for Internal and Judicial Affairs under the National People's Congress, observed that:

> In the main, Chinese judiciaries, including judges, prosecutors and police, have noticeably upgraded their performance of duties, but we cannot simply afford to neglect the problems of extended detention and forced confession that exist in many places....While a number of those already under extended custody before the new law was enforced have not been released, new instances of the same kind are occurring...they [lawyers] have difficulties in meeting their clients and accessing court files relating to their cases, and their reasonable petitions have more often than not been rejected.

The National People's Congress investigation teams attributed the problem to a lack of understanding of the Criminal Law and the law being "too advanced" for China.[121]

The Minister of Public Security, Jia Chungwan, issued the National People's Congress investigation report in November of that year. On this occasion, Cao Zhi, vice-chairman of the National People's Congress Standing Committee, observed: "Since cleaning up the police force is a great concern of the public and a long-term task, the legislature will for a long period of time list it as a key part of legislative supervision over government and judicial work." The National People's Congress cited major areas of concern: "Situations of unfair and illegal law enforcement, abuse of power, and rudeness to the people are mostly perpetrated by police and staff in grassroots police stations." Police abuse of powers and dereliction of duties were blamed on a failure to observe existing laws, regulations, and charters pertinent to police work and on the dereliction of duty by leaders of the police departments in supervising the officers in a conscientious manner. Police corruption and abuse were attributed, in part, to a lack of resources; inadequate funding and poor equipment in some areas aversely affected normal operations of the police departments, as police officers resorted to corruption to supplement their income. Since then, the National People's Congress and its Standing Committee have taken measures to more closely supervise the conduct of the country's 1. 5 million policemen.[122]

According to Cao Zhi, the National People's Congress primary supervisory activities include examination of government and judiciary reports, launching law-enforcement inspection tours, and organizing people's deputies to assess government and judicial work.

To facilitate better and more effective police supervision, Cao called for more concrete measures, including detailed rules on the recruitment, training, assessment, promotion, and dismissal of policemen.

At the same time, Li Peng, chairman of the Standing Committee of National People's Congress, asked that the public security and judicial departments take more effective measures to implement the PRC Criminal Procedure Law. Particularly, it was necessary to take steps to safeguard the citizens' legitimate rights and root out police malpractice and abuse of power, such as detaining suspects for excessive periods of time and inquisition by torture. A number of steps should be taken to ratify the situation. Police and judicial personnel should enhance their legal awareness. They should pay more attention to legal procedures instead of just being concerned with substantive results. Laws, rules, and regulations should clearly define the duties of the public security department, court, and procuratorate. The political and professional quality of police and judicial personnel had to be improved so they would use the correct legal procedures to fight crime and protect the legitimate rights of the general public.[123] In 2000, the National People's Congress Law Committee and the Commission of Legislative Affairs of the National People's Congress Standing Committee also sent investigation teams to the provinces of Guangdong, Yunnan, and Hainan to gather suggestions from official departments and foreign trade companies regarding the performance of and abuses by customs officials.[124]

To exercise its supervisory role and responsibilities, the National People's Congress has taken a number of high-profile supervisory actions against various law enforcement agencies.[125] In the past, the police have been asked to collect illegal fees and fines on behalf of townships and villages. To address this problem, the National People's Congress took two legislative actions. The law enforcement panel at the National People's Congress Standing Committee, in conformity with the Township Enterprise Law, recommended that the State Council abolish 2035 illegal fees levied on township enterprises which amounted to 1 billion yuan in 2000. The State Economic and Trade Commission pledged to remove all illegal fees and fines by June 2001. Also, the National People's Congress appropriated more money for police and security to discourage police officers from engaging in the collection of illegal fees and penalties. The National People's Congress budgeted an additional 5.6 billion yuan for army, armed police forces, and procurator, judicial, and public security organs.[126]

To control police misappropriation of funds (e.g., tapping fines and fees for operational expenses), the National People's Congress set out strict financial accounting and auditing systems:

> First, supervision and management of funds should be tightened....Second, we should continue to implement the central government's regulations on managing administrative fees, fines and confiscated funds according to the principle of separating revenue from expenditures....We should fully implement a method whereby relevant organs make out invoices for administrative fees and fines which must be paid to a bank account under the unified management of a government finance department to ensure that those who determine the amounts of fees and fines or make out invoices cannot collect them or use them themselves. Third, the Accounting Law should be conscientiously implemented....Fourth, we should lose no time in rectifying public accounting and auditing firms and other intermediary organs to standardize their business operation and strengthen self-discipline to provide objective, fair and highly efficient services to the public. Fifth, financial laws should be further improved and enforcement of these laws should be strengthened....Greater efforts should be made to ensure that financial affairs are handled in accordance with the law.[127]

To facilitate police supervision by local elected officials, the National People's Congress strengthened grassroots control by promulgating the Law on the Organization of Village Committees in 1998 to allow for direct election of village officials.[128] It was hoped that this democratic process would improve management and enhance supervision.[129] In 1999, the Forest Law Enforcement Inspection Group of the Chinese National People's Congress Standing Committee directed the Forest Law enforcement departments (State Forestry Administration, State Development Planning Commission, Ministry of Finance, Supreme People's Court, Supreme People's Procuratorate, and the MPS) to enforce the Forest Law with due diligence.[130] Also, the National People's Congress increased supervision of customs enforcement. It vowed to stamp out smuggling by increasing the power of customs officials and to stop corrupt activities of customs officials by supervising them more closely. In 2000, the 15th Session of the Standing Committee of the Ninth National People's Congress amended the Customs Law to increase supervision of customs personnel. The National People's Congress wanted to give customs officials more power to enforce the law to make them more effective, but it also wanted more powers to supervise the customs officers to hold them more accountable. Specifically, the National People's Congress added a clause that said: "Customs and their staff should accept supervision by supervisory departments when they conduct their administrative law enforcement; anti-smuggle police should accept supervision by the people's procuratorate when they conduct investigations." Another clause reads: "Auditing departments should conduct auditing and supervision on the financial income and expenditure of customs in accordance with law and have the right to carry out special auditing and investigation on matters that are related to the financial income and expenditure of the State."[131]

Responding to the National People's Congress' call, local public security officials stepped up their supervisory measures. The Hainan PSB chief, Wang Heping, confirmed that his bureau established a special supervisors program (*teyao jiandu yuan zhidu*) to coordinate all other forms of supervision, including Party supervision, legal supervision, public supervision, and public opinion supervision. The 15 Hainan special supervisors, after inspecting Hainan public security operations, made the following observations: (1) Overall, the public order and crime situation in Hainan was acceptable, but there were specific areas of concerns; the public security bureaus needed to form task forces to deal with these areas of concern. (2) The quality of the frontline officers was low, and law enforcement activities were not uniform. (3) Traffic control only dealt with cars, not people. (4) There was a need to improve communication between the police and press, such that the press would not be second guessing what the police were doing or reporting distorted news.[132]

In 2006, the National People's Congress passed the Supervision Law of Standing Committees of People's Congresses at Various Levels.[133] The Supervision Law gave the National People's Congress more powers to supervise administrative agencies, government functions, and official activities. The drafting and passage of the Supervision Law took 10 years. The National People's Congress gathered 222 motions from 4044 National People's Congress deputies seeking improvement and passage of the law. It was first submitted to the Standing Committee for passage in 2002. It was finally passed after four discussions[134] and several rounds of revisions.[135] Immediately after passage of the Supervision Law, legislature and staff met to learn about its implementation and problems and issues that might arise.[136]

Legal Supervision

Overall, police reform in China since 1979 has been moving steadily toward institutionalization (*zhidu hua*), standardization (*guifan hua*), and legalization (*fazhi hua*)[137] to make police work more uniform, predictable, and accountable. Legalization of police work means that policing—policy, process, decision, and action—must be guided and restricted by laws and regulations. The objective is to have "laws to follow" (*you fa ke yi*), "laws that must be followed" (*you fa bi yi*), and "laws that must be implemented sternly" (*zhi fa bi yan*), in addition to holding those who violate the laws responsible (*wei fa bi gou*).[138] This notion of police law (*yifa zhijing*) is a direct derivative of the rule of law (*yifa zhiguo*).[139] In 1998, *yifa zhijing* became a constitutional principle. *Yifa zhijing* means that:

> The masses, under the leadership of the Party, and in accordance with the Constitution and law, manage state, economic, social business in various means and ways. It is to make sure that the state's various businesses are conducted by law to realize the ideas of democratization, institutionalization, and legalization. It is to make sure that the system does not change due to changes in leadership, ideas, and focus.[140]

In carrying out their duties, the PRC police are expected to follow increasingly sophisticated and detailed laws, rules, and regulations, most of them published after 1979: (1) PRC Constitution promulgated by the National People's Congress; (2) laws concerning public security organization, functions, and processes promulgated by the National People's Congress; (3) laws and decisions concerning public security organization, functions, and processes promulgated by the Standing Committee of the National People's Congress; (5) administrative regulations concerning public security promulgated by the State Council and restrictive regulations published by the MPS;[141] (6) local laws concerning public security promulgated by the National People's Congress or Standing Committee of respective provinces, autonomous regions, and municipalities under direct rule; and (7) self-governing laws and local regulations concerning public security work promulgated by autonomous regions' people's congresses or their standing committees.[142] Finally, there are disciplinary policies, rules, and regulations promulgated by the Communist Party.[143]

In spite of increased police laws and regulations, the goal of achieving legalization of the police has been an elusive one. In 1999, the State Council promulgated their "Decision regarding Full Implementation of Administration in Accordance with the Law" ("*Guanyu quanmian tuijin yifa xingzheng jueding*") and observed openly that progress toward policing in accordance with the law was afflicted with difficulties.

Problems with police legal reform in China can be attributed to a number of factors. Historically, the Chinese people have had no concept of the rule of law. They have accepted the autocratic rule of the state and authoritarianism of the emperor. They have grown used to the idea that the law does not apply to officials. People have a tendency to prefer utility over the law (*zhongli qingfa*), to prefer individual and local interests over collective and national interests, and to humanize (*renqing fa*) and individualize (*gexing fa*) the law.[144]

Problems Confronting Legal Supervision of Police

Public security leaders are not competent in and have little understanding of the law. When supervising police work, they prefer to rely on their own personal experience and subjective judgment. They routinely condone and actively promote inappropriate police conduct, such as illegal use of force and the collection of illegal fees and charges. Police leaders and officers in the field often do not follow the law in the execution of their duties. Instead, they try to take advantage of their position by seeking bribes—in other words, offering their police power to the highest bidder. They collect fees and impose punishment at the behest of the local Party secretary and involve themselves in economic cases on behalf of the local rich and powerful (*difang zhuyi*). The police prefer substantive justice to procedural fairness; coerced confessions and illegal extended detention in pursuit of justice are the norm. The law is enforced and cases are decided based on personal relationships (*guanxi*) and individual favors owed (*ganqing*)—in other words, human factors (*renqing*). The police supervision system is not operating in an efficient and effective manner, as the National People's Congress and judiciary seldom exercise their legal powers to supervise the police; these supervisory agencies and processes exist on paper only. The police legal system is facing new challenges. The PRC has signed international conventions on torture and human rights and 17 other international agreements, but PRC police law has yet to integrate these international laws and conventions into their system of prohibitions and regulations.

Police Work Supervision[145]

Police work supervision (*jingwu ducha*) is a specialized form of internal police supervision unique to China. Philosophically, police work supervision is grounded on Confucius' ideal of self-cultivation. Theoretically, police work supervision is informed by legal supervision doctrines.[146] Historically, police work supervision recalls the venerable *yushi jiandu* system in imperial China.[147] Comparatively, police work supervision resembles internal affairs units in major police departments in the United States. Currently, little research has been conducted into the police accountability system in the PRC, and none on police work supervision specifically.[148]

Origin and Development

The need for police work supervision is a result of the Chinese reform process, which introduced the rule of law to China. Its development is very much driven by the dynamics and outcome of the reform; that is, the reform raised the standards of the police and heightened the expectations of the public, who have called for greater police discipline. The police supervision system was considered necessary in the reform era to ensure that the police operate according to the rule of law. Also, such a system was necessary to establish the legitimacy of the police, to gain the confidence of the people, and to properly and effectively execute the will of the Party and the policy of the state. The police work supervision system was intended to curb police abuses and avoid incompetence that might have an impact on social, political, and economic stability. Long before the police work supervision movement and ever since the beginning of the reform, the Party and public security leadership have consistently called for reining in abusive and improper police conduct through

Party oversight and police discipline. The impetus of a police work supervision system can be traced to the "sternly discipline the police by law" (*yi fa chongyan zhijing*) campaign. In 1991, the Communist Party of China Central Committee issued their "Decision to Strengthen Public Security Work," which highlighted the need to establish a system and processes to guide, train and regulate police work. The MPS and the State Council Legal System Office then drafted "Public Security Organ Supervision Regulations."[149] In 1995, the Eighth National People's Congress Standing Committee, at its Second Plenary Meeting, passed the People's Police Law of the People's Republic of China.[150] Section 47 of the law specifically provides that an internal police supervision system must be established: "Public security organs shall establish a supervisory system to supervise the enforcement of laws and regulations and observance of discipline by the people's policemen of public security organs."

Establishment of the Police Supervision Committee (*Gongan ducha weiyuanhui*)

In 2001, the Ministry of Public Security formed the national Police Supervision Committee (*Gongan ducha weiyuanhui*). The Committee was established under the "Public Security Organs Supervision Regulations" ("*Gongan jiguan ducha tiaoli*"). Reporting to the MPS, the Supervision Committee is responsible for the organization, administration, and supervision of all police supervision organs and strategies nationwide. The duties and responsibilities of the Supervision Committee include:

1. Supervise MPS organs and police officers in their execution of duties in accordance with law.
2. Organize and plan public security supervision.
3. Issue decisions and instructions regarding public security supervision work.
4. Examine and approve annual police supervision reports.
5. Receive reports of the MPS and Police Supervision Bureau in a timely manner.

The Supervision Committee is made up of staff members of the Police Supervision Bureau, Supervision Bureau, Audit Bureau, Administrative Office, Personnel Training Office, Propaganda Office, Public Order Management Office, Border Management Office, Fire Management Office, Transportation Management Office, Legal System Office, and Party Committee Cadres.

Ideas on How to Establish a Modern Supervision System

The modern police supervision system is a 24/7, comprehensive, proactive supervision system. It involves supervising police activities from administration to operations, from planning to implementation, from procedure to conduct, in process and outcome, openly and secretly. The purpose of supervision is not to punish wrongdoing by finding fault but to prevent police abuses by discovering weaknesses and promoting best practices, developing good procedures, and inculcating exemplary police attitudes and sound habits. Modern police supervision utilizes multiple means to supervise the police, from unannounced inspections to observing their operations. Police supervision is focused on solving problems and improving performance. It relies upon advance planning and tight coordination with other supervisory, regulatory, and disciplinary agencies. Modern police supervision must work with these units to improve police work and should not interfere with the other units' jurisdictions or functions. Police supervision should not only focus on finding faults but also pay attention to exonerating innocent police officers and promoting good practices. Police supervisors and police officers should work together to subject themselves to a lawful supervision process. The modern supervision system should work on perfecting the complaint system by honoring and allaying people's concerns. Currently, police supervision can be activated by: (1) citizens' complaints, (2) media exposure, (3) public security scrutiny, (4) Party inquiry, or (5) self-reporting. There is an impression that citizens' complaints are not taken seriously, and there are legitimate concerns with conflicts of interest and covering up complaints.[151] The modern police supervision system should be able to ensure the integrity and effectiveness of such an inspection system.[152]

Onsite Supervision

To carry out onsite supervision properly and effectively, police supervisors must pay attention to three things:

1. The target of supervision must be properly identified and clearly stated. The targeted police activities to be supervised must be taken into consideration in planning and organizing the supervision.
2. The supervisor must adjust its tactics and react to particular situations. In criminal cases, supervisors must react quickly and decisively. In cases where citizens are complaining about ongoing police abuse and misconduct, the supervisors should act quickly to correct the situation (e.g., illegal detention). When citizens are not happy with police administrative decisions, the supervisors should allow the police an opportunity to resolve any differences with the citizens.
3. The supervisor should insist on the "double service principle" (*xiangxian fuwu yuanze*). Police supervisors are there to supervise the police and protect the rights of citizens, but the supervisors also have another duty. They are there to make sure that the police are doing their job and to shield them from trivial and malicious citizen allegations.

To carry out supervision efficiently, supervisors must coordinate and cooperate with other disciplinary functionaries or supervision departments. They have to work with the Party Commission for Inspection Discipline (*Jilu Jiancha Weiyuanhui*) and the Police Discipline and Supervision Department (*Jijian Jiangcha Bu*). The former is responsible for the education, punishment, supervision, and protection functions of the Party. The latter is responsible for investigating citizens' complaints for public security bureaus. The Police Work Supervision Team has a different mission. It is there to monitor and supervise police procedures and activities to make them conform to the law and be held accountable to the people. It has a more practical charter and comprehensive coverage. There is also a difference in methods and focus. The Police Work Supervision Team should be responsible for initial investigations into citizen complaints. After a complaint case is established, however, it should be transferred to the Police Discipline and Supervision Department for action. Alternatively, when either the Party Commission for Inspection Discipline or the Police Discipline and Supervision Department is actively involved in an investigation or processing a complaint, the Police Work Supervision team should back off.

To conduct police supervision smoothly, the supervision teams should be firm but fair and should not unduly intimidate the officers involved. They should not give criminals or offenders the opportunity to avoid the legal process because of the presence or involvement of police supervision. Supervisors must watch out for any signs of cover-ups and must stand firm against any undue influence from senior officers or Party cadres.[153]

Strengthening and Improving Police Supervision

To strengthen and improve upon police supervision efforts, it is important to focus on maintaining the ideological purity, integrity, discipline, and work style of the supervision team. The quality (political, moral, professional, cultural, and personal) of supervising police officers must be improved. Also, supervising police officers should be properly trained in police supervision to develop the required expertise. Such instruction and training must be relevant and useful. The instruction must integrate theory with practice. The instruction and training must occur under field conditions and be subject to validation from the field. A systematic, comprehensive, and stringent assessment process should be in place to be sure that supervision is being conducted as designed.[154]

Public Opinion on Police Work Supervision Program

Generally speaking, and especially in the beginning, the police work supervision program has not been well received by the police. Some consider it to be a nuisance that is looking for trouble. Over time, however, frontline officers have found that the police supervisors can, in fact, be helpful, such as when they defend them against frivolous complaints and clear their name. Guangxi Province, for example, reported a total of 9450 complaints about police not doing their job properly or enforcing the law properly; however, upon investigation, only 3320 cases were substantiated.[155]

Assessment of the Police Work Supervision Program

In 2001, the MPS organized a national police supervision conference in Shenzhen Municipality, Guangdong Province, to discuss implementation of the police supervision system. The Shenzhen meeting defined the spirit of the supervision program and was used as a reference for local police leaderships in setting up their own police supervision programs. Since then, police supervision programs and activities have spread all over the nation. The lessons derived from the conference included the fact that supervision work has become more sophisticated. It has moved from being concerned with appearance, manner, and style to more substantive issues, such as how cases are handled and what outcomes have been achieved. Supervision is becoming more constructive than negative; thus, instead of inspecting and investigating to find fault, inspectors try to alleviate the underlying problems giving rise to the police misconduct. Also, supervision is becoming more proactive in anticipating citizens' concerns rather than reacting to citizens' complaints. Still, though, many problems with police supervision remain to be addressed and resolved:[156]

1. Local police leadership is still reluctant to embrace the concept of police supervision because of a lack of understanding of the role and functions of inspectors.
2. Some local police leadership has not followed the spirit of Shenzhen in establishing the required supervision program as instructed by the MPS.

3. For some police organs, the establishment of police inspector units has not been accompanied by the necessary regulations; that is, police supervision has not been properly institutionalized. Establishment of the police inspector program is necessary to give force and effect to the public security organ's internal regulations (*Gongan jiguan renmin jingcha naiwu tiaoli*) and for actualization of the "three items of education" initiative.

An Inspector's Reflection on Supervision

A criminal investigator with ten years of experience reflected upon her term as a police inspector. The supervision teams (*ducha dui*) have been viewed by a majority of the public as an alternative avenue for filing police complaints (*xinfang ke*). The public and police seek out supervision teams when they have problems with each other. The inspectors often find themselves caught in between. Depending on the decisions made and actions taken, their decisions are going to offend one of the two parties, sometimes both. This is particularly so when the inspectors have to investigate and sanction their fellow officers (*xiongdi*), but it is a task that must be carried out with integrity and professionalism. This investigator noted the utility of inspectors in clearing the names of fellow police officers.[157]

Issues and Problems with the Supervision System

An inspector with the Ruian Municipality PBS, Zhejiang Province, brought up a number of problems with the police supervision system. Of primary importance is an apparent confusion regarding roles and functions:

1. Police organs treat police inspectors as reserve officers (e.g., as task force or emergency unit officers). Police inspectors are made to function as operational officers when deemed necessary. Theoretically and by law,[158] police inspectors should act as independent and objective observers. In practice, due to the nature and reality of police work, police inspectors are rarely able to function independently. They are not able to stay free and clear of ongoing police operations. Police inspectors routinely are involved in emergencies, and they often are called upon when police resources at the scene of a crime or emergency are not adequate to deal with the problem.
2. The police inspectors themselves are not sure what their own duties and responsibilities are under the law, such as the "Police Organ Supervision Regulations" ("*Gongan jiguan ducha tiaoli*") and the "Implementation Methods for Police Organ Supervision Regulations" ("*Gongan jiguan ducha tiaoli shishi banfa*"). Inspectors usually come to identify with the officers they are supervising and otherwise share in their work effort (e.g., license inspection or criminal investigation).
3. Other Party and government units charged with police oversight (e.g., CPC Supervision and Disciplinary Committee) do not understand what police supervision is and what police inspectors do. The Supervision and Disciplinary Committee often passes along complaints filed with the Party to police inspectors for investigation. The police inspectors call upon the Supervision and Disciplinary Committee members or other police officers (e.g., traffic police) to engage in supervision. There is no common understanding regarding who is in control and what process applies in resolving cases.

Also, the supervision work is not conducted with sufficient competency or professionalism:

1. Most of the time, police supervision work is conducted in a very superficial and perfunctory manner. Inspectors are often more concerned with the outward appearance of police officers (e.g., uniform and bearing) than with the substance of police work (e.g., legality of criminal procedures, effectiveness of administrative procedures).
2. The inspectors have few of the skills and techniques required to pursue inspector work (e.g., they seldom work with others, they are more critical than constructive). They do not set a good example themselves nor are they able to show the police another, better ways of doing things.
3. The inspectors have few rules to follow. They seldom prepare their cases beforehand or in an adequate manner. They usually react to complaints instead of taking proactive actions. They seldom solve problems but are quick to point out mistakes. They seldom engage in the promotion of supervision work or educating police officers as required by the "Police Organ Supervision Regulations" and "Implementation Methods for Police Organ Supervision Regulations."

The police supervision teams are grossly understaffed, undertrained, and inadequately resourced. According to the MPS and law requirements, inspectors are supposed to be on duty 24 hours a day, with at least two people on duty for each shift. There are not enough inspectors to go around. Most of the inspectors are not adequately trained for the job. Except for the team leaders, most of the inspectors do not have the necessary education or training. Some do not even have on-the-job training. As a result, their knowledge of police and public security work is not adequate and they do not have specialized police supervision skills. The inspectors do not have their own offices, interview rooms, or detention facilities. They do not have a full complement of investigative tools.

The inspectors also suffer from personal attitude problems. Some inspectors consider themselves over and above other officers. This arrogance has led to abuse and resentment. Some investigators, especially the younger ones, are afraid of offending people, and older inspectors do not have the drive to solve the world's problem. Many of the inspectors have not been called upon to demonstrate proficient professional skills and the legal knowledge necessary for criminal investigation, public order management, household administration, and community supervision.

The inspectors are affected by external constraints. Police leaders do not understand the importance and necessity of inspectors and treat them as a supplement to internal supervision. Police leaders themselves are not familiar with the "Police Organ Supervision Regulations" and "Implementation Methods for Police Organ Supervision Regulations." They fail to define roles, functions, duties, and authority clearly. They often assign inspectors to routine police duties.

Lowering the admission standards allows second officers or retired officers to assume police inspector posts. Sometimes inferior officers at police posts are appointed. There are great differences between supervision units nationwide and even within different parts of a province. Some supervision units are very well established but others do not even have office space and little equipment at their disposal. Some work alongside the Party Supervision and Disciplinary Committee, but others work by themselves.

Countermeasures for these problems in implementing police supervision include the following: (1) Political and police leadership must understand and appreciate the roles, functions, importance, and necessity of the inspectors. Inspectors must be treated with appreciation, support, and, most importantly, respect. (2) Inspectors must be given the necessary staff and resources. (3) The inspection process should be institutionalized and standardized. There must be a supervision system with a clear mission, detailed procedures, specific guidelines, and a structured data system. Every effort should be made to strengthen police supervision teams by improving team members' understanding of politics and by improving their quality through science and technology and by providing the necessary resources, as well as by being stern and strict.[159]

According to the official police work supervision activities report for 2000, 1.5 million written notices (*tongzhi shu*), recommendations (*jianyi shu*), and decisions (*jueding shu*) were issued, with 1906 offending police officers being relieved of their duties and another 1124 being restricted to working in the office (*jinbi cuoshi*). Police supervision was also used to make sure that national, central, and universal policies were being implemented. Police work supervision uncovered and corrected 6718 cases involving failures to follow rules or regulations when establishing cases or when processing permits and collecting fees. It addressed 3.2 million calls to the 110 call system reporting police illegality and impropriety, leading to the correction of 3758 cases on the spot and 2577 cases later. The system corrected an erroneous public image 7.4 million times and handled 3.6 million claims of inappropriate use of equipment.[160]

Judging by such preliminary data (3.2 million calls involved police misconduct but only 6335 of these were resolved), the police supervision program has not been very successful. The reasons for such lackluster performance can only be surmised; perhaps police supervisors are not trusted by the public and are resented by the police officers, so they do not have a mandate from the people and the support of the officers necessary to carry out their responsibility effectively. Not being able to appease the public and earn the respect of their officers, supervisors turn to the only thing they can do—inspecting uniforms and checking equipment.

Media Supervision

Post reform, the media have increasingly served as a bridge between the Party and the people. The media play a supervisory role over government officials and are a communication tool between the government and public. Beginning in 1998, the media took on the important function of airing public opinion regarding the government and its actions. In doing so, they are able to provide something of a check on government functions and abuses.[161] The National Committee of the Chinese People's Political Consultative Conference (CPPCC) strongly supports media supervision as a means to promote democracy and guarantee the rule of law.[162] The CPPCC has asked for laws and regulations to protect journalists. Many journalists have been met with a lack of cooperation and a good deal of obstruction. A few of them have been attacked and arrested for doing their job.[163] An exception is Dalian, in northeastern Liaoning Province, which embraces the idea of media supervision. Dalian has encouraged and supported local news media to report on activities of government departments, enterprises, and non-government groups. The Dalian city publicity department has issued circulars encouraging the media to expose official bureaucracy and dereliction of duty and to report major problems related to people's work and life. More significantly, these circulars prohibit any government officials from refusing to cooperate with reporters or assertively intervening with media work.

Media Supervision Mandate

When Premier Zhu Rongji visited China Central Television (CCTV) in 1998,[164] he said that the PRC government and the CPC considered media supervision to be very important in building a democratic and legal system in China. Zhu implored all levels of government to accept media supervision and to cooperate with journalists nationwide in their investigations of government waste, corruption, and abuse. To emphasize the point, the Premier described the role of CCTV as: "media supervision, voice of the people, reference for the government, and vanguards in the reform." Premier Zhu's view was echoed a short time later by National People's Congress Chairman Li Peng. When a German correspondent asked Li about democratic conditions in China, Li declared that the media (e.g., CCTV) had a very important role to play in uncovering social problems, government corruption, and political abuses.[165]

In 2000, members of the National Committee of the CPPCC urged the media to play a bigger supervisory role and asked that relevant laws and regulations be formulated to protect the legal rights and interests of journalists. The Committee also validated the importance of media supervision in a socialist democracy and as an instrument to help enforce the rule of law. That same year, Luo Ming, then vice president of CCTV, confirmed and reiterated at the Asia News Forum that the Chinese government attaches great importance to the role played by media in supervising government bodies and officials. Media supervision is considered as important as, if not more important than, supervision from the masses and from within the Party. "Focus" is a CCTV program aimed at exposing social problems, including abuses of power, neglect of responsibility, corruption in administrative affairs, and so on committed by government departments or officials.[166]

Implementation of Media Supervision

Increasingly, police accountability has been achieved through media supervision.[167] In 1998, a police chief in Chengdu Municipality, Sichuan Province, related a complaint of the public to the press to heighten awareness and spearhead reform. The Chengdu Evening News began running a permanent feature called "Public Opinion and the Police" ("*Renmin minyi danwei he minjing*") to foster public discussion of police performance. When it reported that certain police posts were infested with crime, the report caught the attention of municipal officials and police leadership, and actions were taken to remedy the problem.

Implementation Benefits

Qi Deyuan, a police officer, related how he came to write newspaper articles promoting the police image. He thought that the newspapers were devoting too much time to negative reporting of the police, and he wanted to change that, so he began writing about police work and police officers to promote a different image of the police. He cited the case of Sun Mengda, a police wife, who drew attention to the working conditions of her husband by writing an open letter to the Guangdong Province political and police leadership: "I am the wife of a police officer. When the phone rings at night, I am afraid. When I read about police officers being killed in the line of duty, my heart breaks." The story attracted nationwide attention and support.[168]

Implementation Difficulties

Sensationalism

One major problem with media supervision is that media accounts of the police, especially police dramas, are not always accurate. To attract a larger audience, more and more television stations are airing police shows, but they are not all that realistic. In a show called "Police Line" ("*Jingjie xian*"), for example, a local public security official (a deputy police department head and section head of the criminal investigation) was able to drive up to a detention center and take a prisoner without following proper procedures. This situation is unrealistic and ignores proper legal and administrative procedures. In such cases, the media have created distorted images of the police.[169]

Rejection by Police

The police accuse the media of not being fair and balanced in their coverage of them. In Ruichang Municipality, Jiangxi Province, police official Zhou Qiyuan questioned why the media paid so much attention to police corruption. After all, police officers make mistakes, just like everyone else. He came to the realization that the police are singled out for a number of reasons: (1) The police are law enforcement officers who have to face the public every day. Most of the time, people call the police or the police have to intervene in various types of conflicts. When stressed, the public is more inclined to direct their frustration and dissatisfaction toward the police, and it is impossible for the police to keep everyone happy all the time. (2) The police deal with newsworthy events every day, and the media tend to report such bad news more often than good news. Zhou illustrated this point with a case concerning the theft of cows. Villagers arrested a person for stealing cows, but the thief refused to talk to the police. Officers had to gather evidence against the thief, but the villagers complained that the officers were deliberately dragging their feet and not wanting to press charges. It turned out that, through the hard work of the officers, they were able to recover the 19 stolen cows.[170]

Controlling Police Use of Firearms

This chapter ends appropriately with an investigation into how police use of firearms is controlled by law. It serves as a summary and conclusion of sorts. The police, or public security (*gongan*), in the People's Republic of China are given extensive power to execute their duties, the most formidable of which is the right to bear arms ("PRC Measures for the Control of Weapons"[171]) and to use deadly force ("Provisions for the Use of Weapons"[172]). To date, other than occasional news reports of egregious cases of the illegal use of firearms by the police, few data and few published research studies on police use of deadly force in China are available. The author has observed that, "Until very recently (1990s), research in China was handicapped by unavailability of sources, inaccessibility to places/people, scarcity of bilingual researchers, and incompatible scholarship style."[173] This section provides an overview of the legal framework regulating the police use of firearms in China, from the Chinese perspective.

Nature of the Problem

In 2001, the MPS held a television/telephone conference (National Police Inspector Conference on Abusive Use of Firearms) to strengthen supervision efforts to stop the use of firearms in violation of the law. The meeting was attended by Minister of Public Security Jia Chunwang; Deputy Minister of Public Security Luo Feng, and Party Disciplinary Committee Secretary and Chief of Inspectors Zhu Chunlin. Jia Chunwang observed that police illegal use of firearms had increased substantially, resulting in injury and deaths to civilians. This affected the police image and public relations. The abusive use of firearms pointed to a rise in bureaucracy (i.e., abuse of power, slack discipline, and lack of supervision). The suggested remedy was more political education and stricter supervision and discipline.[174]

Shooting of Dr. Yin Fangming

On November 13, 2007, at 4.55 a.m., Dr. Yin Fangming was shot dead in his car by a police officer near the hospital where he worked in Guangzhou, after an altercation resulting from a routine traffic inquiry.[175] The shooting quickly gained the attention of the news media, foreign and domestic, and stirred the emotions of the public, both locally and nationally. In this section, we will investigate the facts, circumstances, and laws pertinent to this case to better understand how Chinese police shooting accountability is working in the reform era.

Facts of the Shooting

On November 13, 2007, Dr. Yin Fangming went out on the town with a former classmate, Wang Yanming, who had just returned from Germany. Afterward, the two ended up talking in the doctor's car, which was parked near Zhujiang Hospital, where Dr. Yin worked. At about 4.55 a.m., two patrol officers from the Haizhu District (in Guangzhou, the capital of Guangdong Province) came upon the parked vehicle, which had both of its license plates covered with newspaper. It turned out that the car had expired military plates. Later investigation after the incident uncovered two sets of civilian plates in the trunk, one from Hainan and the other from Guangzhou.

One of the police officers demanded identification. Dr. Yin, the driver refused and asked for the police officer's identification instead. There was an altercation, but the police officer did produce his identification. Dr. Yin grabbed it and started to drive away. In the process, he backed up and hurt the officer in the knee. The officer held onto the car door handle and was dragged a few meters. The other officer pulled out his service revolver and fired two shots at Dr. Yin. One bullet pierced his heart, and another hit him in the head, killing him instantly. Immediately after the incident, the Guangzhou police placed the sole witness, Wang Yanming, under "protective custody" for investigation purposes for days. The Guangzhou police chief promised a speedy investigation and public accounting. A joint investigation team was set up that included the local political and legislative committees, the procuratorate, and the Public Security Bureau. The Propaganda Department of Guangdong Province ordered a news blackout. Within days, the MPS launched an independent investigation.

Other relevant information should be considered here to fully understand the incident. Physician Yin Fangming, 43, was an associate professor, medical expert, and accomplished researcher. He had published more than 40 medical papers and participated in five key medical programs. He had won prizes from Guangdong Province for his achievements. He was also considered to be a good-natured colleague at Zhujiang Hospital. The officer was a rookie who had been on the job for 3 months. He had worked at Zhujiang Hospital and might have known Dr. Yin. At the time of the shooting, Guangzhou was suffering from rising crime rates and violence. Zhang Guifang, deputy Party secretary of Guangzhou, encouraged police officers "not to be afraid of shooting criminals when their lives or the lives of the common people are seriously threatened. Otherwise, it would be deplorable for the Chinese police force." Officers were even paid for shooting fleeing felons. The shooting policy was hugely popular with the public.

Public Reactions

Public reactions to the shooting online were mixed. Some thought that the police had the right and, indeed, the duty to inquire and to shoot when met with resistance. Others thought that the police had been acting too rashly, even when a case could be made for shooting. Some condemned the police for taking liberties with their authority. Others simply did not trust the police. Overall, there was no consensus or even a majority opinion among the online comments:

- Police should do what is necessary to keep the public safe: "Good killing. There are many false military vehicle licenses nowadays. This has created many dangers for the public, many unsafe roads."
- Police should act more prudently with warning shots: "According to what I know, shooting should be aimed at the sky, do not know why this could cause death… there is no explanation for killing someone with a warning shot!"
- Police superiority feelings should be checked: "Need to stop this kind of business. First we need to restrict police powers by law. Then we need to remove the idea that the police are superior and are our rulers."
- The professor was flaunting his status and acted above the law: "Think being a professor is such a hot shot? Snatched police ID, drove car away, hit people.…If I were a police officer I too would have opened fire."
- The police officer had a right to conduct an inquiry at night and shoot if need be: "Police inquiry is normal. Under those circumstances, in the middle of the night, the deceased acted suspiciously. If the police had not opened fire he would not have lived up to the expectations of the people. He is not fit to be a police officer."
- A quick investigation into the incident is needed: "Quickly publish the investigation report."
- The Party can be trusted to do justice: "We believe that our Party and our government will do justice for the police and the professor."
- The professor was not above the law: "Do not think of being a professor as being a big deal. The people's police are sacred and should not be interfered with."
- Police have no right to act on whim: "When the police are unhappy, they can shoot and kill. What is the need for procuratorate, court, and labor reform organs and areas? If the police can kill bad people who do wrong things, our country can save a lot of police, prosecutor, and court resources and people's tax money. However, that life being terminated might be your friend or family."
- Police should not investigate the case due to a conflict of interest: "When the police are suspected of a crime, the local police investigates itself and detains key witnesses who are in the know. Does this mean that China has no rule for

avoidance in such investigations? If not, we strongly request the NPC to make laws to restrict law enforcement's criminal investigation activities, to protect the public's right to know."

- The police are in the wrong: "The police have a problem, intuitively."
- Police should have respect for people's lives: "After reading most of the comments, it makes me scared. The commentaries reflect a low regard and a lack of respect for human life in our contemporary education. The police shot a citizen who should not have paid with his life. This kind of cold attitude toward life not only did not serve people's understanding, but attracted society's condemnation. I do not know where we can find harmony in our society. If the most basic harmony between police and citizens cannot be found, then how can we talk about harmony between man and nature, man and animal, man and environment? There is no mistake-free life with people. Society progresses as a result of people's mistakes. A healthy society is one that tolerates citizens' mistakes and also accepts citizens' errors....If people do not condemn police who act without conscience, it is a hopeless society, and everyone will face the dire prospect of being shot. Those who support police killing today will be exposed to police killings tomorrow. I rather wish the police had a loving, compassionate, and respect for life."
- The police frequently abuse their powers: "Currently, there is a lot of police abuse of power. I have also experienced police abuses."
- The case has many unanswered questions: "Not only does the family have questions about the Guangzhou PSB's announcement, but I do, too. The reason being, the announcement said that the military license plates were covered with newspaper. Does that not attract attention by itself? If it is a fake license, why would people do that? On top of that, whether the license was false or not, it should have been left to the traffic division to deal with."
- Police officers are too young, inexperienced, and trigger happy: "I am of the opinion that the present day police force is too young which has resulted in a drop in quality overall. This is a problem that cannot be ignored. They use arms whenever they want. More to the point, they like this kind of stuff."
- Police should be punished—a life for a life: "A life for a life, serious punishment for the killer."

Social Context

Police use of firearms in China against the masses was unheard of before reform. According to Mao, contradictions among the people are best resolved through education and with reason, not by force and coercion.[176] During Deng's reform, the use of deadly force was sanctioned to effect arrest,[177] to suppress disturbances,[178] for self-defense,[179] and when deemed necessary (i.e., Deng's doctrine of security and stability above all).[180] Since 2000, the right to use deadly force has been a topic of heated debate in China. Issues regarding the use of deadly force were brought to the forefront by high-profile wrongful killings of civilians by police officers, either on or off duty, and by repeated citizen assaults on police officers. In response, the MPS took several actions to deal with the problem, including publishing bright-line rules ("Five Prohibitions"), adopting zero-tolerance policies (strict liability),[181] and mounting national gun control campaigns.[182]

TABLE 6.19   Nationwide Police Injuries and Deaths in the Line of Duty

Year	Injuries	Deaths
2001	3429	68
2002	3663	75
2003	4000	84
2004	3786	48
2005	1932	27
2006 (January–May)	160	11
Total	16,970	313

Police Perspective

Understandably, police officers feel vulnerable, impotent, and frustrated in the face of belligerent challenges and violent attacks in the line of duty. According to MPS data (see Table 6.19), from 2001 to 2006[183] there were at least 313 deaths and 16,970 injuries among police officers while on duty due to obstruction of and resistance to police authority.[184] On February 13, 2006, for example, a Tianjin traffic officer tried to stop a vehicle for making an illegal U-turn. The driver knocked the officer over, but the officer hung onto the hood while the vehicle sped away. The officer was finally thrown off the vehicle and seriously injured.[185]

A field study conducted in 2006 on why police did not defend themselves in the face of attacks found that the officers were afraid of offending the people.[186] Particularly, the police were instructed by their superiors to "be hit without reacting and yelled at without responding" ("*da bu huan shou, ma bu hua kou*"). Police officers are subject to strict and uncompromising rules against the use of force. The potential for administrative discipline, criminal sanctions, and civil lawsuits is in the back of an officer's mind every time he draws a gun.

The police want more liberal and clearly defined deadly force authority to enforce the law and protect personal safety. As noted earlier, Zhang Guifang, deputy Party secretary of Guangzhou, became a folk hero when he advocated the use of force to stop crime on April 4, 2006: "Police officers must not be afraid of shooting criminals when their lives or the lives of common people are seriously threatened. Otherwise, it would be deplorable for the Chinese police force. Police officers often encounter great dangers in face-to-face fighting, and the use of guns is a powerful approach to combating crime."[187] A substantial majority of the public also support giving the police more powers. A self-selected online survey in China in 2006 drew a total of 217,000 votes. Of these, 86.41% supported police shooting offenders to deter crime, but only 9.19% were concerned about police abuse of firearms.[188]

Police Internal Study

In 2008, an internal police study openly admitted to a police gun control problem:

> In the last three years, there were instances of public officials having their guns lost or stolen and violating gun control rules in injuring and killing others. Staff did not relinquish or return their guns after retirement; leaving the post; being transferred or terminated, including staff who were under investigation; being suspended from duties or while in custody; and after receiving Party discipline and administrative sanctions. Officers suffering from family conflicts, economic disputes, or work pressures are emotionally unstable. Other violations of regulations are also deserving of removal of the right to bear arms.[189]

A typical case serves to highlight the nature of the problem. On April 26, 2007, Wang Hongwu, a 32-year-old unlicensed "black taxi" driver was soliciting business at the Xiongyuecheng train station. Wang got into an argument with police officer Su Kai after he stepped into a prohibited zone. Su chased Wang away, but Wang had convulsions and fell 100 yards away. Wang's 29-year-old wife, Wang Jing, and his 62-year-old father, Wang Changyuan, went to see Officer Su over the incident and had an argument. Wang, Sr. fainted and had to receive medical attention. At around 3 p.m., Wang Hongwu, Wang Wang Jing, and Wang Changyuan went to the duty room of the Xiongyuecheng PSB to seek compensation from Officer Su. Su shot all three of them. The crime scene was closed and a complete media blackout was maintained, although the incident was briefly reported by local papers on April 28. National reporting was prohibited. Three days later a deputy director of the Dalian Railroad PSB met with the family of the victims to settle the case.[190] This and other cases call for greater oversight on the use of firearms,[191] as they reflect deep-seated dissatisfaction with police abuse of powers in the reform era.[192]

The Police Right to Bear Arms

In China, there is no constitutional or common law right to bear and use arms. The manu-facturing,[193] distribution,[194] transport,[195] possession, and use[196] of firearms are comprehen-sively regulated[197] and strictly controlled.[198] Nevertheless, the Chinese population remains one of the most heavily armed in the world,[199] despite repeated attempts of the police to purge the private holding of guns. As a practical matter, police in China rarely carry guns on duty for ideological (Mao), moral (Confucianism), legal, bureaucratic, and resource con-siderations. A commenter online observed: "I grew up in a small town and then lived and worked in a mid-size city in China. I've never seen police carry guns and have never seen police patrol the streets except for traffic cops."[200]

In China, the police right to bear arms is specifically provided by Article 5 of the Law of the People's Republic of China on Control of Guns: "People's policemen of the public security organs…when performing their functions pursuant to law and when it is defi-nitely necessary for them to use guns, should be armed with guns for the discharge of official duties."[201] A close examination of Article 5 reveals that the police right to bear and use arms is dependent on the following principles:

1. There is no general right to bear arms, only special empowerment based on func-tion (e.g., security organs) and contingent on needs (e.g., discharge of duties).
2. The right to bear arms does not presuppose the right to *use* arms. Guns should only be used by officers "when performing their functions…and when…definitely necessary."
3. The right to bear arms and use force is subject to strict State Council and MPS administrative rules.

Control of Police Use of Deadly Force

Police use of deadly force is subjected to three kinds of legal control:

- Accessibility control
- Use control
- Administrative sanctions

Accessibility Control

Accessibility control is codified in the "Regulations on Public Security Organs' Use of Guns in the Provision of Civil Service"[202] (referred to as Gun Management Regulations) and includes functional control, capacity control, activities control, disqualification control, prudential control, and custodial control. In terms of *functional control*, only officers who are on active duty and have functional or operational needs are entitled to bear arms. Article 3 of the Gun Management Regulations provides that: "Public security organ service guns are to be assigned based on work necessity principle; if there is no work-related need, guns will not be assigned. People's police who are not on active duty are strictly not allowed to carry and use service guns." Thus, the police are allowed to bear arms when their job requires or during certain operations (e.g., riot control).

In terms of *capacity control*, Article 17 of the Gun Management Regulations state that only qualified officers are entitled to carry arms—those who are politically dependable, professional, responsible, personally law abiding, psychologically sound, and without drinking habits. Beyond that, officers must be properly trained, qualified, and well versed in gun laws and regulations. Officers must have 1 year of service and have no disciplinary problems before they can be certified. Thus, police officers are allowed to carry guns when they can be trusted to do so safely.

In terms of *activities control*, Article 18 of the Gun Management Regulations state that police officers are not allowed to carry and use guns while off duty; while in prohibited areas; while drinking; while in restaurants, plazas, ballrooms, or entertainment areas; or for hunting. Furthermore, police officers are not allowed to rent, loan, exchange, or give away service guns. They are not allowed to place service guns in the possession or custody of civilians. Article 19 further prohibits officers from carrying their service guns into airports, except with permission. Police officers are absolutely forbidden to carry service guns while in Beijing and when on assigned security guard duties. Thus, the police right to bear arms is strictly monitored to make sure weapons are not found in the wrong place (e.g., Beijing), in the wrong hands (e.g., criminals), or at the wrong time (e.g., after work).

In terms of *disqualification control*, Article 20 provides that guns must be returned upon retirement or transfer, after being disqualified from using guns, or having failed in the theory and practice of shooting. Article 21 requires surrendering service guns on the following grounds: when the officer is under criminal investigation or facing disciplinary proceedings, when the officer has violated gun control laws or regulations, when the officer's gun is stolen or lost, or when the officer has been terminated or detained. Thus, the police right to bear arms is subject to continuous monitoring.

In terms of *prudent control*, Article 22 stipulates that police officers are not allowed to use guns under the following conditions: when dealing with routine public order matters, peoples' petitions, and citizens' disputes; in crowed streets, commercial markets, public entertainment centers, or dangerous goods areas; while on patrol and accosting suspects who do not resist or attack; during major gathering and events; while on traffic duty or when issuing tickets; or when arguing with others. Thus, gun use is not allowed when the situation is not volatile, if the place is too dangerous to do so, if the incident is too minor, or if heightened emotions are involved.

In terms of *custodial control*, Article 25 provides for centralized storage and control in county and above organs, except for criminal investigators and patrol officers, who can keep their service guns in police posts. Article 26 requires officers to turn in their guns when they are on vacation, on sick leave, or on personal business; when they are on training duty; or when they are reassigned to other non-gun-using posts or activities (e.g., attending conferences).

Not everyone in public security is entitled to bear arms. In fact, there are not enough guns go around. Ultimately, the right to bear arms depends on police jurisdiction (e.g., urban vs. rural), police functions (e.g., officer staff vs. operational officers), and specialization (e.g., generalist vs. specialist). In terms of who within the public security has the right to bear arms, Article 5 of "Public Security Organ and Guard Department Gun Control Provisions" ("*Gongan jiguan he baohu bumen qiangzhi guanli guiding*") provides that, in small and medium size municipalities and county-level police bureaus, all operational officers (*ganjing*), not including administrative staff, and police post officers are entitled to bear arms. In larger city police departments, only political security officers, economic security officers, public security officers, criminal investigators, guards, and preliminary examiners who are on duty are entitled to bear arms. In railroad, traffic, airline, and forest police stations, only political security officers, public security officers, criminal investigators, security guards, preliminary examiners, and police post officers are entitled to bear arms. Among prefecture public security divisions, provincial public security offices, Ministry of Public Security, Ministry of Transport, Ministry of Aviation, and Ministry of Forest, only those police officers responsible for surveillance and public order and security guards are entitled to bear arms. Under Article 5, every one of these designated officers on duty is entitled to carry one gun.

Article 6 limits the availability of guns for police command; thus, large municipality police bureaus and sub-bureaus might have only one gun for every three officers. Police posts will have one gun for every two officers, and traffic police will have one gun for every three officers. Detention, arrest, and preliminary examination center officers will have one gun for every two officers. Other types of police personnel will have one gun for every three officers, except for police colleges (one for every five) and officers stationed at the MPS and other ministries who do not require guns as part of their work routine. The idea here is to restrict the total availability of guns to a minimum but also to have a sufficient reserve for unexpected contingencies.

Use Control

In China, the police right to use deadly force is based on the legal doctrine of "legitimate self-defense" (*zheng dang fang wei*). According to Article 3(4) of "Provisions regarding People's Police Legitimate Self-Defense Conduct in the Line of Duty," police not only have the right but also the duty to protect the rights of people and property of the state. The basic principles of legitimate self-defense are spelled out in Article 20 of the PRC Criminal Procedure Law: "Criminal responsibility is not to be borne for an act of legitimate defense that is undertaken to stop present unlawful infringement of the state's and public interest or the rights of the person, property or other rights of the actor or of other people and that causes harm to the unlawful infringer."[203] The exercise of legitimate self-defense must be based on these five basic factors:[204]

1. Causality (*qiyin tiaojian*)—There must be an illegal harmful act in actual existence (i.e., no preemptive attacks allowed).
2. Time (*sijian tiaojian*)—The harmful act must be in progress (i.e., no self-defense after the fact).

3. Target (*dui xian tiaojian*)—Legitimate self-defense must be directed toward the dangerous actor (i.e., self-defense must be focused, not random).
4. Purpose (*zhuguan tiaojian*)—Legitimate self-defense must be intended to protect national or public interests or the rights of self or others from harm (i.e., self-defense must avoid causing collateral damages).
5. Limits (*xiandu tiaojian*)—Legitimate self-defense must be proportionate to the potential harm (i.e., no wanton or reckless self-defense).

The self-defense provisions in Article 1 of the "Provisions regarding People's Police Legitimate Self-Defense Conduct in the Line of Duty" set forth the conditions when the use of force for self-defense is allowed: violent attacks on transports; use of transports to harm the public; acts that endanger public safety, such as arson, explosion, murder, or robbery; police protective targets under attack; forceful resisting arrest; escape from lawful custody; attacks on the police; and struggles for arms. Police use of force must stop when an illegal attack has been prevented or stopped or when the attackers have been incapacitated. The "Provisions regarding the Use of Police Implements and Arms by the People's Police" (adopted by the State Council on July 5, 1980) authorize the police to use deadly force to prevent crime and protect life proportionately, as a last resort, and with prior warning (Article 4). More specifically, the police can use deadly force under the following circumstances (Article 3):

1. Resisting arrest
2. Escaping from apprehension
3. Stealing police service weapons
4. Attacking police officers while being arrested or detained
5. Violent crime and dangerous acts in progress
6. Attacking a police-guarded object
7. Group raid of a prison
8. Prisoners escaping, rioting, murdering, or stealing guns from security officers
9. Threatening the life of a police officer

In the reform period, all aspects of police authority are governed by the People's Police Law of the People's Republic of China.[205] Article 10 governs the use of deadly force: "The people's police of public security organs may, in accordance with the relevant regulations of the state, use weapons in case of emergencies such as resisting arrest, rebellion, escaping from prison, grabbing firearms, or other acts of violence."

As a general rule, under Article 4 of "Regulations on Police Use of Weapons and Complements,"[206] police can use arms to stop criminal activities and prevent harm to people and property; as a first principle, the police should seek to avoid harm and damage to people and property as much as possible. Article 9 specifies particular situations when the police can use guns, such as when public safety is threatened (e.g., arson, plane hijacking, theft of guns or explosives) or when crimes are being perpetrated with guns or explosives (e.g., armed robbery). Guns may also be used to prevent the destruction of strategic and infrastructural assets, such as a telecommunications network. Deadly force can be used to protect personal safety and public order from violent attack (e.g., murder), to defend secured sites (e.g., Congress) from attack, to foil gang robbery or armed robbery, or to disperse unruly crowds or uncontrollable riots (but as a last resort). Guns can be used to protect police officers in the line of duty, including attacks on the police. They can also be used to prevent the escape of prisoners, to arrest felons and dangerous criminals, to confront criminals armed with guns or other dangerous weapons, and in any other circumstances allowed by law.

Administrative Regulations

In 2003, the MPS adopted a zero-tolerance policy toward the abuse use of guns on and off duty and issued its "Five Prohibitions":

1. *Strict prohibition against violating gun control regulations* (violators are to be disciplined, and officers should resign or be terminated when their violations result in serious consequences)
2. *Strict prohibition against carrying arms while drinking* (violators should resign, and officers should be terminated when their violations result in serious consequences)
3. *Strict prohibition against driving after drinking*
4. *Strict prohibition against drinking on duty*
5. *Strict prohibition against participating in gambling*

The "Five Prohibitions" provide administrative sanctions, including transfer, resignation, and termination, for the violator, immediate supervisor, and senior leadership. When violations lead to death or gun crimes, the immediate supervisor and other major leaders are to be removed from office. In all cases with serious circumstances and consequences, the immediate supervisor and senior leadership will be asked to resign or will be removed from office. Finally, if cover-ups are found, the supervisors and leaders responsible will be held strictly accountable.

Remedies[207]

Under the PRC Constitution,[208] Chinese citizens harmed by government officials are entitled to restitution or compensation for harm done. Article 37 of the PRC Constitution provides that: "The freedom of person of citizens of the People's Republic of China is inviolable.... Unlawful deprivation or restriction of citizens' freedom of person by detention or other means is prohibited." Article 41(4) further provides that: "Citizens who have suffered losses through infringement of their civil rights by any state organ or functionary have the right to compensation in accordance with the law." Consistent with international norms,[209] victims of police abuse can expect compensation as a matter of right under PRC criminal law and civil law. Article 31 of the PRC Criminal Procedure Law establishes a right for crime victims to secure compensatory damages: "Where the victim has suffered economic loss as a result of a criminal act, the criminal, in addition to receiving criminal sanctions according to law, shall in accordance with the circumstances be sentenced to pay compensation for the economic loss." Article 121 creates a legal liability on the police to address official wrongdoings: "If a state organ or its personnel, while executing its duties, encroaches upon the lawful rights and interests of a citizen or legal person and causes damage, it shall bear civil liability."[210]

Finally, Article 3 of the Law of the People's Republic of China on State Compensation[211] creates a special cause of action against police for harm caused by unlawful use of firearms: "The victim shall have the right to compensation if an administrative organ or its functionaries, in exercising their administrative functions and powers, commit any of the following acts infringing upon the right of the person of a citizen:…(4) Unlawfully using weapons or police restraint implements, thereby causing bodily injury or death to a citizen." To recover damages, victims of police abuse must show the following:

1. The officer must have been acting in an official capacity, under the "color of law" and in the line of duty.
2. The police's exercise of authority was illegal.
3. The police action caused harm.

In cases of injury or death, compensation is provided in accordance with Article 27 of the State Compensation Law:

1. Out-of-pocket medical expenses are to be reimbursed.
2. Loss in income due to missed work will be compensated up to five times the State average yearly pay of staff and workers in the previous year.
3. Loss of working capacity, in whole or in part, will be compensated a maximum of ten times the State average salary; for total loss, the maximum compensation will be twenty times plus living expenses for life.
4. If death results, compensation for death and funeral expenses will be paid; the total amount will be twenty times the State average yearly salary. Living expenses will be paid to dependents with no working capacity.

Conclusion

This chapter was primarily about police laws on the books, not policing on the streets. How the law is applied and to what effect were not the object of this study; nevertheless, this outline of the legal framework governing police use of deadly force should help us to understand what PRC policymakers think about the best way to control the police. The lesson we learned here is that, consistent with Chinese thinking regarding comprehensive crime control, the Ministry of Public Security's control of the use of guns by police officers is conducted in a comprehensive, systematic, and holistic manner. The MPS spends as much time regulating gun availability (how many guns are made available) and entitlement (who can bear arms) as it does regulating how guns are used and how offenders should be sanctioned. It is important to note that internal administrative control is given more weight than external legal control. Finally, it is clear that Chinese administrators consider prevention to be better than a cure.

The regulatory framework requires modification in at least two ways. First, legal ambiguities must be removed. This can be achieved by refining the law to make room for more structured and guided police discretion in the use of arms, such as detailing the critical risk factors contributing to the decision to shoot, or specifying what warning steps should be taken before the use of force is allowed. Second, greater legal protection is necessary for street officers encountering belligerent citizens and violent attacks. This could be accomplished by introducing a citizen's accountability doctrine that takes into account contributory negligence when determining compensatory damages in wrongful shooting cases.

It is clear that the overwhelming evidence compiled in this book shows that the Chinese political and police leadership cares deeply about the integrity and performance of the police in meeting the expectations of the public, the nation, and (of late) the world. This does not mean that the leadership is always successful in reforming the police in the image of the Party, much less in meeting the needs of the people. In fact, evidence suggests that, in spite of their efforts, the leaders are struggling to reform the police in a way that keeps pace with the radical economic, social, and cultural changes occurring today. Despite this, three things are readily apparent: (1) Chinese leadership is comprised of dedicated and competent police reformers, (2) Chinese policing has changed for the better, and (3) much remains to be done to transform the Chinese police from a revolutionary force to an order maintenance and public service institution. I hope this book has been as effective in debunking myths and revealing prejudices about China as it has been in opening up minds ("seeking truth from facts"), liberating spirits ("crossing the river by feeling the stones"), and touching on feelings ("harmonious society") as ways of discovering and in time embracing what policing with Chinese characteristics is all about.

Notes

1. "China's Political Life Featuring Openness, Supervision," *People's Daily Online*, March 15, 2000 (http://english.peopledaily.com.cn/english/200003/15/eng20000315N103.html).
2. Jiang Xueqin, "China's Powerful Police," *Wall Street Journal*, July 9, 2002
3. Laws and regulations are cited on the origination and to demonstrate the scope of police powers, not current legal regime and application.
4. *How People Deal with the Public Security* [*Renmin ruhe yu gongan da jiaodao*], Falu Chubanshe, Beijing, 1990, pp. 4–6.
5. "Regulations of the People's Republic of China on Administration of Traffic Safety in Inland Waters," adopted at the 60th Executive Meeting of the State Council on June 19, 2002; promulgated by Decree No. 355 of the State Council of the People's Republic of China on June 28, 2002; and effective as of August 1, 2002.
6. "Regulations on Civil Aviation Security of the People's Republic of China," promulgated by Decree No. 201 of the State Council of the People's Republic of China on July 6, 1996, and effective immediately.
7. "Regulations of the People's Republic of China on Implementing Customs Administrative Penalties," adopted at the 62nd Executive Meeting of the State Council on September 1, 2004; promulgated by Decree No. 420 of the State Council of the People's Republic of China on September 19, 2004; and effective as of November 1, 2004.
8. "The Procedures of Birth and Death Registration for Aliens in China," Article 26 of the "Rules Governing the Implementation of the Law of the People's Republic of China on the Entry and Exit of Aliens," which stipulates that the parents of an alien infant born in China or their agent shall, within one month after the child's birth, report to the local Public Security Bureau (PSB) with the birth certificate and complete registration procedures.
9. (a) "PRC Household Registration Regulations," adopted at the 91st Meeting of the Standing Committee of the First National People's Congress on January 9, 1958, and promulgated by the President of the People's Republic of China on January 9, 1958. These regulations require citizens to register with public security upon birth (Article 7), death (Article 8), moving in (Article 13), and moving out (Article 10). Public security is put in charge of maintaining local *hukou* systems (Article 3). (b) Michael R. Dutton, *Policing and Punishment in China*, Cambridge University Press, Cambridge, UK, 1992, p. 221. (c) Xiaogang Wu and Donald J. Treiman, "The

Household Registration System and Social Stratification in China: 1955–1996," *Demography*, 41(2), 363–384, 2004. Registration is a prerequisite to receiving social welfare. Without registration, it is not possible to enter school, gain employment, participate in elections, serve in the armed forces, or marry. Without registration, citizens are not able to arrange housing, take up an allotted grain ration, or obtain a supply of cotton.

10. (a) "Interim Procedures for the Control of Chinese Citizens Who Travel to and from Hong Kong and Macao on Private Errands" ("*Zhongguo gongmin yin sishi wanglai Xianggang dequ huozhe Aomen dequ de zhanxing guanli banfa*"), approved by the State Council of the People's Republic of China on December 3, 1986, and promulgated by the Minister of Public Security on December 25, 1986. Article 11 vested public security with the authority to process applications to emigrate to Hong Kong and Macao (Article 7, 10). (b) Kam C. Wong, "Testing the Limits of 'One Country, Two Systems': An Overview of the 'Right of Abode' Case," *Australian Journal of Law and Society*, 15, 164, 2001.

11. (a) "Regulations for People's Republic of China Assemblies, Parades, and Demonstrations," approved by the State Council of the People's Republic of China on May 12, 1982, and promulgated by the Minister of Public Security on June 16, 1992. (b) Kam C. Wong, "Law of Assembly in the People's Republic of China," *Journal of Civil Rights and Social Justice*, 12(2), 151–181, 2006.

12. Certain businesses are heavily regulated by public security. Shooting ranges are regulated by "Rules for the Control of the Shooting Sites Installations" ("*Shejichang sheji guanli guicheng*"), approved by the State Council of the People's Republic of China on February 24, 1958, and promulgated by the Minister of Public Security on March 29, 1958. The hotel industry is regulated by "Procedures for the Maintenance of Public Order at Hotels" ("*Luguanye zhian guanli banfa*"), approved by the State Council of the People's Republic of China on September 23, 1987, and promulgated by the Minister of Public Security on November 10, 1987. The printing industry is regulated by "Interim Provisions for the Administration of Printing, Molding, and Carving Industries" ("*Yin, zhu, kezi ye zhanxing guanli*"), approved by the Political-Legal Committee of the Government Administration Council and promulgated by the Minister of Public Security on August 15, 1951. Dangerous chemical goods manufacturing, storage, and transportation are addressed in "Regulations for the Management and Safety of Dangerous Chemical Goods" ("*Huaxue weixian wupin anquan guanli tioali*"), promulgated by the State Council of the People's Republic of China on February 17, 1987. Firearms sales are regulated by "Regulations of the People's Republic of China for the Control of Weapons" ("*Zhonghua renmin gongheguo qiangzhi guanli banfa*"), approved by the State Council of the People's Republic of China on January 5, 1981, and promulgated by the Minister of Public Security on April 25, 1981. All businesses are subject to fire inspections; see generally "Fire Protection Regulations of the People's Republic of China" ("*Zhonghua renmin gongheguo xiaofang tioali*"), adopted at the Fifth Meeting of the Standing Committee of the Sixth National People's Congress on May 11, 1984, and promulgated by the State Council on May 13, 1984. These regulations established public security as fire supervision bodies that supervise and inspect fire protection activity in accordance with the regulations. These regulations can be found in *The Laws of the PRC (1983–1986)*, Foreign Languages Press, Beijing, 1987, pp. 139–145.

13. "Regulations of the People's Republic of China Governing Road and Traffic Control" ("*Zhonghua renmin gongheguo daolu jiaotong guanli tioali*"), promulgated by the State Council on March 9, 1988.

14. Laws of the PRC on the Control of the Exit and Entry of Citizens (*Zhonghua renmin gongheguo gongmin chujing rujing guanli tioali*), adopted at the 13th Meeting of the Standing Committee of the Sixth National People's Congress; promulgated by Order No. 32 of the President of the People's Republic of China on November 22, 1985; and effective as of February 1, 1986. Article 5 provides that, "Chinese citizens who desire to leave the country for private purposes shall apply to the public security organs of the city or country in which their residence is registered. Approval shall be granted except in cases prescribed in Article 8 of this law." These regulations can be found in *The Laws of the PRC (1983–1986)*, Foreign Languages Press, Beijing, 1987, pp. 197–201.

15. (a) "Resident Identity Card Regulations" ("*Zhonghua renmin gongheguo jumin shenfenzheng tiaoli*"), adopted at the 12th Meeting of the Standing Committee of the Sixth National People's Congress; promulgated by Order No. 29 of the President of the People's Republic of China on September 6, 1985; and effective immediately. Article 13 provides that, "When performing its duties, the public security organ shall have the power to examine a citizen's resident identity card, and the citizen shall not refuse to be examined." These regulations can be found in *The Laws of the PRC (1983–1986)*, Foreign Languages Press, Beijing, 1987, pp. 188–196. (b) As to what constitutes performance of duties, later regulations ("*Zhonghua renmin gongheguo jumin shenfenzheng tiaoli shuixi xiji*") approved by the State Council on November 3, 1986, and promulgated by the Ministry of Public Security on November 28, 1986, provide that public security can inspect a resident's identity card while: (1) fighting crime (e.g., investigation of a crime, pursuing a prisoner, confronting a suspect); (2) maintaining order (e.g., keeping order on public transport, in public places, and when dealing with public order violators); (3) handling major catastrophes and at the site of emergencies; and (4) conducting and auditing household registrations (Article 41(c)). (c) See also *How People Deal with the Public Security* [*Renmin ruhe yu gongan da jiaodao*], Falu Chubanshe, Beijing, 1990, p. 73.

16. "Provisions for the Use of Weapons and Police Instruments by the People's Police" ("*Renmin jingcha shiyong wuqi he jingxie de guiding*"), approved by the State Council of the People's Republic of China on July 5, 1980, and promulgated by the Ministry of Public Security on July 15, 1980. These regulations allow the police to use lethal weapons and, if necessary, to maim and kill, under a limited set of "self-defense" situations (Article 3).

17. "Regulations of the People's Republis of China for the Control of Weapons" ("*Zhonghua renmin gongheguo qiangzhi guanli banfa*") (see Note 12). Firearms are only available for limited categories of government workers, including public security, on an as-needed basis. Examples include court, procuratorate, border, and remote coastal government officials; provincial party transportation officers; border county and city communication officers; custom officers; and military factory guards.

18. Sarah Biddulph, *Legal Reform and Administrative Detention Powers in China*, Cambridge University Press, Cambridge, UK, 2007.

19. Sarah Biddulph, "The Production of Legal Norms: A Case Study of Administrative Detention in China," *UCLA Pacific Basin Law Journal*, 20(2), 217–277, 2004.

20. "Regulations of the People's Republic of China on Administrative Penalties for Public Security" ("*Zhonghua renmin gongheguo zhian guanli chufa tiaoli*"), adopted at the Fourth Session of the 17th Meeting of the Standing Committee of the Sixth National People's Congress on September 5, 1986, and revised in accordance with the "Decision on Revising the Regulations of the People's Republic of China on Administrative Penalties for Public Security," adopted at the Seventh Meeting of the Standing Committee of the Eighth National People's Congress on May 12, 1994; promulgated by Order No. 24 of the President of the People's Republic of China.

21. People's Republic of China Administrative Punishment Law (*Zhonghua renmin gongheguo xingzheng chufa fa*), adopted at the Fourth Session of the Eighth National People's Congress on March 17, 1996; promulgated by Order No. 63 of the President of the People's Republic of China and effective October 1, 1996.

22. Mineral Resources Law of the People's Republic of China, adopted at the 15th Meeting of the Standing Committee of the Sixth National People's Congress on March 19, 1986; revised in accordance with the "Decision of the Standing Committee of the National People's Congress on Revising the Mineral Resources Law of the People's Republic of China" and adopted at the 21st Meeting of the Standing Committee of the Eighth National People's Congress on August 29, 1996.

23. Water Law of the People's Republic of China, adopted at the 24th Meeting of the Standing Committee of the Six National People's Congress on January 21, 1988; promulgated by Order No. 74 of the President of the People's Republic of China on August 29, 2002; revised at the 29th Meeting of the Standing Committee of the Ninth National People's Congress on August 29, 2002.

24. Law of the People's Republic of China on the National Flag, adopted at the 4th Meeting of the Standing Committee of the Seventh National People's Congress on June 28, 1990; promulgated by Order No. 28 of the President of the People's Republic of China on June 28, 1990; and effective October 1, 1990.

25. Kam C. Wong, "Chinese Jurisprudence and Hong Kong Law," *China Report*, 45(3), 213–239, 2010. The indeterminacy of the law, with it the discretionary application of rules, advances more than subverts justice in China. Chinese jurisprudential thinking finds rule-bound justice to be sterile, as it does not take into consideration the multitude of potential considerations, chief of which are natural (law), moral (imperative), personal (status), social (relations), and situational (dynamics). Chinese jurisprudence considers circumstances, reason, and law (*qing, li, fa*) before coming to judgment on a case. The vagaries of the law are also strategically deployed to accommodate differences in local conditions and developmental needs.

26. See the People's Republic of China Administrative Punishment Law (*Zhonghua renmin gongheguo xingzheng chufa fa*), Chapter III, "Acts Violating the Administration of Public Security and Penalties," for details of administrative penalty offenses.

27. Internal public security guidelines and policies restrict unfettered imposition of fines.

28. Online conversations at police websites, such as *Tianya*, suggest that tariffs differ for various crimes; for example, out-of-town drivers are often treated differently than local drivers.

29. Sarah Biddulph, "The Production of Legal Norms: A Case Study of Administrative Detention in China," *UCLA Pacific Basin Law Journal*, 20(2), 217–277, 2004; especially see Note 82.

30. Michael R. Dutton and Tianfu Lee, "Missing the Target? Policing Strategies in the Period of Economic Reform," *Crime and Delinquency*, 39, 316–333, 1993.

31. For a discussion of how to apply such open-ended criteria, see Chapter 4, "The Appropriate Application of Public Security Administrative Penalty" ["*Zhian xingzheng chufa de shiyong*"], in Shi Zhongzheng, *General Treatise on Public Security Administrative Punishment* [*Zhian xingzheng chufa tonglun*], Zhongguo renmin gongan daxue chubanshe, Beijing, 2002, pp. 60–70.

32. See the People's Republic of China Administrative Punishment Law (*Zhonghua renmin gongheguo xingzheng chufa fa*) for other process arrangements: Article 34, "Summons, Interrogations, Obtaining Evidence, Rulings"; Article 36, "Payment of Fines"; Article 37, "Receipt and Disposition of Confiscated Property"; Article 38, "Discharge of Reparation"; Article 39, "Protest and Appeal"; Article 40, "Ruling Effective on Appeal"; Article 41, "Impartiality and Recourse"; and Article 42, "Public Security Bureau Mistakes."

33. *Compendium of People's Republic of China Public Security Law* [*Zhonghua renmin gongheguo gongan falu quanshu*], Jilin Chubanshe, Jinlin, 1995, pp. 382–384.

34. In contrast to, for example, the *Federal Sentencing Guidelines Manual and Appendices*, U.S. Sentencing Commission, Washington, DC, 2010.

35. Hu Yanfei, "A Discussion on Public Administrative Discretion" ("*Lun gongan xingzheng zhiyou cailiang quan*"), *Public Security Studies*, 59, 49–51, 1998. Police exercise wide and boundless discretion with little recourse in their administration.

36. Jing Changling, "Current Status and Legislative Proposal for Public Security Administrative Punishment ["*Gongan xingzheng chufa chengxu guifan de xianzhuan yu lifa jianyi*"], *Public Security Studies*, 59, 52–53, 1998. There is a need to standardize PSB administrative procedures and the various branches of police (custom, border, and regular police).

37. Ibid.

38. Laws are deliberately drafted vaguely to afford flexibility of application. It serves the purpose of accommodating changes in circumstances over time.

39. Deng admonished that having a bad law is better than having no law.

40. Zhang Guang and Li Mingqi, "Police Discretion: How to Control Effectively? An Analysis of Police Administration" ["*Jingcha ziyou cailiang quan: ruhe youxiao de guanli cong jingcha xingzheng guanli de jiaodu fensxi*"], *Journal of Chinese People's Public University* (*PSU Journal*), 95, 48–50, 2002.

41. "Regulations of the People's Republic of China on Settlement of Labor Disputes in Enterprises," adopted by the State Council of the People's Republic of China at the Fifth Executive Meeting on June 11, 1993; promulgated by Decree No. 117 of the State Council of the People's Republic of China on July 6, 1993; and effective August 1, 1993.

42. Zhang Guang and Li Mingqi, "Police Discretion: How to Control Effectively? An Analysis of Police Administration" ["*Jingcha ziyou cailiang quan: ruhe youxiao de guanli cong jingcha xingzheng guanli de jiaodu fensxi*"], *Journal of Chinese People's Public University* (*PSU Journal*), 95, 48–50, 2002.

43. See also Xie Xiao-jian and Pi Te-yan, "Criminal Detention Operation: Theory and Practice" ["*Xingshi juliu yunzuo: lilu yu shijian de bofan*"], *Journal of Chinese People's Public University* (*PSU Journal*), 128, 85–100, 2007. Pi Te-yan was the Deputy Procurator of the Yi Chun Municipal People's Procuratorate and later the Mayor of the Gao An Municipality, Jiangsu Province.

44. Zhang Chao, "Investigation Report on Criminal Detention Terms Enforced by the Police" ["*Gongan jiguan shisi xingshi juliu qixian zhuang kuuang tiaocha baogao*"], *Journal of China Lawyer and Jurist*, 25, 1–12, 2007. Wuhan Law School is known for their pioneer work on social justice and, more famously, for providing legal services to the poor. The project was assisted by Professor Lin Lihung, Director of the Center for Protection for the Rights of Disadvantaged Citizens of Wuhan University, and by professors from Hubei Police Officers College and Heinan Public Security College.

45. Ibid., p. 2.

46. Olivia Yu and Lening Zhang, "Under-Recording of Crime by Police in China: A Case Study," *Policing: An International Journal of Police Strategies & Management*, 22(3), 252–263, 1999.

47. Actually, as noted elsewhere, Chinese policymakers, especially with regard to the police, have routinely gathered substantial data about crime and policing and conducted special investigations, but such data and analyses are not readily available to outsiders. Occasionally, they are mentioned in passing in newspapers, journal articles, or policy pronouncements, but more often than not they are deliberately obscured such that they are of little use to researchers. Of late and under the Hu–Wen administration, we have experienced a new round of openness. The latest sign of this trend is a series of before and after studies in the Renmin Gongan Bao regarding "Three Represents" initiatives between 2004 and 2007. Another is a series of national surveys carried out from 2008 to 2009 by local Communist Party of China (CPC) branches to study the attitudes and work styles of young police officers. Finally, several surveys have been conducted by the *PSU Journal* in association with *Police Post Magazine* on various aspects of police post work and leisure.

48. Zhang Chao, "Investigation Report on Criminal Detention Terms Enforced by the Police" ["*Gongan jiguan shisi xingshi juliu qixian zhuang kuuang tiaocha baogao*"], *Journal of China Lawyer and Jurist*, 25, 1–12, 2007. See Tables 10 and 11.

49. (a) Kam C. Wong, "Studying Policing in China: Some Personal Reflections," *International Journal of the Sociology of Law*, 35(3), 111–126, 2007. (b) Kam C. Wong, *Chinese Policing: History and Reform*, Peter Lang Publishing, Bern, Switzerland, 2009, Chapter 1.

50. (a) For a comparable study, see Zhang Chao, "Investigation Report on Criminal Detention Terms Enforced by the Police" ["*Gongan jiguan shisi xingshi juliu qixian zhuang kuuang tiaocha baogao*"], *Journal of China Lawyer and Jurist*, 25, 1–12, 2007. (b) An e-search of a Chinese academic journal database uncovered 150 articles on criminal detention, 30 of which are on police detention. All of them deal with philosophy, law, and practice issues. An Internet search using the key term *chao qi juliu* ("extended detention") uncovered 20,000 items, none of which provided empirical data on extended detention by police. Of note, though, is a master's thesis by Yu Aomen, "Empirical Research into Current Conditions of Our Nation's Criminal Detention Operations and Process" ["*Guanyu woguo xingshi juliu yunxing xiangzhuang de shizheng yanjiu*"], School of Law, Sichuan University, 2005.

51. Zhang Chao, "Investigation Report on Criminal Detention Terms Enforced by the Police" ["*Gongan jiguan shisi xingshi juliu qixian zhuang kuuang tiaocha baogao*"], *Journal of China Lawyer and Jurist*, 25, 1–12, 2007. See Table 1.

52. Ibid., Table 2.

53. Ibid., Table 3.

54. Ibid., Table 4.

55. Ibid., Table 5.

56. Ibid., Table 6.

57. Ibid., Table 7

58. Ibid., Table 8.

59. Ibid., Table 9.

60. Ibid., Table 10.

61. The selection criteria are neither disclosed nor mandated.

62. Zhang Chao, "Investigation Report on Criminal Detention Terms Enforced by the Police" ["*Gongan jiguan shisi xingshi juliu qixian zhuang kuuang tiaocha baogao*"], *Journal of China Lawyer and Jurist*, 25, 1–12, 2007.

63. Ibid.

64. Ibid.

65. (a) The Criminal Procedure Law of the People's Republic of China was adopted by the Second Session of the Fifth National People's Congress on July 1, 1979, and amended pursuant to "Decision on Amending the Criminal Procedure Law of the People's Republic of China," adopted by the Fourth Session of the Eighth National People's Congress on March 17, 1996. (b) Criminal investigative detention is also regulated by the Supreme People's Court, Supreme People's Procuracy, Ministry of Public Security, Ministry of National Security, NPC–Legal System Work Committee's "Regulations regarding Certain Questions in the Implementation of Criminal Procedure Law" ("*Guan yu xingshi susong fa shishi zhong rugan wenti de guiding*"); "Supreme People's Court, Supreme People's Procuracy, Ministry of Public Security; by the "Notice regarding Stern Execution of Criminal Procedure Law in Resolute Ratification of Overextended Cases Concerning Criminal Suspects and Accused" ("*Guangyu yange zhixing xingshi susong fa guanyu dui xianyi fan bigo ren jiya qixian de guiding jiandu zhixing chaoqi jiya wenti tongzhi*"); by the Ministry of Public Security's "Regulations regarding Processing Criminal Case Procedures" ("*Guanyu banli xingshi anjian chengsu guiding*"); and by a clarification of the Ministry of Public Security's "Regulations regarding Processing Criminal Case Procedures" ("*Guanyu 'Gongan bu guanyu banli xingshi anjian chengsu guiding' de suoming*").

66. Liu Jihua, "Detention and Arrest System Reform and Improvement Proposal," *People's Prosecutorial Semimonthly*, 14, 12–18, 2007.

67. It would be of interest to compare samples of detention cases with nondetention cases.

68. In 2006, the author was consulted by Mr. So, an executive manager of a German electronics company, who was detained by public security for over 2 years to obtain a financial settlement over a contract dispute.

69. This is the same situation with setting speed limits at 55 and expecting people to do no more than 65.

70. Zhang Chao, "Investigation Report on Criminal Detention Terms Enforced by the Police" ["*Gongan jiguan shisi xingshi juliu qixian zhuang kuuang tiaocha baogao*"], *Journal of China Lawyer and Jurist*, 25, 1–12, 2007.

71. Effective application for approval refers to one that follows laws and regulations.

72. Zhang Chao, "Investigation Report on Criminal Detention Terms Enforced by the Police" ["*Gongan jiguan shisi xingshi juliu qixian zhuang kuuang tiaocha baogao*"], *Journal of China Lawyer and Jurist*, 25, 1–12, 2007.

73. Ibid., Note 11.

74. One way to evaluate police performance is through their peers. In the Chinese criminal justice system, the procuratorate supervises the police (e.g., approves arrests and conducts prosecution). The procuracy should have a very good grasp of the nature of police work. On May 5, 2007, a procuratorate posted a blog entry offering his observations and advice to police officers (http://www.tianya.cn/techforum/content/158/543695.shtml). The procuratorate said that he had worked with the police for a long time. He found that most of the police officers were good. They do not earn a high income but they have to work under high pressure. He was quick to point out, though, that police officers suffered from low professional standards at work and high opinions of themselves when working with others (e.g., prosecuratorate's office): "1. Please work hard to enhance your professional competency by ensuring case processing quality. In dispatch cases for arrest supervision and prosecution, many public security personnel are content with arresting suspects. The evidence accompanying these cases is seriously lacking. Take testimonial evidence, for example; questions that should be asked are not asked. Some of the questions that need not be asked were asked in abundance. My own opinion is that many police officers do not have a basic understanding of what constitutes a crime. They often compile a case based on common sense. They only have a very vague idea that certain conduct could be criminal and proceed to make an arrest. As a result, arrests cannot be prosecuted due to lack of basic requirements, causing a waste of valuable judicial resources. 2. Police comrades, please be a bit more humble. As a matter of fact, the procurators' legal knowledge and understanding are actually greater than police officers' due to the special nature of our work. Regrettably, many public security officers do not understand this. Many dispatched cases are full of mistakes. When asked to reinvestigate and refile these cases, they are most unhappy. When they are told what kind of supplementary investigation is required, they do not listen. As a result, the supplementary materials are of little use, and this is the more responsible ones. Many of them just throw the file aside, and when the time comes to submit their reinvestigation, the original file is resubmitted without changes and with the comment 'cannot be supplemented.'" We do not know how valid these observations of police incompetency are, but they certainly ring true, notwithstanding the obvious inter-agency antagonism. The complaints here pointed out that bureaucratic infighting is fierce in China, to the point of obstructing normal functioning of the judicial process. Procuratorate legal supervision over the police is real, and procurators do reject cases for a lack of compliance with the law; however, formal prosecuratorate supervision over the police is not working, due to a lack of enforcement powers. In many cases, police make arrests not based strictly on legal criteria but on other considerations, political or moral.

75. For another study, see Xie Xiao-jian and Pi Te-yan, "Criminal Detention Operation: Theory and Practice" ["*Xingshi juliu yunzuo: lilun yu xijian de bofan*"], *Journal of Chinese People's Public University* (*PSU Journal*), 128, 85–100, 2007.

76. Ibid., p. 98.

77. *Cheung Tse-keung* can be translated into *Cheung Chi-keung* in Cantonese or *Zhang Zi-qiang* in Mandarin (Pinyin). I have used Cheung Tse-keung throughout this article because this is the version most often used in the media and among the public. Here, "Big Spender" refers to the case, and Cheung Tse-keung (or sometimes Cheung) refers to the person. "Big Spender" is an alias of Cheung Tse-keung; it is a translation of *da fu hao*. For an account of the lifetime exploits of the legendary Cheung Tse-keung ("king of thieves"), see *Next Magazine*, November 6, 1998, pp. 38–58. A highly acclaimed television documentary on the life and criminal career of Cheung Tse-keung aired on November 19, 1998, on the Asian Television (ATV) investigative show, "Looking Closer Today." Another documentary, "King of Thieves of the Century: The Final Chapter," was produced by the PRC Phoenix Station, and "King of Thieves of the Century: Cheung Tse-keung" was produced by the People's Liberation Army Television Broadcast Centre.

78. (a) Tommy Lewis, "Trial of Big Spender to Start Next Week," *South China Morning Post*, October 17, 1998. (b) Ng Kang-chung, "Troops on Alert for Start of 'Big Spender' Trial," *South China Morning Post*, October 20, 1998. (c) "The Prosecutor's Case," *South China Morning Post*, November 6, 1998.

79. For the purposes of this chapter and ease of reference, I have used PRC or China to refer to the PRC government as a distinct legal and political entity, excluding Hong Kong. I have used Hong Kong Special Administrative Region (hereinafter HKSAR or SAR) to refer to Hong Kong as a distinct legal and political entity. I have used Mainland to refer to the territorial limits of the PRC, excluding Hong Kong. I have used Hong Kong to refer to the territorial limits of HKSAR. For a superlative discussion on the geopolitical boundary of the PRC vs. HKSAR see Roda Mushkat, *One Country, Two International Legal Personalities*, Hong Kong University Press, Hong Kong, 1997, especially Chapter 2, pp. 44–84.

80. For a summary of charges, see *Ta Kung Po*, November 13, 1998, p. A9. See also "Big Spender Case: The Rest of the Gang," *South China Morning Post*, November 13, 1998.

81. The formal arrest of Cheung signified the end of the police investigative phase and the beginning of the prosecution stage. On July 21, 1998, the official PRC news agency, *Xinhua*, broke the news that the "Big Spender" gang has been arrested and Cheung had confessed.

82. Cheung was arrested on January 25, 1998, and interrogated on January 26, 1998. He did not disclose his true name or address until the middle of June 1998. For an account of the police interrogation of Cheung, see *Tian Di*, 48, 85–90, 1999.

83. Article 126 specifies that, if an investigation cannot be concluded within the time limit specified in Article 124 of the law, then an extension of 2 months may be allowed upon approval or decision by the People's Procuratorate of a province, autonomous region, or municipality directly under the Central Government. Article 126 refers to (1) serious and complex cases in outlying areas for which transportation is most inconvenient; (2) serious cases that involve criminal gangs; (3) serious and complex cases that involve people who commit crimes in more than one place; and (4) serious and complex cases that involve various locations and for which it is difficult to obtain evidence.

84. For a discussion of PRC investigative detention powers, see Kam C. Wong, *Sheltering for Examination (Shoushen) in the People's Republic of China: Law, Policy, and Practices*, Occasional Papers/Reprints Series in Contemporary Asian Studies, School of Law, University of Maryland, Baltimore, 1997, pp. 26–30.

85. Cheung was not a common criminal. He was the target of an investigation coordinated by the MPS in Beijing. Cheung's identity and characteristics were known in advance to the interagency work group consisting of the Ministry of Public Security, the Ministry of State Security, and the Guangdong Province Public Security Bureau. More significantly, it was clear that the PRC interrogators were certain of Cheung's identity, notwithstanding his less than effective denial, as early as January 26, 1998.

86. At the time of the arrest, the PRC police had accumulated a substantial amount of information about the personal background and criminal activities of Cheung and his gang. The office space dedicated to the "Big Spender" case investigation contained 80 volumes of files, 2 meters high.

87. On April 10, 1998, one of the gang members, Cheung Chi-fung, started to talk and identified Cheung as the leader of the criminal gang.

88. Kam C. Wong, "Police Powers and Control in the PRC: A Reflection on the Lok Yuk Sing Case," unpublished paper on file with the Chinese Law Program, Chinese University of Hong Kong, November 1999.

89. The new Criminal Procedure Law, adopted by National People's Congress in March 1996 and effective October 1997, introduced the principles of *presumption of innocence* and the *right to have a lawyer*.

90. "Extended Detention, Forced Confession Still Salient in Chinese Judiciary: Report," *People's Daily Online*, December 28, 2000 (http://english.peopledaily.com.cn/200012/28/eng20001228_59073.html).

91. "Clearing of Extended Detention, Remove the Obstacle to Judicial Justice," *Legal Daily*, October 30, 2003. In May 2003, a detective team leader, Ye Junting, was charged with illegal detention of a criminal suspect for over 6 days. Ye was convicted and sentenced to 6 months of supervision. On March 12, 2003, a case of explosives and detonators was reported stolen in Henan Province. Ye Junting was arrested for detaining a farmer, Mr. Zhao, for investigation and interrogation on the night of March 12, 2003. The suspect was not released until March 21, 2003, long after the 48 hours he could be legally detained. There was a great debate as to the legality and appropriateness of the conviction of Ye Junting. One school of thought was that the overly extended detention was administratively inappropriate but not illegal, as the person had been arrested legally. This extended detention was simply an administrative problem. Others believed that such extended detentions are as much a criminal act as any other illegal detention.

92. "Clearing of Extended Detention, Remove the Obstacle to Judicial Justice," *Legal Daily*, October 30, 2003. The longest detention case cleared was that of Xie Hungwu, a farmer. He was arrested by the police on June 24, 1974, and declared innocent on December 23, 2003. He spent over 28 years in jail for an unsubstantiated charge.

93. "China Clears Up Detention Cases," *YuanDaily.com*, November 19, 2004.

94. "Clean-Up of Extended Detention: Procuratorate Issued New Extended Detention to 85 People in 2007," *ChinaCourt.com*, March 10, 2008 (http://www.chinacourt.org/html/article/200803/10/290917.shtml).

95. Liaowang Zhoukan, "An Yuan Ding: Beijing Interdiction of Visits, 'Black Prison' Survey," *Southern Metropolitan Daily*, September 24, 2010. "Black prisons" (*he jianyu*) run by private security firms are springing up in Beijing to house "letter and visit" (*xinfang*) petitioners arriving at the Capitol. According to internal reports, provinces and cities have established 73 "black prisons" to interdict and return petitioners to their homes. Such interdiction centers can be found at, for example, hotels.

96. Constitution of the People's Republic of China, adopted at the Fifth Session of the Fifth National People's Congress and promulgated for implementation by Proclamation of the National People's Congress on December 4, 1982 (http://english.peopledaily.com.cn/constitution/constitution.html).

97. "CPC Central Committee Proposal for Formulating Tenth Five-Year Plan (Summary)," *People's Daily Online*, October 18, 2000 (http://english.peopledaily.com.cn/200010/18/eng20001018_52942.html).

98. The reform agenda included consolidating and strengthening the primary status of agriculture; speeding up restructuring, transformation, and upgrading of the industrial sector; vigorously developing the service sector; accelerating construction of an information infrastructure for national economic and social development; further enhancing infrastructure construction in such sectors as water conservancy, communications, and energy; implementing the strategy of developing the western region to promote coordinated development among different regions; actively promoting urbanization in a reliable manner; promoting scientific and technological advancement and creation; tapping human resources and quickening the cause of education; enhancing management of population and resources, attaching importance to ecological construction and environmental protection; further deepening reform and improving the system of a socialist market economy; further opening up to the outside world and developing an open economy; actively expanding employment and improving the social security system; improving the life of urban and rural residents; advancing socialist ethical and cultural progress; and strengthening construction of the socialist democracy and legal system.

99. "CPC to Strengthen the Democratic Legal System," *People's Daily Online*, October 18, 2000 (http://english.peopledaily.com.cn/200010/18/eng20001018_52960.html).

100. "Top Legislator Calls for Sound Legal System in Rural Areas," *People's Daily Online*, June 15, 2001 (http://english.peopledaily.com.cn/200106/15/eng20010615_72660.html).

101. "Full Text of Premier Zhu's Government Work Report (1)," *Report on the Work of the Government* by Premier Zhu Rongji delivered at the Fifth Session of the Ninth National People's Congress on March 5, 2002, *People's Daily Online*, March 17, 2002 (http://english.peopledaily.com.cn/200203/16/eng20020316_92211.shtml).

102. "Premier Wen Jiabao Discusses Rule of Law with University Students," *Legal Daily*, December 4, 2009. "Editor's Note: On May 4th, 2008, Wen Jiabao, Premier of the People's Republic of China, paid a visit to the China University of Political Science and Law (CUPL) for Youth Day. In the Law Library, Premier Wen had a cordial talk with the students on the rule of law. Today, at the time of National Law Publicity Day, the *Legal Daily* here presents for its readers the full text of Premier Wen's conversation with the students."

103. K. Drinhausen, "Hu Xingdou: Wen Jiabao, Hero of the Chinese People," *China Geek*, October 30, 2010 (http://chinageeks.org/2010/10/hu-xingdou-wen-jiabao-hero-of-the-chinese-people/).

104. People's Police Law of the People's Republic of China, adopted at the 12th Meeting of the Standing Committee of the Eighth National People's Congress on February 28, 1995; promulgated by Order No. 40 of the President of the People's Republic of China on February 28, 1995, and effective immediately.

105. Article 37 of the PRC Constitution states: "The freedom of person of citizens of the People's Republic of China is inviolable. No citizen may be arrested except with the approval or by decision of a people's procuratorate or by decision of a people's court, and arrests must be made by a public security organ."

106. (a) Commensurate powers are given to the local people's congresses in Article 99 of the PRC Constitution: "Local people's congresses at various levels ensure the observance and implementation of the Constitution and the law and the administrative rules and regulations in their respective administrative areas." Article 104 provides that, "The standing committee of a local people's congress at or above the county level…supervises the work of the people's government, people's court, and people's procuratorate at the corresponding level." It turned out that local people's congresses are playing a more assertive and effective legislative and supervisory role over government functions, including justice administration. (b) Young Nam Cho, *Local People's Congresses in China: Development and Transition*, Cambridge University Press, Cambridge, UK, 2008. In 2000 and 2001, the Gonghe County People's Congress in Qinghai Province and the Shenyang Municipal People's Congress, respectively, voted on annual work reports of the courts, marking the first time that local people's congresses demanded a meaningful voice in how government should be run.

107. Article 67(1) of the PRC Constitution provides that the Standing Committee has the function and power to "interpret the Constitution and supervise its enforcement."

108. Article 57 of the PRC Constitution states: "The National People's Congress of the People's Republic of China is the highest organ of state power. Its permanent body is the Standing Committee of the National People's Congress."

109. Chen Yong, "Several Problems with Checking on Law Enforcement" ["*Guanyu zhifa jiancha de jige wenti*"], *Chinese Legal Science* (*Zhongguo falu*), 2, 61–67, 1994. Theoretically, the National People's Congress can of course act as the main body (*zhuti*) for legal inspection, but in practice it is not easy to do so. The National People's Congress meets only once a year, but inspection and supervision of the legal system are ongoing; thus, it is difficult to deal with unconstitutional and illegal acts in a timely way. Furthermore, because the meetings are short and burdened with a heavy schedule, participants cannot pay adequate attention to legal enforcement work. Before 1993, various attempts were made to address the inadequacy of law enforcement inspection and supervision; for example, the Seventh Standing Committee working paper called for selective exercise of its inspection and supervisory powers over the implementation of important laws; any unconstitutional and illegal conditions discovered should be reported to responsible state organs for correction. The working paper also called for establishing *ad hoc* investigative committees (*teding wenti de tiaocha weiyuan hui*) to deal with special lapses in law enforcement.

110. "Provisions of the Standing Committee of the National People's Congress on Strengthening Inspection and Supervision of Law Enforcement," adopted at the Third Meeting of the Standing Committee of the Eighth National People's Congress on September 2, 1993.

111. In his address at the Third Meeting of the Standing Committee of the Eighth National People's Congress on September 2, 1993, Qi Shi, Committee Chairman, observed that regulations on law enforcement inspection and supervision are necessary to fight corruption (*fubai*), as many of the existing laws on corruption, bribery, smuggling, prostitution, and drug use are not enforced properly or followed literally.

112. For a discussion on the legislative intent of the regulations, see Cao Zhi, Chief Secretary to the Eighth Standing Committee, "Clarification regarding the Standing Committee's Certain Regulations on Reinforcing Inspection and Supervision over Actual Implementation of the Law (Draft)" ("*Guanyu quanguo renmin daibiao dahui changwuweiyuanhui guanyu jiaqiang dui falu shishi qinquan de jiancha jiandu ruogan guiding* [*caoan*] *de suoming*"), in PRC National People's Congress Standing Committee Promulgations, 1993.

113. Special committees are provided for by Chapter III of the Organic Law of the National People's Congress of the People's Republic of China, adopted at the Second Session of the Fifth National People's Congress and promulgated for implementation by proclamation of the National People's Congress on December 2, 1982. Article 35 provides that, "The National People's Congress shall establish…such other special committees as may be deemed necessary by the National People's Congress." Article 37 further details the work of these special committees: "To investigate and propose solutions to issues that are related to the special committees and which fall within the scope of functions and powers of the National People's Congress or its Standing Committee."

114. "National People's Congress Deputies Strengthens Supervision," *People's Daily Online*, March 13, 2000 (http://english.peopledaily.com.cn/200003/13/eng20000313N112.html).

115. This law was first drafted in 1987. It was submitted to the top legislature for review in August 2002 and finally passed in August 2006. (a) Supervision Law of the Standing Committees of the People's Congresses at Various Levels, adopted by the 23rd Meeting of the 10th National People's Congress Standing Committee, August 27, 2006; effective January 1, 2007. (b) "Top Legislature Adopts People's Congress Supervision Law," *Xinhua*, August 28, 2006.

116. "Backgrounder: NPC's Power of Supervision," *Xinhua*, March 4, 2011 (http://news.xinhuanet.com/english2010/database/2011-03/04/c_13760917.htm).

117. "China Makes Legislative Efforts to Protect Human Rights," *Xinhua*, December 9, 2010 (http://www.china.org.cn/china/2010-12/09/content_21511049.htm). In March 2010, Wu Bangguo, chairman of the 11th Standing Committee of the National People's Congress, said that the country's top legislature would ensure that the goal was achieved by the end of the year, as scheduled.

118. Administrative Supervision Law of the People's Republic of China, adopted at the 25th Session of the Eighth National People's Congress Standing Committee and promulgated by President Jiang Zemin on May 9, 1997.

119. "China Amends Law to Tighten Civil Servants Supervision," *China Daily*, February 24, 2010 (http://www.chinadaily.com.cn/china/2010-02/24/content_9498885.htm).

120. "Inspection Teams to Tour Country, Check Law Enforcement," *China Daily*, February 24, 2010 (http://www.chinadaily.com.cn/china/2010-02/24/content_9498885.htm).

121. "Extended Detention, Forced Confession Still Salient in Chinese Judiciary: Report," *People's Daily Online*, December 28, 2000 (http://english.peopledaily.com.cn/200012/28/eng20001228_59073.html).

122. "Chinese Legislature to Take up Supervision of Police Conduct," *People's Daily Online*, November 5, 1999 (http://english.peopledaily.com.cn/199911/05/eng19991105Y108.html).

123. "Top Legislator on Enforcing Criminal Procedure Law," *China Daily*, November 20, 2000 (http://www.china.org.cn/english/2000/Nov/4242.htm).

124. "China to Intensify Supervision over Customs," *People's Daily Online*, April 26, 2000 (http://english.peopledaily.com.cn/200004/26/eng20000426_39702.html).

125. "Top Legislative Body Strengthens Supervision over Law Enforcement," *People's Daily Online*, December 14, 2000 (http://english.peopledaily.com.cn/english/200012/13/eng20001213_57740.html).

126. "Report on the Implementation of the Central and Local Budgets for 1999 and on the Draft Central and Local Budgets for 2000. Part II. The Draft Central and Local Budgets for 2000," *People's Daily Online*, March 6, 2000 (http://english.peopledaily.com.cn/features/financebudget/2.html).

127. "Report on the Implementation of the Central and Local Budgets for 1999 and on the Draft Central and Local Budgets for 2000. Part III. Deepening Financial Reform, Standardizing Management of Revenue and Expenditures, Stepping Up Efforts to Handle Financial Affairs in Accordance with the Law and Striving to Implement the Budget for 2000," *People's Daily Online*, March 6, 2000 (http://english.peopledaily.com.cn/features/financebudget/3.html).

128. The Organic Law on Villager Committees was adopted on November 4, 1998. In June 2001, the Law Enforcement Program of the Standing Committee of the National People's Congress organized a tour to inspect implementation of the law. Representatives visited five provinces and autonomous regions (Shandong, Fujian, Hainan, Jilin, and Xinjiang), and the four provinces of Heilongjiang, Henan, Guangxi, and Yunnan were authorized to conduct their own inspection tours. Ministry of Civil Affairs (MCA) officials briefed the inspection team on implementation of the law in advance. The inspection group went to a total of 45 prefectures, cities, and counties; listened to 27 reports; visited 48 villages; and convened 65 forums with people's congress deputies, township and village cadres, and village representatives. They also used other methods such as interviews with villagers at home and examinations of village files and bulletin boards for the open administration of village affairs. The investigation suggested that democratization of the villages had been successful. See *Report of the National People's Congress Inspection of the Implementation of the Organic Law on Villager Committees in China* (Jamie P. Horsley, transl.), August 29, 2001.

129. "Ambassador Defends China's Human Rights Situation in 1999," *People's Daily Online*, March 31, 2000 (http://english.peopledaily.com.cn/200003/31/eng20000331W111.html).

130. "National People's Congress Strengthens Supervision over Forest Law Enforcement," *People's Daily Online*, December 15, 1999 (http://english.peopledaily.com.cn/199912/15/eng19991215E101.html).

131. "China to Intensify Supervision over Customs," *People's Daily Online*, April 26, 2000 (http://english.peopledaily.com.cn/200004/26/eng20000426_39702.html).

132. "Hainan Listened Attentively to Special Supervisor's Comments," *China Police Daily Online*, March 29, 2002 (http://www.cpd.com.cn/xxlr.asp?menulb=039%C8%CB%C3%F1%B9%AB%B0%B2%B1%A8&id=14467).

133. Supervision Law of Standing Committees of People's Congresses at Various Levels, adopted at the 23rd Session of the Standing Committee of the Tenth National People's Congress, effective January 1, 2007.

134. "Legislature's Supervision Draft Law Discussed," *Xinhua*, June 26, 2006 (http://www.china.org.cn/english/government/172720.htm).

135. "China's Top Legislature Adopts People's Congress Supervision Law," *Xinhua*, August 28, 2006 (http://english.peopledaily.com.cn/200608/28/eng20060828_297335.html).

136. "China's Legislature Holds Training Class for Implementing Supervision Law," *Xinhua*, September 26, 2006 (http://english.peopledaily.com.cn/200609/26/eng20060926_306317.html).

137. Luo Feng, Deputy Minister of Public Security, "Rule the Police by Law and Enforce Law Strictly Is the Strategy of Public Security in the New Century," *Public Security Studies*, 88, 1–4, 2000, pp. 1–4.

138. Kam C. Wong, "Govern Police by Law," *Australian New Zealand Journal of Criminology*, 37(4), 90–106, 2005.

139. There is an ongoing debate as to the meaning of the rule of law (*yifa zhiguo*). Does it mean the promotion of "rule *by* law" or "rule *of* law"?
140. Xu Peixing, "A Discussion about the Concept, Dilemma, Causes, and Countermeasures to Rule the State According to Law," *Journal of Shanghai Public Security Academy*, 9(6), 1–6, 1999.
141. In his keynote address, "Preventive Measures and Strategies against Corruption Adopted by Chinese Police," given in January 2003 at the ICAC–Interpol Conference, Yu Yong, Deputy Director of Inspection Committee, Ministry of Public Security, PRC, and Director of Supervision Bureau, Ministry of Supervision to Ministry of Public Security, PRC, said: "To prevent corruption, MPS has promulgated the following rules and regulations: Interior Service Regulations of People's Police of Public Security Organs, Professional Code of Ethics of People's Police, Procedures and Rules on Handling Criminal Cases by Public Security Organs, Rules on Assessing and Appraising the Quality of Law Enforcement of Public Security Organs, Code of Law Enforcement and Practice of Local Public Security Office, Professional Code of Post Responsibilities of Vehicle Control Office, Ten Forbidden Acts of Public Security Officials and Police Officers under Public Security Organs, and Rules on Occupation of Family Members of Leading Cadre of Public Security Organs….To enhance inspection and supervision, the Ministry of Public Security has relied on the following laws and regulations: People's Republic of China Administrative Supervision Law, Public Security Organs Supervision Regulations and Public Security, Organs Internal Audit Interim Provisions, and state supervision authorities….Finally, to establish an internal inspection system, the following rules and regulations have been promulgated: Rules on Supervision of Internal Law, Enforcement of Public Security Organs, Rules on Responsibility for Law Enforcement Faults of Public Security Organs and People's Policemen, Interim Rules on Receiving Accusations and Complaints by Public Security Organs, Interim Rules on Taking Action against Leaders by Public Security Organs, and Rules on Enforcing the Order of Suspension from Office and Closure by Public Security Organs."
142. Chinese Police Studies Association, *Research into Public Security with Distinctive Chinese Characteristics* [*Zhongguo teshe gongan zhi yanjiu*], Qunzhong chubanshe, Beijing, 1996.
143. These rules include the following: Declaration of Incomes of Public Officials, Registration of Gifts Accepted by Officials, Avoidance of Close Relatives Working in the Same Unit, Disciplinary Action Rules of the CPC, Implementation Measures on Intraparty Supervision, Ethical Code of CPC Cadres, Regulations on System Responsibility to Conduct Party's Atmosphere and Clean Government Construction, Rules against Luxury Spending, and Administration Supervision.
144. Xu Peixing, "A Discussion about the Concept, Dilemma, Causes, and Countermeasures to Rule the State According to Law," *Journal of Shanghai Public Security Academy*, 9(6), 1–6, 1999.
145. "Henan Public Security Organ Faces Society and Employs Specially Monitoring Inspectors," *news.dayoo.com*, May 12, 2006 (http://china.dayoo.com/gb/content/2006-05/12/content_2502484.htm). Internal police supervision is supplemented and complemented by specially appointed external supervisors (*ducha jiangdu yuan*). These external supervisors are selected from among the public, and they generally are local lawmakers, political committee persons, professors, and labor union representatives. They have the authority to render opinions on supervision, inquire about law enforcement processes and conduct, listen to public concerns and suggestions, participate in inspection of work, and to correct and question police appearance and manners.
146. Jin Po (Ed.), *The Theory and Practice of Legal Supervision* [*Falu jianju de lilun you shijian*], China Procuratorial Press, Beijing, 2005.
147. Charles O. Hucker, *The Censorial System of Ming China*, Stanford University Press, Palo Alto, CA, 1966.
148. Inside China, there are many published treatises, books, and articles on this topic. The standard text on the subject matter is *Public Security Police Work Supervision* [*Gongon jingwu ducha*], Zhongguo renmin gongan daixue chubanshe, Beijing, 2004, which was written for the training and development of political cadres and professional officers.

149. "Public Security Organ Supervision Regulations" ("*Gongan jiguan ducha tiaoli*"), adopted by the State Council of the People's Republic of China at the 57th Meeting on June 4, 1997. For a reprint of the law, see http://www.86148.com/chinafa/shownews.asp?id=698.

150. People's Police Law of the People's Republic of China, adopted at the 12th Meeting of the Standing Committee of the Eighth National People's Congress on February 28, 1995; promulgated by Order No. 40 of the President of the People's Republic of China on February 28, 1995, and effective immediately.

151. "Ideas on Establishing Modern Supervision System" ["*Jianli xiandai ducha jizhi de sikou*"], *China Police Daily Online*, January 8, 2002.

152. "Explaining On-Site Supervision" ["*Jieshi xianchang ducha*"], *China Police Daily Online*. November 18, 2001.

153. "On-Site Police Supervision Implementation and Coordination" ["*Jiancha ducha shishi yu xietiao*"], *China Police Daily Online*, February 5, 2002.

154. "Reflecting on How to Strengthen Police Supervision Ranks" ["*Jiaqiang ducha duiwu jianshe de sikao*"], *China Police Daily Online*, March 26, 2002.

155. "People's Police Changed Perception of Police Work Supervision" ["*Guanxi minjing zhuanbian dui jingwu ducha de kanfa*"], *China Police Daily Online*, April 15, 2002.

156. "Focus on Police Who 'Police' the Police: A Summary Account of Police Inspection Work for the Nation after the Shenzhen Meeting" ("*Zhumu 'guan' jingcha de jingcha: Shenzhen huiyi yihou quanguo jingcha ducha gongzuo zongshu*"), *China Police Daily Online*, November 18, 2001.

157. "The State of Mind of an Inspector" ["*Ducha xinqing*"], *China Police Daily Online*, March 29, 2002.

158. "Police Organ Inspection Regulations" ("*Gongan jiguan ducha tiaoli*") and "Implementation Methods for Police Organ Inspection Regulations" ("*Gongan jiguan ducha tiaoli shishi banfa*").

159. "Currently Existing Problems and Countermeasures with Police Inspection" ["*Dangqian ducha gongzuo cunzai de wenti ji duice*"], *China Police Daily Online*, April 9, 2002.

160. "Police Inspection Work 2000" ["2000 *nian jingwu ducha gongzuo*"].

161. "Supervised by Public Opinion vs. Supervising 'Mass Media,'" *People's Daily Online*, April 15, 1999 (http://english.peopledaily.com.cn/199904/15/enc_990415001011_HomeNews.html).

162. "Media Should Play Bigger Watchdog Role: CPPCC Nat'l Committee," *People's Daily Online*, March 9, 2000 (http://english.peopledaily.com.cn/200003/09/eng20000309L107.html).

163. David Bandurski, "Why Are More Reporters Beaten and Arrested in China?" *Southern People Weekly*, January 18, 2010 (http://cmp.hku.hk/2010/01/20/4086/).

164. "Chinese Premier Visits CCTV," http://english.peopledaily.com.cn/199810/08/head.htm.

165. "National People's Congress Chairman Li Peng on Several Questions by German Correspondent," *People's Daily Online*, December 12, 1998 http://english.peopledaily.com.cn/199812/02/lipeng.html.

166. "Coastal City Protects Media Rights," *China Police Daily*, July 30, 2000 (http://english.peopledaily.com.cn/200007/30/eng20000730_46851.html).

167. "Open Supervision: Blow Away the Husk and Reveal the Grain" ["*Gongkai jiandu, chuikang jianmi*"], *China Police Journal*, January 6, 2001, p. 1.

168. "Thirty Years Learning the Art" ["*Sansi nian xue yi*"], *China Police Daily Online*, April 3, 2002.

169. "The Disappearance of Minor Details" ["*Shi zhen de xijie*"], *China Police Daily Online*, April 3, 2002.

170. "Please Have Mercy with the Pen" ["*Quan jun bixia liuqing*"], *China Police Daily Online*, April 4, 2002.

171. "PRC Measures for the Control of Weapons," adopted by the State Council of the People's Republic of China on January 5, 1981; promulgated by the Ministry of Public Security on April 25, 1980.

172. "Provisions for the Use of Weapons and Police Instruments by the People's Police," approved by the State Council of the People's Republic of China on July 5, 1980; promulgated by the Ministry of Public Security on July 15, 1980.

173. Kam C. Wong, *Chinese Policing: History and Reform*, Peter Lang Publishers, New York, 2009, Chapter 1.

174. "*Gonganbu zhaokai dianshi dianhua huiyi jiaqiang jingwu ducha gongzuo ezhi xie chuang weifa, weiji,*" *China Police Daily Online*, October 19, 2001. The MPS organized television and telephone conferences to improve inspection work with regard to stopping the use of firearms in violation of the law and disciplining such occurrences.

175. Ibid.

176. Mao Tse-tung, "On the Correct Handling of Contradictions among the People," speech given February 27, 1957, at the Eleventh Session of the Supreme State Conference.

177. Zheng Caixiong, "Police Shooting of Suspects Sparks Debate," *China Daily*, April 6, 2004 (http://www.chinadaily.com.cn/china/2006-04/06/content_561164.htm). Zhang Guifang, deputy Party secretary of Guangzhou in charge of public security, encouraged other officers to take aim when criminal suspects resisted arrest.

178. "China's Official Media Says 3 Died in Police Crackdown on Village," *Asian Political News*, December 19, 2005. On December 6, 2005, 3000 military police surrounded Dongzhou village in Guangdong Province and opened fire on 1000 villagers returning home from a protest; three men died.

179. "Three Chinese Police Officers Killed in Gunfight Near Border," *People's Daily Online*, March 27, 2007 (http://english.peopledaily.com.cn/200703/27/eng20070327_361173.html). Three officers died in a shootout with drugs traffickers.

180. Andrew Scobell, *China's Use of Military Force: Beyond the Great Wall and the Long March*, Cambridge University Press, Cambridge, UK, 2003, especially pp. 163–164.

181. "PSB Chief Charged with 'Illegal Possession of Gun Ammunition' Attracts Debate" ["*Gongan juchang beipan 'feifa chiyou danyao' yinqi zhengyi*"], *Dongfang Fayan*, July 1, 2008 (http://www.dffy.com/sifashijian/al/200807/20080701063820.htm). A police chief with a long and meritorious service record was sentenced to jail for possessing 270 out-of-date bullets.

182. "Bao You Municipality Public Security Bureau, Jiuyuan Sub-Bureau, Proposal for Special Campaign on Control of Use of Service Guns" ("*Bao Tou Shi Gongan Ju Jiuyuan Qu Fenju gongwu yongqiang shiyong zhuanxiang zhengli xingdong gongzuo gongan*"), March 6, 2008.

183. From 1990 to 2005, a total of 6819 officers were killed in the line of duty, averaging 1.2 officers a day, and 120,783 officers were injured in the line of duty, averaging 20.7 officers per day. See *People's Daily*, July 24, 2006, p. 10.

184. Resistance to and obstruction of police duties are complex social problems that require extensive study and comprehensive treatment. "MPS Will Soon Draft Regulations on the Obstruction of People's Police Carrying out Their Duties" ["*Gonganbu jiang zhiding guizhang chuzhi zuai minjing zhixing zhiwu xingwei*"], *e.north.com.cn*, July 20, 2006 (http://news.enorth.com.cn/system/2006/07/20/001363275.shtml).

185. "Dragged Traffic Police for Two Kilos before Absconding" ["*Tuodai jiaojing liang gongli hou taoyi*"], *e.north.com.cn*, February 14, 2006 (http://news.enorth.com.cn/system/2006/02/14/001232249.shtml).

186. "The Status, Cause and Response to Obstruction of Police in the Execution of Duties" ["*Dangqiang zuai renminjingcha zhixing zhiwu xianzhuan, chengyin ji duice*"], Provincial Legislative Affairs Office, August 30, 2007.

187. "Police Should Only Shoot as Last Resort," *GOV.cn, Chinese Government's Official Web Portal*, April 12, 2006 (http://english.gov.cn/2006-04/12/content_251575.htm).

188. See Note 1 to "The Protection and Limitation of Police Right to Open Fire" ["*Jingcha kaiqiang de baohu yu xianzhi*"].

189. "Bao You Municipality Public Security Bureau, Jiuyuan Sub-Bureau, Proposal for Special Campaign on Control of Use of Service Guns" ["*Bao Tou Shi Gongan Ju Jiu Youang Qu Fenju gongwu yonqiang shiyong zhuanxiang zhengli xingdong gongzuo gongan*"], March 6, 2008.

190. Guo Qiao, "Dalian Police Committed Murder; Media Forbidden to Report," *Asia Weekly* (via Observechina.net), May 3, 2007 (http://www.zonaeuropa.com/20070504_1.htm).

191. (a) "Associate Professor Shot; Legal Experts Believe the Regulations Must Be Refined" ["*Fu jiaoshou bei qiangji an*: *Falu zhuanjia yingwei youguan tiaoli bixu xihua*"], *Xinhua*, November 15, 2007 (http://news.xinhuanet.com/legal/2007-11/15/content_7078010.htm). (b) Zhu Zhe, "Police Should Only Shoot as Last Resort," *China Daily*, April 12, 2006 (http://www.chinadaily.com.cn/china/2006-04/12/content_565656.htm).

192. Mark O'Neill, "China's Bad Comrade Cops," *Asia Sentinel*, November 22, 2007 (http://www.asiasentinel.com/index.php?Itemid=31&id=892&option=com_content&task=view).

193. Law of the People's Republic of China on the Control of Firearms, promulgated on July 5, 1996, and effective October 1, 1996; see Chapter 3.

194. "Regulations of the People's Republic of China on the Administration of Militia Equipment," promulgated and effective on June 3, 1995; see Chapter 3.

195. Law of the People's Republic of China on the Control of Firearms, promulgated on July 5, 1996, and effective October 1, 1996; see Chapters 5 and 6.

196. Law of the People's Republic of China on the Control of Firearms, promulgated on July 5, 1996, and effective October 1, 1996; see Chapter 4.

197. (a) Law of the People's Republic of China on the Control of Firearms, promulgated on July 5, 1996, and effective October 1, 1996. (b) "Regulations of the People's Republic of China on the Administration of Militia Equipment," promulgated and effective on June 3, 1995. (c) "Regulations of the Chinese People's Liberation Army on the Administration of Military Equipment," promulgated and effective on January 12, 1995.

198. "China Reiterates Stance on Gun Control," *People's Daily Online*, April 23, 2007 (http://english.peopledaily.com.cn/200704/23/eng20070423_368861.html?q=gun&button.x=23&button.y=6&button=Dic). The MPS launched a nationwide crackdown on illegal gun possession and use in 2006. Between June and September 2006, police confiscated about 178,000 illegal guns, 3900 tons of explosives, 7.77 million detonators, and 4.75 million bullets.

199. (a) Graduate Institute of International Studies, *Small Arms Survey 2003: Development Denied*, Oxford University Press, London, 2003, p. 86. (b) "Guns in China: The Wild East," *Economist*, November 8, 2001.

200. Buxi, "Chinese Police Adopt New Form of Self-Defense," *Fool's Mountain: Blogging for China*, July 9, 2008 (http://blog.foolsmountain.com/2008/07/09/chinese-police-new-self-defense/).

201. Law of the People's Republic of China on Control of Guns, adopted at the 20th Meeting of the Standing Committee of the Eighth National People's Congress on July 5, 1996; promulgated by Order No. 72 of the President of the People's Republic of China and effective as of October 1, 1996.

202. "Regulations on Public Security Organs' Use of Guns in the Provision of Civil Service" ["*Gongan jiguan gongwu yongqiang guanli shiyong guiding*"], *ChinaLawEdu.com*, October 9, 1999 (http://www.chinalawedu.com/news/1200/22598/22604/22711/2006/3/xu925383958112360025662-0.htm).

203. Criminal Law of the People's Republic of China, adopted by the Second Session of the Fifth National People's Congress on July 1, 1979, and amended by the Fifth Session of the Eighth National People's Congress on March 14, 1997.

204. Liang Zhaojung, "Research into Conditions of Legitimate Self-Defense" ["*Zhengdang fanwei tiaojian de yanjiu*"], *Free Thesis Net*, September 5, 2006.

205. People's Police Law of the People's Republic of China, adopted at the 12th Meeting of the Standing Committee of the Eighth National People's Congress on February 28, 1995; promulgated by Order No. 40 of the President of the People's Republic of China on February 28, 1995, and effective immediately.

206. "Regulations on Police Use of Weapons and Complements," promulgated by Order No. 181 of the State Council of the People's Republic of China on January 8, 1996.
207. Gao-Feng Jin, "The Protection and Remedies for Victims of Crime and Abuse of Power in China," in *Resource Material Series No. 70* (pp. 163–169), United Nations Asia and Far East Institute for the Prevention of Crime and the Treatment of Offenders (UNAFEI), Fuchu, Tokyo, Japan, November 2006 (http://www.unafei.or.jp/english/pdf/PDF_rms/no70/p145-155.pdf).
208. Constitution of the People's Republic of China, adopted at the Fifth Session of the Fifth National People's Congress and promulgated for implementation by Proclamation of the National People's Congress on December 4, 1982 (http://english.peopledaily.com.cn/constitution/constitution.html).
209. United Nations Declaration of Basic Principles of Justice for Victims of Crime and Abuse of Power, General Assembly resolution 40/34, annex, of November 29, 1985.
210. General Principles of the Civil Law of the People's Republic of China, adopted at the Fourth Session of the Sixth National People's Congress on April 12, 1986; promulgated by Order No. 37 of the President of the People's Republic of China on April 12, 1986; and effective January 1, 1987.
211. Law of the People's Republic of China on State Compensation, adopted at the Seventh Meeting of the Standing Committee of the Eighth National People's Congress on May 12, 1994; promulgated by Order No. 23 of the President of the People's Republic of China on May 12, 1994; and effective January 1, 1995.

Reflections

7

More than ten years ago, I started investigating police reform in China. In 2002, I published my first article on the subject matter.[1] This was followed in 2009 by *Policing in China: History and Reform*, which provided, in broad strokes, an introduction to the origin, history, culture, education, reform, and theory of policing in China. In the 2002 article, I drew three conclusions regarding the current status of police reform in China, its future prospects, and difficulties associated with researching it. With the passage of time and increasing knowledge of the field, these aspects of police reform deserve a second look. This final chapter affords such an opportunity to reflect. With respect to the current status of police reform, I said in 2002 that:

> The Chinese public security system is changing in fundamental ways. It is in the process of re-generating itself. The impetus of reform has come from within as well as without the organization. The forces of change have been both economic and social, though political considerations have invariably played a part. The direction of reform has been toward more rationalization, institutionalization, and legalization of police service. That much is clear from the above discussion.

With respect to the future prospects of police reform, I raised the follow questions:

> Less clear is what does the future hold for police reform in China? In this regard, there are two questions that are of most concern: the durability of past changes and the direction of future reform. For example, will the police reform process sustain itself? How fast, how deep, and how comprehensive will the reform process be? In what direction and manner will the reform process move in the short and the long term? More significantly, what will the public security system "with Chinese characteristics" look like?

With respect to the research problem, I made the following observation:

> In this first attempt to investigate police reform in China we find that: we know more about stated objectives and espoused purposes than unarticulated priorities and hidden agendas; we know more about public commitments than private ambitions; we know more about what the Party and central government wanted than what the professional officers and local administrators desired; we know more about official pronouncements than common understanding; we know more about theory, policy, laws, and regulations than social reality, street practices, and individual idiosyncrasies; and last, but certainly not least, we know more about reported compliance and noted successes than hidden defiance and undisclosed failures. In sum, we know more about the formal and official aspects of the reform, to the exclusion and at the expense of the more important (for our purpose of analysis) unofficial and informal accounts of changes that transpired. An informed and balanced judgment on the future prospect of the current reform process has to wait for more objective information and properly conducted surveys, not to mention an enlightened perspective and seasoned analysis.

In the remaining pages, I will revisit these three observations about police reform in China in light of current research findings reported in this book. I will then close the book with a section I have fittingly titled "Voices of the Police," which looks into what police officers themselves have to say about the reform process. I chose to end this book with "Voices of the Police" because, once again, I want to remind readers that there is a different and better way to investigate and understand Chinese policing—that is, by listening to what the Chinese people "think" and "feel" about their police.

Status of Police Reform

Much that was said about the status of police reform in 1990s still holds true today; that is, Chinese policing has changed in fundamental ways and is in the process of regenerating itself. As stated earlier, "The direction of reform has been toward more rationalization, institutionalization, and legalization of police service." Our current discussion is an extension and elaboration of the 2002 study theme, but with a different focus and approach. The 2002 study was an overview of police reform in China compiled mainly from Chinese open-source materials, such as *Gongan Yanjiu* and *Gongan Bao*. At that time, I reported on what was known about police reform in China in a systematic way—that is, its mission, values, power structure, status, organization, process, and leadership.

The main purpose of the 2002 study was to give China watchers and foreign criminologists a sense of what has been happening in China with respect to police reform. That article contributed to drawing attention to a field of study that has long been neglected, in spite of China's historical importance and recent fast ascent. Here, though, we take on a completely different intellectual project altogether, one that seeks to lay the necessary foundation for the healthy development of Chinese police research and discourse by debunking myths, proposing methods, offering perspectives, raising issues, and supplying data.

This book has an even more ambitious agenda. It is not content with reporting on what is known about police reform in China but rather reveals how little we know about Chinese policing, in theory and especially in practice (see Chapter 3). We know very little, for example, about the theoretical and empirical relationships, necessary or contingent, among Chinese political and ideological development, leadership (personality transition, socioeconomic change), Ministry of Public Security (MPS) strategy, Public Security Bureau (PSB) policing tactics, and frontline officer behavior. How does a change of political ideology from revolutionary communism (Mao) to socialism with Chinese characteristics (Deng) impact the direction of police reform (see Chapter 3)? How will successive generations of political and police leadership change affect police work (see Chapter 1)? How has the Internet changed the organizational structure and process at the MPS? How have officers reacted to the MPS and PSB "Strike Hard" (Deng), "Three Represents" (Jiang), and "harmonious society" (Hu) doctrines? How has mass line policing changed from Mao's time to Hu's era? How has the "Strike Hard" campaign style of law enforcement changed from Deng to Jiang to Hu?

We know very little about what policing with Chinese characteristics is all about (see Chapter 5). In what ways is it similar and to what extent is it different when compared with other Asian police agencies, such as in Hong Kong? How is community policing (e.g., in the United States) different from mass line policing in China? We also know very little about what Chinese people "think" and "feel" about their police, such as with regard to corruption (see Chapter 5), joining the police, or marrying police officers (see Chapter 6).

In any study of policing, determining what the people "think" and "feel"[2] matters, and the latter is more important to understand than the former.[3] In theoretical terms, it is more important to understand the police based on the people's perspective (below) than on the state's pronouncements (above). This is so because police in the eyes of the people are neither a gun nor the law; they are neither a political resource nor an instrument of the state but are a social resource in existence to meet people's expectations of all kinds.[4]

We know very little about how police insiders view police reform from the bottom up, although see Chapter 3 for discussions on police overtime and see Chapter 6 for "32 Classical Police Sayings." What is the role of frontline PSB officers in the formulation of MPS strategy? What has been the impact of police reform on police officers (see Chapter 1)? How do police feel about the deteriorating police–public relationship (see Chapter 4)? How do the police react to public challenges to police authorities ("hit without reacting and be yelled at without responding"; see Chapter 4)? What is the opinion of the police regarding traditional management practices, such as inspection and self-assessment?

Second, building upon *Policing in China: History and Reform*, I propose changing the way we investigate and in turn understand Chinese policing. Specifically, I argue that at the current stage[5] of Chinese police study development, we need to adopt a more cultural–anthropological approach,[6] rather than a strictly scientific survey approach to study Chinese policing.[7] This means examining Chinese history, culture, and social conditions, what the Chinese called *guoqing* (literally, "national circumstance"), to provide context[8] and more importantly to make sense of what is going on.[9] In this regard, Dutton's work is exemplary and trend setting in linking the past with the present to study the "history of the present."[10]

Finally, when studying Chinese policing it is best to adopt an inside-out, bottom-up approach. Research projects should be driven by an indigenous perspective (*qing, li, fa*; see Chapter 1) and informed by empirical data.[11] Researchers should have a bicultural orientation, if not qualifications (e.g., language facility, cultural emersion).[12] The research focus should be more on data collection than theory development, more on description than evaluation, more on analysis than on proselytizing, and more on understanding than critique.

What has been achieved in police reform to date, compared to what occurred up through the 1990s, includes the following:

1. *Discovery of a secular police reform ideology*—Over the years, there has been a gradual but distinctive shift of political ideology from Deng's "two hands" reform doctrine (i.e., one hand on development and the other on stability) to that of Hu's "scientific development perspective" and a harmonious and humanistic approach (see Chapter 1). This has taken police reform from a reactive mode to a proactive mode.
2. *Embrace of evidence-based policymaking*—Policymaking now draws upon Marx's dialectical materialism philosophy, Mao's "in practice" action learning theory, and Deng's "seeking truth from the facts" thinking. This has put police reform policymaking on a factual and rational basis, amenable to factual disputation, accessible to logical analysis, and capable of empirical assessment, a far cry from the earlier ideological straightjacket (see Chapter 5).
3. *Consolidation of the police reform plan*—Police reform today links political ideology with reform strategies and police operations under the Communist Party of China Central Committee's "Decision regarding Strengthening and Improving Public Security Work" ("*Guanyu jin yi bu jiaqiang gaijin gongan gongzuo de*

jueding"), which was issued on November 18, 2003. Police ideology now has to come to terms with emerging problems and issues in a systemic, comprehensive, and coherent manner.

4. *Use of both scientific study and trial and error*—The Party and MPS leaders are becoming seasoned reformers with the experience and confidence to match. Chinese police reform is moving into a new phase, from fighting brush fires to drawing up plans for change.

5. *Coming to terms with structural "contradictions" plaguing the reform process*— There seems to be no end in sight for such "contradictions," including the spread of mass incidents (see Chapter 4).

6. *Actualization of policing by the rule of law (yifazhi jing)*—Since 1990, the focus has been on stringent enforcement of police law. Effective implementation of the legal supervision of police began with educating people and officials on the importance of the law (i.e., building up a legal culture).

The single most significant development in the last decade on the actualization of policing by the rule of law is the advent of expressing public opinion on the Internet. In 2009, in a year-end review of notable media-related events, this development emerged as one of the most important. To many people in China, being able to express one's opinions on the Internet is democracy in action.[13] To the socially aggrieved, economically oppressed, and legally wronged, the Internet allows public "supervision" of officials[14] and virtual justice by those participating.[15]

In November 2009, for example, someone came upon a set of government documents showing official travel expenditures. He circulated them on the Internet, with the note, "I accidentally uncovered this expenditure list for a civil servant's foreign inspection tour." The list and 37 accompanying photographs created quite an Internet buzz and has since come to be known as "Inspection-gate." The officials involved were from the Xinyu and Wanzhou municipalities in Jiangxi Province. The documents showed that 11 members of the Xinyu human resource inspection group spent a total of 35,000 yuan in 13 days, and the Wanzhou training group of 23 members spent a total of 65,000 yuan in 21 days. Both groups of officials were immediately investigated and disciplined. The officials also were required to repay their expenditures personally.[16]

In early 2008, in Suzhou Municipality, Jiangsu Province, Quanshan District Political Committee Secretary Dong Feng's wife sought out China Mineral University Professor Wang Peiron and gave Wang evidence of Dong Feng's economic and personal work style problems. Wang dispatched these materials to the CPC Inspection and Discipline Department by express mail, but there was no reply for 2 months. Professor Wang posted a blog entry entitled, "The nation's most corrupt and shameless district committee secretary." The forum master followed up with an essay entitled, "Jiangsu Xuzhou, District Committee Secretary, directs and performs an incredulous 'one husband two wives' act." This posting was picked up and spread by many other websites. When Suzhou Municipality learned of the Internet exposé, they decided to investigate and take disciplinary action. In July of that year, Dong was suspended from his duties and was formally disciplined by the Party and government. In August, Dong was arrested.[17]

The power and utility of Internet supervision were confirmed by a public opinion survey conducted in January of 2009. In March of 2009, *People's Daily* reported the results of the online survey regarding the popularity and influence of the Internet as a public opinion and monitoring (*wanluo jiandu*) tool. The survey revealed that the Internet was the preferred mode for supervising officials and expressing opinions; in fact, 51% of the respondents answered "yes" to the question "Do you think Internet supervision is necessary?" The Internet was considered to be a "very necessary supplement to traditional public opinion supervision." While recognizing the importance of the Internet, 41% thought that it was illegitimate. As to necessity, 7% believed that people could do with it or without it, but some thought it should be integrated into mainstream public opinion channels.[18] More tellingly, 93.3% of the respondents responded positively to the question, "When you observe a socially undesirable event, would you select to expose it on the Internet?" Finally, when asked whether they paid attention to Internet public opinion, 87.9% said that they paid it a lot of attention; 7.1%, average; 2.2%, sometimes; and 2.6%, no attention.[19]

Future of Police Reform

With respect to the future of police reform, a number of issues present themselves. Ideologically, policing with Chinese characteristics still escapes clear and definitive articulation. That remains an unfinished but ongoing police reform project. If it is ever going to come to pass, policing with Chinese characteristics is likely to be defined from the bottom up rather than from the top down, with the "top" providing the necessary leadership and the "bottom" setting the basic parameters. Furthermore, policing with Chinese characteristics, to be meaningfully understood, needs to be contextualized within a specific time–space milieu. That said, consistent with CPC governance philosophy and mass line policing theory, it is anticipated that under a broad rubric of policing with Chinese characteristics there would be many varieties, depending on the region and size of city, that would defy unified treatment by policymakers and warrant different research strategies.

Philosophically, can revolutionary policing exist side by side with professional policing? It is now clear that Chinese leadership, especially during the Hu–Wen era, is seeking to reinvent the police by adopting a bureaucratic/legal/professional paradigm ("professional" policing), without explicitly reconciling it with the revolutionary model. Three assumptions are at work to support this marriage of convenience between the revolutionary ideal and professional policing: (1) The Party leadership considers the professional police to be an instrument of the state to serve revolutionary ends, without inherent conflicts, such as in the case of resolute suppression of Falun Gong and negotiated peacemaking with mass incidents. (2) With the Party in the lead, police bureaucracy, law, and professionalism are not allowed to stand above the Party or the masses nor can the police be an autonomous institution with entrenched values and culture to match. In this way, a professional officer is first and foremost a revolutionary cadre; for example, a professional officer is one who is responsive, responsible, fair, competent, good mannered, and working selflessly for the people, just as Lei Feng would. (3) Inasmuch as *revolutionary* policing is a strategy and style and *professional* policing is an organizational principle, there is no conflict between the two; for example, *yanda* can be carried out by professional police according to law.

Theoretically, we must consider to what extent police reform in China, in process and outcome, will follow the transitional police reform model or path.[20] If we were to look at transitional police reform literature, the study of transitional police reform is the study of progressive changes from authoritarian control to democratic governance. Specifically, in order to move from the past to the present, or from backwardness to progressiveness, one must be prepared to give up informal social control in favor of bureaucratic, legal, and professional policing. A number of consequences follow from this understanding. First, there is only one path to reform, from the old (backward) to the new (forward). Second, there is only one way to reform: from informal to formal control. Third, the most effective way to achieve reform is by mimicking the West, from the importation of ideals (democratic governance) and ideas to the adoption of institutions (rule of law) and processes (procedural justice).

Looking at some of the research findings in this book, it is clear that China does not neatly fit the existing transitional state police reform model. Transitional police reform presupposes a failed state (diminished capacity) or dysfunctional ideology (anomie) that is in search of a replacement, with democratic institutions coming to the rescue. China is not a failed state. Communism (at least from the perspective of the leaders) is not a dysfunctional ideology. Most importantly, China (neither its leaders nor its people) is not looking for political reform. Finally, China's understanding of the role and nature of democratic values and institutions is different from that of transitional police reform. Chinese police leaders, for example, do not embrace the Western form of human rights, but a Chinese version of humanity (e.g., Hu's people orientation, or *yi ren wei ben*) encompasses social welfare and physical safety. Practically, can top-down police reform be sustained without bottom-up support? It is clear that top-down police reform has been met with dissent, resentment, and obstruction from down below. From web blogs, we have learned the following.

Grassroots officers display animosity toward "white-collar" police. In 2009, a web discussion began with a solicitation for the opinions of "basic-level" officers about "white-collar" officers: "Police brothers from the basic level, how do you view 'white-collar' police from agencies?"[21] Specifically, the forum master observed that the terms and conditions of employment are much better at the office level than the street level. This is a clear sign of interagency rivalry. One participant observed:

> There are many people who want to climb to the top at all costs, because when agency cops come down to the basic level their work is inspection and instruction. They are at the same rank as the basic unit members, but they consider themselves to be the boss and give us instructions here and there. In reality, they do not understand basic-level circumstances, and they do not care about the difficulties and bitterness of the basic level police.[22]

Whereas such interagency rivalry is common in the Western world, it is rare (or rarely discussed) in communist China. Publicly, Communists preach common goals and egalitarian rule, police officers are taught to emulate Lei Feng and sacrifice themselves for the common good, and it is politically incorrect to compete with each other over welfare and incentives. China under CPC rule is an administrative state, where police agencies have well-defined roles and responsibilities. Tight coordination and strict discipline are the rule, allowing no room for interagency competition. Despite this, interagency rivalry has arisen due to changes in administrative philosophy, organizational culture, and ethics. China has moved away from micromanagement by the Party toward macro control by the law. Instead of management by result, it is now management by process and outcome. Loyalty to one's own agency comes before obedience to the Central authority. A common saying is *"Shang you zhengce, hayou duice"* ("There are policies from above and countertactics from below"). In terms of work ethics, to each his own.

Police leaders are not respectful of the dignity and rights of prison officers.[23] A prison police officer offered up this comment on police leadership:

Prison is beginning to conduct body searches again!! A few "inspectors" were stationed on two sides of the road inside the main gate. They held metal detectors and searched every prison police officer coming in and out, and occasionally they searched the pockets of the officers to see whether they had cell phones. Since the order disallowing cell phones in prisons, this kind of scene occurs frequently. The dignity and respect for prison police officers disappear completely with such "raising hands, undoing clothes"! Our nation's Constitution, Article 37, clearly states that the freedom of person of citizens of the People's Republic of China is inviolable.

The commenter further suggested that, if police administrators do not respect prison police officers and continue to violate the Constitution, it would set a bad example for the officers and inmates. This post reveals that frontline police officers are not in agreement with police leaders. Time and again, officers are suspicious of the intent and competency of their leaders when making good decisions. The distance between police leaders and those being led is growing wider. Their relationship is much more strained than in Mao's days when police officers and their leaders were brothers in arms struggling for a common cause: building a strong and prosperous China. As a Chinese saying goes, police leaders and line officers are odd bedfellows, "sharing a bed, each with a different dream." Whether or not sharing the same bed is enough to achieve the goals of reform is the ultimate question. Evidence gleaned from this study suggests tremendous resistance among most frontline officers.

Research

Among all the areas of police reform, Chinese police research and its publication have made the greatest improvement (see Chapter 3). Reading through national and provincial police journals reveals both an increase in output and an improvement in the quality of police research. As early as 1992, the MPS began collecting survey data on public fear of crime. Through the years, Chinese government research institutes (e.g., Chinese Academy of Social Sciences), police think tanks (e.g., MPS Fourth Research Institute), police colleges (e.g., Public Security University), police scholars (e.g., *Wang Danwei*), and academic units (e.g., Center for Protection for the Rights of Disadvantaged Citizens of Wuhan) have been conducting theoretically driven, empirical studies on various aspects of policing in China, from extended detention (see Chapter 6) to public opinion on torture.[24] In essence, there is no shortage of data and empirical findings to make some preliminary assessment of police reform in China. What awaits is for Chinese police researchers to analyze these data and provide context with case studies (see Chapter 6).[25]

Voices of the Police

Call for Reactions to Police Reform and Ideas

It is appropriate to close this book by listening to what police officers have to say about the police reform process. In 2005, as a result of his involvement in an internal public security reform exercise, a forum master[26] posted a blog on *Tianya* inviting discussion of public security reform.[27] The public security reform exercise addressed deploying more officers to the frontline.[28] In the words of the forum master: "Explore a little the issues regarding organization reform and *jingli xiaqin*, the downward sinking [deployment] of police power."[29]

The blog attracted 3147 visitors who provided 177 comments.[30] This forum originally focused on how public security organization could be restructured to deploy more police to the frontline, but in the process it turned into a wide-ranging discussion of how police reform should be directed and undertaken. The forum master invited honest feedback: "I sincerely hope to hear different grassroots viewpoints. I believe there are differences of opinions, from public security organs above to bottom-level posts."[31] He urged his colleagues to speak their minds in a forthright, but circumspect, manner after a commenter dismissed such self-organized, grassroots feedback as a waste of time:

> Change entails changing fundamental matters. But what fundamentals should be changed? Under current situations, what can be changed and what cannot be changed? I sincerely hope that every one of you changes the habit of just grumbling without making concrete suggestions! Do not wait for others to change or tolerate others not to change. If there is time to grumble, why not use one's limited energy to discuss something concrete!!![32]

Control of Police Reform

One of the first commenters observed that police reform in China cannot be successful without central direction and control:

> I am all for PS system reform. But currently only local [agencies] are changing this and that, here and there. This kind of reform is futile. Reform must be led by the MPS. There needs to be comprehensive investigation in different locations. The MPS needs to propose a reform plan. Local agencies cannot be trusted to launch and manage the reform. The first thing to do is to have a central budget from above. The second is central, direct control over personnel and operations.

The forum master agreed but suggested that the directive for and direction of change must come personally from the Minister of Public Security, Zhou Yongkang:

> The three levels of public security organs—province, county, and city—should seriously investigate the issue of a downward shift [of personnel, responsibilities, and authorities] at critical points and propose concrete plans and feasible methods for strengthening frontline policing through consolidation—simplification and reduction—of police strength at the three levels of police organs so as to achieve 2/3 police strength at the frontline and avoid being top heavy and bottom light. In establishing the organization structure, there should be a special policy. Provinces, self-administered prefectures, directly administered city PSBs, and city and county organs should all design their own organizational structure according to their operational needs, without necessarily matching units above or below. There is a need to encourage shifting of the center of gravity downward to the frontline by comprehensively integrating policy, income and benefits, expenditures, and equipment. The ultimate goal is to truly shift police strength downward to the grassroots, not stay congested at the three levels of public security organs—provincial, city, and county.

Police Reform and Vested Interests

According to one observer, theoretically there are substantial differences between top-down and bottom-up reform:

When reform is top down, people with a vested interest voluntarily share their interest with those who have interest and those who have not. When reform is from the bottom up, people without a vested interest force those with a vested interest to share benefits.[33]

Because police reform in China is basically a top-down affair directed by the Party, front-line officers should not expect to enjoy reform benefits until and unless senior officials are willing to give them. This is consistent with Deng's theory of economic reform—those who get rich first will create wealth for those to follow. Whereas Deng's theory was built upon expanding the economic base, thus creating more wealth for all to share, the theory proposed here is premised on the redistribution of existing resources (e.g., police ranks).

Form over Substance

It was also observed that true organization reform would not come if it was in form only (i.e., moving people around from the top to the bottom) and not in substance (i.e., curtailing the movement of administrative work to the bottom):

> The difficulty with reform and the downward movement of police strength is that the reduction of troops is not followed by a corresponding reduction in administration. Many units with police organs still maintain this or that function. With the abolition of a department, the workload of units above has no corresponding department below to be assigned to. The conventional saying is "thousands of threats [above], a single needle [below]." As long as these threats are not reduced, the grassroots level must expend the energy to deal with them. Also, basic unit workload expands exponentially with the lowering of rank.

> When a certain central leader (CL) speaks, the MPS and Central Political Legal Committee (CPLC) must study the leader's speech. The Public Security Offices (PSOs) will then have to study three speeches: those of the CL, the MPS, and the COLC. Public Security Bureaus then have to study five speeches: those of the CL, the MPS, the COLC, the PSO Chief, and the Provincial Legal Committee. Finally, the Police Post ends up having to study 11 speeches.

Police Reform and the Rule of Man

One participant observed that reform is futile without changing the culture and practices of the citizens: "Can you change the rule of man? If not, why bother to talk?" Another commenter was quick to point out that, if the current dictatorial system was not changed, then there would never be any respect for human rights by frontline officers and thus no reason to discuss the matter further: "If the system is unchanged, it is a waste of time!…If the view on human rights under the system is not changed, there will never be any change in perspective. Dictatorial government will not create democratic human rights!"[34]

Police organization reform was introduced to streamline police operations, to make the police more efficient and effective, responsive and responsible. Technically, it is not reform regarding the rule of man or rights of the people. Still, police organization reform in China cannot be viewed, still less understood, in isolation from other police reform objectives—for example, govern the country by law (*yifa zhiguo*) and to put people first (*yi ren wei zhu*). Viewed in this light, putting more police on the frontline results in greater police protection and better service to the people.

Another more important point that should be noted here, in line with the observation regarding form over substance, is that police reform is less about changing structure and more about changing organizational culture; less about moving people and more about changing personal attitudes. Top-down, directed reform done in a bureaucratic and militaristic way has a tendency to put form over substance, structure over culture. That has been the problem with Chinese police reform all along.

Incrementalism as a Strategy of Reform

In reply to the suggestion that police system change is not going to be effective without a change in the rule of law, aggressive incrementalism was proposed—that is, struggle for incremental change under the current system and keep the dialog going:[35]

> I feel that although it is not possible to change [the rule of man], we should talk about it.[36] I have always proposed to fight for the most interest from the reform process under the current system. After all, we cannot be brothers to the upstairs and come out directly against the government.[37]

Incrementalism has three things to offer the reformers and supporters. First, proponents (young, educated pragmatists) and detractors (old, revolutionary ideologues) of police reform are not likely to settle their differences. Incrementalism buys time to bring about a gradual change of view on both sides. Incrementalism allows the Party, the engineer of reform, to slowly prime the reform to adjust to the people, through a dialectical exchange process. Second, incrementalism is in line with Deng's call for experientialism ("crossing the river by feeling the stones"), which allows learning from one's mistakes and building upon experience. Third, incrementalism prevents the radicalization of views and provides for changes with continuity, order, and stability. In these ways, incrementalism fits in with Deng's idea of reform: pragmatism, experientialism, experimentation, incrementalism, and due regard for continuity, order, and stability—more simply, police reform with Chinese characteristics.

Conclusion

The above online discussion allowed us to listen to the voices of police officers. In my 2002 article, I complained about the lack of data. This is what I said:

> In this first attempt to investigate police reform in China…we know more about what the Party and central government wanted than what the professional officers and local administrators desired; we know more about official pronouncements than common understanding; we know more about theory, policy, laws, and regulations than social reality, street practices, and individual idiosyncrasies; and last, but certainly not least, we know more about reported compliance and noted successes than hidden defiance and undisclosed failures. In sum, we know more about the formal and official aspects of the reform, to the exclusion and at the expense of the more important (for our purpose of analysis) unofficial and informal accounts of changes that transpired.

The police voices tell us about the top-down vs. bottom-up reform debate and that personal fortunes and individual ambitions are riding on the outcome. They also tell us that major obstacles to reform are the people and culture, not structure and process. In not so many words, the police voices told us that the future of police reform in China most likely rests on the people and their culture, values, and interests; thus, studying policing in China is perhaps better suited for cultural anthropologists than lawyers or social scientists.

Notes

1. Kam C. Wong, "Policing in the People's Republic of China: The Road to Reform in the 1990s," *British Journal of Criminology*, 42(2), 281–316, 2002.
2. Variously known as "hearts and mind" in military jargon.
3. In daily life, people's "sense and sensitivity" matter more than reason and rationality. (a) "Sense and Sensitivity," *Economist*, August 17, 2010. (b) "Sense and Sensitivity," *Times of India*, May 8, 2010.
4. Kam C. Wong, *Policing in China: History and Reform*, Peter Lang Publishing, Bern, Switzerland, 2009, Chapter 8.
5. We need both qualitative as well as quantitative research to understand policing in China, but in the beginning state of building a Chinese police study discipline it is more important to focus on particularized (through case study) and contextualized (historical and cultural) study to improve our understanding of China sufficiently to generate research questions and interpret research data. This is particularly important to understanding policing reform, the development of which is very much driven by history and informed culture. In the case of China, history and culture have left a strong imprint on police and policing. See Chapters 2 and 3 in *Policing in China: History and Reform*.
6. Karl N. Llewellyn and E. Adamson Hoebel, *The Cheyenne Way: Conflict and Case Law in Primitive Jurisprudence*, University of Oklahoma Press, Norman, 1941.
7. Jeff Ferrell, "Kill Method: A Provocation," *Journal of Theoretical and Philosophical. Criminology*, 1(1), 1–22, 2009.
8. Philip C. C. Huang, "Theory and the Study of Modern Chinese History: Four Traps and a Question," *Modern China*, 24(2), 182–208, 1998.
9. *Cultural Cognition Project Study Examines Why "Scientific Consensus" Fails to Create Public Consensus*, Yale Law School, New Haven, CT, 2010 (http://www.law.yale.edu/news/12248.htm).
10. (a) Michael R. Dutton, *Policing and Punishment in China*, Cambridge University Press, Cambridge, UK, 1992. (b) Kam C. Wong, *Policing in China: History and Reform*, Peter Lang Publishing, Bern, Switzerland, 2009, Chapter 1.
11. Kam C. Wong, "Studying China Policing: Some Personal Reflections," *International Journal of Sociology of Law*, 35(3), 1–20, 2007.
12. Philip C. C. Huang, "Biculturality in Modern China and in Chinese Studies," *Modern China*, 26(1), 3–31, 2000.
13. "'Grassroots' Internet Supervision Power Emerges, Realization of Progress in Democracy," *Ben Yue Kan*, January 23, 2009 (http://news.xinhuanet.com/zgjx/2009-01/23/content_10707844.htm).
14. Xiao Yuhen, "Officials' 10 Commandments Should Be Taken Seriously," *China Daily*, December 4, 2009 (http://www.chinadaily.com.cn/metro/2009-12/04/content_9118298.htm).
15. Yang Gengshen, Ji Huitao, and Han Xue, "Do Netizens Have the Right to Take the Law into Their Own Hands?" *Beijing Review*, June 18, 2007 (http://www.bjreview.com.cn/print/txt/2007-06/18/content_66593.htm).

16. Ibid.

17. "'Grassroots' Internet Supervision Power Emerges, Realization of Progress in Democracy," *Ben Yue Kan*, January 23, 2009 (http://news.xinhuanet.com/zgjx/2009-01/23/content_10707844.htm).

18. "Over 90% of Netizens Care about Web Exposure, Web Supervision: Need Regulations while Blossoming," *Xinhua*, March 3, 2009 (http://news.xinhuanet.com/politics/2009-02/03/content_10753429.htm).

19. "2009: Reflection on Chinese New Medium" ["2009: *Xinwen ye hui wan*"], *People's Net*, December 4, 2009 (http://media.people.com.cn/GB/40628/10514756.html).

20. Mark Shaw, "Crime, Police and Public in Transitional Societies," *Transformation: Critical Perspectives on Southern Africa*, 49, 1–24, 2002.

21. With regard to "white collar" agency police (*Jiguan bailing jingcha*, 机关白领警察), the forum master had the following to say: "All police brothers from the basic level, how do you all view 'white collar' police from agencies? I think the treatment (welfare and benefits) is bad at the basic level, and the salaries of agency police are no less than ours, but they assume fewer risks. We have to confront the masses and the criminals. Law enforcement risks are high, work days are long." For the forum master, agency work referred to office work with no street assignments, such as crime scene technicians who go to crime scenes to collect evidence for office analysis.

22. Office cops, for example, are regular officers, but they tend to assume the role of boss when examining and instructing frontline staff without knowing what is going on down below.

23. "All Prison Guards at Hujian Chongshang Prison Were Searched?!" ("*Hujian Chongshang jianyu quanti ganjing shangbanshi bi shoushen*"), http://www.tianya.cn/techforum/content/158/549365.shtml.

24. (a) Lin Lihong, Zhao, Zhao Qinflin, and Huang Qihui, "Investigation Report on Social Cognitive State of Extorting a Confession by Torture, Part 1," *Law Review*, 24(4), 119–137, 2006. (b) Lin Lihong, Zhang Chao, and Yu Tao, "Investigation Report on Social Cognitive State of Extorting a Confession by Torture, Part 2," *Law Review*, 24(5), 124–141, 2006. (c) Kam C. Wong, "How Chinese People 'Think' and 'Feel' about Xingxun Bigong," January 10, 2010 (online discussion).

25. For another study, see Xie Xaio-jian and Pi Te-yan, "Criminal Detention Operation: Theory and Practice" ["*Xingshi juliu yunzuo: lilun yu xijian de bofan*"], *Journal of Chinese People's Public University* (*PSU Journal*), 128, 85–100, 2007. Pi was the Deputy Procurator of Yi Chun Municipal People's Procuratorate and later the Mayor of Gao An Municipality, Jiansi Province.

26. In China, the person who authors a blog is the forum master (*lauzhu*, or LZ).

27. 警察天地　[意见建议]公安体制改革大家来谈　(http://www.tianya.cn/techforum/content/158/537543.shtml).

28. The proper deployment of frontline officers has been debated since as early as 1989. The issue is how to serve the masses better by making the police more accessible (geographically) and available (personally). The issue is one of having more police posts (within a short distance) vs. more police officers (available around the clock) vs. more intimacy (officers with local bonds).

29. 在这里希望求得各位广开言路，探讨一下机构改革和警力下沉中存在的问题.

30. 访问数.

31. 很希望能在这里听到不同层面的看法，下到基层科所队，上到公安部机关，相信每个人都会有不同的见解.

32. "If the fundamentals are not changed, no matter what LZ said it is a waste of time. The most that could be said is improvement." ("根本的东西不改，楼主说得再多也白搭，顶多算是改良.")

33. 改革是自上而下的，是既得利益者向利益和未受益者主动让利革命是自下而上的，是未得利益群体强迫既得利益者让利.

34. 体制不改，啥都白搭！人权观在体制不变的情况下，不可能完全改观。专制政府从来不会产生民主人权.

35. 我觉得虽然不能改变，也应该谈一下.

36. 我向来主张在现有体制下，争取改革受益的最大化.

37. 毕竟我们不能向楼上的兄弟那么直接的跳出来反对政府.

Index

C

Q

R

S

A Call for Authors

Advances in Police Theory and Practice

AIMS AND SCOPE:

This cutting-edge series is designed to promote publication of books on contemporary advances in police theory and practice. We are especially interested in volumes that focus on the nexus between research and practice, with the end goal of disseminating innovations in policing. We will consider collections of expert contributions as well as individually authored works. Books in this series will be marketed internationally to both academic and professional audiences. This series also seeks to —

- Bridge the gap in knowledge about advances in theory and practice regarding who the police are, what they do, and how they maintain order, administer laws, and serve their communities
- Improve cooperation between those who are active in the field and those who are involved in academic research so as to facilitate the application of innovative advances in theory and practice

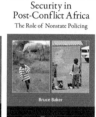

The series especially encourages the contribution of works coauthored by police practitioners and researchers. We are also interested in works comparing policing approaches and methods globally, examining such areas as the policing of transitional states, democratic policing, policing and minorities, preventive policing, investigation, patrolling and response, terrorism, organized crime and drug enforcement. In fact, every aspect of policing, public safety, and security, as well as public order is relevant for the series. Manuscripts should be between 300 and 600 printed pages. If you have a proposal for an original work or for a contributed volume, please be in touch.

Series Editor
Dilip Das, Ph.D., Ph: 802-598-3680
E-mail: dilipkd@aol.com

Dr. Das is a professor of criminal justice and Human Rights Consultant to the United Nations. He is a former chief of police and, founding president of the International Police Executive Symposium, IPES, www.ipes.info. He is also founding editor-in-chief of *Police Practice and Research: An International Journal* (PPR), (Routledge/Taylor & Francis), www.tandf.co.uk/journals. In addition to editing the *World Police Encyclopedia* (Taylor & Francis, 2006), Dr. Das has published numerous books and articles during his many years of involve-ment in police practice, research, writing, and education.

Proposals for the series may be submitted to the series editor or directly to —
Carolyn Spence
Acquisitions Editor • CRC Press / Taylor & Francis Group
561-998-2515 • 561-997-7249 (fax)
carolyn.spence@taylorandfrancis.com • www.crcpress.com
6000 Broken Sound Parkway NW, Suite 300, Boca Raton, FL 33487

For Product Safety Concerns and Information please contact our
EU representative GPSR@taylorandfrancis.com Taylor & Francis
Verlag GmbH, Kaufingerstraße 24, 80331 München, Germany